THE PELICAN GUIDE TO ENGLISH LITERATURE

7

THE MODERN AGE

Boris Ford read English at Cambridge before the war. He then spent six years in the Army Education Corps, being finally in command of a residential School of Artistic Studies. On leaving the Army, he joined the staff of the newly formed Bureau of Current Affairs and graduated to be its Chief Editor and in the end its Director. When the Bureau closed down at the end of 1951, he joined the Secretariat of the United Nations in New York and Geneva. On returning to England in the autumn of 1953, he was appointed Secretary of a national inquiry into the problem of providing a humane liberal education for people undergoing technical and professional training.

Boris Ford then became Editor of the *Journal of Education*, until it ceased publication in 1958, and also the first head of School Broadcasting with independent television. From 1958 he was Education Secretary at the Cambridge University Press, and in 1960 he was appointed Professor of Education and Director of the Institute of Education at Sheffield University. In 1963 he became Professor of Education and subsequently Chairman of Education at the University of Sussex. He is Editor of *Universities Quarterly*.

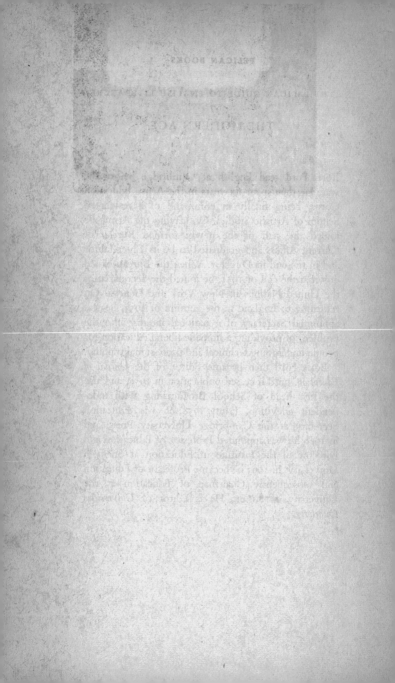

The Modern Age

VOLUME

7

OF THE PELICAN GUIDE TO ENGLISH LITERATURE

★

EDITED BY BORIS FORD

THIRD EDITION

PENGUIN BOOKS

Penguin Books Ltd, Harmondsworth, Middlesex, England
Penguin Books Inc., 7110 Ambassador Road, Baltimore, Maryland 21207, U.S.A.
Penguin Books Australia Ltd, Ringwood, Victoria, Australia
Penguin Books Canada Ltd, 41 Steelcase Road West, Markham, Ontario, Canada
Penguin Books (N.Z.) Ltd, 182–190 Wairau Road, Auckland 10, New Zealand

—

First published 1961
Second edition 1963
Reprinted with revisions 1964
Reprinted 1966, 1967, 1969 (twice), 1970, 1972
Third edition 1973
Reprinted 1974, 1975

—

—

Made and printed in Great Britain
by Hazell Watson & Viney Ltd,
Aylesbury, Bucks
Set in Monotype Bembo

CONTENTS

PART IV

COMPILED BY JOAN BLACK

GENERAL INTRODUCTION

THIS is the final volume of the *Pelican Guide to English Literature*. Inevitably the project as a whole has taken a good deal longer to carry out than was originally planned, with the result that a number of the earlier volumes in the series have already been through several impressions. Indeed, from the point of view of sales the *Guide* seems to have done very well, at any rate well enough to modify the comment made in the original General Introduction that 'this is not an age which is altogether sympathetic to such an undertaking'.

Yet though the sales of Pelican books undoubtedly signify something (if only a guilty conscience about the topics that one has always meant to 'take up'), they cannot of themselves dispel one's sense of the 'deep-seated spiritual vulgarity that lies at the heart of our civilization', in L. H. Myers's phrase. Other ages have no doubt suffered from their own kinds of grossness and vulgarity, which (and it would be a legitimate criticism) the earlier volumes of the *Guide* have not always sufficiently emphasized. The reason for this, perhaps, was that ultimately the critical preoccupation of these volumes was with the meaning of literature for our own age and for the non-specialist and non-historical reader of today, who might be glad of guidance to help him to respond to what is living and contemporary in literature. For, like the other arts, literature has the power to enrich the imagination and to clarify thought and feeling. Not that one is offering literature as a substitute religion or as providing a philosophy for life. Its satisfactions are of their own kind, though they are satisfactions intimately bound up with the life of each individual reader and therefore not without their bearing on his attitude to life.

This attempt to draw up an ordered account of literature that would be concerned, first and foremost, with value for the present, has meant that the *Guide* has been a work of criticism rather than a standard history of literature. And if this was so in the case of the earlier historical volumes, it was always certain that when it came to offering guidance about the literature of this century, the work would have to be conducted in an unusually critical and yet exploratory spirit. Of all the volumes, this last was bound to be the hardest to assemble, for the major writers are still very much part of our time and yet they are just sufficiently in the past for it to have become fashionable to find some of them unfashionable; and at the same time, the profusion of lesser writers have a certain inescapable currency that makes it very hard, in a volume designed for the wide-ranging contemporary reader, to disregard them altogether

In the event this final volume has had to accept a measure of compromise between critical rigour and what one might call sociological indulgence. A variety of extra-literary factors may give much of the writing of one's own day a certain genuine life, even though one comes to the conclusion that it will be comparatively short-lived. Both these evaluations need to be made, for only in this way can one avoid the prevailing sins of much week-end criticism, which is not that it gives too much space to lesser writers but that it tries to justify this space by concocting an unconscionable number of masterpieces. Though this volume of the *Guide* has not uncovered any new masterpieces or master-writers, it has done its critical best not to take a narrow or unsympathetic view of things. But in the end the standards of reference have been a few writers who seem, on re-examination, to have made a profound contribution to our literature, and a few critics who have made a determined effort to elicit from this literature what is of living value today. Together, they have managed to re-establish a sense of literary tradition and they have defined the high standards that this tradition implies.

It is in this spirit that this final volume of the *Guide* offers its contour-map of the literary scene to the general reader. Like its predecessors, it provides the reader with four kinds of related material:

(i) An account of the social context of literature in the period, attempting to answer such questions as 'Why has the literature of this period dealt with *this* rather than *that* kind of problem?', 'What has been the relationship between writer and public?', 'What is the reading public like in its tastes and make-up?'. This section of the volume provides, not a potted history, but an account of contemporary society at its points of contact with literature.

(ii) A literary survey of this period, describing the general characteristics of the period's literature in such a way as to enable the reader to trace its growth and to keep his bearings. The aim of this section is to answer such questions as 'What *kind* of literature has been written in this period?', 'Which authors matter most?', 'Where does the strength of the period lie?'

(iii) Detailed studies of some of the chief writers and works in this period. Coming after the two general surveys, the aim of this section is to convey a sense of what it means to read closely and with perception, and also to suggest how the literature of this period is most profitably read, i.e. with what assumptions and with what kind of attention. In addition, this section includes a few general studies of such topics as

Criticism, the Prose of Thought, the Best-Seller, and the Mass Media.

(iv) Finally an appendix of essential facts for reference purposes, such as authors' biographies (in miniature), bibliographies, books for further study, and so on.

Thus, this volume of the *Guide* has been planned as a whole and should be read as a whole. The individual essays have not been written to a single formula, some of them being more detailed and some more discursive than others; but this seemed the best way of giving the reader a varied understanding of the literature of the period. The contributors have been chosen as writers who would be inclined and willing to fit themselves together into this common pattern and this has meant that they are people whose approach to literature is based on common assumptions; for it was essential that the *Guide* should have cohesion and should reveal some collaborative agreements (though inevitably, and quite rightly, it reveals disagreements as well). They agree on the need for rigorous standards, and they have felt it essential to take no reputations for granted, but rather to examine once again, and often in close detail, the strength and weaknesses of our contemporary literature.

In conclusion I should like to express my personal thanks to three people in particular: to Professor L. C. Knights and Mr G. D. Klingopulos for their frequent advice and guidance; and to Mr L. G. Salingar, who helped to plan the *Guide* in the early stages and has given me a most generous amount of assistance and encouragement since then.

BORIS FORD

INTRODUCTION TO THE THIRD EDITION, 1973

IT is now twelve years since *The Modern Age* was first published, and nine since it was last revised. In a seven-volume publication beginning with *The Age of Chaucer*, that is a short period; but because this is the period in which we are living, it is long enough to see significant changes, both factual changes such as new publications or deaths, and changes of critical viewpoint and fashion. For this reason, while the Bibliographies on the first six volumes have been fairly regularly brought up to date, in the case of this contemporary volume the up-dating has inevitably been a rather larger business, which in 1963 and now in 1973 has amounted to publishing a new edition.

In this 1973 edition some of the chapters have been considerably rewritten, and two of the original chapters have been replaced altogether. In addition, the Bibliography has been re-done. The number of authors included is virtually the same as before, though the list has changed. But the number of references provided has been greatly increased, and they have been brought up to the year 1972.

But even now, this volume does not offer itself as a comprehensive reference-book: it is still a *guide* to the literature of the twentieth century.

BORIS FORD

PART
I

THE SOCIAL AND INTELLECTUAL BACKGROUND

G. H. BANTOCK

Professor of Education, University of Leicester

Introduction: The writer's predicament

WHEN Logan Pearsall Smith confessed to Henry James that he wished to do the best he could with his pen, James replied that, if such was the case, 'There is one word – let me impress upon you – which you must inscribe upon your banner, and that word is Loneliness.' James caught at the eremitic implications of Pearsall Smith's pursuit of 'the best' at a time so inimical to a display of the finest awarenesses. If, then, two basic themes of 'modern' literature have been those of 'isolation' and of 'relationship' within what has been considered a decaying moral order, they have reflected a sense, on the side of the writer, of alienation from the public, an alienation reinforced by indifference or hostility on the part of the community at large. I refer, of course, to the greatest writers and critics rather than to those who have preferred the equivocations necessary in audience-seeking – the 'associational process' as James called it – to the renunciations implicit in the lesson of the Master. Though even these latter have recently shown a tendency to exploit a fashion for 'outsiders' and 'drop-outs' which is at the opposite pole to James's exacting regard for the life of the artist.

The fact that, in our times, really serious literature has become somewhat peripheral may induce a feeling that the writer's diagnosis of moral confusion or perplexity is suspect, springing from a wounded ego or dramatizing a self-pity. Though many eminent Victorians had regarded their age as one of transition, for the great unthinking the Edwardian week-end was little disturbed by intimations of 'chaos' and 'multiplicity', such as afflicted Henry Adams; and Henry James's comment to A. C. Benson in 1896, 'I have the imagination of disaster – and see life as ferocious and sinister', would have fallen strangely on many ears at that time. Yet it is clear that by the mid twentieth century every newspaperman had become aware of a 'crisis', a translation into journalese of Adams's intimation of moral confusion, ushered in, as he saw it, by the final triumph of the Dynamo over the Virgin. Two world wars and an accelerated degree of social change have produced profound alterations from even the nineteenth-century ethos, which we now know to have been less stable and free from doubt than was once imagined.[1] Nor has the serious artist remained aloof from social movements or indifferent to moral dilemmas. Rarely, indeed, can there have been a time when 'background' more readily obtrudes as an essential part of foreground. For all the comparative indifference with which they have been received, writers have less and less felt able to retreat into private worlds; instead, they have become increasingly committed to social, political, and therefore public comment. Indeed, one of our great twentieth-century novelists, in a television interview, explained his recent lack of fecundity as being due to precisely such altered pressures:

> ... I think one of the reasons why I stopped writing novels is that the social aspect of the world changed so much. I had been accustomed to write about the old-fashioned world with its homes and its family life and its comparative peace. All that went, and though I can think about the new world I cannot put it into fiction. (E. M. Forster)

Economic and social change

The later years of the nineteenth century saw the almost final breakdown, in the limited areas in which it still survived, of a pre-industrial way of life and economy. The agricultural depression of those times (1870–1902) hit particularly hard the landed aristocracy and the agricultural labourer; and it was then that the 'change in the village' denoted the end of rural England on any significant scale; as Lawrence noted, even the countryman became a 'town bird' at heart. Of the 45 million inhabitants of the United Kingdom in 1911 (an increase of 14 million in 40 years), nearly 80 per cent lived in England and Wales; and, of these, again roughly 80 per cent came to live in urban districts. The development of the American wheat prairies and the importation of refrigerated meat from the Argentine meant that four million arable acres, £17 millions of landed rents, 150,000 agricultural labourers disappeared during a period of forty years – some place the numbers a good deal higher. Free Trade, and the increasing urbanization it provoked, 'gorged the banks but left our rickyards bare' (Rider Haggard).

'Agriculture', as G. M. Trevelyan has said, 'is not one industry among many, but is a way of life, unique and irreplaceable in its human and spiritual values.' The decline of the rural way of life has certainly been reflected in the tenuousness of this century's nature poetry and in the veering of interest, noted by Dr Holloway, towards urban and cosmopolitan themes. The profound human implications of its loss have been mourned by Hardy, George 'Bourne', Richard Jefferies, Edward Thomas, and others, though as a way of life it had a shadier side to it than they always confessed. For the evidence of Commissions on the state of the rural poor ought not to be forgotten in assessing the implications of rural depopulation. The Rev. J. Fraser, reporting on the eastern counties for the Royal Commission on Women and Children in Agriculture (1867–70), said that 'The majority of the cottages that exist in rural parishes are deficient in almost every requisite that should constitute a home for a Christian family in a civilized community'. Certainly, then, the 'organic community' of rural England may not have existed quite as its more naïve exponents believe; in re-animating the past it is easy to omit the stresses that are inseparable from the human condition. Nevertheless, this idealization of rural values is important because many writers have accepted its essential truth and have involved it, if only as a nostalgia, in their work. The theme of the past golden age, over the last century and a half, has manifested itself, in one of its important guises, as a yearning for a simpler, more 'organic' (a modern hurrah-word) society, to provide a refuge in this 'much-divided' civilization. The pervasive feeling certainly is that any material gain must be balanced against a perceptible spiritual loss, and it is the spiritual loss which has received the literary attention, even though one realizes in saying so that the division itself over-simplifies the situation.

The altered social emphasis following on urbanization extended the encroachment of a changed pattern in social relations already to be found over the greater part of the country throughout the century. Considering the enlarged role of money in the new village economy, George 'Bourne' points to the alterations necessitated by the slow but remorseless enclosure of the commons after 1861, a phase which in his area lasted until 1900:

> ... the common [was], as it were, a supplement to the cottage gardens, and [furnished] means of extending the scope of the little home industries. It encouraged the poorest labourer to practise, for instance, all those time-honoured crafts which Cobbett, in his little book on Cottage Economy, had advocated as the one hope for labourers.
>
> (*Change in the Village*, 1912)

With the enclosure of the common, 'the once self-supporting cottager turned into a spender of money'. The implications of this struck at the very heart of his human relationships; what emerged was a new ethic, familiar enough by then in the towns but less known in the country, the ethic of competition. The effect of this had been to reduce man to the level of economic man, one whose community relationships were at the mercy of the cash-nexus, and whose psychological motivations were thought of mostly in terms of self-interest. (There had been protests, of course, but not on a socially significant scale.) In such circumstances, '"the Poor" was regarded not as a term descriptive of a condition of society but of the character of a group of people' (Beatrice Webb, *My Apprenticeship*). Darwinian notions, interpreted by Herbert Spencer and others, helped to afford a set of fortuitous economic arrangements with the force of an apparent natural law. The chance interaction of economic atomic particles pursuing their rational self-interest was regarded as the inevitable and exclusive model of social behaviour. Notions of a public morality in terms of a diffused public good hardly existed among ordinary people – as C. F. G. Masterman's *Condition of England* (1909) makes clear.

Private morality, at least on the face which it turned towards the world, was authoritarian and taboo-ridden. Serious personal oddity was dismissed as a sign of degeneracy, not diagnosed as neurosis. The bringing-up of children, as Samuel Butler bore witness, was strict; and the overt decencies of family life and relationship were maintained, whatever went on under the surface. The 'great ladies of the day' sent for Lord Templecombe when the question of divorce arose, in Miss Sackville-West's *The Edwardians:*

> 'Noblesse oblige, my dear Eadred', they had said: 'people like us do not exhibit their feelings; they do not divorce. Only the vulgar divorce.'

The twentieth century has seen the break-down of the old familiar authoritarian pattern in private and social, as opposed to political, life. A similar type of moral questioning to that which, in the later eighteenth and nineteenth centuries, undermined the old hierarchic political order, affected many of the assumptions of family and social life. By way of compensation, private dilemma provoked, or at least went along with, a growth of public concern, particularly a developing guilt over wealth. Divorce today carries no moral stigma comparable to that of exploiting the poor, or of ill-treating a child. To some extent, indeed, the realm of the public has expanded at the expense of the private, almost as if the pressure of uncertainty had been resolved by a transfer of responsibility. The individual and the social ('the social' understood to imply the primary sub-group as well as society at large) have come to seem inter-dependent to a degree which would have appeared strange to a Victorian, to the detriment of that individual atomization inherent in Victorian economic arrangements, and of that sense of individual self-responsibility which characterized the morally earnest Victorian ethos. As Lord Annan has pointed out:

> Nothing marks the break with Victorian thought more decisively than modern sociology – that revolution at the beginning of this century which we associate with the names of Weber, Durkheim, and Pareto. They no longer started with the individual as the central concept in terms of which society must be explained. They saw society as a nexus of groups; and the pattern of behaviour which these groups unwittingly established primarily determined men's actions.
> ('The Curious Strength of Positivism in English Political Thought', 1959)

It may be that, in Lord Annan's meaning of the terms, positivist and sociological notions still vie for ascendancy in our political thinking. What is certain is that man's private behaviour has been profoundly affected, both by the atmosphere of moral perplexity within which he lives and by the expansion of the public realm which characterizes our age.

Moral perplexities

A theory basically economic had considerably affected social and political thinking about relationships in society for nearly a century, then. In its replacement, the empirical, sceptical spirit of science played a large part and helped in the dissolution of old social acceptances based on *a priori* assumptions. Beatrice Webb refers to the

> ... belief of the most original and vigorous minds of the seventies and eighties that it was by science, and by science alone, that all human misery would be ultimately swept away.

The scientific approach affected also the field of economics and social investigations. From trying 'to solve the largest possible problems from the least possible knowledge' (Postan), Cambridge economists from Marshall to Keynes have infused their theoretical constructions with particular observations of reality. No Gradgrind could have pursued facts more relentlessly than the investigators into social conditions at the end of the nineteenth century. The wife of Charles Booth, whose *Life and Labour of the People of London* (1891–1903) was one of the first great social surveys, stated clearly in a *Memoir* of her husband's life:

> The *a priori* reasoning of political economy, orthodox and unorthodox alike, fails from want of reality. At its base are a series of assumptions very imperfectly connected with the observed facts of life. We need to begin with a true picture of the modern industrial organism.

'The primary task [is] to observe and dissect facts,' urged the Webbs. Education and other aspects of social life were similarly affected.

The Enlightenment view of the world of men as constituting simply a part of the natural world and hence offering precisely similar opportunities for scientific investigation is nowhere better illustrated than in the rapidly developing study of psychology and particularly in the work of Freud. Freud worked within the framework of nineteenth-century assumptions – deterministic, materialistic, and rationalistic. At the same time, there were also features of his work which to the careless reader seemed to point to a considerable scepticism about the findings of reason. Rooted in a theory of biological instincts, Freud's view of the developing psyche placed a great emphasis on the power of the unconscious to affect conduct; intellectual convictions seemed to be rationalizations of emotional needs – 'rationalization' being a word introduced by Freud's disciple, Ernest Jones. Freud's teleology was firmly rooted in nineteenth-century hedonism; but the discovery that man's actions could be 'motivated' by forces of which he might know nothing introduced a probable irrationality into human behaviour which was profoundly disturbing. This 'entirely unsuspected peculiarity in the constitution of human nature', as William James not quite accurately called it, meant that a new dimension in the assessment of human behaviour had to be taken into account. The 'normal' scale of events demanded a new measuring rod, for analysis might reveal a profound significance in the apparently trivial. The firm line which nineteenth-century psychiatrists had drawn between the normal and the abnormal, the latter of which they explained largely in terms of degeneracy, disappeared; dreams and slips of the tongue, if nothing else, showed that we all displayed neurotic symptoms. Above all, the implied criticism of the traditional model in terms of which reason ruled the will in the interests of moral behaviour, and the discovery that the super-ego could profoundly distort the ego, so that 'in our therapy we often find ourselves obliged to do battle with the super-ego, and work to moderate its demands', had a profound effect on twentieth-century moral attitudes. Rationalist though Freud was, therapeutically speaking, his 'ego' is a feeble thing, fighting for its life against the encroachments of the super-ego and the id. And then, of course, there was the enormous importance, in the theories of instincts, placed on the demands of libido (those, that is, of sexuality), particularly on those manifested in the Oedipus phase.

Thus a blow seemed to be struck at men's sense of self-responsibility and at the ordered emphases of behaviour on which he had come to depend: the consequences for fiction can be sensed in the comments of Virginia Woolf, who knew of psycho-analytic doctrine early because of her affiliations with the Strachey family:

> ... the accent falls differently from of old; the moment of importance came not here but there ... Let us not take it for granted that life exists more fully in what is commonly thought big than in what is commonly thought small.
>
> ('Modern Fiction' in *The Common Reader*, 1919)

The results in the spheres of private and family relationships were profound, especially during the twenties and thirties. Jealousies were recognized where no such imputations would previously have been made. Mothers, particularly, were suspect as seeking to devour their sons; *Hamlet* was interpreted in terms of an Oedipus situation. The theme of sexual renunciation practically disappeared as subject for a novel; the dilemma of Isabel Archer *vis-à-vis* Gilbert Osmond no longer appeared real. Interest in perversion has grown. The relation between the generations has profoundly altered; and the Freudian phenomenon of infantile sexuality, though initially received with horror, has focused attention on the importance of early developments and given childhood a status it had only previously had in the pages of Rousseau and the writings of other 'progressives'. Before the First World War, male hegemony had suffered a reverse in the rise of the 'new woman' and the suffragette movement. Shaw's analysis of feminity in *Man and Superman* and *Candida* implies an error in the conventional nineteenth-century assessment of the relative role of the sexes. Little wonder that D. H. Lawrence, writing in 1913, found in the relations between man and woman '*the* problem of today, the establishment of a new relation, or the readjustment of the old one...'; and that, where parents and children were concerned, there was a break-up of the old authoritarian pattern. For Ronald Knox's sister, Lady Peck, parents had been 'a race apart'. To Robert Graves, during the twenties, his children were 'close friends with the claims of friendship and liable to the accidents of friendship'.

The traumatic event which hastened, though it did not initiate, the dissolution of familiar boundaries was the First World War of 1914–18. The conflicts between the generation too old to fight and the generation of the trenches did a great deal to re-shape the old authoritarian pattern. Those in authority – the politicians and generals – had, many of them, been wasteful and incompetent. Nor did their mutual recriminations help to preserve the façade of authority.

The peace of Versailles seemed, to a generation which distrusted the politicians as much as it had learnt to despise the generals, simply to play the old imperialist game: 'oil was trumps', as Dos Passos put it in *Nineteen Nineteen*. The war has been the subject of a hundred memoirs, defining in their varied terms its impact on the shocked nerves of a generation. What in essence died, Lawrence tried to reveal:

> It was in 1915 the old world ended. In the winter 1915–16 the spirit of the old London collapsed; the city, in some way, perished, perished from being the heart of the world, and became a vortex of broken passions, lusts, hopes, fears, and horrors. The integrity of London collapsed and the genuine debasement began, the unspeakable baseness of the press and the public voice, the reign of that bloated ignominy, *John Bull* ... The well-bred, really cultured classes were on the whole passive resisters. They shirked their duty. It is the business of people who really know better to fight tooth and nail to keep up a standard, to hold control of authority. *Laisser-aller* is as guilty as the actual stinking mongelism it gives place to.
>
> (*Kangaroo*)

The reaction of the post-1918 world was to suspect too easily all manifestations of authority. The twenties was the era of 'revolt' against signs of the assertive will. Acton's dictum about power corrupting became so popular that it came to symbolize the unease of a generation. The temper of the age was anti-heroic; Oxford in the thirties, for example, refused to fight for King and Country. E. M. Forster pointed to an early reaction against the moral imperatives of the war period when he commented in 1917:

> Huysmans' *À Rebours* is the book of that blessed period that I remember best. Oh, the relief of a world which lived for its sensations and ignored the will – the world of des Esseintes. Was it decadent? Yes, and thank God. Yes; here again was a human being who had time to feel and experiment with his feelings, to taste and smell and arrange books and fabricate flowers, and be selfish and himself. The waves of edifying bilge rolled off me, the newspapers ebbed.

The 'will' (the instrument of the moral 'super-ego') had, then, in some degree exhausted itself in the war effort; it was, in any case, suspect through its association with Victorian strenuousness and the subtle dominations of family relationships. Lawrence was insistent on its power to cramp and thwart in the field of personal relationships between 'men and women' – the 'insensate love will' marred the intimate growth of psychic uniqueness. He saw in it, too, the motive force behind developments in machine technology, dehumanizing in the industrial field.[2] Strength became a questionable value and 'success' in a worldly sense was only for the insensitive – Babbitt on Main Street. The theme was not by any means entirely new, of course, as witness Gissing's *New Grub Street.* And, further back, there was Blake's 'Damn braces; bless relaxes', not to mention Wordsworth's 'wise passiveness'. But there is an increasing tendency, in the inter-war years, for the hero in novels to be a person to whom things happen, rather than someone who to any extent imposes his will on life – Eustace rather than Hilda – a whimper replaces a bang. In the thirties, the life of action itself (except, of course, in defence of the Workers' Republic) is often suspect; *The Ascent of F6* poses the dilemma of action and contemplation.

In the social sphere increasing knowledge tended only to confirm and strengthen intimations of moral unease and to destroy faith in the essential and unquestioned rightness of Western ways of behaviour. Advances in anthropology, for instance, helped to undermine the absoluteness of religious and ethical systems in favour of a more relativistic standpoint. Westermarck's *Ethical Relativity*, denying the objectivity of moral judgements, was followed by Frazer's *Golden Bough* (1890–1915), beneath which, as Noel Annan puts it, 'runs the theme that all Christian ceremonies are merely sophistications of savage rituals and that as magic was superseded by religion, so religion will vanish before reason'. Further developments conceived primitive societies as integrated structures, 'patterns of culture', and, in this way, a large variety of different ways of organizing a society was demonstrated. The myth of a universal human nature was finally exploded; modes of behaviour obviously varied immensely in different environments. To grow up in Samoa was obviously not the same thing as to grow up in, say, Chicago. Ruth Benedict herself pointed out, whilst she deprecated, a typical Western reaction to these findings:

> The sophisticated modern temper has made of social relativity ... a doctrine of despair. It has pointed out its incongruity with the orthodox dreams of permanence and ideality and with the individual's illusions of autonomy.
>
> (*Patterns of Culture*, 1934)

Behind all these manifestations of confusion and uncertainty there lies a deeper and more profound problem – the inability to arrive at a commonly accepted metaphysical picture of man. To Freud man is a biological phenomenon, a prey to instinctual desires and their redirection in the face of 'harsh' reality; he is, therefore, in the Darwinian tradition, simply a part of nature. To Marxists he is the outcome of economic and social forces, the product of an evolutionary necessity as rigid as any to be found in the natural world. The declining, but still powerful rationalistic picture of man derived from the liberal, *laisser-faire* tradition rests upon an assumed harmony among men's varying rational desires, which, when not interfered with, reflect the pre-established harmonies to be found in nature; this view is derived, in part, from the optimism of the Enlightenment. A pessimistic scientific humanism sees man's aspirations and hopes as 'but the outcome of chance collocations of atoms' (Bertrand Russell). The Christian notion of man as inherently the child of sin, as belonging at once to the natural and to the transcendent world, and owing his possibilities of salvation to the Grace of God, a man whose essence is free self-determination and whose sin is the wrong use of his freedom, retains only an echo of its former vitality. Though Christianity, especially in its more extreme Catholic forms, underwent spasmodic revivals of influence – witness Chesterbelloc, T. S. Eliot, Graham Greene – or was sometimes condescended to by sociologists as fulfilling a social 'function' – religious controversy no longer vitally affects public issues. Many of the greater writers, however, like D. H. Lawrence and L. H. Myers, have found empirical accounts of experience totally insufficient to the ultimate mystery of human existence; certain theologians like Kierkegaard have enjoyed spells of popularity because they depicted an *Angst* which echoed the emotional despair of our times.

Nor are these uncertainties removed or lessened by current theorizing in philosophy or ethics, where the tendencies, on the whole, have been anti-metaphysical. True, philosophy, after avoiding system-building and becoming linguistic and analytical, once more allows some of the great questions. Yet, in general, philosophers have become more conscious of a professional expertise and have shown a concern for rigour of argument, which has replaced rhetoric and eloquence.

In the early years of the century, Bradley's absolute idealism began to give way to the realism of Russell and Moore. Russell urged in 1914 that philosophers 'should give an account of the world of science and daily life'; Moore put forward the claims of common sense. From this and from Moore's practice of clarification and analysis implicit in the *Principia Ethica* (1903) and *Ethics* (1911), through the aridities of logical atomism and logical positivism, developed the current concern with the analysis of ordinary language. On the way, metaphysics was repudiated, as could be seen in A. J. Ayer's *Language, Truth and Logic* (1935). The later Wittgenstein, in the *Philosophical Investigations*, dismisses any desire to reveal *the essential* function of language and seeks to investigate *how* language is used in daily existence. During the sixties there was a revived interest in metaphysics. But, in general, the tendency of the dominant school of English philosophy over the last fifty years has been '... not to increase what we know ... but to rectify the logical geography of the knowledge we already possess' (Gilbert Ryle, *The Concept of Mind*).

This changed focus of philosophical discussion has been accompanied by the belief that moral statements do not constitute genuine propositions. With the decline of intuitionism, the view of the American C. L. Stevenson, that ethical judgements had 'no objective validity whatsoever ... (but) are pure expressions of feeling and as such do not come under the category of truth or falsehood', was widely accepted among ethical theorists in the late thirties and forties and reflected a widespread scepticism about the objectivity of moral judgements. Ethics, for many moral philosophers, became 'the logical study of the language of morals' (R. M. Hare, 1952). Latterly, ethical statements have been reinstated as being supportable on rational, and not merely on emotive, grounds; though ethical judgements are, strictly speaking, neither true nor false, they can be better or worse. Recent developments, too, have shown some interest in the psychology of moral decisions. Nevertheless, the ethical philosopher still largely denies that his job is to tell us what we ought to do:

> Generalization [about moral advice] is possible only in so far as men are psychologically and biologically similar ... it is vain, presumptuous, and dangerous to try to answer these questions without a knowledge both of psychology and of the individual case. (P. H. Nowell-Smith, *Ethics*, 1954)

Something of the same spirit has infected the field of political philosophy. Political and party propagandists and left-wing theorists like the British Marxist, the late Harold Laski, have continued to discuss or imply the function of the state. But, after the generation of Hobhouse, Lindsay, and Ernest Barker, academic political theorists have either, like Michael Oakeshott, reacted against ideological system-builders, finding in the pursuit of 'intimations' a sufficient guide to political action, or urged, like T. D. Weldon, the uselessness of attempting to discover *the* ideal purpose of the state and assigned to the philosopher a subordinate role as 'consultant' (*The Vocabulary of Politics*, 1953). Though writers such as Collingwood have not been totally neglected nor the work of foreign existentialists unknown, the empiricists have increasingly dominated the native philosophical scene, bringing with them an element of scepticism: 'in science there is no "*knowledge*" in the sense in which Plato and Aristotle understood the word, in the sense which implies finality' (K. Popper: *The Open Society*). Certainly, twentieth-century physical scientists have abandoned their claim to depict 'reality' as something independent of the observer's position and of the conceptual system adopted for the purpose of interpretation. In any case, the implications of the scientific approach confirm an attitude which is public and egalitarian rather than esoteric and hierarchic; for facts are publicly inspectable and open to revision in a way in which *a priori* moral postulates are not. Hence, moral philosophers have avoided the deduction of abstract schemes of human betterment from axioms within a postulational system, and the bolstering up of existing systems by similar means. They too, then, have played their part in the gradual dissolution of authority and certainty.

At the practical political level the development of Imperial relations strikes the note of moral dilemma and uncertainty full in the hearing of autocracy and power. The period from 1883, when Seeley's *Expansion of England* proclaimed the Imperial Mission, to the present day, when Empire has dissolved into Commonwealth, represents a time of remarkable political transformation concerning notions of Imperial hegemony and white superiority. By 1900 the Empire had reached nearly 13,000,000 square miles and 370,000,000 people; the colonies were being used as sources of raw materials, markets, and incomes, and outlets for emigration. But the Boer War went a long way to puncture British complacency. The developing conception of Imperial relations is exemplified most clearly in the history of India where the high promises of Empire, in Kiplingesque terms, take on an increasingly hollow emphasis amidst the twentieth-century hatreds and discordances: 'We have', wrote Lord Chelmsford to George V on 4 October 1918, 'an educated class here, 95 per cent of whom are inimical to us, and I venture to assert that every student in every university is growing up with a hatred of us.' After the Amritsar shootings in 1919, Gandhi transformed 'an intellectual agitation into a mass revolutionary movement'. Political struggle and negotiations lasted off and on for nearly thirty years, until on 15 August 1947 India and Pakistan became independent within the Commonwealth. More recently, we have seen emergent Africa.

The trend of events in India and elsewhere has been assisted by the pervasive scepticism about political power among writers and intellectuals. Political subjection was repugnant to those, like George Orwell, in whom it aroused strong feelings of guilt, and like E. M. Forster, who thought in terms of personal relationships based in equality and the feeling heart. About Ronnie, his complacent young Anglo-Indian in *A Passage to India* (1924), Forster says:

> One touch of regret – not the canny substitute but the true regret from the heart – would have made him a different man, and the British Empire a different institution.

This criticism involved a comment on a whole ethos, one far transcending the comparatively local manifestations of imperial relations. It was a protest of the 'heart', solicitous for a fellow feeling where social and political subjection have no place, against the divisive implications of the will-to-power and of that 'intellectual hatred' which, as Yeats has reminded us, 'is the worst'. Forster proclaimed, scandalously, that:

> I hate the idea of causes and if I had to choose between betraying my country and betraying my friend, I hope I should have the guts to betray my country.
>
> ('What I believe', 1939)

For the world, he believed, 'is a globe of men who are trying to reach one another ... by the help of goodwill plus culture and intelligence' – a remark which betrayed a true English insularity in the era of Freud (*homo homini lupus*) and Hitler; though it is to Forster's credit that he recognized the echo in the Marabar caves as a threat to his liberal rationality. He does not plumb, but he is aware of, the demonic depths; he receives intimations from the dread goblins who, for him, stalk through Beethoven's Fifth Symphony.

Furthermore, in the middle and late sixties, there has grown up something of a nostalgia for the lost certainties and glories of Empire – part, perhaps, of the general revival of interest in Victoriana. It may be, it is surmised, that the present disorientation of youth springs, in part at least, from lack of opportunity for commitment and pride such as, at its best, the Empire provided. The Empire, it has been discovered, was held together by bluff, born of supreme self-confidence. How otherwise could a handful of men dominate almost a fifth of the globe? And did not this imply perhaps rather more good will on the part of the governed than had previously been assumed? Was there not, indeed, more of *service* implicit in what is usually described as 'exploitation' than had been suspected by the critics? Granted imperialism remains an atrocious concept was there not a certain graciousness in the manner of imperial dissolution of which we can be – almost – proud?

The new social ethic

It was, however, the sudden frightening awareness of a level of human behaviour the ordinary liberal, rationally inclined intellectual usually managed to ignore which, in the thirties, provoked a fairly widespread but uncharacteristic liaison with a continental authoritarian creed. Marxism combines in a curious way a moral relativism which fitted the sceptical mood of the times with a historical necessitarianism which evoked a comforting political absolutism. The nature of such an absolutism was not understood, in the main; it simply provided a refuge from the all too pressing horror of nearer, more visible absolutisms which threatened the safety of Europe. (Russia, in any case, appeared the natural enemy of German expansionist ambitions.) For a writer like L. H. Myers – and there were a number like him in this – a sentimental Marxism provided at once a tool of sceptical analysis of the prevailing class structure and a vision of a New Society. Such writers found themselves agreeing that:

> ... all former moral theories are the product, in the last analysis, of the economic stage which society had reached at that particular epoch. And as society has hitherto moved in class antagonisms, morality was always a class morality.
>
> (Engels, *Anti-Duhring*)

Positively, Marxism filled an uncomfortable vacuum which liberalism – 'a movement not so much defined by its end, as by its starting point', as Eliot observed – had left. Lacking the continental *feel* of absolutism, many hastened to abet the new manifestations of Necessity, the victory of the proletariat.

Yet the temporary success of Marxism merely served to highlight in dramatic form the slow, uncertain emergence of a new ethic which, in so far as contemporary movements are discernible to those who live through them and who therefore lack historical perspective, would seem to compensate in some measure for the private dilemmas we have analysed. The Protestant, individualistic, liberal outlook seems to be giving way to a social group ethic, in no way universally accepted, even though it had been developing spasmodically during the nineteenth century, but providing considerable evidence of a trend. The old atomization has met the challenge of new key concepts: 'organic', 'integration', 'relation', 'adaptation'. The new hell is to be that of other people. The empirical philosopher often speaks as if disagreement springs from inadequate factual data; the 'organization man' suspects a break-down in communication. The solution involves 'imprisonment in brotherhood' – or at least 'Speaking to Each Other'.

Indeed, there would be reasons for thinking that some of the earlier questionings in the private sphere arose out of a changing social awareness. The nineteenth century, of course, had a long minority tradition of comment and criticism unfavourable to the cultural and social consequences of industrialization and commercialism. Cobbett, Robert Owen, Dickens, Matthew Arnold, Ruskin, William Morris had all, with a variety of stresses, pointed to the human unsatisfactoriness of the dominant trends. At the end of the century, a number of circumstances combined to bring this minority criticism into greater prominence. Signs of a relative decline *vis-à-vis* certain foreign nations, the exclusion from certain primary markets by the imposition of heavy duties, a decline in the birth rate, and an increase in emigration induced unaccustomed uncertainties into the economic situation. The third Reform Act of 1884 and the County Councils Act of 1888, together with the development of universal education after 1870 and the rise of the grammar schools after 1902, implied a change in political balance; the lower middle classes were arriving. Though the predominant class structure was still strongly authoritarian, it came to be realized that the boasted 'freedom' extended only to the employer of labour; the implications of 'water plentiful and labour docile' were examined and found wanting.

There were signs that the upper classes were no longer quite what they had been. Henry James bluntly referred to the 'clumsy conventional expensive materialized vulgarized brutalized life of London', and found the state of the upper class in England 'in many ways very much the same rotten and *collapsible* one of the French aristocracy before the revolution'. The old aristocracy of birth and inheritance was being replaced by one of wealth and economic power during all the Victorian period. By its end, even the degree of 'respectability' exacted, in moral and sexual terms, was, as Beatrice Webb saw, graded to the degree of social, political, or industrial power exercised. Ramsay MacDonald proclaimed that 'the Age of the Financier' had come and expressed the belief that 'such people' (they included 'the scum of the earth which possessed itself of gold in the gutters of the Johannesburg market place') 'did not command the moral respect which tones down class hatred'.

What was distasteful in this society to the sensibilities of the writer was the total lack of concern for personal relationships, the judging of people by exclusively 'social' standards; though, perhaps, what was new was the sensitivity of the artist rather than the behaviour of exclusive social sets:

> What was demoralizing ... because it bred a poisonous cynicism about human relations, was the making and breaking of personal friendships according to temporary and accidental

> circumstances in no way connected with personal merit: gracious appreciation and insistent intimacy being succeeded, when failure according to worldly standards occurred, by harsh criticism and cold avoidance. (Webb, op. cit.)

This diagnosis was confirmed from the early years of the century by L. H. Myers who, with his aristocratic affiliations, was able to observe the ethics of the 'cult of first-rateness', as he calls it in *The Pool of Vishnu*, at close quarters. His letters betray his profound hatred of upper-class life in precisely Beatrice Webb's terms. Miss Sackville-West's *The Edwardians* affords further evidence; the people of whom she wrote knew only, she suggests, that they '[needed] plenty of money and that they must be seen in the right places, associated with the right people ... Whatever happens, the world must be served first'. Forster, with his theory of the undeveloped heart, has linked this insensitivity to 'persons', in contrast to extreme awareness of social atmospheres, with the public school outlook. Such analyses should perhaps warn us against accepting sureness of values as in itself a virtue. The value of the values, so to speak, is also in question.

Politically, the aristocracy, with the passing of the Parliament Act of 1911, suffered a great loss of direct influence. And when George V, after much anxious thought and consultation, accepted the advice of Lord Balfour and, in 1923, sent for Stanley Baldwin in preference to Lord Curzon to form the new Conservative ministry, the highest political office in the land was forever closed to a member of the House of Lords as such. At the same time, the persistence of what has been termed an 'Establishment' – a network of social-political-commercial and economic relations involving the decision-makers of our generation – has been amply demonstrated in an article by T. Lupton and C. Wilson published in *The Manchester School*. The network of family, school, club, and personal relationships there revealed, together with some significant remarks at the Parker Tribunal, would suggest that personal influence has not given way before the insistent claims of the new social Meritocracy as much as might have been thought. Even in the Labour Party, after the first generation of members had passed, a public school education at Haileybury or Winchester proved no bar to advancement; and though Lloyd George had proclaimed 'the day of the cottage-bred man', the personnel of the House of Commons remains obstinately middle class. Nevertheless, there has been a considerable increase in social mobility; and the struggle for status, based on education not birth, has become a characteristic mid-century phenomenon. This has both accompanied and sustained a predominance of the economic motive.

Beatrice Webb's father, she recalled, had no conception of 'general principle ... no clear vision of the public good'. The new ethic of which she herself was symptomatic was to be much concerned with 'public good'; state action was to replace the 'freedom of the market' but without fundamentally altering the anti-traditional, rationalistic basis of political behaviour. For the spirit of Bentham rather than that of Burke still triumphs; indeed, both *laisser-faire* liberalism and socialism stem from the ideas of the Enlightenment. The new sense of 'community' is dependent very much on the functioning of the 'upper centres' as Lawrence would have put it. Old custom was to be replaced, after the nineteenth-century vacuum, by positive law as the guiding force of the new communal spirit: at this level, relationship was willed rather than the result of a genuine 'organic' growth, though to say that is not to deny it a strong positive value.

Several groups at the end of the century demanded change: the Marxist Social Democratic Federation under A. M. Hyndman provided the revolutionary element, though its influence was not great. The Socialist League produced Morris, even if otherwise its effect was slight. Above all, the Fabian Society, which started out in revolutionary terms, became the 'symbol of social democracy, of gradualism, of peaceful permeation, of avoidance of revolution'. Wedded to fact-finding, its empirical approach forbade the enveloping philosophical theory and substituted a detailed programme of action based on the careful collection of factual data. As Helen Lynd put it, the Fabians 'applied the method of social engineering to questions hitherto left to the realm of sentiment'. The only common principle was the 'condemnation of the profit motive [which condemnation] was the G.C.M., the greatest common measure, of socialists'.

The Gladstone Parliament of 1880–85 was 'the "no-man's land" between the old Radicalism and the new Socialism'. The new spirit not only manifested itself in a spate of social legislation and royal commissions, but received theoretical justification at the hands of T. H. Green and the neo-Hegelian philosophers in the universities. The stage was set for the predominant twentieth-century developments, both in social philosophy and legislation. 'Every period has its dominant religion and hope,' as Arthur Koestler says, 'and "Socialism" in a vague and undefined sense was the hope of the early twentieth century.' The changing attitude was reinforced by developments in social psychology – notably in the American Charles Cooley's *Human Nature and the Social Order* (1902) – which, in Dewey's phrase, conceived 'individual mind as a function of social life'. Even Freud, who started from a firmly rooted theory of biological instinct, came latterly to see the importance of the social environment.

But not all were satisfied with the Fabian purview or the Fabian rate of progress. H. G. Wells, who so interestingly represents a facet of modern rationalistic political thinking, was struck by the wastefulness of contemporary conditions, the Victorian formlessness, and welcomed the forces tending to 'rationalize' and systematize, those which tend

> to promote industrial co-ordination, increase productivity, necessitate new and better-informed classes, evoke a new type of education and make it universal, break down political boundaries everywhere and bring all men into one planetary community. (*Experiment in Autobiography*)

The effects of this, in terms of immediate personal relations, Wells approvingly defines as a 'progressive emancipation of the attention from everyday urgencies ... conceptions of living divorced more and more from immediacy'. Though he deprecated any repudiation of the 'primaries of life' – personal affection and the like – he admitted the desire to control them in order to 'concentrate the largest possible proportion of my energy upon the particular system of effort that has established itself for me as my distinctive business in the world'. Modern conditions admitted the revolutionary question: ' "Yes, you earn a living, you support a family, you love and hate, but – *what do you do?*" ' What *he* did he summed up: 'We originative intellectual workers are reconditioning human life.'

The mechanical, abstract basis of community relationship could hardly be more clearly illustrated. We can see why D. H. Lawrence had to ask:

> Why do modern people almost invariably ignore the things that are actually present to them? ... They certainly never live

> on the spot where they are. They inhabit abstract space, the desert void of politics, principles, right and wrong, and so forth ... Talking to them is like trying to have a human relationship with the letter X in algebra. ('Insouciance', 1928)

The reconditioning process involved an appreciation of the planned world state as the answer to Victorian untidiness. Fabian interpenetration was rejected as a 'protest rather than a plan'. Wells thinks in terms of large administrative units rather than of the adaptation of existing governmental machinery. 'I listened to *Arms and the Man* with admiration and hatred. It seemed to me inorganic, logical straightness and not the crooked path of life': Yeats's comment is equally applicable to Wells's utopian schemes.

Many others took up the notion of the planned, particularly as the moral climate concerning personal responsibility for misfortune and poverty changed so that, as Professor Titmuss put it: 'Inquiry [moved] from the question "who are the poor" to the question "why are they poor"' (*Essays on 'The Welfare State'*). The progress of events – war, unemployment, economic depression – favoured the concentration on social and economic problems. Alfred Marshall, in his *Principles*, had already urged that there was 'no moral justification for extreme poverty side by side with great wealth'. Maynard Keynes, in the twenties, resisted the hereditary 'lethargy' of the orthodox view of *laisser-faire*:

> It is *not* true that individuals possess a prescriptive 'natural liberty' in their economic activities. There is *no* 'compact' conferring perpetual rights on those who Have or on those who Acquire. The world is *not* so governed from above that private and social interest always coincide ...
>
> (J. M. Keynes, *End of Laisser-faire*, 1926)

and so on. The need was to distinguish, more comprehensively but in Bentham's terms, the *Agenda*, and the *Non-Agenda*, of government.

Keynes, of course, was not a socialist planner; he aimed rather at 'improvements in the technique of modern Capitalism by the agency of collective action'. Others, during the economic crisis of the thirties, were much more forthright in demanding full planning. The example of Russian planned economy was frequently invoked, sometimes with a cautious warning against the violent means employed, as in Barbara

Wootton's *Plan or No Plan*, sometimes with an acceptance of the inevitable possibility of violence, as in John Strachey's *The Theory and Practice of Socialism*. The Webbs visited Russia and proclaimed its virtues: A New Civilization.

For, indeed, as Kingsley Martin pointed out in his biography of Harold Laski, the effect of the 1931 crisis, when MacDonald, Snowden, and Thomas defected from the Labour party and the National Government was set up, was to change the philosophy of a large part of the Labour party. Previously, among the intellectual strands which had gone to form British Socialism, 'including Chartist Radicalism, Owenite optimism, Christian Socialism, William Morris romanticism, Fabianism and Marxist materialism, the last had been the least important. After 1931 it became dominant, not yet in action, but as a matter of increasingly accepted theory.'

Arthur Koestler has evoked, in his autobiography, the emotional impact and the intellectual attraction of Marxism:

> ... born out of the despair of world war and civil war, of social unrest and economic chaos, the desire for a complete break with the past, for starting human history from scratch, was deep and genuine. In this apocalyptic climate dadaism, futurism, surrealism and the Five-year-plan-mystique came together in a curious amalgam. Moved by a perhaps similar mood of despair, John Donne had begged: 'Moist with a drop of Thy blood my dry soule.' The mystic of the nineteen-thirties yearned, as a sign of Grace, for a look at the Dnieper Dam and a three per cent increase in the Soviet pig-iron production.

The age of anxiety evoked, in some hearts, a desire for the comforts of a simplifying formula or of a closed system, like Marxism, providing all the answers. R. H. S. Crossman refers in his introduction to *The God that Failed* to the attractions of an 'unquestioned purpose', the peace of intellectual doubt and uncertainty in subjecting one's soul to the 'canon law of the Kremlin'. Symptomatically, many disillusioned communists turned to the Catholic church. Marxism as a serious force amongst intellectuals did not survive the post-war political behaviour of Russia; disillusionment had already been expressed before the war by writers like Orwell and Gide, though war-time exigencies temporarily silenced doubts. Nevertheless, the concern for social improvement which was one of the motive forces of the 'pink decade' continued, in psychological as well as economic terms. 'Security', as defined by Beveridge, rather than simply 'wealth' – the cash-nexus – becomes politically important. 'Want, Disease, Ignorance, Squalor, and Idleness' were the giants against which Beveridge tilted: the terms in which Ignorance was tackled represent, even if rather tritely, the extent to which we have moved beyond the cynicism of educating our masters:

> In the development of education lies the most important, if not the most urgent, of all the tasks of reconstruction. The needs of civilized man are illimitable, because they include the wise, happy enjoyment of leisure!

The section in which this appears is headed, symptomatically, 'Social Conscience as Driving Force'.

The attempted organization of the state in terms of community 'needs' rather than for individual 'exploitation' has been paralleled in a number of other fields, where two somewhat contradictory principles have been at work: a socio-political egalitarianism and a scientistic assessment of the importance of the group – particularly the primary group – in human contentment. Notions of permissiveness, to replace the older more authoritative patterns and influenced, perhaps, by a model derived from free-association techniques in psycho-therapy, are much mooted. The resultant gain in personal freedom, however, has been matched by new manifestations of group tyranny. Modern psychology stresses group dynamics rather than individual behaviour, the total configuration rather than the isolate. Group therapy appears alongside individual treatment; group methods involving 'projects' are recommended in schools to replace the old individualistic competitive pattern. The comprehensive experiment in education urges the benefits of social intermingling in the same breath that it plays up the needs of the Meritocracy. Business men with advanced views proclaim industry as fulfilling a social as well as an economic function. The notion of 'adjustment' to society comes to play an important part as a value concept. Diseased aspects of society or a variety of other external causes, rather than individual wickedness, have for long been blamed for increased delinquency and crime; as Barbara Wootton puts it in her *Social Science and Social*

Pathology (1959), 'the logical drive, in modern social science, away from notions of individual responsibility is very powerful'. A social psychologist, like J. A. C. Brown, can write that 'the primary group is the basic unit of society, not the individual' (*The Social Psychology of Industry*, 1954).

Though the movement in England is as yet fitful, tentative, and spasmodic, and has not yet warranted the riposte it has earned in William H. Whyte's *Organization Man* in America, the book can be appreciated here in terms of contemporary trends. The problem of the old ethic was man's indifference to man; that of the new, man's too confident and complete assumption of concern. With typical insight and brilliance de Tocqueville foresaw the dilemma:

> In the principle of equality I very clearly discern two tendencies; the one leading the mind of every man to untried thoughts, the other inclined to prohibit him from thinking at all. And I perceive how, under the dominion of certain laws, democracy would extinguish that liberty of the mind to which a democratic social condition is favourable; so that, after having broken all the bondage once imposed on it by ranks or by men, the human mind would be closely fettered to the general will of the greatest number.
>
> (*Democracy in America*)

At the same time, warnings against the totalitarian implications of state interference have grown apace since 1945. There has been *1984* and *The Yogi and the Commissar*. Karl Popper's *The Open Society and its Enemies* reasserted liberal values, and his *Poverty of Historicism* protests against notions of historical inevitability. F. A. Hayek's *Road to Serfdom* was anti-Left in attitude; and when, in 1951, Michael Oakeshott replaced Harold Laski in the chair of Political Science at the London School of Economics, so long associated with socialist views, a philosopher in the Burke tradition replaced an English Marxist. Nevertheless, the growing classlessness of the young points to a homogenization of social attitude which bodes ill for the future. The new élite are essentially anti-élitist.

Problems of popular culture

The problem de Tocqueville saw has not, contrary to some expectations, been assuaged by the new literacy of the masses and their consequent political and social emancipation. The commercial development of various media of mass communication has fostered further that trading spirit which de Tocqueville diagnosed as having already affected literature by 1840. Since the aim, cynically overt or sententiously wrapped up, is so often quick profits, the tendency has been to appeal at a low level of public taste on the assumption that this will bring about the largest quantitative return.

The case for the new age of industrial democracy has been stated by John Dewey: he is pointing out how learning is no longer a 'class matter':

> ... as a direct result of the industrial revolution ... this has been changed. Printing was invented; it was made commercial. Books, magazines, papers were multiplied and cheapened. As a result of the locomotive and telegraph, frequent, rapid and cheap intercommunication by mails and electricity was called into being ... The result has been an intellectual revolution. Learning has been put in circulation ... Stimuli of an intellectual sort pour in upon us in all kinds of ways.
>
> (*School and Society*, 1900)

His near contemporary, Henry James, would hardly have agreed that these advantages necessarily produced that intellectual renaissance Dewey seemed to be expecting. And the more relevant diagnosis seems to be that implicit in F. R. Leavis's remark: 'It is as if society, in so complicating and extending the machinery of organization, had lost intelligence, memory, and moral purpose.'

The coming of universal literacy, following the Education Act of 1870, indeed, produced no such anticipated advances in rationality as the utilitarian theorists had prophesied. Indeed, our current educational dilemmas merely serve to highlight our inability to find an adequate substitute for the old culture of the people – expressed in folk song and dance, rustic craft and natural lore – which industrialism has destroyed. Where the secondary modern curriculum has been concerned, for instance, neither the encouragement of that 'practical' bent said to characterize those of inferior intellectual capacities nor the more 'democratic' suggestion of the common core curriculum meets the case satisfactorily. Hence the move towards de-schooling.

Where popular reading is concerned – here the effect of the new literacy can be assessed – there would seem to be some evidence of a decline in quality.[3] Certainly, popular reading matter of the twentieth century has demonstrated a distressing poverty in the imaginative life of the people. The sort of cultural and moral desiccation represented by the attitudes of a Northcliffe and those of his heirs reveals itself in a variety of ways. What is almost worse than the vulgarity, triviality, and sensationalism implicit in the sort of emphases the news receives and in the methods of exploitation and presentation, is the standard of human relationship tacitly accepted in the journalist's search for news. Harold Laski described his humiliations during the libel case he brought in 1946 in a bitterly felt account of what modern publicity entails:

> ... the photographers – a merciless and determined race – await you as you enter the big doors of the Courts, begging you to pose ... They run in front of you as you approach the bus ... The notion that you have some right to privacy either does not enter their minds, or is mercilessly thrust on one side in the knowledge that your temporary publicity is the basis upon which they may earn an extra half-guinea...

If the ethics of business enterprise with its consequent emphasis on material consumption are accepted, advertising has a necessary place in the economy; yet its effect in creating stereotypes, in stimulating the baser aspects of human nature – fear of social nonconformity, snobbery, resentment at the demands of work – must rank high in any assessment of deleterious influences on the twentieth-century consciousness. In the same way, the various forms of popular literature – crime or love stories – are to be condemned, not because they incite to violence and rape, but because the attitudes they involve in important matters of human relationship and moral choice are obstructive to finer or more subtle responses. The expectations about human behaviour aroused by the ordinary work of popular fiction or popular magazine story involve grossly over-simplified stereotypes which, to addicts, must to some extent interfere with their ability to understand those with whom they have to live in close personal contact, as in family life. At the very least, they debase the medium of social intercourse, language, and when that happens, 'the whole machinery of social and individual thought and order goes to pot', as Ezra Pound put it.

Again, twentieth-century technical developments have produced a variety of mass media of communication – the cinema, the television, the wireless – of, as yet, unmeasured potency, though it is already clear that the radio and television are of some political effectiveness. As important is the fact that night after night a selection of programmes of inane triviality seems to be acceptable to millions of people. And these, it is necessary to remind ourselves, are the 'educated' and literate descendants of the people who produced the folk song and the folk tale, who built the parish churches and nourished Bunyan.

The whole problem of the effects of bad art has indeed become one of incalculable importance in our times. I. A. Richards wrote in *Principles of Literary Criticism* (1924),

> At present bad literature, bad art, the cinema, etc., are an influence of the first importance in fixing immature and actually inapplicable attitudes to most things. Even the decision as to what constitutes a pretty girl or a handsome young man, an affair apparently natural and personal enough, is largely determined by magazine covers and movie stars.

In recent years a good deal of work has been done in America, and latterly in this country, in an attempt to measure these influences in more precise terms than those provided by the 'moralizing literati' of the last two hundred years. Effects, it has been realized, are matters of some complexity; a simple extrapolation from content analysis is insufficient. The manifestations of popular culture need to be seen as influences working amid other factors in a total configuration; in the words of a social scientist:

> ... the effects of communications can be many and diverse, they may operate at different levels and in different strengths, they may manifest themselves in different ways or they may be latent, and they may derive from different aspects of the content and different parts of the communication process. However, in spite of these difficulties and with due allowance for the incomplete nature of the evidence, it will be seen that what evidence there is suggests that the media have effects and that it would be wrong to assume that these effects are wholly good.
>
> (J. D. Halloran, *The Effects of Mass Communication*, 1964)

Indeed, evidence of the deleterious effects of the cheaper manifestations of the media is growing, even though it is realized that these effects differ in relation to the predispositions of the receiving agent. At best there is often the negative result of wasted opportunities and emotional energies dissipated in unselective television viewing; for instance:

> The defenders of television are ever ready to claim that the medium can improve and widen tastes and stimulate interests in creative activities. The evidence available does not support these claims. (ibid.)

Positive effects on some recipients, as in matters of personal dress, hair style, make-up and house furnishing, as well as in some of the intimacies of human behaviour, such as love making, have been recorded. The implication is that, at times at least, many people live fantasy existences derived from the shadow lives of the screen; they acquire, if only temporarily, models of behaviour. It may be that 'conclusive evidence about communication effects is still inadequate'; but there is enough to show that the 'moralizing literati' have a case. In any case, Marshall McLuhan has caused us to suspect that even the medium itself may have unsuspected implications: the medium, as well as the content, 'is the message'. This at a time, too, when the nature of the work performed by the masses stimulates less and less to a sense of reality, to a grappling with the intractable nature of materials and substances in the individual and personal creative effort of the craftsman to induce form on the formless. The impersonal machine functions instead. Hannah Arendt's indictment has behind it a complex and powerful analysis of the development of modern attitudes: it is, she writes,

> ... as though individual life had actually been submerged in the over-all life process of the species and the only active decision still required of the individual were to let go, so to speak, to abandon his individuality, the still individually sensed pain and trouble of living, and acquiesce in a dazed, 'tranquillized', functional type of behaviour ... It is quite conceivable that the modern age – which began with such an unprecedented and promising outburst of human activity – may end in the deadliest, most sterile passivity history has ever known. (*The Human Condition*, 1958)

Certainly there is a danger of a positive 'fixing' of psychic expectation and 'idea'.

> The girl who is going to fall in love knows all about it beforehand from books and the movies ... she knows exactly how she feels when her lover or husband betrays her or when she betrays him: she knows precisely what it is to be a forsaken wife, an adoring mother, an erratic grandmother. All at the age of eighteen. (D. H. Lawrence)

Growth, then, is fixated. Mr Hoggart was diagnosing something similar when he noted that so much popular music consists of

> strictly conventional songs; their aim is to present to the hearer a known pattern of emotions; they are not so much creations in their own right as structures of conventional signs for the emotional fields they open.
>
> (*The Uses of Literacy*)

Constant Lambert, in his *Music Ho*, made the same point. To use Lawrence's terminology, such 'idealization' implies the death of the dynamic personality. By contrast it has seemed to many critics of the twentieth century that it is precisely the function of great literature to foster growth, to break down such stereotypes: in Dr Leavis's view, to speak out for 'life'.

Part of the trouble, of course, has been the increasing 'rootlessness' of the modern world – one which the modern 'angries' exploited:

> 'Was that,' my friend smiled, 'where you "have your roots"?'
> No, only where my childhood was unspent,
> I wanted to retort, just where I started. (Philip Larkin)

Greatly increased mobility has implied a lack of continuity of environment and a consequent superficializing of relationships. The antagonism between the generations, a theme as old as the gods, has become more overt and uncontrolled owing to the moral uncertainties of the older generation, the acceptance of adolescence as a time of 'revolt', and the insidious exploitation of young people for commercial and political reasons by affording them a spurious 'importance'; hence the development of the teen-age market and the granting of votes at eighteen. Symptomatic of the moral rootlessness is the kaleidoscopic progression of fashions, intellectual and otherwise, which characterizes our age:

> The generations are extraordinarily short-lived. I can count up the intellectual fashions that have taken and held my students for a brief space. When I began in 1907 there was a wave of social idealism. Then ... suffrage, then syndicalism, then the war ... then Freud ... It's lost labour to refute these things – they just die out in time. (L. T. Hobhouse)

For some time it has become fashionable to attack this general view of cultural malaise on two grounds: that it springs from a sentimentalization and over-estimation of a past which only *seems* to offer more coherent and preferable standards – things have never really been different – and that it underestimates the very real advantages of the present and ignores 'growing-points' of our civilization. Moral uncertainty, it is argued, is a positive gain: 'It is precisely our uncertainty which brings us a good deal closer to reality than was possible in former periods which had faith in the absolute' (K. Mannheim). There have been immense strides in material well-being and in the banishing of poverty. In a world increasingly aware of the dangers of over-specialization, the relative popularity of the agencies for cultural dissemination – the work of the Arts Council, the Third Programme (now defunct), the encouraging sales of good-quality paperback books and classical gramophone records, and so on – seems to indicate a more widely diffused seriousness of interest. Vigorous experiment in the fields of music, painting, architecture, and industrial design is cited as evidence of vitality, change being thought a mark of cultural vigour rather than a symptom of break-down of cultural continuity. Science provides an alternative culture – C. P. Snow's Two Culture theory. Raymond Williams points to our misuse of the notion of the 'masses' and notes signs of cultural vitality within the working classes. The current interest in education is said to indicate a concern for values beyond the purely material.

Furthermore, surely, in very recent years there have been signs of a general renaissance at the more popular levels. Entertainment has no longer been so passive – witness 'rock', skiffle, and beat music. The popular music of the sixties has been defined by Professor Hoggart as 'muscular'; he compares its vital working-class characteristics with the insipidities of middle-class popular music of earlier years of the century very much to the advantage of the former. Interest in folk music has spread and a new 'folk' related to the social and political problems of the sixties has arisen. Young people especially are no longer willing to accept the conventions and restrictions of our society – students protest and revolt against a materialistic profit-ridden view of society; they wage war on want and inveigh against the inhumanity of Vietnam and Biafra. The minority *avant-garde* has forged links with popular cultural manifestations – as the Lichtenstein exhibition at the Tate Gallery and the wooing of 'pop' in the quality Sunday weeklies, to mention but two among a number of manifestations, would seem to indicate.

The complexities of assessing the relative movements of a whole civilization are so immense that it is only right that such counter-charges should be carefully noted. Certainly, that my indictment has been repeated from Wordsworth and Coleridge to Lawrence and Leavis seems to indicate a continuity of awareness which is encouraging and does something to nullify the charges made – this one can grant. Yet, some writers and critics might reply, the new complacency sidesteps the assumption on which their work is based, that great literature is not peripheral, but remains, after the decay of organized religion, one of the few means through which we can appraise the nature and quality of our lives and is therefore vital to any strenuous attempt to define the nature of the good life. Indeed, it cannot be a matter of indifference that earlier in our period practically no writer of major stature failed to lament an isolation enforced on him by public apathy or even hostility. (There are today – 1972 – no longer any major writers of this stature left to lament.) Nor, if literature is accepted as a presentation of 'felt' life, is it possible to brush aside as mistaken the testimony of its most powerful practitioners on a matter so fundamental as their relationship with their audience. For the nature of their analysis is of a very different sort from that of Johnson's easy and unselfconscious appeal to the 'common voice of the multitude, uninstructed by precept and unprejudiced by authority', or Dryden's complacent comment on his Elizabethan predecessors: 'Greatness was not then so easy to assess, nor conversation so free, as it now is.' It may be that this is the price of democratization; it is no use, however, burking the fact that there is a price and that it is a serious one. Today, there is none of that interpenetration of artistic, social, and political life that characterized the Augustan age. And this at a time when the implications of C. P. Snow's 'scientific revolution' of 'electronics, atomic energy, automation' with its repercussions for work and leisure are being forced upon us as part of the foreseeable future.

Indeed, the pleading to which I have just referred could in itself be regarded as symptomatic of a weakening of consciousness, if not always necessarily of conscience. The notion of 'Mass Civilization and Minority Culture' has been attacked on the grounds of its inadequate formulation of the complexities inherent in 'mass' civilization. It would be as relevant to note that the 'minority', in the literary field alone, subdivided, proliferated, and disagreed. Bloomsbury's all too self-contained aestheticism, *Scrutiny*'s reassertion of the puritan, ethical virtues, and 'Eng. Lit.'s' academic cohorts intent on the claims of scholarship, indicated a serious cleavage in what was still exiguous opinion. *Scrutiny* (1932–53) contained major revaluations over a wide range of literature in addition to challenging repudiations of 'aesthetic' and 'academic' values manifest, one in the belle-lettrist tradition and the other in scholarship uninformed by critical sensibility, and of the 'associational process' which accompanies both. This brought it into conflict with Bloomsbury, which countered with charges of a 'scientific' intrusion into the proper work of aesthetic criticism, and with certain academics, who flung charges of inadequate learning against a few of *Scrutiny*'s historical reassessments. Latterly, the 'minority' weeklies and monthlies have suffered a further debilitation of standards which is manifest in the staggering judgements too often perpetrated in their pages. That this is not exactly a new phenomenon – witness the late-nineteenth-century craze for Marie Corelli in unexpected places – does not warrant our failing to see in, say, the astonishing reaction to the Beatles in the quality press (cf. the notorious comments of *The Times* critic among others) an unhappy portent.

There is, indeed, little reason to attach much significance to the current protests of young people against the mechanical and materialistic nature of our civilization. Superficially correct though their indictment may seem to be, it is to be remembered that not all protests are the same protest; the informed, carefully detailed criticisms of great artists, balanced by acceptable positive affirmations of substance and quality, constitute a very different form of result from the naïve dissentient views of student agitators or the opting out of the 'hippies' and the drug takers. Seemingly united in protest against something – one is tempted to write 'anything' – positively their suggestions are thin and unconvincing; and their protests afford evidence of a widespread and growing repudiation of the disciplines necessary for civilization – even for civility – rather than reveal any profound penetration into the ills of a declining culture. Beat music, Neo-dadaism, the cult of the working classes revealed in speech and dress (a modern form of romantic pastoralism), the acceptance of the anti-hero, instant art in the guise of the ready-made, or at the behest of chance, permissive sex, the flight into alcohol and drugs, all manifest a common basis in the repudiation of effort and sacrifice, the search for momentary sensations, the acceptance of the anti-rational and the mindless. The 'revolt' in the terms in which it has defined itself is as stultifying as the mechanical order against which it is protesting. They constitute different sides of the same coin: a point made by Christopher Booker in *The Neophiliacs*. Here he explains the revolution of English life in the fifties and sixties in terms of the acceptance of a collective 'dream image', arising out of a fusion of *avant-garde* and popular culture, and sustained by '"liberal intellectuals", many of whom were beginning to see in the rebelliousness, the disregard for authority and the frantic search for thrills, an image of powerful attractions'. Even if the book in fact employs the very techniques of sensational utterance it is concerned to deprecate, its documentation is not unimpressive. And what it points to is an element of fantasy and neurosis in our collective life of dangerous implications. On the one hand we have been taken up with the technological dream of mastery over the environment; on the other hand we have succumbed to the libertarian dream of ridding ourselves of our inhibitions and impressions, becoming 'trousered apes':

> ... the former ... by in some way distorting man's views of his place in nature and reducing his civilization to an even more unnatural and mechanical conformity, produces the latter, made up of all the individual and group-fantasies of a society in disintegration.

The writer's response to his age

The high degree of social and experiential awareness on the part of the modern writer enables us, without much difficulty, to relate social and intellectual background to the nature of literary preoccupation in the twentieth century. The matter can be approached through a realization that such 'awareness' manifests itself in very different guise in the great creative artist from what it does in, say, the social scientist, whose increased importance has been noted above. What the writer ideally commits himself to, in effect, is a process of defining the implications of experience as a prerequisite to the right ordering of personal and social life. Particularly is he the enemy of those abstractions which have clogged our consciousness as a result of the rationalist, positivist tradition. Thus he pursues his sense of the 'real' beneath the level attainable (as yet, at least) by the scientific sociologist; where the latter conceptualizes, the former, at his best, attempts to employ a more unified interplay of feeling and intellect, one which defines itself through the emotive complexities of language. He *feels into* situations rather than subjects them to rational and therefore extraverted analysis. He is essentially the practitioner of '*Verstehen*'.

Lawrence, indeed, in the name of that ultimate spark of spontaneity, the essential uniqueness, the essential untouchable naïvety at the centre of all true human beings, rejected both the false 'individuality' of the liberal tradition and the increasing socialization of his times. His triumph was to see them as joint manifestations of the same basic outlook, involving the elevation of the '*ego* or spurious self, the conscious entity with which every individual is saddled' – the conceptualizing self, not the unified sensibility. In essence, too, this was his case against the positivist assault. In reaction against the abstraction of the intellect, the failure of 'reason' to capture adequately the sheer flux and flow of experience, there has been a counter-assertion of the need to convey emotional immediacy, a grasping after the moment, a subjective insistence on the force of inner feeling, what Dr Holloway, in his survey, describes as the Romantic preoccupation.

T. S. Eliot's notion of the 'dissociation of sensibility', whatever it may indicate about certain movements of consciousness in the seventeenth century, reveals a diagnostic impulse of the twentieth-century poet in positing an unhealthy split between 'thought' and 'feeling'. Eliot's summing-up of Donne's sensibility: 'An idea was an experience; it modified his sensibility' implies a contemporary criticism of the conceptualizing ego. Part of its tyranny has been over the tool of the artist, language: so that Yeats repudiates the Ibsenite tradition, the drama of idea, as that of those who 'write in the impersonal language that has come, not out of individual life, nor out of life at all, but out of the necessities of commerce, of parliament, of Board schools, of hurried journeys by rail'; and this 'death of language, this substitution of phrases as nearly impersonal as algebra for words and rhythms varying from man to man, is but a part of the tyranny of impersonal things'. Yeats, in praising Synge for being 'by nature unfitted to think a political thought', had in mind the same sort of criterion as had Eliot in appraising Henry James for having too fine a mind for it ever to be violated by an idea.

Yet, in accepting Eliot's diagnosis of 'dissociation', we are still in a world where the 'idea' is acknowledged – even if as something to 'touch and stroke', to '*feel*' rather than to inter in conceptualization. What he – and Lawrence, for that matter – advocate is the *unified* sensibility; the aim is to catch 'the whole man alive' in terms of the feeling intellect, not the surrender to pure emotion. There have, however, been more extreme manifestations of irrationality – in line with a movement 'which in its various hues may be called irrationalism, vitalism, pragmatism or pure empiricism' – all of which Santayana diagnoses as 'extreme expressions of romantic anarchy':

> Immediate feeling, pure experience, is the only reality, the only fact ... Truth, according to Mr Bergson, is given only in intuitions which prolong experience just as it occurs, in its full immediacy; on the other hand, all representation, thought, theory, calculation, and discourse is so much mutilation of the truth, excusable only because imposed upon us by practical exigencies. (*Winds of Doctrine*, 1912)

D. H. Lawrence, with his protests against 'idealization' and his assertion of the poetry of 'the immediate present' which has 'no perfection, no consummation, nothing finished', asked:

> The ideal – what is the ideal? A figment. An abstraction. ... It is a fragment of the before and after. It is a crystallized aspiration, or a crystallized remembrance: crystallized, set, finished. It is a thing set apart, in the great storehouse of eternity, the storehouse of finished things.

> We do not speak of things crystallized and set apart. We speak of the instant, the immediate self, the very plasma of the self. (Preface to *Poems*)

Though his practice, in the main, belied his theory, for in Lawrence the intelligence usually accompanies the feeling, nevertheless such formulations point to an influential notion of experience as a continuum rather than as something divisible into discrete entities. William James, the pragmatist, from whom the notion of 'stream of consciousness' partly derives, thus defines consciousness:

> ... consciousness, then, does not appear to itself chopped up in bits ... It is nothing jointed; it flows. A 'river' or 'stream' are the metaphors by which it is most naturally described. In talking of it hereafter, let us call it the stream of thought, of consciousness, or of subjective life.
> (*Principles of Psychology*)

Psychological atomism, inherent in associationist ideas, has been challenged by 'gestalt' theories. The relationship between mind and world becomes one of 'transaction' in John Dewey's sense of the term, not 'interaction' with its implications of discreteness. To William James, as we see, experience, reality constituted a continuum. (It is relevant to remember that Henry James, after receiving his brother's book, confessed to having been a pragmatist all his life.)

> I found myself compelled to *give up* logic, fairly, squarely, irrevocably ... It has an imperishable use in human life, but that use is not to make us theoretically acquainted with the essential nature of reality ... I find myself no good warrant for even suspecting the existence of any reality of a higher denomination than that distributed and strung along and flowing sort of reality we finite beings swim in. That is the sort of reality given us, and that is the sort with which logic is so incommensurable. (op. cit.)

These tendencies, important in the development of 'stream of consciousness' fiction, were reinforced by Bergson and his assertions of the superior claims of intuition over intelligence in the apprehension of reality; the artist 'becomes the flag-bearer of intuition in its interminable struggle against logic and reason'. Where the use of words is concerned,

> The truth is that the writer's art consists above all in making us forget that he uses words. The harmony he seeks is a certain correspondence between the movements of his mind and the phrasing of his speech, a correspondence so perfect that the undulations of his thought, born of the sentence, stir us sympathetically; consequently the words, taken individually, no longer count. There is nothing left but the flow of meaning which pervades the words, nothing but two minds, without the presence of an intermediary, which appear to vibrate sympathetically. The rhythm of speech has, then, no other object than the reproduction of the rhythm of thought.

Bergson praised music as the finest of the arts, and notions of *leitmotiv* and counterpoint greatly affect writings in the earlier years of the century – for example, those of Virginia Woolf and Huxley in this country and Proust abroad. The analogy is often repeated – Forster calls music the novel's 'nearest parallel'.

The Freudian unconscious, too, represents a continuum unmodified by the abstracting power of logical thought; and in an ill-guided moment, Freud referred to the unconscious as 'the true psychic reality'. The dream reveals its functioning as nearly as the 'censor' will allow; and the dream displays a curious blending and intermingling of experiences, a telescoping of time and place which only the significantly named technique of 'free association' can, by delving below the normal levels of logic and rationality in waking life, expound. When free analysis fails, a form of symbolism is brought into operation which implies a continuity between the individual consciousness and the life of the race; and Freud linked this symbolism with that found in 'fairy tales, myths, and legends, in jokes and in folklore'.

The prevalence of such notions encouraged a number of efforts to transcend the abstracting, configurating force of the rational ego. In essence they provoke a series of 'raids on the inarticulate', the basic function of which is to seek an answer to the question, 'Who am I and what is the nature of my experience?' They represent, that is, extreme varieties of the romantic mode. The most successful, because the most intelligently controlled, can be noted in Lawrence's attempt to probe below 'the old stable *ego* of the character', noted in a letter commenting on *The Rainbow*.

Those who employed a form of stream of consciousness technique, Dorothy Richardson, James Joyce, to some extent Virginia Woolf, and the inferior hangers-on, like Gertrude Stein, the Dadaists, the Futurists, the more naïve symbolists and surrealists in writing and in painting, the abstract expressionists, all stem from the same root, even if the fruits they brought forth vary immensely in richness. In a world of increasing socialization, standardization, uniformity, the aim was to stress uniqueness, the purely personal in experience; in one of 'mechanical' rationality, to assert other modes through which human beings can express themselves, to see life as a series of emotional intensities involving a logic different from that of the rational world and capturable only in dissociated images or stream of consciousness musings. They represent the counter-culture before the term was invented. The 'beats' and 'angries' and the hippies, in somewhat different terms, repeat in the post-war world the essential element of social repudiation. 'Opting out', in the middle and late sixties, has become an occupational hazard where the young are concerned; in its most extreme form it manifests itself in the 'trip' induced by drug-taking.)

Two comments can perhaps be made. The notion of 'experience' as a 'transaction' between subject and object implies the abandonment of the two-world theory inherited from Greek distinctions between 'appearance' and 'reality'. This may explain the concern for surfaces which has characterized a good deal of the writing of the last forty years – 'I am a Camera'. 'Posters, shop windows, anything stuck on the walls around us. I believe these images constitute our profundity,' M. Alain Robbe-Grillet said in a newspaper interview. 'The essence of modern man ... is no longer to be found within a hidden soul, but plastered on hoardings.' Recent developments in the cinema – Godard, Fellini, etc. – bear out this diagnosis. The appearance, the 'image', *is* the reality. The modern writer and the scientist both agree at least to the extent that both see life as Process and Flux, and both admit a degree of personal choice in the handling of 'experience'.

The other point is that one sees in such reassertions of the psychic balance against the influence of mechanization attempts to heal the rift which lies at the heart of our modern consciousness. It is true that the extremer forms – surrealism, surrender to the passing emotion, *avant-gardism* – are as life-destroying as the disease they seek to cure. Nevertheless, in a 'much-divided civilization', one, moreover, where the claims of technology are becoming increasingly insistent, the role of the greatest writers, where intellect is suffused with emotion and emotion controlled by intelligence, points a way to 'unity of being' – or, as the modern idiom has it, psychic wholeness and health. In such a fusion, intuitive insight and moral control coalesce. Obviously, it is necessary to insist (I quote Dr Leavis), 'a real literary interest is an interest in man, society, and civilization'.

The last twelve years

I have been interested to discover, as I have revised this chapter nearly twelve years after it was originally written, how comparatively little I have needed to alter other than to amplify the account of trends already noted by citing more immediate examples. But in one respect the cultural situation has become more alarming than it was twelve years ago; and as this is a central issue in a book devoted to the literature of a period it seems advisable to spell out what I mean more explicitly. What I refer to is the further dissolution of the minority: the obliteration, indeed, of the ideals of the Renaissance.

I have already noted earlier that the minority had 'subdivided, proliferated and disagreed'; what was not so apparent twelve years ago was the *extent* to which it was proposing to abdicate. In some respects, of course, the minority has become more and more sophisticated. Many scientific and technical triumphs have been recorded during the last decade, of which the conquest of space and the heart transplants have only been the most widely publicized. In other words, where expertise has been concerned there has been rapid, in some cases, spectacular advance. But the specialized triumphs, it is becoming increasingly apparent, have been bought at the expense of general cultivation. The reasons why advocates of liberal education from Aristotle through Castiglione to but yesterday have continually opposed virtuosity, a narrow expertise, as inimical to true liberality have become all too clear.

What I am getting at has been admirably diagnosed by Saul Bellow in an article in the *Observer* (8 December 1968):

> In the 17th and 18th centuries the public was small, but highly educated and cultivated.... In the 19th century there appeared a mass public, the readers of Dickens, Thackeray and Trollope. By the end of that century, there had appeared a second and very small public interested in Baudelaire, Mallarmé, and, a little later, Proust and Joyce. There were two publics. Now

> again we have a single public. The methods of the small-public masters have been generally assimilated. Even the mass media employ the techniques of Joyce. ... In fact, all the traditions of art have been absorbed into the movies, television, fashion and smart journalism. Our new public is by now university-educated, but it would be incorrect to compare it to the aristocratic public of the 18th century. University education has not instilled good taste, has not refined the judgement of readers. The literary conversation of educated people can frighten a writer to death.

What Mr Bellow perhaps fails to bring out with sufficient explicitness is that this absorption has been a two-way process. If the techniques of the *former* 'advanced' writers and painters (Joyce, Picasso) have been absorbed and utilized by the mass media and the world of fashion (thus undoubtedly helping to make the mass public more alert and quicker witted), it is equally true to say that the present *avant-garde* has increasingly looked for its source material and its emotional circumambience within the world of popular culture. The minority and the majority, in fact, have drawn together: Lichtenstein uses the strip cartoon, and the Beatles produced pastiche of Joyce or Dylan Thomas. The necessary outcome of this process is, in the sphere of the arts, a homogenizing of emotional range; and indeed, it is this which has become increasingly apparent during the last few years. The themes chosen by 'serious' writers have more and more exploited violence and an interest in the cruder forms of sex. The net result has been to display a restricted and inadequate account of human possibility and potentiality; and human beings are correspondingly diminished. Thus we have seen the heroic deprecated, pride and honour under a cloud, decorum and grace ignored; in becoming assimilated to the largely corrupt world of popular art, the writer with serious pretensions has forgotten the first rule of artistic integrity, the need for fidelity to the range of man's potential rather than a surrender to a temporary vehemence. (This is what Keats implied by 'negative capability'.) Otherwise he becomes sentimental and eccentric; and this, in fact, is just what he has become. To display the world as totally disruptive, violent, and regressive is to distort the human situation even in an era which is marked by a good deal of violence, disruption, and regression. Furthermore, it is to reduce man to the level of a 'Trousered Ape', to evoke the title of a recent book by Professor Duncan Williams.

A hundred years ago Matthew Arnold expressed certain doubts about Swiss democracy: it had become, he said, 'socialistic, in the sense in which that word expresses a principle hostile to the interests of true society – *the elimination of superiorities*'. What indeed is needed in even a democratic society, if it is to survive, is 'superiority' in two senses; superiority of insight on the part of writers, so that the worst *and the best* can be faced without distorting emphasis on the one or the other; and superiority of manners as a part of general social behaviour so that literature has a context in which it can perform its traditional function of refining understanding and assisting moral discrimination. The two processes, of course, are interdependent; literature both feeds and is fed by the social process. When, however, literature focuses its attention, for reasons of profit or fashion, on a restricted aspect of the social situation it both offends against its own nature and furthers the disintegration of civility which rests, at even the best of times, on slender and brittle foundations. The net effect of the last few years has been to demonstrate – if further demonstration was necessary after the cultural *débâcle* of Nazi Germany and of Soviet Russia – the vital need for the preservation of a sense of cultural continuity (so that the eccentricities of the present can be more fully realized) and of loyalty to the circumstances of artistic integrity as opposed to those of fashion and over-anxious though selective social commitment – the 'fashionable conscience', as *The Times* leader has dubbed it (May 1970). It is now apparent, to an extent which was not true twelve years ago, that the isolation I referred to in the opening paragraphs of this essay was a source of strength as well as of weakness. Interest in the arts, it is true, has grown, though it is often the dealers' shops and the coffee tables that have benefited; the values implied are commercial and social rather than deeply personal. As Professor Quentin Bell has said:

> The art of painting has today something in common with *haute couture*: the artist need shrink from no audacity so long as he is audacious in a socially acceptable way and so long as his inventions have the charm of novelty.
>
> (*Crisis in the Humanities*, ed. J. H. Plumb)

I have referred above to the 'obliteration of the ideals of the Renaissance'. Certainly the penetration of high culture by popular and proletarian models points to the decay of élitism, a decay symbolized in the attacks on the private education system, the destruction of the grammar school and the 'massification' of higher education and of the universities. In education, the first great revolution of the Renaissance enthroned the ideal – essentially élitist – of the literate man of affairs; the second – that of our own century – has rejected such 'amateurism' in favour of a narrow expertise (so that we are faced with the brutality of minds that know a great deal about a little but not much about anything else). In *avant-garde* culture itself there is a reaction against tradition and memory in favour of individual sensation, discontinuity, chance, and the denial of form. The lack of an informed public invites any eccentricity that can make itself heard. The crisis of our times is not only a crisis at popular level; it has permeated all of our society. Sporadically – witness the Black Papers in education – there are signs of an attempted re-assertion of traditional standards, but the forces of change and instability are powerful and in accord with the overwhelming economic aspirations of the age.

NOTES

1. Cp. W. E. Houghton, *The Victorian Frame of Mind, 1830–1870*.

2. Cp. the rationalization of the coal mines by Gerald Crich in *Women in Love*. It may be that what Lawrence was getting at was 'Taylorism' or 'scientific management', which was a near-contemporary industrial manifestation. On the whole question of modern industrialism and its implications for work satisfaction and human relationships, the reader is strongly recommended to read Georges Friedmann's *Industrial Society*. One of the best attempts to characterize the nature of the mental climate induced by the machine is to be found in Chapter IX in Thorstein Vehlen's *The Theory of Business Enterprise*, where it is recognized that 'The discipline exercised by the mechanical occupations ... is a discipline of the habits of thought.' These habits of thought are defined at some length by Vehlen.

3. Professor Webb's article in the sixth volume of the *Guide* warns against over-emphasis on the homogeneity or seriousness of the Victorian reading public. Yet Miss Dalziel, in her *Popular Fiction 100 years Ago* (1957), considers that there are grounds to support Mrs Leavis's contention, made in *Fiction and the Reading Public* (1932), that there has been a deterioration in the quality of popular literature over the last hundred years, though those grounds are not quite the ones Mrs Leavis herself expresses.

PART
II

THE LITERARY SCENE

JOHN HOLLOWAY

Professor of Modern English, University of Cambridge

Introductory

THERE are certain things which the reader should bear in mind throughout this Survey, as fundamentals in the literary scene of the last sixty or seventy years. The first is that this has been a period in which, as a result of developments in the religious, political, economic, military, and other fields, men have more and more lost faith in certain traditional ways of seeing the world. This is not a change which began in 1900. Something like it is a great feature of the cultural life of the whole nineteenth century. It has gone conspicuously further, however, in the period which concerns this chapter: a period which has seen some writers reach an ultimate point along the line of bewilderment and disillusion, and others (or indeed, the same ones at another stage or in another phase) making a new start, and hammering out the terms of life afresh.

This is a fact about the period which has spread so wide, that it would be important for a survey of any aspect of its life; and it has been discussed at length in the preceding chapter. The second fundamental fact also spreads far beyond literature, but it concerns the literary scene quite as much as the first. It is that the age under review has conspicuously been one of popularization and commercialization. As a fundamental of modern life, this has also received attention by Professor Bantock. It has meant that literature and serious literary standards have had to survive in, and to one sense adapt themselves to, a world which has been largely alien to the attitudes, values, and assumptions that they most naturally require. Again, this development has a history throughout the nineteenth century. Wordsworth, Ruskin, and Matthew Arnold – to name only three of many – all noticed it as a deep-rooted feature of English life in their time. But the changes that they noticed have proceeded further; and serious writers, with those who most seriously care for literature and the continuance of literature, have been confronted with a society which in part relied, half-indifferently, upon the stock literary judgement, the best-seller, and the polite verse anthology, but which had forgotten that literature could touch life at both its deepest, and its most exhilarating.

These are familiar ideas. They have already been put forward by some of the more notable critical or social studies of our time.[1] Less often commented upon (if commented upon at all) is something which has arisen strictly within the field of serious literature and serious thinking about it, and which has given these wider facts about the mass nature and the commercialized nature of modern society a quite special importance. This is, that the period under review is one in which most important new work in literature has lent itself especially little to general consumption, or to a relaxed taste, or a taste influenced by non-literary interests. The main body of outstanding work written in the last half-century has been written under a special kind of influence which has necessarily made that work unfamiliar and difficult. This has been the influence of contemporary literature abroad; and, in the case of poetry especially, of a foreign school of poetry, that of certain late-nineteenth-century French writers, whose work was uniquely condensed and obscure.

Comparison with the mid nineteenth century may make this point clearer. Poets like Tennyson and Rossetti, prose writers like Arnold, novelists like George Eliot were not of course devoid of acquaintance with foreign writing: such a suggestion would be absurd. But their interests were not concentrated on, or even much directed to, truly contemporary and *avant-garde* authors abroad. Moreover, knowledge or interest is one thing, and seeking to learn massively about fundamental questions of writing, to naturalize new basic techniques and insights, is another. These are the processes which, over the last two generations, have so often been important. Relatively speaking, the mid-Victorian period was one in which English literature pursued a self-contained course. Certainly, this contrast may be over-simplified; it is not a black and white contrast. On the other hand, in seeing the period of this survey as one of major influence from abroad, we see in it something which has been recurrent in the development of our literature over centuries. More than once in the past, a period of comparative native independence has been succeeded by a period of major influence from continental Europe; this has been assimilated, and once again our literature has temporarily become more self-contained in its development. Indeed (to anticipate the whole argument of this chapter), it is on just this note of partial assimilation, and increasing independence, that this survey will close.

The opening scene

With these guiding ideas in mind, it is time to come to some details which may throw the changes of the last seventy years into relief; and to begin with, to reconstruct as a starting point something of the world, so different from our own, of the turn of the century.

Yeats, retrospecting in 1936, recalled the change at this very time. His tone does not invalidate what he says:

> Then in 1900 everybody got down off his stilts; henceforth nobody drank absinthe with his black coffee; nobody went mad; nobody committed suicide; nobody joined the Catholic Church; or if they did I have forgotten.
>
> (Introduction to *The Oxford Book of Modern Verse*, p. xi)

But the literary scene of the nineties spread far wider than the Rhymers' Club (their intentions, if not their achievement, being more down-to-earth than is usually realized)[2] and the 'Nineties Poets'. It spreads out to the whole opulent plutocratic social world of the time. This means the great country houses (James was an habitué) with their fashionable weekends; the great town houses (Lancaster Gate in *The Wings of the Dove*, Princes' Gate in real life, where Leyland the Liverpool shipping merchant collected his Japanese blue-and-white china, and Whistler created the famous 'Peacock Room'); and artistic Chelsea where Whistler, Wilde, Henry James, and Sargent were all near neighbours. It means also the reign of the 'actor-managers' in the London theatre (Irving at the Lyceum, Beerbohm Tree at His Majesty's giving Easter Shakespeare seasons – *A Midsummer Night's Dream* with real woods, bluebells, rabbits, *Macbeth* with witches that flew on wires and real guardsmen from Chelsea Barracks for the battle scenes); of the Leicester Square Alhambra, with its Moorish dreamland architecture and lavish shows, and the adjoining Empire with its notorious promenade, and the 'Gaiety

Girls' who married into the peerage (model wives, usually). Again, it means the great divorce scandals – Dilke, Parnell, Lady Colin Campbell. The third of these gave Frank Harris's scandal-journalism its first great opportunity and doubled his paper's circulation, all of them perhaps did something to strengthen the new preoccupations of Hardy's *Jude the Obscure* (1896) – though Hardy's concern with these matters is visible in *The Woodlanders* (1887) – and certainly supplied the scene for Pinero's *The Second Mrs Tanqueray* (1893) and Wilde's ironically named *An Ideal Husband* (1895). It is against this richly varied background, and as in a real sense not only the critic but also the chronicler of this world, its chronicler with unrivalled fullness, insight, and humanity, that Henry James must be seen.

The Spoils of Poynton (1897) is James's dramatization of the conflict between what Arnold would have called the 'Barbarian' aspect of this plutocracy, and the 'Aesthetic' one: first the vulgarizing, Edwardianizing Mona Brigstock, with her aspirations to transform the house of priceless art treasures by installing a winter garden and a billiard room; second Mrs Gareth, the 'treasure hunter' as James called her, yet herself a vulgarian in conduct (albeit an elegant one) and conscious of the fineness only of fine 'Things'. James makes it clear enough that Poynton in no way stands for the traditions of a true and enduring aristocracy. It has no special claim to its 'Spoils'. They are spoils in the full, satiric sense; the work of another Lord Duveen. The fire which destroys the house at the end (it is one of James's few triumphs purely as a descriptive writer) is no mere re-using of the closing move of Meredith's *Harry Richmond* (1871) or Hardy's *A Laodicean* (1881). James is making clear, finally, the worth as he sees it of 'Spoils' in life.

By the same token, *The Awkward Age* (1899) is not a title which refers merely to the dawning womanhood of its heroine. It is the age as a whole which is awkward: the reign of a plutocracy (shoe magnates, aristo-bureaucrats, an upper class whose chief media of living are elegant talk and the *liaison*) in which an older, plainer kind of integrity is neither possible nor, save to the peculiarly astute, even recognizable. In several of James's more important short stories, the plutocracy of his time is studied from the point of view of the writer: over and over again James reveals his conviction, sometimes with bitterness, that the social world of his time at bottom had little to offer the artist save a velvet-gloved exploitation and the kind of hollow applause which destroyed his real life and real work. *The Lesson of the Master* (1888) and *The Author of 'Beltraffio'* (1884) show writers spoilt through eagerness for pretty wives and the social veneer in which they mainly shone; *Broken Wings* (1900), a man and a woman writer who, for the illusory opulence of a life of country-house visits and the rest, have bartered away not only their best work but also their real lives as lovers. In *The Death of the Lion* (1894) the demands of the literary hostess upon her 'lion' are ultimately those of a homicide. *The Coxon Fund* (1894) shows the other side of the coin: literary patronage issues from a world without grasp or standards ('fancy constituting an endowment without establishing a tribunal – a bench of competent people – of judges') and can therefore do nothing but first select a largely bogus talent and then corrupt it. These two stories were both first published in *The Yellow Book* (1894–7): a fact which serves as reminder that James was nearer to the 'Aesthetic Movement' than one might now assume from the massive moral seriousness of his work; and that, for him, aesthetic perfection and moral significance were not opposed but – as in truth they are – complementary aspects of a single reality.

The interest of James, in this context, does not quite stop there. That one after another of his stories is about story-writing itself is an index, perhaps, that the world in which he moved did not give him as rich a field of real life as he craved for on behalf of the novelist.[3] Deeply and strongly as he saw into that world and grasped its limitations, those limitations elusively grasped him as well. This survey is not the place to enter into a full evaluation of the varied body of James's work. The problem here is of how that work belongs to and reflects its period: its place in a general scheme. In regard to this it seems as if what is best in James's work points mainly back to his American origin; and that the British (or in part European) scene of the turn of the century, as he used it in his later works, gave him something which in part he could turn to good effect, but not wholly so. James's distinction lies in the quick yet strong intelligence which unremittingly controls his work; in the clarity and nobility of his moral vision; and in his great sense of the richness and beauty of what at least is potential in human life. These qualities of intelligence, integrity, and idealism, this sense of what life can offer, are forcibly remininscent of what was best in the culture of New England, Boston,

Harvard, and New York in which James grew up. James's earlier work is largely set in America; and in it these qualities are intact (*The Europeans*, 1878; *Washington Square*, 1880). His genuineness is completely and splendidly reassuring in the larger and more ambitious *Portrait of a Lady* (1881). The work of his closing years, however, cannot be seen in quite the same light. He saw deficiencies in the kind of complexity and refinement which characterized this later period; yet these very things seem to colour his later work. As his world becomes more multitudinously self-reflecting and variegated, a doubt more and more preoccupies the reader. The doubt is, whether James's many-dimensional kaleidoscope of surfaces is after all a true revelation of deeper life in the characters, or only a wonderful simulacrum of deeper life. Nor can that doubt but be strengthened by James's growing tendency to invest his interplaying surfaces with all the grandiosity of Edwardian opulence; his growing dependence on words for his characters and their doings like 'fine', 'lovely', 'beautiful', 'tremendous', 'large', 'grand' ('they insisted enough that "stupendous" was the word': *The Wings of the Dove*, 1902, chapter 34); and this not as part of a total view, admire-but-judge, but rather of characters whom he endorses out and out. In the end, one is inclined to conclude that James and Sargent were not near neighbours quite for nothing. Nor is to perceive this to deny James's exhilaration and indeed his greatness; but to recognize that he was of his time.

Conrad has, as his strongest link with James in literary terms, his sense of life as a sustained struggle in moral terms: an issue between good and evil, in the fullest sense of these words, which individual men find they cannot evade. But James and Conrad should be seen together in the period in which they wrote, because the latter, with the former, is registering, and searchingly criticizing, basic realities of his time. Moreover, Conrad's realities relate to those which preoccupied James. *Nostromo* (1904), unquestionably Conrad's masterpiece, provides the definitive picture of how Western financial imperialism (that its roots are American makes no difference), proffering to bring to an equatorial American society material advancement and an end to the picturesque banditry of the past, in fact brings only spiritual emptiness and an unnoticed compromise with principle, or progressive blindness to it.

It may seem wilful to link, to Conrad's richness of substance, deep humanity of insight, and comprehensive, almost faultless control, the name of Kipling. Yet to see in Kipling only a vulgar Imperialist is crude. His values are largely the mid-Victorian ones of earnest effort and personal genuineness (*The Mary Gloster* or *MacAndrew's Hymn*, 1894). His chief aversion was to the smooth representatives of plutocracy who both censure and exploit the pioneering generation (*Gentleman Rankers*, 1892; *The Explorer*, 1898; *The Pro-consuls*, 1905). His chief fear, the point of *Recessional* (1897), was that the exploiters, the parasites, were winning. What limits his achievement is that he submits to the trend of his time. Even as a poet, he writes for the audience to which his journalistic years directed him, and the result is an embarrassingly buoyant heavy-handedness under which the finer distinctions disappear and the plainest issues of good and evil seem without weight. This applies also to his prose, though it must be remembered that in *Kim* (1901), at least, there is an immediacy, richness, and exactitude which put Kipling high among the chroniclers of British expansion.

Kim's Russian agents were in the Himalayas. Other writers were to sense, nearer home, some of the threats to the world of opulent liberalism. Conrad's *Under Western Eyes* (1911) depicts the nineteenth-century Russian police state with the brilliance of one who knew it at first hand; and is little less outstanding in dealing with the extremist exiles from it in Western Europe. In *The Secret Agent* (1907) it is not the terrorists themselves, but the (thinly disguised) Russian embassy and its *agent provocateur* which preoccupy the author. James's *The Princess Casamassima* (1886) cannot be seen as dealing successfully either with Bakuninism or with the life and mind of the London poor. But that James of all writers should have taken up the subject is itself illuminating; it is a forcible reminder of how widely the writers of the closing years of the nineteenth century were aware of all that existed in their society outside its circle of opulence. One can see, in this work, an awareness in James of those forces which were soon to bring sweeping social changes, and in the end, contribute decisively to the transformed social scene of two generations later. If the *fin-de-siècle* or Edwardian periods were opulent, it was an opulence which arose out of a sea of poverty. General Booth's *In Darkest England* (1890) began with an account of the opening up of Central Africa, only to point out that there was a social jungle, with its three million slaves to destitution, at home. Hardy, in both his prose and verse, reflected the rural side of poverty and deprivation. Gissing (*The Unclassed*, 1884) revealed a London which seemed to have lost the variegatedness it had for Dickens, and to have become a sea of undifferentiated anonymity which destroyed all the individual's vital energies.

New influences in fiction

One section of Gissing's most forceful work, *New Grub Street* (1891), is particularly helpful in throwing light on what was happening in English fiction towards the close of the century. In Chapter 10 of this book, several of the characters discuss the kinds of novel they would like to write. Among them, they stress the importance for fiction of new ideas in natural history (above all, Darwin) and religious thinking. This fact is helpful in that it is a brief reminder of how English fiction had for several decades been coming to deal with new and more 'intellectual' subjects; had been gaining, as with Hardy and indeed Meredith, a dimension which might almost be called philosophical. George Eliot, in real contrast to Thackeray or Trollope, and superficially (though not fundamentally) in contrast also to Dickens, based her fiction on a comprehensive, systematic sense of society and the inter-relations within it; a sense which must owe something to her early study of the social sciences and contact with the circle of the *Westminster Review*. The trend had been going on for some time, and it remains important for a twentieth-century writer like Bennett. The debate in *New Grub Street*, however, also throws something else into relief; and this new factor is one which rapidly became more important towards the end of the century. As they discuss the fiction they would like to write, Gissing's characters not only decide that Dickens's treatment of common life is lacking in seriousness because of his leanings towards humour and melodrama; they also consider Zola's treatment of common, everyday life – dry, patient, comprehensive, seemingly non-committal – as a contrast and a superior alternative to Dickens.

Here, in this interest in, this impact of, the continental model, is a basic and enduring new influence. Zola's *L'Assommoir* (1877) was the detailed model not only of the Victorian melodrama *Drink* (1879: arranged by Charles Reade) but also for George Moore's *A Mummer's*

Wife (1888), the first serious attempt in English at fiction like Zola's; and to some extent (though the influence of Dickens is also asserting itself) for Maugham's first novel, *Liza of Lambeth* (1897). Arnold Bennett's work displays not only the influence of the new, systematic, intellectual approach to fiction ('Herbert Spencer's *First Principles*, by filling me up with the sense of causation everywhere, has altered my whole view of life ... you can see *First Principles* in nearly every line I write,' Bennett says in his *Journals* for September 1910) but the French influence as well. 'I ought during the last month to have read nothing but de Goncourt,' he wrote when *Anna of the Five Towns* was begun; or again, 'The achievements of the finest French writers, with Turgenev and Tolstoy, have set a standard for all coming masters of fiction' (*Journals*, September 1896, January 1899). James and Conrad, as will transpire later, in part belong to this story also.

The newer influences were not only French. It is not a long step from the realism of Flaubert or Zola to that of Ibsen; and when Ibsen decisively 'arrived' in the 1891 season of G. T. Grein's Independent Theatre Group,[4] Shaw not only decided that Ibsen's topical concern with current abuses was his most conspicuous achievement (*The Quintessence of Ibsenism*, 1891), but himself followed at once in the same direction as a writer. Admittedly, we do not now see this kind of topicality as Ibsen's chief merit: but the point at issue for the present is the importance of continental influences, and Shaw's response to Ibsen is another aspect of this. *Widowers' Houses* (1892) was staged the year after the Ibsen season (by the same director and company in the same theatre) and it was the first in a series of plays which were Ibsenite in dealing with questions and abuses of the day, though by no means in the Irish rodomontade with which they did so. These included *Mrs Warren's Profession* (written 1893), *Man and Superman* (1903), and *Major Barbara* (1907); the two latter works reflecting Ibsen's own particular interest in problems connected with the 'New Woman'.

Ibsen was also the recurrent point of reference (reference largely, though by no means wholly, by opposition)[5] for Yeats as he developed his ideas of poetic drama in the 1890s and early 1900s. Long before, James in a number of critical essays had struggled repeatedly with what he saw as the radical defect of the whole French school, its preoccupation with the drab intricacies of mere material or sensuous or narrowly sexual realities at the expense of genuinely humane and spiritual insight. Moreover, James studied foreign literature deeply, but he was clear that learning from abroad had to go with continuing to learn from what had been done at home. He pointed to George Eliot as a writer who had achieved the massive and integrated richness of external or material facts of writers like Flaubert or Zola, without forfeiting realism in a richer sense, the realism which sees into psychology, character, and moral values.

On the other hand, he had stressed how Turgenev had also achieved this richer, more human realism in some respects more successfully than George Eliot. It is important to see how the native strand and the foreign were working together. George Eliot was also singled out for just such praise in the first decisive Western European recognition of the greatness of Russian fiction, de Vogüé's *Le Roman russe* (1886, translated 1913); and this work began to exercise an immediate effect on English thinking about fiction. George Moore wrote the Introduction for a re-issue of Dostoyevsky's *Poor Folk* (1894), and Edward and Constance Garnett's translations from Turgenev began to appear during the nineties. In Galsworthy's *Villa Rubein* (1900) and Conrad's *Under Western Eyes*, the influence of Turgenev is clear; though Conrad's novel may in part satirize what it draws on. Tolstoy's influence dates also from this period, which is that of Arnold's essay on him (1887); his *Kreutzer Sonata* (1889) helped to intensify the questioning of the marriage institution in the 1890s, and its radical thinking on art and society were influential too. The vogue of Dostoyevsky came later, among the sufferings and disorientation of the 1914–18 war. All in all, the Russian impact was a profound one. It related to matters of technique, at one extreme, and of the spirit in which both art and life were conducted at the other.[6]

It is difficult to sum up in specific detail what was acquired from abroad by each individual writer. In James, French influence shows in such things as his reproving Trollope for lack of detachment in portraying character (Trollope was too much the Thackerayan 'puppet-master'); in his intense interest in self-conscious construction, controlled tone, and calculated effect ('Ah, this divine conception of one's little masses and periods in the scenic light – as rounded Acts'); or in his repeated imitation of how Flaubert in *Madame Bovary* (1857), say, shows the whole course of the novel from the standpoint of the central character. If James's immense admiration for Turgenev can be localized in his work, it lies in the poetry, tenderness, and tact with which he handles some of his scenes – the heroine's tea-party in *The Awkward Age*, for example. Bennett, despite his admiration for the Russians, seldom has this deep feeling, restraint, and dignity; the humanity of his characters (*Riceyman Steps*, 1923) illustrates this well) tends to be submerged in analysis of how they are the creatures of their environment. But Bennett's sense of half-impersonal historical continuity (notably in *The Old Wives' Tale*, 1908), and his accumulation of factual detail to produce a dense and rich, if limited, context for the action, are achievements of no mean order; and the point, in the present context, is that such an achievement as they represent must certainly be related to the influence of Zola.

Conrad's rigid economy of style, his taut and sequacious construction, his effects that seem so carefully timed, have their counterparts in Flaubert or Stendhal rather than in any Victorian novelist. Lawrence in a letter of 1 February 1913 likens his own work to that of Chehov in contrast to 'the rule and measure mathematical folk' – Shaw, Galsworthy, Barker. He is in fact speaking of plays; but the parallel and the contrast are plain enough in his short stories also Moreover, there is a poetry and symbolism, a poignant strangeness, and often a seemingly disjointed surface creating in the end a deep inner unity, which are plain in his work as they are also, in different terms, in that of Virginia Woolf or Ford Madox Ford. Such qualities have no clear counterpart in mid-nineteenth-century English fiction; though they have, undoubtedly, in Dostoyevsky. In the end, however, these suggestions must be taken as explanatory: the detailed work in these fields has still in large part to be done.

Tradition and experiment in poetry

Late-nineteenth-century French literature had not been Realist only. If it had included Zola and the brothers Goncourt, it had also included Rimbaud and Mallarmé and Laforgue; and the early-twentieth-century movement in English poetry which came to terms with these writers should be seen as part of a whole continental impact. But there is a prior question: what sort of poetry occupied, as it were, the field? Upon what in English poetry did the influence of continental models impinge?

Just as in discussing developments in fiction it was important not to oversimplify the picture of the mid-nineteenth century in England, and necessary to remember that that period included George Eliot just as much as it did Dickens, so it is important to remember the complexity and variety of the situation in poetry. Dr Leavis has said: 'Nineteenth-century poetry was characteristically preoccupied with the creation of a dream-world.'[7] This points forcefully to much of the poetry of the later years of the nineteenth century.

> Sunlight from the sun's own heart
> Flax unfolded to receive
> Out of sky and flax and art
> Lovely raiment I achieve
> Summer is time for beauty's flowering
> For the exuberance of day,
> And the cool of the evening,
> Summer is time for play,
> And for joy, and the touch of tweed.

That, without a word altered, is part of a poem from the closing pages of the *Oxford Book of Victorian Verse*, and part tailor's advertisement (*c.* 1950) from a Sunday newspaper. It brings out not merely what was worst in the verse of the later nineteenth century, but also how that tradition of bad poetry was something which created an established taste for itself: a taste, a taking-for-granted, which could later be exploited by the world of commerce because it was in no way essentially different from that world. One can glimpse in the very possibility of amalgamating those two passages, some of the underlying causes why the poetry of Pound and Eliot should have seemed, to the man in the street and also to much organized literary taste, an affront to what was truly poetic.

Yet to think of the later nineteenth century as typically represented by 'Sunlight from the sun's own heart' and rubbish like it would be to oversimplify here; and later, when this survey moves forward to the period after Eliot, to render the task of comprehension and integration much more difficult. ('Not all of the poetry, or all of the poets,' Dr Leavis added to his remark just quoted.) 'Dream-world' is a term which does not bring out the strength – though one must add at once that it was a modest strength – of much later nineteenth-century verse; and once that relatively sound and strong kind has been identified, it can be seen as a tradition of English verse which is firmly in being before the time of Pound and Eliot, and which runs steadily through, and after, the years in which they were making their impact.

This other tradition of verse displays a use of language which is unquestionably vernacular, but rather too deliberate (one might put it) to be termed colloquial; an intimate, personal, yet unassertive tone: a modest lyric artistry; and a thoughtful receptivity before the poet's environment, especially nature seen in a somewhat domestic way, by the cottage, not on the mountain. Later developments in English poetry will prove baffling to those who do not recognize the quality and provenance of this kind of verse, and its strength as a tradition in being at the close of the nineteenth and in the early twentieth century. Here it is in Hardy's *An August Midnight* (1899):

> A shaded lamp and a waving blind,
> And the beat of a clock from a distant floor:
> On this scene enter – winged, horned, and spined –
> A longlegs, a moth, and a dumbledore;
> While 'mid my page there idly stands
> A sleepy fly that rubs its hands ...

Hardy, it must be remembered, was writing verse steadily from the 1860s; and, with its plain vernacular language, and its strong (if nostalgic) awareness of everyday life, his large body of verse forcibly invites us to see nineteenth-century poetry itself in other than 'dream-world' terms. But Hardy is not the only poet to represent, at the turn of the century and just after, the tradition of writing described above. Edward Thomas does so as well:

> And yet I still am half in love with pain,
> With what is imperfect, with both tears and mirth,
> With things that have an end, with life and earth,
> And this moon that leaves me dark within the door.
>
> (*Liberty*, *c.* 1915)

So does Lawrence, for example, in *End of Another Home Holiday* (*c.* 1913):

> When shall I see the half-moon sink again
> Behind the black sycamore at the end of the garden?
> When will the scent of the dim white phlox
> Creep up the wall to me, and in at my open window?

and finally, with a slight yet salient difference in the closing lines, to which the discussion must revert, so does Robert Graves's *Full Moon*, written (before 1923) at a time when Pound and Eliot were beginning to dominate the scene:

> As I walked out that sultry night,
> I heard the stroke of one.
> The moon, attained to her full height,
> Stood beaming like the sun:
> She exorcized the ghostly wheat
> To mute assent in love's defeat,
> Whose tryst had now begun.

Those who see how the first of these passages is reminiscent of Wordsworth's *Green Linnet*, say, or the second of the opening lines of Keats's *Endymion* and the simple, more introspective passages of his *Epistles*, or the fourth of *The Ancient Mariner* (though the links are not all equally strong), will recognize that this kind of verse was no isolated or merely local freak of poetic development, but had a good deal of English poetry behind it. But what is also clear is that the range of experience which lies behind this verse was mainly a traditional and rural one. It did not easily come nearer to the city than the suburban garden.

Because of this, the verse of Hardy, Edward Thomas, and also D. H. Lawrence in his first years as a poet, for all its soundness and modest strength, was not abreast of the time; and could barely develop to meet its challenges. The centre of life had moved away from what was rural. This shows earlier, and later too, in the declining quality of the rural inspiration. There is a note of retreat, of weariness, even in Richard Jefferies; but the indications elsewhere are clearer. They are clear, for example, in some of the townified versions of rurality which were poeticized for the Georgian Anthologies (1912–20); in Wells's picture in *The History of Mr Polly* (1910) of the countryside as a place for afternoon bicycle excursions or escapist idylls; and in the fragile, fey quality which colours the achievement of a fine talent like that of Walter de la Mare. Most revealing of all, perhaps, is the work of T. F. Powys. Here a deep sense of the total round, rich fertility and sour brutality of rural life, and a command over both fable and symbol as fictional vehicles, seem recurrently to be marred by relapses into a kind of jasmine frailty or coy whimsy, or a response to sex and to cruelty which not infrequently seems disquietingly ambivalent. So devious, so various, are the signs that a way of life can no longer abundantly sustain a body of literature.

The new poetry which came into being from about 1910 did not modify the English tradition which has just been discussed, but departed sharply from it. This new poetry looked not to the countryside, but to the great city.[8] Already, in this fact alone, the complex story of its affiliations begins to emerge. From one point of view, Eliot's 1917 poems (*Preludes, Rhapsody on a Windy Night*) stand in a loose continuity with Laforgue, with Rimbaud's *Illuminations*,[9] and above all with the *Tableaux Parisiens* of Baudelaire, probably the first poet in Europe to take his stand as the poet of the '*Fourmillante cité, cité pleine de rêves*' of which the poet can say '*tout pour moi devient allégorie*'. As Eliot said, '(Baudelaire) gave new possibilities to poetry in a new stock of images from contemporary life.'[10] The new poetry was also a city poetry, however, in a rather special sense. After all, verse like Hardy's 'A Wife in London' or Henley's 'London Voluntaries' was about city life. The new poetry goes much further. It is written by, and for, a metropolitan intelligentsia. This explains the polyglot, cosmopolitan interests which lie behind it, and of which its continuity with French poets[11] is only one part; for Pound's attention to the literature of the Far East, Eliot's Sanskrit and Hindu studies, are others.

Moreover, there is a further way in which this body of verse belongs not to the modern city in general, but rather to one distinctive group within it. To a greater or lesser extent it rests upon a repudiation of the broad city middle class, the commercial bourgeoisie. This was the class which for several reasons, but in particular for its failure to respond to the work of the Abbey Theatre, notably Synge, in Dublin during the 1900s, had disgusted Yeats. That modern poetry started with this repudiation of the broad city middle class affords a link between the new poets of the 1910s and those of the Aesthetic Movement of the 1890s, and helps one to see how it was natural enough that Pound's earliest verse should have *fin-de-siècle* qualities, or that like the nineties poets Pound should have had a special interest in Old French or Provençal. The point also emerges in early essays of Yeats like *What is Popular Poetry?* (1901) or *The Symbolism of Poetry*

(1900) written under the immediate influence of Arthur Symons's *The Symbolist Movement in Literature* (1899); itself the first book significantly to introduce English readers to French Symbolists, even if it a little tinged these with Celtic twilight in the process. For Yeats, poet and peasant could come together (and Yeats reflected the distinctive quality of Irish life and of the Irish peasantry in the ease with which he envisaged that); but grocer and politician were in another world. This amounted in practice to a firm repudiation of what was seen by Yeats as the whole Tennysonian stance, the poet as public figure writing for the broad middle class and diluting his poetry until that class could take it in.

Repudiating this particular social status for poetry seems actually to underlie the more technical features of the new verse. It issued, in the first place, in the demand that social respectability should not be allowed to impose restrictions of subject-matter upon the poet, nor literary convention impose restrictions of diction or emotion. This is why Jules Laforgue particularly interested both Pound and Eliot. Again, this change in social orientation led to an insistence on the supreme virtue of economy and concentration: poetry was not to be made easy for the relaxed general reader. Yeats in his early essays made it clear that, for him, refusing to do this underlay dropping what binds normal discourse tidily together: a sequacious logic, a self-explaining easy-to-follow train of thought.[12] This repudiation of tidy logical exposition in poetry brought with it perhaps the most characteristic quality of all, a constant laconic *juxtaposition* of ideas, rather than an ordering of them in a banally lucid exposition.

Again, the immediate roots of this principle of style are foreign; but though they are partly from France, they are not wholly so. Pound himself did not speak of juxtaposition, but of 'the mode of superposition', which he recognized above all in the Japanese seventeen-syllable poems, the *hokku*.[13] Ernest Fenollosa's brilliant *The Chinese Written Character* (finished before his death in 1908, published by Pound in 1920) finds a paradigm for this, the true poetic texture, in the very nature of Chinese as a language. But T. E. Hulme, an influential member of the circle of Pound's intimates, goes clearly back for his conception of the truly poetic use of language to the contrast which Bergson drew between the order of logic and the continuity of life; and when Eliot, in 1920, writes that certain lines of Massinger

> exhibit that perpetual slight alteration of language, words perpetually juxtaposed in new and sudden combinations, meanings perpetually *eingeschachtelt* into meanings

he is writing in the tradition of Mallarmé's *Crise de vers* (1895):

> l'œuvre pure implique la disparition élocutoire du poète, qui cède l'initiative aux mots, par le heurt de leur inégalité mobilisés; ils s'allument de reflets réciproques comme une virtuelle trainée de feu sur des pierreries.[14]

Indeed, this also has an affinity of thought with the best known of Rimbaud's letters, the 'Lettre du Voyant', written to Démeny on 15 May 1871.

When, further, Eliot distinguishes in *Tradition and the Individual Talent* (1917) the radically non-logical nature of the poetic process, he draws heavily on Rémy de Gourmont's *Le Problème du style* (1902). 'Sensibility' and 'fusion' were the key terms for both in their account of the working of the poet's mind; and it is in de Gourmont that we find a classic account of what probably lies at the centre of recent British thinking about poetry, the power, depth, and suggestiveness of metaphors.[15] If this whole sense of the intricate surface and deeper evocativeness of poetry could be related to music (as it was), that goes back ultimately to the especial reverence of Mallarmé and those who followed him for the music of Wagner, and their recognition of Wagner's peculiarly intricate and comprehensive inter-relatedness of texture. But it goes back further to Wagner's own idea of what this enabled the artist to achieve: nothing less than a half-mystic glimpse of true Reality behind Appearance.[16] The idea chimed in well with the Neo-Platonist and occultist strains which were plain enough in the work of the French poets; and indeed, it is this idea that the ostensible subject of the poem may be the key to an ulterior Reality which is really the justification for calling them 'Symbolists'.[17] The term is less helpful in discussing English literature, because (save with Yeats) this train of thought was usually dropped when their ideas were imported. This dropping-out of the idea of deeper truth behind the sharply focused surface fact is especially clear in the *Imagist Manifesto* (1913), where the stress is laid upon economical presentation of a brilliant visual reality. But the Imagists, apart from

Pound, and also Lawrence who had a slight and brief connection with them, have no importance.

From these considerations, and from the fact that Eliot had completed *Prufrock* and *Portrait of a Lady* by 1914, it is clear enough that so far as the central creative work of this circle went, the articles of their creed had been established well before 1920, and Eliot's work at that time on Jacobean literature constituted the development of them in one particular field, rather than homage to the decisive source of inspiration. Some distinctions, in fact, need to be drawn at this point. The new qualities of Eliot's earlier verse have often been seen as standing in very close connection with his special interest in early-seventeenth-century dramatic and lyrical verse, especially Donne. In reality, this interest now seems to show more prominently in Eliot's critical work (it should be remembered that he by no means began the revival of Donne)[18] than in his verse. Close study reveals that there is surprisingly little sign of a direct and detailed influence of Donne on Eliot as a poet; less so, indeed, than on Yeats.[19] Again, the fact that Eliot broke sharply with nineteenth-century verse does not mean that Pound did so to the same extent. The continuity in his case has already been touched on (p. 71), and in an important letter of May 1928 he relates it also to one of the greatest of Donne's nineteenth-century admirers: '*überhaupt ich stamm aus Browning. Pourquoi nier son père?*' though he adds that his father in poetry was a Browning '*dénué des paroles superflues*'.

Poetry and the war crisis

These were the trends: to what sort of poetic achievement did they lead? On the surface, to writing which was brilliant and exhilarating for its intelligence and complexity; in essence, to what was much more powerful and moving than the conventional verse of the time, because its many-sidedness could touch and move the whole depth and capacity of the mind. As an example, here are the closing stanzas of the first part of Pound's *Hugh Selwyn Mauberley*:

> His true Penelope was Flaubert,
> He fished by obstinate isles;
> Observed the elegance of Circe's hair
> Rather than the mottoes on sundials.

Unaffected by 'the march of events',
He passed from men's memory in *l'an trentiesme*
De son eage; the case presents
No adjunct to the Muse's diadem.

The sub-title is *E. P. Ode pour l'Election de son Sepulchre*: that is to say, a dryly ironical imitation of Ronsard becomes the vehicle by which the minority poet will express his sense of failure in a society which is radically hostile to serious art ('a half-savage country'). But the astringent compression, the powerful suggestiveness of these widely ranging but tightly juxtaposed references to literature, mythology, and public life, pass beyond intellectual excitingness to achieve true and deep feeling. The 'elegance of Circe's hair' image, picked up again in the 'Muse's diadem', conveys Pound's service to a destructive enchantress; but this is, at one and the same time, true devotion to Penelope, his faithful mate and equal. Again, the poet is seen at once as the wily Odysseus and a crafty fisherman ('obstinate isles'), and also, through the terse reference implied in '*l'an trentiesme de son eage*', as the hapless, hopeless Villon. The mottoes on sundials which he misses are not only those about transience, but those about happiness too. His acute predicament emerges movingly from these seeming-fragments, dry and sophisticated.

But something has been omitted from this account of development. What has been said so far can largely explain *Hugh Selwyn Mauberley* ('an attempt to condense the Jamesian novel', Pound called it),[20] and still more so the new astringency, bluntness, irony, many-sidedness, vernacular quality – and emotional charge – of such poems as Yeats's *The Fascination of What's Difficult*, or Eliot's *Mr Apollinax*. But Yeats's *The Second Coming* (1921) or Eliot's *The Waste Land* (1922) strike a new note, and one that contradicts Yeats's early ideas, or those of the French poets discussed above.

'On Margate Sands.
I can connect
Nothing with nothing.
The broken fingernails of dirty hands.
My people humble people who expect
Nothing.'

la la

To Carthage then I came

Burning burning burning burning
O Lord thou pluckest me out
O Lord thou pluckest

burning

Using much the same method of terse and esoteric reference as Pound's, these closing lines of the third part of *The Waste Land* provide the very title of the poem. 'To Carthage then I came' are the opening words of Book III of St Augustine's *Confessions*: and he closed the preceding book with the words 'I wandered, O my God, too much astray from Thee my stay, in these days of my youth, and I became to myself a *waste land*'.[21] But this, and the echo of Amos 4:11 which follows it in the poem, and leads into the title of the section ('The Fire Sermon'), do not merely create a satirist's vision of society or an artist's private sense of personal predicament. They go with the terse indications of humble Thames-side scenes ('la la' is the strumming of a mandoline) to evoke a genuinely prophetic vision (none the less real because it comes, as in poetry such things almost must come, with an intensely personal and subjective vibration) of a break-down in life itself: a waste land, general to humanity, in which nothing connects with nothing. Here is no notion of keeping art free from middle-brow preoccupations like social reality; but an anguished concern to register a sick world and to make contact with something which might restore the springs of human goodness and vitality.[22]

This radical shift becomes easier to understand if one remembers that Yeats and Pound were studying the Japanese plays, and the latter exercising his commanding influence on *The Egoist* and *The Little Review*, during the years of the Great War. This traumatic experience marked a decisive phase in British civilization, and was registered in the emergence, over the years following, of several outstanding war autobiographies: Blunden's *Undertones of War* (1928), Graves's *Good-bye to all That* (1929), Wyndham Lewis's *Blasting and Bombardiering* (1937). Similarly, the length and intensity of the 1914–18 experience brought it about that English poetry of the more traditional and indigenous kind itself underwent a remarkable change, and one which ran parallel to those now more conspicuous changes initiated by Pound and Eliot.

The early war poets are among the weaker representatives of a poetic line which has already been discussed (pp. 69–70 above). At bottom, lyricism and rurality were there to guide them:

> The fighting man shall from the sun
> Take warmth, and life from the glowing earth.

Julian Grenfell wrote in *Into Battle*. England gave Rupert Brooke's *Soldier* 'her flowers to love, her ways to roam'; and Edward Thomas's *A Private* (who had been a ploughman) suggests that, decisive as are the differences in other respects, Thomas is part of this picture. But after the holocausts of the middle war years these poets gave place to others, such as Siegfried Sassoon; and now a style prominent from his time to our own (1960) may be seen in the very act of breaking out of the shell of the old:

> I see them in foul dug-outs, gnawed by rats,
> And in the ruined trenches, lashed with rain,
> Dreaming of *things they did with balls and bats*
> And mocked with hopeless longing *to regain*
> *Bank holidays and picture shows and spats*
> *And going to the office in the train.* ('Dreamers')

But the laconic diction (tautened everywhere by paradox) and the restless, evocative rhythm of Wilfred Owen's *Exposure* represent a much more distinguished achievement; they also show an unexpectedly interesting flowering, it might be claimed, of *Imagisme*, and an expression of tense yet aimless awareness coming near to some purely civilian scenes in *The Waste Land*:

> Our brains ache, in the merciless iced east winds that knive us ...
> Wearied we keep awake because the night is silent ...
> Low, drooping flares confuse our memory of the salient ...
> Worried by silence, sentries whisper, curious, nervous,
> But nothing happens.

War and crisis in fiction

The most remarkable record in fiction of change and disruption from the Great War is surely Ford Madox Ford's 'Tietjens' tetralogy (*Some Do Not, No More Parades, A Man Could Stand Up, Last Post*; 1924–8). The sheer bulk of Ford's minor output, and his early prominence in the literary scene as an editor (see below, p. 96), have concealed his achievement as a novelist. *The Good Soldier* (1915) resumes the trend of French influence touched upon earlier (see the reference to Conrad, p. 67 above). The seeming casualness of tone and randomness of organization in this book are in fact remarkable displays of judgement and insight exercising themselves through technical artistry.

If this novel has an underlying defect, it is one to which one might also point in works by Arnold Bennett. Both novelists, inclined to seek a representation of life which is more complete, sensitive, and humane than what they found in de Maupassant or Zola, were a little inclined to do so on too easy terms. The result is a certain relaxing of detachment and control, a manipulatory holding up of the characters and their situation for comprehension, sympathy, a feeling of pathos even, which betrays the general influence of Dickens or Thackeray in the background. The Tietjens books probably lack the delicacy of perception and movement of indisputably great fiction. But in their large, loose organization, their outstanding resilience and vitality, and their comprehensive, unflinching grasp of a complex pattern of cultural change, they are very notable works; and they suggest that Russian fiction (with its assured achievement in displaying how near the order of art can come to the disorder of life, and how novels may have poignant compassion, sympathy, and insight without manipulation or straining for emotion) was once again exerting its influence upon English.

Virginia Woolf put this better. Speaking of the novels of Turgenev she said: 'They are so short and yet they hold so much. The emotion is so intense and yet so calm. The form is in one sense so perfect, in another so broken.'[23] In her own complex of affiliations, the Russian one is clear enough; but a complex it certainly is, and other links are clearer. Behind her emphatic repudiation of the pedestrian, in a sense the peripheral realism of Bennett or Wells,[24] lies not only a more sharply differentiated concern for art as such, but also a sense of the inexhaustible interest and significance and *goodness* of experience, even at its most immediate and transient, which connects her with G. E. Moore (in a work like *Principia Ethica*, 1903), and with Walter Pater. This side of Virginia Woolf, at its slightest, can be disconcerting. It leads occasionally to a kind of perky incompleteness in her criticism, and an almost dithery brightness in her fiction, in which there is even a streak of vulgarity ('somehow or other, loveliness is infernally sad': *Jacob's Room*, 1922).

Yet to say no more than that is to caricature. Her preoccupation with the immediate and always-changing surface of life is based upon substantial grounds. These are much the grounds which Bergson would have offered for the same preference: and it is noteworthy that her well-known remark in the essay on *Modern Fiction* (1919), 'life is not a series of gig-lamps symmetrically arranged; life is a luminous halo, a semi-transparent envelope', seems to be following a passage in Bergson's *Introduction to Metaphysics* (1904).[25] But if the lamps are Bergson's, the luminous halo and the envelope may come from Henry James's *Art of Fiction* (1884).

Another possible link, this time with painting, must also be noticed. Virginia Woolf's concern for surface impression and immediacy brings Monet to mind, and the infiltration of the Impressionist painter's vision at least into poetry is something which may be often traced in English poetry from the 1880s on: but she was also in the circle of Roger Fry, whose main achievement was to introduce English taste to the first generation of Post-Impressionist painters (Cézanne, Van Gogh, and the rest) in the famous London exhibitions of 1910 and 1912. Virginia Woolf is no Cézanne, but if Cézanne used the discoveries of earlier Impressionist painters in order to capture not the surface but the essence of his subjects, it is not altogether pointless to liken her to him. Her best work embodies a vision of how richly the immediacy of experience engages also what is substantial in experience; a sense reminiscent of James (though flimsy by comparison) that life's delicate surfaces reveal what T. S. Eliot has called 'the boredom and the horror and the glory' which can be just below them. Virginia Woolf brings to the more aesthetic or Impressionist side of her work an interest in human values which plainly shows the influence of her father, Leslie Stephen. The 'stream of consciousness' which her writing endeavours to capture (and for this purpose she was no inconsiderable technical innovator) reflects a genuine humanity, a real and compassionate concern for what makes life rich and what dries it up.

Finally, her position in these matters fits properly into its historical context. It is the position of the liberal intellectual surviving in the post-war world. Fullness of individual life stands over against brutal dominance. *Mrs Dalloway* (1925) is polarized between the abundant if uninsistent life of the heroine, and the sheer not having of experience of Sir William Bradshaw, the doctor who drives his shell-shocked patient to suicide. In *To the Lighthouse* (1927), life and the self-assertive negation of life interact within the experiences of Mr Ramsay, of his children, even of Mrs Ramsay herself.

If there is a lack in Virginia Woolf's work, it is that she has also the weakness of the liberal intellectual. It is a lack not of values but of confidence, ultimately of vitality. What she cares for is always made tentative and exploratory, and – she is typical of the period after 1918 in this – it survives within a perimeter of threatening violence, deeply feared and half-understood. The meaningless death of the hero of *Jacob's Room* in battle, the thread of tragedy and brutality running so close to life's most exquisite striations in *Mrs Dalloway*, the suppressed vindictiveness of *To the Lighthouse*, the spiritual deprivation, squalor, physical violence, that everywhere surround the village pageant in *Between the Acts* (1941), all at bottom reflect the plight of the liberal in the modern world. It is surely significant that the same two attitudes – a care for the immediacy of private living, a sense of its being surrounded and threatened by meaningless violence – combine prominently in the work of E. M. Forster. It shows that the plight of the liberal was one which could be diagnosed before 1914; and in Forster's works also, the pervasive sense is of how the good of life, ordinary kindly private living, is everywhere surrounded by unpredictable violence, the product of random change or of uncomprehending self-assertiveness. If Forster, in the end, is a less exciting but more reassuring novelist than Virginia Woolf, it is because, though he lacks her exuberant subtlety of sensuous perception, he never radiantly obscures what is central to his purpose by technical virtuosity. His integrity is always, sometimes even a little nudely, in view. Moreover, he ranges further than Virginia Woolf, and is more aware than she of how the goodness of private experience is something which the individual shares with others. *A Passage to India* (1924) has a humanity and modesty, a plain and strong sense of values, and at the same time a half-poetic imaginativeness, which put it far above his other works, and above anything of Virginia Woolf's also.

The works of Forster and Virginia Woolf represent an early phase in a probing and challenging of that polite liberal culture which, more and more, came to seem radically incommensurate with the challenges confronting it in the twentieth century. That it did so has been a fundamental reality of the period, and a recurrent feature of its fiction. In the novels of Huxley, too, there is a sense of a world of cultivated people closely surrounded by a bigger world of horror and brutality: 'At this very moment ... the most frightful horrors are taking place in every corner of the world ... screams of pain and fear go pulsing through the air ... after travelling for three seconds they are perfectly inaudible'; 'The Black and Tans harry Ireland, the Poles maltreat the Silesians, the bold Fascisti slaughter their poorer countrymen: we take it all for granted. Since the war we wonder at nothing' (*Crome Yellow*, 1921).

But in Huxley the doubts have entered deeper than in Forster or Virginia Woolf. They impugn the centre itself; and leave in his works a paradoxical central emptiness, in that the writer seems still to believe in the elements of the culture he knows (music, art, rational conversation) but sees only a restless sterilized fatuity in those who transmit that culture. It is, indeed, the world of one part of the 1920s: that of the first jazz, the Charleston, the first sports car. In Huxley's later novels (as in *Eyeless in Gaza*, 1936, where a dog falls from an aeroplane to bespatter the liveliest intimacies of two roof-top lovers) the sense of circumambient violence has become obsessive; and in the novels of Evelyn Waugh (e.g. *Decline and Fall*, 1928) a further stage still may perhaps be traced. Here, the social group is an élite of money rather than ostensible culture, but even so it is not far remote from Huxley's; yet now the elements of culture are themselves valueless. There is nothing for a world of absurd violence either to surround or threaten; the result is to make violence both ubiquitous and insignificant.

Wyndham Lewis's later work throws his earlier work into a new focus, and shows him not only as one of the major destructive critics of our time, but as seeing in fundamental terms what the writers just discussed saw in isolation or did not see so much as merely use.[26] In *The Apes of God* (1930) Lewis does little more than toy disgustedly with the social levels that also half repulsed Huxley. But in *The Revenge for Love* (1937) and still more in *Self Condemned* (1951), what threatens life is seen not as among the preoccupations of a class, but as having its roots deep in the modernity of the modern world, committed as this is to the rhythms of the great city and the machine.

The machine, moreover, can take control of men's lives because in the end there is something of the mechanical even about men themselves; the idea is already clear enough in *Tarr* (1918) and in the outstanding short stories published in *The Wild Body* (1927). The same insights are prominent in Lewis's remarkable paintings. There are things to be said against his sprawling works and his largely (not wholly) negative vision, but it must also be said that Lewis is the only English writer who establishes his full comprehension of the basic realities of life in a mid-twentieth-century society, that of a mass civilization, wholly mechanized and essentially megalopolitan. His last important work, *The Human Age* (1955), is perhaps the most memorable picture, in the form of fable rather than realistic fiction, that we have of our own time.

Lewis was no isolated phenomenon: he was one of the great seminal creative group of whom the main figures were Eliot, Epstein, and Pound. His work, straddling literature and the visual arts, reproduced the range of interest of the group as a whole; and Pound's immediate recognition of his power (*Letters*, 9 March 1916) should be known:

> Lewis has just sent in the first dozen drawings ... the thing is stupendous. The vitality, the fullness of the man! Nobody has any conception of the volume and energy and the variety ... It is not merely knowledge of technique, or skill, it is intelligence and knowledge of life, of the whole of it, beauty, heaven, hell, sarcasm, every kind of whirlwind of force and emotion.

Probably the most enigmatic associate of this group, however, remains to be mentioned. It was Joyce. Like Pound, Joyce has a link with the Aesthetic Movement of the nineties, and it shows in his early poems and in some of the most evocative passages of his early short stories (*Dubliners*, 1914). The independent reality of art is endorsed in *A Portrait of the Artist as a Young Man*, which Pound published in *The Egoist* in 1916; but that work is also a searchingly realistic picture of intense emotion and decisive spiritual development. Moreover, although Joyce took his stand as a rebel against Irish life and the Roman Catholic religion which dominated it, this novel shows how deeply his own mind had been influenced by both. The combined variety and shabbiness of the social milieu, and the rich facility and inventiveness of language, point to Joyce's emergence from a distinctively Irish society; the pervasive sense of incessant sinfulness and incessant redemption point to his roots in Catholicism. All these things retain their importance (indeed, they extend further) in his later fiction.

Joyce's admiration had also gone out to the realism that gave ample place to the sordid: he found it in Ibsen, and it led him to his own play *Exiles* (1918). Again, his frequent residences in France and consequent contact with French experimental writing, as also his connections with Pound and Eliot, brought him to a turning away from logic, to a reliance upon laconic juxtaposition as the staple ordering principle of contemporary literature, and to a densening verbal texture, until the kaleidoscopic inter-relatedness and inter-suggestiveness of his work make it, in some respects, a clearer example of the linguistic idea of Symbolist writers than anything else in English.

Thus, many lines of origin and development help to create the difficulty of Joyce's case. Taken even at its simplest, there is a problem about the consciousness of reality revealed by his chief novel: *Ulysses* (1922). This work, first published in part in *The Little Review*, with which Pound was connected, carries realism to the length of an encyclopedic portrayal of one single day, pursued by the author with dogged yet inexhaustible vitality. The result is a unique picture of life, seen (paradoxically) with disillusion and delight at one and the same time. Joyce stands as the last and in some ways unquestionably the most gifted of a line of novelists, running back through the previous century, who sought to depict the inner radiance of what is most ordinary and commonplace in how men live. His compassion and insight enter life at its littlest, its most trivially prurient. This prurience can even seem to infect the writer (Lawrence spoke of his 'dirty-mindedness'): but his vitality and many-sided awareness sustain a true sense of human sympathy and genuine care for life at the very same time.

Yet to leave the account there would be to omit what Joyce himself would have seen as of major significance. There is a core of truth in the aesthetic ideal that Joyce early encountered. 'Art for great art's sake,' one might perhaps put it. The idea is relevant to *Ulysses*. Like all great art, this novel is no mere picture of reality, but a re-making of reality into the unique reality of the work; a re-making where substance and medium cannot be divorced, where almost a new world of language, a progressive energizing and then debilitating of style sustained in an extraordinary way over the whole book, and an unhesitating medley of pastiche, quotation, extravaganza, dramatization, complex literary allusion, all interfuse with story and character and grotesque realistic immediacy so as to create the richness and heterogeneity of a new cosmos. *Ulysses* itself is an undoubted masterpiece: whether *Finnegans Wake* (1939), which pushes much further in the same directions, is a success, the present writer had best admit that he cannot say: the book is beyond him.

The search for values in poetry

There is a diagnosis, a representation of life, in both Huxley and Joyce; though it is much more impressive in the latter than in the former. But literature can be something which is distinguishable from a representation of life. It can offer to re-invigorate the very forces which lend life validity. T. S. Eliot made clear his own concern for this function of literature in his essay on *The Pensées of Pascal* (1931). Here he implicitly contrasts his own position with that of 'the unbeliever' who

> ... is, as a rule, not so greatly troubled to explain the world to himself, nor so greatly distressed by its disorder; nor is he generally concerned (in modern terms) to 'preserve values' ...

The Waste Land (1922) is, from the point of view of its substance, an attempt, articulated with peculiar clarity, to diagnose the 'disorder'; to render its challenge inescapably insistent; and in its final section to deliver a 'message' emphasizing certain human values, on the strength of which the poet can add, 'Shall I at least *set my lands in order*?' Admittedly, there is something a little arbitrary or bookish about Eliot's solution, which suddenly makes its appearance from the Upanishads; but this is representative of a certain negativeness or distaste in the face of experience which runs widely through Eliot's earlier work.

Yeats goes far beyond the present train of thought. He does not have his roots in the Aesthetic Movement for nothing, nor for harm only; and if he had never written a line of 'prophetic' verse, he would still be a major poet for his great body of lyric and dramatic poems

(*The Cold Heaven*, 1914; *An Irish Airman Foresees his Death*, 1919; *Leda and the Swan*, 1928; *Long-legged Fly*, 1939, are merely a few among many). Moreover, as perhaps the last of these poems makes clear, Yeats's outlook and philosophy (and his philosophy of history) are sometimes present in his verse when they do not dominate it. Those who rightly see Yeats's knowledge of the Neo-Platonist tradition widely in both his later verse and later drama should bear in mind that Yeats chiefly valued the philosophy for the poetry, not conversely:

> ... ours is the main road, the road of naturalness and swiftness, and we have thirty centuries on our side. We alone can 'think like a wise man, yet express ourselves like the common people'. These new men are goldsmiths, working with a glass screwed into one eye, whereas we stride ahead of the crowd, its swordsmen, its jugglers, looking to right and left. 'To right and left' – by which I mean that we need, like Milton, Shakespeare, Shelley, vast sentiments, generalizations supported by tradition.[27]

Here may be seen Yeats's enduring sense of the poet as taking up a stance and sustaining a role. That in its turn should probably be seen as one aspect of Yeats's distinctive position: not an English but an Irish poet. Sometimes, as with Joyce, language could also for him be a rich and splendid and even intoxicating thing. Yeats's adaptation of the minority views of the French poets to the special conditions of Ireland, with its archaic Western peasantry that still had something of the Homeric about them, has already been noticed (p. 72 above). Essentially Irish too were his points of reference in history, from his early attachment to the Irish Heroic Age, to his later admiration of the eighteenth-century Ascendancy. Nor did his attachment to the Irish Heroic Age give place to a merely 'Anglo-Irish' awareness as the eighteenth century. Much as Yeats admired the Ascendancy of that time, and checked as he inevitably was by his family background and his virtual ignorance of the Irish language, he nevertheless acquired (largely through Douglas Hyde) some vivid glimpses, anyhow, of Irish culture in the Penal Age; and these entered intimately into some of his later poems.[28] *An Irish Airman Foresees his Death* brings out in how un-English a way Yeats naturally saw the events of the 1914–18 war which had so affected English poets; and if it is true that he, as much as any writer, saw the quality of nightmare in his own time, it is true also that he did so through distinctively Irish realities:

> Things fall apart; the centre cannot hold;
> Mere anarchy is loosed upon the world,
> The blood-dimmed tide is loosed, and everywhere
> The ceremony of innocence is drowned ...
>
> (*The Second Coming*, 1921)

To this awareness Yeats was brought not by the 1914–18 war but (as *Nineteen-Nineteen* or *Meditations in Time of Civil War* set beyond doubt) by the period of 'Troubles' in Ireland which were a direct consequence of that war, coinciding with it and prolonged after it. Yet if Yeats's more or less esoteric philosophy of history explains and dramatizes both good and evil in the world, it is not this philosophy which his work advances as a source of re-invigoration, so much as an intense energy which goes into creating the poem as an elaborate artefact at the same time as, with fierce intimacy, it takes hold of the validity of life itself: a validity of which the living moment is the sole and decisive warrant. This is the conviction which blazes out in *A Dialogue of Self and Soul* (1933):

> What matter if the ditches are impure?
> What matter if I live it all once more?
> I am content to live it all again
> And yet again, if it be life to pitch
> Into the frogspawn of a blind man's ditch –

and in *The Gyres* (1939):

> What matter though dumb nightmare ride on top,
> And blood and mire the sensitive body stain?
> What matter? Heave no sigh, let no tear drop,
> A greater, a more gracious time has gone;
> For painted forms or boxes of make-up
> In ancient tombs I sighed, but not again;
> What matter? Out of cavern comes a voice,
> And all it knows is that one word 'Rejoice!'

The 'cavern' may be the Neo-Platonic Cave of the Nymphs, but its message is not of return to the Heavenly world: it is of a universal, joyous transformation and energy within which both evil and good belong to a greater good. Moreover, this vital conviction, imposed for Yeats by the act of life itself, underlies all his findings when he looked to his own Irish scene for abiding points of reference and sources of vitality. Two more quotations will make this clear. The immediate all-deciding vigour of life is known as much to the beggar-woman in *Crazy Jane Grown Old looks at the Dancers* (1933):

> God be with the times when I
> Cared not a thraneen for what chanced
> So that I had the limbs to try
> Such a dance as there was danced –
> *Love is like the lion's tooth.*

– as it is in *Ancestral Houses* (1928):

> Surely among a rich man's flowering lawns,
> Amid the rustle of his planted hills,
> Life overflows without ambitious pains;
> And rains down life until the basin spills,
> And mounts more dizzy high the more it rains ...

Yeats's stature is not self-evident. He wrote enough for a number of his poems to be unimportant or unsuccessful, and an element of grandiose silliness appears in some of his ideas, parts of his life, and a little of his verse. His work exposes itself to cavil more openly than that of a more circumspect writer like Eliot. But the range and variety of what he has done in prose and verse, and, at the best, its splendid vitality, its humanity and positiveness, and its irresistible artistry, set beyond question his greatness as a writer, and his supremacy in this century as a poet.

Values in fiction

Of all the writers of this century, D. H. Lawrence was the most impassioned and persistent in seeking to diagnose some of the psychic dangers besetting his society, and the potential sources of strength from which they might be combated. His position on the literary scene may, in external terms, be plotted easily enough:

> I hate Bennett's resignation. Tragedy ought really to be a great kick at misery. But *Anna of the Five Towns* seems like an acceptance – so does all the modern stuff since Flaubert.
> (Letter to A. W. McLeod, 6 October 1912)

Here is Lawrence's revulsion from the French Realist tradition. His indebtedness to the more spiritual realism of the Russian novelists shows in a letter to Catherine Carswell of 2 December 1916:

> ... don't think I would belittle the Russians. They have meant an enormous amount to me; Turgenev, Tolstoi, Dostoievski – mattered almost more than anything, and I thought them the greatest writers of all time.

(That by the date of this letter he could go straight on to condemn Russian fiction does not affect the issue.) He may, in loose terms, be connected with the same nonconformist Midlands as George Eliot; though he was not intimate with anything comparable to the radical intellectual circles of her early years (see p. 64 above). But Lawrence has a clearer literary continuity with Hardy's less systematized and more poetic conception of the novel, and with the deep sense pervading Hardy's work of man's life as one with its environment in nature. Richard Jefferies's link with Lawrence is also strong: it involves not merely the Hardyesque qualities of Jefferies, but the fact that the terse yet offhand rhythms, and the flexible, sarcastic, slightly truculent tone of much of Lawrence's polemical prose seem also to go back directly to Jefferies.[29]

While Hardy was preoccupied with a rural world in decline, however, Lawrence saw one in the more characteristically modern condition of transformation to industry and urbanism. This runs steadily through *The Rainbow* (1915). Little by little, the Brangwen circle move out from a life bounded by the rhythms of the traditional farmer's year, into more modern worlds: to the local high school, to London 'into a big shop' or to study art, to a working-class town school, to a Teachers' Training College where folk-song and morris-dancing appear, their own ghosts, in the curriculum, to 'a fairly large house in the new, red-brick part of Beldover ... a villa built by the widow of the late colliery manager'. 'Out into the world meant out into the world.'

Thus *The Rainbow* registers how a wider, looser, more complex, more ambitious pattern of life came in; and recognizes also that the archaic springs of strength could no longer meet its needs. Most of what Lawrence was to write after *The Rainbow* conducts the search, in fictional terms, for a new source of vitality. What Lawrence, in fact, saw himself as discovering was that in any individual there is a unique and inexpungable source of vitality lying deep in the psyche; and his concern with the intimacies of sex is best seen as a derivative from this belief, a conviction simply that in sex the central psychic forces can most abundantly flow and most easily and naturally assume their uninsistent yet powerful kind of control. Much of his outstanding later work may be seen as an exploring of the essential difference between the sham strength of those who lack this kind of integration, and the essential reality of those who have it. Particularly is this true of the short stories: for example, *St Mawr*, *The Captain's Doll*, *The Fox*, *Sun*, *The Virgin and the Gipsy*.

Moreover, the psychic ideal – an inner, intangible, relaxed but sinew-strong integrity and unity – becomes a literary one; and the topicality of this fact will by now be plain. The 'old stable ego' of character disappears,[30] and so does that of plot. 'Tell Arnold Bennett that all rules of construction hold good only for novels which are copies of other novels.'[31] In *Women in Love* (1920), his most clearly unique achievement,[32] the characters are caught in all their disjointed wholeness; and the wavering episodic movement, the abrupt transitions of the story, leave the book itself with the same kind of unity – massively and cumulatively present in spite of much that would seem at first to preclude it. Lawrence's personal quality is insistent throughout, to be sure. But there is more to say. The abrupt transitions, the calculated disjointedness, the organic kind of unity, belong to the period, and (leaving the differences for the moment aside) have affinity with the modes of organization of Eliot's *Love Song of J. Alfred Prufrock* or of *Ulysses* (see pp. 72–4 and 83–4 above).

Lawrence's verse follows a similar course. The more traditional inspiration of the passage quoted above (p. 69) gives place, even before 1914, to a progressively freer verse style, to the new, looser kinds of transition and unity which have just been discussed in his prose, and to a related overriding concern for the essential, individual reality of living things. Finally, the *Preface* which Lawrence wrote for the 1927 edition of his poems shows him clearly as one who, from the point of view of the period, should be seen in relation to Bergson, to Imagism (although it is an Imagism taken to new and transforming depths), and in general to the new sense, both of life and of technique, which had entered English poetry.

It is the quality of Lawrence's interest in life which justifies his claim: 'Primarily I am a passionately religious man'. But with the clarity of the great artist he went straight on, in the same sentence, to make clear how a struggle against difficulties, a struggle indeed to overcome weaknesses, is integral to his work:

> ... and my novels must be written from the depth of my religious experience. That I must keep to because I can only work like that. And my Cockneyism and commonness are only when the deep feeling doesn't find its way out, and a sort of jeer comes instead, and sentimentality, and purplism.
>
> (Letter to Edward Garnett, 22 April 1914)

Lawrence becomes a master in fiction through the struggle to become master of himself. If self-absorption is an evil, he was not wholly free of it. A few months before the battle of the Somme he could write:

> ... I will not live any more in this time ... as far as I possibly can, I will stand outside this time, I will live my life, and if possible, be happy, though the whole world slides in horror down into the bottomless pit ... What does it matter about that seething scrimmage of mankind in Europe?
>
> (Letter to Lady Ottoline Morrell, 7 February 1916)

And if *Women in Love* exposes the self-assertive determination of one human being to dominate another, one should have in mind that Lawrence can also write:

> Frieda says I am antediluvian in my positive attitude. I do think a woman must yield some sort of precedence to a man ... I do think men must go ahead absolutely in front of their women, without turning round to ask for permission or approval from their women. Consequently the women must follow as it were unquestioningly.
>
> (Letter to Katharine Mansfield, December 1918)

Above all, it is necessary to recognize that Lawrence's deep sense of how modern man may become rootlessly cut off from the proper springs of his vitality is not a calm and magisterial diagnosis of weakness in others, but a brave and persevering response to the challenge of his own predicament:

> We're rather like Jonahs running away from the place we belong ... So I am making up my mind to return to England during the course of the summer. I really think that the most living clue to life is in us Englishmen in England, and the great mistake we make is in not uniting together in the strength of this real living clue – religious in the most vital sense.
>
> (Letter to R. P. Barlow, 30 March 1922)

Five years later Lawrence is still writing in much the same way:

> It is our being cut off that is our ailment, and out of this ailment everything bad arises. I wish I saw a little clearer how you get over this cut-offness. ... Myself, I suffer badly from being so cut off. But what is one to do? ... One has no real human relations – that is so devastating.
>
> (Letter to T. Burrow, 3 August 1927)

It may be that this alienation from his own country ('the thought of England is entirely repugnant,' he wrote in 1921; he never really abandoned this position and never returned save as a fleeting and dissatisfied visitor) lies behind another achievement in Lawrence which is close to his own weakness. If we value him as the writer who, more than any other in this age, has striven to affirm and renew life, we should remember that this was in response to his own tendency to indiscriminate exasperation and disgust, to something not unlike the 'doing dirt on life' that also disgusted him in his other phase. 'This filthy contemptible world of actuality' in a letter of 1 April 1917 is both echoed, and controlled, in the words of the Lawrentian hero of the last novel:

> When I feel the human world is doomed, has doomed itself by its own mingy beastliness, then I feel the colonies aren't far enough. The moon wouldn't be far enough, because even there you could look back and see the earth, dirty, beastly, unsavoury among all the stars: made foul by men. Then I feel I've swallowed gall, and it's eating my inside out, and nowhere's far enough away. But when I get a turn, I forget it all again. (*Lady Chatterley's Lover*, Chapter 16)

If Lawrence is the greatest English writer of the century (Yeats, in this respect, stands nearest to him) it is largely because art feeds upon the tensions in the artist as well as on their resolution; and the tensions hinted at by the above quotations are what help to give Lawrence's people their rich and flexible complexity and their astonishing vitality. Thus it is exactly as an artist that Lawrence is so greatly superior to, say, a writer with serious and sensitive interests in human personality like L. H. Myers (*The Clio*, 1925; *The Root and The Flower*, completed 1935; *Strange Glory*, 1936). Myers's preoccupation with what is real and what is hollow in life is akin to Lawrence's, but the best part of his work specifically as fiction is his rendering of the equatorial forest as expressing rich relaxed spontaneity. Aside from this, there is a recurrent tendency for the action of the books to become progressively divorced from what is most seriously at issue in them, and to degenerate into a kind of slow-moving and wooden intrigue.

Largely, it is also Lawrence's talent as a writer, in a comparatively conventional sense, that makes him more satisfying than an important though still much neglected novelist of his period, John Cowper Powys (*Wolf Solent*, 1929; *A Glastonbury Romance*, 1933; *Weymouth Sands*, 1934). Powys, like Lawrence, responded as a moralist to the needs of the modern world (see his long prose essay, *In Defence of Sensuality*, 1930). His highly idiosyncratic kind of sensualist Manichaeism is sometimes a trifle ridiculous; but so, one must surely admit, is Lawrence at his most speculative and dogmatic. Powys's sense of life, though crabbed and contorted, can be powerfully vivid; and his awareness of natural beauty is deeply moving, and reminiscent of both Lawrence and Hardy. It must also be said in his favour that he was not an alienated writer as both these were in part. His work never displays either melancholy, or waspish despair; and is confident and zestful, with a kind of tempestuous geniality. But it is also usually awkward and (despite its almost Dickensian elaboration) curiously same, with characters and incidents that can be both wooden and forced. Surprisingly, the immediately striking contrast with Lawrence is in respect simply of literary competence. Viewed generally, Powys's work leaves the impression of a lifelong amateur of gigantic ambition and real if ill-directed genius. All in all, however, he requires fuller treatment than he can receive here.

Many will remain dubious of Powys's ragged immensities; and in the context of the present discussion will find a more congenial figure in Joyce Cary. Cary, though, has something important in common with Powys. Also a moralist, he is also no 'Modernist'. In his work too, a loose episodic structure and a boisterous sense of character are akin to Dickens rather than Lawrence. His predilection for the chronicle novel, straddling several generations, hints at Galsworthy, and there is little that is cosmopolitan and sophisticated about it – it is the resumption of a homely and traditional form. But as this discussion proceeds, it will transpire that this does not make Cary an isolated throw-back. On the contrary. It is what makes him belong to the period in which we now live ourselves: for this, it will be seen, turns out to be a period when the cosmopolitan influence has spent itself, and English writers are resuming certain – for a time neglected – links with the native past.

Cary's political novels (*Prisoner of Grace*, 1952; *Except the Lord*, 1953) have something in common with a work like Wells's *The New Machiavelli* (1911) in their sense of the contrast between the corruptions of public life and the restoring strength of private affection; but Cary's sense of this is easily the fuller, and his rendering of it correspondingly more substantial. At its richest his work is almost poetic in its imaginative apprehension of life and its lyrical expression of this in metaphor. A novel like *A Fearful Joy* (1949) is deeply impressive for its sense of the continuing collapse of traditions in the social revolutions of the two wars; and yet at the same time of this as urgent transformation rather than mere decline, of life continually reasserting itself through its own deepest, strongest, yet crudest drives. Finally (to revert to Lawrence) at one point Cary is strong where Lawrence is weak. Throughout his work runs a confident sense, made real in the fiction itself, of how each man or woman lives and thrives by virtue of bonds with many others; of how everyone is a unit in the whole social fabric of the family and of society. Lawrence is very different. Birkin says to Ursula, 'I don't want a definite place ... it is a horrible tyranny of a fixed milieu'.[33] Mellors and Connie (*Lady Chatterley's Lover*, 1928) find their fulfilment in isolation in an unsympathetic world. Great as are the differences, the reader of Lawrence will sometimes find himself recalling Arnold's *Dover Beach*:

Ah, love, let us be true
To one another! for the world ...
Hath really neither joy, nor love, nor light,
Nor certitude, nor peace, nor help for pain;
And we are here as on a darkling plain. ...

Developments in literary criticism

The development of literary criticism in this period is a topic which receives detailed discussion later, and what is said here is by way of preliminary to that. Perhaps it is as well to indicate at the start, in broad terms, the two interests which have lain behind what has been new and forward-looking in criticism since Eliot began his career. Of these one has started from the fact that a literary work is nothing other than certain words in a certain order; and it has taken the form of a close and detailed concern with how the verbal texture of the work, through the exact quality and interplay of its details, creates the richness and depth of meaning of the whole work. This, as is suggested by the comparison between Eliot and Mallarmé (made on pp. 72–3 above), largely derives from the ideas and theories about poetry of the late-nineteenth-century French poets and critics who have already been discussed.

The other guiding idea – the best critics have necessarily seen both in the closest inter-connection – has spread much wider, and run parallel in fact to the writers' concern with how society has been disrupted and endangered. Reacting from the idea (as sometimes expressed by Wilde, say) that literature, being art, stood apart from life, critics have insisted that literary values were ultimately one with those of living itself. From this point of view, critical issues are inseparable in the end from general cultural ones. Serious writing has been seen as one of the major forces sustaining general cultural health; and the weakening of society, the decline of its standards of discrimination through the spread of either commercial or scientific values beyond their proper spheres, stood out as matters directly concerning the critic. Moreover, much that is distinctive of criticism in the modern period has developed along with the development of English literature as a major part of higher education (at school or university) in the humane, non-vocational 'cultural' sense (see pp. 36–8).

It is Matthew Arnold who stands at the point of origin of this way of studying literature; and his reasons for stressing its value help to explain how criticism (with literature itself) has in fact been reaching forward to a new social role. 'More and more mankind will discover', Arnold wrote in 1880, specifically with the decline of religion in mind, 'that we have to turn to poetry to interpret life for us, to console us, to sustain us.' Some of the implications of this for the function of the critic emerge from what the most important of modern teacher-critics, F. R. Leavis, has said in the context of Arnold:

> Many who deplore Arnold's way with religion will agree that, as the other traditions relax and social forms disintegrate, it becomes correspondingly more important to preserve the literary tradition.[34]

In part, literary criticism and the educational institutions associated with it have been moving towards some of the social functions – such as sustaining an awareness of cultural tradition and moral values – once chiefly exercised, and in part still exercised, by organized religion. Criticism has been gaining a place which spreads wider in society, and goes deeper, than might at first appear.

In turning from these general matters to brief detailed illustration of them, the main point is that there has been no sudden break in development. Throughout the nineteenth century, there was a strong tradition (Ruskin, Coventry Patmore, and Leslie Stephen have their places in it, besides Arnold) that the values of life and art were ultimately one. The critical writings of A. R. Orage (editor of *The New Age*, 1908–21) constantly take up problems of moral wholeness ('moral decadence may be discovered in style itself... its sign-manual in style is the diffuse sentence, the partial treatment, the inchoate vocabulary, the mixed principles'[35]) and also of cultural decay, commercialization, shortage of serious criticism, and debasement of standards. Moreover, they insist steadily on the critic's duty to distinguish decisively between the first-rate and the second-rate, and they employ both crushing irony and also close poetic analysis. They point clearly backwards to Arnold (whom Orage constantly praises, and whose method of 'touchstones' in poetic criticism he regularly employs) and forwards to more recent criticism. Not only in singling out a writer like George Bourne for commendation, but also in its *bêtes noires* (the military critic of *The Times*, 'the frivolous Professor Murray', the Poetry Society, Masefield, Landor, polite essayists like 'Alpha of the Plough', popular reviewing, literary weeklies, and the 'kept Press') Orage's work seems to radiate out almost equally towards Arnold, Eliot, and Leavis. As his work becomes better known, Orage is now proving to be one of the decisive figures in the continuity of criticism over the last century.

A number of others, however, must also be taken into account. Ford Madox Ford (or Hueffer) was a more relaxed and less incisive critic, but he deserves mention in the same context as Orage, and the columns of his *English Review* (he edited this from 1908) often dealt seriously with central issues of criticism and culture, even if Orage's *New Age* was ill-satisfied with how they did so. Before 1912, T. E. Hulme had repudiated 'romantic' poetry and the primacy of emotion, and had stressed how writing which is not trivial uses words precisely and concretely.[36] J. Middleton Murry's *The Problem of Style* (1922) was also something of a landmark, for it brought clearly together the ideas that literature is the expression of the writer's whole response to life seen in its deepest terms, and that it is so through its exploratory and creative use of language and especially of metaphor. Moreover, Murry anticipated much later work in insisting that the greatness of Shakespeare himself lay precisely here.[37] Eliot's importance and influence must be gauged not only by his early critical essays, but also his editorship (1922–39) of the *Criterion*, which published important critical work by Pound, Hulme, and Eliot himself, and stressed such ideas as that literature is an integral part of life, that it should show a response in particular to the facts of contemporary life, that humane culture is threatened by the spread of a crudified scientific outlook and that a loss of standards has occurred through the invasion of literature by commerce. 'The almost impregnable position ... that one should write in some way that will not depreciate the value of the electro-plates now possessed by the elder British publishing firms', Pound put it in the opening issue. As the *Criterion* went on, however, its editorial commentaries proved more stilted in tone, and less concerned with critical than with ecclesiastical, architectural, theatrical, or publishing issues.

Much superior to it as a critical journal was *The Calendar of Modern Letters* (1925–7), edited by Edgell Rickword and Douglas Garman.

This not only published essays of central importance like Lawrence's *Art and Morality* and *Why the Novel Matters*, but spoke out, with consistency and often with pungent asperity, against the 'annihilating of standards' ('the subservience of criticism to publishers' advertisements') as reflected by certain literary weeklies, the literary 'Establishment', or the modern section of the *Oxford Book of English Verse*; and also against the harmful influence, in the sphere of spiritual values, of science. On the positive side, much that is best in later criticism was already fully developed in the *Calendar*: its contributors are consistently clear, for example, on the claim of satire to a high place in literature, the ultimate identity of 'poetic and real values', and the fact that in all literature (fiction as much as verse) it is the organization of language, 'the verbal and differentiated qualities of writing', which should determine the critic's judgement. To turn from A. R. Orage or the *Calendar* to *Scrutiny* (1932–53), which with the writings of its editor F. R. Leavis is the outstanding critical achievement of the century in English, is to see that *Scrutiny*'s merits lie less in bringing original and powerful new ideas into criticism than in the comprehensive and detailed working out of ideas which had already been formulated, and in a recognition, sustained over several decades, of what makes a significant argument in critical matters, and what a trivial one.

The technique of detailed 'analysis' was developed in several important books of the 1920s. I. A. Richards's *Principles of Literary Criticism* (1924) supplied an elaborate (if in the end inadequate) theory on which analysis could be based, and that theory also gave poetry a central place as contributing not merely to amusement, but also to fundamental cultural health. *A Survey of Modernist Poetry* (1927), by Robert Graves and Laura Riding, was a pioneer work anticipating much later writing, now better known, in the field of poetic ambiguity.[38] Finally, G. Wilson Knight began his detailed if often erratic analyses of poetry and symbolism in Shakespeare just before 1930.

At about that time, indeed, a change begins to come over the critical scene. The period 1910–30 was one in which a whole series of fundamental ideas in English criticism were either brought into being, or re-expressed so as to be endowed with quite fresh power. With them had already come a new sense of what was important in English literary history – Milton, the Romantics, Victorians, and especially

'Georgians' counting for less, Pope, Dryden, and especially the early-seventeenth-century poets counting for more.[39] The last twenty or thirty years have seen the full working out of those fundamental ideas, or their extension to new fields (for example, to medieval literature). This is not to depreciate the value of the later work: Leavis's best poetic analyses (they vary greatly in merit) are the best in the language, Empson's studies of ambiguity are much more systematic and elaborate than Graves's. It is to point to the kind of importance which this later work has had. In a period when literature was threatened by many difficulties, a major critical effort did much to maintain serious standards, and also to make a great body of original and difficult creative work understood and valued by the front line of serious readers. Eliot, Joyce, and Lawrence are now comprehended and valued by thousands who have never known the appearance of baffling strangeness which these writers presented a generation ago. But the fact of a basic contrast between the best critical work of the last generation, and that of the generation before it, remains.

The closing years of an age

This situation in criticism closely follows the situation in original writing: and naturally so, for in large part the former was made both possible and urgent by the latter. It is at this point that the reader should recall what was said above about Cary (p. 93); and that the general picture of literary development over the past fifty years – one of which no clear and full impression has yet, I think, been suggested anywhere – starts to become clear. From 1930 onward the *avant-garde* writers of the two preceding decades begin to retire from the scene. Pound had left England and wrote in comparative isolation abroad; Lawrence, Joyce, and Virginia Woolf were removed by death, and Eliot produced no verse (other than his plays) after *Four Quartets*, completed by the early 1940s. A number of new writers appear, and the question is of the relation which they have to the outstanding figures who preceded them. Again, it is probably best to suggest an answer in broad terms, before attempting to illustrate it.

Two forces seem to have been at work. First, a number of the younger writers, especially poets, were affected by, and in part conformed to, the literary and critical ideas which this survey has associated with Eliot. On the other hand, when younger writers have been at their most individual or original, it has often been on lines independent from Eliot, and perhaps even taking up something in our past literature which was set in the background by his views, rather than brought into the foreground. Two contrasting and yet interrelating trends have therefore to be distinguished. One is represented by a measure of deference to the attitudes which came from the period 1910–30 (and which were now sometimes seen in simplified form); the other by various more or less tentative efforts to write independently of those attitudes or to reach back to areas and traditions of our literature which they depreciated or condemned.

On the question of relative value, the answer is simple. The 1910–30 period was one of the great epochs of English literature. It stands with 1590–1612, or 1710–35, or 1798–1822. What has been written since then does not bear comparison with it for a moment. The trends which have been referred to, however, throw light not on the quality of recent development, but on its direction. They suggest, in fact, that Eliot and Pound must surely leave a permanent mark on English verse, but did not re-orientate it once and for all.

To turn, for example, to Auden, Spender, and the other 'political' poets of the 1930s (though they were not writers of political verse only) is at once to encounter work which is very far from continuing the traditions of Pound and Eliot. Certainly, their concern about social and cultural disorder is reminiscent of *The Waste Land*:

> In unlighted streets you hide away the appalling;
> Factories where lives are made for a temporary use
> Like collars or chairs, rooms where the lonely are battered
> Slowly like pebbles into fortuitous shapes.
>
> (*The Capitol*, 1940)

But the resemblance is a strictly limited one. Eliot's gaze was upon the culture and society of his own time, but he saw it in the abiding terms of one whose ultimate solutions were spiritual and universal. Topicality in the work of these new poets was at once sharper, less portentous, and more limited: the counterpart of a less serious or at least less solemn conception of verse, as also of an interest in left-wing politics, combined with the mounting political tension created by the Slump, the rise of Hitler, the war in Spain, and the unemployment and industrial policies of the government (see pp. 33–4). These differences of attitude and approach show clearly in the texture of their verse. Auden does not employ Pound's 'mode of superposition', but an organization which, in both logic and syntax, is like that of ordinary discourse. Moreover, his work draws on a very much narrower range of cultural reference, and offers a much narrower range of emotion, at least within the single poem. He reflects the new admiration for dryness, irony, easy vernacular diction, and self-deflation in verse; but because his mode of organization was, in several respects, different from that of Pound or Eliot, his verse lacks the poignant intensity of those poets, though it offers something instead.[40]

Indeed, Auden to some extent drew upon the very cast of thought – external, scientific, classifying – which lay behind the social organizations he condemned: perhaps the most distinctive feature of his verse is the almost uninterrupted succession of class-words (plural nouns, or singular nouns employed with plural force) which run through it. 'Streets', 'Factories', 'rooms', 'the appalling', 'the lonely', make this decisively clear in the passage quoted above. All this is to say that the continuity with Pound and Eliot was superficial rather than profound. Certainly, from 'Lay your sleeping head, my love' to *The Shield of Achilles*, there is a more lyrical side to Auden's work; one which grew more prominent in quantity, if not quality, as his later verse ceased to be political, and became personal and religious. But this spare lyrical poignancy, musical though vernacular, can in no way be referred back to Eliot. Influenced perhaps by Yeats, it points mainly to Hardy, and is a partial resumption of the tradition of verse discussed above on pp. 69–70.

The work of Dylan Thomas often conspicuously conforms to Eliot's guiding ideas. These lines are from *A Refusal to Mourn the Death, by Fire, of a Child in London*:

> Never ...
> Shall I let pray the shadow of a sound
> Or sow my salt seed
> In the least valley of sackcloth to mourn
> The majesty and burning of the child's death.
>
> I shall not murder the mankind of her going with a grave truth
> Nor blaspheme down the stations of the breath
> With any further
> Elegy of innocence and youth.

'Valley of sackcloth', 'stations of the breath', 'mankind of her going', and several other turns of phrase in this passage bring to mind Eliot's 'words perpetually juxtaposed in new and sudden combinations, meanings perpetually *eingeschachtelt* into meanings' (see above, p. 73). But when he wrote this, Eliot was discussing a passage from Tourneur, and pointing to the firm-set muscularity of its language. Thomas's conformity to Eliot's principle is superficial. In these lines it appears as a harmless idiosyncrasy of diction; often elsewhere as mere distracting cleverness. His strength (and it must be remembered that he was the most obviously gifted poet – the words imply clear reservations – to appear in the last thirty years) lay elsewhere: in a half-naïve, half-mystical, delighted sense of the livingness of man's environment and his oneness with it, which emerges in a few only of his poems, such as *A Refusal ...*, *Poem in October*, and 'Especially when the October Wind'. But again, though in a different way, the case is one of a poet who conforms on the surface to Eliot's dicta, but is independent in substance; for this deeper and more genuine side to Thomas does not point at all towards Eliot, Pound, Donne, or the *Symbolists*, but to Hopkins and still more to Blake, poets whom Eliot ignored or disparaged.

The important poet of this period who seems to have been decisively influenced by Eliot was William Empson. His case is a very different one, but in the end, surprisingly, it seems to bring out the same general direction of change. In his slender though distinguished production of verse there is a dry but impassioned or half-tortured intellectuality which indeed looks back to Donne; and with that, often, a coolness and casualness of tone which seem to stem from the criticism of Eliot or Richards:

> It is the pain, it is the pain endures.
> Your chemic beauty burned my muscles through.
> Poise of my hands reminded me of yours.
>
> What later purge from this deep toxin cures?
> What kindness now could the old salve renew?
> It is the pain, it is the pain, endures. ('Villanelle')

Moreover Empson, as these lines show ('Poise of my hands', 'this deep toxin'), has a particularity of apprehension and of language which Auden lacks. Yet although Empson has been an important influence on later writers of verse, his influence has not been contrary to that of Auden so much as parallel to it. This is because Empson's recondite, contorted, and powerful poems (*Arachne*, say, or *High Dive*) have not been imitated. Later writers have taken their direction rather from those of his poems, like *Villanelle* and *Aubade*, where an adroit and suave easiness prevails – where, indeed, Empson is nearest to a kind of verse which Auden both practised, and identified as 'the fencing wit of an informal style'. The result has been that Empson at his most distinctive has been least influential: and most influential at his most Audenesque. John Wain, for example, has claimed to have followed Empson's lead; but this must be seen in the light of a characteristic poem of Wain's like *Who Speaks my Language?*:

> Ah, no. It seems the simplest words take fright
> And shape themselves anew for every ear,
> Protected by a crazy copyright
>
> From ever making their intention clear.
> And yet one cannot blame the words alone ...

The nearest parallel is not in Empson at all, but Auden, and it is decisively close:

> Verse was a special illness of the ear;
> Integrity was not enough; that seemed
> The hell of childhood: he must try again.
> (*Rimbaud*, 1940)

Empson's work, that is to say, has a very distinctive place for its intrinsic qualities, but as an influence it has contributed to the general direction of movement rather than made against it.

It thus transpires that recent verse has not been under the dominant influence of what was most distinctive and remarkable in Eliot and Pound. It has picked up many different threads of poetic development, including some from that immediate past with which they broke fairly sharply, and others from phases of English literature which they repudiated or ignored. Among other recent writers, Philip Larkin's respect for an early-nineteenth-century poet like Praed, and Donald Davie's tribute to the purity and decorum of eighteenth-century poets like Cowper, point in a similar direction; as does the crisp elegance of a rather older poet, Roy Fuller, who has written his best work in the 1960s, and the measured, scrupulous limpidity of Charles Tomlinson at his best. Graves and Muir also have their place, in this context. The former has emerged more and more clearly in recent years as a poet who has made a substantial contribution to English literature while eschewing the revolutionary techniques of Eliot and Pound; and the latter's best verse (written late in his life) stresses yet another link with the poetry of the past, in that the chief English influences upon it have been Blake and Wordsworth.

Perhaps this perspective will become clearer if the reader refers again to the poetic continuity noticed (pp. 69–70) in Hardy, Edward Thomas, Lawrence, and Graves. The full point of the dry, witty tone in the closing lines of Graves's stanza may now be seen: it shows, at an early stage, what has emerged as a very definite change in that continuity, but not (as could have been argued twenty years ago, say) something like a lasting repudiation of it. The impact of Eliot and Pound and all that they stood for has been profound. English poetry will be slow to lose the power for astringent intellectuality, or wide cultural reference, or satire and vernacular, which have extended its potentialities during the last forty years. But it remains true that Eliot and Pound now seem to have constituted a highly distinctive *phase* of poetic history, one which was at bottom a continental impact, rather than the decisive restoration of a central English tradition; and recently, the English traditions these writers displaced have been reasserting themselves. If any poet has continued unquestionably in the tradition of Eliot and Pound (though raising also the matter of certain independent, Celtic modes of writing and sensibility), it is David Jones.[41]

Something of the same shift may be traced in the recent history of the novel. Since Cary, the most remarkable and original writer of fiction in English has undoubtedly been Samuel Beckett (*Murphy*, 1938; *Watt*, 1953, written much earlier; *Molloy*, *Malone meurt*, and *L'Innommable*, French versions 1951–3, subsequently published in English versions by the author himself). But Beckett is perhaps more of a French than an English writer, and he is also (though the point cannot be pursued here) profoundly an Irish one, as is Flann O'Brien (*At Swim-Two-Birds*, 1939; *The Third Policeman*, written 1940, published 1967). Apart from Beckett, the years since the war have produced fiction of strictly limited interest. But if the question is one of detecting a direction of movement, then it is worth while noticing that many of the novels which have attracted attention (those of Snow, Amis, and Wain for example) have been written in more or less conscious revolt from all that is *avant-garde* and cosmopolitan, and have re-established a degree of continuity with more conventional writers like Wells and Bennett.[42] Lawrence Durrell's tetralogy of novels (*Justine*, 1957; *Balthazar* and *Mountolive*, 1958; *Clea*, 1960) has been based on the idea that human affairs illustrate the Einsteinian principle of relativity. But the chief impression which these works leave (for all their richness, poignancy, and local colour) is of a pervasive negativeness and deprivation which is surprising in a work intended to explore the variety of human love; and as narratives they are straightforward and traditional rather than experimental or *avant-garde*. Anthony Powell's long novel, *The Music of Time* (1951–), unfolds as less and less Proustian in essence with each new volume; and Iris Murdoch, one of the more interesting talents of the last twenty years, has if anything become less conspicuously *avant-garde*.

More important, because of the quality of their writings, is the fact that the later work of both Pound and Eliot falls into place in this picture of gradual and partial change. Pound, writing after 1920 on his own in Italy, seems to have continued in the *Cantos*,[43] with extraordinary consistency, to work in the vein of 1920. There is the same principle of structure through juxtaposition, the same dislocating medley of references, the same density and compression, the same constant extension into new meanings (reaching in the end to the Chinese character and the Egyptian hieroglyph), the same emphatic shifts of voice, often the same casual yet sarcastic tone. That the *Cantos* seem as a whole to be a profound quest, blocked out through example after example taken in all its fullness, for the qualities which can validate public life and thus make true art possible, does not affect the question of continuity. Pound has gone on in a direct line from how he began.[44]

By contrast, Eliot has spent his later years in England, more and more as an established landmark in its literary scene. His later work shows it. Already by the 1930s he was praising, in his prose:

> poetry so transparent that we should not see the poetry but that which we are meant to see through the poetry, poetry so

transparent that in reading it we are intent on what the poem points at, and not on the poetry; this seems to me to be the thing to try for.

With these points in mind, certain features of *Four Quartets* (1935–42) take on a special interest. Among these are the clear-cut yet buoyant quality of several of the lyrics; the sombre lucidity of expression going with an elusiveness not of subtle evocation but rather of argument and idea; the acceptance of something like philosophical generalization; the notable absence of abrupt and cryptic juxtapositions such as are so frequent in *The Waste Land*; and the tone, seldom satirical or throw-away, but often quiet, sincere, intimate, unhappy – sometimes reminiscent of the meditative verse of Arnold. These things make it clear that from several points of view the *Four Quartets* are traditional poems in a sense of that word which Eliot's 1917 essay, *Tradition and the Individual Talent*, implicitly condemned. They have a continuity with areas of English literature from which that essay turned away. This is neither to praise nor to condemn them, but to point towards the kind of work which they comprise. Eliot's later plays are clearly among his minor works; but if their nature, rather than their merit, is considered, they afford another item of evidence to show how far he has moved from where he stood in 1920; and the direction of that movement seems to have been not unlike the general movement of the last decade or so which has been the subject of this whole last section of 'The Literary Scene'.

NOTES

Notes 22, 26, 40, and 41 below refer to publications by the present writer.

1. See Q.D. Leavis, *Fiction and the Reading Public* (1932); F. R. Leavis and D. Thompson, *Culture and Environment* (1933); George Orwell, 'Boys' Weeklies' (1939), and 'Raffles and Miss Blandish' (included in *Critical Essays*, 1946); M. Dalziel, *Popular Fiction 100 Years Ago* (1957); Richard Hoggart, *The Uses of Literacy* (1957).

2. W. B. Yeats, 'The Rhymers' Club' (1892), in *Letters to the New Island* (1934): see especially pp. 144–6.

3. See his essay 'The Art of Fiction' (1884; in *Partial Portraits*, 1888, and *Henry James and Robert Louis Stevenson*, ed. Janet Adam Smith, 1948).

4. For sporadic earlier productions see Una Ellis-Fermor, *The Irish Dramatic Movement* (1939), Appendix B; and the *Guardian*, 28 November 1959, p. 6.

5. *Plays and Controversies* (1923), pp. 157–8; but compare pp. 12 and 155.

6. See Gilbert Phelps, *The Russian Novel in English Fiction* (1956); a short but illuminating book.

7. *New Bearings in English Poetry* (1932), p. 10.

8. Some confirmation of this is given by references in Pound's *Letters*, ed. D. D. Paige (New York, 1950), pp. 90, 239.

9. See, e.g., Wallace Fowlie, *Rimbaud's 'Illuminations'* (1953), p. 109n; also, among the *Illuminations* themselves, 'Villes I and II', and 'Métropolitain'(which may be a source for Eliot's description of the fog in *Prufrock*).

10. *Selected Essays* (1932), p. 373.

11. See Pound's series of essays and notes on recent French poets (*Little Review*, 1918; reprinted in *Make it New*, 1934).

12. See the essay, 'What is Popular Poetry?' (1901), reprinted in *Ideas of Good and Evil* (especially p. 7, 1914 ed.).

13. Earl Miner, *The Japanese Tradition in British and American Poetry* (Princeton, 1958); an informative book, despite its improbable title.

14. Eliot, *Selected Essays*, p. 209; Mallarmé, *Œuvres* (Pléiade, 1945), p. 366.

15. F. W. Bateson, 'Dissociation of Sensibility', *Essays in Criticism*, July 1951; *Le Problème du style* (13th ed., 1924), especially pp. 91–101.

16. Wagner, *The Music of the Future* (1861); *Prose Works*, trans. W. A. Ellis (1894), Vol. III, pp. 317–18; and Vol. V, p. 65, on Schopenhauer's 'Platonic' theory of music.

17. See Gwendoline Bays, *The Orphic Vision* (1964).

18. See, e.g., K. Tillotson, 'Donne in the Nineteenth Century' (in *Essays Presented to F. P. Wilson*, 1960).

19. J. E. Duncan, *The Revival of Metaphysical Poetry* (Minnesota, 1959), especially Chapters VI–VIII.

20. Letter of 9 July 1933.

21. Augustine, *Confessions* (trans. E. B. Pusey, 1930), pp. 53–4.

22. 'The Waste Land Revisited', *Encounter*, August 1968.

23. 'The Novels of Turgenev' (1933), in *The Captain's Deathbed* (1950), p. 54.

24. See her essays, 'Modern Fiction', in *The Common Reader* (1925), and 'Mr Bennett and Mrs Brown', in *The Captain's Deathbed.*

25. But compare J. W. Graham, 'A Negative Note on Bergson and Virginia Woolf', *Essays in Criticism*, January 1956.

26. I have discussed these points more fully in 'Wyndham Lewis: the Massacre and the Innocents', *Hudson Review*, Summer 1957; reprinted in *The Charted Mirror*, 1960.

27. Letter to Dorothy Wellesley, April 1936; in Yeats's *Letters*, ed. A. Wade (1954), p. 853.

28. 'Yeats and the Penal Age', *Critical Quarterly*, 1966.

29. See for example *Amaryllis at the Fair* (1887), Chapter 27, or the closing pages of Chapter 32.

30. Letter to Edward Garnett, 5 June 1914; in the context, it is relevant to note, of several foreign writers, Russian or Italian, as possible guides or models.

31. 16 December 1915; *Letters*, ed. Aldous Huxley (1932), p. 295.

32. It was described as 'Mr Lawrence's most significant and most characteristic novel' by E. D. McDonald as early as 1925 (*Centaur Bibliography*, p. 49).

33. *Women in Love*, Chapter 26 (Phoenix ed., 1954, p. 348).

34. 'Arnold as Critic' in *Scrutiny*, 1939, Vol. VII, p. 323.

35. A. R. Orage, *Selected Essays and Critical Writings*, ed. H. Read and D. Saurat (1935), pp. 13–14.

36. See *Speculations*, ed. H. Read (1924), pp. 113–40; and also *Further Speculations*, ed. S. Hynes (Minnesota, 1953), especially pp. 79–80.

37. *The Problem of Style* (1922; lectures, 1921), pp. 26–31; 83, 97–9; and 13 and elsewhere.

38. See also, however, Graves's earlier pamphlet, *Contemporary Techniques in Poetry* (1925).

39. On Milton, see *The Problem of Style*, p. 109; and also Read's 'The Nature of Metaphysical Poetry' (*Criterion*, 1923; reprinted in *Reason and Romanticism*, 1926).

40. 'Auden: The Master as Joker', *Art International*, January 1969.

41. 'David Jones: A Perpetual Showing', *Hudson Review*, Spring 1963, reprinted in *The Colours of Clarity*, 1964.

42. I have discussed this suggestion more fully in 'Notes on the School of Anger' (*Hudson Review*, Autumn 1957, and *The Charted Mirror*).

43. *A Draft of XXX Cantos*, 1933; *Cantos XXXI–XLI*, 1934; *The Fifth Decade of Cantos*, 1937; *Cantos LII–LXXI*, 1940; *The Pisan Cantos* (LXXIV–LXXXIV), 1949; *Section: Rock Drill* (*Cantos LXXXV–XCV*), 1957; *Thrones* (*96–109 de los cantares*), 1960.

44. Pound's splendid but in a certain sense traditional translations from the Chinese *Classical Anthology* (1956) should however be noted.

PART III

HENRY JAMES: THE DRAMA OF DISCRIMINATION

HENRY GIFFORD

Winterstoke Professor of English, University of Bristol

'I HAVE made my choice, and God knows that I have now no time to waste.' This memorandum of 1881, written for his own eye, reveals the essential Henry James in his power of lonely decision and his uncommon ardour. The particular choice was to live in England: a step often deplored but, given the peculiar genius of James, strictly logical. In taking it he overcame the last of his disabilities. Almost from infancy he had known his talent – that of 'the visiting mind', to gather impressions and to read aspects – but for making use of it he needed faith in his own lights. The elder Henry James, his father, thought little of 'mere' literary men, since any kind of 'doing' was a restriction on 'being'. William James teased and harassed his younger brother with cordial insensibility until at length – in 1905 – Henry rejected his point of view as too 'remotely alien' for the beginnings of appreciation. He waged a further struggle with his American environment. An essay in *French Poets and Novelists* (1878) speaks of Turgenev as 'having what one may call a poet's quarrel' with his native land. 'He loves the old, and he is unable to see where the new is drifting.' James recognized this 'poet's quarrel' as necessarily his own, though for him the conditions were even less favourable. Turgenev at least could rejoice in the wealth of type under his eye, whereas the American novelist had still like Hawthorne to content himself with coldness, thinness, and blankness. 'It is on manners, customs, usages, habits, forms, upon all these things matured and established, that a novelist lives ...' In the second chapter of his *Hawthorne* (1879), James drew up a list of 'the items of high civilization' missing from American life: a court, an aristocracy, an established church; country houses, cathedrals, old universities and schools; the arts, a political society, a sporting class. Another kind of novelist – Melville, for instance, of whom James apparently knew nothing – may live immensely without these things, or on their sparest counterparts. But for James, with his indefeasible sense of Europe, America gave too little suggestion. He coveted the 'deep, rich English tone' of George Eliot, and the density of Balzac's France. Instead, America offered too often scenes like this in *The Bostonians* (1886):

> the desolate suburban horizons, peeled and made bald by the rigour of the season; the general hard, cold void of the prospect; the extrusion, at Charleston, at Cambridge, of a few chimneys and steeples, straight, sordid tubes of factories and engine-shops, or spare, heavenward finger of the New England meeting-house. There was something inexorable in the poverty of the scene, shameful in the meanness of its details ... loose fences, vacant lots, mounds of refuse, yards bestrewn with iron pipes, telegraph poles, and bare wooden backs of places.

The activity these things betoken meant very little to James. He pleaded ignorance of the business world – which formed, on his own reckoning, nineteen-twentieths of American life. His family and friends were all among the 'casually disqualified', so that eventually, like White-Mason in *Crapy Cornelia* (1909), he would find himself shut out from 'the music of the future', together with

> the few scattered surviving representatives of a society once 'good' – *rari nantes in gurgite vasto.*

But that predicament – seen in terms of 'social impossibilities' – was reserved for Edith Wharton to render. James's concern, growing over the years, is more profound. Like Hawthorne, he came to know the pains of the separated artist: the American writer who lived for discrimination and his own approval was forced to contend against the current of national life.

If his experience was narrow – and the James children had scarcely seen a clergyman, a military man, or a politician – he had the advantage of a 'formed critical habit'. There are times when 'critic' and 'creator' are for James interchangeable terms. The critical impulse, as T. S. Eliot long ago pointed out, was remarkably strong in him. We may accept from Mr Eliot that James stands nearer to Hawthorne than to any foreign novelist[1]; but what enlarges his scope beyond Hawthorne's, enabling him to read similar problems with more subtlety, was perhaps the study of Sainte-Beuve and Arnold. These latter displayed (what he might find also in George Eliot and Turgenev) the values of intelligence and irony and of the finely disinterested mind. The young Henry James, according to a letter he wrote in 1867, even had visions of himself as a Sainte-Beuve in English letters.[2] Doubtless it was Sainte-Beuve's marked novelistic sense – his desire to present the whole man in his proper setting – that appealed to James. *Partial Portraits* (1888) owe more than their title to Sainte-Beuve, two collections of whose 'portraits' James had reviewed earlier in the *Nation*. It may even be that there is a hint of derivation, however remote, in *The Portrait of a Lady*.

The American privilege, as James saw it then, was to 'pick and choose and assimilate and in short (aesthetically etc.) claim our property wherever we find it'. Deprivation at home caused a hunger to appropriate and claim possession. Fullness of life was something promised in books, as the small boy discovered from reading *Punch* on the hearth-rug in 'medieval New York'. There he saw the varieties of English life; subsequent visits to Europe beset him thickly with recognitions. Henry James had, like T. S. Eliot and Ezra Pound, the *instructed* imagination, proceeding from books to life and holding the two in mutual enrichment.

* * *

The 'necessity of his case' brought James to the international theme: a restless childhood divided between Europe and America fitted him perfectly for this kind of counterpoint. 'It was as if I had, vulgarly speaking, received quite at first the "straight tip" – to back the right horse or buy the right shares.' The 'mixture of manners', their contrast, the possibilities of a higher civilization than either hemisphere could show by itself – these interests held his attention from the beginning, and never wholly passed out of sight. The sense of Europe involved him, as it had involved Cooper, Hawthorne, and Melville, in a continuing dialectic between present and past, present and future, between innocence and experience, good and evil.[3] Usually he preferred to try 'the bewilderment of the good American, of either sex and of almost any age, in presence of the "European" order'. European bewilderment in presence of America he found less treatable: such attempts as *An International Episode* (1879), *Pandora* (1884), and *Lady Barbarina* (1884) could not be renewed indefinitely. There was in fact a risk of monotony: they had too little to confront. Far more numerous, and generally more rewarding, are the studies of American innocence in a fascinating but more or less corrupt Europe. A brief comparison of *The Europeans* (1878) with *The Portrait of a Lady* (1881) will show what each end of the relation had to offer him.

In presenting the American scene to European eyes he needed to avoid 'the poor concussion of positives on one side with negatives on the other'. Just this difficulty arose in the working of *Washington Square* (1880), which is a provincial story, *mœurs de province*, revealing a corner of the past, 'medieval New York', with a light, caressing irony. Though James's subject is a bad case of parental despotism, it receives something of an idyllic frame. *The Europeans* gains by bringing the European values – merely implied in *Washington Square* – into an active relation with those of Boston. Felix Young and the Baroness not only provide two differing registers of the scene, two projections of European intelligence: they must in their turn face criticism from the Wentworths, they too are weighed in James's fine balance. The author himself, as F. R. Leavis has demonstrated in his alert commentary,[4] does not directly intervene. His sympathies may well lean to the American order – homely, pious, frugal, earnest, candid – but nothing is made simple or schematic. We are called upon to appraise various notes. There is the note of Mr Wentworth and Mr Brand: New England sense of duty; the note of Gertrude Wentworth: a shy originality not altogether at ease in Zion; the note of the Baroness: European worldliness and lack of scruple; the note of Felix: a free intelligence at play, too ingenuous to be wholly European, too light for New England. The comedy of manners, then, defines tacitly an ideal of civilization, where wit shall be tempered with morality, and morality enlivened with wit.

James's own loyalties, it should be stressed, were to patrician New York.[5] As a young man at Newport he had felt a 'particular shade of satisfaction' in 'being in New England without being of it'. He is therefore the impartial onlooker at his comedy in this novel. Boston had struck him as still a rural centre: in the Harvard Law School he used to study his professors for 'type', and, Sainte-Beuve assisting, divined 'those depths of rusticity which more and more unmistakably underlay the social order at large'. That is the style of the Wentworths ('It's primitive,' Felix informs the Baroness, 'it's patriarchal; it's the *ton* of the golden age'). The first encounter with Gertrude staying at home from church on a fine Sunday morning in springtime conveys this exactly. It is done by exhibiting 'the simple details of the picture' to form 'the items of a "sum" in addition'. 'A large square house in the country'; 'neatly-disposed plants' over against a muddy road; doors and windows thrown open 'to admit the purifying sunshine' – here is order, confidence, a quiet joy in 'the abundant light and warmth'.

> It was an ancient house – ancient in the sense of being eighty years old; it was built of wood, painted a clean, clear, faded grey, and adorned along the front, at intervals, with flat wooden pilasters, painted white.

The specification of eighty years is not wholly ironic. Almost the same span in *The Jolly Corner* (1908) provides the sense of continuity over three generations. Here it serves as a passport into the eighteenth century – General Washington had slept there. It belongs to the past in which James felt at ease; the more remote past was 'dusky' for him, the past of Hawthorne's House of the Seven Gables and of iniquitous feudal Europe. But the 'big, unguarded home' in its cleanliness and sobriety has no guilty secrets: it reflects faithfully its master, also 'a clean, clear, faded grey'.

James may have been helped to this vision by certain passages in Turgenev (behind which one discerns the second chapter of Pushkin's *Onegin*). Mr Wentworth is perhaps seen with the aid of George Eliot: a more sympathetic, an unselfish if still pedantic kinsman of Mr Casaubon. Certainly the notation is similar:

> It seemed to him he ought to find [the materials for a judgment] in his own experience, as a man of the world and an almost public character; but they were not there, and he was ashamed to confess to himself ... the unfurnished condition of his repository. (*The Europeans*)

> Hence he determined to abandon himself to the stream of feeling and perhaps was surprised to find what an exceedingly shallow rill it was. (*Middlemarch*)

When a page or two later Felix offers to paint Mr Wentworth 'as an old prelate, an old cardinal, or the prior of an order', we may recall

Ladislaw's idea of Mr Casaubon as a model for Aquinas. Felix indeed is a Ladislaw properly conceived – a convincing and not wearisome Bohemian (something George Eliot could never do). Such derivations often suggest themselves in James's work – there is a hint of another when he says that Turgenev's heroines 'have to our sense a touch of the faintly acrid perfume of the New England temperament'. The art of working the American scene depended on a faculty for relations: hence the critical vision turning to literature for perspective. What he required was the appropriate tone. One might say that his delicacy is Hawthorne's, his mild asperity – the light brush of satire – George Eliot's. But the 'very atmosphere of the mind' that 'takes to itself the faintest hints of life' was entirely his own. Henry James brought an abundant gift of consciousness, controlled in part by what he read, but never submitting to mere imitation.

In *The Europeans* his scrutiny of manners is serious but gentle. The novel was called by him a sketch: it has the brightness of the American air, and its values are put in with a light dexterity. Mr Wentworth's 'doctrine ... of the oppressive gravity of mistakes'; Gertrude's puzzling out of the unfamiliar concept, to 'enjoy'; the Baroness's attitude towards 'fibbing': these revelations of character and social ethos are in their essence playful. The Baroness quits the scene, a superior woman disabled by American rural worth. Like Lord Lambeth in *An International Episode*, and the Prussian Count in *Pandora*, she had expected to conquer. But American simplicity holds the field.

The Portrait of a Lady carries on the debate in much graver terms. The tone has utterly changed:

> She could live it over again, the incredulous terror with which she had taken the measure of her dwelling. Between those four walls she had lived ever since; they were to surround her for the rest of her life. It was the house of darkness, the house of dumbness, the house of suffocation.

Isabel Archer's situation might be compared with Catherine Sloper's in *Washington Square*. Each is the victim of a domestic tyrant, each has been deceived in her generous affections. Isabel, of course, is the more finely aware, and that makes for a higher intensity. But she also matters more for James: her plight deeply engages. There is Ralph Touchett to focus our anxiety for her; and sinister apparitions lurk along her path – Madame Merle at the piano that rainy afternoon, Osmond waiting in the villa which 'had heavy lids, but no eyes'. The symbolism obtrudes: the 'silent, motionless portal' in the Albany house leading in her imagination to 'a region of delight or of terror'; the reminder

> that there were other gardens in the world than those of her remarkable soul, and that there were moreover a great many places which were not gardens at all – only dusky pestiferous tracts, planted thick with ugliness and misery.

The sense of Isabel's predicament seems to be Hawthorne's: her native innocence cannot brook the uncleanness of Osmond. 'She was not a daughter of the Puritans, but for all that she believed in such a thing as chastity and even as decency.' It was Hilda of *The Marble Faun* – a trusting and exalted American girl in guilt-laden Rome – who told the priest in St Peter's after confession: 'I am a daughter of the Puritans'; and James regarded that scene as one of the great moments in Hawthorne's novel.

Isabel, of course, stems from a proved social reality. She is the unique American girl, 'heiress of all the ages', and for her as for Milly Theale in *The Wings of the Dove* (1902), a novel that returns upon this theme, there must be 'a strong and special implication of liberty', to bring out the poignancy of her case. The American girl in Europe – 'a huge success of curiosity' who had 'infinitely amused the nations' – confronted the old order with an entire freedom: she was not 'placed' socially, and wealth made its own privileges. Ralph Touchett sees to it that Isabel receives wealth. Thereby he fosters her illusion of being superior to conditions.

Isabel's self-regard, her habit of 'treating herself to occasions of homage', her 'confidence at once innocent and dogmatic', are grievously punished, and thus James may be seen to explore the American theme of spirit and refractory circumstance. At the same time he offers Isabel a choice between representative men: Lord Warburton the English magnate, Caspar Goodwood the New England entrepreneur, Osmond the American divorced from the native values by long residence in Europe, Ralph Touchett the American who has become in Mr Eliot's sense 'a European – something which no born European, no person of any European nationality, can become'. *The Portrait of a Lady* is indeed brilliant on its social surface. Keen observation; the surest of touches in placing Osmond, Madame Merle, Henrietta Stackpole, the Countess Gemini, Lord Warburton; so much of control, intelligence, the large critical view and sense of relations: having all these, it is justly celebrated as a magnificent novel. In our gratitude for such mastery, we may not recognize the presence of an undertow, pulling James into a region where the intelligence can be blinded. Two jottings from his notebook scenario point this weakness:

> Isabel awakes from her sweet delusion – oh, the art required for making this delusion natural! – and finds herself face to face with a husband who has ended by conceiving a hatred for her own larger qualities.
>
> Ralph's helpless observation of Isabel's deep misery ... This to be a strong feature in the situation.

These notes give too much away. As a matter of fact, Isabel's 'sweet delusion' never is made quite convincing. Both her martyrdom and Ralph's 'helpless observation' seem things contrived, things James needed to bring about for the expression of some deep personal theme. His mind was fixed on suffering and renunciation.

* * *

Popularity – never very certainly in his grasp – deserted James altogether in 1886, the year of *The Bostonians* and *The Princess Casamassima.* If *Daisy Miller* (1878) – an exhibition of the American girl made, as he admits, in poetical rather than critical terms – won him a fairly wide success, *The Bostonians* blighted his fortunes with the public at home. It happens that James's intentionally 'very *American* tale' started to run in the *Century Magazine* for February 1885 which was then publishing two other fictions deeply American: *The Rise of Silas Lapham* by W. D. Howells, and Mark Twain's *Huckleberry Finn.* Howells, the old friend and editor of James, had set his novel also in Boston, and what he produced – a clean square of local colour, rendered with acuteness and sympathy – couldn't fail to please the American reader looking out for the depiction of national type. Lapham, the simple and stubborn Yankee who found his fortune in a paint-mine on the old farm, was well understood by Howells, and the novel has survived much of his other work. *The Bostonians* – a daylight raid on an unsuspecting city, merciless and complete – is brilliant in a manner quite beyond Howells (who has marked affinities with the author of, say, *Washington Square* or *A New England Winter* (1884)). Understandably, its brilliance did not appeal to Mark Twain. Although *Huckleberry Finn* shares at least one of James's preoccupations – the incorruptible young mind, and Huck is, like Maisie Farange, wiser than the adults – Mark Twain and Henry James differ in their knowledge, their irony, their divinations, and their beliefs. The spell of *Huckleberry Finn* arises from two things, Huck's intimacy with the river, and the native resource of his language. The world of the frontier was closed to James; and Huck's range of expression (so suggestive to later American novelists) could not be his: it wasn't his birthright. 'The lightning kept whimpering'; 'it was a steamboat that had killed herself on a rock' – the truly American force of such phrases is bound up with attitudes even hostile to James. (Mark Twain 'would rather be damned to John Bunyan's heaven than read' *The Bostonians*.) A very large side of American life James had to take on trust. All the camp-meeting background of Selah Tarrant is supplied, perhaps, from a book he once reviewed, Nordhoff's *Communistic Societies*; and there is, of course, as F. R. Leavis has noted, a real debt in *The Bostonians* to *Martin Chuzzlewit*. Yet James's novel, even beside a nonpareil like *Huckleberry Finn*, at once folk-tale and poignant record of the American prime, doesn't appear what one might expect, artificial and 'genteel'. It is extremely animated, and it strikes hard.

James knew very well the intellectual tone of Boston (he made one year later a compensatory gesture in his portrait of Emerson); the absurdities of the lecture hall and the passions of female insurgence did not escape his eye searching for the 'salient and peculiar'. He noted 'the situation of women, the decline of the sentiment of sex' as an index to the whole society, and chose therefore to organize his drama of conflicting values around 'a study of one of those friendships between women which are so common in New England'. The battle for Verena Tarrant's soul between the implacable female zealot, Olive Chancellor, and the rude Southern knight-errant, Basil Ransom, enacts in passionate and personal form a conflict of ideas – between North and South, reform and reaction, the feminine and the masculine principles. The periphery is richly comic – a world of queer female missionaries under the gas lamps, of fraud and exaltation and selfless service and crude publicity. But the centre is otherwise conceived:

> There was a splendid sky, all blue-black and silver – a sparkling wintry vault, where the stars were like a myriad points of ice. The air was silent and sharp, and the vague snow looked cruel. Olive now knew very definitely what the promise was that she wanted Verena to make ...

This might almost be the desolate world of ice and snow in which Gerald Crich dies. Lionel Trilling has read a Laurentian meaning into James's novel, and 'fear of the loss of manhood' may be among the promptings to James's imagination.[6] But more essentially – and here too he is akin to Lawrence – James is concerned with the will to dominate. Olive Chancellor is a more awful Hermione Roddice, white-hot and armed with a gospel.

The Princess Casamassima, a novel in which divination frankly replaces the inward knowledge of *The Bostonians*, is in certain ways a companion piece. Its thesis, however, remains somewhat abstract, and James's rendering lacks the complete assurance of *The Bostonians* (Miss Birdseye is given far more circumstantially than Lady Aurora). Again, a group with a fixed design (here they are anarchists) wish to make use of a gifted but immature being. Ransom's words to Verena – 'you are unique, extraordinary ... outside and above all vulgarizing influences' – are even more true of Hyacinth Robinson. But this latter is the conscious artist; and when he too betrays the cause, he does so not as a hustled captive to superior force like Verena, but of his own deliberate choice. Hyacinth's dilemma somewhat resembles that of Nezhdanov in *Virgin Soil*, whom James in a review of Turgenev's novel had characterized as 'drifting ... into the stream of occult radicalism' and then finding himself 'fastidious and sceptical and "aesthetic" '. Nezhdanov kills himself through a sense of his own ineptitude and unworthiness: Hyacinth, because the ideal no longer convinces him. Lionel Trilling in a most persuasive essay[7] has sought to show that James hit off the revolutionary movement of his time with a 'striking literary accuracy', and that every detail of his picture could be 'confirmed by multitudinous records'. Even so, Hyacinth himself – who 'sprang up ... out of the London pavement' – isn't appropriate for the kind of novel – 'grainy and knotted with practicality and detail' – that Mr Trilling makes out *The Princess Casamassima* to be. He springs (as Mr Trilling also argues) from a necessity of James's own spirit. One has the sense that the author imposes a scheme upon his story, perhaps in part unrecognized by himself. 'The dispute between art and moral action', from which Hyacinth at last escapes into death, had its unhappy familial side for James. And the theme of the exquisite nature cut off in its first flowering was to return with Milly Theale.

James's possession of 'the great grey Babylon' (with some help from Dickens) proves how little time he had lost in assimilating the English scene. He was also alive to the drawbacks of his situation. Powerful and privileged Englishmen cared little for ideas: Lord Canterville's 'den' in *Lady Barbarina* was part office and part harness-room – 'it couldn't have been called in any degree a library'. James admired the massive confidence and unconcern of these people, but he became increasingly aware that they missed their opportunities. The young American sister-in-law in *A London Life* (1888)

> marvelled at the waste involved in some human institutions – the English landed gentry for instance – when she noted how much it had taken to produce so little ... all that was exquisite in the home of his forefathers – what visible reference was there to these fine things in poor Lionel's stable-stamped composition?

James clung to the forms of English life, but his sense of alienation grew, in a society where art received every kind of empty homage: 'the line is drawn ... only at the importance of heeding what it may mean'.

In the last decade of the century he wrote numerous stories about the ordeal of the modern artist. These proclaim the duty of sacrifice, of abiding by the 'inspired and impenitent' choice. Two of his most deeply felt tales on this theme, *The Death of the Lion* and *The Middle Years*, came out in the volume called *Terminations* (1895). Only a few months before, James's desperate fling at the theatre had been ended by the miscarriage of *Guy Domville*. These five years of deluded endeavour betray something like a failure of nerve. He had dropped the writing of long novels after *The Tragic Muse* (1890) to win wealth and glory as a dramatist. He found neither: and it is difficult to see what he gained from the whole misadventure except perhaps 'the divine principle of the scenario', which enabled him to project an entire novel in its articulation before rendering it. A novelist whose public begins to desert him is bound to meet the temptation of confronting them more directly, either through the theatre or, as Dickens did, through public readings. James wanted to receive acclamation in person. He swallowed his pride; he made too many concessions; he even put himself in the hands of George Alexander, who on relinquishing James took up Oscar Wilde. *Guy Domville* had some merits, as A. B. Walkley recognized. But 'fastidious, frugal quietism' does not make good theatre. Henry James returned to attempt the work of his life, with no illusions about his solitude.

* * *

R. P. Blackmur has well said that 'James made the theme of the artist a focus for the ultimate theme of human integrity'. This engaged him very often during his English years: Laura Wing in *A London Life*, Rose Tramore in *The Chaperon* (1891), Fleda Vetch in *The Spoils of Poynton* (1897) all face temptations of the wilderness, in which 'the free spirit' is put to proof. Nanda Brookenham in *The Awkward Age* (1899) is left at the end to muster her courage and 'let Van down easily'; Maisie Farange endures in *What Maisie Knew* (1897) a culminating ordeal of moral responsibility to which only an angelic child would be equal. James cannot remit these fierce probations. The sins of greed, the rages of a ruling passion, prey on his mind. Mrs Gereth suffers 'the torment of taste'; the researchers in *The Aspern Papers* (1888) and *The Figure in the Carpet* (1896) that of an obsessed curiosity: the eyewitness in *The Sacred Fount* (1901), for whom 'the condition of light' is 'the sacrifice of feeling', exposes the common case. All these figures are living in what might be Dante's hell. Mr Eliot was surely wide of the mark in referring once to James's 'idealization' of English society. *What Maisie Knew* fixes with unfaltering verve and scorn the barbarities of a world at once feral and ridiculous.

The three major explorations of moral responsibility which James now undertook – *The Ambassadors* (1903), *The Wings of the Dove* (1902), *The Golden Bowl* (1904) – are notorious for their difficulty – a difficulty which first declared itself in *The Sacred Fount*. The notation is almost excessively fine, the issues often appear tenuous, the atmosphere has been pumped 'gaspingly dry'. Readers who delighted in the pictorial brilliancy of his earlier work and its neatness of style, must now grope in a world where for all the animation of James's figurative speech both meaning and action often hang in suspense; they must give unremitting attention to a new kind of discourse – the passional language of disembodied intelligences. And yet – is the later style really so cumbersome? F. O. Mathiessen examined the revisions made in *The Portrait of a Lady* for the New York edition:[8] almost every one is a gain in dramatic power and lucidity. A few random samples from *The Pension Beaurepas* illustrate this: I give the earlier version in brackets:

> 'Poor Mr Ruck [who is extremely good-natured and soft] who's a mush of personal and private concession ...'
>
> Mrs Church [looked at me a moment, in quickened meditation] with her cold competence, picked my story over.
>
> But if he ate very little, he [talked a great deal; he talked about business, going into a hundred details in which I was quite unable to follow him] still moved his lean jaws – he mumbled over his spoilt repast of apprehended facts; strange tough financial fare into which I was unable to bite.

The abounding images – in *The Golden Bowl* there is the Palladian church in the Piazza (ch. vii), the Pagoda in the garden (ch. xxv), the 'tortuous stone staircase' of Prince Amerigo's moral sense in contrast to the high-speed elevator of Mr Verver's (ch. ii), and the overworked device of the bowl itself – are all planted as 'aids to lucidity'. Often they give a patterning to the whole work. Their effect is that of the classical simile as Johnson saw it, which 'must both illustrate and ennoble the subject'. They yield always an explicit meaning: 'the breakage [of the golden bowl] stood not for any wrought discomposure among the triumphant three – it stood merely for the dire deformity of her attitude toward them'. Such images must necessarily be inferior to those which, like the moon in a difficult chapter of *Women in Love*, compose meanings in no other way to be apprehended. They are expository, for the most part brilliantly contrived, but seldom, one feels, forcing their way up from the deepest levels of imagination.

The Golden Bowl in particular makes heavy demands on the reader's willingness to suspend disbelief. Princes and innocent millionaires and sublime little American girls, acting out between them a drama of wonderful intensity, stand a poor chance with the contemporary reader. Meticulously charting the course, James leads Maggie Verver to a kind of Gethsemane: seeing her father, her father's wife, and that wife's lover – her own husband – at cards from the darkness outside, she divines their appeal to save them; to contrive a relation; to lighten them of their sins, like the scapegoat. James's theme of redemption has its moments when high drama breaks out – Maggie, for instance, confronting Charlotte, the uncaged beast, in her splendid and dangerous pride. Yet the conclusion of the novel, with Charlotte safe in the silken halter, worries our sense of fitness. Adam Verver, the saint of acquisition; Maggie herself, in that fug of filial piety (the two Ververs, like the James family, being most of the time 'genially interested in almost nothing but each other'); and the Prince as final trophy and reward – are they quite credible? Such apparent allegories, which confront evil and yet seek to resolve it through the fearless innocence of youth, are essentially romantic: they proceed by 'the beautiful circuit and subterfuge of our thought and our desire'. One might see a distant parallel to Shakespeare's final plays, his 'romances'. It should not be pushed too far, because James demands from his reader the kind of acceptance that every novel tied to actualities must be given. The only magic he can use is that of operative virtue, in his heroines. And this must inevitably meet with scepticism. *The Golden Bowl*, like its two companion novels, didn't quite enact the intended truth.[9]

* * *

Those who are dissatisfied with these novels should not forget that James was still to write excellent smaller pieces (as in that collection of 1910, *The Finer Grain*, to which Ezra Pound gave especial praise). Much could be said in a discussion of James's pre-eminent skill in the slighter thing – the short story and *nouvelle*. After his visit to America in 1904 he began a moving 'interrogation of the past', originally in the pages of *The American Scene* (1907), where the daunting present drove him to 'felicities of the backward reach'; next in the Prefaces written for his New York Edition, where he narrated the story of each story; and finally in the volumes of autobiography prompted by his brother's death. If these last describe the 'growth of a poet's mind', and the Prefaces trace the processes of that mind in particular acts of creation, *The American Scene* itself is the most beautiful long poem yet to have come out of America. From his first appalled view of the villas on the New Jersey shore – loneliness and inanity written all over them – to the tragic plea on his last page, James displays a gift of divination which seldom fails him. Wells's book of the same time, *The Future in America*, for all its acuteness and verve, looks flimsy indeed beside James's deeply felt record of a signal experience.

The world war found him no better prepared than most of his contemporaries. At one moment he cried out in panic that 'the subject-matter of one's effort has become *itself* utterly treacherous and false – its relation to reality utterly given away and smashed'. He abandoned *The Ivory Tower*, which nevertheless showed the keenest sense of realities – the black dishonoured roots of colossal fortunes flaunted in contemporary Newport. James in this last phase of social understanding (attained through the experience of *The American Scene*) stands not very far from Conrad. Though the outward forms of the civilization he knew have largely decayed, his meaning is still actual; very little in the vast body of his work can be disregarded. He has become widely recognized as a pattern of the dedicated artist, who exists to create values, to extend life, 'to be finely aware and richly responsible'. In the last of his Prefaces he claimed for himself the title of poet. There is nothing extravagant in this claim, since poets, no less than novelists, have much to learn from him. Henry James is a master for all who prize (in Marianne Moore's words) 'certainty of touch and unhurried incision'.

NOTES

1. Eliot's essay on 'The Hawthorne Aspect' and the detailed exploration by Marius Bewley in *The Complex Fate* set James firmly in his native tradition: Balzac, Turgenev, George Eliot, Dickens seem to have been *consciously* assimilated, Hawthorne's hold on his imagination was not perhaps perfectly clear to him.

2. Both James and T. S. Eliot in early manhood wrote review articles greatly outnumbering their attempts at original work. This allowed each to think over the bases of his art. James's fullest statement on this subject before the Prefaces was 'The Art of Fiction' (1884), reprinted in *Partial Portraits*.

3. On the significance of these themes for the American novelist of the nineteenth century see *The Complex Fate* and its sequel *The Eccentric Design*.

4. In 'The Novel as Dramatic Poem (III): *The Europeans*', *Scrutiny*, Vol. XV (1948).

5. W. D. Howells defined 'New Yorkishness' as 'a sort of a Bostonian quality, with the element of *conscious* worth eliminated, and purified as essentially of pedantry as of commerciality'.

6. See his preface to *The Bostonians* in the Chiltern Library edition (London, 1952); reprinted in *The Opposing Self*.

7. In *The Liberal Imagination*.

8. See his appendix to *Henry James: The Major Phase*, entitled 'The Painter's Sponge and Varnish Bottle'.

9. Quentin Anderson in *The American Henry James* takes them rather as a 'divine novel', in which James sought to dramatize the religious views of his father. One may readily acknowledge Mr Anderson's insight into the delicacies of James's moral sense. It goes without saying that James like his father abhorred greed and domination; and we must treat with caution the view that his moral sense in these later novels surrendered to ambiguities. One can only enter here the plea that it is preposterous to conceive of father and son as standing perpetually in the same Swedenborgian pew. Mr Anderson has suffered the novelist's mind to be violated by an idea.

FROM *HEART OF DARKNESS* TO *NOSTROMO*: AN APPROACH TO CONRAD

DOUGLAS BROWN

CONRAD'S art has its limitations. It does not explore human relationship; it offers few triumphs of feminine portraiture; it lent itself to a good deal of plainly inferior work, and two or three even among the masterpieces are flawed – *Lord Jim*, for instance, and *Chance* and *Victory*. But there is no point in making much of the limitations, for Conrad's astonishing *range* of achievement is part and parcel of them. To testify to that variety, there are successively *The Nigger* (1897), *Lord Jim* (1900), *Heart of Darkness* (1902), *Typhoon* (1903), *Nostromo* (1904), *The Secret Agent* (1907), *Under Western Eyes* (1911), *The Secret Sharer* (1912), *Chance* (1913), *Victory* (1915), and *The Shadow-Line* (1917).[1] Consider what distinction of styles separates the affirmative eloquence of much of *The Nigger* from the discomposing astringency of *The Secret Agent*; what distinction of scale separates the epitomizing *The Secret Sharer*, and *Nostromo*. The Congo terrain of *Heart of Darkness*, the London streets of *The Secret Agent*, the South American province of *Nostromo*, and the Gulf of Siam and the shipboard life of *The Shadow-Line* call to mind the Polish expatriate, his adventurous and disordered youth and early manhood, seemingly at the beck of some compulsion to make terms with the sheer multiplicity of the world. In his own experience he knew both far-ranging styles of life and nature, and a strict commitment to one tested tradition – that of the mercantile marine. It was a unique equipment for a novelist; moreover, behind his subtle judgement of appropriate style and scale and method, lay his equally strict service of his artistic vocation, once the decision for that new *métier* was taken. It meant 'the intimacy and strain of a creative effort in which mind, and will, and conscience are engaged to the full'.

So the organization of his novels and tales is not to be taken lightly: it expresses a scrupulous, sceptical intelligence. Several of the finest use a present moment, still not oversure of its perspectives, to look back into past experience and recreate it, its immediacy still vivid but its meaning enlarged and clarified by distance. The recurring figure of the raconteur, his experience separated from the novelist's own, or the aligning of a series of distinct attitudes, deny the reader simple certitudes. *Nostromo*, supremely, exhibits this structural scepticism. Now it reflects back from a forward point in time, when consequences have become evident; now contemporary events reach us through a variety of distinct consciousnesses established at various points along the chronological route; now one style of appraisal – Decoud's, now another – Mitchell's; now meditation and now drama. Add the oppressive presence of darkness or shadow through so much of the novel, and we are kept steadily in mind of the insufficiency of anyone's comprehension. Reading, we lack orientation. Nobody is thoroughly understood, no situation is perfectly clear. And the scepticism tapers off – is it the sardonic manner? or the elliptical method? – into the enigmatic. It is to the point that the novel's pivotal figure, Nostromo, is an enigmatic figure.

It may be right to associate this facet of Conrad (1857–1924) with the expatriate wanderer. Other elements in his art express the commitment of the sailor. His artistic manifesto, the Preface to *The Nigger*, speaks of imaginative creation that shall address the senses irresistibly and so reach down to 'the secret springs of responsive emotions'. The process does not stop there; it calls into being our sense of our involvement in mankind. Conrad shares with George Eliot a concern for 'the latent feeling of fellowship', 'the subtle but invincible conviction of solidarity'. They share also the concern to give imaginative authority to the sense of obligation and rectitude, to the word 'ought' which surmounts the noise of the gale on Macwhirr's lips. So Conrad's best work gives full play to disquieting scepticism, yet celebrates fidelity and heroic discipline. It probes anxiously at traditional moral sanctions; it preserves something nearer to respect than to confidence; we move along a tightrope. Each vantage point in *Nostromo* questions or invalidates some other, no focus for authority emerges. Yet the sense of quest for some such focus prevails: the novel's structure insists upon it. It seems, on one hand, that no traditional or social code withstands the catalyst of the silver, or that other catalyst of solitude and darkness towards which repeatedly the narratives tend. But even the unillusioned cynic Decoud, who trusts nothing but the truth of his sensations, finds he desires at the crisis to leave behind him a true record of his acts. It's a sort of desolate gesture to human solidarity. And there is always some note of compassion, or regard, for those in Sulaco who do live by 'some distinct ideal'. Conrad's preoccupation with betrayal is itself suggestive: betrayal in his world has social roots, it presumes a collaborative morality – people to fail, dues to forfeit. It is affirmative. Jukes's experience in *Typhoon* presents the sway between anarchy and discipline in plainer terms. On one side of him is Macwhirr's unshakeable commitment to the demands of his tradition: on the other, the typhoon's immeasurable and destructive potency. It saps resolve, and the sense of obligation, and self-respect. As the novels and tales lead out of the nineteenth century and into our own, we are made to feel more of the limited, contingent validity of moral claims and of collaborative endeavour. We are confined in a gleaming engine-room while natural forces beyond imagination wreak havoc on the deck above and threaten to overwhelm the ship. Or, with Jukes, we suffer 'the thick blackness which made the appalling boundary of his vision', or discover in the Placid Gulf of *Nostromo* 'the limitations put upon the human faculties by the darkness of the night'.

Conrad's art addresses our senses, then, and goes on from there. 'The yarns of seamen have a direct simplicity, the whole meaning of which lies within the shell of a cracked nut. But ... to him the meaning of an episode was not inside it like the kernel but outside, enveloping the tale which brought it out only as a glow brings out a haze.' This is Marlow, the protagonist of *Heart of Darkness*, whose memory pieces together and re-lives the journey into the Belgian Congo. The image is important. A kernel can be extracted and the shell discarded: and recently there has been a good deal of such extraction from Conrad's work – symbols, and Jungian motifs, and so forth. The effect is to falsify and simplify the truth and depth of his art, and not surprisingly the plain force of his tales often gets obscured too.[2] We are to attend, rather, to the luminous quality of the tale itself, its 'glow'; we are to depend on the evidence of our senses, and our power to respond delicately enough to the story-teller's arrangement of his scenes, and to his tone of voice. (Though he was Polish by birth, Conrad became a master of our speech. He learnt it from the talk of seamen first, as he learnt our language generally from manuals of navigation, entries in ships' logs, as well as studies in our literature. He felt 'a subtle and unforeseen accord of my emotional nature with its genius'.) His artistic austerity led him to present no more than was necessary. Even through the vast span of *Nostromo*, one comes to feel that a thorough sifting has already taken place. There is point in every paragraph, and though there is lightness and humour, there is no give in the prose. At every moment it matters whose voice we are listening to or whose tone is prevalent. And if the *montage*, the shifting viewpoints, impose a condition of incertitude upon the reader, they also elicit an activity of clarification. Evidence confronts us and we are drawn to judge, and implicate ourselves in the consequences of judgement – or of incapacity to judge. Frequently the way of the narrative itself suggests this: as the *Patna* inquiry does, or the circle of auditors to whom Marlow relates his Congo ordeal as if testifying; as the manner of the young captains in *The Secret Sharer* and *The Shadow-Line* does, in no way solemn, yet seeming to bear witness before some ultimate tribunal. (*The Shadow-Line* is sub-titled 'A Confession'.) *Nostromo*'s key figure – if such it has – Dr Monygham, lives under the same constraint.

Beyond question, *Nostromo* is Conrad's greatest achievement. Yet its very magnitude and cogency sometimes obstruct readers; and it does not yield the measure of its worth at one reading, though it offers rewards enough to be going on with. It has certainly not lacked critical advocacy and no detailed fresh appraisal would earn its place here.[3] An appraisal of *Heart of Darkness* perhaps may. It is a novel that can be read, considered, and re-read in a short time; and once engaged with, it is not likely to leave a reader alone until *Nostromo* and *The Shadow-Line* have had their say. It has received rather less than its due of respect and understanding although it is characteristic Conrad and includes passages that are by common consent among his very finest. Most important, and when due regard has been given to its dramatic fibre, it exhibits – like *The Shadow-Line* – a profoundly personal art: both tales handle distressing personal experience such as extends a man's knowledge of himself and of what the world is like. It is safe to say that Conrad's own Congo journey and its attendant breakdown were decisive in confirming him in his vocation as an imaginative artist. His own laconic remark prepares us for what the novel is about: 'before the Congo I was only a simple animal'.

Marlow's journey is an initiation into a fuller scale of human being. Jukes's ordeal, in *Typhoon*, relates to it, as do those of the later captains of ships. In *Nostromo* such ordeal is absorbed into and changed by a more extensive pattern, but it counts. In Sulaco, where yet more various political and economic forces are at work than make their presence felt in the Congo, Nostromo at first commits his whole identity to his public role. He is the common folk's mysterious chieftain, the creator and devotee of a cult of public fidelity. The ordeal of the pitch-dark night on the Gulf marks the point of his awakening to the nature of his city, and its silver, and his part in both. Like the adolescent in ritual, he goes out into the night and sleeps alone. In solitude he must forge an adult identity for himself. Then he puts on a man's strength and resolve and returns to his city. But Sulaco has the complex and entangling character of modern civilization, and in Sulaco Nostromo cannot escape what he has been, nor the pressures of the silver. They bear even more strongly and corruptingly upon the adult. Soon he is romanticizing his new manhood, his resentful duplicity, his subtlety, and his power. He plays alternately the hero and the villain of some adventure story of his own contriving. The enigmatic knight-errant of the silver-grey mare becomes a sort of corrupt Robin Hood: fittingly, he ends half highwayman, half cavalier.[4]

Adult manhood is not simple or unconfined in Conrad; confusions, tensions, disappointments, and corruption strengthen their hold. Growth brings to the Marlow of *Heart of Darkness* a radical discomposure of the self. But the feeling of growth and fuller participation in the human condition carries its own worth. Conrad appears to have altered little the biographical data from his own past. His creative energy goes into acts of selection and juxtaposition, into sensuous prose, and into the provision and use of Marlow: so securing a holdfast upon the discomposure, a detached view of the changing self.

> 'I don't want to bother you much with what happened to me personally,' he began. ... 'Yet to understand the effect of it on me you ought to know how I got out there, what I saw, how I went up that river to the place where I first met the poor chap. It was the farthest point of navigation and the culminating point of my experience. It seemed somehow to throw a

> kind of light on everything about me – and into my thoughts. It was sombre enough, too – and pitiful – not extraordinary in any way – not very clear either. No, not very clear. And yet it seemed to throw a kind of light.'

There is a subtle command of the tone of voice. A slightly mannered colloquial unpretentiousness, nervous hesitations and reticences, alert the reader, and give authority to that 'farthest point of navigation'. Navigation, and the duty of the helm, and the experience of dangerous or uncharted waters, 'glow' continually in Conrad with issues of direction, of responsibility, of purpose. A memorable line runs through Singleton in *The Nigger*'s storm and Hackett ('fixed to look one way') in *Typhoon*'s, through the nearly blind Whalley of *The End of the Tether*, and the African steersman here, through Nostromo at the helm for Decoud on the Placid Gulf; towards those later vindications of responsible purpose, the terrified but obedient helmsman of *The Secret Sharer*, and the sharing of the helm at the end of *The Shadow-Line* between the captain himself and the frail, indomitable Ransome. As for Marlow's 'farthest point of navigation', the hint finally takes us to the presiding figure of Captain Giles, imagined with such serene humour in *The Shadow-Line*, who 'had his own peculiar position. He was an expert. An expert in – how shall I say it? – in intricate navigation. He was supposed to know more about remote and imperfectly charted parts of the Archipelago than any man living.'

The novelist himself is among the group of listeners to Marlow's voice, aboard the yawl that night on the Thames. His eyes see Marlow as an object, 'sunken cheeks, a yellow complexion, a straight back, an ascetic aspect', and his mind prepares to contemplate one of 'Marlow's inconclusive experiences'. The laconic note indicates a considered distance from the raconteur, and Marlow's own variety of tone and nuance secures a further perspective. A grim or playful sardonic understating manner remains Marlow's staple; but it becomes liable to a jarring flippancy here, a callowness there, that register the disturbing power of the memories; and later still, to a vacant rhetoric symptomatic of evasive fears and embarrassments, of memory working upon a nervous disorder. Conrad's art is that of a consummate stylist, and to read his novels well is to cultivate the utmost sensitivity to style, style as moral imprint, and to the implications of tone and arrangement. Arrangement, here, includes the company director – 'our captain and our host' – the lawyer, and the accountant, alongside the novelist, comprising Marlow's audience. For the codes and vocations of all these are implicated in the tale to come, and the novel sharpens in many ways our perception of such involvements.

Using style and arrangement like this, and by abundant sensuous life, the opening pages begin to connect many modes of exploration. We experience a movement towards the dead of night, and towards an indistinct region in which London – its lights brilliant on the water – and the Thames of now and of earliest history, and the Congo river, become one; and the various darknesses merge. Conrad purposes not only to penetrate the tenebrous moral and physical world of the Congo, and to trace the web that joins it to London's Thames, and joins its present with our past; his art is also to vibrate with the potentialities of the self that the exploration releases, to suggest the tremors suffered by the stable and complacent levels of judgement. Not that the tale is to become a mere image for the soul's 'night-journey' (after Jung): any more than the Leggatt encountered in the night of *The Secret Sharer* emanates from the psyche of the young captain. These are real meetings with people and the natural world, that so disturb the sensitive regions of the self as to require some new orientation. So far as *Heart of Darkness* records a journey into the darks of the self, those darks awaken at the touch of the actual Congo experience, and what it brings of confusion, fascination, guilt, the sense of nightmare. 'It seemed to throw a kind of light upon everything about me – and into my thoughts.'

Then there is a grandiose note, too, in these opening pages, to be discountenanced by the progress of the tale, like the initial complacencies of *Nostromo*, or the overweening confidence in the securities of the naval tradition in *The Secret Sharer* and *The Shadow-Line*. A boyish review of the piratical, the expeditionary, and the colonizing glamour in the British past follows the path of the Thames: and Conrad traces another filament of the all-connecting web. And there is one more note, perhaps the most significant. The prose suggests many forms of stillness and inertia blent with the darkness: a brooding immobility accompanies and lures on the unfolding tale. The Conrad of *The Nigger* and *Typhoon* is still recognizably a nineteenth-century novelist;

what threatens the human order with tragedy appears as storm, and invites heroic resistance. The twentieth-century Conrad of *Nostromo* and *The Shadow-Line* expresses a profounder and more disturbing intuition of menace, under the image of becalmed or stagnant conditions, with the collapse of the power or the will to act. This is more insidious, it turns the mind in on itself to probe at the rationale of living and question its own identity. Decoud at the time of his suicide is the extreme term, pointing to nihilism. More positively there are the diary entries in *The Shadow-Line* and the hours just before the rain comes. *Nostromo* tends to reflect one focal image from episode to episode, as though the human condition in Sulaco is perpetually this: a lighter loaded with the silver that all factions and individuals adjust themselves to, suspended motionless in pitch darkness on a motionless Gulf. There are three figures abroad, Hirsch, impotent with fear, Decoud, impotent with nihilism, and Nostromo at the helm: a steersman whose whole identity has been bound up with public endorsement, and who can accomplish nothing in that Gulf. They are there to serve the instincts of acquisition or of power. And this 'Night of the Gulf' pervades the whole novel. It continues all the while, whatever men or factions may believe. This is what Charles Gould's activity amounts to in the end; and his wife's impotent grief – as the poignant chapter at the end of the book discloses. One reason why the narrative line has often to fall below the surface is to prevent the apparent form of men's doings from concealing the lighter on the Placid Gulf from us. Nostromo's hands seem still to be on that tiller when he lies dead.[5]

Heart of Darkness is heavy with brooding at the outset, and still and sombre gloom seems to be the agent, as much as the setting, of the unfolding experience. But just before the first uttered words draw everything together, 'the stir of lights going up and down' catches the eye. Energy and movement continue through the novel to stand over against inertia and stillness. Here, the ordered navigation of ships about their business momentarily sets off the dark places of the earth, and of history, and of human being – undeveloped or deranged. (Just so, the last light to go out in *Typhoon* before anarchy is unloosed is 'the green gleam of the starboard light', the navigation light for ocean traffic.) ' "And this also", said Marlow suddenly, "has been one of the dark places of the earth".' The weight falls memorably on the first three words. Marlow's mind is already active in the Congo and in the past: the brooding stillness promotes that activity. So the grim speculations upon the bygone Roman invasion of *our* interior, added to that 'also', seem to be both a pertinent tableau of the invasion of Africa, and a disconcerting shift in the point of view. At the same time Marlow's uneasy tone suggests memories so disruptive that he has now to re-live them deviously, and diminish the tremor by reference to common historical experience. What the experience has done to Marlow, how it has wounded him – this, as much as the journey itself, is Conrad's subject. The sardonic, the mordant, or the facetious note in the raconteur's manner preserves detachment: but there is something else. The caustic flippancy with which he recounts his predecessor's death, for instance, conveys some insecurity. For the fatal eruption of rage in that quiet Danish skipper hints at a transformation of the ego under the pressures set up 'out there' by the jungle and the trading milieu. It is another filament of the web; Marlow discerns himself in his predecessor; their roles are the same. The episode makes an embryo of things to come. Both the naval community and the African community disintegrate: 'The steamer Fresleven commanded left also in a bad panic, in charge of the engineer, I believe ... The village was deserted, the huts gaped black, rotting, all askew within the fallen enclosures ... The people had vanished.' It presages the eventual arrival at Kurtz's trading station; it offers the first sight of crazy physical destruction; and 'black' goes on to attach itself to one thing after another – another filament of the web. Marlow, replacing the Danish skipper, finds his way to the shadowed and deserted Company Offices, to the two women knitting black wool and 'guarding the door of darkness'. And so the web has him. His interview with the doctor, if it adds an ingredient of observant humour, quickens our apprehension of quiescent unbalance 'The changes take place inside, you know.'

With the voyage towards the Congo, forms of immobility and of activity group themselves on either side. We observe in a more extended passage such as this, how the Trading Company's new representative encounters the Africans: he idle, isolated, deluded, they zestful and purposeful. The 'lugubrious drollery' of the French warship aimlessly firing into the continent – the power behind the trade – seems like energy warped, slowing to a standstill. 'The merry dance of death and trade goes on in a still and earthy atmosphere like that of an overheated catacomb.'

> The idleness of a passenger, my isolation amongst all these men with whom I had no point of contact, the oily and languid sea, the uniform sombreness of the coast, seemed to keep me away from the truth of things, within the toil of a mournful and senseless delusion. The voice of the surf heard now and then was a positive pleasure, like the speech of a brother. It was something natural, that had its reason, that had a meaning. Now and then a boat from the shore gave one a momentary contact with reality. It was paddled by black fellows. You could see from afar the white of their eyeballs glistening. They shouted, sang; their bodies streamed with perspiration; they had faces like grotesque masks – these chaps; but they had bone, muscle, a wild vitality, an intense energy of movement, that was as natural and true as the surf along their coast. They wanted no excuse for being there. They were a great comfort to look at. For a time I would feel I belonged still to a world of straightforward facts; but the feeling would not last long. Something would turn up to scare it away. Once, I remember, we came upon a man-of-war anchored off the coast. There wasn't even a shed there, and she was shelling the bush. It appears the French had one of their wars going on thereabouts. Her ensign dropped limp like a rag; the muzzles of the long, six-inch guns stuck out all over the low hull; the greasy, slimy swell swung her up lazily and let her down, swaying her thin masts. In the empty immensity of earth, sky, and water, there she was, incomprehensible, firing into a continent. Pop, would go one of the six-inch guns; a small flame would dart and vanish, a little white smoke would disappear, a tiny projectile would give a feeble screech – and nothing happened. Nothing could happen. There was a touch of insanity in the proceeding, a sense of lugubrious drollery in the sight ....

This has poetic force; and so has Conrad's command of *montage* and juxtaposition. A mordant commentary rises from within, needing no further expression, as episode and attitude draw power from contiguity. Consider as a sequence the scenes and impressions that follow immediately upon Marlow's arrival at the trading station. If there is a connecting thread, it is his instant reflection as the chain-gang moves by: 'I foresaw that in the blinding sunshine of that land I would become acquainted with a flabby pretending weak-eyed devil of a rapacious and pitiless folly.' First, a scene of desultory mess: the half-buried boiler, the railway truck with its wheels in the air, the dilapidated machinery. Then the sound of blasting (quite purposeless, it soon appears) recalls the warship pouring out its shells. The chained gang of forced labourers comes very close, in one of the most incisive and pitiful paragraphs anywhere in our fiction. The eye fastens again on material disorder: a heap of broken drain-pipes, 'a wanton smash-up' in a quarry dug for no purpose and abandoned. Then, to draw these sights and sounds into the larger web of the novel, comes an extraordinary impression simultaneously of violent motion and infernal stillness in the African scene. Next, the pity owing to the human victims of this wanton smash-up is summoned by a painful closeness of vision to sick African labourers cast aside to die. Sounds of the objectless blasting go on. As the eye accustoms itself to the gloom of the grove, the 'black shadows' define themselves poignantly as individual human beings. To complete the sequence, there comes into sight the absurd, immaculate figure of the company's chief accountant. 'I saw a high starched collar, white cuffs, a light alpaca jacket, snowy trousers, a clean necktie and varnished boots. No hat. Hair parted, brushed, oiled, under a green-lined parasol held in a big white hand. He was amazing, and had a penholder behind his ear.'

The horror out in the grove gives place to an equal horror indoors, where the impeccably kept trading accounts deflect in turn every human claim. The scenes have the same quality of significant series. The emergence of that accountant, and all that transpires in his office, point up Conrad's creative relationship with Dickens, at the same time as they exhibit a sensuous animation, a rendering of the external, that seem uncanny. Appropriately, it is on this accountant's lips that Marlow first hears Kurtz's name. Kurtz seems to emanate from trade distorted into crass lust of gain; from 'the work of the world' distorted into a perfect accountancy of predatory spoliation; and from the presence there, in that room, of a dying agent. The later and more shameful horrors that gather about him adhere to his function, agent for the Company, who 'sends in as much ivory as all the others put together'. The manager's account of him comes next, and adjoins Marlow's finding the steamer he should command, wrecked and half-submerged. The effect is to locate Kurtz in this crassness that smashes pipes and overturns trucks and abandons steamers and dissolves human solidarities. He is both the instrument and the consequence of power at the service of greed. He personifies the exploiter's disavowal of moral obligation towards the African community, whether in trade, law, or financial probity. (We may recall that circle of auditors to Marlow's tale.)

Hence the peculiarly suggestive force of ivory. It serves as a point of focus like the silver in *Nostromo*. That is mercantile wealth and a focus for acquisitiveness. As the silver of the mine involved in the operations of finance houses and eventually breeding industrial strife, it is a focus for human labour. As the silver of the mountain Higuerota it focuses power; and as the contemporary equivalent for the 'legendary treasure' it fastens upon the mind, possessing those who seek to possess it. As the 'incorruptible metal that can be trusted to keep its value for ever' it is the emblem all rally to, it holds the question of final ends continually before us. This is not to expand symbolic levels but to respond to the pressures of Conrad's art: the silver manifests itself in all these ways. The ivory of *Heart of Darkness* is the raw material of wealth: raw, for its resonance affects one more intimately than mineral silver. This is bone that was once part of the living animal, it is more and other than natural resource for human plunder. And then particularly ivory is the material of luxury, the ornament of civilization. Raw or refined, it evokes pallor, personality gone bloodless and impenetrable. By its use for fetish and idol it insinuates the religious quest, devotion or possession or idolatry – and these may distort or corrupt the mind and appetite. The very first pages of the novel propose this issue. What, they ask, is the 'ideal' that sustains colonial enterprise? What may the apparent ideal conceal? – The lust of power? Greed of gain? Or may it really be 'a humane idealism, a civilizing mission'? What do these men (the phrase is Marlow's) 'bow down to'? The raconteur himself sits there motionless, like an idol, presenting the question to his listeners. All the suggestions latent in the ivory, and this last especially, come together in the sardonic designation of the waiting traders and agents at that station: the pilgrims. From now on Marlow never sees them as anything else. 'The word "ivory" rang in the air, was whispered, was sighed. You would think they were praying to it. A taint of imbecile rapacity blew through it all, like a whiff from some corpse.' While he waits, dejected and inactive, the suggestions implicit in the ivory increase and become more distinct. At the same time through rumour and surreptitious gossip and the story-teller's hints of what is to come, Kurtz also becomes more distinct: what he does and what he has become. 'The wilderness had patted him on the head, and, behold, it was like a ball – an ivory ball; it had caressed him, and – lo! – he had withered ... Ivory? I should think so. Heaps of it, stacks of it ... It was no more fossil than I am; but they call it fossil when it is dug up ... We filled the steamboat with it, and had to pile a lot on deck. Thus he could see and enjoy as long as he could see ... You should have heard him say, "My ivory."' Marlow's eventual first sight of him he remembers as 'an animated image of death carved out of old ivory'. 'I saw him open his mouth wide – it gave him a weirdly voracious aspect, as though he had wanted to swallow all the air, all the earth, all the men before him.'

As the actual appearance of Kurtz to Marlow's memory comes nearer, his style of narrative loosens its hold. The sardonic manner still maintains some foothold in these shifting nightmare-like places. But more and more he lapses into mordant quirks, spasmodic advances and withdrawals, and a hollow rhetoric like that of Kurtz's report for the International Society for the Suppression of Savage Customs, 'vibrating with eloquence, but too high-strung, I think'. The yells of a beaten African get into his mind, words like 'jabber' and 'fantastic' recur, there are tremors of hysteria. The novelist chooses this place, therefore, to return to the actual present, the night on the Thames, the equable circle of listeners; and significantly he does so twice more before the tale is done. For the unstable and hectoring quality of the narrative as we approach Kurtz are Marlow's, they register its renewed impact upon his memory: they are not Conrad's. And Marlow's tone, too, can suddenly adjust itself to our normality:

> 'Do you see the story? Do you see anything? It seems to me I am trying to tell you a dream – making a vain attempt, because no relation of a dream can convey the dream-sensation ...'
>
> He was silent for a while.
>
> 'No, it is impossible; it is impossible to convey the life-

> sensation of any given epoch of one's existence – that which makes its truth, its meaning – its subtle and penetrating essence. It is impossible. We live, as we dream – alone.'
>
> He paused again as if reflecting, then added –
>
> 'Of course in this you fellows see more than I could then. You see me whom you know.'
>
> It had become so pitch dark that we listeners could hardly see one another.

There are limits to what can be communicated of the farther reaches of Marlow's memories, except obliquely. And part of the obliquity is this way the prose has of giving the resurgence of Kurtz and his fascination in a style of absurd vehemence. 'The man presented himself as a voice.' 'What carried the sense of his real presence was his ability to talk, his words.' The horror of Kurtz is in part an evil done upon style; upon the decorum and usefulness of language – that lucidity of speech that makes for relationship and clear perception. During the journey downriver we find that at any moment the ordinary detail of work to be done, or the sensory facts of wilderness and river, may re-establish their equilibrium. And other vital parts of the horror of Kurtz, too, may be defined with sardonic vigilance. The extravagant rhetoric is no artistic accident: it gives part of the memory's response to the experience itself, and it indicates the quality of the fascination which so subtly disturbs Marlow's own moral categories at that time with the menacing 'and yet'. In him, too, during the ordeal, and drawing him towards the corrupted trader, it is a rhetoric to bolster egotism, even at the hideous price of proposing something 'moral' about Kurtz's final state.[6] The final scenes concerning him suggest something insupportable in the direction and purpose given to life by the hallowing or authorizing of economic forces at work beneath the ostentation of a civilizing mission, and by the 'wanton smash-up' of primitive communities. It is Conrad's achievement to communicate a powerful sense of sacrilege, independently of any traditional religious sanctions. Sacrilege, essentially, against human dignity. The black shadows of diseased and cast-off African workers first call it into play, and that grotesque parody of what collaborative work ought to be, the chain-gang. And in Kurtz himself we get the maniacal assertion of the self against traditional morality, integrity in human dealing, and law. The diversity of race and nation drawn into the novel's web, and the interlocking responsibilities of warships, soldiers, traders, and seamen, provide authority for the claim thrown out as if accidentally – 'All Europe contributed to the making of Kurtz.' The predatory lust that possesses him takes support from the objects of the Company he serves, and that Company is felt in a ghastly way to be active on behalf of all acquisitive Europe, requiring its civilized ivory luxury, and disengaging the human ties in pursuit of wealth for power, power for more wealth, without end.

This is not all that needs to be said of the darkness, the horror, that Marlow encounters; but this is its plain force, and to minimize it is to read glibly, in Kurtz's own fashion. Other darknesses, too, inhabit the jungle interior, and something especially sinister seems to emanate from the collision between what the traders are, and bring with them, and what they find already there. And again, inhabiting those voids of rhetoric and anxiety on Marlow's later pages is the sense of delusion, of nightmare. There is an abyss at hand, the human tenure of any moral categories feels insecure. We are nearing the darknesses and solitudes of *Nostromo*, the shadow of Koh-ring and the uncharted seas of *The Secret Sharer* and *The Shadow-Line*. In *Heart of Darkness*, this particular insecurity seems partly to lurk in the wanton disregard of the smaller, traditional morality, operative in the charted places. These suggestions, then, are present, but the plain meaning stands. The novel's first movement opened with the grim tableau of the Roman expeditionary force penetrating our own interior. The movement ends with the return from the African interior of the Eldorado expedition. Conrad never wrote a page more laconically savage.

But the rivets are quite another matter. By contrast with the ivory and the darkness there is the salvage of the steamer, the order of work and purpose. The need of ships to be under way, in other Conrad tales, is to enable seafaring activities and skills to be exercised in purposeful collaboration. So here, the work of repair. 'Waiting for rivets' Marlow 'stuck to his salvage night and day'. Those rivets are a characteristic triumph: the symbolism proposes itself perfectly naturally. The salvage briefly restores the social bonds that rapacious folly disrupts, and it resists the paralysis all round it. Marlow doesn't relinquish the sardonic manner altogether, but respect prevails. A man can 'find himself' in such work, it is life-enhancing; and the self he finds in work for and with others is both a social reality, and yet a profound private reassurance. As soon as Marlow's work begins, here, relationships grow between mechanics, foreman, boiler-maker, and Marlow himself. The only real human relationships the novel records come of the work of repair and the work of navigation – and the finding of a manual of seamanship. As they go downriver, the skill demanded, and the collaboration, repeatedly offset the hints of nightmare, the darknesses, or the Kurtz rhetoric. And there is work to be done, with the same effect, before and after the actual death of Kurtz: leaky cylinders to mend, connecting rods to straighten, the helm to look to.

Taking this aspect of *Heart of Darkness* with such things as Singleton's unrelieved thirty hours at the helm through the storm of *The Nigger*, Macwhirr's all-sufficient 'He isn't on duty' after his second mate's insubordination, or the marvellous pages that follow the coming of rain at the climax of *The Shadow-Line*, we are left in no doubt of the place of 'the work of the world' in Conrad's art. It is honoured; but by a sceptical intelligence. If Macwhirr's ship goes down, the gleaming engine-room with its harmonious power and 'builders – good men' behind it, and disciplined engineers within it, go down too, and the man at the helm: and this at the behest of a captain's obstinate folly in misjudging nature's potencies by simple reference to his own experience and code. The selfless work Charles Gould gives to the mine in *Nostromo* has to subserve forces beyond his control; and Marlow's spiritual bravado in making the steamer seaworthy is offset at once by the appearance of the dreadful Eldorado expedition. What, the juxtaposition asks, is the work *for*? And later, where is the helmsman steering to, and why? In a sense the purposeful work only obscures a grim reality of the kind insinuated by stillness and inertia. The slow voyage up the Congo 'crawled towards Kurtz, exclusively', towards 'this Kurtz grubbing for ivory in the wretched bush'. When Marlow comes upon Towson's manual of seamanship and feels 'its singleness of intention, an honest concern for the right way of going to work which made these pages luminous with another than a professional light', the 'delicious sensation of having come upon something unmistakably real' can only be enjoyed in a moment's oblivion of 'the jungle and the pilgrims'. At once he catches sight of the manager and traders, puts the book in his pocket, and 'started the lame engines ahead', now and again picking out a tree 'to measure our progress towards Kurtz by'.

So energy takes more grotesque and irrational forms, activity becomes more sluggish, as the ulterior purposes they serve loom clearer. The superb movements of Africans paddling their boats from the shore: the merry dance of death and trade: the chain-gang: the jig Marlow dances with the foreman in the hope of rivets: jungle dwellers capering wildly, fighting crazily: and at last the orgy round Kurtz at dead of night. Even navigation becomes (in Marlow's grim phrases) 'monkey-tricks' and 'performing on a tightrope'. As we approach the shrine, the last trading station, we experience many penetrations at once: into a distinct and fearful African territory; into the darks of time; into mingled social forms, neither barbaric nor civilized but profoundly disordered and spoiled; into the darks of moral anarchy; and into the darks of the self that the sense at once of repulsion and fascination disturbs. We could take for close reading in this light the pages immediately following the finding of the manual, and leading to that wild cry of despair with which the jungle dwellers greet the approaching traders, and which they take to be the war cry of attacking savages.[7] Such subtly organized sequences, with their questioning ironies, their variety of vocal nuance, their tentative hints at the protagonist's instability and suffering and his disintegrating confidence – above all, with their discomposing particularity – have no superior in Conrad's work, and may stand as the essence of his contribution to our fiction. Inevitably, this experience of penetration, of absorption, this loss of moral clarity and of certitude, feels sluggish: the very voyage a kind of paralysis:

> The current ran smooth and swift, but a dumb immobility sat on the banks. The living trees, lashed together by the creepers and every living bush of the undergrowth, might have been changed into stone, even to the slenderest twig, to the lightest leaf. It was not sleep – it seemed unnatural, like a state of trance. Not the faintest sound of any kind could be heard. You looked on amazed, and began to suspect yourself of being deaf – then the night came suddenly, and struck you blind as well. About three in the morning some large fish leaped, and the loud spash made me jump as though a gun had been fired.

> When the sun rose there was a white fog, very warm and clammy, and more blinding than the night. It did not shift or drive; it was just there, standing all round you like something solid.

It is the kind of experience we have at the scene of Decoud's suicide, and again as Mrs Gould suffers her own death-in-life desolation at the end of *Nostromo*. Its last form is the embodied intuition of 'a sense of finality' just before the rain falls in *The Shadow-Line*. But even upon the horror of that paralysis there supervenes 'the seaman's instinct alone survived whole in my moral dissolution'. The contrary forces stand over against each other: that of the gulf, the typhoon, the wilderness, beyond the scope of moral certitudes and obligations, isolating and dissolving personal consciousness; and that of traditional human codes, reciprocal service, vocation, the sense of the human bond. On either side they stand at the culmination of Marlow's journey, and the needle still swings between them in Conrad's next major achievement: 'Both the typhoon and Captain Macwhirr presented themselves to me as the necessities ... '[8]

There is a fine ease about the later parts of Conrad's best work, which is the earned ease of genius. One thinks of the last stages in the relationship of Leggatt and the young captain in *The Secret Sharer*; of the pages just before the final onslaught of the typhoon; of the handling of Ransome towards the end of *The Shadow-Line*. Having worked so hard for his imagined world, having so profoundly gauged and charted its significances, Conrad has finally only to log accurately and in order the physical and the spiritual facts. So it is with the coming upon Kurtz himself at last, the nocturnal orgy, the return journey, and the superb scene of Kurtz's death. That outing at dead of night, and the orgy, draw all the filaments of the web visibly together. This is the dance of death and trade: like the lighter on the Placid Gulf in the greater novel, this is what has happened throughout, manifestly or covertly. Everyone seems to be a part of it: the manager, the pilgrims ('squirting lead in the air out of Winchesters held to the hip' so that we remember the crass violence of those warships), the Africans, Marlow, Kurtz himself, even the Company's head offices – 'the knitting old woman with the cat ... a most improper person to be sitting at the other end of such an affair'.

The achievement of the closing pages is more equivocal. The

collision between the Congo wilderness, and the elegances and proprieties of the Europe at the other end; the sepulchral city replacing the ivory pallor – this is well managed. But it seems that Conrad tries to accomplish too much, after enough has already been done for the scale of his invention, when the deceptions and speculations and moral somersaults perceptible through the haze of memory as it works over the experience of nervous breakdown, occasion the scene of Marlow's visit to Kurtz's fiancée, and of his romantic lies to her. The absurd vein of sentimental heroics fits the unhinged adventurer with the diseased imagination all right; but the reader is hard put to it to find and keep his bearings. Not until we reach the equable tones of the last paragraphs does the grotesque ardour of Marlow's account fall into perspective. The final sentence is often quoted, but those that precede it have as distinct a place in the total economy of the novel:

> Marlow ceased, and sat apart, indistinct and silent, in the pose of a meditating Buddha. Nobody moved for a time. 'We have lost the first of the ebb,' said the Director, suddenly. I raised my head. The offing was barred by a black bank of clouds, and the tranquil waterway leading to the uttermost ends of the earth flowed sombre under an overcast sky – seemed to lead into the heart of an immense darkness.

NOTES

1. See, for critical guidance on most of these, F. R. Leavis: *The Great Tradition*.
2. For example in parts of the writing on Conrad of A. J. Guerard, R. W. Stallman, Robert B. Haugh, and a number of other American critics; and such essays by English critics as those on *The Secret Sharer* by D. Hewitt (*Conrad: a reassessment*) and J. Wain (*London Magazine: Conrad Symposium*).
3. Notably by F. R. Leavis, A. Kettle (*Introduction to the Novel*, vol. II), and D. Hewitt.
4. See chapter 8 of 'The Lighthouse'.
5. *Nostromo* pp. 465–8 – Nostromo's return to Viola's Inn – gives very poignantly this omnipresence of the Gulf.
6. It seems perverse and sentimental to attribute to anyone except Marlow the notion that Kurtz represents a character to be admired, or his end some sort of 'moral victory': a Marlow, moreover, recording the disorder and fascination remembered from a state of nervous collapse. Yet a good deal of criticism appears to suppose simply this to be Conrad's own view of the matter.
7. *Heart of Darkness* pp. 100–14.
8. *Typhoon:* Preface.

HARDY, DE LA MARE, AND EDWARD THOMAS

H. COOMBES

GEORGIAN poetry derives unduly, that is to say with a minimum of significant modification, from early- and later-nineteenth-century romantic poetry. From that poetry it mostly took over the weaker characteristics such as vague emotion, inexpressive sing-song rhythms, emphasis on surface verbal music for its own sake, and the tendency to fantasy or dream without any very strong human interest. We can usefully make discriminations, but it remains generally true that the Georgians allowed themselves only a limited range of feelings and mostly stereotyped techniques. Hardy, de la Mare, and Edward Thomas (who is often associated with the Georgians though he never appeared in Edward Marsh's Georgian Books) stand out by their refusal to wear the label of a category.

Of the three poets of permanent value to be here considered, Walter de la Mare (1873–1956) is the most readily assimilable to nineteenth-century techniques and habits of thought and feeling, but to say this is not to question the individuality of his poetic gift. And if, as is likely, the factor of 'escape' must come into our final estimate of de la Mare, we shall nevertheless be wise not to insist on 'reality' as in all conditions a fixed and all-redeeming criterion. It is indisputable that most of his poetry evades reality in various important ways. Yet precisely because of his evasion, his gifts being what they were, he created a body of exquisite minor poetry.

He was, of course, perfectly aware of the dream-like quality of his poetry: he cultivated fantasy, he aimed consciously at entrancement. But he was not wholly aware of the hazards for a poet in postulating, as he repeatedly does, a dichotomy between 'the day's travail' and 'the garden of the Lord's' in which he is enchanted by the dream that brings poetry:

> Ev'n in the shallow, busy hours of day
> Dreams their intangible enchantments weave.

Happy childhood, harsh adult world, happy recollections of childhood, pleasure and profit in dreaming, beauty and transcendental worth of nature, the duty to love: this seems a reasonably fair account. An innate tenderness saved de la Mare from the danger Yeats saw in such a creed:

> We had fed the heart on fantasies,
> The heart's grown brutal from the fare.

But the habit did involve for him a certain narrowness of sympathetic response as well as repetition and monotony. And though his general delight in flowers, trees, insects, birds, streams is unquestionable, his apprehension of the natural world is nothing like so full or delicate as Hardy's or Edward Thomas's.

There is validity in the common view of de la Mare's poetry as 'making the actual magical and the magical actual': the issue here is one of the magic of dream and of the child's world. This does not mean that it is a poetry of the nursery, though much of it does in fact delight children. Many readers feel 'that beneath the murmur of childish voices we hear a more ancient and wiser tongue, the language of myth and fairytale, dream and symbol'.[1]

There is little need here to point to de la Mare's skill in creating atmosphere idyllic or foreboding (*Nod*, *The Tailor*, *At the Keyhole*, *Never-to-be*), or the aptness of his rhythms in various kinds of narrative and situation (*The Dwelling-Place*, *Off the Ground*, *Nicholas Nye*), or the wistful or humorous fancies (*Sam*, *The Quartette*, *Where*), or the small pathetic pieces (*The Silver Penny*, *All But Blind*, *Fare Well*); these are plain for all to see. But his habit of mind, impelling him to handle his themes in a particular way, does involve him too often in a dependence on a 'verbal magic' which is overmuch a matter of dexterity with vowels and consonants. And in moving about his world – green shadows, cool clear water, slim hands, unfolding buds, starry tapers, steps on stairs, dark hair and shining eyes, moths at evening, dew, faint shrill cries of birds, sailors' bones, tranquil dreams, dying fires, woods, musicians – we do need to discriminate between the genuine poetry and a routine use of the properties.

Our concern as adult readers is finally with adult poetry, with those poems in which an interesting play of mind accompanies the enchanted atmosphere and the word-music. *Old Shellover* is one of many poems, slight but real, which do not wholly rely on power to charm with mystery. The snails and the scene have their own small reality, and a touch of feeling implicit in the dialogue makes the poem just that little more than a 'pretty fancy':

> 'Come!' said Old Shellover.
> 'What?' says Creep.
> 'The horny old Gardener's fast asleep;
> The fat cock Thrush
> To his nest has gone,
> And the dew shines bright
> In the rising moon;
> Old Sallie Worm from her hole doth peep;
> Come!' said Old Shellover.
> 'Ay!' said Creep.

The Witch tells how her pack of spells and sorceries, as she slept under the churchyard wall, was plundered by the dead who thereupon assumed the shapes of wild creatures. The poem is lively with crisp action and has genuinely created atmosphere; everyday 'unromantic' terms – 'jerked it off her back', 'squats asleep' – play their part in a final effect of 'romantic' economy:

> Names may be writ; and mounds rise;
> Purporting, Here be bones:
> But empty is that churchyard
> Of all save stones.
>
> Owl and Newt and Nightjar,
> Leveret, Bat and Mole
> Haunt and call in the twilight,
> Where she slept, poor soul.

Sometimes, as in *John Mouldy*, atmosphere is subtly achieved with a minimum of supernatural story. Mould in a cellar has moved the poet to a creation lightly but convincingly sinister:

> I spied John Mouldy in his cellar,
> Deep down twenty steps of stone;
> In the dark he sat a-smiling,
>   Smiling there alone.

He read no book, he snuffed no candle,
The rats ran in, the rats ran out;
And far and near, the drip of water
  Went whispering about.

The dusk was still, with dew a-falling,
I saw the Dog Star bleak and grim,
I saw a slim brown rat of Norway
  Creep over him.

I spied John Mouldy in his cellar,
Deep down twenty steps of stone;
In the dark he sat a-smiling,
  Smiling there alone.

Here a variety of elements, of facts and things with widely dissimilar associations, have been brought into unity. The subject has engaged the poet; the word-music serves imagination.

The Ghost and *The Song of the Mad Prince* are two of those poems in which the poet aims at expressing more profoundly personal emotion. Both deal with love and loss. In the first of them a dialogue between the man and the ghost, movingly dramatic within the 'wistful' range, is followed by the characteristic de la Mare 'magic':

Silence. Still faint on the porch
Brake the flame of the stars.

In context the self-conscious poeticality is effective enough, but then the gloom is laid on heavily, and the poem ends with 'vast Sorrow', and the ghost of the loved one has become almost an occasion for indulgence in the 'sweet cheat' of illusion. The reality of sharp personal feeling has in the end been evaded. In *The Song of the Mad Prince* the idealization is purposive and seems a quite natural movement of feeling in the totality of the poem:

Who said, 'Peacock Pie'?
  The old King to the sparrow:
Who said, 'Crops are ripe'?
  Rust to the harrow:
Who said, 'Where sleeps she now?
  Where rests she now her head,
Bathed in eve's loveliness'?
  That's what I said.

Who said, 'Ay, mum's the word'?
  Sexton to willow:
Who said, 'Green dusk for dreams,
  Moss for a pillow'?
Who said, 'All Time's delight
  Hath she for narrow bed,
Life's troubled bubble broken'?
  That's what I said.

The mad prince is of course the poet as well as Hamlet, and in the seemingly inconsequential images he makes a comment on life which contains his feeling. The echoes of *Hamlet*, and the suggestions of colour and feasting, harvest and the passage of the seasons, death, both intensify the poignancy of lost love (stressing its universality too) and serve with their width of reference as a check to disproportionate indulgence in grief. If we feel some uneasiness at the underlining that occurs in the last but one line of the poem, it will be at least lessened if we think of the incantation of the Weird Sisters in *Macbeth*. *The Song of the Mad Prince* is perhaps the strongest poem that de la Mare wrote.

A reading of the whole of de la Mare's poetry would reveal many shortcomings: a tendency to repetition which shows that enchantments can become stale; flat emotional commonplaces in explicit terms like 'heart's vacancy' and 'anguished sigh'; portentousness and melodrama in his treatment of such actualities as (say) a prisoner in the dock; simple horror-reactions to evil; excess of self-pity and of yearning for rest and peace; clichés and poeticalities when women and beauty are the set themes; over-elaboration of the idyllic and the eerie; ponderous moralizing about time and eternity; a lack of experience to guarantee the solidity of his affirmations of the value of love and beauty; a sensuousness which is too often the effect of accumulating items from other poets. This is an alarming list. It is a measure of de la Mare's gifts that when all has been said in question of his total achievement, there remain poems of his fine enough and numerous enough to ensure him a permanent place among twentieth-century poets.

Thomas Hardy (1840–1928), also a prolific poet, needed in a high degree the quality we commonly designate as 'courage to live'. His writing has almost nothing of the dream about it, and in his rare evocations of childhood it is never the magic that he emphasizes. His sense of change and of bereavement was exceptionally acute; furthermore he was dogged by a view of life which could afford him no illusory comforts. And the power of these agencies in his life was the stronger because his interest in humanity and in phenomena was great and lasting. He was a humane, sensitive man who could not entertain any suggestion of a Deity other than an indifferent or a malevolent one, and who did not believe in any form of personal survival as it is usually understood; who yet had deep loves in his life and who keenly observed and seriously pondered. Out of his beliefs and the tensions generated between his beliefs and his intimate feelings sprang his poetry, first-rate and third-rate alike.

Perhaps his one escape is to be found in the pertinacity with which he held to his conception of a Vast Imbecility or a neutral Spinner of the Years or a sightless Mother presiding over a mankind endowed (or cursed) with sentience; this pertinacity led him often into heavy protests, portentous and uttered with a prosy clumsiness which, while unquestionably sincere, is too simply explicit to impress deeply:

AN ENQUIRY

A Phantasy

Circumdederunt me dolores mortis. – Psalm XVIII

I said to It: 'We grasp not what you meant,
(Dwelling down here, so narrowly pinched and pent)
By crowning Death the King of the Firmament:
The query I admit to be
One of unwonted size,
But it is put to you sorrowingly,
And not in idle-wise.'

Or he was betrayed – if the phrase is appropriate to writing that was so completely deliberate – into anecdotes and episodes which reveal a perverse preoccupation with 'life's little ironies' and a prepossession with gloom: the young Parson in *The Curate's Kindness* has succeeded in persuading the Guardians of the Workhouse to annul the regulation separating man and wife, but the narrator is dismayed when he hears about it:

'I thought they'd be strangers aroun' me,
  But she's to be there!
Let me jump out o'wagon and go back and drown me
  At Pummery or Ten-Hatches Weir.'

And it is a fixed, unalive cynicism that calls in despair for a return of human impercipience:

Ere nescience shall be reaffirmed
  How long, how long?

Sometimes the language corresponds in luridness or inflation to the melodrama of the subject; at other times it is merely metrical and low-pitched rhymed prose. A failure in self-criticism leads him sometimes into humourless solemnities and bathos.

Yet the bent of Hardy's mind is ultimately conditioned by a sympathy for human and animal suffering and usually even the banalities, in their context, have saving sincerities. There are, moreover, many poems (*The Sleep-Worker*, for instance) which, though we may consider their prompting idea to be unduly partial, show a steady progression of thought which is impressive.

The case that Hardy makes out for 'pessimism' in the Apology to *Late Lyrics and Earlier* (1922) cannot at any rate be dismissed on the ground of insincerity: 'What is today,' he writes, 'in allusion to the present author's pages, alleged to be "pessimism", is, in truth, only "questionings" in the exploration of reality, and is the first step towards the soul's betterment, and the body's also.' He claimed that his poems were 'a series of fugitive impressions', and not the expression of anything like a systematized view of life. This is certainly true of a limited number of the poems, but if they are taken altogether most readers will feel that there was a certain amount of self-deception in the claim.

But despite being based too often on a view of life which seems to inhibit a free responsiveness, Hardy's poems provide an abundance of people and incident and perceptions; they are the work of a man who is also a novelist. Eye and ear are delicate and vigilant: he notes 'the smooth sea-line with a metal shine', and May's 'glad green leaves ... Delicate-filmed as new-spun silk'. In *Old Furniture*, where he thinks with characteristic affection of the hands that have owned and handled the 'relics of householdry', he imagines a finger setting the hands of the clock right,

> With tentative touches that lift and linger
> In the wont of a moth on a summer night.

Moments of everyday life are seen and presented with a quite individual intimacy:

> Icicles tag the church-aisle leads,
> The flag-rope gibbers hoarse,
> The home-bound foot-folk wrap their snow-flaked heads.

This intimate knowledge of village and small town life, rendered as it is with a deep regard for its value simply as life, is one of the 'positives' in Hardy's poetry. He does not of course attempt, as he does in some of the novels, any big or sustained account of the rural civilization which he saw changing and decaying. But there is enough of church and churchyard and music gallery, ballroom and pub, lovers' walks, sea-port, watering-place, tea under the trees, fields and woods and barns, and it is given in such a way as to impress itself on us as a profound element in Hardy's personal history. He appreciates the deftness of the turnip-hoer as he does the 'junketings, maypoles, and flings'; cider-makers and field-women and fiddlers catch his interest. He can be humorous on the 'ruined maid' (see the poem of that name) from the country. When William Dewy, in *Friends Beyond*, is recalled from the past and made to say 'Ye mid burn the old bass-viol that I set such value by', an ancient way of life is woven into the poet's feeling and habit of thought. When Beeny Cliff, Yell'ham Wood, Mellstock Churchyard, and so on come into Hardy's poetry it is normally with a strongly personal note: places are important to him, his feeling for them is one of his buttresses against the gloom of his general view of life and the universe.

The middle range of Hardy's poetry – lying between, on the one hand, patriotic jingles and banal-darksome tales and simplified love-idylls and heavy explicit statements of his 'philosophy', and on the other the small number of his wonderful best poems – displays in general the Hardy stoicism and truthfulness in the face of uncomforting experience. *Afterwards*, speculating on what people will say about him after his death, makes the quietest of claims for the gifts of loving observation and kindness to living things, at the same time envisaging with detachment his 'bell of quittance'; the poem is full of particular perceptions played off beautifully against the idea of death. In *An Ancient to Ancients*, tone and movement are more formal, but there remains a distinctive pathos in his account of the changes of fashion in dancing, opera, painting, poetry. *His Visitor* pictures the ghost who has 'come across from Mellstock while the moon wastes weaker' to revisit her home; disappointed by the changes she sees, she leaves 'to make again for Mellstock to return here never And rejoin the roomy silence ...': the tone is low-pitched and the rhythms (though regular) unemphatic, and the feeling comes from the quiet manner of conveying the sense of the importance to the ghost of the domesticities whose changes now trouble her. The feeling, it should be said, is comparatively unsubtle, as it is in *Beeny Cliff, March 1870–March 1913* and in *Five Students*, two other moving 'middle-range' poems with a poignant significance for the writer.

What justifies the use of 'wonderful' near the beginning of the previous paragraph is the extraordinary power and originality with which Hardy records in his best poems a tragic sense derived from intense personal experience. In these poems we have the stoicism which has not involved any evasion of the felt multiplicity and force of life. There is none of the simplifying division into ideal and actual which Hardy was prone to fall into, no over-spiritualization of women. The actual in these poems is imbued by the fineness of Hardy's spirit with a profound significance. Most, though not all, concern a man-woman relationship. All are an outcome of intensely pondered experience. There is simultaneously a vivid evocation of the past and a vivid rendering of the feeling of the present moment.

The grey bleakness of loss is conveyed as strongly in *Neutral Tones*, written in his twenties, as in *The Voice*, written in his seventies, though the earlier poem has a note of bitterness not present in the later one. Both poems make wonderful use of the natural scene: in the first, 'the pond edged with greyish leaves', and in the second

> the breeze, in its listlessness,
> Travelling across the wet mead to me here

are powerful agents of feeling.

The Self-Unseeing, in the space of twelve short lines, gives the scene now before the poet, with recollection of the fiddler and the dance and the woman, and realization of their failure to live that past moment to the full. The bareness of

> Here was the former door
> Where the dead feet walked in

combines with the momentary strong glowing excitement of

> Blessings emblazoned that day

to produce a rich economy. In contrast, though equally poignant, is *A Broken Appointment*: nothing of the scene is given except a suggestion of the clock striking the hour which should have brought her, and the poem rests upon the steady painful recognition of the significance of her non-appearance and the quiet rebuke which the poet offers with such delicacy:

> ... But, unto the store
> Of human deeds divine in all but name,
> Was it not worth a little hour or more
> To add yet this: Once you, a woman, came
> To soothe a time-worn man; even though it be
> You love not me?

In *After a Journey* the poet is at the edge of the sea, at night, communing with the 'ghost' of the woman he had been there with forty years before. The long deliberate lines suggest exact contemplation in memory, and the loved memory of the dead woman is simultaneously present with the sense of irretrievable loss. The remembered mist-bow above the waterfall and the present voice of the cave below are elements of the natural scene which are at the same time images charged with particular emotions. Unbeglamoured truthfulness conveys the profound loyalty of the poet, and as dawn comes the 'ghost' is as nothing to the creatures, who carry on life as if she had never been: 'The waked birds preen and the seals flop lazily.' In a superb analysis of the poem[2] F. R. Leavis has shown how the apparently awkward phrases are actually felicities aiding in the revelation of a rare integrity: 'The real focus for me,' he shows Hardy as saying, 'the focus of my affirmation, is the remembered realest thing, though to remember vividly is at the same time, inescapably, to embrace the utterness of loss.'

During Wind and Rain is hardly less fine and moving, though less intensely personal, than *After a Journey*. Here again the past is vivid in consciousness. In each of four stanzas a warmly recalled moment or scene is brought sharply up against a refrain-like line whose burden is 'the years', and this is followed by a last line which gives with great force and immediacy a detail of the wild autumn day now before the poet. The deliberation of the stressing in the final line of the poem,

> Down their carved names the rain-drop ploughs,

clinches, with precisely that implication of mortality, the poet's confrontation of reality in the beauty and vividness of art.

The epic-drama, *The Dynasts* (1903–8), has been claimed by some admirers to be Hardy's greatest work. But while it is impressive by its manifestation of the peculiar strength and quality of its author's character, it seems in its magnitude to be more a matter of determined accumulation for preconceived ends than of impulsion from Hardy's deepest emotional being.

It is one of the triumphs of Edward Thomas (1878–1917) that with the character and temperament he possessed he could move quite away from the kind of shadowiness that marks de la Mare's poetry, and also out of the landscape that Hardy too often colours with his own greyness of spirit, into an open and fresh air. When we call him a poet of minute particularity and fidelity we have in mind both phenomena and mood. His poetic output, compared with that of Hardy and de la Mare, is small, but a high proportion of it bears his characteristic excellences. The fact that he did not start writing poetry until he was thirty-five accounts in part for a degree of self-awareness and self-criticism that served him well. He knew from the start that there were certain things he wished to avoid in his poetry, and it was because he was an original poet with the original poet's disturbing power that editors to whom he submitted poems were almost unanimously discouraging.

Reviewing Robert Frost's *North of Boston* in 1914 Thomas wrote: 'These poems are revolutionary because they lack the exaggeration of rhetoric.' This is a way of saying that he welcomed a departure from at least some of the aspects of nineteenth-century poetry. His own poems were alleged, by friends during his lifetime and by many critics after his death, to lack 'form'. He was felt to be disturbingly different from the typical Georgian poets (several of whom he was friendly with). His refusal to take the influential Edward Garnett's advice to 'chisel' *Lob* is characteristic of his steady perseverance in the way he wanted to go. We can now see Edward Thomas as a poet of great distinction, English in a profound sense, a voice that is contemporary in the middle of the twentieth century.

It is only on the superficial ground of broad similarity of subject-matter that Edward Thomas can be assimilated to the Georgians. Nature and the countryside, though intensely and exquisitely appreciated for their own sake, are mainly in his poetry an occasion for exploring and presenting his mood and character and a whole mode of experiencing; while his best love poems are quite personal. The presentment is quiet, delicate, and strong, and the quality of the man profoundly interesting.

He had the gift of putting character, mood, attitude to life, into a seemingly small situation, into a moment's perceiving. And the records he unassumingly offers will enhance the more our own power of experiencing because he is in close and vitalizing touch with the natural world. He can give us enlightenment on sincerity and beauty.

This poem is entitled *A Tale*:

> There once the walls
> Of the ruined cottage stood.
> The periwinkle crawls
> With flowers in its hair into the wood.
>
> In flowerless hours
> Never will the bank fail
> With everlasting flowers
> On fragments of blue plates, to tell the tale.

A small poem, as serious though not as powerful as Wordsworth's *A Slumber Did My Spirit Seal*. The cottage and scene are actual and now; but what they tell is not simply the tale of themselves but *the* tale of man's life, of nature and change, of disappearance and also of relics that are emblems of endeavour. Thomas perceives a depth in the seen. In another small poem, *The Hollow Wood*, a goldfinch flits and feeds on thistle-tops at the edge of a wood, while other birds pass to and fro inside the wood: we can abstract an idea-feeling if we wish from the juxtaposition in the poem of the known and bright with the strange and dark. But what is essentially communicated is a way of seeing and feeling that has depth and innerness while still remaining fresh and physical.

'Forest' or 'wood' is a recurring symbol in Edward Thomas, and its introduction is invariably a spontaneous and unforced item of the experience he is describing. With its various significances – obscure regions of human experience not wholly susceptible to rational explanation, or the gulf 'where nothing is But what is not', or thoughts of death – it is connected in Thomas's poetry with his well-known melancholy. But he does not simplify and narrow down; his poetic analysis of his feeling is finer than (say) the typical Victorian or Georgian piece in being immeasurably more than an expression of regret or sorrow or apprehensiveness. There are no inert or merely weary poems in Thomas. He never fails in sharp sensuous perceiving and rarely in a precision of phrasing which retains a hauntingly natural manner.

In *The Gypsy* he goes home at night after the Christmas fair and market, carrying with him the image of what he has seen and heard:

> ... Not even the kneeling ox had eyes like the Romany.
> That night he peopled for me the hollow wooded land,
> More dark and wild than stormiest heavens, that I searched and
> scanned
> Like a ghost new-arrived. The gradations of the dark
> Were like an underworld of death, but for the spark
> In the Gypsy boy's black eyes as he played and stamped his tune,
> 'Over the hills and far away', and a crescent moon.

The feeling of a dark unknown immensity is very powerful, but it is not all-conquering: against the blackness and the words of the tune (suggesting an ever farther recession) there are the spark, the strength of stamping, the new moon. Even in the most stark among the poems, *Rain* for instance –

> Rain, midnight rain, nothing but the wild rain
> On this bleak hut, and solitude, and me
> Remembering again that I shall die ...

– and in the poems, such as *Lights Out*, where he seems near to surrender, there is no defeat and no flaccidity. A sensitiveness of movement and an exactness of statement show the poet to be in full and alert control.

In many of the poems it is a subtle intermingling of diverse sense-impressions and delicate observations that is largely effective in conveying a feeling of elusive experience which the poet has nevertheless firmly caught. *Ambition* has an extraordinary interplay of images of energetic life with a sense of silence and emptiness. *The Brook* has child paddling and man seated, butterfly on stone, silent bird and silent man, a horse galloping and a horse at rest. The dualities in Thomas's poetry – clear and misty, near and far, sound and silence, present and past, movement and stillness, thought and sensation, and so on – are never posited by the poet. We may or may not note them consciously as we read, but they have their effect in a seemingly inevitable whole.

What is in fact subtly organized poetry sounds often like the poet speaking easily but with beautiful precision, revealing an inner life by a remarkably sensitive account of the outer world. The second half of *March* follows on a vivid rendering of a bitterly cold day of hail and wind, with the sun now near the end of the day filling earth and heaven with a great light, but no warmth:

... What did the thrushes know? Rain, snow, sleet, hail,
Had kept them quiet as the primroses.
They had but an hour to sing. On boughs they sang,
On gates, on ground; they sang while they changed perches
And while they fought, if they remembered to fight:
So earnest were they to pack into that hour
Their unwilling hoard of song before the moon
Grew brighter than the clouds. Then 'twas no time
For singing merely. So they could keep off silence
And night, they cared not what they sang or screamed;
Whether 'twas hoarse or sweet or fierce or soft;
And to me all was sweet: they could do no wrong.
Something they knew – I also, while they sang
And after. Not till night had half its stars
And never a cloud, was I aware of silence
Stained with all that hour's songs, a silence
Saying that Spring returns, perhaps to-morrow.

To appreciate this in all its rich significance, it would of course be necessary to see it with the first half of the poem. But the extract may show how the feelings and perceptions, the thankfulness that overcomes the distress of the cold, the exquisite way the silence comes into his consciousness, the sense that the Spring of the poem is happiness (without ceasing to be Spring), are given – to use Thomas's words about Frost – 'through fidelity to the postures which the voice assumes in the most expressive intimate speech'.

His language is quite free from stale poeticalities. It frequently has, it is true, words common in 'romantic' poetry of nature and love and disillusion – sweet, solitary, once, strange, hidden, vainly, happy – but they are never simply exploited for their stock emotional content; they are *used* as an essential item, modifying and modified by other items. He makes good use also, with a sort of homely vividness, of phrases which were deemed unpoetical by many of his contemporary readers: his thrushes *pack* into an hour their 'unwilling *hoard* of song'. It is ultimately his complete lack of condescension, his openness to impressions, which give his language (like his rhythms) a certain easy breadth; the breadth contributes to a total complexity born of a rare union of fastidiousness and democratic sympathy, including humour:

> Women he liked, did shovel-bearded Bob,
> Old Farmer Hayward of the Heath, but he
> Loved horses. He himself was like a cob,
> And leather-coloured. Also he loved a tree.

A certain robustness-with-shrewdness, like that which he portrays with such a light touch in Old Jack (to use one of Lob's several folk-names), is an ingredient of his own character:

> He is English as this gate, these flowers, this mire.
> And when at eight years old Lob-lie-by-the-fire
> Came in my books, this was the man I saw.
> He has been in England as long as dove and daw ...

Old Man, *The Glory*, *The Other*, are among the finest of many poems that present a self-questioning which does not preclude a wealth of outgoing feeling, and a reaching for fulfilment which we feel cannot for him be dependent upon any possible creed or any group-support. The nature of the statement and the self-searching that we get in the following superb lines from *The Glory* are quite different from Hardy's expressions of solid views and attitudes:

> The glory of the beauty of the morning –
> The cuckoo crying over the untouched dew;
> The blackbird that has found it, and the dove
> That tempts me on to something sweeter than love ...
>
> Or must I be content with discontent
> As larks and swallows are perhaps with wings?
> And shall I ask at the day's end once more
> What beauty is, and what I can have meant
> By happiness? And shall I let all go,
> Glad, weary, or both? Or shall I perhaps know
> That I was happy oft and oft before,
> Awhile forgetting how I am fast pent,
> How dreary-swift, with naught to travel to,
> Is Time? I cannot bite the day to the core.

Thomas was sharply aware not only of the difficulty of fulfilment in human relationship but also of the impact of new knowledge and of the destructive effects of certain new attitudes on many of the things he cared for.

Prufrock appeared in the year Edward Thomas died. But though the externals of Mr Eliot's urban world are probably the more relevant now to the majority of readers (and poets), those of Edward Thomas's are in some important aspects still with us and must continue to be so. Furthermore the partial supersession of the rural civilization which he himself saw declining, does not affect his status as a poet, for fundamentally he deals with permanent things in human nature. Although he does not offer either a fullness like that of Keats's *Autumn* or the kind of dramatic force and concentration that Hopkins won from his self-division, he has his own delicate richness and his own explored stresses. If he had lived longer he might have widened his range, perhaps making discoveries that would have enabled him to present more of himself and of life. As it is he remains a remarkable original poet.

NOTES

1. William Walsh, in *The Use of Imagination* (London, 1959).
2. In *Scrutiny*, Vol. XIX, No. 2.

THE LITERATURE OF THE FIRST WORLD WAR

D. J. ENRIGHT

THOUGH Wilfred Owen and Siegfried Sassoon may not have contributed to the establishment of what we call 'modernism', the poetry of the First World War has a clear right to be considered part and parcel of modern poetry. It would be strange were this not so; for the experience of the War was emphatically one which could not be conveyed in debilitated nineteenth-century poetic conventions. Owen's poetic antecedents and personal tastes were of the nineteenth century; he was in no sense a conscious innovator of the kind of T. S. Eliot or Ezra Pound or even the Imagists; he was not a literary intellectual, he was probably unaware of any poetic crisis, quite possibly he had read neither the Jacobeans nor the Metaphysicals. Simply, the War, a great non-literary event, forced him, as a poet and an honest man, to find another way of speaking.

The compulsion behind this War poetry, that is to say, was one of subject-matter. This is particularly true of Sassoon, whose style, when one becomes aware of it, is unashamedly old-fashioned. In the more successful War poetry, the style capitulated to the subject-matter; in the best of it, and predominantly in Owen's work, the style was *in* the subject-matter.

Since the reputations of the War writers are by now variously established, this essay will largely take the form of an anthology accompanied by a minimum of commentary. We begin with a brief comparison between Rupert Brooke (1887–1915) as old-style war poet and Wilfred Owen (1893–1918) as new-style war poet, which, though hackneyed, is still useful. For one thing, the comparison serves as a simple illustration of a basic difference between early-twentieth-century 'traditional' poetry and modern poetry: the abandonment by the latter of nice-mindedness, of prescribed 'romantic paraphernalia, of the conception of poetry as 'dream'. But the

War only accelerated the development of modern poetry: it did not instigate it. What the difference between

Safe shall be my going,
Secretly armed against all death's endeavour;
Safe though all safety's lost; safe where men fall;
And if these poor limbs die, safest of all
(Brooke: *Safety*)

and

One dawn, our wire patrol
Carried him. This time, Death had not missed.
We could do nothing but wipe his bleeding cough.
Could it be accident? – Rifles go off . . .
Not sniped? No. (Later they found the English ball.)
(Owen: *S.I.W.*)

implies is three years extra of war – and, of course, their effects on a poet who, whatever his earlier allegiances, was able to perceive and follow the new directives of experience.

There is little compulsion behind Brooke's peace-time poetry: apart from some pleasant light verse, it is only accomplished, self-consciously graceful, and vaguely portentous within the bounds of good manners, except when setting out to be bad-mannered and turning into schoolboy cynicism. It is his war poems we are concerned with, however: the sequence of sonnets entitled *1914*.

Sonnet I, *Peace*, propounds the idea that war is clean and cleansing, like a jolly good swim. A grand change, in fact, from 'all the little emptiness of love' (whose love?) and from 'half-men, and their dirty songs' (who are they? Was one obliged to listen to their songs?). The only thing that can suffer in war is the body. (Enough, one might think – and later writers showed how wrong Brooke was, at that.)

Sonnet II, *Safety*, testifies in a cloud of witness to the safeness of war. War may even lead to death, which is the safest of all shelters against the dangers of life. (These dangers are not specified: they may be the 'dirty songs' of the preceding poem.)

Sonnet III, *The Dead*, is a conventional trumpet-piece, free from the utter irrationality of the first two sonnets, though later poets were not so sure about the grand abstractions of the sestet: 'Honour has come back, as a king, to earth . . .'

Sonnet IV, *The Dead*, has none of the petulant anti-life feeling of

I and II; indeed, the octave concerns the past life of the dead, rather affectedly described but not perverse. The sestet describes water which has frosted over, and seems to have nothing to do with the octave.

Sonnet V, *The Soldier* (amusingly summed up in a student's comment in the Asian library copy before me as 'frank and unashamed peace of patriotism'), I quote in full, as it is certainly Brooke's most celebrated poem and probably still more widely read than Owen's *Strange Meeting*.

> If I should die, think only this of me:
> That there's some corner of a foreign field
> That is for ever England. There shall be
> In that rich earth a richer dust concealed;
> A dust whom England bore, shaped, made aware,
> Gave, once, her flowers to love, her ways to roam,
> A body of England's, breathing English air,
> Washed by the rivers, blest by suns of home.
>
> And think, this heart, all evil shed away,
> A pulse in the eternal mind, no less
> Gives somewhere back the thoughts by England given;
> Her sights and sounds; dreams happy as her day;
> And laughter, learnt of friends; and gentleness,
> In hearts at peace, under an English heaven.

In its simple-minded flamboyant way, it seems successful enough, a pleasant period piece, 'frank and unashamed'. But a second reading suggests that a little shame could well have leavened the frankness. The reiteration of 'England' and 'English' is all very well; but an odd uncertainty as to whether the poet is praising England or himself – 'a richer dust' – remains despite that reiteration. Moreover, the 'mysticism' of the sestet, whereby the treasures enumerated in the octave are to be given back ('somewhere', to somebody), is hardly more convincing, though obviously better educated, than the pathetic desiderations found in the 'In Memoriam' column of any local newspaper.

In short, Brooke's war poetry is typically pre-War poetry. And what has been said above is no more than was said, with far more authority, by a number of poets within a short time of Brooke's death. Charles Sorley (1895–1915; he died six months later, but those months had been spent on the Western Front) had said: 'The voice of our poets and men of letters is finely trained and sweet to hear ... it pleases, it flatters, it charms, it soothes: it is a living lie.'[1] He made the radical criticism of Brooke's work: 'He has clothed his attitude in fine words: but he has taken the sentimental attitude.' And in a sonnet Sorley makes an explicit rejoinder to Brooke's *1914* sequence:

> When you see millions of the mouthless dead
> Across your dreams in pale battalions go,
> Say not soft things as other men have said,
> That you'll remember. For you need not so.
> Give them not praise. For, deaf, how should they know
> It is not curses heaped on each gashed head?
> Nor tears. Their blind eyes see not your tears flow,
> Nor honour. It is easy to be dead.

Sorley's attitude to the conflict – an attitude which grew stronger in later writing, where the conflict came to seem one of soldiers against politicians rather than nationality against nationality – was already far more thoughtful, humane, and accurate than Brooke's:

> ... in each other's dearest ways we stand,
> And hiss and hate. And the blind fight the blind.

Relevant on this point is Sir Herbert Read's (b. 1893) remark in *Annals of Innocence and Experience*:

> It must be remembered that in 1914 our conception of war was completely unreal. We had vague childish memories of the Boer War, and from these and from a general diffusion of Kiplingesque sentiments, we managed to infuse into war a decided element of adventurous romance. War still appealed to the imagination.

A little later it was to appeal, violently, to the senses, and the old imagination was blown to pieces. There are the few poems of Arthur Graeme West (1891–1917) to show how that imagination was exploded:

> Next was a bunch of half a dozen men
> All blown to bits, an archipelago
> Of corrupt fragments ...
>
> (*Night Patrol*, March 1916)

In a letter written early in 1917 Owen comments, '... everything unnatural, broken, blasted; the distortion of the dead, whose unburiable bodies sit outside the dug-outs all day, all night, the most execrable sights on earth. In poetry we call them the most glorious.' Finally, there is Robert Graves (b. 1895), in *Goodbye to All That*, reporting a conversation with Siegfried Sassoon in November 1915:

> ... he showed me some of his own poems. One of them began:
>
> 'Return to greet me, colours that were my joy,
> Not in the woeful crimson of men slain ...'
>
> Siegfried had not yet been in the trenches. I told him, in my old-soldier manner, that he would soon change his style.

In considering the real poetry of the War, or the poetry of the real War, we may most conveniently begin with Siegfried Sassoon (1886–1967), the one major war poet (one would not include Robert Graves or Edmund Blunden, b. 1896, in the category of war poets) to survive the War.

The great compulsion here, as to a lesser extent in Owen's work, was to communicate reality, to convey the truth of modern warfare to those not directly engaged in it. For this was the first modern war, in respect of destructive power; at the same time it was (for the British people at least) the last of the old wars in which the civilian population were at a safe distance from the destruction. As Professor de S. Pinto reminds us, by 1916 a change had taken place in English society whereby a vertical division, cutting across class distinctions, separated the Nation at Home from the Nation Overseas (i.e. the armies on the Continent). Inevitably civilian attitudes were, to use Herbert Read's term, largely Kiplingesque. Information and correction were necessary, and all the more so in view of the romantic lies of the politicians, the nobility-in-absentia of the newspapers, and the vicarious altruism of the profiteers. The common soldier could not speak for himself, and the casualty lists apparently did not speak plainly enough. Thus the writers in the trenches felt it a duty, not simply to write poems or prose, but to write about the trenches.

The mood in Sassoon's early verse of

> War is our scourge; yet war has made us wise,
> And, fighting for our freedom, we are free
>
> (*Absolution*)

was soon replaced by a sober documentary manner:

> He was a young man with a meagre wife
> And two small children in a Midland town;
> He showed their photographs to all his mates,
> And they considered him a decent chap
> Who did his work and hadn't much to say ...
>
> (*A Working Party*)

And in turn this manner was pushed aside by the angry violence of the collection entitled *Counterattack* (1918):

> 'Good-morning; good-morning!' the General said
> When we met him last week on our way to the line.
> Now the soldiers he smiled at are most of 'em dead,
> And we're cursing his staff for incompetent swine.
> 'He's a cheery old card,' grunted Harry to Jack
> As they slogged up to Arras with rifle and pack.
>
> . . .
>
> But he did for them both by his plan of attack.
>
> (*The General*)

Counterattack is first-class propaganda, and rather more: angry polemical verses, technically simple, rough and ready, concerned only with the obvious meanings of the words used, never suggesting more than is actually said, but never suggesting less than is said:

> I knew a simple soldier boy
> Who grinned at life in empty joy,
> Slept soundly through the lonesome dark,
> And whistled early with the lark.
>
> In winter trenches, cowed and glum,
> With crumps and lice and lack of rum,
> He put a bullet through his brain.
> No one spoke of him again.
>
> . . .
>
> You smug-faced crowds with kindling eye
> Who cheer when soldier lads march by,
> Sneak home and pray you'll never know
> The hell where youth and laughter go.
>
> (*Suicide in the Trenches*)

Not poetry, perhaps? But did that matter? The poetry – to adapt a phrase from Owen – is in the anger. While its impact would have been more powerful, or more permanently powerful, had the mode of satire been more controlled, more calculated, and had Sassoon drawn these victims less sketchily, we must yet admit that in the best of his poems it is the spontaneity, the lack of calculation, which impresses us. They were so clearly written out of honest rage and decent indignation.

Perhaps it is significant that since the War Sassoon has only written so forcefully when remembering it. One of his best pieces was provoked by the erection of the great War Memorial near Ypres, *On Passing the New Menin Gate, 1927*:

> Who will remember, passing through this Gate,
> The unheroic Dead who fed the guns?
> Who shall absolve the foulness of their fate, –
> Those doomed, conscripted, unvictorious ones?
> Crudely renewed, the Salient holds its own.
> Paid are its dim defenders by this pomp;
> Paid, with a pile of peace-complacent stone,
> The armies who endured that sullen swamp ...

There is also the satirical collection, *The Road to Ruin*, written in the early thirties: a prefigurement of similar ambitions, euphemisms, and lies, leading to another great war, with greater weapons and more radical destruction. The opening poem describes the Prince of Darkness standing with his staff at the Cenotaph, 'unostentatious and respectful', and praying, 'Make them forget, O Lord, what this Memorial means ...' The best is probably *An Unveiling*:

> The President's oration ended thus:
> 'Not vainly London's War-gassed victims perished.
> We are a part of them, and they of us:
> As such they will perpetually be cherished.
> Not many of them did much; but all did what
> They could, who stood like warriors at their post
> (Even when too young to walk). This hallowed spot
> Commemorates a proud, though poisoned host.
> We honour here' (he paused) 'our Million Dead;
> Who, as a living poet has nobly said,
> "Are now forever London" ...'

Its effectiveness is much increased by memories of the poet's earlier piece on the New Menin Gate and of Brooke's *Soldier*, reincarnated in the form of a civilian casualty list.

Yet Sassoon's poems of 1949 revert to Brooke in sentiment, though they are far less lush in language and rhythm. *Silent Service* –

> Now, multifold, let Britain's patient power
> Be proven within us for the world to see

– is no more than a dash of Winston Churchill in an ocean of water; and one turns with relief to Herbert Read's poem, *To a Conscript of 1940*:

> But you, my brother and my ghost, if you can go
> Knowing that there is no reward, no certain use
> In all your sacrifice, then honour is reprieved.

If Brooke has played the war poet for those who are fascinated by the 'idea' of poetry, Wilfred Owen is the war poet for those who desire the reality. For an account of his life and thought there is the excellent memoir by Edmund Blunden, affixed to *The Poems of Wilfred Owen.*[2] Owen began to write poetry at an early age and, as Blunden points out, the influence of Keats, to whom he was devoted, is clear in his first poems. Along with imitation of the late-nineteenth-century 'decadents', the Keatsian influence ('Five cushions hath my hands, for reveries;/And one deep pillow for thy brow's fatigues') remained in force up to and some little way beyond his enlistment in 1915. In January 1917 he wrote from the Somme, 'I can't tell you any more Facts. I have no Fancies and no Feelings ...' A few days later: 'Those "Somme Pictures" are the laughing-stock of the army – like the trenches on exhibition in Kensington ... The people of England needn't hope. They must agitate. But they are not yet agitated even.' And in August 1917, in hospital near Edinburgh, he refers thus to Tennyson's personal unhappiness:

> as for misery, was he ever frozen alive, with dead men for comforters? Did he hear the moaning at the Bar, not at twilight and the evening bell only, but at dawn, noon, and night, eating and sleeping, walking and working, always the close moaning of the Bar; the thunder, the hissing, and the whining of the Bar? – Tennyson, it seems, was always a great child. So should I have been, but for Beaumont Hamel.

While convalescing from his 'neurasthenia', Owen met Sassoon, and the two became close friends. Sassoon's example confirmed Owen in his resolve to speak out against the War, in harsh, clear, and unpleasant words, unsoftened by any poetic or patriotic euphemisms. He entered his brief brilliant maturity.

These two extracts come from a poem called *Disabled*:

> One time he liked a blood-smear down his leg,
> After the matches, carried shoulder-high.
> It was after football, when he'd drunk a peg,
> He thought he'd better join. – He wonders why ...
>
> . . .
>
> Some cheered him home, but not as crowds cheer Goal.
> Only a solemn man who brought him fruits
> *Thanked* him; and then inquired about his soul.
> Now, he will spend a few sick years in Institutes,
> And do whatever things the rules consider wise,
> And take whatever pity they may dole.
> Tonight he noticed how the women's eyes
> Passed from him to the strong men that were whole.
> How cold and late it is! Why don't they come
> And put him into bed? Why don't they come?

It may be that this poem found its originating impulse in anger; but it goes far beyond anger. Just as much as the best poems of Sassoon, this is the expression of a lacerated moral sensibility: even so, it is poetry of a different and higher order. The success of Sassoon's anti-war verse depends to a great extent upon the reader's personal attitude: you will only *agree* with what is said if you are already tending towards the same opinion. The power of Owen's poetry is greater. It can create an attitude, starting from nothing: it can impel agreement by the depth, the 'density', of its expression. The 'he' of *Disabled* has a life, a presence, which is only hinted at in the convenient satirical shorthand of Sassoon's 'Harry' and 'Jack'. Sassoon's most interesting poetry is composed of what have been called the 'negative emotions' – horror, anger, disgust – and outside that field he inclines to become sentimental in a conventional way. (Robert Graves hits the nail on the head in saying, 'Modernism in Mr Sassoon is an intelligent, satiric reaction to contemporary political and social Bluffs; it is not a literary policy.'[3]) In Owen's work, the 'positive emotions', of love, compassion, admiration, joy, are present as well, and their co-existence strengthens the poetry.

These comments should not be taken to suggest that Owen ever reverted to the simple-minded romanticism of Brooke or Julian Grenfell (1888–1915). (It is touching to read in the Appendix to his *Poems* that he was collecting photographs of war wounds, mutilations, and the results of surgical operations.) On the contrary, some of his poems are almost unbearably painful, in that they permit us no escape into cursing or self-righteousness or other satisfactions afforded by the squib or lampoon. The quiet accurate accounts of gas casualties, men who have gone mad, men who are technically alive although their bodies have been destroyed – these are in the end a more powerful indictment of war than Sassoon's fluent indignation. And they do not 'date'.

Anthem for Doomed Youth is one of his best-known poems:

> What passing-bells for these who die as cattle?
> Only the monstrous anger of the guns,
> Only the stuttering rifles' rapid rattle
> Can patter out their hasty orisons.
> No mockeries for them from prayers or bells,
> Nor any voice of mourning save the choirs, –
> The shrill, demented choirs of wailing shells;
> And bugles calling for them from sad shires.
>
> What candles may be held to speed them all?
> Not in the hands of boys, but in their eyes
> Shall shine the holy glimmers of good-byes.
> The pallor of girls' brows shall be their pall;
> Their flowers the tenderness of silent minds,
> And each slow dusk a drawing-down of blinds.

The opening seems obvious in its intention: the poet protests at the discrepancy between the suffering of the Nation Overseas and the smugness of the Nation at Home. The 'cannon-fodder' *cliché* hovers near. But the third line demonstrates the poet's ear: 'the stuttering rifles' rapid rattle': and sends us back to see (or hear, rather) whether the second line really is a *cliché*. The word 'patter', similarly, when listened to as well as looked at releases an unexpected complexity of meaning. The following lines appear to be an obvious and easy success in the line of sarcasm: 'no mockeries for them from prayers or bells...' But Owen was too much of a poet to be content with resting on those laurels. There is, paradoxically, a kind of glory in the next two lines:

The shrill, demented choirs of wailing shells;
And bugles calling for them from sad shires,

though a very different kind of glory from the official one. Then, when we arrive at the sestet of the sonnet, the bitterness of the opening has faded, and what prevails is the quiet restrained sorrow appropriate to a tragic close. (The quietness of tone may prevent us from noticing what a risk Owen took in his last line, how narrowly he brought it off.)

It is instructive to set side by side a poem of Owen's and one of Sassoon's, the originating impulses of which were clearly similar:

The Bishop tells us: 'When the boys come back
They will not be the same; for they'll have fought
In a just cause: they lead the last attack
On Anti-Christ; their comrades' blood has bought
New right to breed an honourable race,
They have challenged Death and dared him face to face.'

'We're none of us the same!' the boys reply.
'For George lost both his legs; and Bill's stone blind;
Poor Jim's shot through the lungs and like to die;
And Bert's gone syphilitic: you'll not find
A chap who's served that hasn't found *some* change.'
And the Bishop said: 'The ways of God are strange!'
(Sassoon: '*They*')

I mind as 'ow the night afore that show
Us five got talking, – we was in the know, –
'Over the top to-morrer; boys, we're for it.
First wave we are, first ruddy wave; that's tore it.'
'Ah well,' says Jimmy, – an' 'e's seen some scrappin' –
'There ain't more nor five things as can 'appen; –
Ye get knocked out; else wounded – bad or cushy;
Scuppered; or nowt except yer feeling mushy.'

One of us got the knock-out, blown to chops.
T'other was hurt like, losin' both 'is props.
An' one, to use the word of 'ypocrites,
'Ad the misfortoon to be took be Fritz.

Now me, I wasn't scratched, praise God Amighty
(Though next time please I'll thank 'im for a blighty),
But poor young Jim, 'e's livin' an' 'e's not;
'E reckoned 'e'd five chances, an' 'e 'ad;
'E's wounded, killed, and pris'ner, all the lot,
The bloody lot all rolled in one. Jim's mad.

(Owen: *The Chances*)

'*They*' is one of the poet's most effective outbursts, but as a poem it is weakened by the too-amenable Bishop: Sassoon has shot, right through the heart, a sitting duck. We feel less indignant than the poem wants us to feel. *The Chances* – one of the very few successful English 'proletarian' poems, incidentally – is an altogether richer piece, a poem which will hold even though every bishop should take a vow of pacifism or silence. The humour in the speaker's style – with the implied modesty of one who has no intention of 'preaching' – lays the reader open to the full onslaught of the last short sentence. As for anger: that is not in the poem, it is in the reader.

Blunden quotes a friend's description of Owen: '... an intense pity for suffering humanity – a need to alleviate it, wherever possible, and an inability to shirk the sharing of it, even when this seemed useless. This was the keynote of Wilfred's character ...' It is also the keynote of his poetry. An instance is the fine lyric, *Futility*, as bare and cool and natural in its English as the poetry of Edward Thomas:

Move him into the sun –
Gently its touch awoke him once,
At home, whispering of fields unsown.
Always it woke him, even in France,
Until this morning and this snow.
If anything might rouse him now
The kind old sun will know.

Think how it wakes the seeds, –
Woke, once, the clays of a cold star.
Are limbs, so dear-achieved, are sides,
Full-nerved – still warm – too hard to stir?
Was it for this the clay grew tall?
– O what made fatuous sunbeams toil
To break earth's sleep at all?

And the note sounds, more explicit, in the last stanza of *Insensibility*, beginning 'But cursed are dullards whom no cannon stuns':

> By choice they made themselves immune
> To pity and whatever moans in man
> Before the last sea and the hapless stars;
> Whatever mourns when many leave these shores;
> Whatever shares
> The eternal reciprocity of tears

– a passage sufficient in itself to prove that Owen is a poet, not a war poet alone. His use of assonantal rhyme should be remarked on here: deriving from his reading of French poetry, it afforded the measure of formal control he desired without the too melodious and (in view of his subject-matter) inappropriate chime of pure rhyme. Simultaneously, and notably in *Strange Meeting* and *Exposure*, it contributes a telling music of its own, ominous in its intonations:

> Watching, we hear the mad gusts tugging on the wire,
> Like twitching agonies of men among its brambles.
> Northward, incessantly, the flickering gunnery rumbles ...

In August 1918, his convalescence over, he returned to France, feeling that life there could not be harder to bear than 'the stinking Leeds and Bradford war-profiteers now reading *John Bull* on Scarborough Sands'. There was a more positive reason for his readiness to go back to the trenches: 'there', he wrote, 'I shall be better able to cry my outcry'. It was this compulsion to speak so as to be understood which guarded him against his Keatsian taste for rich sensuous language. In a letter to Sassoon, he declared: 'I don't want to write anything to which a soldier would say *No Compris*!'

When Owen was killed on 4 November, among his papers was found a draft preface to a future volume of poems. It is the best commentary on the work he left:

> This book is not about heroes. English poetry is not yet fit to speak of them.
>
> Nor is it about deeds, or lands, nor anything about glory, honour, might, majesty, dominion, or power, except War.
>
> Above all I am not concerned with Poetry.
>
> My subject is War, and the pity of War.
>
> The Poetry is in the pity.

> Yet these elegies are to this generation in no sense consolatory. They may be to the next. All a poet can do today is warn. That is why the true Poets must be truthful ...

In the table of Contents, against *Strange Meeting*, possibly the last of his poems, and the finest, is written: 'Foolishness of War'. This poem is no doubt 'allegorical', but it succeeds through its sheer concretion: 'it is a dream only a stage further on than the actuality of the tunnelled dug-outs', as Blunden remarks, if indeed we think of it as a dream at all –

> It seemed that out of battle I escaped
> Down some profound dull tunnel ...

He rouses one of the 'encumbered sleepers' there:

> And by his smile, I knew that sullen hall,
> By his dead smile I knew we stood in Hell.

The other speaks of the wastage of life, of the ambition, which now cannot be realized, to help humanity by warning, by telling the truth:

> For by my glee might many men have laughed,
> And of my weeping something had been left,
> Which must die now. I mean the truth untold,
> The pity of war, the pity war distilled ...

The poem has its weaknesses, which the poet would surely have dealt with had he lived. The reference to 'chariot-wheels', even though we take the implication that 'all wars are one war', is out of place in the Hindenburg Line; the words 'mystery' and 'mastery' are vague where they need to be precise; and 'trek from progress' is a rather abject concession to the exigencies of rhyme. But again and again the poet scores a bull's-eye: 'lifting distressful hands as if to bless', 'foreheads of men have bled where no wounds were', and the extracts quoted above and below. The poem ends:

> I am the enemy you killed, my friend.
> I knew you in this dark; for so you frowned
> Yesterday through me as you jabbed and killed.
> I parried; but my hands were loath and cold.
> Let us sleep now ...

Isaac Rosenberg (1890–1918) was the other indubitable poetic loss incurred in the War; he was killed at the age of twenty-eight. Though his work is undigested, it is still impressive: isolated lines blaze with energy and colour. For example, the image of the 'dead heart' in *Midsummer Frost* –

> A frozen pool whereon mirth dances;
> Where the shining boys would fish

– or the opening of *Day*:

> The fiery hoofs of day have trampled the night to dust;
> They have broken the censer of darkness and its fumes are lost in light.
> Like a smoke blown away by the rushing of the gust
> When the doors of the sun flung open, morning leaped and smote the
> night ...

'Scriptural' and 'sculptural' are the adjectives by which Sassoon describes Rosenberg's muscular use of language.[4] True, the lines quoted are undisciplined, but one would not demand discipline at the age of twenty-two. His best-known poem, *Break of Day in the Trenches*, is a more mature and integrated work, yet less individual, perhaps a little too 'white with the dust' of the trenches.

I have not included Edmund Blunden and Robert Graves in the province of war poets, though memories of the War have haunted their poetry ever since. They must feature here as the authors of the two finest prose works to deal with the War. Blunden's *Undertones of War*, an established classic, is a work gentler in tone than those we have been chiefly concerned with (it was written in 1928), with literature and the English countryside never very far away, yet accurate and detailed in observation of the War scene and its human figures. *Goodbye to All That*, Robert Graves's 'autobiography' (written at the age of thirty-three), dealing largely with his War experience, is the lively sort of writing we have come to expect from the author, racy without being careless, crammed with short stories and brilliant character sketches, a little too casual and almost callous at times, but continuously readable. With these first-class accounts we must group Sassoon's *Memoirs of an Infantry Officer*, a more painful work characterized by sensitive and minute documentation; and two shorter pieces by Herbert Read, *In Retreat* ('A journal of the retreat of the Fifth Army from St Quentin, March 1918') and *The Raid*[5]. David Jones's (b. 1895) *In Parenthesis* (1937) is a consciously 'literary' work: its style, tapestried and 'modernistic' at the same time, is at odds with its subject-matter (infantry life on the Western Front), and the allusions to ancient Welsh poetry and Celtic myths with their explanatory but not always justificatory footnotes rob the account of most of its immediacy.

If less urgently than the poets, the prose writers too were under the compulsion to report, to inform, and (however indirectly) to warn. All were affected by the new human experience of the War: the relationship between officers and men, with its 'depth of understanding and sympathy for which I know no parallel in civilian life', as Herbert Read puts it: 'the relationship was ... like that of a priest to his parish'.[6] These writers were not only (as officers) priests, they were also interpreters.

NOTES

I have been much indebted to Edmund Blunden's pamphlet, *War Poets 1914–1918* ('Writers and their Work' Series, London, 1958) and to the short but substantial chapter on 'Trench Poets' in V. de S. Pinto's *Crisis in English Poetry 1880–1940* (London, 1951).

1. Compare this comment and the following comments on the need for a change in poetic style with Ezra Pound's remark: 'the poetry which I expect to see written during the next decade or so ... will, I think, move against poppy-cock, it will be harder and saner, it will be ... "nearer the bone" ... its force will lie in its truth' (*Poetry Review*, February 1912).

2. Complete edition, edited by Edmund Blunden and first published in 1931. *Poems*, edited by Siegfried Sassoon and published in 1920, consisted of a selection.

3. 'Modernist Poetry and Civilization', *A Survey of Modernist Poetry* (with Laura Riding, 1927). This essay is reprinted in *The Common Asphodel* (London, 1949).

4. In the foreword to Rosenberg's *Collected Works*, edited by G. Bottomley and D. Harding (London, 1937).

5. Included in the enlarged edition of *Annals of Innocence and Experience* (London, 1946).

6. 'The Impact of War', *Annals of Innocence and Experience.*

THE LATER POETRY OF W. B. YEATS

GRAHAM MARTIN

Reader in Literature, The Open University

THERE seem to be two distinct kinds of difficulty in Yeats's major poems. One, the focus of much discussion, is the relevance of Yeats's beliefs to his verse, and the sometimes cryptic symbolism with which – some claim and some deny – he succeeded in expressing these beliefs. The second has received less attention, and is certainly less easy to identify. Yeats's major work (i.e. from 1918 to his death in 1939) appeared during a period in which the combined influence of Eliot's poetry and criticism was more and more felt to have superannuated the tradition out of which Yeats grew. Whatever the rights of this view, there is no doubt that to go to Yeats from the Eliot 'quatrain' poems – if I can use them to pinpoint one pervasive influence on a modern reader – entails as thorough a revision of critical expectancy as to go from Pope to Wordsworth. In what follows, I have tried to approach Yeats with this particularly in mind.

The first section of this chapter discusses 'Meditations In Time Of Civil War', the poem in which Yeats most fully expresses his attitude to the common nightmare of his time: in Pound's phrase, to the 'botched civilization'. This allows a useful contrast with Eliot; but more importantly, it details the way in which a specifically Irish event is the stimulus to Yeats's meditation on the common theme in terms which have an honourable nineteenth-century pedigree. Yeats's romantic inheritance is not simple. When in about 1903 he began to re-formulate his poetic idiom in a way that was soon to impress the young Ezra Pound, he seems to be reaching forward into the new century. 'My work has got more masculine. It has more salt in it' ... 'the error of late periods like this is to believe that some things are inherently poetical' ... 'I believe more strongly every day that the element of strength in poetic language is common idiom.'[1] But he is also reaching back into the deeper meanings of the complex relationship between the romantic artist and society which the late Victorian period of his youth had simplified and narrowed. The Irish situation was to provide in his life, and by metaphor in many poems, the arena in which Yeats recapitulated that relationship with unique intensity.

In the second section, I have concentrated on two issues: the question of Yeats's 'philosophy', on the way in which ideas enter into his poems, and the kind of importance – limited in my view – which they have; and the particular quality of feeling many of his lesser poems evoke. This seems to me to be sufficiently unlike any other twentieth-century poet to require some stress. The complex, self-aware, meditative poems like 'Among Schoolchildren' and 'Sailing to Byzantium' are very fine, but it is difficult not to feel that they owe something of their prominence in Yeats's criticism to the fact that they are mostly easily discussed in the critical tradition represented by, for example, Cleanth Brooks's *The Well Wrought Urn*. But 'Those men that in their writings are most wise Own nothing but their *blind, stupefied* hearts'[2] – that is quite commonly Yeats's centre and, in the twentieth century, not the least either of his challenges or of his claims to greatness.

* * *

'And no one knows, at sight, a masterpiece.
And give up verse, my boy,
There's nothing in it.'
... Don't kick against the pricks,
Accept opinion. The 'Nineties' tried your game
And died, there's nothing in it.[3]

There was certainly not much in it for Yeats – 'never ... more than two hundred a year ...' he noted of his early career, 'and I am not by nature economical'[4] – and without Lady Gregory, without the Irish movement as a whole, it is unlikely that he would have reached even this precarious independence: which is not, of course, to say that he had anything to learn from Mr Nixon. Yeats knew what image 'the age demanded'. As much as Eliot, Yeats lived through 'the beating down of the wise';[5] even, in a biographical sense, more. Born in 1865, he was old enough to have had very different hopes about the twentieth century from those entertained by his younger contemporaries. 'New from the influence, mainly the personal influence, of

William Morris, I dreamed of enlarging Irish hate, till we had come to hate with a passion of patriotism what Morris and Ruskin hated... We were to forge in Ireland a new sword on our old traditional anvil for the great battle that must in the end re-establish the old, confident, joyous world.'[6] With memories like these, it is not surprising that the tone of Yeats's dealings with the 'filthy modern tide' has little in common with the mordant commentaries of Eliot and Pound. And in all of Yeats's mature poems, it is *tone* – in an exact sense – that one immediately notices.

> What shall I do with this absurdity –
> O heart, O troubled heart – this caricature,
> Decrepit age that has been tied to me
> As to a dog's tail?
>
> ('The Tower', 1927)

> A tree there is that from its topmost bough
> Is half all glittering flame and half all green
> Abounding foliage moistened with the dew;
> And half is half and yet is all the scene;
> And half and half consume what they renew,
> And he that Attis' image hangs between
> That staring fury and the blind lush leaf
> May know not what he knows, but knows not grief.
>
> ('Vacillation', 1932)

> Come, fix upon me that accusing eye.
> I thirst for accusation. All that was sung,
> All that was said in Ireland is a lie
> Bred out of the contagion of the throng,
> Saving the rhyme rats hear before they die.
> Leave nothing but the nothings that belong
> To this bare soul, let all men judge that can
> Whether it be an animal or a man.
>
> ('Parnell's Funeral', 1934)

> No dark tomb-haunter once; her form all full
> As though with magnaminity of light,
> Yet a most gentle woman; who can tell
> Which of her forms has shown her substance right?
>
> ('A Bronze Head', 1939)[7]

Self-mockery, visionary exaltation, contemptuous defiance, elegy – Yeats's consistently public tone accommodates an extraordinary range of feeling. It presupposes a listener of even wider experience than that humanistic figure, 'the normal active man',[8] that the poet set himself to express in 1909 when he began to wither into the creative disillusionment of his major work. To write like this out of 'a botched civilization'[9] certainly argues a very surprising command of his own experience, and even when contemporary barbarism is his theme, it is still Yeats's *command* that one principally notices.

> The cloud-pale unicorns, the eyes of aquamarine,
> The quivering half-closed eyelids, the rags of cloud or of lace,
> Or eyes that rage has brightened, arms it has made lean,
> Give place to an indifferent multitude, give place
> To brazen hawks. Nor self-delighting reverie,
> Nor hate of what's to come, nor pity for what's gone,
> Nothing but grip of claw and the eye's complacency,
> The innumerable clanging wings that have put out the moon.
>
> I turn away and shut the door and on the stair
> Wonder how many times I could have proved my worth
> In something that all others understand or share;
> But O! ambitious heart, had such a proof drawn forth
> A company of friends, a conscience set at ease,
> It had but made us pine the more. The abstract joy,
> The half-read wisdom of daemonic images,
> Suffice the ageing man as once the growing boy.
>
> ('Meditations In Time Of Civil War', 1923)

Yeats is writing in the syntax and idiom of ordinary discourse – elaborated only at moments of intensity, and then very slightly – of an experience which on the face of it seems likely to make ordinary discourse impossible. Even though, as he states in the earlier verses, this estranging vision evokes 'monstrous familiar images' which 'bewilder [and] perturb the mind', the mind continues to act, to define, to persuade. 'Brazen hawks' and 'the innumerable clanging wings' point towards nightmare, but the effect – hawks are not made of brass, brazen usually applies to hussies, wings do not clang – of conscious trope is not to draw us into the experience of an alienated mind, but to warn (perhaps to remind) us of the possibility. The tone unites us with the 'I' of the poem, over against his prophetic insight: on the one hand, the hawks, urgent and dreadful; but on the other, the precisely judged '*indifferent* multitude'; and again, 'the eye's *complacency*' balances 'grip of claw', the critical observation is intensified, not obliterated by the monstrous image.[10]

Yeats wrote 'Meditations In Time of Civil War' during the summer of 1922 - the war broke out in June - and, significant enough in his country's history, the event had a particular meaning for the poet. He had already (certainly by 1922, but the following passage was probably drafted in 1916–17) come to accept the fact that 'the dream of my early manhood, that a modern nation can return to Unity of Culture, is false; though it may be we can achieve it for some small circle of men and women, and there leave it till the moon bring round its century'.[11] He had, that is, given up hope that Ireland would produce, and that he would contribute to, an art both major and popular. What remained was the limited achievement of writing for a sympathetic coterie, and the verse-plays of *Four Plays for Dancers* (1921) are precisely that. 'In writing these little plays I knew that I was creating something which could only fully succeed in a civilization *very unlike ours*'[12] - Yeats is adjusting his ambitions to the restricted community of 'some fifty people in a drawing room', and the achieved content is correspondingly thin. But in 'Meditations', the old dream reasserts itself in a painful yet fruitful way. The fact that Ireland is no exception to the historical rule has come true in the most tragic terms: the fact of the war resurrects in Yeats's mind the whole structure of youthful hopes, and involves him in a more thorough abandonment of those hopes than he had expected.

Thus, the poem is not only a generous humanitarian response to the war, but stimulus to a far-reaching personal examination, and it was this because the 'Irish' dream was a moving force in the development of Yeats's major poetry. Yeats's sense of his own identity and function as a poet begins to take shape in the context of Irish nationalism, out of his deliberate and many-sided effort to provide the movement with some finer motive than mere hate of the English. He complains in 1909, for example, that 'the political class in Ireland – the lower-middle class from whom the patriotic associations have drawn their journalists and their leaders for the past ten years – have suffered through the cultivation of hatred as the one energy of their movement, a deprivation which is the intellectual equivalent to a certain surgical operation. Hence the shrillness of their voices. They contemplate all creative power as the eunuchs contemplate Don Juan as he passes through Hell on the white horse.'[13] The function of the Abbey was to supply 'loftier thought, Sweeter emotion';[14] to dramatize 'the Ireland of men's affections [as] self-moving, self-creating'.[15] '... in the work of Lady Gregory, of Synge, of O'Grady, of Lionel Johnson, in my own work, a school of journalists with simple moral ideas could find right building material to create a historical and literary nationalism as powerful as the old and nobler. That done, they could bid the people love and not hate.'[16] The journalists, however, refused to be taught, and it was the recognition of this, forced upon Yeats by the reception of Synge's *Playboy*, and later, by the Hugh Lane controversy, that provoked him to the new powers of expression, evident in *The Green Helmet* (1910) and *Responsibilities* (1914). (In the latter volume, the significant group of poems is Nos. 2 to 8: see Yeats's note on the 'three public controversies',[17] with which he associated them.)

By 1922, all this deep personal and artistic significance was a matter of accepted history; but to foresee the failure of a dream, and to live through a consequence of that failure are different things. In 1916, for example, Yeats could describe the bloody Easter Rising which destroyed a good part of O'Connell Street, as having given birth to 'a terrible beauty'.[18] But the violence of the Troubles had a different aspect.

> Now days are dragon-ridden, the nightmare
> Rides upon sleep: a drunken soldiery
> Can leave the mother, murdered at her door,
> To crawl in her own blood, and go scot-free;
> The night can sweat with terror as before
> We pieced our thoughts into philosophy,
> And planned to bring the world under a rule,
> Who are but weasels fighting in a hole.
>
> ('Nineteen Hundred and Nineteen', 1921)

Yeats felt responsible for the Troubles as he had not done for the Rising, and an acute sense of guilt is at the poem's heart:

We, who seven years ago
Talked of honour and of truth,
Shriek with pleasure if we show
The weasel's twist, the weasel's tooth.

As the over-emphasis indicates, the shock goes deeper than he is able to control, and in the poem's argument – that the particular catastrophe mirrors both a metaphysical condition ('Man is in love and loves what vanishes, What more is there to say?') and a historical process (see poem VI) – there is a complementary vagueness. The opening stanzas, for example, assert a bond between the 'ingenious lovely things' of art, and 'a law indifferent to blame or praise': 'the nightmare' of violence and terror destroys both, and for Yeats, these are newly significant interconnexions. But the poem leaves them unexplored, concentrating instead on the plight of 'He who can read the signs', and upon his emotions of moral outrage and despair.

'Meditations' is an advance on this. The political catastrophe appears not as an unexplainable revelation of man's state, but as the inevitable period to a whole phase in Irish history. The 'I' of the poem is less a person (confused by double loyalties) than a poet with a clear function, the unambiguous witness not of 'many ingenious lovely things' but of 'life's own self-delight'.

There are seven sections to the poem. In the first, 'Ancestral Houses', Yeats evokes only to discard a familiar image for Unity of Culture, the house-and-garden of eighteenth-century Anglo-Ireland.

... now it seems
As if some marvellous empty sea-shell flung
Out of the obscure dark of the rich streams,
And not a fountain, were the symbol which
Shadows the inherited glory of the rich.

The very excellence of past creations has exhausted the creative energies, and the present impulses have yet to crystallize. In poems II to IV, he erects symbols appropriate for a poet isolated by destructive social change. In poems V and VI, he shows his response – part-envy, part-revulsion – to the actual business of war. Finally, in poem VII he prophesies the threatening future which 'the indifferent multitude' is likely to command. Here, then, is Yeats's 'waste land', his most extended meditation on the contemporary theme, written shortly before the first appearance of Eliot's poem in October 1922. One major difference is clear at once. In both poems the identity of the observer is comparable: both are poets, both witnesses of threatened cultural traditions; but in Eliot's poems, the observer is not distinct from what he observes – we see a state of mind as much as a social condition – whereas in Yeats's what the poet diagnoses exists on its own public and historical terms. This distinction enters each poem's detail, and leads to others:

DA
Dayadhvam: I have heard the key
Turn in the door once and turn once only
We think of the key, each in his prison
Thinking of the key, each confirms a prison
Only at nightfall, aethereal rumours
Revive for a moment a broken Coriolanus.[19]

We are closed in, and the key is turned
On our uncertainty; somewhere
A man is killed, or a house burned,
Yet no clear fact to be discerned:
Come build in the empty house of the stare.

The points of comparison are clear enough: the common metaphor, the common condition of isolation, uncertainty, fear, the common prayer for deliverance (though that is too emphatic a term for the Eliot passage). But it is the differences that matter. Eliot's verse – and in this respect, the lines are typical – is wholly given over to defining the subtle condition, the lost identity, and listless self-involvement which are both cause and effect of this condition. Eliot's 'I' is incapable of experience, because incapable of the self-definition which precedes it; and his 'we' is an aggregate of such lost souls. Yeats's lines follow a different direction: the fear and menace are there (who turned the key?), but opposing them is 'uncertainty' – the condition has a name; 'somewhere A man is killed or a house burned' – it has nameable causes; and though 'no clear fact [is] to be discerned', still, 'facts' exist, and 'discernment' is possible. In the full context, these differences become more exact:

'The Stare's Nest by My Window'

The bees build in the crevices
Of loosening masonry, and there
The mother birds bring grubs and flies.
My wall is loosening; honey-bees,
Come build in the empty house of the stare.

We are closed in, and the key is turned
On our uncertainty; somewhere
A man is killed, or a house burned,
Yet no clear fact to be discerned:
Come build in the empty house of the stare.

A barricade of stone or of wood;
Some fourteen days of civil war;
Last night they trundled down the road
That dead young soldier in his blood:
Come build in the empty house of the stare.

We had fed the heart on fantasies,
The heart's grown brutal from the fare;
More substance in our enmities
Than in our love; O honey-bees,
Come build in the empty house of the stare.

The prison is both actual and metaphorical, a place as well as a condition of mind, and these two meanings co-exist without interfering with each other. Correspondingly, the lines hold two distinct attitudes in a single tension: the fear of inner collapse in 'My wall is loosening'; and the creative purposefulness of 'build', 'mother-birds', and 'house'. The subsequent stanzas develop this contrast, and the last one generalizes it. The firm syntax, the detailed report, the ballad refrain work an effect wholly opposite to that of the Eliot lines; they protest against the condition of 'We are closed in', rather than state its fullness, so that the isolation of Yeats's prison becomes not a paralysis, so much as an opportunity for diagnosis and judgement. Moreover, the war – literal cause of the imprisonment – is the appropriate occasion for these thoughts. It involves the poet because the utopian 'fantasies' which brutalize the heart lead through war to 'That dead young soldier in his blood'. The poet's 'We' involves him in that death (contrast the 'we' of the Eliot lines), and this gives conviction to his prayer. Yeats's 'O honey-bees, Come *build* ...' grows from the metaphor which demonstrates his sickness. The invocation is not applied to the situation, it is his intimate response to it. Comparably, Eliot's 'Dayadhvam' is part of the diagnosis, an Olympian comment.

Now the argument which links the various poems in 'Meditations' identifies culture, with the poet as witness, with the fountain of 'life's own self-delight'. Just as the 'golden grasshoppers and bees' of 'Nineteen Hundred and Nineteen' are, in comparison with the 'honey-bees' of the above verse, merely beautiful objects; so, in the later poem, 'culture' means no longer 'Many ingenious lovely things ... That seemed sheer miracle to the multitude', but the self-moving self-creating energies of life itself.

> Surely among a rich man's flowering lawns,
> Amid the rustle of his planted hills,
> Life overflows without ambitious pains;
> And rains down life until the basin spills ...
>
> ... Mere dreams, mere dreams! Yet Homer had not sung
> Had he not found it certain beyond dreams
> That out of life's own self-delight had sprung
> The abounding glittering jet ...

The poem shows that two kinds of change threaten the poet's ability to give proper voice ('Homer') to this meaning. First, there is the superannuation of the old social forms which throws the poet upon his own resources of personal symbol – 'My House', 'My Table', 'My Descendants', and

> An ancient bridge, and a more ancient tower,
> A farmhouse that is sheltered by its wall,
> An acre of stony ground,
> Where the *symbolic* rose can break in flower. [*my italics*]

This change the poet has to accept, because 'if no change appears No moon; only an aching heart Conceives a changeless work of art'. The real source of life is 'the obscure dark of the rich streams' of history, and the poet must remain sensitive to this. It is because he does, that the calamity outlined in the quoted stanzas of 'The Stare's Nest' is also a source of new life.

But there is another change which the poet cannot turn to account: the portentous vision of poem VII *I see Phantoms of Hatred and of the Heart's Fulness and of the Coming Emptiness.* Faced with 'Nothing but grip of claw, and the eye's complacency', with a future 'indifferent' not simply to the delicacies of art, but callous, insentient, uninvolved in life itself, the poet can find no possible identity. His towered isolation becomes therefore the refuge of 'life's own self-delight' from 'the coming Emptiness'.

And I, that count myself most prosperous,
Seeing that love and friendship are enough,
For an old neighbour's friendship chose the house
And decked and altered it for a girl's love,
And know whatever flourish and decline
These stones remain their monument and mine.

'Seeing that love and friendship are enough', 'The mother birds bring grubs and flies' – if we think of *The Waste Land* these may seem simple formulas; but they do not emerge from any turning away from the contemplated present; and the strength which makes them convincing is not simple. The central appeal is underwritten by the clear statement of what 'poet' and what 'culture' mean in this situation. Yeats is evoking in terms of his particular experience a traditional protest,[20] less subtly than Eliot, but with a satisfying freedom from hesitation and ambiguity. *The Waste Land's* use of literature as a means of definition and perspective ('a broken Coriolanus'), and so a shorthand statement of attitude, often gives questionable status to covert 'personal' judgements, to feelings that the poet seems unwilling to declare. Yeats, on the other hand, as the closing lines of poem VII suggest, includes his own failure in the total analysis. Similarly, his '*We* had fed the heart on fantasies' is wholly candid: one sign of his own involvement in the whole historical event.

But the main point is not whether or not Yeats is more 'positive' than Eliot - whose strength in *The Waste Land* is, after all, in being 'negative', in showing what happens when you go beyond the limit of 'brazen hawk' into the experience it points to – but in the different response to the contemporary nightmare. For Yeats, there are established positions, and his response to the threat is to state these. That is not to say that he comes to the event with a ready-made answer:

the difference between 'Nineteen Hundred and Nineteen' and 'Meditations' shows that it took the severe pressure of the whole experience to arrive at the control and understanding of the later poem. There is, in these poems, and in the movement between them, an interplay of individual attitude and public event which it is not easy to parallel; and this participation between Yeats and 'events' - intimate, yet principally on Yeats's own terms, so that the events re-emerge in what people call Yeats's *myth* - is central to his development as a poet. You cannot understand this process simply in terms of a literary tradition, working itself out; simply in terms of maturing 'personal' experience.

> You that would judge me, do not judge alone
> This book or that, come to this hallowed place
> Where my friends' portraits hang and look thereon;
> Ireland's history in their lineaments trace;[21]

The point needs stressing if only to underline that the ubiquitous assurance of the public 'tone' arises from a genuinely public, a genuinely social poetry - the fact is important whatever final assessment the social ideas and insights require – and if the tone marks Yeats off from Eliot, then his right to it, as the upshot of a continuing relationship with the history of his own country, marks him off from Auden. (Auden often takes over the manner, but he could not inherit the relationship, nor did he create one of his own: compare 'Nineteen Hundred and Nineteen' with 'Spain 1937'.) Yeats's audience, his capable listener, was neither a fiction nor a coterie ('parish of rich women' as Auden called it).[22] It was, at least in the first instance, a group for whom Ireland was the common theme, the public issue in whose terms Yeats could address himself as a poet and expect to be heard.

> All day I'd looked in the face
> What I had hoped 'twould be
> To write for my own race
> And the reality; ...
> Suddenly I began,
> In scorn of this audience,
> Imagining a man ...
>
> ('The Fisherman', 1916)

But scorn is a relationship, and the tension between the flawed reality and the ideal Unity of Culture was enough for Yeats to work on. In that relation, Yeats could write 'as a man speaking to men' – in, at any rate, a richer, more immediate relation than any other poet of the century.

* * *

Yeats's identification of the poet with the affirmation of 'life's own self-delight' offers a useful perspective on his work as whole, and in particular, on those poems which seem to attempt a different complexity. There is, for example, 'The Second Coming' (1920).

> ... Things fall apart; the centre cannot hold;
> Mere anarchy is loosed upon the world,
> The blood-dimmed tide is loosed, and everywhere
> The ceremony of innocence is drowned;
> The best lack all conviction, while the worst
> Are full of passionate intensity.
>
> ... The darkness drops again; but now I know
> That twenty centuries of stony sleep
> Were vexed to nightmare by a rocking cradle,
> And what rough beast, its hour come round at last,
> Slouches towards Bethlehem to be born?

As often with Yeats's prophetic or visionary poems (where the reciprocal relationship of 'a man speaking to men' is qualified by the poet's special 'disposition to be affected *more than other men by absent things as if they were present*; [his] ability of *conjuring up in himself passions*, which are indeed far from being the same as those produced by real events')[23], these lines suggest something unsettled in the poet's final attitude. Louis MacNeice ascribed this ambiguity to the fact that 'Yeats had a budding fascist inside himself'[24] and therefore heralded 'the rise of this tide ... with a certain relish'. But this is to confuse Yeats-and-his-reader with Yeats-and-his-subject. The poem's intensity depends primarily upon our familiarity with ideas like 'the Second Coming ... a rocking cradle ... Bethlehem'.[25] Yeats, that is, in order to express 'his vision of absent things' lays hold of the only available public language, and adapts it in a number of bold paradoxes. The magus foresees, but it is the poet who urges, and here, at the polemical level,[26] lies the difficulty. The poem's tone is not coherent. Beside the memorable restraint of 'The best lack all conviction, while the worst Are full of passionate intensity', the rhetorical attack of the final lines is crude – it exploits the previously established relationship – and with this in mind, it is possible to feel that the famous 'The ceremony of innocence is drowned' is a discreeter example of the same exploitation. There is more anxiety than insight in the line. The poet claims an assurance that he does not feel – this is one way of putting it; and – crucial in a polemical poem – what he is not sure about is whether the sanctities invoked in 'sleep ... vexed ... cradle' can or cannot withstand the future.

It is helpful to relate this uncertainty, if not to the actual details of 'A Vision', then certainly to the question of its determinism, a point which Yeats had not settled in 1919, if indeed he ever did settle it. (The 1925 edition implies a complete determinism, but the 1937 edition develops one of the original suggestions into an explicit allowance of free-will.) By means of the first line 'Turning and turning in the widening gyre', the poem invokes this 'determinism' at one level only to effect a moral protest at its implications at another. Like so many political statements, the poem both hopes and fears at once. This ambiguity recurs in a poem like 'The Gyres' (1938), or 'The Statues' (1939), and its extreme form is the desperate idealizing of the 'heroic' Irish in the late writing. Yeats seems to have combined a very powerful sense of immediate history with a restricted historical equipment for relating present insight to the determining past. The evidence for the historical patterns of 'A Vision' is almost entirely drawn from the arts, and while this may help to organize and project a chosen structure of loyalties and predispositions, it is not much help when it comes to predicting the probable future. In 'The Second Coming', Yeats has tried to generalize his immediate foreboding into a historical statement, but since the historical idea ('gyre') is itself ambiguous, it simply ratifies the confusion of fear and hope from which the poet begins. This is then transmitted in the uncertain tone, and unjustified variation of intensity in the rhetoric. Uncertain of his own position, Yeats turns, so to speak, on his listeners. There should not, finally, be any question as to where Yeats stands in relation to the rough beast. The companion poem to his prophecy is, after all, the restrained and assured 'A Prayer for My Daughter' (1919).

A more straightforward unevenness in the third section of 'The Tower' (1927) shows again that 'ideas' in Yeats are sometimes his way of refusing to think out his position. In this poem, he is stating his final attitude about old age and approaching death.

> Now shall I make my soul,
> Compelling it to study
> In a learned school ...

and at 'learned', we naturally refer back to the earlier declaration. What is the relation between the two 'learnings'?

> And I declare my faith:
> I mock Plotinus' thought
> And cry in Plato's teeth,
> Death and life were not
> Till man made up the whole,
> Made lock, stock, and barrel
> Out of his bitter soul,
> Aye, sun and moon and star, all,
> And further add to that
> That, being dead, we rise,
> Dream and so create
> Translunar paradise.
> I have prepared my peace
> With learned Italian things
> And the proud stones of Greece,
> Poet's imaginings
> And memories of love ...

When Yeats begins to sound like 'the annual scourge of the Georgian anthology' (T. S. Eliot), it seems fair to protest. What is the basis of this swashing dismissal of Plotinus and Plato? – a quasi-religious idiom ('rise ... create ... paradise'), a clerical boom ('I have prepared my peace'), and a comically unembarrassed display of culture-totems ('proud stones', etc.). Take away these trappings, and there is not much left, certainly not a philosophy, so that it needs to be stressed that the attitude with which the *poem* (as distinct from the poet) faces death is very different.

In a learned school
Till the wreck of body,
Slow decay of blood,
Testy delirium
Or dull decrepitude,
Or what worse evil come –
The death of friends, or death
Of every brilliant eye
That made a catch in the breath –
Seem but the clouds of the sky
When the horizon fades;
Or a bird's sleepy cry
Among the deepening shades.

A sustained metaphor underlies this conclusion. 'wreck ... decay ... delirium' register the pain of physical ageing; 'dull decrepitude' qualifies the protest with a contemptuous resignation which anticipates the final acceptance. The digression enlarges the perspective to include the death of the poet's friends, and of what he values ('every brilliant eye'), so that his merely personal extinction has disappeared from view by the time you reach the main verb ('seem') and the concluding recognition that death is a natural process, not to be gainsaid. The teaching of the 'learned school' is not new (cf. the last stanza of Keats's 'Ode to Autumn'); and if it is profound, then not in the sense in which some of Yeats's critics – certainly encouraged by the poet in some parts of his work – use the term. There is nothing profound about Yeats's 'translunar paradise'. The elaborate paraphernalia of 'ideas' masks nothing more complicated than an instinctual refusal-to-die. When in the final lines, this instinct is confronted with the equally simple fact of death, a genuine 'idea' does emerge: individuals die, but nature, the species, does not. But what matters is not this 'philosophy', but the controlled rehearsal of the approach to death, beside which the earlier protest is a comparatively frivolous display of 'style'. As Yeats's father said to him, 'You would be a philosopher and are really a poet',[27] and the *would be* is often the point for the critic. Yeats's profundity is rarely a matter of complex or intricate thinking about human experience. Ideas enter his poetry in the form of large generalizations which focus with unique intensity a particular group of experiences:

... Endure that toil of growing up;
The ignominy of boyhood; the distress
Of boyhood changing into man;
The unfinished man and his pain
Brought face to face with his own clumsiness;
The finished man among his enemies ...
('A Dialogue of Self and Soul', 1929)

Assume the pain of growth, carry it through the detail of experience, and we get this concentrated statement: 'endure ... toil ... ignominy ... distress ... pain ... clumsiness ... enemies'. In the poetry of 'thinking', idea and detail interact; each alters the other, exists in terms of the other. But in Yeats, the detail of experience does not question, it illustrates the ideas (as the poems on the Troubles show), which have, so to speak, been decided upon outside the poem. Adopt, then, another assumption about 'growing up', and we get these famous lines:

That is no country for old men. The young
In one another's arms, birds in the trees
– Those dying generations – at their song,
The salmon-falls, the mackerel-crowded seas,
Fish, flesh, or fowl, commend all summer long
Whatever is begotten, born, or dies.
('Sailing to Byzantium', 1927)

It is not the greater complexity that is my point, but the different idea – growth as a rich blind trustfulness – the point of view with which in some argument, one might oppose undue insistence on the '*toil* of growing up'. It is by debate, argument, the confrontation of different ideas and so of the different experience each idea engages that Yeats arrives at his most varied insights. And it is the inclusive generalizations of 'thought' ('gyres', 'translunar paradise') which involve him in simplification and ambiguity.

Another group of poems which bear on this occurs in *Michael Robartes and The Dancer* (1920), where the enemy of life is not the historical process, or the 'indifferent' future, but what Yeats calls 'thought' or 'opinion'. He remarks elsewhere that 'A mind that generalizes rapidly, continually prevents the experience that would have made it feel and see deeply',[28] and 'thought' in those poems is the neurotic hypertrophy of this condition. The amusing title poem (1920) announces the theme:

He ... and it's plain
The half-dead dragon was her thought,
That every morning rose again
And dug its claws and shrieked and fought.
Could the impossible come to pass
She would have time to turn her eyes,
Her lover thought, upon the glass
And on the instant would grow wise.
She You mean they *argued* ... [*my italics*]

This maladjustment of 'thought' and experience links the subsequent poems on love, in which some abstracting fantasy interferes with the relationship, with the better-known political poems.

Maybe the bride-bed brings despair,
For each an imagined image brings
And finds a real image there;
Yet the world ends when these two things,
Though several, are a single light,
When oil and wick are burned in one;
('Solomon and The Witch')

Hearts with one purpose alone
Through summer and winter seem
Enchanted to a stone
To trouble the living stream.
('Easter 1916', 1916)

Did she in touching that lone wing
Recall the years before her mind
Became a bitter, an abstract thing,
Her thought some popular enmity ... ?
('On A Political Prisoner', 1920)

My mind, because the minds that I have loved,
The sort of beauty that I have approved,
Prosper but little, has dried up of late,
Yet knows that to be choked with hate
May well be of all evil chances chief.
... An intellectual hatred is the worst,
So let her think opinions are accursed.
('A Prayer for my Daughter', 1919)

As the various dates show, Yeats has here brought together unpublished and previously published poems which apply a common insight to different situations and relationships. The insight is not explored, nor is it fully realized in any one instance, but provides rather the organizing centre for a number of experiences of introspection or observation. A poem of a decade later shows how such a key-emphasis can resurrect itself, still 'undeveloped', yet just as vital:

> I know not what the younger dreams –
> Some vague Utopia – and she seems,
> When withered old and skeleton-gaunt,
> An image of such politics.
> Many a time I think to seek
> One or the other out and speak
> Of that old Georgian mansion, mix
> Pictures of the mind, recall
> That table and the talk of youth,
> Two girls in silk kimonos, both
> Beautiful, one a gazelle.
>
> ('In Memory of Eva Gore-Booth and Con Markiewicz', 1929)

Here it is not a metaphor so much as the beautifully managed cadences of the final lines (from 'Pictures') that judges 'such politics'. For dreams of the 'vague Utopia' – and 'vague' is the important word – Yeats offers the precise alternative of his delicately stated feeling for what has gone. This is the stress: the actuality of human interchange, however transient or imperfect, is of 'the living stream', and therefore a test for the questionable truths of 'thought'. Whether the result is heroic, degrading, or even a spiritual certainty, 'thought' distracts from, where it doesn't deform, the difficult intricacy of life. It is at best a superior compensation for failing to live, and with this in mind, the force of saying that Yeats's poetry works from ideas rather than through them should be clear.

A related impulse is important in the unique series of occasional poems which extend from about 1912 till Yeats's death. Yeats's 'modernity' may properly begin with *The Green Helmet* (1910) – though its anticipation in one or two poems (subsequently added to) in *In The Seven Woods* (1903) is clear; see for example 'Never Give All The Heart' first published in 1905 – but his first unquestionably great poem is 'In Memory of Major Robert Gregory' (1918). One difference between this poem and, say, 'To A Shade' (1913) has been well underlined by Professor Kermode. It is the first poem fully to incorporate

Yeats's romantic inheritance.[29] But it is also the first in a long line of occasional celebrations and laments: 'All Souls' Night' (1921), 'A Prayer For My Daughter' (1919), 'Coole Park and Ballylee, 1931' (1932), and 'The Bronze Head' (1939), and this coincidence is important. 'The self-conquest of the writer who is not a man of action is style',[30] and the style of these poems – formal, elaborate, yet easy and humane – can be said to state Yeats's responsibility as a poet to the central human experiences they commemorate.

> He had much industry at setting out,
> Much boisterous courage, before loneliness
> Had driven him crazed;
> For meditations upon unknown thought
> Make human intercourse grow less and less;
> They are neither paid nor praised.
> But he'd object to the host,
> The glass because my glass;
> A ghost-lover he was
> And may have grown more arrogant being a ghost.
> ('All Souls' Night')

The stanza is the poetic expression of what Yeats in 'A Prayer For My Daughter' calls 'courtesy': it reconciles the criticism of 'arrogant' with the appreciation of 'boisterous courage'. The sensitive adjustments of feeling depend wholly upon the changes in pace which the elaborate verse and rhyme scheme makes possible. The directness reacts with the formality so that the first is not blunt, and the second not stiff. The poet disappears, so to speak, into the poetry, and the poetry into the permanent experience of what Blake called 'the severe contentions of friendship'.

If one senses the writer's 'self-conquest' in the style of all these occasional poems, it is even more evident in the actual structure of the Gregory elegy.

> I had thought, seeing how bitter is that wind
> That shakes the shutter, to have brought to mind
> All those that manhood tried, or childhood loved
> Or boyish intellect approved,
> With some appropriate commentary on each;
> Until imagination brought
> A fitter welcome; but a thought
> Of that late death took all my heart for speech.

'We are not required to accept as true the statement that Yeats had intended a longer poem,' wrote Peter Ure in his explication of the poem. 'All is device and formality, a mask on the face of grief.'[31] But this, with its suggestion of hidden tears, a suppressed catch in the throat, is a little misleading. The point of the final trope is to dissolve the 'personal' voice with which the poem has been speaking into anonymity, without losing the sense of an actual relationship between the writer and the dead man. The poet's business is to express not his own feelings, but other people's as if they were his own: 'whatever's written in what poets name The book of the people'.[32] The elegy needs an obituary voice, that is still not 'official'. The effect of the last stanza after what has preceded it is to achieve this adjustment of attitude, this difficult generality. The presentation of Robert Gregory who is 'a man of action' and 'all life's epitome' takes place in this context: the projection of the romantic figure who burns his life out is by means of the poem accommodated to the 'damp faggots' of ordinary living – Yeats's term in this poem for himself and for the continuity he is affirming.

The formal elaboration of these poems expresses, then, an important part of their meaning: the terms on which we share in the commemorated experience, but even in much simpler poems, rhetorical device is prominent, and it serves a similar purpose. One can express this roughly by saying that many of Yeats's poems express a familiar general emotion, but in a strange, even an eccentric way. Yet the difficulties are superficial; they do not belong to the experience, so much as guard it from misunderstanding or too-easy acceptance. The experience is very often 'what oft was thought', but the expression sheers off the encrustations of habitual response, and protective staleness. Feeling in Yeats is, in general, not complex: i.e. not realized with all the contradictions and qualifications which any particular emotion actually involves; but 'simple': 'disengaged, disembroiled, disencumbered, exempt from the conditions we usually know to attach to it'.[33] The process of disengagement is undertaken in several ways. There is the discreet wit in phrases like: 'that discourtesy of death', 'casual comedy,' 'popular rage', 'civil rancour'[34] – where one word discriminates the general emotion suggested by the other. The effect is to invite one's cooperation in the critical refinement (cf. Pope's and Dryden's similar fondness for the construction). More generally, there is the rhetorical syntax which plays off 'artificial' against 'natural' speech rhythms; and the use of dramatis personae or Masks, and of named occasions and situations for the particular experience. To take a familiar example:

'Easter 1916'

I have met them at close of day
Coming with vivid faces
From counter or desk among grey
Eighteenth-century houses.
I have passed with a nod of head
Or polite meaningless words,
Or have lingered awhile and said
Polite meaningless words,
And thought before I had done
Of a mocking tale or a gibe
To please a companion
Around the fire at the club ...

The lofty opening rhythms quickly give way to the loose 'casual' movement of the later lines, and this follows the contrast of the 'vivid faces', and the commonplace gossip which the poet retails about them. But before that happens, there is the memorable dissonance of 'faces/houses', forcing its way against the secure 'day/grey', like some flattened seventh in a full statement of the key. The clash has its point. It underlines the heroic opening – by slightly departing from it, that is, it makes an individual statement of this note. The note is essential; the very title demands it; but of course, Yeats's view of the heroism of Macdonagh and Macbride and Connolly and Pearse is very specific and he only adapts the banal emotion of the political tub-thumper because he wants it on his own terms. Admittedly, these are not as clear or satisfactory as they might be: but 'terrible beauty', whatever its failings, sufficiently shows how Yeats *insisted* on his own particular view of 'the heroic emotion'. The title, then, is a first approximation to Yeats's own definition: it is not just a piece of information, but part of the poem's language.

Another example is the first poem of *Supernatural Songs*, 'Ribh at the Tomb of Baile and Aillinn' (1934), a title whose strangeness immediately contrasts with the opening familiarity of 'Because you have found me in the pitch-dark night/With open book you ask me what I do'. But Ribh is not a character, and if he is a Mask, that is not because he delivers any special necessary meaning. What he says makes its own point:

> ... when such bodies join
> There is no touching here, nor touching there,
> Nor straining joy, but whole is joined to whole;
> For the intercourse of angels is a light
> Where for its moment both seem lost, consumed.
>
> Here in the pitch-dark atmosphere above
> The trembling of the apple and the yew,
> Here on the anniversary of their death,
> The anniversary of their first embrace,
> These lovers, purified by tragedy,
> Hurry into each other's arms; these eyes,
> By water, herb, and solitary prayer
> Made aquiline, are open to that light.
> Though somewhat broken by the leaves, that light
> Lies in a circle on the grass; therein
> I turn the pages of my holy book.

The natural leaves interfere with the supernatural light; but this light is a metaphor for an ideal love-in-nature. Ribh's eyes see by the light, but *what* he sees is not 'the intercourse of angels', but his 'holy book'. The effect is to interpenetrate the categories of real and ideal fulfilment in an extraordinarily delicate relationship; to convey Ribh's ponderings about the completion beyond death of the full relationship life denies to the lovers without suggesting compensatory nostalgia, or spiritual voyeurism about a love he never experienced. The poem's outworks – Ribh, Baile, Aillinn – make the experience strange, not because it is difficult, complex, and mysterious (as, for example, the rejections and projections of Eliot's 'Marina' are) but because it must be very exactly defined. It is the essential heart of the condition which the poem conveys, and in order to insist on this its language (again the title is part of the language) prunes away implication and suggestivity. Yeats's claim that his mind was 'sensuous, concrete, rhythmical'[35] is not more important than the complementary statement '...I, whose virtues are the definitions Of the analytic mind'[36] – and the analysis progresses towards general emotions exactly defined. Even where the emotion is 'complex', Yeats arrives at the complexity by accumulating a number of distinct strands. These lines from 'The Man and The Echo' (1939) provide a miniature instance:

> O Rocky Voice,
> Shall we in that great night rejoice?
> What do we know but that we face
> One another in this place?
> But hush, for I have lost the theme,
> Its joy or night seem but a dream;
> Up there some hawk or owl has struck,
> Dropping out of sky or rock,
> A stricken rabbit is crying out,
> And its cry distracts my thought.

Each strand – hope for happiness after death, stoical acceptance of human ignorance, sympathy for the suffering of created life – has a separate identity, and they co-exist in such a way as to sharpen that identity. Out of context, for example, it is impossible to know how to read lines 3–4: gloomily? toughly? with suppressed self-pity? Only in relation to the other lines can one say: the stoicism is not tough, but a simple statement ('all we can be certain of is ...'); not gloomy, because the 'great night' – impressive rather than terrifying – offers the possibility of joy; nor self-pitying because the sympathy goes wholly to 'the stricken rabbit'. The effect of the context is to do away with the usual blur of feeling that accompanies the direct commonplace question, to make it more direct without making it any the less commonplace, and so genuinely the question of the generic Man in whose name the poem is written. It need hardly be insisted that this ability, in a culture that has driven the wedge between artist and the 'commonplace' experience of men as deeply as ours has, is uniquely important. Like any great poet, Yeats offers many satisfactions, but there seem to me good grounds for rating the simple direct centrality of much of his work as the most lasting.

NOTES

1. *The Letters of W. B. Yeats* (ed. Allan Wade, 1954), pp. 397, 460, 462.
2. *Collected Poems* (1950), p. 182. My italics.
3. Ezra Pound, 'Hugh Selwyn Mauberley', *Selected Poems* (1948), p. 179.
4. *Autobiographies* (1955), p. 409.

5. 'The Fisherman', *Collected Poems* (1950), p. 167.

6. *Essays* (1924), pp. 307–8.

7. The dates given for these and subsequently mentioned poems are those of the first publication – in some cases earlier by several years than the date of the collection in which the poem finally appears in *Collected Poems*. See Allan Wade, *A Bibliography of the Writings of W. B. Yeats* (2nd ed., 1958). For a list of probable dates of composition, see Richard Ellmann, *The Identity of Yeats* (1954).

8. *Autobiographies* (1955), p. 492.

9. *Hugh Selwyn Mauberley*, ibid., p. 176.

10. Cf. 'And bats with baby faces in the violet light
Whistled, and beat their wings
And crawled head downward down a blackened wall'. T. S. Eliot, *The Waste Land*, *Collected Poems 1909–1935* (1936), p. 76.

11. *Autobiographies* (1955), p. 295.

12. *Four Plays For Dancers* (1921), pp. 105–6. My italics.

13. *Autobiographies* (1955), p. 486. See also 'On Those That Hated "The Playboy Of The Western World", 1907', *Collected Poems* (1950), p. 124.

14. 'To A Shade', *Collected Poems* (1950), p. 123.

15. *Autobiographies* (1955), p. 361.

16. Ibid., p. 494.

17. *Collected Poems* (1950), p. 529.

18. 'Easter 1916', ibid., pp. 202–5.

19. *The Waste Land*, ibid., p. 77.

20. Discussing the contribution to the total meaning of 'culture' made by the Romantic poets, Raymond Williams notes 'an emphasis on the embodiment in art of certain human values, capacities, energies, which the development of society towards an industrial civilization was felt to be threatening or even destroying'. ... 'The whole tradition can be summed up in one striking phrase used by Wordsworth, where the poet, the artist in general, is seen as "an upholder and preserver, *carrying everywhere with him relationship and love*".' *Culture and Society 1780–1950* (1958), pp. 36, 42. My italics.

21. 'The Municipal Gallery Revisited', *Collected Poems* (1950), p. 370.

22. 'In Memory of W. B. Yeats', *Collected Shorter Poems 1930–44* (1950), p. 65.

23. 'Preface to Lyrical Ballads (1800)', W. Wordsworth. My italics.

24. L. MacNeice, *The Poetry of W. B. Yeats* (1941), p. 132.

25. Allen Tate has pointed out, correctly I think, that this is more generally true of Yeats's esotericism than most critics admit. See *The Permanence of Yeats* (ed. Hall and Steinemann, 1950), p. 111.

26. That the poem is, in a deep sense, polemical, I take the following letter to indicate. '... as my sense of reality deepens ... my horror at the cruelty of governments grows greater ... Communist, Fascist, nationalist, clerical, anti-clerical, are all responsible according to the number of their victims. I have not been silent; I have used the only vehicle I possess – verse. If you have my poems by you, look up a poem called *The Second Coming*. It was written some sixteen or seventeen years ago and foretold what is happening. I have written

of the same thing again and again since. This will seem little to you with your strong practical sense, for it takes fifty years for a poet's weapons to influence the issue.' (April 1936.) *The Letters of W.B. Yeats* (ed. Allan Wade, 1954), p. 851.

27. *J. B. Yeats, Letters to his son ... 1869–1922* (ed. J. Hone, 1944), p. 97.

28. *Essays* (1924), pp. 406–7.

29. Frank Kermode, *The Romantic Image* (1957), pp.30–42.

30. *Autobiographies* (1955), p. 516.

31. Peter Ure, *Towards A Mythology* ... (1946), p. 40.

32. 'Coole Park & Ballylee, 1931', *Collected Poems* (1950), p. 276.

33. The phrase is from Henry James's 'Preface to *The American*', *The Art of the Novel* (1953), p. 33.

34. *Collected Poems* (1950), pp. 150, 203, 319, 320 respectively.

35. *Autobiographies* (1955), p. 434.

36. 'The People', *Collected Poems* (1950), p. 170.

IRELAND'S CONTRIBUTION

GRATTAN FREYER

AROUND half a century ago it would have been appropriate to entitle this chapter 'The Irish Movement'. Today writers who work or were born in Ireland are not conscious of belonging to any 'movement'. Irish independence, for which the earlier writers – under the all-pervasive influence of Yeats – struggled to create a cultural consciousness, is a fact. Yet it is still useful to refer to a distinctive Irish contribution to the mainstream of writing in the English language this century. The present chapter will, therefore, consider first the Irish movement proper and then give some account of the contemporary situation among Irish writers. Yeats's own work has been dealt with in an earlier chapter, so will only be referred to, where necessary, in passing.

Ireland forms part of the British Isles, yet the Irish have never really formed part of the British nation. Race, religion, history, and the ensuing social and economic development have all helped to keep the two peoples distinct. The majority of the Irish have remained Roman Catholics, and though many of her leading writers have come from the Protestant minority, the traditional faith colours the background from which they spring. There is a relative absence of individualistic and class distinctions, and a sense of community and social fluidity in Ireland, which has long since ceased to exist in England. This is an asset of particular interest to the dramatist. In Synge's plays, when a stranger enters, he shares naturally in the conversation; no introduction is necessary. It is sometimes suggested that this community feeling arose from the unity of the Irish people in their historic struggle against British occupation. Yet this is not entirely true, since even the margin between the British 'ascendancy' – the descendants of those who were given land when the native Irish were dispossessed – and the local people was never a sharp one. In Yeats's early novel *John Sherman* (1889), the principal character, who is a member of the lesser gentry, observes: 'In your big towns a man finds his minority and knows nothing outside its border ... but here one chats with the whole world in a day's walk, for every man one meets is a class.' The capacity of the Irish to absorb their invaders and make them 'more Irish than themselves' is proverbial. It is the more remarkable in that, unlike the Chinese or even the French, there was never any well-defined or sophisticated civilization into which the invaders were fitted.

This amorphousness of class structure is closely related to another feature of the Irish scene – the easy-going character of the Irish people, at least in those parts that now form the Republic, which, though less marked today than formerly, never fails to strike an outside visitor. This, however, has a negative aspect as far as literature is concerned. There has been an almost complete lack of social purpose or moral earnestness, and writers such as Bertrand Russell or Sartre would be as alien in Ireland as men from Mars. Even Shaw, strangely enough, hardly aroused a flicker of interest in his native country. Irish writers generally are 'uncommitted'. Moreover, a substantial portion of English writing has depended on exploring the sensibilities and situations to which a well-defined class structure gives rise – one thinks of Waugh or E. M. Forster, but it is equally true of those like Kingsley Amis who are eager to demolish class. The counterpart of this preoccupation in Ireland is perhaps the relationship of the writer to the dominance of the Catholic church, which will be considered below.

It will be appropriate here to refer briefly to the only native culture Ireland possessed, the ancient Gaelic civilization. Ireland became Christian in the fifth century, and the golden age of Gaelic culture lasted from the seventh to around the twelfth century. The language declined steadily under the British occupation, and by the first half of the nineteenth century Irish had ceased to exist as a tongue for the educated. What survived were a number of peasant dialects, spoken along the western and southern seaboards. A movement to revive the language began at the turn of the present century, and after the Irish Free State came into being in 1921, teaching of the language – and wherever possible in the language – was made compulsory in the schools. It is common knowledge today that this policy has met with scant success and lately it has come in for strong criticism. Nevertheless the language has had considerable influence on speaking and writing in English. Synge wrote nothing in Irish, but the English he used drew its peculiar quality from being frequently a direct translation of Gaelic idiom.

With Liam O'Flaherty (b. 1897), who is an Aran islander born and so a native speaker, the influence is even stronger. His first book, *The Black Soul*, appears to have been written in Irish and then translated. Just as in Conrad, there are passages which suggest an extremely vivid but not a native command of English. Most of the later generation of writers had a competence in Irish. Frank O'Connor, Seán O'Faoláin, Donagh MacDonagh, Thomas Kinsella, all published translations from the Gaelic. Brendan Behan's riotously lyrical play, *The Hostage*, which caused a sensation in London in 1958, was originally performed in Irish.

There is one eighteenth-century Gaelic poem of some length which possesses such unique liveliness and interest that it has drawn forth no fewer than four contemporary translations into English, and it deserves mention here. This is Brian Merriman's *Midnight Court*, and it deals in racy and often ribald language with a peculiarly Irish problem even today: the difficulty of persuading eligible bachelors to marry! The translations of Ussher, O'Connor, Longford, and Marcus all have merit. I quote at random from Marcus's very free rendering to show a rhythm and manner which is directly brought over from the original – the lady is beginning the catalogue of her neglected charms:

> My mouth is sweet and my teeth are flashing,
> My face is never in need of washing,
> My eyes are green and my hair's undyed
> With waves as big as the ocean tide,
> And that's not a half, nor a tenth, of my treasure:
> I'm built with an eye to the maximum pleasure.

Two other translations of unusual interest are Tomas O'Crohan's *The Islandman* and Maurice O'Sullivan's *Twenty Years A-growing*. Both these are autobiographies by peasants from the Blasket Islands off the far south-western tip of Kerry. They portray men whose everyday way of life was not greatly different from that of Homer's fishermen or the Icelanders of the sagas. The value of O'Crohan's book is enhanced by the fact that he was deeply conscious of the new civilization which was soon to engulf them. He states his purpose in writing as 'to set down the character of the people about me so that some record of us might live after us, for the like of us will never be again'.

The surge of creative writing in Ireland around the opening of this century has often, with mild exaggeration, been spoken of as the Irish Literary Renaissance. Though Ireland's population is less than one-tenth that of Great Britain, she produced in Yeats (1865–1939) and Joyce (1882–1941) two out of the half-dozen or so major writers of this period. She contributed at least her fair share of minor writers, and in the field of the English-speaking theatre was the principal medium for a revolution in dramatic writing and acting technique. What was responsible for this sudden outpouring of talent?

It is neither easy nor necessary to give a precise answer to that question. The troubled history of Ireland and the complete absence of settled, wealthy, middle-class patronage seem responsible for the lack of any tradition in painting or music. Apart from architecture, literature, in fact, was the only art form which did appear under these conditions. But during the greater part of the nineteenth century the enthusiasm and idealism of the country tended to politics rather than literature. In 1890 political nationalism received a sudden and unusual check when the movement was split from top to bottom over Parnell's divorce case. Historical detail would be out of place here, but a glimpse of the anguished disillusion caused among ordinary people is given in Joyce's short story 'Ivy Day in the Committee Room', included in *Dubliners*, and in the family quarrel depicted in the early part of *A Portrait of the Artist as a Young Man.* The point to note here is that in Yeats's and Joyce's formative years nationalist fervour was seeking an outlet outside politics. The Gaelic League, which was the movement to revive the language, and the national theatre movement were the principal beneficiaries. Both date from this time.

Five or six individuals were responsible for launching the new theatre movement, and, quite naturally, their aims were not identical. Yeats was interested from his early days in dramatic verse; he had already had a verse play performed in London. Edward Martyn's (1859–1924) enthusiasm was in direct opposition to Yeats's; he admired Ibsen, and though there was a poetic side to Ibsen which appealed to Yeats and Joyce, it was the aspect of his work dealing with problems of local politics – in 'joyless and pallid words', as

Synge later put it – which Martyn wanted to apply to Ireland. Martyn's cousin, George Moore (1852–1933), had some practical experience of plays and players in Paris and London, a genuine interest in the Irish countryside and her people, and a natural attraction towards a new medium of self-expression. Moore and Martyn were Catholic landlords from the West, and they met with Yeats in the home of a Protestant neighbour, Lady Gregory (1852–1932), who contributed a little money, several short plays, and much diplomacy to the venture. (A lot was needed.) These were people of letters. From the theatrical side came the Fay brothers, William and Frank, who had for some years been acting in amateur and badly paid productions in Dublin and the provinces. The Fays, in fact, were looking round for more serious plays to perform than the romantic melodramas[1] then current, at the same time as the literary men were seeking an outlet in the theatre. The Fays approached the poet AE (George Russell, 1867–1935) and Douglas Hyde (1862–1946), the founder of the Gaelic League. AE put the Fays in touch with Yeats.

The Irish National Theatre Society was founded in 1901 with Yeats as president. Two years later – owing to the financial support of an English drama enthusiast, Miss Horniman – a small theatre seating 500 was acquired. At first, productions were entirely amateur. But the need for professionalism inevitably asserted itself, though it led to the loss of some enthusiasts. The Abbey Theatre Company came into being with Yeats, Lady Gregory, and later Synge as directors. William Fay was its first manager.

From the start the Abbey aroused intense interest and controversy at home. But it was the acclaim and financial success of visits to London, Cambridge, Oxford, Manchester, Glasgow, and other British cities which kept the company solvent. Plays were invariably 'by Irish authors on Irish subjects', but it was the style of acting which took English audiences by storm. The essentials of this style were realism in scenery, dress, and language (except for the verse plays), a refusal to allow any 'star' acting to dominate the group, and a studied absence of unnecessary gesture. (It is said that at one time Yeats tried to get the actors to rehearse in barrels.) This was a style of acting which had just been introduced in France by Antoine with his *théâtre libre*, which the Fays enthusiastically admired. Retrospectively, the scenic realism of the Abbey appears overdone, producing a fresh cramping convention in its turn; but the new purity of diction was to be a lasting innovation which cleared the way for later developments on the English stage.

It is sometimes supposed that the fierce quarrels which broke out in Dublin over the subject-matter of the new plays showed a straightforward cleavage between an enlightened band of artists and patriots and a priest-led mob. This was in fact far from the case. William Fay wrote in his memoirs that every play had to face two questions: Was it 'an insult to the faith'? Was it 'a slander on the people of Ireland'? Most serious plays failed in one test; some, such as *The Playboy*, failed in both. But leading patriots were as concerned over these questions as anyone else and were often opposed to Yeats's vision of artistic integrity within a nationalist mould. Arthur Griffith, the Sinn Fein chief, poured invective on the whole Abbey venture. The pacifist Francis Sheehy-Skeffington signed the protest against Yeats's *Countess Cathleen* – in which a philanthropist sells her soul to the devil to provide for her people in time of famine. And Maud Gonne, who had played the leading role in this play, herself walked out in protest against Synge's *In the Shadow of the Glen*, which she regarded as an attack on the purity of Irish womanhood. Patrick Pearse, however, who was later executed for his leadership of the 1916 insurrection, was in favour of Synge. Many times it looked as though the theatre would be forced to close either by mob violence or by a newspaper-led boycott. Yet somehow it weathered the storm. A small army of policemen had to be on hand to allow *The Playboy* to finish its first week and even then no audience was permitted to hear the play through. Further riots greeted O'Casey's plays after the First World War. The wheel turned, and a few years later two young men forced their way on to the stage to protest against the irreverent way in which one of O'Casey's masterpieces had been acted!

The plays written by the Abbey dramatists reflected the contrasting ideals of the theatre's founders, which have already been mentioned. Yeats wrote one expressly patriotic play: *Kathleen ni Houlihan*, an allegory in which the spirit of Ireland is personified by an old woman who rouses her people to the national struggle. This was a moving play to an Irish audience, but fell flat elsewhere. Yeats's other contributions offered an astonishingly wide range in theme and treatment from the prose farce of country life, *The Pot of Broth*, through the beautiful, but theatrically unsuccessful *Four Plays for Dancers*, which utilized the conventions of Japanese Noh drama, to an extraordinarily dramatic and intellectually satisfying play on Swift, *The Words upon the Window-pane*. All are one-act plays. Lady Gregory, who had never written a line before middle age, translated Molière successfully into West of Ireland dialect, and wrote a number of slight peasant comedies. One short play, *The Rising of the Moon*, with its intermingling of high patriotic seriousness and comedy – the Quixote formula, which was to be so often repeated – has been consistently popular. Her other plays fell into disfavour soon after her death, but are now attracting increasing critical attention.[2]

Many playwrights have dealt in the Ibsen manner with the typical problems of modern Irish life: the hunger for land (Padraic Colum); the frustrated ambitions of provincial life (Lennox Robinson, Seán O'Faoláin); the asperities of peasant life (T. C. Murray); the role of the priests (Joseph Tomelty, Paul Vincent Carroll); emigration and late marriages (M. J. Molloy). And a new stage Irish comedy emerged in George Shiels and others. Most of these plays were too topical to last, or to hold interest for non-Irish audiences. But there are two Abbey dramatists whose work forms part of the wider theatre – Synge and O'Casey.

More than any other writer, J. M. Synge (1871–1909) may be said to have been the creation of the Abbey Theatre. Yeats describes in one of his autobiographies how he met Synge in Paris, supplementing a small private income by giving English lessons and making translations from French poets into Anglo-Irish dialect. He advised Synge to return to his own country, learn Irish, and write plays for the new theatre. Synge followed his advice to the letter. It is doubtful if even Yeats anticipated the consequences of this advice.

The plays of Synge rise head and shoulders above the dramatic conventions of his fellow-playwrights. They are not purely poetic plays, nor peasant plays – though they have something of both; still less are they problem plays. The greatest of them, *The Playboy of the Western World*, was soon to be performed in half a dozen European languages. This is the story of a peasant boy who flees home under the impression he has killed his father. He is acclaimed as a hero, and under this acclaim becomes a hero – until his 'murdered da' reappears! Synge's strength, like that of Cervantes, lies in the juxtaposition of the most earthy realism with the highest flights of fancy. His characters speak a language which is imaginative and exuberant, just as sixteenth-century English was, because it was not cramped by industrial conformity or newspaper emotions:

> Bravery's a treasure in a lonesome place, and a lad would kill his father, I'm thinking, would face a foxy divil with a pitchpike on the flags of hell.

We forget the wild improbability of the story, because it is both possible and probable at a certain level of the imagination. The patriot hysteria which greeted early productions in Dublin depended on the conviction that no decent Irish country girl would admire a murderer. Yet there is a primitive element in all human nature which is eternally ready to rejoice in the heroic, amoral act – until the civilized inhibitions clamp down. Synge's world is not the conventional world of modern living, but a small pre-civilized world of the imagination. Within this small world, his characters are completely convincing and enormously alive. It is absurd to try to disentangle any 'message' from so unpolitical a writer; what does perhaps emerge is the nostalgia of a lonely and sick man for vital living. Synge died at the age of thirty-eight.

There is a measure of similarity between the work of Synge and Sean O'Casey (1880–1964) in that both rejected the 'joyless and pallid words' of the naturalist drama, but that is as far as the parallel goes. Whereas Synge was bred a country gentleman of small means and educated at Trinity College, Dublin, O'Casey was an autodidact from the Dublin slums. Moreover, a radical change had come in the Irish scene in consequence of the First World War, the Irish fight for independence, and the civil war which ensued between those who wished for a compromise within the British empire, and those who, like de Valera, wished for an independent republic. Each of O'Casey's three great Irish plays, *The Shadow of a Gunman*, *Juno and the Paycock*, and *The Plough and the Stars*, is set in the poorer parts of the city in which the playwright was born, and in each there is a background of armed fighting and revolutionary catchcries.

A writer using such material started with an initial advantage. His theme is the impact of war and of a national ideal embodying courage and self-sacrifice on lives that would otherwise be merely sordid and without dramatic interest. All these plays verge on melodrama, but the intensity of a real experience, which was shared by the author and his early audiences, saves them from being quite that. The dominant motif is pity, pity for suffering humanity. The necessity of the national struggle is accepted, it is felt to be as inevitable as birth or death. Yet the heroes of these plays are not its soldiers, but their womenfolk who show courage of a different sort – who fight without sentiment and without conscious idealism to aid the suffering and afflicted, and to protect their own.

After the last of these plays, O'Casey left Ireland for England, and though some of his later work is set in Ireland it belongs primarily to the English stage. There is a complete difference of opinion between most Irish and non-Irish critics about the value of O'Casey's later work. In the Irish view there is a diffuseness and maudlin sentimentality about both the plays and the four volumes of autobiography which begin with *I Knock at the Door* (1939): the theme is still pity and admiration for the common people, but it is drowned in sardonic and indiscriminate contempt for the upper classes, which soon becomes monotonous. It is relieved only occasionally by the old vitality of language. There is a basic failure of organizing intelligence. By this time O'Casey, who had been a syndicalist and follower of Larkin and Connolly in his youth, was a vociferous supporter of the British Communist Party. Few of the later plays have been staged in Ireland and none have been successful. But *Cock-a-Doodle Dandy* ran well in London, and an American critic, Robert Hogan, in *After the Irish Renaissance* has emphasized that these plays belong to the central tradition of English pastoral comedy and that it is irrelevant to compare them with the early plays – a view apparently authenticated by O'Casey himself during the controversy[3] over *The Bishop's Bonfire* (1955). The theme, as in Shakespeare's *Winter's Tale*, is the innocence of bucolic love pitted against the hypocrisies of state and church, with modern Ireland as a rather special Aunt Sally.

In several of his writings setting out the ideals of the Abbey Theatre Yeats had mentioned that he hoped its work would be complemented by a move to make the classics of world drama available to Irish audiences. After the First World War this hope materialized. In 1918 a new theatrical grouping was established, the Dublin Drama League, with just this intention. Plays by Pirandello, Eugene O'Neill,

D'Annunzio and others were performed. In 1928 this group led to the founding of the Dublin Gate Theatre by Hilton Edwards and Michael MacLiammoir. The work of the Gate was not limited to non-Irish plays. The wider perspectives offered made it also a forum for Irish work which could find no place in the increasingly narrow conventions of the Abbey. The Gate's most notable discovery was Denis Johnston (b. 1901). The title of his earliest play, *The Old Lady says 'No!'*, refers to its rejection by the Abbey directors. This play, together with *A Bride for the Unicorn* and *The Golden Cuckoo*, used an expressionist technique, similar to that of Toller and Brecht. Unfortunately, they depend for their full effect on a close acquaintance with Irish history and tradition and the emotional undertones this involves.

Johnston's most successful play, *The Moon in the Yellow River* (1931), which was welcomed in London and New York as well as in Dublin, is a straight play within the Chehov-Ibsen tradition. It deals with the impact of material progress on a countryside still dominated by easy-going traditionalism and romantic nationalism. As in O'Casey, there is conflict between an advancing ideal and human nature, and once more comedy and tragedy are juxtaposed. But unlike O'Casey the conflict is presented with full intelligence instead of with despairing pity. It is seen as part of a wider context: the 'message' of the play is to reflect a genuine perplexedness, which is as relevant to Russia or China (from which the title comes) as to Ireland. After the Second World War Johnston concentrated increasingly on work for the BBC and television. For the last several years he has fallen silent, living in America where he teaches drama at a New England university.

The great days of the Abbey run from its foundation to the early 1920s, those of the Gate dominate the '30s and '40s. 1939 marked both the death of Yeats and a split in the Gate Theatre Company between the artistic directors, Edwards and MacLiammoir, and the sixth Earl of Longford, who had contributed generous financial support and since 1931 been chairman. Two companies, Gate Theatre and Longford Productions, succeeded the older company with an agreement each to use the theatre for six months of the year and tour the remainder. Lord Longford and Lady Longford produced plays of their own successfully for several more years, but there was a gradual falling-off in experimental work.

The rather humble original Abbey premises burned down in 1951 and were only replaced by a modern government-subsidized building in 1966. Meanwhile a proliferation of miniature theatre groupings had taken place in Dublin and its suburbs. In 1957 the first Dublin Theatre Festival was held. After teething troubles, notably an acrimonious controversy with O'Casey,[4] which led to him refusing permission for any more of his plays to be performed in Ireland, and a decision by Samuel Beckett to withdraw a play in sympathy, the Festival has settled down as an annual event which provides the main outlet for new work and experiment. Two playwrights in particular, John B. Keane (b. 1928) and Brian Friel (b. 1929), have come to the fore since the Festival was established. Keane is a Kerryman by birth and a publican by trade. As might be expected from this background, his varied characters are bursting with vitality and perform with devastating naturalism, though their language sometimes runs to hyperbole. *Sive*, a most popular play for amateur productions, is a poignant re-use of an old theme – the young girl driven by parental greed to marriage with a rich farmer twice her age. *The Highest House on the Mountain*, another tormented play of rural tensions, was the great success of the 1960 Theatre Festival. Brian Friel is a Northerner, living until recently in Derry. Two of his plays, *Philadelphia, Here I Come!* (1964) and *The Loves of Cass McGuire* (1967), have been successful in New York as well as Dublin. Both deal imaginatively with the impact of emigration on Irish life, the first with the despair and frustration which drive a young man out of Ireland, the second with the disillusion greeting the returning exile.

Beckett's plays, together with his novels, will be discussed later in this chapter.

The influence of cultural nationalism was strongest in the theatre. It was marked in poetry and least strong in prose fiction. It used to be felt indeed that the novel was the weakest art-form in Irish letters. Joyce, of course, is a case apart: his work transcends the Irish scene, and it has a separate place in this volume. George Moore wrote some fine novels portraying, with a tinge of anti-clericalism, life in the Mayo countryside, together with many grossly-overwritten ones, contemporary with the great days of the Abbey. After that there is a hiatus until a crop of vivid short story writers appeared soon after independence. In recent years, however, several novelists of talent have made their presence felt. These writers do not constitute a cohesive group. Nevertheless they stand out from their English and American contemporaries, less perhaps by a distinctive style than by their use of characteristic themes.

Four main themes seem to be important in Irish prose writing this century and our discussion is best grouped round these – the nature theme, the historical theme ('the Troubles'), the Catholic novel, and the comic novel. The latter leads to a subsidiary theme, that of the experimental novel.

The finest example of a writer utilizing nature themes is Liam O'Flaherty, who has already been mentioned. A fellow-writer, Seán O'Faoláin, tells in his autobiography how, when O'Flaherty arrived in London fresh from the Aran Islands and determined to be a writer, he attempted a novel of society ladies and their love-affairs. A perspicacious publisher recognized the talent behind it, but advised him to write of things he knew from personal experience. 'But I only know about fields, rocks and cows' was O'Flaherty's unhappy answer. 'Then write about them.' He did, and produced the exquisite tales of country life collected in the volumes *Spring Sowing* (1924), *The Tent* (1926) and *The Mountain Tavern* (1929). It would be hard to think of any European writer with the same power to place himself imaginatively into the anguish of a cow looking at her injured calf or a baby seagull just learning to fly.

The bloodshed which took place in Ireland during the years 1916 to 1923 was a shattering experience for all sensitive Irishmen. For English and continental writers who experienced the First World War, it was the futility and anonymity of mass-slaughter which horrified. In the Irish struggle, particularly in the civil war, personal relationships were tragically close: often a family was divided against itself, and even where this was not so, the existence of a common language between the English soldiery and the Irish insurrectionaries gave it a more private character. The title-story of Frank O'Connor's (1903–66) first book, *Guests of a Nation* (1931), well illustrates this. Seán O'Faoláin (b. 1900) produced a first collection on the same theme at the same period, *Midsummer Night Madness* (1932); and Liam O'Flaherty caught the vivid detail of the revolutionary war in such short novels as *The Informer* (1925) and *The Martyr* (1933), some of which were filmed. All these writers were young men who had participated in the fighting they depicted. History had been kind to the poet Yeats in that he reached maturity before the nationalist movement passed from words to acts: he was both involved and detached and so able to produce great reflective poetry, such as the 'Meditations in Time of Civil War'. By contrast these youngsters were caught and hurt by the raw experience which they could record but not place in any settled perspective. It has often seemed surprising that Ireland produced no novel of wide canvas to depict the drama of these years. But it should be remembered that *War and Peace* was written nearly sixty years after the events it describes and which Tolstoy knew principally from grandfathers' tales. Michael Farrell's *Thy Tears Might Cease* (1963) is an only partially successful attempt to do the same for Ireland.

It was not easy for men whose formative years had been spent in guerrilla war to settle to the humdrum business of the middle-class state that emerged from the Irish revolution. The early years of the Irish Free State were still troubled politically, and the absence of any established background to society has been blamed for the failure to produce any novelist of distinction in these years. It might be felt that the Catholic church should have been able to offer such a background. But Irish Catholicism had such a narrow and parochial character as to prove rather a millstone round the neck of any creative writer. One of the first actions of the new government was to impose a censorship of books on moral grounds, which soon made Ireland the laughing stock of intellectual Europe. Few writers of world repute failed to figure on the censored list, and Irish writers were under special scrutiny. It was not pleasant for men like O'Faoláin to find themselves branded in their native land as pornographers. O'Faoláin's *Come Back to Erin* and Brinsley MacNamara's *Valley of the Squinting Windows* reflect the straitjacketing of the times. In recent years, happily, the censorship has been considerably relaxed.

One novel of maturity and distinction, promptly banned in Ireland, did appear in these years – Seán O'Faoláin's *Bird Alone* (1936). A subtle and sensitive novel in its own right, it also highlights an important question: What is the Catholic novel? The central character is an old man who in youth, as the story little by little reveals, got a girl with child. The girl dies in childbirth, tormented by her sin. The struggle of carnal desire against Catholic precept is told with immense delicacy and sympathy, and the implied background of transcendental values sets this novel in a world apart from the slice-of-life fiction contemporary in America and England. In the more open Ireland of the 1960s a new group of Irish writers has tackled similar themes – John McGahern in *The Barracks* and *The Dark*, Brian Moore in *The Lonely Passion of Judith Hearne, The Luck of Ginger Coffey* and *I am Mary Dunne*, Patrick Boyle in *Like Any Other Man*. In a different key, Edna O'Brien has pictured vivaciously the unexpected outcome of a Catholic upbringing in *The Country Girls, Girl with Green Eyes* (originally *The Lonely Girl*), *Girls in their Married Bliss*, and a series of later novels, which perhaps fall prey to a bright sensationalism.

The hardest genre to discuss is the comic novel, because too often the effect of analysing humour is to lose it. But if, in spite of that, one dare venture a definition, Irish humour seems characterized by the juxtaposition of seedy, earthy realism with abstruse flights of metaphysical fancy. This is the nature of much of the humour in *Ulysses* and *Finnegans Wake* and in the early writings of Beckett. It is found in unadulterated form in the novels of Brian Nolan, alias Flann O'Brien, alias Myles na gCopaleen (1911–66), the most outstanding of which are *At Swim-Two-Birds* and the posthumous *The Third Policeman*. These two are also rare precursors of the anti-novel in English. 'One ending and one beginning for a book was a thing I did not agree with', announces the protagonist of *At Swim-Two-Birds*. 'A good book may have three openings entirely dissimilar and inter-related only in the prescience of the author, or for that matter one hundred times as many endings.' It is easy to imagine where this doctrine leads.

The titan figure of Yeats inevitably dominated the Irish poetic scene even well into the years following his death. This did not make it easy for younger men to find distinctive voices. F. R. Higgins (1896–1941) and Padraic Colum (1881–1972) owe something to the early Yeats and more to the older ballads. Colum's fine lyric 'She Moved through the Fair' evokes the anonymity of the bardic tradition and reminds one of Yeats's observation that the country people are fond of verses and stories that 'keep half their meaning to themselves'. Donagh MacDonagh (1912–68) broke new ground by contributing to the Dublin stage two ballad-comedies, *Happy as Larry* (1946) and *God's Gentry*. These are in the manner of Brecht's *Beggar's Opera* and were forerunners of Behan's *The Hostage* and the musical adaptation of

The Playboy as *The Heart's a Wonder* which achieved passing fame in the 1950s.

Two powerful Catholic poets, Austin Clarke (b. 1896) and Denis Devlin (1908–59), emerged in the 1930s. Clarke owes much to Yeats, to the verbal tricks of Gaelic poetry, and to a Jansenist-tinged vision of the early Irish church. His later collections *Flight to Africa* (1963) and *Old-Fashioned Pilgrimage* (1967) include clipped, sardonic satire on issues Irish and foreign. His long *Mnemosyne Lay in Dust*, perhaps his finest work, agonizingly depicts a nervous breakdown. Denis Devlin was a member of Ireland's diplomatic corps and much of his work was published abroad. His imagery and subject-matter are correspondingly wide. He was better known in Italy and America during his lifetime until the posthumous *Collected Poems* appeared in 1963. Neither Clarke nor Devlin can approach their deity with Hopkins's fearful, but positive, apprehension, but if Clarke's approach is Jansenist, Devlin's is Kierkegaardian:

> It being essential to the gall he tasted
> That bitterness only bitterness can share.

But the most original poet to appear since the death of Yeats was Patrick Kavanagh (1905–67). Born on a poor farm near the Ulster border, the opening lines of his longest poem, 'The Great Hunger', portray this land:

> Clay is the word and clay is the flesh
> Where the potato-gatherers like mechanized scarecrows move
> Along the side-fall of the hill – Maguire and his men.
> If we watch them an hour is there anything we can prove
> Of life as it is broken-backed over the Book
> Of Death?

Any forerunner here is D. H. Lawrence, not Yeats. Kavanagh's unromantic picture of grinding toil in the pocket-handkerchief fields of his homeland is closer to Lawrence's stories of the collieries than to any of the English nature-poets:

> Watch him, watch him, that man on a hill whose spirit
> Is a wet sack flapping about the knees of time.

The poet who wrote that had himself worn an old sack for a cheap apron on muddy work. Here once more we find the problem of Ireland's lonely bachelors, fearful to marry lest they overcrowd the land, this time seen from the inside. The 'hunger' of the title is both the hunger for land and the hunger for life, both finally unappeased:

> ... he is not so sure now if his mother was right
> When she praised the man who made a field his bride.

When this Guide was first published, twelve years ago, Thomas Kinsella (b. 1927) was alluded to as the youngest poet of promise. With his last collection, *Nightwalker and Other Poems* (1968), he has amply fulfilled this. A rare devotion to craftsmanship, a scholar's knowledge of Gaelic tradition, and an almost unbearably poignant personal vision are his strength. For the last few years, like many other Irish writers, his home has been America, but in 1968 he returned to Ireland on a Guggenheim fellowship. He devoted this to preparing a complete rendering in prose and verse of the great epic of Ireland's golden age, the *Tain*, published – with illustrations by Louis le Brocquy – in 1969. A near contemporary of Kinsella is Richard Murphy. His talent has been slower to mature, but *The Battle of Aughrim* (1968), a long poem on a historic theme, marks his breakthrough to the first rank.

From other young and middle-aged poets writing today, it is difficult to select those whose contribution will last. Brendan Kennelly (b. 1936) has published eight collections and two novels to date. He has shrewd observation and the memorable phrase, but might profit from recalling that facility is often the enemy of talent. John Montague and Seamus Heaney (b. 1939) are Ulster poets with directness of vision: whether there's a message is to be questioned. Eavan Boland (b. 1946) made a stir with her first collection, *New Territory* (1967); her writing offers the deft, unexpected phrase linked with a penetrating intellect, but her energies seem currently directed to political journalism.

We come, finally, to the most enigmatic Irish writer of all: Samuel Beckett. Catapulted to fame by the international success of *Waiting for Godot* soon after the last World War, his reputation has grown steadily. In the last decade critical commentary[5] around his work threatens to rival the Yeats and Joyce 'industries', and many would not hesitate to rank Beckett as the most significant writer of present times. In 1969 he was awarded a Nobel Prize.

The critic faces a certain difficulty of approach. While preceding authors may be discussed in terms of conventional literary criticism, elucidating the references and symbolism, evaluating the philosophy behind, Beckett can not. Painstakingly, this author has whittled away the literary façade of modern writing, until what remains is an experience which, if we approach him at all, we must only share. Nevertheless, some biographical data and certain pointers in his development may be useful here to those who approach his work for the first time.

Beckett was born in Dublin in 1906, of moderately well-to-do parents. His upbringing was 'almost Quaker', he once told an inquirer. He graduated at Trinity College in 1930, briefly held a lectureship there, then travelled and studied in Germany, England and France before settling in Paris in 1937. These were years in the wilderness. He lived in Joyce's circle and was sometimes referred to ironically as 'le petit Joyce'. He published a long poem, *Whoroscope*, in 1930, a short study, *Proust*, about the same time, a book of short stories, *More Pricks than Kicks* (1934), and a novel, *Murphy* (1938). The Second World War found him in Ireland visiting his mother, but he hurried back to his Paris flat. As an Irish national he first felt himself neutral, but the Nazi occupation changed his opinions. He joined the French resistance and spent two years collating intelligence, then when his group was betrayed took refuge, with his wife, in Vichy France; he lived in disguise as an agricultural labourer and wrote *Watt* (not published till 1953). *En Attendant Godot*, produced in Paris in 1953, secured sudden critical acclaim and the English translation, *Waiting for Godot*, repeated this in London, Dublin, and New York. To his own humble astonishment, Beckett had 'arrived'. A trilogy of novels followed, *Molloy*, *Malone Dies*, *The Unnameable*, and a whole series of plays for theatre, radio and television, of which the most important are *All That Fall*, *Endgame*, *Krapp's Last Tape*, *Happy Days*, and *Play*. A further novel, *How It Is*, appeared in 1964. Many of these were written in French, then translated, but recently Beckett has returned to writing in English. It is not irrelevant to mention that many stories circulate of Beckett's immense personal kindness to simple friends and acquaintances. This quality of character is not over-common among intellectuals, though Beckett shared it with Camus; compassion is a strong element in both their writings.

Belacqua, the classic procrastinator of Dante's *Purgatorio*, is the name given to the central character in the early stories, and this seedy, idle, Dublin iconoclast is the precursor of the tramps or down-and-outs in *Watt* and *Godot* and of Krapp. It is as if Beckett wished to show human nature stripped of the veneer of modern civilization, long before the hippie movement became a mass culture. The early books show that Beckett could write both lyrically and descriptively. Poetry is still present in *Godot*:

ESTRAGON: All the dead voices.
VLADIMIR: They make a noise like wings.
ESTRAGON: Like leaves.
VLADIMIR: Like sand.
ESTRAGON: Like leaves.
Silence.
VLADIMIR: They all speak together.
ESTRAGON: Each one to itself.
Silence.

The progressive purging of this to the unadorned prose of *How It Is* and the later plays is a deliberate achievement. It is the literary counterpart of the process by which Beckett's characters, his 'people' as he prefers to call them, have already been whittled back to the elementals of the universal human condition. The names given to the 'people' in *Godot*, Vladimir, Estragon, Pozzo, and Lucky, evoke the four points of the European compass. In this play they are still mobile, though that takes them nowhere, but in the novels and subsequent plays they are usually crippled or captive. For Beckett the antithesis between the infinity of man's mental processes and the finiteness of his worldly condition appears literally hopeless.

There is humour of the Irish kind, as already stated, in the early Beckett. Often comic effect is incidental to the Swiftian disgust his people evince at carnal love, or their Eliotian *ennui* for the preliminaries. But the overall vision progresses in bleakness. *Godot* has Christian overtones. One of the thieves was saved, one of the thieves was damned, we do not know why, suggests a further pointer to the human condition. In *Endgame* and *Happy Days* there is a faltering hint that we may be saved by love. But the bleakness of *Krapp's Last Tape* or *How It Is* seems unrelieved. Yet the effect on the viewer or reader (one would like to say on the 'experiencer') is anything but depressing. If we relax, we experience a deep catharsis. Another Irishman, Brendan Behan, is reported as saying: 'I don't know what his plays are about, but I enjoy them. I don't know what a swim in the ocean is about, but I enjoy it. I enjoy the water flowing over me.'

Compiling in the early 1970s a survey of this kind on Irish writing is peculiarly difficult; because an important part of the country is currently in political turmoil, which may well spread to the whole island. Whatever the outcome, things will not be the same as in the half-century of relative stability which followed the settlement of 1921, and this must have consequences for literature, just as the earlier unrest did. Yet it is early to discern where these developments will lead. Two long poems by writers already referred to must certainly be signalled: John Montague's *A New Siege* (1970)[6] is a historical meditation which parallels the events in Londonderry's Bogside of the previous year with the famous siege of the city by Jacobite forces in the seventeenth century. Thomas Kinsella's *Butcher's Dozen* (1972) is a savage tract of the times in the tradition of Swift and Dante: it evokes the accusing shades of the thirteen unarmed Derry citizens who were shot by British paratroopers on 13 January 1972.

It seems appropriate at this point to mention another writer of Northern background whose work has hitherto been widely ignored. Francis Stuart was born in 1902 of Protestant stock. He married Maud Gonne's natural daughter, Iseult, turned Catholic, and took the extreme Republican side in the Irish civil war. Later he spent the Second World War in Germany, and its aftermath in France, only returning to Ireland in the mid-1960s. Though he never propagandized for the Nazis, he lived through the bombing of Berlin and its occupation by the Russians. Probably he is the only novelist of stature writing in English to bring such experiences to bear on his work. His finest novels, *The Angel of Pity* (1935), *Redemption* (1949) and *The Flowering Cross* (1950), reflect the problems of suffering once posed by Dostoyevsky, and a Catholicism that anticipates the Second Vatican Council. A strange work, *Blacklist Section H* (1971),[7] part autobiography, part historical fiction, is felt by some critics to be a seminal work in understanding the subterranean forces now shaping the Ireland of the future.

NOTES

1. The old melodramas were scorned for half a century, but have lately become popular again. Dion Boucicault's *The Shaughraun* and *Arrah na Pogue* have run to enthusiastic audiences at the Abbey in the last ten years, and a handsome edition of the three Irish plays, *The Dolmen Boucicault* (edited by David Krause), was published in Pennsylvania and Dublin in 1965.

2. See Elizabeth Coxhead, *Lady Gregory* (revised edition, 1966), and Ann Saddlemyer, *In Defence of Lady Gregory, Playwright* (1966).

3. See Gabriel Fallon, *Sean O'Casey: The Man I Knew* (1965), for details; also Robert Hogan, *After the Irish Renaissance* (1968).

4. See previous note.

5. The best short introduction in English is Richard N. Coe, *Beckett* (1964). See also Hugh Kenner, *Samuel Beckett: A Critical Study*, and Alec Reid, *All I can Manage, More than I could: An Approach to the Plays of Samuel Beckett* (1968). The latter apparently has Beckett's *imprimatur.*

One of the best discussions of the religious implications of *Godot* is still the contemporary notice in *The Times Literary Supplement*, 10 February 1956. They are also discussed in Coe, Kenner and Reid – see above.

6. Incorporated with other meditative historical poems in *The Rough Field* (1972).

7. Published by Southern Illinois University Press, Carbondale, U.S.A. At time of going to press no Irish or English publisher had ventured on this book.

SHAW AND THE LONDON THEATRE

T. R. BARNES

Bishop Wordsworth's School, Salisbury

> DRAMATIC art has long seemed to me a kind of *Biblia Pauperum* – a Bible in pictures for those who cannot read the written or printed word; and the dramatic author a lay preacher, who hawks about the ideas of his time in popular form – popular enough for the middle classes, who form the bulk of theatrical audiences, to grasp the nature of the subject without troubling their brains too much. The theatre, accordingly, has always been a board-school for the young, for the half-educated, and for women, who still retain the inferior faculty of deceiving themselves and allowing themselves to be deceived: that is to say, of being susceptible to illusion and to the suggestions of the author. Consequently, in these days, when the rudimentary and incompletely developed thought-process which operates through the imagination appears to be developing into reflection, investigation and examination, it has seemed to me that the theatre ... may be on the verge of being abandoned as a form which is dying out, and for the enjoyment of which we lack the necessary conditions ... in those civilized countries which have produced the greatest thinkers of the age – that is to say, England and Germany – the dramatic art ... is dead.
>
> (Strindberg, Preface to *Miss Julie*, 1888)

The passage is well known, but it has seemed worth quoting at length, not only because it so well typifies the climate of opinion in which Shaw (1856–1950) began to write plays, but because it remains so extraordinarily apposite a description of his own work and of much that has been written since. Consider for example, this account, by F. C. Burnand, of the audience at the Royal Court Theatre, during the famous Barker-Vedrenne regime, 1903–6: 'The female element predominates over the inferior sex as something like twelve to one. The audience had not a theatre-going, but rather, a lecture-going, sermon-loving appearance.' And it is easy to compile a list of worthy plays, from *Strife* to *Thunder Rock* or *A Sleeping Clergyman* or *Johnson Over Jordan*, which are, in essence, lessons for Strindberg's 'board-school'.

The attack on the imagination is also relevant. Curiously old-fashioned though it may sound today, it is characteristic of much thinking about the drama at the end of the nineteenth century. There was a naïve belief that the literature of naturalism was, for the first time, revealing the truth. '*Dans l'enfantement continu de l'humanité,*' declared Zola magniloquently in the preface to the dramatized version of *Thérèse Raquin*, '*nous en sommes à l'accouchement du vrai.*' This truth was to be 'scientific'. 'What we wanted as the basis of our plays', wrote Shaw, 'was not romance, but a really scientific natural history'; and this basis was to be arrived at by thinking: 'there is flatly no future now for any drama without music, except the drama of thought'. Strindberg would seem to imply that if all we have is 'reflection, investigation, examination', we 'lack the necessary conditions for the enjoyment' and also, presumably, for the creation, of the drama. It seems to be a popular procedure in *avant-garde* criticism to cut off the branch you are sitting on – Ionesco and Beckett are contemporary examples – and Strindberg's practice belied his theory; but in the attitude to literature expressed in these remarks, above all in the exaltation of the intellect at the expense of the imagination, in the insistence on scientific method and on thought, lies the reason why so much of the well-intentioned, thought-provoking, socially-directed drama of the Shavian period seems so dead today.

Shaw claimed to be in the tradition of Molière. 'My business as a classic writer of comedies', he said, 'is to chasten morals with ridicule'; and part of his technique was to reintroduce to the drama 'long rhetorical speeches in the manner of Molière'. There can be no doubt that his plays amused, stimulated, exasperated, and shocked his contemporaries; that no plays since Congreve's (it is Mr Eliot's opinion) have more pointed and eloquent dialogue, that he was a man of great intelligence and immense seriousness of purpose, and that only one of his contemporaries, in one play, *The Importance of Being Earnest*, can hold a candle to his best work. But if we compare his work with that, say, of Lawrence, of Forster, or of Eliot, can we say that it still lives for us as much as theirs does, that we can return to it, as we can to theirs, and find new values in it? Does not the reference to Molière, which was seriously meant – it is not a mere piece of Shavian rodomontade – make us feel a bit uneasy?

Consider these fragments of dialogue:

> *Madelon* (one of the Précieuses Ridicules):
> *La belle galanterie que la leur! Quoi! Débuter d'abord par le mariage?*
> *Gorgibus* (her father):
> *Et par où veux-tu donc qu'ils débutent? Par le concubinage?*

> *Don Luis* (speaking to his son, Don Juan):
> *Apprenez enfin qu'un gentilhomme qui vit mal est un monstre dans la nature....*

> *Mme Jourdain: ... Il y a longtemps que vos façons de faire donnent à rire à tout le monde.*
> *M. Jourdain: Qui est donc tout ce monde-là, s'il vous plaît?*
> *Mme Jourdain: Tout ce monde-là est un monde qui a raison, et qui est plus sage que vous.*

> *Mendoza:* I am a bandit. I live by robbing the rich.
> *Tanner:* I am a gentleman. I live by robbing the poor. Shake hands!

> *Undershaft:* Poverty, my friend, is not a thing to be proud of.
> *Shirley*. Who made your millions for you? Me and my like. Whats kep us poor? Keepin you rich. I wouldn't have your conscience, not for all your income.
> *Undershaft:* I wouldn't have your income, not for all your conscience, Mr Shirley.

All these bits depend for their impact on the weight of certain key words – *galanterie*, *mariage*, *nature*, *monde*, gentleman, poverty, riches, conscience, and so on. If Molière's terms have much greater weight than Shaw's, and I think it could be shown that they have, this is because his audience spoke the same language as he did, because values were shared between them, because Molière's culture supported him, so that he could assume an understanding on the part of his audience more complete than any contemporary playwright can count on. The fact that this sort of understanding no longer exists makes 'chastening morals with ridicule', as Molière or Ben Jonson understood the matter, most difficult, if not impossible; since before morals can be chastened we must agree on what they are, and by what standards they are to be judged.

This difficulty cripples the dramatist more than any other writer, because he must move a group. The novelist or poet, who addresses the individual, can forge his own language, and hope that his readers will learn it. The dramatist must speak in terms they already understand; he has to use the language of his age, and this language reflects the condition of the society that speaks it. Our society and our language are such that it is far more difficult to produce truly creative and original work in a medium like the drama, which depends for its effect on immediate public consent, than it is to do so in the comparatively private media of poetry and fiction. The dialogue in which Shaw's characters discuss the ideas about society and politics and justice which he wanted his audience to respond to remains brilliantly clear: we have only to turn over the pages of *Strife* or *The Madras House* to see how vastly better he was than his contemporaries. Yet many critics, from A. B. Walkley onwards, have felt that there was something 'wrong' with Shaw's plays. They certainly wear less well than those of his near-contemporaries, Ibsen and Chehov. The reason lies in his curiously ambivalent attitude to art and literature.

Shaw proclaimed himself uncompromisingly a Puritan: 'My conscience is the genuine pulpit article: it annoys me to see people comfortable when they ought to be uncomfortable; and I insist on making them think in order to bring them to a conviction of sin.' 'For art's sake' he would not 'face the toil of writing a sentence'. Yet literature is part of 'the struggle for life to become divinely conscious of itself', he writes. In *Man and Superman* he makes Tanner explain to Tavy that 'the artist's work is to show us ourselves as we really are. Our minds are nothing but this knowledge of ourselves; and he who adds a jot to such knowledge creates new mind as surely as any woman creates new men.' A noble definition, expressed with the rhythmic precision and clarity which Shaw's best dialogue always exhibits; but when we remember the whole scene, and the context of this speech, we also remember that it is Tavy who is supposed to be the 'artist', and he is a refined well-to-do version of the usual *vie de Bohème* stereotype that Shaw always represents the artist as being, and of which Marchbanks and Dubedat are the classic examples. It is

Tanner whose work is important, and he is no 'mere artist' but an 'artist philosopher' – the phrases were used by Shaw to describe the author of *Everyman*; his literary ancestor is not Shakespeare but Bunyan. Shakespeare, 'who knew human weakness so well, never knew human strength ...', but Bunyan 'achieved virtue and courage by identifying himself with the purpose of the world as he knew it'.

If, then, we are to judge the value of Shaw's work, we must estimate what he has added to our knowledge of ourselves, and how he has explained the purpose of the world. But he has made it very difficult for us to do this on his own terms, because in his view such knowledge is always going out of date, and the purpose of the world (magniloquent but empty phrase) would appear to be always changing. Consider these remarks, from the Preface to *Man and Superman*:

> Effectiveness of assertion is the Alpha and Omega of style. He who has nothing to assert has no style and can have none: he who has something to assert will go as far in power of style as its momentousness and his conviction will carry him. Disprove his assertion after it is made, yet its style remains. Darwin has no more destroyed the style of Job nor of Handel than Martin Luther destroyed the style of Giotto. All the assertions get disproved sooner or later, and so we find the world full of a magnificent débris of artistic fossils, with the matter-of-fact credibility gone clean out of them, but the form still splendid. And that is why the old masters play the deuce with our mere susceptibilities.

How did a man whose specific judgements on music and drama were so often so acute, come to write such irrelevant nonsense when he generalized about the arts? Because, I believe, he was uneasily conscious of his talent's limitations. As a wit and a pamphleteer he was impressive: as a creative artist only a minor figure. The epithet he applies to our susceptibilities gives the game away; it gives evidence, like his digs at Shakespeare, of an underlying, perhaps unconscious envy of qualities he knew to be outside his scope. *St Joan* was his attempt at a great play. Its discussions of political motives and class antagonisms are lively; its efforts to move our 'mere susceptibilities' are failures. Shaw commands only the language of assertion and dialectic; when he deals with emotion there is only cliché: 'if only I could hear the wind in the trees, the larks in the sunshine, the young lambs crying through the healthy frost, and the blessed, blessed church bells'. One is reminded of Yeats's remarks about the realistic drama: 'Except when it is superficial, or deliberately argumentative, it fills one's soul with a sense of commonness as with dust. It has one mortal ailment. It cannot become impassioned, that is to say vital, without making somebody gushing and sentimental.'

Shaw advised us to 'get rid of reputations: they are weeds in the soil of ignorance. Cultivate that soil, and they will flower more beautifully, but only as annuals.' But since, presumably, we cannot agree with this, or with the idea that past works of art are 'fossils', preserved in 'style', we must ask what elements in Shaw's work are still living. His assertions about the Life Force, tolerable in a light-hearted performance like *Man and Superman*, become boring in the over-long and pretentious *Back to Methuselah*; his admiration for the great man, stimulating and even ennobling in *Caesar and Cleopatra*, degenerated into dangerous and sentimental weakness; but his wit, his gaiety, above all his passion for justice, remain undimmed.

Shaw was a pioneer in the matter of publishing plays. 'He realized', says Mr St John Ervine, 'that no one would read a prompt copy of a play unless he had to.... *Plays Pleasant and Unpleasant* was, therefore, issued in a form which was a mixture of novel and play ... the emotions of the characters at a particular point were described.' The same authority tells us that 'dull people imagined that G. B. S. in writing these accounts was naïvely revealing his inability to write plays at all'. Think, for a moment, of the brillant paragraph which, at the beginning of *Man and Superman*, describes Roebuck Ramsden in his study:

> He wears a black frock coat, a white waistcoat (it is bright summer weather) and trousers, neither black nor perceptibly blue, of one of those indefinitely mixed hues which the modern clothier has produced to harmonize with the religions of respectable men ...

If we remember anything about Roebuck it is likely to be this joke about the colour of his trousers. The specimen is pinned down for our leisurely inspection, its habitat sketched in, and its prejudices, social, political, economic, and aesthetic, neatly indicated. 'Against the wall opposite him are two busts on pillars: one, to his left, of John

Bright; the other, to his right, of Herbert Spencer ... autotypes of allegories by Mr G. F. Watts (for Roebuck believes in the fine arts with all the earnestness of a man who does not understand them) ...' Our pleasure in this detached and comic portrayal is increased by symbolic and humorous exaggeration. The polish on Roebuck's furniture, made possible by the labour his money can buy ('it is clear that there are at least two housemaids and a parlourmaid downstairs, and a housekeeper upstairs who does not let them spare elbow grease'), is transferred to his bald head: 'On a sunshiny day he could heliograph orders to distant camps by merely nodding.' Shaw's debt to Dickens in passages like this is obvious. But to think of a novelist, is to think that this whole passage might well come from a novel, though it is in fact a stage direction; yet when we consider it from that point of view we see at once that most of it is quite irrelevant, for no audience can be expected to recognize photographs of George Eliot and busts of John Bright and draw from them those conclusions about Roebuck's character which Shaw so neatly deduces.

Mr St John Ervine's dull people were, of course, wrong when they thought Shaw couldn't write plays; but the point they might have made about this description of Ramsden is simply that it is not in the play at all, and that no matter how cunning the scene designer, or how skilled the actor, it can't by any means be got into it. And they might also add that in great drama 'the emotions of the characters at a particular point' are not described, but expressed. Shaw's dialogue, his style, his rhythms, his imagery, though admirably suited to dialectic or pedagogy, won't do for everything he has in mind to put in the plays; and this is largely true of naturalistic drama in general. We need not, in way of comparison, invoke the shades of Shakespeare or Molière: Congreve, Sheridan, Beaumarchais, or even Wilde will do. We don't need elaborate descriptions of Ben the Sailor, or Sir Benjamin Backbite, or Figaro (compared with him how poverty-stricken a character is Henry Straker), or Lady Bracknell, because their creators have expressed them fully and exactly through the speeches and rhythms they have created for them.

In the Preface to *Plays Pleasant and Unpleasant* Shaw discusses stage directions, complains that there are none in Shakespeare's plays, and goes on to say:

> It is for want of this elaboration that Shakespeare, unsurpassed as poet, story-teller, character draughtsman, humorist, and rhetorician, has left no coherent drama, and could not afford to pursue a genuinely scientific method in his studies of character and society.

If Shaw's drama *is* intellectually coherent, its coherence can only be grasped by a reader. We must agree with Shaw when he says that he has 'never found an acquaintance with a dramatist founded on the theatre alone ... a really intimate and accurate one'; but we may also wonder whether any drama is truly great that depends as much as his does on extra-theatrical considerations.

When we turn from the plays of Shaw to those of his contemporaries and successors who used the naturalistic convention to depict and discuss society and its problems, we find little of permanent interest. Much work, like that of Barrie or Coward, for example, is merely sentimental, frivolous, or trivial. Attempts by such writers as Galsworthy, Maugham, Bridie, or Priestley to deal with serious themes seem already dated. There is a good deal of honest and earnest work, some flashes of humour and fantasy, and useful discussion – for Shaw's success undoubtedly opened the theatre doors to the drama of ideas – but there is nothing truly creative. These writers all handle ideas we have heard before, and manipulate situations and feelings already familiar. They are not trivial, they do not lack a 'worthy purpose', but they are not creative. If effective enough in the theatre, their works do not repay reading; their dialogue is for the most part invincibly dull: words fail them.

Not all voices at the beginning of the century acclaimed naturalism: Yeats, for example, had very different ideas. He had been told, he said, that 'the poetic drama has come to an end, because modern poets have no dramatic power'; but this explanation didn't convince him. He found it 'easier to believe that audiences, who have learned ... from the life of crowded cities to live upon the surface of life, and actors and managers who study to please them, have changed, than that imagination, which is the voice of what is eternal in man, has changed'. 'The theatre', he maintained, 'began in ritual, and it cannot come to its greatness again without recalling words to their ancient sovereignty.'

It would, I think, be true to say that most plays of any literary merit produced during the last half-century exhibit the influence of what we might call the Shavian or the Yeatsian points of view. Though naturalism was dominant, there were many besides Yeats who were dissatisfied with what they felt to be the imaginative poverty of realism, and who tried to bring poetry back to the theatre. Mostly they failed, and it is usually thought that they did so because they knew nothing of the stage, or play construction, or how to write dialogue, and this is partly true; but the real reason for their failure is linguistic. Their verse was merely decorative, their idiom devitalized, their rhythms flaccid. They pleased what Lawrence called the 'habituated ear' of the public whose taste approved the Georgian Poetry anthologies, but their plays could only lead a brief obscure theatrical existence in private performances or in occasional appearances in the lists of the more adventurous repertory companies. Believing the naturalistic conventions to be sterile, determined to get away from 'plays with pink lamp-shades', from 'patent leather shoes on Brussels carpets', from a stage dedicated to picturing 'life on thirty pounds a day, not as it is, but as it is conceived by the earners of thirty shillings a week', they escaped for the most part into romantic unrealities. Their works might well have been written by Marchbanks or Tavy.

In the thirties, W. H. Auden, in collaboration with Christopher Isherwood, tried to assimilate elements of the popular theatre into plays which should embody a serious comment on the contemporary situation. The result was an uneasy mixture of satire and nostalgia, of moral indignation and self-pity, seasoned with tags from Freud and Marx, but it had at least a certain energy; it evinced a genuine concern for the human situation, and tried to express that concern in a poetic idiom tough enough to work on the public stage.

That the poet should try to make use of the forms of the commercial theatre, instead of turning his back on them in despair or disgust, was an important departure which has obvious bearings on the dramatic work of Mr Eliot. We are now no longer surprised that a play in verse should have a run in the West End. Audiences have begun to welcome verbal exuberance and rhetoric, after a starvation diet of the dullest prose, and some of them seem to be beginning to share Yeats's views (thirty or more years after he wrote them) on the 'play about modern educated people'. Indeed, Mr Rattigan, our top practitioner in that line, has dignified this development of taste by describing it as 'a revolution in the contemporary theatre, begun a few years ago by T. S. Eliot and Christopher Fry', which 'has rescued the theatre from the thraldom of middle-class vernacular in which it has been held, with rare intervals, since Tom Robertson, and given it once more a voice'.

It is characteristic of the confusion of critical values today that Mr Rattigan, and many others with him, should imagine that the voices of Mr Eliot and Mr Fry have anything in common. Mr Fry is certainly exuberant. His verse, with its tumbling imagery, almost batters an audience into submission. But if we examine his lines in detail, we find they resemble those of 'poet-dramatists' like Gordon Bottomley, though Fry's idiom is, of course, more fashionable:

Thomas: Oh no!
You can't postpone me. Since opening-time I've been
Propped up at the bar of heaven and earth, between
The wall-eye of the moon and the brandy-cask of the sun
Growling thick songs about jolly good fellows
In a mumping pub where the ceiling drips humanity,
Until I've drunk myself sick, and now, by Christ,
I mean to sleep it off in a stupor of dust
Till the morning after the day of judgement.
So put me on the waiting-list for your gallows
With a note recommending preferential treatment.
Tyson: Go away; you're an unappetizing young man
With a tongue too big for your brains. ...

The Lady's Not For Burning is not really about anything; it is a sort of conjuring trick – the quickness of the word deceives the ear – and the images, unrelated to any over-all pattern of meaning, remain a series of disconnected bright ideas. A similar criticism may be made of the ingenious phrases:

Cain. ...
a huskular strapling
With all his passions about him ...
Old Joe Adam all sin and bone ...

which decorate a more serious work like *A Sleep of Prisoners.*

Mr Eliot, we know, has long envied the music-hall comedian his direct contact with his audience: and we would, I think, be justified in assuming that one of his reasons for turning to the drama was the desire to break out of the cultural isolation from which the modern poet suffers. 'Our problem should be', he wrote in *The Possibility of a Poetic Drama*, 'to take a form of entertainment of a crude sort and subject it to the process which would leave it a form of art.' The form of entertainment he has chosen is the drawing-room comedy, that 'sets a piece of the world as we know it in a place by itself'. The list of characters in *The Family Reunion*, for example, would suit a play by Maugham or Coward or Rattigan; it is patently 'a play about modern educated people'. The 'process' to which this 'form' is subjected is twofold: first the story or action refers to a Greek original; it has a skeleton of myth, presumably to help represent 'what is eternal in man', though this can be of use only to the author, for he cannot rely today on an audience understanding such an allusion, and Mr Eliot has himself recorded that he had to 'go into detailed explanation' to convince his friends that the source of *The Cocktail Party* was the *Alcestis* of Euripides. Second, the dialogue is written in verse. ('Surely there is some legitimate craving, not restricted to a few persons, which only the verse play can satisfy.') This verse has 'a rhythm close to contemporary speech'; the lines are 'of varying length and varying number of syllables, with a caesura and three stresses', and the whole is intended as 'a design of human actions and words, such as to present at once the two aspects of dramatic and musical order'.

Few can doubt the value of Mr Eliot's experiments, and of the acute analyses he has made of the problems of poetic drama. But in spite of the care, the skill, the intelligence that has gone to their making, these plays lack vitality because they are not informed with human sympathy. In the arbitrary hierarchy of spiritual values that the characters represent there is no charity. We are shown their actions, we are told about their motives, we see their progress to the solution Mr Eliot has arranged for them, but we do not feel any of this. It is impossible to believe in Colby Simpkins's future ordination, or to be convinced by the martyrdom of the young lady in *The Cocktail Party*. This lack of warmth and energy is strikingly brought out if we compare a page or two of any of these plays with that remarkable fragment *Sweeney Agonistes* – surely the finest piece of dramatic verse Mr Eliot has ever written. We might apply to it his own remarks on Yeats's last play, *Purgatory*, 'in which ... he solved his problems of speech in verse, and laid all his successors under obligation to him'. When we think of *Prufrock* and *Gerontion*, where verse follows with insidious intent and exhilarating vigour the quirk of character, the shift of mood and feeling, we may feel like applying to Mr Eliot the remarks he makes about Browning, in the essay entitled 'Three Voices of Poetry':

> What personage, in a play by Browning, remains alive in the mind? On the other hand who can forget Fra Lippo Lippi, or Andrea del Sarto ... It would seem without further examination, from Browning's mastery of the dramatic monologue, and his very modest achievement in the drama, that the two forms must be essentially different. Is there ... another voice ... the voice of the dramatic poet whose dramatic gifts are best exercised outside the theatre?

It may be significant that Mr Eliot's most successful play should be *Murder in the Cathedral*, which was written for the Canterbury Festival, and was therefore intended to fufil a specific social purpose, a purpose, moreover, with which the drama has still a living and real, if tenuous, connexion – the performance in aid of the parish funds. The poet was here playing a traditional role; his gifts served a cause and commended beliefs which he shared with his audience, and this situation seems to have liberated energies which have given the play strength enough to dominate an audience in a public theatre, a greater strength, it seems to me, than is exhibited in any of the plays which use the conventions of drawing-room comedy.

Shaw once said that what was wrong with 'the drama of the day' was that it was 'written for the theatres instead of from its own inner necessity'. The sort of play that Shaw was complaining about is still the staple fare in the West End theatre. But thanks to him that fare now usually includes a few dishes more nourishing than any he had to feed on in the days when he was a dramatic critic. His precepts and his example have had their effect. Shaw cannot be considered a major artist (he ranked himself about number ten among English playwrights); but we can with some justice claim that our best dramatic work is livelier, more serious, more deeply concerned with life than it has been at any time since the days of Fielding. In so far as any one man is responsible for this, that man is Shaw.

THE COMEDY OF IDEAS: CROSS-CURRENTS IN THE FICTION AND DRAMA OF THE TWENTIETH CENTURY

R. C. CHURCHILL

THERE has been a great deal of interest taken recently in Henry James's abortive flirtation with the drama, it being widely recognized that this experience was one of the chief influences behind the intensely dramatized form of his later novels. What has not been remarked is the curious fact that at the same time as James was trying to get the dramatic virtues into the novel, Bernard Shaw, who had started as a novelist and had the same failure in fiction as James had on the stage, was trying to get the virtues of the novel into the drama. Shaw was to become the leading platform debater, as well as the leading dramatist of ideas, of the twentieth century; and there was nothing that James liked better, whether in writing or in conversation, than to discuss the problems of his art. Yet, though the two men did correspond on this subject, no record of a full-scale debate has survived.

We can, nevertheless, imagine roughly how it would have gone. In the correspondence of James and H. G. Wells[1] we have the classic case of the literary artist versus the journalist, summed up by Wells when he wrote: 'To you literature like painting is an end, to me literature like architecture is a means, it has a use ... I had rather be called a journalist than an artist, that is the essence of it.' He was to satirize the literary artist of the James type in *Boon* (1915), as he had satirized the sociologist of the type of the Webbs in *The New Machiavelli* (1911). Both James and Wells, however, were inclined to exaggerate their position. In reaction against Wells's immense international reputation,[2] James over-emphasized his own unpopularity. He was not in fact so unpopular as he frequently lamented. One of his novels, *The American*, appeared in Nelson's Sevenpenny Library, as 'an example of the best work of one who is regarded with justice as among our greatest living novelists ... as one of the most perfect examples of Mr Henry James's remarkable art'.[3] On his side, in reaction against the beliefs of the James-Conrad–Ford circle, Wells was inclined to over-emphasize the reliance of his fiction on the topics of the moment, saying that most of his work would survive only so long as their ideas remained current. This view is obviously correct in regard to such novels as *Ann Veronica* (1909); but in the best of his social comedies, such as *Kipps* (1905) – which James thought his masterpiece – and in the best of the scientific romances and short stories, like *The Time Machine* (1895) and *The Country of the Blind* (1911), he attains the stature of a literary artist of a minor but decidedly original kind. The 'idea' is still the mainspring, but it involves the moral idea of the novel proper and, though most of such stories had a 'use' in their time, it would be untrue to say that they are now readable only as period pieces.

Shaw in retrospect is connected with Wells: we see them as embattled Socialists and Evolutionists debating endlessly, on platform and in print, with the Distributism and the Christian Liberalism of Hilaire Belloc and G. K. Chesterton, all four very much in the public eye. And he would have echoed many of Wells's remarks in his controversy with James. An inner distinction is there, nevertheless, as well as an outward resemblance. Wells was a teacher of science and a writer of scientific textbooks before he became a novelist; Shaw was a music critic, and one of the best in modern times, before he won fame as a playwright. We are apt to think of him as merely the propagator of Ibsen (or William Archer's Ibsen) and Samuel Butler; we forget his love of music and the fact that his writing was always deeply influenced by the four masters of his youth: Bunyan, Blake, Dickens, and Ruskin. Wells in his novels of ideas may have 'rather been called a journalist than an artist'; in his dramatic criticism and his drama of ideas Shaw would have queried the distinction.

He was convinced that the 'new drama' must compete in elaboration with the contemporary novel. He was thinking of Meredith, Hardy, and Gissing rather than of James,[4] and James of course was writing novels like this:[5]

> 'She gave me a lot of money.'
>
> Mrs Wix stared. 'And pray what did you do with a lot of money?'
>
> 'I gave it to Mrs Beale.'
>
> 'And what did Mrs Beale do with it?'

'She sent it back.'

'To the Countess? Gammon!' said Mrs Wix. She disposed of that plea as effectually as Susan Ash.

'Well, I don't care!' Maisie replied. 'What I mean is that you don't know about the rest.'

'The rest? What rest?'

and was soon to graduate to this:[6]

'... I can bear anything.'

'Oh "bear"!' Mrs Assingham fluted.

'For love,' said the Princess.

Fanny hesitated. 'Of your father.'

'For love,' Maggie repeated.

It kept her friend watching. 'Of your husband?'

'For love,' Maggie said again.

That is the novel partaking of the dramatic emotion of the stage play. Shaw, at the same time, was writing plays with enormous stage directions, being convinced that the time had gone by when one could just say, like the Elizabethans, 'another part of the field', and leave it at that. Shaw not only set his scene in the utmost detail, but gave his actors an embarrassment of help by describing both the outward appearance and the personality of his characters:

Major Sergius Saranoff, the original of the portrait in Raina's room, is a tall romantically handsome man, with the physical hardihood, the high spirit, and the susceptible imagination of an untamed mountaineer chieftain. But his remarkable personal distinction is of a characteristically civilized type. The ridges of his eyebrows, curving with an interrogative twist round the projections at the outer corners; his jealously observant eye; his nose, thin, keen, and apprehensive in spite of the pugnacious high bridge and large nostril; his assertive chin would not be out of place in a Parisian salon, shewing that the clever imaginative barbarian has an acute critical faculty which has been thrown into intense activity by the arrival of western civilization in the Balkans. The result is precisely what the advent of nineteenth-century thought first produced in England: to wit, Byronism. By his brooding on the perpetual failure, not only of others, but of himself, to live up to his ideals ... (etc., etc.: continues for twenty more lines in the collected edition).

This massive detail,[7] to say nothing of his lengthy prefaces, makes his plays something of a cross between dramatic literature and the novel; assisted by the accident of his becoming famous in print first, then on the stage afterwards. James's move in the opposite direction was partly due to his irritation at the sprawling habits of the Victorian three-volume novel, particularly those previously serialized in magazines, the novelist padding out his numbers against the clock. It cannot be denied, however, that most of James's later novels, for all their dramatic merits, make heavier reading than he intended; nor that, despite the readability as well as the theatrical qualities of the early Shaw, there was a corresponding limitation in the Shavian conception of the dramatic art.

This is best seen in his view of Shakespeare. Shaw the music critic spoke well of the 'orchestration' of Shakespeare's verse; but his portrait of Shakespeare in *The Dark Lady of the Sonnets* (1910) is one that could only have been produced by a writer who combined a deep appreciation of music with a total misconception of dramatic poetry. His Shakespeare carries a notebook about with him and when anyone utters a 'strain of music' he copies it down for future use. Thus, when the Beefeater exclaims: 'Angels and ministers of grace defend us!', down it goes in Shakespeare's 'tablets' for future use in *Hamlet*! The limited truth behind this misconception is, of course, that the Elizabethan drama, like the Authorized Version of the Bible, was based on the common speech of the time; but what Shaw failed to realize was that poetic drama is not drama with poetry added to it but a separate species in which the drama and the poetry are one and the same.[8] A related point is that Shaw romanticized a poet in *Candida* (1894) and a painter in *The Doctor's Dilemma* (1906), both highly unconvincing figures; he would not have made the same mistake with a composer.

I cannot myself see entire success either in the majority of James's later 'dramatic' fiction or in most of Shaw's early 'novel-plays'. They were written at roughly the same time, *c.* 1890–1910, and they have, I believe, different but related weaknesses. James's intention was so to dramatize the novel that all extraneous matter could be eliminated and the attention of the reader fixed throughout on the main scenes, like a spectator in the theatre; Shaw's intention was to provide plays with so extensive an elaboration that they could bear intellectual comparison with the novels of a Meredith. We cannot doubt the limited success of these endeavours, James's later novels being on as lofty a level compared with the average Victorian three-decker as Shaw's early plays compared with the average Victorian melodrama or farce. But do such novels as *The Awkward Age* and *The Golden Bowl* compare favourably with *Middlemarch* or with the best of James's own earlier work? Is not their comparative unreadability partly due to a misconception of form, similar to Shaw's lack of dramatic art compared with Shakespeare or Synge? It is with the results of this curious juncture in mind that I should like to make some observations on the position of the literature of ideas in the twentieth century.

* * *

We can imagine roughly, as I say, the arguments used by James and Shaw in justification of their contrary proceeding. Much of their debate would have been talking at cross-purposes, but not all of it; for James was as profoundly versed in painting as Shaw was in music, so that each had a standard in a different art to which literature could profitably be compared. James's analogies with painting, in the prefaces to the novels, are as frequent as Shaw's orchestral analogies in the prefaces to the plays. Sooner or later, however, they would, as it were, have come to blows: they would have started hurling Dickens at each other, and both would have been justified in their ammunition.

For we cannot proceed very far in any discussion of the relation of the English novel to the English drama without bringing in Dickens. He is the most dramatic of our novelists, though he did not deliberately incur the dramatic responsibilities in the manner of James. In his autobiographies James gives him the title of 'Master' along with George Eliot, and he had the privilege of meeting both Masters personally.[9] There are perhaps two main currents in the English novel, the one flowing from Fielding and Smollett to Scott and Dickens, the other from Richardson and Jane Austen to George Eliot and James. We need not discuss the minor links; it is sufficient for our purpose to note that the novel proper in the twentieth century has mostly stemmed from the latter source, the novel of ideas from the former. There is a tradition of comedy in English fiction which originally sprang from the drama, which reached its highest point in

Dickens, and which in our time is principally found in the novel of ideas from Wells to Orwell and in the novel-drama of Shaw. They are the inheritors here, not only of the comic richness and the concern for social justice of Fielding and Dickens, but of that looseness of art in the general run of eighteenth- and nineteenth-century literature against which writers like James and Conrad reacted. They were right so to react; but we must not put all the righteousness on the one side. What a sprawl is *Chuzzlewit* compared with James's *Lady* or Conrad's *Nostromo*! If James had written *Chuzzlewit*, we can be sure that the novel would have been a unified work of art, as Dickens's novel is not; but there would have been no artistic necessity for such characters as Mrs Gamp or Young Bailey, or indeed for the whole Columbian business, and it is precisely there that the comic genius of *Chuzzlewit* mainly resides. Mrs Gamp, like Sam Weller, was an afterthought, a sudden flush of comic inspiration; and when you write a novel on the principles of Flaubert or James you keep to your original plan, with no afterthoughts permitted.[10] It was the practice of James, particularly after his dramatic experience, to draw up what he called 'a really detailed scenario, an intensely structural, intensely hinged and jointed preliminary frame'; it was the practice of the early Dickens to draw up a rough plan and improvise the details as he went along – a practice encouraged by publication in instalments. It is the whole achievement of the work of art which we admire in James (though some of his novels, including *What Maisie Knew*, were serialized in magazines); in Dickens we often forget the over-all plan in our admiration of the details.

I submit the following proposition: that the literature of ideas in the twentieth century is mainly Dickensian, both in its virtues and in its vices, and that to criticize it by the standards of Henry James is beside the point. It is the English tradition of comedy, both in its admirable detail and its casual sprawl, which is inherited by writers like Shaw, Wells, Chesterton, Huxley, and Orwell. In *Unto This Last* Ruskin praised 'the essential value and truth of Dickens's writings', singling out *Hard Times* ('to my mind, in several respects, the greatest he has written') and advising us not to 'lose the use of Dickens's wit and insight, because he chooses to speak in a circle of stage fire'.[11] This is eminently just and reasonable, but nevertheless it was that disparaged fire which produced Mrs Gamp and most of the other memorable Dickens characters as well as the melodrama and the sentimentality which Ruskin rightly deplored.

Paraphrasing Ruskin, I would say: let us not lose the wit and insight of the best of our literature of ideas because these virtues are embodied in writings which, as works of art, do not stand comparison with even the lesser productions of our major literary artists. Compared with Synge, Shaw seems as insecure an artist as Wells compared with James, or Huxley compared with Lawrence; but Shaw on the stage, though comparable at his best with Sheridan and Oscar Wilde, is not the whole Shaw: he has a further dimension in non-dramatic literature, as the novels and essays of Wells, Belloc, Chesterton, Huxley, and Orwell are variants of the same species. The literature of ideas in our time is a very untidy business; but no more so than in the novels (or assorted scrapbooks) of Peacock, Disraeli, and Samuel Butler.

Proportion is the essence of the serious literary artist; comic exaggeration, if often for a serious purpose, is the keynote alike of Dickens and the twentieth-century literature of ideas: exaggeration in all its forms, of speech and idea and procedure. Where Dickens in the preface to *Little Dorrit* cannot write simply of 'a small boy carrying a baby' but must needs write 'the smallest boy I ever conversed with, carrying the largest baby I ever saw'; so in *The Truth about Pyecraft* (1903), Wells writes of the '*British Encyclopaedia* (tenth edition)', where the edition is absolutely irrelevant; in *Arms and the Man* (1894) Shaw puts his ideas about Byronism into a stage-direction and writes a preface to the gigantic *Back to Methuselah* sequence (1921) which is itself a hundred pages long and the wittiest summary of the Darwinian controversy ever written; Chesterton pads out to novel length the simplest of short stories, like *Manalive* (1912), as if Hans Andersen had taken three volumes to tell the story of the Ugly Duckling; Huxley in *Brave New World* (1932) cannot resist the temptation to quote the nursery rhymes of the future: 'Streptocock-Gee to Banbury T, to see a fine bathroom and W.C.', etc.; and Orwell in *1984* (1949) inserts some notes about modern idiom he had previously discussed in the essay *Politics and the English Language*. ... In all these cases, and any reader will supply a dozen more, there is evidently no premeditation, but ideas springing to the mind of the writers as they go along, too rich to be left out, too absorbing not to be carried to the bitter end. Equally, it is in these details, as it is in Mrs Gamp in *Chuzzlewit*, that the value of their writings mainly resides.

Huxley himself, under the thin disguise of the character Philip Quarles in *Point Counter Point* (1928), discussed the difference between the novelist of ideas and what he termed the 'congenital' novelist. And in that novel he made an attempt to proceed from being the former into being the latter. I believe we should be grateful that the attempt was, on the whole, a failure. Compared with the best of Forster or Lawrence, the novel does not rank very high as a work of art. Huxley has since gone back to his early style, producing novels of ideas like *Brave New World* and *After Many a Summer* (1939), which, like the early Peacockian Huxley, make up for their artistic weaknesses in the exuberance of their ideas and the fertility of their comic invention. Huxley and Orwell were to the generations of the twenties, thirties, and forties what Shaw, Wells, and Chesterton were to the pre-1914 public; comparison with a James is as irrelevant as comparison with a Joyce. They are writers like Wells's Mr Britling, who have 'ideas about everything ... in the utmost profusion', and proceed to pour them out in an unending series of novels, essays, and pamphlets. It is a matter of comparative unimportance for them whether their views are expressed in fictional or non-fictional form: a state of mind incomprehensible to a literary artist like James or Conrad. Whole chunks of Huxley's novels could be printed as separate essays with only a little alteration; the opening of Chesterton's *Napoleon of Notting Hill* (1904) could have developed into an essay with equal plausibility, and some of the essays in *Tremendous Trifles* (1909) could have developed quite easily into stories.

The literary artist in fiction is interested above all in the personal relations of his characters: 'I have never taken *ideas* but always *characters* for my starting point', wrote Turgenev. 'I never attempted to "create a character" if in the first place I had in mind an idea and not a living person.'[12] The writer of the novel or the drama of ideas is apt to conceive of his ideas first, then to invent characters to embody them. We remember *Ann Veronica* as a novel about the condition-of-woman question; it is difficult to recall anything about Ann Veronica Stanley as an individual woman. Wells, like Shaw, however, has something of the Dickensian gift for comic speech; if we do not commonly remember his characters as persons, more often as the mouthpieces of the author, we do sometimes recall their characteristic idiom.

There is a related difference in real life between the literary artist and the novelist or dramatist of ideas. The latter are apt to be 'characters' in themselves, often public figures known to everyone in rough outline, as Shaw the flamboyant Irishman, Wells the Cockney prophet, Chesterton the rolling English rover, Orwell the Old Etonian tramp ... We do not conjure up such a vision, or such a caricature, of writers like Synge, James, or Forster: their personalities are more private, their art more impersonal. It must be difficult for a writer who is a 'character' in his own right to keep himself out of his work, and the plays of Shaw are as full of Shavian figures as the novels (and biographies) of Chesterton of Chestertonian eccentrics. Comstock in *Keep the Aspidistra Flying* (1936) and Bowling in *Coming Up for Air* (1939) are composite figures, composed in equal parts of the ordinary man as seen by Orwell and Orwell himself; this actually makes them very 'uncomstock',[13] liable to speak as often in their creator's character as in their own.

There is subtle, ironic comedy in the work of such writers as James and Forster. But the kind of laughter that Dickens often provokes – 'Laughter holding both his sides' – is more frequently found in our time in the literature of ideas. It is the kind of laughter provoked by the deliberately absurd and exaggerated: qualities – which can so easily become vices – that we do not associate with the literary artists of our age, but rather with those who, like the early Dickens, think of their best strokes as they go along. The most memorable line in Orwell's *Animal Farm* (1945), for instance – the revised revolutionary slogan: 'All animals are equal but some animals are more equal than others' – was evidently, like Mrs Harris, an inspiration of the moment.

'Heavens, how we laughed!' wrote Murry, reflecting on the impact of Wells on his generation.[14] This seems to me the right attitude to adopt, and many readers of a later generation would echo Murry's words in relation to Huxley or Orwell. One would not claim too much for such writers; the distinction between the literary artist and the journalist still holds true. At the same time, we must not forget the significance of James's failure in the theatre and the relative failure of most of his later 'dramatic' novels; Shaw's 'novel-drama' has a similar limitation as literary art. Yet our literature of ideas as a whole has managed to carry on something of the Dickensian tradition of English comedy. In an increasingly cosmopolitan literary world, that is an achievement by no means to be despised.

NOTES

1. *Henry James and H. G. Wells*, ed. L. Edel and G. N. Ray (1958). For the less extensive correspondence between James and Shaw, see *The Complete Plays of Henry James*, ed. L. Edel (1949).

2. '... he had become the chief representative of English literature upon the European continent. In every bookshop in France you would see, in the early years of this century, the impressive rows of his translated works ... I believe it was on the immense sales of his early scientific stories and romances that the success of the great French publishing house, the Mercure de France, was mainly founded.' (J. M. Murry, *Adelphi*, October 1946; reprinted *Little Reviews Anthology*, 1948, p. 188.)

3. I quote Nelson's advertisement.

4. Meredith is the novelist he actually mentions. See Preface, *Plays Pleasant and Unpleasant* (1898), Vol. I, p. xxi.

5. *What Maisie Knew* (1897, p. 544), ch. xxv. Written 1896–7.

6. *The Golden Bowl* (1904), Book IV, ch. VI.

7. The example is from *Arms and the Man* (1894), Act II.

8. To paraphrase Granville-Barker. Eliot has made much the same point. Shaw complained that the Folio 'gives us hardly anything but the bare lines'! If only, he wrote, Shakespeare 'instead of merely writing out his lines' had prepared his plays for publication 'in competition with fiction as elaborate' as that of Meredith, 'what a light they would shed ... on the history of the sixteenth century!' (ref. Note 4 above).

9. See *Autobiography* (1957), reprint in 1 vol. of *A Small Boy and Others* (1913), *Notes of a Son and Brother* (1914), and the unfinished *The Middle Years* (1917).

10. In *The Maturity of Dickens* (1959) Monroe Engel, whose object is 'to insist that Dickens can and should be read with pleasure and no restriction of intelligence by post-Jamesian adults', treats Mrs Gamp simply as 'an example of the callous brutality bred by poverty'.

11. *Unto This Last*, Essay I, note to para. 10: World's Classics edition, p. 26.

12. Two separate quotations here juxtaposed: cited in Miriam Allott, *Novelists on the Novel* (1959), p. 103.

13. The name Comstock is an interesting anticipation of the 'Newspeak' of *1984*. The opposite would be 'uncomstock' – a serious crime in Oceania.

14. J. M. Murry, *Adelphi*, October 1946; reprinted *Little Reviews Anthology*, 1948, p. 189.

THE PROSE OF THOUGHT

E. W. F. TOMLIN

Professor of Philosophy and Literature, University of Nice

It is a commonplace that the behaviour of language in prose is different from its behaviour in verse; what the difference is may not be so apparent. As with many distinctions so fine as to resist precise formulation, an example may illuminate it. The lines are from Yeats's *The Crazed Moon*:

> Crazed through much child-bearing,
> The moon is staggering in the sky.

The image, a brilliant one, is to be seized in itself. The thought behind the image enjoys no independent existence, affords no additional satisfaction. Concept and intuition are one, but only in the sense that the distinction has not yet arisen. The language of prose, though not without this inner quality, enjoys at the same time a kind of external existence; it lives for something beyond itself, namely the communication of a meaning or idea. It is a means to an end. In prose we first become aware of the distinction between what is said and what is meant; and this is evidently a stage which has something to do with man's attainment, if always uncertain grasp, of his 'humanity'. Hence some of the repetitiveness of prose, and the still greater repetitiveness of conversation. The writer or speaker has to struggle to maintain intelligibility – 'I mean ...', 'What I mean is ...', etc. Furthermore, within all rational exposition there exist two elements, mutually opposed and therefore generative of tension. These elements may be called the *dialectical* and the *eristical*. Dialectical exposition is that which elucidates its subject after the manner of dialogue. There is statement, counter-statement, and conclusion; the primary appeal is to reason. Eristic has not merely a different but usually a concealed aim; it seeks not to persuade but to impose; and this it does by deliberate appeal to sentiment and prejudice. As the Oxford Dictionary says, the aim of eristic is not truth but victory. The ideal prose of thought would be that in which the two elements were in equilibrium.

Given this definition, the prose of thought might be expected to find its most perfect embodiment in works of philosophy. For philosophy, since the time of its systematic development, is committed to the putting forward of arguments; and arguments are valid only in so far as they conform to rational canons of inference. It is true that Hume, and in our century Dewey, tried to demonstrate that inferential thinking arose not from some rational constraint in the mind, but from acquired habit or custom; but in Hume's philosophical works, and in Dewey's logical treatises, the exposition clearly lays claim to be rational; these thinkers are stating a case, not simply reflecting a vagrant 'state of mind'.[1] Nor is conceptual thinking to be regarded as the monopoly of civilized peoples: Lévy-Bruhl came to abandon his idea of a 'pre-logical' stage of thought, and the conceptual ability of primitive peoples has been stressed recently by Lévi-Strauss. A work such as the 'Memphite Drama', which dates from the fourth millennium, is at least as well argued as many later theological treatises, and remains more intelligible than some; and the myths of the Bushmen and the Ainu, to name two peoples who until recently followed a Neolithic way of life, are not irrational, if by that is meant devoid of sense. Any society in which there is a recognizable legal system, or a set of regulations not arbitrarily to be set aside, must be capable, in its exposition and administration of the law, of the prose of thought.

The analogy with jurisprudence is, as we shall see, strictly relevant; for the task of the courts is not merely to expound the law but to sustain a case. Style is needed. And the same is true of philosophy, or the rational inquiry into the basic principles of any field of speculation. Ideally, the task of philosophy would be, in Brand Blanshard's words, 'to see what is the case' rather than 'to make out a case'.[2] If the case were judiciously and honestly stated to perfection, it would at the same time be 'made'. In practice, however, since every word of philosophy has a polemical aspect and arises in a context of argument, the function of style is not merely to present but to persuade; and that is why the prose of thought cannot dispense with an element of eristic.

Certainly, British philosophy, to take that alone, can claim its masters of style. Even those who remain indifferent or allergic to their thought may find Berkeley, Hume, Mill, and Bradley satisfying and elegant writers. Latterly, we have witnessed a revolution in the idea of philosophy, at least in Britain; and this has affected the way in which philosophy has come to be written. One of the tenets of this new view is that certain philosophical problems, especially those termed metaphysical, arise from intractable elements in language. In other words, our common language is riddled with ambiguity. Artificial languages need to be constructed for the assertion of rational truth. A purely referential or scientific language would presumably be one voided of every ambiguity, every emotive element. There would be no 'style', no verbal opacity; merely the transparent revelation of thought. Moreover, it would be a *fixed* language. What is called the analytical or linguistic movement in philosophy has a double aim. First, it seeks to achieve the purification of language, even to the point of trying to escape from common language altogether. Secondly, it seeks to effect the liquidation of systems of thought held to batten upon linguistic ambiguity. The 'elimination of metaphysics', to use the common phrase, is the consequence of the supposed elimination of a flaw in language.

The justification for referring thus early to a particular philosophical movement is that the theory behind it has exerted considerable influence outside the sphere of philosophy proper. Works on theology, history, literary criticism, law, even political theory and economics, reveal the influence of the linguistic movement. Without the early writings of Russell, G. E. Moore, and Wittgenstein, such works as Richards's *Principles of Literary Criticism* and its offspring Empson's *Seven Types of Ambiguity* might never have been written. The same applies to more recent studies such as Frazer's *Economic Thought and Language* (1936), Weldon's *Vocabulary of Politics* (1953), and the symposium *New Essays in Philosophical Theology* (1955).

By contrast, we find that, in countries in which the analytical movement has failed to take hold, philosophy and theology are still written in the traditional manner. To take France as an example, the *Revue de Métaphysique et Morale* (January–March 1952, p. 69) refers to the British analytical school as '*un mouvement imparfaitement connu en France*'. The philosophical writings of Sartre, Marcel, Merleau-Ponty, and Bachelard, however revolutionary they may be, belong to the orthodox classico-literary tradition. There is a stylistic link between these writers and Bergson, just as there is a link between Bergson and Maine de Biran. The last great English philosophical writer in this tradition, if we exclude McTaggart, is F. H. Bradley. Much of Bradley's writings can be classed as *belles lettres*; they remain a quarry for the anthologist. Bradley is distinguished from Arnold on the one hand and from his fellow-idealists on the other, by his greater analytical powers and his mastery of logic. Yet it would seem that people today read *The Principles of Logic* (1883) less for instruction than for the spectacle of a sustained literary and polemical performance.

The decay of idealism, which set in many years before Bradley's death in 1924, is visible as much in the abstraction-ridden prose of Lord Haldane as in the basic poverty of his thought. (It is only fair to say that Haldane disliked the term idealist; but it is not what one likes to be called, it is what one is.) Similarly, the balance and precision of such an early work as Moore's *Principia Ethica* (1905) marks a new departure in philosophy, the birth of a New Realism. The 'philosophy of common sense', which Moore initiated, needed a medium of expression radically different from that of the idealists; it needed plainness, an approximation to common usage. Stripped of its conventional arguments, the idealism of the neo-Hegelian variety consisted for the most part in a prolonged hymn to the Absolute. The flowing periods, the incantatory rhythm, the outbursts of lyricism, were all part of a metaphysical ritual. To embrace Reality-as-a-whole, as Bradley sought to do in *Appearance and Reality* (1893), was necessarily to have recourse to the grand manner. Theology in the nineteenth century was likewise nurtured in the neo-Hegelian tradition; Edward Caird was a theologian as well as a philosopher, and so was T. H. Green. Thus the sermon, once capable of inspiring excellent prose, has suffered degeneration no less from its worn-out phraseology than from the absence of trained congregations. It is surprising to what extent much modern theology has remained linked to a form of philosophy long outmoded.[3] Moral exhortation does not always make for good prose, though it may provide material for rhetoric and for inferior poetry.

By way of illustrating the difference between the old and the new prose of thought, it may be illuminating to compare an extract from Bradley with a passage from Moore. Here is Bradley (*Appearance and Reality*):

> Reality is one experience, self-pervading and superior to mere relations. Its character is the opposite of that fabled extreme which is barely mechanical, and it is, in the end, the sole perfect realization of spirit. . . . Outside of spirit there is not, and there cannot be, any reality, and the more that anything is spiritual, so much the more is it veritably real.

And further:

> Spirit is the unity of the manifold, in which the externality of the manifold has utterly ceased.

Here is Moore (*Principia Ethica*):

> My point is that good is a simple notion, just as 'yellow' is a simple notion: that, just as you cannot, by any manner of means, explain to anyone who does not already know it, what yellow is, so you cannot explain what good is. Definitions of the kind that I was asking for, definitions which describe the real nature of the object or notion denoted by a word, and which do not merely tell us what the word is used to mean, are only possible when the object or notion in question is something complex. You can give a definition of a horse, because a horse has many different properties and qualities, all of which you can enumerate. But when you have enumerated them all, when you have reduced a horse to its simplest terms, then you can no longer define those terms ... And so it is with all objects, not previously known, which we are able to define. They are all complex, all composed of parts, which may themselves, in the first instance, be capable of definition, but which must in the end be reducible to simplest parts, which can no longer be defined. But yellow and good, we say, are not complex; they are notions of that simple kind, out of which definitions are composed and with which the power of further defining ceases.

I have deliberately chosen Bradley, and not the most rhetorical example of Bradley at that, because the selection of a more impassioned piece, such as one taken from Stirling's rarefied work *The Secret of Hegel* (1865), would scarcely have been fair. Even so, this brief extract, despite its apparent simplicity, is found on examination to be blurred by imprecise terminology and to be informed with an undercurrent of rhetoric. 'Self-pervading', which has meaning in Whitehead's philosophy of organism, acts here rather like a plug of emotive cotton-wool. The use of 'mere' to qualify 'relations', like the use of 'fabled' to qualify 'extreme', is a calculated thrust at less lofty philosophies. 'Veritably' as qualifying 'real' is superfluous. Moreover, in the final sentence, the words 'utterly ceased', besides being curiously inept in the context, form a kind of pseudo-eschatological climax; we are in the world of the *Upanishads*. By comparison, the passage of Moore makes a direct appeal to the reader's intelligence; it is turned outwards, following patiently, perhaps a little pedestrianly, the movement of thought. Its peroration, if such it can be called, is addressed not to the emotions but to the reason. This is demonstrated in the use it makes in conclusion of the same verb, 'ceases', as that which terminates the passage from Bradley.[4]

Moore is a transitional writer; he remains, for all his commonsense, a stylist. He has balance and decorum. As we know, he exerted no small influence on the aestheticism of Bloomsbury;[5] there is even a stylistic link between him and J. M. Keynes. The effort towards plainness, towards the lowering of temperature to that of cold statement, is best observed in certain early associates, though not always disciples, of Moore. Of these, one of the most interesting is Cook Wilson. *Statement and Inference* (1926), a posthumously selected volume of Wilson's lectures and notes, gives the surface-appearance of meticulous, orderly, but essentially 'deflating' expression. A more powerful and complex thinker, likewise reluctant to publish, was Wittgenstein himself. With the exception of the *Tractatus Logico-Philosophicus*, which he wrote when a prisoner of war, and the *Philosophical Investigations*, which he composed to deter the plagiarists, Wittgenstein's philosophy took the form of a conversational game, an exercise in verbal dialectic. The *Blue Book* and the *Brown Book* consist of *viva voce* transcripts, but even so the transcription probably dissatisfied him. In the exercise of speaking or thinking aloud, he felt he was less liable to deceive himself, less prone to fall into verbal misrepresentation. 'Consider this example: you tell me to write a few lines, and while I am doing so, you ask, "Do you feel something in your hand while you are writing?" I say, "Yes, I have a peculiar feeling" – Can't I say to myself when I write, "I have *this* feeling"? Of course I can say it'[6] – and so on. This technique of conversational analysis has been developed, and indeed carried to an extreme, by John Wisdom. Here is a typical example:

> You remember it was said – to stop the worry it was said – 'He has the measle germ' just means 'He will give all the measle-reactions'. Now this is incorrect. But that again is not the point. The point is that this answer is too soothing. Or rather not too soothing – nothing could be that, everything's absolutely all right in metaphysics – but it's too sickly soothing. It's soothing without requiring of us that act of courage, that flinging away of our battery of crutches, which is required in order to realize that everything's all right. This phenomenalist answer soothes without demanding this change of heart only by soothing deceptively and saying that this alarming hippopotamus is only a horse that lives in rivers. It's true that the hippopotamus is quite O.K. and not at all carnivorous and won't hurt anybody who treats him right – that treats him like a hippopotamus has to be treated; but it's a mistake to soothe people by telling them he's a horse because, though that may soothe them for a moment, they will soon find out that to treat them like a horse is not satisfactory.
>
> (*Other Minds*, 1952, p. 73)

The point of interest in this passage (which departs so far from philosophical decorum as to betray faint echoes of Gertrude Stein) is that the search for clarity, the unmasking of ambiguity by trying to catch language unawares at its own game, has transported philosophy from the heights of fine writing to the ground level of common speech and even lower. With its nervous colloquialism – there is only one technical term, 'phenomenalist', which seems curiously out of place – it makes use of every device of common speech. Yet such writing has significantly failed to pass through the stage of referential language. Despite attempts to write philosophy in logical notation, that stage has remained not so much an ideal as a chimera; for such language, purged of every emotive element, could not remain a means of communication. Its very fixity would render it ineffective. In the work of the philosophical analysts, and even in the most rigorous of logical positivists, we find not the absence of emotion, not an abandonment of the stylistic screen, but the adoption of studied plainness to convey a particular set of emotions. And these emotions are no less powerful in their way than those expressed by metaphysicians. It is hardly an accident that Cook Wilson, like his disciple Pritchard, not to mention Wittgenstein himself, proved ardent and even intemperate in debate. The *Proceedings of the Aristotelian Society*, together with the issues of the review *Analysis*, provide a wealth of examples of philosophical papers written in the style, at once suave and astringent, customary with linguistic philosophers; but the reader, or better still the listener, comes soon to perceive that this style is meant to convey its own emotional tone. No one is likely to describe the style of Sir Isaiah Berlin, written or spoken, as lacking in emotive power. Indeed it is in such philosophical writers as Berlin that the passion for accuracy, breaking through the fixity imposed upon it by doctrinaire analytical theory, issues once more in a torrent of eloquence.

An example of prose which, avoiding extremes, marshals its ideas with clarity, charm, and the kind of wit without which philosophy may easily fall into pretentiousness, is the following:

> Novelists, dramatists and biographers had always been satisfied to exhibit people's motives, thoughts, perturbations and habits by describing their doings, sayings, and imaginings, their grimaces, gestures and tones of voice. In concentrating on what Jane Austen concentrated on, psychologists began to find that these were, after all, the stuff and not the mere trappings of their subjects. They have, of course, continued to suffer unnecessary qualms of anxiety, lest this diversion of psychology from the task of describing the ghostly might not commit it to tasks of describing the merely mechanical. But the influence of the bogy of mechanism has for a century been dwindling because, among other reasons, during this period the biological sciences have established their title of 'sciences'. The Newtonian system is no longer the sole paradigm of natural science. Man need not be degraded to a machine by being denied to be a ghost in a machine. He might, after all, be a sort of animal, namely, a higher mammal. There has yet to be ventured the hazardous leap to the hypothesis that perhaps he is a man.
>
> The Behaviourists' methodological programme has been of revolutionary importance to the programme of psychology. But more, it has been one of the main sources of the philos-

ophical suspicion that the two-worlds story is a myth. It is a matter of relatively slight importance that the champions of this methodological principle have tended to espouse as well a kind of Hobbist theory, and even to imagine that the truth of mechanism is entailed by the truth of their theory of scientific research method in psychology.

It is not for me to say to what extent the concrete research procedures of practising psychologists have been affected by their long adherence to the two-worlds story, or to what extent the Behaviourist revolt has led to modifications of their methods. For all that I know, the ill effects of the myth may, on balance, have been outweighed by the good, and the Behaviourist revolt against it may have led to reforms more nominal than real. Myths are not always detrimental to the progress of theories. Indeed, in their youth they are often of inestimable value. Pioneers are, at the start, fortified by the dream that the New World is, behind its alien appearances, a sort of duplicate of the Old World, and the child is not so much baffled by a strange house if, wherever they may actually lead him, its bannisters feel to his hand like those he knew at home.

(Gilbert Ryle, *The Concept of Mind*, Chapter X, 'Psychology')

The prose of thought, then, is not prose which lacks emotive ambience; it is prose charged with the emotions most suited to conceptual or dialectical expression. Much hangs on that word 'suited'; it covers not merely 'fitting' but 'sincere'. Bearing in mind our initial distinction between dialectic and eristic argument, philosophy is the subject in which truth must in principle be arrived at; and in order to *arrive* at the truth it is necessary to lay bare every dogma, to unmask subterfuge, to strip away verbiage. Consequently, the movement towards colloquialism in philosophy represents an attempt, if a desperate one, to recapture the true spirit of dialectic, which is realized most effectively in dialogue. For it is only the practice of printing books that obscures the fact that all thought is 'spoken'. By contrast, eristic is an attempt, rarely successful over long periods, to appeal directly to the emotions by by-passing the rational faculty; it is an attempt to manage or manipulate the feelings. A most subtle form of eristic is the kind of writing labelled sentimental. Yet how are we to detect or measure *sincerity* in a writer – a writer not merely on philosophy but on any subject of rational inquiry? If, as T. E. Hulme says, 'style is a way of subduing the reader', we understand again why there must be an eristic element in all style. But we can be subdued in more than one way. We can be made to surrender our rational faculties altogether, or we can be persuaded to compose them in an act of voluntary assent.

In order to approach nearer to the criterion of sincerity, let us shift our attention from philosophy proper to another subject. First we must make a generalization, if only because limitations of space preclude lengthy examples. No writer, whatever his subject, can be judged solely on excerpts. He has his own particular range. In assessing him, this whole range must be taken into account, together with the level on which he deploys his ideas, and his prevailing tone. To know whether a writer rings true, we must sound him at regular intervals. His personality must show coherence; this is revealed often in the degree to which his argument is systematic. If 'personality' is considered too vague a thing to be conveyed by words, we may ask how personality can be expressed otherwise than through language. That is the only true meaning of '*le style, c'est l'homme*'.

The science of economics is of comparatively recent origin; it is an abstraction from political science. Consequently, works on economics show a tendency towards one of two extremes: either, like linguistic philosophy, they seek to employ pure symbolic notation, or, reacting against their own abstractness, they become a branch of 'social studies'. The style will vary accordingly. A work such as Marx's *Das Kapital* oscillates between the two poles; but because it is in the classical tradition of Adam Smith and Ricardo, as well as in the Hegelian philosophical tradition, and equally in the tradition of Hebrew prophecy, it is never, except in some of Part II, pure economic theory. Indeed, the assumption that Marxism is an economic theory instead of a social gospel has misled not merely individual men, but whole nations. In Britain, unlike France, theories such as Marxism, as well as those of Pareto and Henry George, have exerted little attraction, at least for most academic economists. The result is a tradition of writing at once graceful, clear, judicious; Alfred Marshall is still read for the possession of these qualities. With wider culture and greater powers of irony, J. M. Keynes continued the tradition of Marshall; but he combined objectivity with considerable social concern. In his work the eristic element is evident, though well under control: thus one of his volumes was aptly called *Essays in Persuasion* (1931).[7] A writer on economics of remarkable literary gifts was his senior, Philip Wicksteed. Wicksteed's *Commonsense of Political Economy* (1910) represents one of the most successful expositions of ideas, or of a single idea, of modern times. The idea is no less 'philosophical' for being an economic concept, that of Marginalism. Written in prose of sustained elegance, this great book possesses a clarity to be expected of the translator of Dante, though the style recalls that of Newman. There can be few treatises in which successive *sondages* over 800 pages yield such excellence of matter and manner:

> We have seen that a man's economic position depends not only on his powers but on his possessions. These possessions may embody the fresh output of current effort, or they may be accumulations, or they may consist in the control, secured by law, of the prime sources of all material wealth. The differentiation between the taxation of earned and unearned income reminds us that there is a vast revenue that someone is receiving though no one is earning it. Thus it is clear that if no one receives less than his current effort is worth, many receive a great deal more. There seems, then, to be nothing intrinsically monstrous in the idea of looking into this matter. If there are sources from which, apparently, anyone or everyone might receive more than he earns, or is worth to others, no proposal need be condemned simply because it contemplates certain classes receiving more than their output of effort is worth, as certain other classes do at present. Proposals for land nationalization, or for the collective control of the instruments of production, are dictated by the belief that we are in possession of a common patrimony which is not being administered in the common interest. But we should distinguish very clearly in our own minds between saying that a person is 'underpaid for his work', and saying that he has a claim to something more than 'mere payment for his work at its worth'.[8]
>
> (Vol. I, p. 341)

In intellectual works, the temptation of the learned expositor, or the gambit of the charlatan, is the adoption of a tone of unrelieved solemnity. The pedant, the legalist, and often the theologian, are perennial butts of satire; their manner of writing, inflated, lays itself open to parody. The test of sincerity may be not so much prolonged high seriousness or fervour, as the occasional ironic aside, the play of wit. These are means to the preservation of balance and sanity. In all serious writing, a certain elevation of tone is to be expected; flippancy and facetiousness are out of place. But we can be serious without being solemn. The portentousness and aridity of much economic writing, which at one time earned economics the name of the 'dismal science' and Coleridge's epithet 'solemn humbug', may have masked a vagueness about fundamentals, and in the case of those defending the established order a sense of moral uncertainty. Both are characteristic of John Stuart Mill, prior to his mental crisis and before the influence of Harriet Taylor. The muscle-bound prose of the young Mill, modelled on that of his father, contrasts markedly with the fine and flexible medium of the *Essay on Liberty* and the *Autobiography*: a mastery which, save for obvious reasons in the latter work, fell away sadly after the guiding-hand was removed. Today, the revival of economic studies and the liberation of that science from dogmas such as psychological hedonism have been responsible, one may suggest, for an increase in works at once serious and readable. Lord Robbins's well-known essay entitled *The Nature and Significance of Economic Science* (1932) and Mrs Joan Robinson's book *The Economics of Imperfect Competition* (1933), despite their abstract subject-matter, show command of the prose of thought as much by their abundant irony and wit as by their patient analysis of particular doctrines. An example Mrs Robinson's 'Digression on Rent' (Chapter VIII), a topic not as a rule productive of liveliness. Such qualities belong to effective dialectic; the sarcasm characteristic of the unbalanced or wayward personality belongs to eristic. Given space, one would have wished to pursue this investigation in the realm of law and related subjects. Sir Carleton Allen's *Law in the Making* (1927), to take but one example, would be difficult to surpass for sustained lucidity. Indeed, in the work of eminent jurists the prose of thought reaches that temporary equilibrium in which dialectic and eristic enter into partnership.

The course of a man's style can reflect, sometimes with uncanny fidelity, the progress or deterioration of his thought. Whereas the level of writing of such a work as *The Golden Bough* (1890–1912) remains even and steady throughout a succession of volumes, the prose of the last volumes of Arnold Toynbee's *Study of History* (1954) sometimes falls below the level of the earlier part, rallying again in *An Historian's Approach to Religion* (1956), and in the excellent *Reconsiderations* (1961). There is a study to be made of the variations in quality, throughout a long and colourful career, of the prose of Earl Russell. In his middle period, this penetrating thinker seems to have lost his bearings. The result is an excess of eristic writing and some measure of flatness, in contrast to the early superb command of dialectic: whereas some later essays, notably those contained in the volume *Portraits from Memory* (1957), reveal a balance and clarity born of serene and mature reflection.

To suggest that a change in a man's outlook exerts direct or immediate influence upon his style would be to venture too far; but apart from the fact that ideas, if coherent at all, are *expressed* ideas, the movement of a man's thought can and does thus reflect itself. There are not two things, the thought and the style; there is either one thing, or a mere string of words. Nor is this to say that the *manner* necessarily changes; the prevailing manner may remain the same, but transformed into mannerism or caricature. By way of illustration, we may take five modern writers, differing widely in outlook but sufficiently long-lived to have demonstrably exchanged one mood for another. The early prose of W. R. Inge possessed a cutting-edge which, towards the end, had become blunted. A writer who admired Inge's prose, if nothing else about him, was Hilaire Belloc. The Belloc of *The Path to Rome*, the early historical studies, and even *The Cruise of the Nona* (1925), especially the philosophical digressions, wrote eloquent and noble English; the later Belloc often makes heavy and painful reading. Although H. G. Wells was not a professional thinker, he was very much a 'man of ideas'; his early novels and essays have an incandescent quality which lifted their style, otherwise undistinguished, to considerable heights. The Wells of *The World of William Clissold* (1927) was a tired and disillusioned idealist: hence the invective, the sarcasm, the querulous loquacity of much of the later work. Bernard Shaw, after persistent practice, evolved a style so fine and swift that even his sectarian political essays, such as that which he wrote and several times revised for *Fabian Essays* (1889), are still worth reading; but the later plays and their prefaces, for all their violence, are often lifeless.[9] That remarkable philosopher R. G. Collingwood wrote trenchantly about the style appropriate to philosophy, and in such early works as *Speculum Mentis* (1924) and *An Essay on Philosophical Method* (1933) he practised what he preached almost to perfection. Some rift or hesistancy in his thought, due not necessarily to increasing ill-health, makes his work from the *Essay on Metaphysics* (1940) onwards both uneven and erratic.

In the work of all these men we find the style mirroring, however subtly, a change in outlook. The ageing Inge had come to distrust the mysticism to which he was early devoted; Belloc lost not his faith but the sense of beatitude; Shaw's early social idealism gave way to a cynical admiration for despotism; Collingwood fell into the historicism against which he had issued repeated warnings. Consistently enough, the five men came to show a preponderance of the eristic outlook over the dialectic; and this is reflected in the inner quality of their prose.

An essay such as the present must not neglect to take into account a form of prose embodying not so much thought as an attitude to thought. This is reflective prose. In this genre many great writers may be included; two obvious examples are Bacon and Sir Thomas Browne. The twentieth century has witnessed the revival of the essay; but if England has no equivalent to Alain, it has produced some distinguished practitioners of this form; the early essays of Middleton Murry and Aldous Huxley may be cited. Our greatest modern essayists are usually men who imagined they were working in a different genre. The prose works of Wyndham Lewis, particularly *The Art of Being Ruled* (1926) and *Time and Western Man* (1927), fall naturally into separate essays, while such pieces as *The Diabolical Principle and The Dithyrambic Spectator* (1931), despite a marked eristic vein, show a vigorous mind wrestling with new ideas and generating an original prose to embody them, so that Eliot could describe Lewis as 'one of the permanent masters of style in the English language'. Another master of the essay form is Havelock Ellis. Some of the *Little Essays in Love and Virtue* (1922), the two volumes of *Impressions and Comments* (1914–23), and above all *The Dance of Life* (1923) reveal the workings of a fastidious mind, though Ellis could fall into rhetoric.[10] As he confessed in his *Autobiography*, he was essentially a dreamer, viewing life (and sex for that matter) in terms of art; and this quality of reverie, like that of Santayana and Yeats, translated itself into a style of hypnotic charm but often imperfect conceptual realization.[11]

The prose of T. S. Eliot falls naturally into two categories: the reflective and the logical. His studies of individual writers, particularly the Elizabethan poets and Dante, are judicious studies in assessment. To quote Hazlitt, his task is 'to lead the mind into new trains of thought'. But Eliot is likewise a master of logical exposition. Some of the early essays, above all the famous *Tradition and Individual Talent* (1917), or even later works such as *Notes towards the Definition of Culture* (1950) are masterpieces of dialectic. The prose moves forward almost with the movement of thought itself; the result is a succession of illuminations.[12]

> The case for a society with a class structure, the affirmation that it is, in some sense, the 'natural' society, is prejudiced if we allow ourselves to be hypnotized by the two contrasted terms *aristocracy* and *democracy*. The whole problem is falsified if we use these terms antithetically. What I have advanced is not a 'defence of aristocracy' – an emphasis upon the importance of one organ of society. Rather it is a plea on behalf of a form of society in which an aristocracy should have a peculiar and essential function, as peculiar and essential as the function of any other part of society. What is important is a structure of society in which there will be, from 'top' to 'bottom', a continuous gradation of cultural levels: it is important to remember that we should not consider the upper levels as possessing *more* culture than the lower, but as representing a more conscious culture and a greater specialization of culture. I incline to believe that no true democracy can maintain itself unless it contains these different levels of culture. The levels of culture may also be seen as levels of power, to the extent that a smaller group at a higher level will have equal power with a larger group at a lower level; for it may be argued that complete equality means universal irresponsibility; and in such a society as I envisage, each individual would inherit greater or less responsibility towards the commonwealth, according to the position in society which he inherited – each class would have somewhat different responsibilities. A democracy in which everybody had an equal responsibility in everything would be oppressive for the conscientious and licentious for the rest.
>
> (*Notes towards the Definition of Culture*: 'The Class and the Elite')

* * *

A survey of the prose of thought of the twentieth century reveals a certain rhythmic and even cyclic development. In this development we may detect, at each stage, a dialectic and an eristic aspect. This suggests that between the dialectic and eristic elements themselves there operates a higher dialectic. Indeed, without such a higher dialectic, language would constantly be moving towards one or the other extreme and thus failing as a means of communication. The idealist philosophers, taking the Hegelian system as their point of departure, found themselves confronted with the New Realism. Failure to establish communications called out the eristic side of their minds. The analytical school, taking its stand upon empiricism, tended to assume another form of eristic, that directed towards the demolition of speculative systems in general.[13] Having struggled to find a medium of expression transparent to thought, they were finally obliged to re-establish contact with ordinary language. Meanwhile, a more balanced view of philosophy was slowly emerging: A. J. Ayer replaced the eristical prose of his anti-metaphysical manifesto *Language, Truth and Logic* (1935) by the measured urbanity of his *Philosophical Essays* (1954), *The Problem of Knowledge* (1956), and *The Concept of a Person* (1963), where the subject-matter was largely metaphysical. Indeed, there was a remarkable and perhaps significant resemblance between the style of the later Ayer and that of McTaggart. It is now only too clear that Analysis, the weapon of every genuine philosopher, has its own metaphysical assumptions, even if it is only that 'reality' can be conceived as divisible into parts.[14] Moreover, analysis is a process which, in able hands, must be pushed to the limit; but *if* it is pushed to the limit, it finds itself grappling with metaphysical problems. Thus, despite certain signs to the contrary, we may look forward to something in the nature of a metaphysical revival, though not a return to the old idealism. As far as the writing of philosophy is concerned, this will inevitably bring about a resumption of that 'disposition to improvise and create, to treat language as something not fixed and rigid but infinitely flexible and full of life',[15] which has always been characteristic of the best expository prose.

PART THREE

NOTES

1. Cf. Stephen Toulmin, *The Uses of Argument* (1958): 'It cannot be custom alone which gives validity and authority to a form of argument, or the logician would have to wait upon the results of the anthropologist's researches' (p.5).

2. *On Philosophical Style* (1954), p. 23.

3. The point is well brought out in the symposium *Metaphysical Beliefs*, edited by Macintyre and Gregor Smith (1957), p. 5.

4. I make no comment here, or elsewhere, on the *validity* of the argument. The reader who is curious on that point should consult W. D. Ross's *The Right and the Good* (1930), p. 88.

5. See *The Bloomsbury Group*, by J. K. Johnstone (1954).

6. *Preliminary Studies for the 'Philosophical Investigations': generally known as the Blue and the Brown Books* (1958), p. 174.

7. 'It was in a spirit of persuasion that most of these essays were written, in an attempt to influence opinion' (p. v).

8. Observe how, in the hands of less objective writers, this passage could have degenerated into eristic.

9. An exception must be made of the Preface to the World's Classics edition of *Back to Methuselah*, written in his tenth decade and a most spirited performance.

10. E.g. *The Dance of Life*, Chapter III, iv.

11. Cp. in the case of Yeats, the prose of *Per Amica Silentia Lunae* (1917).

12. I have argued elsewhere (*T. S. Eliot, A Tribute from Japan*, Kenkyusha, 1967) that 'the discipline of prose' was that which laid the foundation of Eliot's poetic eminence.

13. E.g. Stuart Hampshire's claim that system-building has been killed 'stone dead' by the 'devastating discoveries of modern linguistic philosophers' (*The Nature of Metaphysics*, edited by D. F. Pears, 1957, p. 25).

14. This is the assumption behind a book by P. S. Strawson, which bears the significant title of *Individuals: an essay in descriptive metaphysics* (1959).

15. R. G. Collingwood, *An Essay on Philosophical Method* (1933), 'Philosophy as a branch of Literature', p. 214.

MR FORSTER'S GOOD INFLUENCE

G. D. KLINGOPULOS

Senior Lecturer in English, University of South Wales, Cardiff

ANYONE familiar with Mr E. M. Forster's* writing for a fair number of years – say a quarter of a century or so – is likely to feel some discontent at his gradual transformation into a 'minor classic'. Such a reader may sit down to write his own account of work he has admired for so long, only to find that the 'major' claim, if it is to be advanced at all, cannot be made to apply to more than one or two of the novels. There is even, he soon realizes, something in the stories themselves which discourages and seems to mock the whole business of careful definition and appraisal. Is he, perhaps, guilty of what his author would regard as a radical fault, a lack of 'humour'?

> Bring out the enjoyment. If 'the classics' are advertised as something dolorous and astringent, no one will sample them. But if the cultured person, like the late Roger Fry, is obviously having a good time, those who come across him will be tempted to share it and to find out how.

Surely these are sentiments to which the bosom of every 'cultured person' returns an echo? Or is Mr Forster himself, in this rare instance, slightly lacking in humour in his anxiety about 'having a good time'? Questioned about this, Mr Forster is almost too ready to see another point of view. 'Were I professionally committed to evaluation, my attitude would of course be different.' The concession is so large that it makes agreement more remote. Is the distinction between the 'professional' and the general reader a sound one, and is not the ideal critic the ideal reader? There appears to be some confusion here about the extent to which criticism, however 'dolorous and astringent', is prescriptive. One is often in the position of thinking: 'I know A is a much finer work than B but it cannot diminish my enjoyment of B.' Mr Forster may only mean to deprecate the simplemindedness which ignores this possibility, a necessary

* E. M. Forster died in 1970.

task but one scarcely worth his insistence. As the justification of a permanent 'unprofessional' attitude it will not do. There is, of course, much more than this to Mr Forster's emphasis on the need for 'humour'.

Much of Mr Forster's, as of Thomas Hardy's, interest and usefulness lies in the challenge presented by all his work to decide how far one *can* go along with him, and how far he *will* do. Whatever the fanciful surface of some of his prose, Mr Forster is a consistent moralist and intellectual. He addresses himself primarily and almost exclusively to those who share his assumptions.

> I distrust Great Men ... I believe in aristocracy though – if that is the right word and if a democrat may use it. Not an aristocracy of power based upon rank and influence, but an aristocracy of the sensitive, the considerate, and the plucky. ... They represent the true human tradition, the one permanent victory of our queer race over cruelty and chaos.

This is the voice that spoke just when many of Mr Forster's readers were embarking in troopships and learning to 'travel light'. They seemed frail words, even, at such a time, slightly absurd, but they represented much of one's ration of moral generalization for the next six years. It was surprising how the timely words travelled and what a good influence they had. Those out of range of the nine o'clock news missed the rhetoric of the Great Men, and when they read about it years later it seemed only rhetorical. The essay 'What I Believe' was the meeting-point for many different sorts of people between 1939 and 1946, and it seemed, with all its frailty and absurdity, exactly right. Anything stronger would have been useless. Some of his other writing became strangely more poignant and meaningful the further one travelled from England. Every so often there were Forster situations, full of his pain, his irony, appearing to demand his invisible participation. For a time his words seemed to point to the immediately hoped for Victory, but once the Liberation had begun it became clear that that could not be what they meant. Their meaning was, roughly, that of Mr Eliot's remark about Arnold: 'We fight rather to keep something alive than in the expectation that anything will triumph.'

This indisputable and long-lasting contemporary importance is, inevitably, the most evanescent part of a writer's achievement. It is what the 'minor classic' accounts of Mr Forster will tend, in time, to take less and less into consideration. A later generation may not easily guess that the thought of this writer's mere being, somewhere in England, has seemed at times, to many people, distinctly reassuring. In a half century which has produced a surfeit of Great Men, bullying, brutality, dogmatism, and noise, Forster has represented an attractive, though not easily imitable, intellectual shrewdness, delicacy, and responsibility. These qualities are not to be explained in terms of Bloomsbury affiliations, and Mr Forster has recently told us that he has never read Moore's *Principia Ethica*. An idealized Cambridge, arising out of an exceptionally lucky imaginative experience of Cambridge,[1] is certainly one source of his charm. He has offered other clues. Jane Austen, obviously, but not, it appears, Meredith, not consciously at any rate. Hardy, as we should expect, is 'my home'. Later there was India which made a deep fusion with some of his earlier attitudes and preoccupations. And the astringent, timeless impact of the Alexandrian recluse Cavafy. One would have guessed the influence of Butler, but not the order of importance which Mr Forster himself gives him. 'Samuel Butler influenced me a great deal. He, Jane Austen, and Marcel Proust are the three authors who helped me most over my writing, and he did more than either of the other two to help me to look at life the way I do.' If the remark implies a slight overestimation of *The Way of All Flesh*, that too is relevant.

The enumeration of influences, however extended, will not add up to an explanation of the impression we have of Mr Forster. Perhaps no literary influences could compare in importance with the world described in *Marianne Thornton* (1956). He is one of the few modern English writers whose work reveals the process of assimilation and growth of a genuine sensibility, by which we mean something different from style, or technique, or learning. It is as rare among poets as among novelists, for determination and a certain amount of verbal skill often suffice for the production of quite reputable verse. It is not manner, though Mr Forster has written much that is only mannered and Lamb-like. It is a quality of interest, sympathy, and judgement which is no more to be achieved by the activity of the will than the idyllic effect of the best of Hardy's prose and poetry. To acknowledge this genuine, experiencing centre in all Forster's work is as important as making up one's mind about the variable quality of the writing in each of his books. Because of this principle of life and growth, he has remained consistently responsive to new people, new books, and new lands, without becoming in the least miscellaneous or indiscriminate. He has not become pompous or, like the scientific progressive H. G. Wells, turned gloomily prophetic in old age.

With all these virtues, Mr Forster might well appear a finely representative 'humanist' and 'liberal', and if he had written only criticism and biography, there would have been no need to go beyond these descriptions which he has frequently applied to himself. But Mr Forster is also and primarily a novelist. The special value of novels, when they rise above ordinary brilliance, is that they enable us to dispense with the labels and slogans which are the currency of professional moralists, philosophers, and politicians, so that we may examine human relationships and motives more inwardly and completely in terms of presented experience. Henry James, it may be recalled, considered the value of a novel to depend directly on 'the amount of felt life concerned in producing it', and thus, ultimately, on 'the kind and the degree of the artist's prime sensibility, which is the soil out of which his subject springs'. The value one puts on Mr Forster's 'sensibility' will decide one's attitude to, for example, his early abandonment of the novel, and to the question whether his gifts really fulfilled their promise.

Some of his earliest short stories are related, though in a slighter mode, to Hardy's theme of Wessex and the consequences of complete industrialization, and one, *The Machine Stops*, is 'a reaction to one of the earlier heavens of H. G. Wells'. In his earlier work, Mr Forster is precariously poised between forms of resistance and of escape – a flight to the Mediterranean world, to 'the other side of the hedge' or to the terminus of the celestial omnibus. Among his short stories, *The Story of a Panic* and *The Curate's Friend* are not far removed from R. L. S.'s slight fantasies.

> Pan is not dead, but of all the classic hierarchy alone survives in triumph; goat-footed, with a gleeful and an angry look, the type of the shaggy world: and in every wood, if you go with a spirit properly prepared, you shall hear the note of his pipe ... It is no wonder, with so traitorous a scheme of things,

if the wise people who created for us the idea of Pan thought that of all fears the fear of him was the most terrible, since it embraces all. And still we preserve the phrase, a panic terror.

(*Virginibus Puerisque*, 1881)

But though Mr Forster has defended 'escape', he was never a whole-hearted escapist. 'I cannot shut myself up in a Palace of Art or a Philosophic Tower and ignore the madness and misery of the world.' Nor has he been tempted to insist on optimism or fatalism or any doctrinal position which would simplify the stresses of life. His slighter works of fantasy must be regarded as attempts to organize and bring to a focus certain intuitions which at first derive from books, and later from experience and from travel. They attempt to open windows for enclosed and regimented men, and to evoke intuitive or childlike memories, as in dreams, of other levels of existence – 'the magic song of nightingales, and the odour of invisible hay, and stars piercing the fading sky'. Criticism is forestalled by the description of Rickie's stories in *The Longest Journey*, but these fragile reworkings of classical myth have their place in any account of Mr Forster's development.[2]

Rickie's stories are, of course, rather ambiguously treated and the novel of which he is the hero has too much of the arbitrary fancifulness of *The Celestial Omnibus* to provide an entirely adequate context of appraisal. *The Longest Journey*, which is the weakest of the novels, is the author's personal favourite, possibly because it contains an autobiographical element which does not have the same value for the reader. The book is about a theme which recurs in all the novels. How can men and women remain loyal to their generous and best impulses in a world which inevitably imposes mere conformity with its coldness, its cowardice and polite deceit? How can men achieve a good relationship with nature and with other men, and avoid the self-sufficiency which is based on various forms of pride or hubris or hardness of will? These themes are as old as European literature, and, recognizing them, we confer importance even on work which embodies them faintly and elusively. They certainly help to give an impression of continuity and completeness to Forster's work, whatever our views of the individual novels may be.

Like everything of Mr Forster's, *The Longest Journey* is immensely readable, but one cannot avoid the impression that a subject-matter requiring some of Lawrence's powers is, in the end, only very sketchily dealt with. The moral disintegration of Rickie and the fulfilment of Ansell's prophecy that Rickie's marriage would fail are never sharply focused. The novelist, one feels, should have given the marriage more of a chance. 'Neither by marriage nor by any other device can men insure themselves a vision: and Rickie's had been granted him three years before, when he had seen his wife and a dead man clasped in each other's arms. She was never to be so real to him again.' Why should Agnes not have become real? The novel does not provide a satisfactory answer, and the business about inherited deformity in Rickie and his child is an evasion, a feeble symbol for over-civilized decadence. Agnes is made unsubtly incapable of realizing that the marriage was a failure. 'She moves as one from whom the inner life has been withdrawn.' Is it much more than a phrase, this 'inner life' which is understood by the philosophizing Ansell and unconsciously represented by Stephen, though only guessed at by Rickie? The novel gives the impression of having been written out of convictions, feelings, and prejudices – about public schools, about townspeople and countrymen and Cambridge – which do not hang together convincingly. The equation between the dead Gerald and the living Stephen as seen by the domineering, disappointed, self-ignorant Agnes, is one of many attempts to 'connect' in Forster which are not quite effective. It is certainly tantalizing. There should have been a deep sense of loss and a tragic song of praise and renewal, but the reader has to guess and invent these for himself because what he is offered is sentimentally vague. Stephen should have had some of the symbolic power of Hardy's Giles Winterborne, but in fact he is not much more substantial than the Pan of the stories. Where the 'pattern and rhythm' which Mr Forster aims at in all his novels, and describes in *Aspects of the Novel*, become conspicuous in set passages of evocative prose, we are reminded not of Hardy but of Meredith:

> The riot of fair images increased. They invaded his being and lit lamps at unsuspected shrines. Their orchestra commenced in that suburban house where he had to stand aside for the maid to carry in the luncheon. Music flowed past him like a river ... In full unison was love born, flame of the flame, flushing

> the dark river beneath him and the virgin snows above. His wings were infinite, his youth eternal: the sun was a jewel on his finger as he passed it in benediction over the world ...

As an attempt to define the 'reality', 'vision', and 'inner life' this is disappointing. The poetic style, though partly insured against bathos by its own exaggeration, appears self-conscious and uncertain in intention. The more elaborate pages of descriptive or impressionistic writing in the earlier novels, especially when they attempt to display the larger significance of events, usually leave a feeling of strain. Only in *A Passage to India* are the descriptive passages deeply evocative, secure, through their real connexion with the novelist's experience, against the incursions of the Comic Spirit or of the little god Pan. The distinction I am making here is not one between 'success' and 'failure'. All the earlier novels remain fresh and individual even after much rereading, and they will probably remain current for a long time to come. But if, despite their deceptive surface lightness, they did not aim at something more than the success of 'light entertainment', they would not require and repay the detailed study which they have received. They have affinities with the novels of Hardy on the one hand, and with those of Lawrence on the other. The affinities are more a matter of differences than of resemblances, yet the differences imply a deeper, though scarcely formulable, connexion with Hardy and Lawrence than the conscious indebtedness to Butler or Proust. If Mr Forster had ever written extensively, as he has at times briefly, about his relation to Hardy and Lawrence he might perhaps have stressed, in the case of Hardy, the ironic contrast of his own birthplace in Melcombe Place, Dorset Square, London, and might have established his own connexion with Lawrence through his sharp awareness that the admirable Victorian liberal outlook 'has lost the basis of gold sovereigns upon which it originally rose, and now hangs over the abyss'. If we cannot claim for Mr Forster the same intensity of moral exploration that characterizes Lawrence, then we must add that it is by no means clear that any modern English writer challenges comparison with Lawrence in this respect.

The continuity between the short stories and the novels is felt most strongly in the two Italian novels, both unquestionable successes. In both, Italian landscape and people enable some English middle-class characters to achieve an increase in freedom and self-knowledge, but confirm the prejudices and self-righteousness of others. At the centre of Mr Forster's hostility is genteel Sawston with its 'culture' and 'principles' and its fear of vulgarity that seems almost a negation of life. Mr Forster does not idealize his Italians to make his point. What he sees in them appears objective and real. Harriet Herriton is blind to this reality. Miss Abbott is transformed by it. The expedition from Sawston to recover the dead Englishwoman's child from its unacceptable Italian father is confused by the living significance of the infant.

> She had thought so much about this baby, of its welfare, its soul, its morals, its probable defects. But, like most unmarried people she had only thought of it as a word – just as the healthy man only thinks of the word death, not death itself. The real thing, lying asleep on a dirty rug, disconcerted her. It did not stand for a principle any longer. It was so much flesh and blood, so many inches and ounces of life – a glorious and unquestionable fact, which a man and another woman had given to the world ... And this was the machine on which she and Mrs Herriton and Philip and Harriet had for the last month been exercising their various ideals – had determined that in time it should move this way or that way, should accomplish this and not that. It was to be Low Church, it was to be high-principled, it was to be tactful, gentlemanly, artistic – excellent things all. Yet now that she saw this baby, lying asleep on a dirty rug, she had a great disposition not to dictate one of them, and to exert no more influence than there may be in a kiss or in the vaguest of heartfelt prayers.

When Harriet succeeded in stealing the baby, she 'dandled the bundle laboriously, like some bony prophetess'. The child is accidentally killed. This violence, like the scuffle which hurries Fielding's departure from the Chandrapore club, reminds us sharply that, though the mode is comedy, Mr Forster is very much in earnest about his subject-matter. Later, this discontent with middle-class manners deepens into a recognition of the difficulty of all good relationship, especially without the mediation of a common religious tradition and vocabulary. Mr Forster's clergymen are all facets of Sawston worldliness and self-importance. He has not attempted to describe religious vocation from the inside – partly because (and not only for Victorian liberals) the 'inside' of modern religious experience tends to be outside ecclesiastical institutions. Like many other observers, Mr Forster doubts the value of the literary Christianity now in fashion. But the satire against the Rev. Mr Eager and the Rev. Mr Beebe in *A Room with a View* would be still more effective if we could be clearer about the rationalist Mr Emerson, with 'the face of a saint who understood'. The fact that the gout-stricken Mr Emerson takes refuge instinctively in the rectory study, its walls lined with black-bound theology, is surely meant to carry meaning, though to Lucy 'it seemed dreadful that the old man should crawl into such a sanctum when he was unhappy, and be dependent on the bounty of a clergyman'. The stock descriptions – 'agnostic', 'liberal sceptic', 'anti-clericalist' – suggest clear-cut attitudes unlike Mr Forster's. He knows when clarity falsifies, and that it is very often better to tolerate muddle as nearer to the actual conditions of intellectual and moral life. But old Mr Emerson is an unimpressive representative of this sort of attitude. Nor can one be quite happy about the kind of generalization Mr Forster makes on very common problems of adjustment to cultural differences within society. Here is an example from Lucy's defence of the priggish London intellectual Cecil:

> 'You can't expect a really musical person to enjoy comic songs as we do.'
>
> 'Then why didn't he leave the room? Why sit wriggling and sneering and spoiling everyone's pleasure?'
>
> 'We mustn't be unjust to people,' faltered Lucy. Something had enfeebled her, and the case for Cecil, which she had mastered so perfectly in London, would not come forth in an effective form. The two civilizations had clashed – Cecil had hinted that they might – and she was dazzled and bewildered, as though the radiance that lies behind all civilization had blinded her eyes. Good taste and bad taste were only catchwords, garments of diverse cut; and music itself dissolved to a whisper through pine-trees, where the song is not distinguishable from the comic song.

The discriminations are not subtle or sharp enough either in these general comments which remind one of Meredith – and of the anxious geniality about critical 'astringency' mentioned in our first paragraph – or in the presentation of Cecil. So that a measure of sentimental vagueness must be tolerated as part of the experience of 'enjoying' the novel. This is also the case in the more substantial work *Howards End*. Here Mr Forster is again concerned with the interaction of cultural levels, and he returns to the attempt made in *The Longest Journey* to analyse and describe the drift of modern English life as it had been transformed by a century of industrialization and imperial expansion. The novel shows the harmonizing, genial, and intensely patriotic sides of the novelist at odds with his radicalism. The date was 1910 and the subject, as Mr Forster has recently put it, 'a hunt for a home'. It is the equivalent in his work of Hardy's *Return of the Native* and is similarly oversimplified. The hunt is genuine enough, but one may well doubt whether the home was ever found. Nevertheless the novel was in some ways a pioneer work and has helped to modify attitudes and educate manners during the last half century. Even *The Times* now prints leading articles weightily agreeing that the British Empire was undermined by bad manners. A future Gibbon

> will have to discover just what part was played in the decline by the behaviour of Englishmen – not to mention Englishwomen – who lived their lives in the East. How much are the angry young men of Singapore a product of an exclusive transplanted Wimbledon?
>
> (*The Times*, 16 September 1959)

The question can be put so calmly largely because *A Passage to India* (1924) made it possible. This major work is, of course, much more than a comment on colonialism, but it is worth saying that one's impression of the courage needed to write it is no less strong now than it was a quarter of a century ago. Democracy has its frivolous side, and questions of principle and moral responsibility for unrepresented populations overseas do not decide parliamentary elections. Mr Forster has done more to educate large numbers of the electorate ('two cheers for democracy') than any English writer of the twentieth century. Because *A Passage to India* has been a best-selling paperback for decades, discussion can dispense with political watchwords and slogans and go straight to the heart of the matter. Written after a silence of fourteen years, the book reveals none of the old Meredithean associations, and the simple pieties of Thomas Hardy have also been outgrown. Seen in relation to Mr Forster's work as a whole, it represents as significant a process of development as any in modern literature. In the earlier novels, the correcting of intellectual arrogance in Cecil Vyse by contrast with Mr Emerson, in Rickie by Stephen, or in the Schlegels by Mrs Wilcox, had left a suggestion of falsity or sanctimoniousness. What Mr Forster recoiled from was clear enough, but his alternatives seemed oversimplified. His last novel does not offer alternatives and solutions. India acts as a solvent not only to the churchy serenity of Mrs Moore (who is related to several other characters in earlier novels) but also to the rationalism and self-confidence of Fielding.

> And he felt dubious and discontented suddenly, and wondered whether he was really and truly successful as a human being. After forty years' experience, he had learnt to manage his life and make the best of it on advanced European lines, had developed his personality, explored his limitations, controlled his passions – and he had done it all without becoming either pedantic or worldly. A creditable achievement, but as the moment passed, he felt he ought to have been working at something else the whole time, – he didn't know at what, never would know, never could know, and that was why he felt sad.

Some readers have seen this novel as essentially pessimistic and 'defeatist', but this seems to be the result of misinterpreting the incidents in the cave. Value must still be affirmed despite the dark rumblings of negation and nullity, and it was the strain of this task which overtaxed Mrs Moore. 'Everything exists, nothing has value.' It was her distinction to have had the experience.

> She had come to that state where the horror of the universe and its smallness are both visible at the same time – the horror of the double vision in which so many elderly people are involved ... In the twilight of the double vision, a spiritual muddledom is set up for which no high-sounding words can be found.

But the experience was also her punishment for having declared earlier, much too complacently, 'I like mysteries, but I rather dislike muddles.' To Adela and Fielding she left a hint of other modes of responsiveness to 'India' than their own. 'Were there worlds beyond which they could not touch, or did all that is possible enter their consciousness? ... Perhaps life is a mystery, not a muddle; they could not tell.'

The Hindu ceremonies with which the novel concludes strike one as the acceptance and sanctification of muddle which appears more tolerable and nearer the truth than more orderly religious systems and patterns of belief. The effect of this conclusion to the elaborate tapestry of the book is positive and far from depressing. And it is naïve to see evidence of a lack of moral vitality in the last words of a novel which, with few reservations, is an impressive structure of carefully pondered experience. 'Love in public affairs does not work', Mr Forster has written in an essay on Tolerance. He is not the first novelist to distrust 'good intentions'. The balance of antipathy and sympathy in *A Passage to India* still seems, after the violence and change of the intervening years, the undistorted response of a mind of rare courage, delicacy, and integrity, and it plays an important part in the total music of this major work.

NOTES

1. It is characteristic of Mr Forster that he should conclude his biography of Goldsworthy Lowes Dickenson (1934) in this way: 'Mephistopheles, who should inhabit a cranny in every biography, puts his head out at this point, and asks me to set all personal feelings aside and state objectively why a memoir of Goldsworthy Lowes Dickenson need be written... The case for Mephistopheles would appear to be watertight, and a biography of my friend and master uncalled for.'

2. See my essay in *Essays in Criticism*, Vol. VIII, No. 2.

VIRGINIA WOOLF: THE THEORY AND PRACTICE OF FICTION

FRANK W. BRADBROOK

Senior Lecturer in English, University College of North Wales, Bangor

THERE are probably no writers whom it is more difficult to discuss with a proper critical disinterestedness than those that one first admired some twenty years ago, as a student. Their influence, however modified by what has been written since, and by one's subsequent reading and experience, remains a deep and permanent one. Moreover, the writers whom one admired in the late thirties have not been outmoded in the sense that H. G. Wells, John Galsworthy, and Arnold Bennett were for Virginia Woolf when she started publishing fiction at the beginning of the First World War. The problem of the relationship between the generations was for her a matter of breaking free from an inadequate technique and a limited vision. Her own achievement may appear now to be a more limited one than it did when her novels were first read, and her lasting contribution to fiction may be reduced to a single novel, *To the Lighthouse*. Yet she had imagination, great sensitiveness, delicacy, wit, and the infinite capacity of genius for taking pains. She, at least, did not curb the spirit, or erect barriers that her followers have had to break down. If one thinks of her limitations, it is only compared with the greatest of her predecessors, Jane Austen and George Eliot, two artists whom she admired and whose work as a whole gives one a sense of achievement and triumph beside which the writings of the twentieth-century novelist, inevitably perhaps, appear, for all the flashes of brilliance, curiously fragmentary and inconclusive.

'That fiction is a lady, and a lady who has somehow got herself into trouble, is a thought that must often have struck her admirers', Virginia Woolf remarks at the beginning of a review of E. M. Forster's *Aspects of the Novel*. There now exist half a dozen books containing essays on the art of fiction and kindred subjects by Virginia Woolf herself. Here one can see the artist working out her technical problems. The essay 'Modern Fiction' in *The Common*

Reader (First Series) is largely taken up with destructive criticism of the Edwardians:

> materialists ... they are concerned not with the spirit but with the body ... they write of unimportant things ... they spend immense skill and immense industry making the trivial and the transitory appear the true and the enduring.

Life escapes H. G. Wells, John Galsworthy, and Arnold Bennett:

> look within and life, it seems, is very far from being 'like this'. Examine for a moment an ordinary mind on an ordinary day. The mind receives a myriad impressions – trivial, fantastic, evanescent, or engraved with the sharpness of steel. From all sides they come, an incessant shower of innumerable atoms; and as they fall, as they shape themselves into the life of Monday or Tuesday, the accent falls differently from of old ... Life is not a series of gig lamps symmetrically arranged; life is a luminous halo, a semi-transparent envelope surrounding us from the beginning of consciousness to the end.[1]

This may be inadequate psychology, it may involve a too passive conception of perception,[2] but it describes what life meant for Virginia Woolf, and it made necessary the creation of new techniques and methods. Plot, character, comedy, tragedy, and the concentration on 'love interest', the old conventional themes and categories, were no longer adequate to communicate the stream of the modern consciousness. Virginia Woolf had certain models for what may be called the 'hit-or-miss' style, such as the Elizabethan novelists, particularly Thomas Nashe, odd eccentrics such as Sterne, and, in her own day, James Joyce. These writers, rather than Thackeray, Thomas Hardy, and Joseph Conrad, whom she also esteemed, provided her with something in the nature of a tradition, though she 'felt the lack of a convention, and how serious a matter it is when the tools of one generation are useless for the next' (*The Captain's Death Bed*). Her attitude is primarily that of the innovator, experimenting, conscious of infinite possibilities, and ready to try anything. There is no such thing as 'the proper stuff of fiction': 'everything is the proper stuff of fiction, every feeling, every thought; every quality of brain and spirit is drawn upon; no perception comes amiss' (*The Common*

Reader, First Series). Such all-inclusiveness has its dangers, and in trying to record everything, in refusing to select and discriminate between the significance and value of different experiences, the novelist may merely end by reproducing the chaos from which it is the function of intelligence to save us.

Virginia Woolf believed that the novelist must 'expose himself to life' and yet be detached from it (*Granite and Rainbow*). Using a vivid image of Ernest Hemingway, she remarks that 'the true writer stands close up to the bull and lets the horns – call them life, truth, reality, whatever you like – pass him close each time' (*Granite and Rainbow*). Life, as she describes it in *A Writer's Diary*, is (this was written in 1920) 'for us in our generation so tragic – no newspaper placard without its shriek of agony from someone ... Unhappiness is everywhere; just beyond the door; or stupidity, which is worse.' Yet it has its moments of happiness, which would be more frequent if 'it weren't for my feeling that it's a strip of pavement over an abyss' (*A Writer's Diary*). 'The Russian Point of View', of which Virginia Woolf was very much aware – her essay with this title is in *The Common Reader* (First Series) – deepened her sense both of the comedy and tragedy of life, but it was supremely embodied in the novels of Tolstoy, whom she saw as a kind of Sir Thomas Browne creating nineteenth-century Slavonic Hamlets who were perpetually asking themselves the question 'Why live?' Modestly realizing her limitations, it was the less massive genius Chehov with whom she tended to sympathize. His art had that economy which she also found in the novels of Jane Austen, who was, in this respect, she thought, superior to George Eliot herself (*The Common Reader*, First Series).[3]

Virginia Woolf was very conscious of her place in the tradition of women writers, and her determination to maintain the dignity of her sex could at times even tempt her into the unartistic faults of stridency, exaggeration, and overemphasis. *A Room of One's Own*, which directly deals with the problems of the woman writer, is interesting and occasionally amusing, but there is a sense of strain and even of viciousness in the attack on various types of masculine pomposity and self-importance in *Three Guineas*. A good case and legitimate attitude are spoilt by an unusual crudity of presentation.[4] Writing about women and fiction in 1929, she prophesied that

> the greater impersonality of women's lives will encourage the poetic spirit, and it is in poetry that women's fiction is still weakest. It will lead them to be less absorbed in facts and no longer content to record with astonishing acuteness the minute details which fall under their own observation. They will look beyond the personal and political relationships to the wider questions which the poet tries to solve – of our destiny and the meaning of life.
>
> (*Granite and Rainbow*)

This 'poetic spirit', together with the concern with the meaning of destiny and life, had been characteristic of Virginia Woolf's own fiction from the first. 'A method essentially poetic and apparently trifling has been applied to fiction', as E. M. Forster has noted (*Two Cheers for Democracy*).

Fiction, for Virginia Woolf, was not a 'criticism of life' in any Arnoldian sense, but rather a re-creation of the complexities of experience. Just as life was a most subtle and complicated succession of experiences, so fiction must be infinitely adaptable and supple in order to catch the 'tones', the light and shade of experience. The art of the novelist was similar to that of the painter, and painting for Virginia Woolf did not mean the Dutch School, who were admired by George Eliot, but Roger Fry and the Post-Impressionists, Van Gogh rather than the Van Eycks, Cézanne, Gauguin, and Matisse. There were various 'phases' of fiction and different types of novelists, equivalent to the different schools of painting, and the task of the modern novelist was to make use of whatever was of value in the past. The truth-tellers, the romantics, the character-mongers and comedians, the psychologists, the satirists and fantastics, and the poets, were like the different paints on the palette. How did one combine their various methods to produce the perfect picture?

Experience is a flux, and the novelist must communicate it. Yet there must be some sort of order in the art by means of which it is presented:

> For the most characteristic qualities of the novel – that it registers the slow growth and development of feeling, that it follows many lives and traces their unions and fortunes over a long stretch of time – are the very qualities that are most incompatible with design and order. It is the gift of style, ar-

> rangement, construction to put us at a distance from the special life and obliterate its features; while it is the gift of the novel to bring us into close touch with life. The two powers fight if they are brought into combination. The most complete novelist must be the novelist who can balance the two powers so that the one enhances the other.
>
> (*Granite and Rainbow*)

Virginia Woolf's values are those of Bloomsbury, the group of writers and artists that included, in addition to Roger Fry, Vanessa and Clive Bell, Duncan Grant, Lytton Strachey, Leonard Woolf, J. M. Keynes, Desmond MacCarthy, and (rather on the fringe) E. M. Forster.[5] The danger of the clique spirit in the modern literary world does not require stressing to anyone who is sufficiently alert and informed to see what goes on, and the Bloomsbury group suffered like any other school of writers from a tendency towards mutual admiration that was merely a form of narcissism. There were also certain blind-spots. Virginia Woolf refers to 'the chants of the worshippers at the shrine of Lawrence', and then, in the following essay, proceeds to chant at the shrine of Roger Fry, who is praised for his honesty and integrity, qualities that he may have owed in part to his Quaker blood. He also went to Cambridge (King's College) and is meant to represent the Cambridge mind at its best. While giving a sympathetic account of *Sons and Lovers*, Virginia Woolf asserts that D. H. Lawrence

> is not a member, like Proust, of a settled and civilized society. He is anxious to leave his own class and to enter another. He believes that the middle class possess what he does not possess ... the fact that he, like Paul, was a miner's son, and that he disliked his conditions, gave him a different approach to writing from those who have a settled station and enjoy circumstances which allow them to forget what those circumstances are. (*The Moment*)

The Lawrence of Virginia Woolf's imagination is not interested in literature, the past, or the present except in so far as it affects the future, or in human psychology, and in comparison with Proust again, he is said to have no tradition behind him. He is lacking in style, civilization, and a sense of beauty.[6] When discussing *A Passage to India*, Virginia Woolf can be more detached because she is talking about the writings of someone with whom she is acquainted and can even be ironical about the place that provided the group with its standards – 'it is a relief for a time, to be beyond the influence of Cambridge' (*The Death of the Moth*). In that 'for a time' there is an unconscious irony.

To pass from Virginia Woolf's theories, ideas, and criticism to the study of her practice as a novelist is to realize how much more conventional she was than she imagined. *The Voyage Out* (1915), her first novel, is quite traditional in form, and the best moments occur when she is being autobiographical. In chapter XIII, Rachel visits the room of Mr Ambrose, her uncle, and one is reminded of the education that Virginia Woolf's father, Leslie Stephen, gave her: 'to read what one liked because one liked it, never to pretend to admire what one did not – that was his only lesson in the art of reading. To write in the fewest possible words, as clearly as possible, exactly what one meant – that was his only lesson in the art of writing' (*The Captain's Death Bed*). There, is the essential strength of Virginia Woolf, the tradition that was to produce Mr Ramsay of *To the Lighthouse*. She did not mean to be prejudiced against the poor, but her intense intellectual life was accompanied by a vein of snobbery, however much she tried to sympathize. George Eliot, the granddaughter of a carpenter, is described as 'raising herself with groans and struggles from the intolerable boredom of petty provincial society'. She was lacking in charm: 'she had none of these eccentricities and inequalities of temper which give to many artists the endearing simplicity of children' (*The Common Reader*, First Series). George Eliot might well reply that the simplicity of children is not always endearing, and that it is the duty of artists to be adult in their attitudes and ideas. When, in *The Voyage Out*, a character called Hewet says 'I want to write a novel about Silence, the things people don't say. But the difficulty is immense', one feels that Virginia Woolf is merely being clever in a Bloomsbury kind of way.[7] George Eliot and D. H. Lawrence could have told her that Bunyan had already done this ('Thus came *Faithful* to his end,' after the trial at Vanity Fair) as had Jane Austen, too ('What did she say? – Just what she ought, of course. A lady always does,' describing Emma's response to Mr Knightley's proposal). The world of Virginia Woolf's characters is supposed to be a sophisticated and cosmopolitan one, yet it, too, has its provincial aspects. Evelyn, in *The Voyage Out*, is going to found a club '– a club for doing things ... It was brains that were needed ... of course, they would want a room ... in Bloomsbury preferably'. There, the essential naïveté of Virginia Woolf manifests itself.

Night and Day (1919), like *The Voyage Out*, is a conventional, realistic story, showing many of the characteristics that Virginia Woolf ridiculed in her criticism of the English realistic novelists. Early in the novel, one is introduced to Katherine Hilbery, 'belonging to one of the most distinguished families in England ... when they were not lighthouses firmly based on rock for the guidance of their generation, they were steady, serviceable candles, illuminating the ordinary chambers of life' (*Night and Day*). She typifies Bloomsbury humanity as well as Bloomsbury snobbery. 'Not to care' is the unforgivable sin. Ralph Denham, whom she eventually marries, is metaphorically united with her towards the end of the novel, and one sees here the beginnings of the later, more subtle use of symbolism and poetic technique: 'an odd image came to his mind of a lighthouse besieged by the flying bodies of lost birds, who were dashed senseless, by the gale, against the glass. He had a strange sensation that he was both lighthouse and bird; he was steadfast and brilliant; and at the same time he was whirled with all other things, senseless against the glass' (*Night and Day*). In Mrs Hilbery's reverie and its conclusion in the statement that 'love is our faith', which is compared by her daughter to the 'breaking of waves solemnly in order upon the vast shore that she gazed upon' (*Night and Day*), there is a foreshadowing of the Mrs Ramsay-Lily Briscoe relationship in *To the Lighthouse*.

Jacob's Room (1922) marks a further development in this poetic method. There are flashes here, too, of that almost vicious, satirical wit, usually aimed at men, and their attempts to think or to keep up the appearance of thinking. Even Cambridge is not lacking in insensitive characters: at George Plumley's luncheon at 'Waverley', on the road to Girton, there were 'on the table serious sixpenny weeklies written by pale men in muddy boots – the weekly creak and screech of brains rinsed in cold water and wrung dry – melancholy papers'. The real culture of Cambridge, however, 'the light of Cambridge', is implicitly opposed to the provincial prudishness of Professor Bulteel of Leeds, who 'had issued an edition of Wycherley without stating that he had left out ... several indecent words and some indecent phrases'. The astringent wit of Virginia Woolf, combined with the quite open snobbery, as in the reference to Soho, 'and so again into the dark, passing a girl here for sale, or there an old woman with only matches to offer', derives from Jane Austen, the Jane Austen of *The Letters*, *Northanger Abbey*, and the ironical observer of the fate with which Jane Fairfax is threatened in *Emma*, though the subject-matter is that of Defoe (cp. the end of the essay on Defoe in *The Common Reader, First Series*). Virginia Woolf also shares with Jane Austen a sense of the importance of the apparent trivialities of life: 'it's not catastrophes, murders, deaths, diseases, that age and kill us; it's the way people look and laugh, and run up the steps of omnibuses' (*Jacob's Room*).

The use of imagery to connect different moments in the novel, and to form patterns apart from character and plot, becomes more confident and consistent in *Mrs Dalloway* (1925). Images, in Virginia Woolf's novels, are even carried over from one book to another. 'Darkness drops like a knife over Greece', in *Jacob's Room*; Mrs Dalloway 'sliced like a knife through everything'; again in *Mrs Dalloway*, Peter Walsh is frequently described as playing with a knife, and it is connected with his habit of 'making one feel, too, frivolous; empty-minded; a mere silly chatterbox'. The image of a knife is also used in *To the Lighthouse*, in connexion with Mr Ramsay, to describe the ruthlessness and insensitiveness of the male intellect, as opposed to the feminine imagination of Mrs Ramsay. (There is, perhaps, too, a suggestion here of Time's 'scythe and crooked knife', one of the themes of Shakespeare's sonnets.)[8] The use of the background of the rhythm of the waves when evoking those isolated, significant moments in experience with which Virginia Woolf is so concerned, appears in *Mrs Dalloway*, looking forward to the extended use of this image in *To the Lighthouse* and *The Waves*. A mood of serenity and resignation is usually conveyed by this image (though sometimes the thundering of the waves can suggest terror). The hypnotic rhythms of the falling waves induce the appropriate response in Mrs Dalloway: '"Fear no more," says the heart, committing its burden to some sea, which sighs collectively for all sorrows, and renews, begins, collects, lets fall'. One cannot help feeling that there is a certain complacency in the novel here, and it appears again in the character of Peter Walsh who, growing old, 'has gained – at last! – the power which adds the supreme flavour to existence – the power of taking hold of experience, of turning it round, slowly in the light'. He, in other words, is another Sir Thomas Browne in modern dress, Hamletizing, as Virginia Woolf imagined the heroes of Tolstoy did, but he makes a comparatively poor showing intellectually. The detachment from life and experience has been too easily won. Clarissa Dalloway is tinged with the same complacency. Living for her parties, she 'could not think, write, even play the piano ... she must be liked; talked oceans of nonsense'. No one liked a party more than Jane Austen's Emma, and she is equally ignorant and undisciplined, but she is only twenty when the novel begins, and has grown up by the end of the story. It is a weakness in Virginia Woolf's novels that her models of mature, feminine wisdom are essentially adolescent – Mrs Ramsay also has an 'untrained mind'. In *Mrs Dalloway*, the macabre Septimus Smith episode is less effective than it would be if Virginia Woolf was more capable of describing the subtleties and complications of normal, mature living.

To the Lighthouse is generally recognized as Virginia Woolf's masterpiece. The combination of autobiographical material with the poetic method of presentation and the larger structural pattern results in the final reconciliation between life and art. The symbolism of the lighthouse, used spasmodically in *Night and Day*, becomes as natural and inevitably right as the

> ever-fixèd mark,
> That looks on tempests and is never shaken.

There is, of course, a danger in making a comparison between a sonnet of Shakespeare (No. 116) and an image used in a modern novel. Yet, *To the Lighthouse* may with justice be described as 'an expanded metaphor', as Wilson Knight has described a Shakespearian play. Here the individual images have the same organic relationship with the allegory of the general theme that we find in Shakespeare's greatest plays. The themes of *To the Lighthouse* are those of the sonnets – time, beauty, the survival of beauty through the means of art, absence, and death:

> Like as the waves make towards the pebbled shore,
> So do our minutes hasten to their end ...
>
> (No. 60)

How with this rage shall beauty hold a plea,
Whose action is no stronger than a flower? ...

(No. 65)

From you have I been absent in the spring,
When proud-pied April, dress'd in all his trim,
Hath put a spirit of youth in every thing ...

(No. 98)

It is, surely, in Shakespeare rather than (as has been suggested) in Bergson that the source of Virginia Woolf's themes is to be found.[9] The method is that of poetry not philosophy, and to discuss *To the Lighthouse* and *The Waves* in terms of mystical experience is equally dangerous.[10] The symbolism of the lighthouse is clear, and Virginia Woolf is no more mystical than E. M. Forster in *Howards End*, where the symbolism of the house performs a similar function and music replaces painting as the source of aesthetic experience. Mr E. M. Forster has, perhaps, been less successful in his 'poetic' effects, but in the way in which he makes use of Beethoven's Fifth Symphony there is an example of the larger rhythm and theme comparable to Virginia Woolf's image of the waves.

These rhythms and themes transcend plot and character, and appear at significant moments during the novels, when the trivialities and pettinesses of ordinary life are surpassed. During isolated moments of intense experience, when 'the miracle happens', life takes on the intensity of art. The long steady stroke of the lighthouse beam is Mrs Ramsay's stroke, and symbolizes the stability and security which her presence imposes on the flux of life. The flashing of the beam is the equivalent in life to the movements of the painter's brush – Mrs Ramsay and Lily Briscoe are equally artists – and the novel ends with the long steady stroke of the brush that also completes Lily Briscoe's picture in the mind, of the perfect woman whom she loves. Both in the novel and in painting, formality and discipline are imposed on the chaos of experience. To make, Virginia Woolf seems to be saying, something of permanent importance out of one's momentary experiences is the aim of the poet, such as Shakespeare in his sonnets, the novelist, the artist in living, such as Mrs Ramsay, and the painter; and in order to express one's personality, one must lose it by absorbing it in something larger and seeing its place in the artistic pattern of the whole: 'losing personality one lost the fret, the hurry, the stir' and gained the peace which passeth all understanding. Virginia Woolf, for once, used directly religious terminology, but the experience she describes frequently occurs in non-religious poetry.

Opposed to this poetic experience is the rationalism of Mr Ramsay, with the endurance, stoicism, and tyranny that it involves. This is the world of Victorian agnosticism:

> We stand on a mountain pass in the midst of whirling snow and blinding mist, through which we get glimpses now and then of paths which may be deceptive. If we stand still we shall be frozen to death. If we take the wrong road we shall be dashed to pieces. We do not certainly know whether there is any right one. What must we do? 'Be strong and of good courage.' Act for the best, hope for the best, and take what comes ... If death ends all, we cannot meet death better.[11]

Such an attitude, of course, can result in self-dramatization which is very far removed from the heroism that it pretends to be (as, for instance, in the conclusion of Bertrand Russell's *A Free Man's Worship*). The greatness of Virginia Woolf's portrait of Mr Ramsay is that she finally acknowledges and succeeds in convincing us of his heroism, despite her prejudice against the tyranny of the male intellect, its essential egoism and pettiness. The contrast between Mr and Mrs Ramsay is comparable to that of Jane Austen's Emma and Mr Knightley: the end of Virginia Woolf's greatest novel also vindicates 'the wishes, the hopes, the confidence, the predictions of the small band of true friends' (the conclusion of *Emma*) as Mr Ramsay reaches the end of his journey to the lighthouse, and Lily Briscoe completes the painting inspired by Mrs Ramsay.[12] The world of prose has been united with those of poetry and of art.

Orlando (1928), though it has brilliant passages, has not the unity of *To the Lighthouse* and the indulgence of fantasy is inclined to pall. Genius, Virginia Woolf remarks,

> resembles the lighthouse in working, which sends one ray, and then no more for a time; save that genius is much more capricious in its manifestations and may flash six or seven beams in quick succession ... and then lapse into darkness for a year or for ever. To steer by its beams is therefore impossible, and when the dark spell is on them men of genius are, it is said, much like other people.

That, unfortunately, is what appears to have happened to Virginia Woolf herself. *The Waves* (1931) deals with the theme of the progress of time, the days, months, and seasons following each other like the waves and ending, for the individual, with death. There are beautiful passages, such as Bernard's final monologue, with which the novel concludes, but no sense of a larger pattern or rhythm. *The Years* (1937) contains, near the beginning, a flash of the old satirical wit in the description of the hypocrisy of Colonel Pargiter and the death, after a painful, protracted illness, of his wife. The novel, as a whole, shows signs of tiredness, and is dull and monotonous. It ends with the sun rising on a new day, 'and the sky above the houses wore an air of extraordinary beauty, simplicity and peace'. It is a conventional, not a strenuously achieved ending, like the serenity of the conclusion of *To the Lighthouse*. There is a reference to 'the heart of darkness', the title of Conrad's tale, and it also appears at the end of the posthumously published *Between the Acts* (1941). The heart had gone out of Virginia Woolf's work.

That her genius had burned itself out is confirmed by the six previously unpublished short stories at the end of *A Haunted House* (1944). Her short stories, despite some brilliancies, tend to confirm the sense of a minor talent. Yet if she is not among the very greatest of English novelists, her fiction leaves one with the impression of a delicate and subtle artist in words, who upheld aesthetic and spiritual values in a brutal, materialistic age. Mr E. M. Forster reminds one of the permanent significance of her work:

> Order. Justice. Truth. She cared for these abstractions, and tried to express them through symbols ... The epitaph of such an artist cannot be written by the vulgar-minded or by the lugubrious ... She triumphed over what are primly called 'difficulties', and she also triumphed in the positive sense: she brought in the spoils. And sometimes it is as a row of little silver cups that I see her work gleaming. 'These trophies,' the inscription runs, 'were won by the mind from matter, its enemy and its friend.'
>
> (*Two Cheers for Democracy*)

To these eloquent words one may, perhaps, add the comment that Virginia Woolf had not only the sensitiveness, poetry, and imagination of Mrs Ramsay. She retained and exemplified the integrity and heroism of Mr Ramsay and of Leslie Stephen, her father.

NOTES

1. The quotations from the works of Virginia Woolf are taken from the uniform edition, published by the Hogarth Press.

2. See D. S. Savage, *The Withered Branch* (1950), quoted by Arnold Kettle in *An Introduction to the English Novel*, Vol. II, p. 105.

3. For the influence of Turgenev on Virginia Woolf, see Gilbert Phelps, *The Russian Novel in English Fiction*, pp. 132–7.

4. See the review by Q. D. Leavis in *Scrutiny*, Vol. VII, No. 2 (September 1938).

5. See Frank Swinnerton, *The Georgian Literary Scene* (Everyman's Library), ch. XIII, and J. K. Johnstone, *The Bloomsbury Group*.

6. Dr Leavis might find in Virginia Woolf's notes on D. H. Lawrence an interesting footnote to his accounts of the social prejudice and intellectual antagonism shown by J. M. Keynes and his circle and others.

7. Perhaps Virginia Woolf is indebted for the idea to Flaubert: 'what I should like to do is to write a book about nothing, a book with no reference to anything outside itself,which would stand on its own by the inner strength of its style, just as the earth holds itself without support in space, a book which would have hardly any subject, or at any rate one that is barely perceptible, if that were possible'. Letter to Louise Colet (16 January 1852), quoted by Miriam Allott, *Novelists on the Novel*, p. 242.

8. Cp. Nos. 95 and 100.

9. J. W. Graham, in 'A Negative Note on Bergson and Virginia Woolf' (*Essays in Criticism* VI, No. 1, January 1956), argues convincingly that the influence of Bergson on Virginia Woolf was both more general and limited than has frequently been assumed.

10. E.g. Peter and Margaret Havard-Williams: 'Mystical Experience in Virginia Woolf's *The Waves*' (*Essays in Criticism* IV, No. 1, January 1954).

11. Fitz-james Stephen: *Liberty, Equality, Fraternity*, p. 353 (2nd ed., London, 1874), quoted by William James, *Selected Papers on Philosophy* (Everyman's Library), p. 124. Virginia Woolf possibly read the passage in William James's *The Will to Believe* (1897), as well as in its original context in Fitz-james Stephen; she was also, of course, a great admirer of the philosopher's brother, the novelist Henry James, to whom there are some interesting references in *A Writer's Diary*. For the intellectual background of the Stephens, see Q. D. Leavis's article on Leslie Stephen, *Scrutiny*, Vol. VII, No. 4, March 1939, and the study by Noel Annan.

12. Two recent American academic studies are 'Mythic Patterns in *To the Lighthouse*' by Joseph Blotner, P.M.L.A., LXXI, September 1956, pp. 547–62, and 'Vision in *To the Lighthouse*' by Glenn Pedersen, P.M.L.A., LXXIII, December 1958, pp. 585–600.

L. H. MYERS AND BLOOMSBURY

G. H. BANTOCK

THE work of L. H. Myers (1881–1944) presents at least two points of interest. There are the novels in themselves – one of which, at least, is of sufficient merit to warrant inclusion among the best of the last fifty years (and the company would not be large); and there is what has happened to the novels – the literary situation in England which, while continuing to find significance in the work of any one of a dozen inferior writers has, after the first mostly adulatory reviews, quietly ignored Myers's work. As might be guessed, the two points are not unconnected; and by defining the attitude to experience that Myers's work entailed and by examining the particular nature of his moral preoccupations, something will already have been done to uncover the motives behind the neglect. Indeed, the use of the word 'moral', necessarily forced upon one in the most preliminary consideration of the novels, may already have provided a clue.

Frederic W. H. Myers, Leo's father, an essayist and poet of minor distinction, was one of the founders of the Society for Psychical Research, in 1882, an undertaking which interested a number of the best minds of late Victorian intellectual society. Thus, Leckhampton House, Cambridge, at which the young Leo was brought up, became a centre of intellectual life attended by many of the distinguished minds of the late Victorian period, Henry Sidgwick, Montagu Butler, Lord Rayleigh, F. W. Maitland, Balfours, Lyttletons, and many others. This was the Cambridge of the Puritan-Whig tradition of common sense and the dry light of reason, as Leslie Stephen described it. Though F. W. H. Myers was subject to a more turgid emotionalism than were many of his friends, his major preoccupation was still primarily rationalistic and moralistic – the attempt to prove, by controlled scientific experimentation, the immortality of the soul.

To the father the common enterprise of psychical research provided an adequate social and intellectual milieu. Given the particular circumstances of the breakdown of dogmatic creeds in the late Victorian era, psychical research was obviously something to engage the united attention of 'serious' minds. This is worth stressing because Leo Myers constantly sought for, and perpetually failed to find, some group which would enable him to achieve at least a tolerable degree of what nowadays is referred to as social integration. As early as at Eton, he reacted strongly against the social tone of his environment. The school provided Myers's first contact with what in his books he called 'the world'; and there is good evidence from friends that he found repugnant the covert insincerities which even this adolescent world demanded. All his life he concerned himself with the Idols of the Market-Place, those which are 'formed by the intercourse and association of men with each other', and the insincerities of behaviour to which men are led by their need to live in society.

Myers was well-to-do and, except for a brief period at the Board of Trade during the First World War, had no regular employment. As a young man, he had a mystical experience in America. Though he had no liking for any orthodox Christian faith, he retained a sense of powers extra-human and transcendental throughout his life. Intellectually he developed late. His first novel, *The Orissers*, took him twelve or thirteen years to write, and was not published until 1922, when he was just over forty. Other novels appeared at regular intervals, until *The Pool of Vishnu* (1940). After that, attempts to write were unsuccessful. An abstract indictment of contemporary society failed, though he attempted at least three versions of it. Just before he died he destroyed an autobiographical study, intended to display the evils of his own social class. He committed suicide in 1944.

As a writer, Myers is much nearer to the practice of, say, George Eliot, than to those modern 'experimental' writers whose aim is to convey experience through the 'stream of consciousness'. He is perpetually aware of the implications of the experience he is conveying. Hence what might be termed the 'literary' flavour of his novels; they are consciously shaped, like Victorian novels, and they seek not to convey the 'moment', but events winnowed and sifted. And the sense which guides and selects is the moral sense. He comments adversely on Proust:

> When a novelist displays an attitude of aesthetical detachment from the ordinary ethical and philosophical preoccupations of humanity, something in us protests ... Proust, for

> instance, by treating all sorts of sensibility as equal in importance, and all manifestations of character as standing on the same plane of significance, adds nothing to his achievement, but only draws attention to himself as aiming at the exaltation of a rather petty form of aestheticism.

Thus Myers seeks to be a 'connoisseur' of character, and criticizes the lack of moral and spiritual discrimination which fails to appreciate the 'deep-seated spiritual vulgarity that lies at the heart of our civilization'.

Hence it is the exercise of the moral judgement which actuates the discriminations among his characters. His novels, though they appear at first sight to be remote in subject-matter, are in fact strictly contemporary; and he worked out in them, after the manner of his own Jali, some of his most pressing personal problems, chiefly the problem which he remembered exercising him from his childhood: 'Why do men choose to live?', and the problem of personal relationships. What he investigated through his 'serious' characters was the possibility of a way of life which should at once stand the test of a morally fastidious taste and end his feeling of social and personal isolation. The books, therefore, are peculiarly autobiographical. Fundamentally, as I have suggested, his mind was of a religious tendency; his major work, *The Near and the Far*, is set in India in the sixteenth century, because this not only allows him the detachment from strictly local and contemporary settings that, significantly, he always needed, but permits him to explore a selection of Eastern and Western approaches to the problem of ultimate 'Being'.

In *The Near and the Far*, Ranee Sita is pointing out to the Brahmin, Gokal, the extent to which she disagrees with her husband Amar's outlook:

> 'I, for my part, shall always affirm what Amar denies. Between us there is a gulf.'
>
> Gokal leaned forward earnestly, 'The gulf lies not between those who affirm and those who deny, but between those who affirm and those who ignore. Listen!' he went on ... 'Fundamentally your mind and Amar's are similar in type; you both raise the same problems and the answers you give are the same in essence, if their substance is not the same. You advocate life's intensification, Amar its extinguishment; but you both recognize imperfection and you both aim at perfection!'

For Myers this distinction between those who affirm and those who ignore – the Fastidious and the Trivial, as he called them – was fundamental. An examination of how these two groups manifest themselves, what characteristics they reveal, and on what terms they exist in society, will take us far in an understanding of Myers's work.

In all his books there is a small group of characters – the Fastidious – who stand over against society as it manifests itself in the life of social classes and institutions. There, standards of conduct are derived, ultimately, not from an apprehension of spiritual forces comprehending something greater than, and apart from, man but from a glorification of society's own spirit, a judgement in terms of its own materialistic values. Most people, he considered, live by appearances; by 'appearances' (illusion, Maya) he usually meant those modes of behaviour, those masks, which a man adopts so that he may find himself accepted. Such a man presents to his companions a recognizable 'personality', a 'persona'; all real genuineness vanishes. Of such are the Trivial.

Myers was always strongly convinced of the reality of the 'Evil Will' in human intercourse. This accounts for his unwillingness to allow for compromise in the conflict between the Trivial and the Fastidious. Such a conflict is the subject of his first novel, which is concerned with the struggle between the Maynes and the Orissers for the possession of the family seat of the Orissers, Eamor. The Maynes represent in their varying degrees of spiritual obtuseness the worldly and material values of that type of society in which Myers moved. Whatever the faults of the Orissers, they recognize a standard beyond social opinion. In the end John Mayne is defeated; and his defeat springs from the forced recognition of a moral obligation. Contact with Lilian Orisser convinces him of his inadequacy; his handing over of the house, Eamor, is the tacit recognition of a standard beyond public opinion and common law, the sources from which the Maynes of the world are accustomed to draw their instinctive self-justification.

Nevertheless, the position of the Orissers is not really satisfactory – and the problem of the Orissers is ultimately Myers's own problem. They are self-isolated; and they are critical enough of their own position to be aware of the fact that to be cut off from 'life', even in John Mayne's interpretation of the word, is not to their advantage. Eamor symbolizes an ordered way of life, uncontaminated by the material spirit of the society of the day; to gain it the Orissers are prepared to offend against the conventional moral code, even to commit murder. Yet, even when they are successful, they feel themselves cut off in Eamor's 'dreadful peace'. If the Orissers are the spiritually aware, they are, nevertheless, aware of themselves as the self-conscious members of an effete and dying social order.

Myers's first novel, then, reveals quite starkly – too starkly – the problem; 'too starkly' because the moral distinctions involved (the dichotomy between the Orissers and the Maynes) are too crudely made – we descend too quickly to melodrama. There is more egotism in the make-up of the Orissers than Myers seems aware of. At the same time, it was right that the concern for standards of conduct should not be regarded as illusory, even as those standards are interpreted in the novel; and Myers does sense that the moral isolation of the Orissers is equivocal, and that such isolation represents a desiccation.

The 'Clio' hardly merits serious consideration; Myers wrote it because he wished to produce something in the Aldous Huxley vein. It is in *The Root of the Flower* (1935), the first three sections of *The Near and the Far*, that the implications of the Orissers are taken up and explored more fully. The Orisser group – the sensitive and fastidious – reappear in the characters of Rajah Amar, his wife, Sita, and their son Jali, together with Amar's brother-in-law, Hari, and a friend, Gokal. Through the 'education' (using the word in the sense in which Henry Adams employed it) of Jali we explore the effect of society on a young and sensitive mind and the pretentiousness of various social and artistic circles is revealed. The Rajah himself, mature and critically aware of the corruptions of the world, seeks to retire from an active to a contemplative life. But his political responsibilities for his small state and the struggle for the throne which is bound to break out between Akbar's two sons, Salim and Daniyal, after the emperor's death, ensure that the contact between the 'fastidious' group and the rest of society shall be much closer than in *The Orissers.* The Rajah believes in an absolute division between the political and spiritual life. He imagines that he can readjust his allegiance in accordance with expediency alone, on the principle of 'Render unto Caesar'. He does not realize that the policy and the person are inextricably bound together. For he feels that, despite his personal distaste for Daniyal, he can side with him on purely abstract grounds.

It is not until Daniyal by a superficially trivial, but brutal, act of cruelty reveals the corruption of spirit which he represents that the Rajah strikes at the prince with his sword. The action is unavailing, but symbolically Myers has indicated that the evil of the world is a quality of the personality and must be met by opposition and action.

There are various gross manifestations of the trivial materialistic outlook in India in the book. Myers's analysis of the Pleasance of the Arts, a meeting place of contemporary aesthetes, has interest beyond the novel, for here he is satirizing a prominent literary group of his times, Bloomsbury.

Daniyal, the leader of the Pleasance, is the 'poet, the Artist, the enraptured lover of Beauty'. The camp glories in its independence of thought, its freedom from conventions, its emancipation from the Philistine and the Prig. It casts off 'dreary actuality' and basks in the glitter of its own pretentiousness. Here everybody flatters himself that he is somebody; 'in artificiality the spirit finds its own true life'; revolt is the order of the day, revolt against the old, outworn conventions, prejudices, and, above all, 'the bullying, nagging disposition of nature'. A closer acquaintanceship with the members of the Pleasance shows, however, that the camp has its own inverted orthodoxy. Not only is the apparent freedom of the camp entirely illusory, for all its inhabitants are bound by a rigid necessity to share the same vices and applaud the same apparently heterodox opinions, but they also depend basically upon a

> solid, shockable world of decorum and common sense. They had to believe that a great ox-like eye was fixed upon them in horror. Without this their lives lost their point.

It is not hard to see why Bloomsbury was distasteful to Myers; for Bloomsbury was aesthetic rather than moralistic, even though its outlook was profoundly influenced by a work on moral philosophy. The last chapter of G. E. Moore's *Principia Ethica*, where his intuitionist moral theory led him to set up personal relations and a sense of beauty as the two supreme goods, formed the starting place for the development of an aesthetic philosophy to which the Bloomsbury intellectuals subscribed with varying degrees of personal emphasis. Mr Clive Bell, in defining what he understood by Civilization, declared that 'Works of art being direct means to aesthetic ecstasy are direct means to good'. The potential value of a work of art lay in the fact that it could 'at any moment become a means to a state of mind of superlative excellence'. The aim of every civilized man was the 'richest and fullest life obtainable, a life which contains the maximum of vivid and exquisite experiences'. Civilized man desired 'complete self-development and complete self-expression'.

What Bloomsbury made of Moore's doctrine, then, was subjectivist and aesthetic, something very different from Myers's transcendentalist position. As Keynes put it in his *Memoir*:

> Nothing mattered except states of mind, our own and other people's, of course, but chiefly our own. These states of mind were not associated with action or achievement or with consequences. They consisted in timeless passionate states of contemplation and communion, largely unattached to 'before' and 'after' ...

The effect was to 'escape from the Benthamite tradition' – there was no place for social effort or moral strenuousness of the Victorian type:

> ... social action as an end in itself and not merely as a lugubrious duty had dropped out of our Ideal, and, not only social action, but the life of action generally, power, politics, success, wealth, ambition ...

The anti-traditional element in all this was strong:

> We claimed the right to judge every individual case on its merits, and the wisdom, experience and self-control to do so successfully ... We repudiated entirely customary morals, convention and traditional wisdom.

The self-regarding mind, then, freed itself from locality and background which might have carried a hint of continuity and obligation. This represents a position very different from that to which Amar came, with its underlying acceptance of social responsibility. But what Myers particularly detested was the Bloomsbury 'tone', the element of communal self-congratulation implicit in the self-conscious spirit of social aloofness and 'difference': 'The life of a first-rate English man or woman', urged Mr Clive Bell, 'is one long assertion of his or her personality in the face of unsympathetic or actively hostile environment.' (*Civilization.*) Roy Harrod, in his book on Keynes, reveals something of the origin and behaviour of the group. It developed from 'The Society' at Cambridge; not all members of Bloomsbury had been members of the Society, but Bloomsbury was, undoubtedly, 'strongly influenced by some who had been members'. Its growth was spontaneous rather than contrived: but frequent meetings and social intercourse induced a reasonably homogeneous outlook. The intimacy of personal relationship manifested itself in a private language; letters and talk between members abounded in esoteric jokes and allusions. It is true that members criticized each other, frequently in a spirit of mockery and raillery, and often displayed considerable differences of opinion; but the criticisms themselves implied a common acceptance of iconoclastic irreverence for all normal taboos and conventions: 'they shared a taste for discussion in pursuit of truth and a contempt for conventional ways of thinking and feeling', admits Mr Bell, while seeking to deny any real homogeneity of outlook (*Old Friends*). Such protestation of liberty of expression and a pervasive scepticism of outlook formed a barrier against an outer world in the grip of superstition and convention. Thus there came to be a Bloomsbury manner – composed of mockery, 'gentle dissection, fun, and ridicule', all 'in the greatest good humour'. There was even a Bloomsbury voice:

> The voice was emphatic but restrained. Certain syllables, or even letters, were rather strongly stressed, but not at all in the manner of a drawl. The presupposition of the cadence was that everything one said mattered. Emphasis had to be applied.
>
> (R. F. Harrod: *The Life of John Maynard Keynes*)

In Bloomsbury, then, it might be said, as Myers so ironically wrote of the Pleasance:

> Here you might come across people of every variety – except one, the commonplace. Dull, conventional people – people who weren't lit by the divine spark, had no chance of gaining admission here. Daniyal had thrown away the shackles of ordinary prejudices and cant.

In this, the reasons why Myers, who had formed many Bloomsbury acquaintances, gradually but effectively dissociated himself from the group become clear. They were both moral and personal.

The Pool of Vishnu, Myers's continuation to and conclusion of *The Root and the Flower*, contains the positive answer to the meretricious materialist world of Akbar's India. In the story of Mohan and Damayanti, Myers reveals the positive nature of a married relationship based on complete candour as between absolute equals working through communion with transcendental powers ... 'All communion', says the Guru, the wise man who defines, too overtly for good novel writing, the moral implications of the book, 'is through the Centre. When the relation of man and man is not through the Centre it corrupts and destroys itself.' This notion, of course, was very similar to that expressed in Martin Buber's *I and Thou*. Personal relationships conceived in such terms – a very different matter from Bloomsbury's conception of them – Myers believed to be capable of infinite extension in a manner which would finally overthrow the old, stratified social order, represented here by Rajah Bhoj and his wife and their cult of first-rateness. And in the relationship between Mohan and Damayanti and their peasants a new brotherhood of man is foreshadowed. At their house Jali discerns a correspondence between the outward things and the inner landscape of his mind – the 'near' and the 'far' coalesce. The material requirements of everyday life are spiritualized in true community. Over all is Vishnu – and Vishnu is a preserver.

This last novel contains Myers's dream of spiritual home. Someone suggested, as he stated, that 'I put serenity into the book instead of finding it in my life'. And he accepted this as being 'shrewd, and, in fact, right'. But he went on, in the same letter, to observe that the Guru does not preach a doctrine of serenity nor do any of the other characters find a resolution of their difficulties and conflicts. A life of effort was always necessary because it implied a transcendence of self in relationship to others. It is this that makes the vision of personal relationships mature and convincing. Here, at any rate, faith and community could combine. In the real world Myers thought that they would manifest themselves in communism; during the last years of his life he became violently pro-Russian. Yet he held such beliefs with the vehemence of desperation. In his own life, he never found the community that he sought. 'Many of my old friends and acquaintances move in a world of thought and feeling that is distasteful to me', he wrote. And in the last five years of his life he withdrew from many long-standing friendships.

It is significant that all the characters in his book inhabit imaginary environments, places to which Myers himself had never been. Their problems are real problems as problems of the mind, but the characters themselves are rootless. Myers did not have, say, George Eliot's capacity, despite the intellectual nature of her mature life, for setting characters in an immediate and closely realized English environment; nor did he, like Lawrence, possess the 'spirit of place'. Myers's characters exist rather as self-consciousness than as intimately observed individuals. He was, in any case, never interested in the setting and he would brush aside praise of his descriptive powers with the remark that he was completely uninterested in description.

Yet Myers remains an important writer. For one thing, he had integrity; behind his work there is a kind of moral honesty which refuses to be taken in by the worldly and the meretricious. His analyses of behaviour are often extremely acute; he realized how very important group appreciation is to man and had an unerring eye for the social insincerity which marks a desire to be approved. He has, in fact, a notion of the civilized life, involving honesty and frankness of relationship, a basic genuineness of personality, which saw beyond the normally accepted criteria of such a life – polite conversation and a dabbling acquaintanceship with the arts. He sees the inadequacy of liberal humanism for the sort of being man is; and one remembers certain scenes – Daniyal's stepping on the cat's head is an example – because they challenge the easy optimism of the liberal tradition. He has, that is, a sense of evil. Had he had more 'imagination' in the Coleridgean sense – a quality necessitating a greater vitality, perhaps – he might have been a great writer. Greatness he misses; but he is never trivial. Fundamentally he is serious, concerned, and intelligent; and in a literary world which seems increasingly to find 'amusing' a term of critical approbation, he has not retained favour. The neglect into which he has fallen invokes a comment on our debilitation of standards; there are not so many with such virtues in our times that we can afford to neglect what he had to say.

D. H. LAWRENCE AND *WOMEN IN LOVE*

W. W. ROBSON

Masson Professor of English Literature, University of Edinburgh

THE object of criticism, it is often said, is to obtain a 'balanced view' of the author criticized. But where the author in question is D. H. Lawrence (1885–1930) this is peculiarly difficult. Lawrence tends to stir up (to use one of his own phrases) a 'bristling rousedness' in his critics, and estimates of him both as a man and as a writer tend consequently to be exaggerated, one way or the other. He is not an easy author for the would-be judicious. The first problem the critic has to face is the daunting mixture of kinds and levels in Lawrence's writing, due to the intimate and complicated relationship in it between the poet-novelist, the prophet-preacher, and the human case. It is easy to make rough-and-ready distinctions: to say, for example, that *The Woman who Rode Away* comes from the artist, *Fantasia of the Unconscious* from the preacher, and the poems in *Look! we have come through* from the man, the 'difficult' husband and lover, the subject for biographical speculation and psychological inquiry amateur or professional. But even in the works mentioned, the relation between the different elements in Lawrence's genius is not altogether simple, and when we come to consider such equally characteristic works as *The Captain's Doll* or *St Mawr* or *The Man who Died* the complexity of the treatment required is obvious. No simple critical formula can be proposed. This is largely because Lawrence is like Byron or Tolstoy, in that it is impossible to separate, for long, his work and his life. The work represents very often the writer's living-through of his personal problems and conflicts, as well as his more general preoccupations; while the life comes to take on the shape of a symbolic story or legend.

In the case of Lawrence the outlines of the 'legend' are very familiar. The childhood of the son of a Midland miner and a woman of marked character, in a country village transformed by the mining industry, which helped to give us *Sons and Lovers* (1913) and *The Rainbow* (1915), with their insights into the emotional and moral problems arising between husband and wife, and between child and parent, in a working-class environment; the youth and early manhood of a provincial elementary-school teacher, with an early success as a writer which distinguished him as one of the most gifted of his time; the union with a German wife of patrician origin, their later marriage which (all difficulties admitted) was to give so much sustenance to the man and subject-matter to the writer; the conflict with the authorities over *The Rainbow*'s alleged immorality (as later over that of *Lady Chatterley's Lover*, 1928); the horrors of the war-time years, the nightmare' described in *Kangaroo* (1923), the petty persecution, the suspicion and fear; the utopian dream of Rananim, with its corollaries partly absurd and partly sad; the years of restless wandering, to all quarters of the earth; the intense, difficult, usually ambivalent personal relationships with men and women, both distinguished and obscure; the temptations to primitivism and Messianism, explored and abandoned; the growing bitterness and depression, illustrated in the satirical quality of so many of Lawrence's later stories, now and then alleviated by flashes of gaiety, sardonic humour, and robust common sense; the long-drawn-out and pathetic struggle with illness, the death in his forty-fifth year – these things have been so much written about that detailed rehearsal of them is unnecessary. But the story will be read over again and probably with more objectivity as the years go by and the personalities and topicalities involved cease to irritate or to divert. Lawrence is a person that future students of English literature and English civilization will have to meet; and it may be said that his 'personality' is the central subject for criticism for the student of his life – not only the Lawrence of anecdote, the brilliant letter-writer, journalist, and travel-book writer, but the wider personality-pattern which informs his creative work. Only one or two facets of Lawrence's 'personality' can be examined here; no comprehensiveness will be attempted, but merely a clearing-away of some of the manifest obstacles to judgement and appreciation.

Many of the works of Lawrence that follow his 'Nottingham' period do present obstacles. Now it should be said at once that where he is most completely a *poet* these seem to disappear; where, for example, he is evoking the life of nature: not merely the 'nature' of nature-poets, but the ancient feeling of the cosmic mystery, the prehuman and inhuman power of the universe, which we may suppose archaic man to have felt, and which Lawrence, with that strong 'archaic' strain in his genius, can make articulate more wonderfully than any other modern writer in English. When this poetry appears in Lawrence – more often in his prose than in his verse – our doubts, objections, and questions are silenced. But Lawrence is a novelist and story-teller as well as a poet of the cosmos, and when he deals in human relationships – and he himself described his own subject-matter as 'the relations between men and women' – we are often disturbed and challenged, and sometimes repelled, by what we sense of the point of view of the author. This is not only because Lawrence preaches to the reader, and many of us dislike being preached to anyway, apart from disliking what he preaches. Even when Lawrence is more fully an artist and makes us feel what he wants us to feel, instead of insisting that we ought to feel it, bafflement and irritation often occur. It is at such times that our attention is drawn away from the work to the man behind the work, and we cannot but deviate into thoughts about those well-known sexual obsessions and social unease which critics and biographers have so much dwelt on. So we lose contact with the world of the author's imagination and find ourselves on the plane of ideas and opinions. It is easy then to discover that Lawrence as a moralist is thoroughly incoherent. Any attempt to institutionalize his moral, social, or political teaching would produce chaos – assuming we could imagine what the attempt would be like. Lawrence is too obviously generalizing improperly, and at times erroneously, from his own case. This is especially clear in the matter of sex. There is obviously self-deception, hence insincerity, in a work like *The Plumed Serpent* (1926), with its insistence that a woman must not seek complete physical satisfaction from the act of sex, but must find contentment instead in a reverent 'submission' to male 'authority'.

But this disagreeable side of Lawrence, though it exists, is relevant to the literary student only in so far as it reflects a failure in Lawrence's art. It is true that this failure is frequent and characteristic – perhaps especially in those post-war years when the suffering and defeated mood of the author is more evident, and coincides with, if it is not indeed partly due to, a decline in his creative powers. But we must be careful to distinguish between those works of his which are disturbing in the wrong way – those which deflect us on to the plane of opinions and arguments – and those which are healthily disturbing, which compel us to a valuable reappraisal, and perhaps readjustment, of our familiar assumptions and attitudes. Roughly speaking, we may say that in his successful works Lawrence makes us *see* the complexity of many of the concrete human situations to which moral judgements are undoubtedly relevant, but which do not lend themselves to description and analysis in straightforward moral terms. Thus (whatever we may think of the success of the novel as a whole) his presentation in *Aaron's Rod* (1922) of the deadlock in Aaron's marriage, the impasse into which Aaron's life has got, is so powerful that we are no more inclined than we would be in real life to pronounce readily on the rights and wrongs of Aaron's decision to leave his wife and children. It is not that we are persuaded to excuse Aaron, though as the novel goes on we soon realize that the author is on Aaron's side. It is rather that, owing to Lawrence's art, we are able to see this sort of situation 'in depth' – in a way that we rarely can, either in our own lives or in the lives of others. When it comes to explaining *why* Aaron took the step that he did, Lawrence is perhaps not able to translate his own convictions about the matter into art – not able to dramatize them; the amateur psychologist may indeed feel that this is because Aaron's decision is not consciously enough related, in the book, to his difficulties revealed there in forming a relationship with *any* woman and his curious quasi-homosexual relationship with the writer Rawdon Lilly. But what Lawrence can and does do is to show *how* it happened. We *see* that the Aaron we meet in his pages would, and did, act in this way. Lawrence's imagination has been sufficient to provide the data, the 'facts' of the situation; though when it comes to interpreting them, his imagination – perhaps because of some personal psychological 'block' – seems to function less powerfully.

Even where Lawrence has clearly fallen into special pleading, we can find this fullness in the presentment of the *données* of the situation which gives us room to make up our own minds. And it should be added that Lawrence's didacticism is characteristically apt to turn into self-questioning; just as those works of his (like *Lady Chatterley's Lover*) where a kind of near-allegorical simplicity is clearly intended, turn into something more complex because Lawrence, in 'becoming' the gamekeeper, cannot but bring into the gamekeeper his own uncertainties and self-mistrust. (A simpler example is the short story *The Daughters of the Vicar*, in the character of the miner Durant, who represents instinctive 'life' in the fable, but who turns out to have intense inner difficulties.) It is notable that Laurentian didactic prose is at its best when it reveals, in its oscillatory, fluctuating movement, this recurrent self-questioning.

Lawrence's over-insistence on 'telling' us things – and sometimes telling us things we cannot accept – should not, then, be allowed to obscure from us the very real extent to which he often succeeds in conveying the feel of actual life and actual human problems. A man who spent so much of his life as Lawrence did in preaching to women, or to one woman, may fail (as Lawrence so often does) to pay due regard to the rules which govern valid argument, illustration, and proof; but this does not mean that he is lacking in the essential intelligence required of a novelist to realize the full human reality of the *people* who argue, puzzle, and suffer. Furthermore, the inner stresses and strains which cause incoherence in the abstract thinker may in the novelist and story-teller provide the creative driving-force.

Perhaps it is something in Lawrence's manner of writing, rather than his matter, which has proved a stumbling-block for many readers. If we take up *The Tales of D. H. Lawrence* – the volume which contains a great part of his most unquestionably successful work as an artist – we will soon be struck by an obvious difference in quality between Lawrence's style and most of the educated English fiction we are accustomed to. Probably a superficial impression of lack of 'style' had counted for much in the opinion, once very common, that Lawrence is an uneducated writer. This opinion, stated baldly, is absurd. Nevertheless, the quality in Lawrence's style which prompts it is certainly there. When Lawrence lapses from his highest level he is apt to move towards Marie Corelli or Rider Haggard, not towards Galsworthy. In his good as in his inferior works he has something in common with the great 'lowbrow' best-sellers: the vitality which they have and the 'middlebrow' novelists have not, though the best-sellers are coarse where Lawrence is sensitive and spiritual. He can use a vocabulary perilously like theirs in which to register his sharpest intuitions into modern civilized life, and allow himself confident generalizations about racial, philosophical, and sexual matters which have a tone and ring uneasily reminiscent of the intellectual underworld of 'British Israel', Count Keyserling, or Max Nordau. This is a pity, because it nourishes the various animosities which ordinary vulgar snobbery, prudery, philistinism, or Bloomsbury superciliousness already have towards Lawrence on other grounds.

But it is now becoming common to praise the directness and vitality of Lawrence's style in general. What seems still an open question, even among his admirers, is whether he succeeded in expressing his full powers in self-sufficient works of art. It is well known that Lawrence rejected the traditional canons of structure and method in the novel. He wanted Arnold Bennett (the 'old imitator') to be told that the principles Bennett invoked held good only for novels that were 'copies' of other novels, and he spoke in exasperation about the 'ossiferous skin-and-grief' form which others wanted to impose on him. Some of what Lawrence said on this subject can be dismissed as mere special pleading. A judicious admirer of Lawrence will not cite *Aaron's Rod* or *Kangaroo* as triumphs of originality of form. They are meandering, repetitious, padded-out. Lawrence, especially in his later years, wrote too much and wrote it too quickly. Nor can the artistic objection to a great part of his work be regarded only as a misguided application of the Flaubertian principles which he rejected. Lawrence allows himself liberties, in what purport to be works of fiction – works of imagination – which are incompatible with the practice of any art, not merely the art of Flaubert. He openly abandons the pretence of dramatic objectivity and admits that this or that character is a mere mouthpiece. He addresses the reader directly, to explain, emphasize, or preach. He permits details from his personal life, not fully coherent with the presented fiction, to get into the book. It is unnecessary to elaborate these faults. Much can be urged in mitigation: the circumstances of Lawrence's life as a professional writer, the treatment meted out to the novels on which he *did* work hard, the growing urgency of his feeling (hence the overwrought, violent, didactic tone so frequent in those later books) about the decadence of modern civilized life. But faults are faults. If Lawrence is to be defended as an original artist of the novel, it will not be on the strength of *Aaron's Rod* or *Kangaroo*. Each has the makings of a good novel: but these are lost in a wilderness of preaching, autobiography, and journalism.

Nor will *The Plumed Serpent* or *Lady Chatterley's Lover* serve to substantiate the artistic claim for Lawrence. These he certainly worked hard on, especially the latter. They are different from one another, and their didactic messages differ. But they have this in common, that the writer is concerned with a single-minded intentness to 'put over' those didactic messages. Certainly his own maxim (in *Studies in Classic American Literature*, 1923) 'Never trust the artist. Trust the tale' applies to those two books. The tale can get the better of the artist. The fantasy-revival of the old Mexican paganism in the one, and the insistent sexual outspokenness in the other, do not make up the whole interest of *The Plumed Serpent* and *Lady Chatterley*. The fables themselves, in important points, do not serve the unequivocal purpose they were meant to serve. *The Plumed Serpent* in places can impress and move the reader who is most convinced that Lawrence's aim in this book was tragically mistaken and perverse – as well as being somewhat absurd. *Lady Chatterley's Lover* can inspire a sympathy with Clifford which was probably not intended, but can be genuinely grounded in what the story tells us. But neither book can be 'lived in': that is, neither book creates an imagined domain in which the reader simply finds himself, and finds *for* himself the moral bearings of the world which the artist has imagined; a world which we are not just told about, but which seems to exist in itself and be discovered by us. In these books, as in other stories of Lawrence, the poles of truth and falsity, good and evil, sickness and health are imposed by the direct moral intervention of the author. The books cohere as wholes and make sense (morally speaking) only if looked at from a point of view already predisposed to accept the author's ideas. Too much of what seems to come out of genuine experience has passed through the moralist's filter. The high proportion in these books of merely sketched, diagrammatic characters is significant.

Now it is easy to show – from explicit remarks of Lawrence's in the novels, as well as in his criticism and in letters and so on – that in this didacticism Lawrence was going against his own proclaimed principles. What is harder to make out is just what *positively* those principles come to: just what is the formal character of the works that do come more or less completely out of 'pure passionate experience'. Some may think that *Sons and Lovers* is the text to choose in order to discover this. It is rightly one of the best known and most popular of

Lawrence's books. But much that is essential to the study of Lawrence would be missed if we took that novel as fully representative. It is certainly the easiest to understand, being the only one of his first-rate books which is like an ordinary novel. Though much of it takes on a fuller significance when we know the rest of Lawrence's life and work, it is self-sufficient and undoubtedly the novel that a reader ignorant of him should begin with. Furthermore, the life-choices that the hero, Paul, makes in *Sons and Lovers* show their consequences in Lawrence's later work. Some have thought that in Paul's failure to see through his mother's pathetically false values, and in the cruelty, due to his mother's thwarting of his development, shown in his attitude to his father and later in his treatment of Miriam, we discover Lawrence himself taking the wrong turning. But however this may be, Paul's choices are self-explanatory within the book itself. If in some respects it seems to be a confessional work, the power of the literary artist is shown in the objectivity with which the confession is treated. Yet *Sons and Lovers* is the work of a potential rather than an actual genius. Its great superiority over Lawrence's previous novels – *The White Peacock* (1911) and *The Trespasser* (1912) – lies in its freedom from literariness. They are over-written: the directness and naturalness of *Sons and Lovers* mark the great *literary* evolution which is the result of Lawrence's decision (encouraged by 'Miriam') to deal directly with urgent personal matter. But by reason of its very merits it cannot be a triumph of imagination. There is little in the book to make us feel that the author's future strength would lie in the imagining of characters and themes outside his immediate personal situation. In this respect it shows no clear anticipation of the best parts of *The Rainbow*.

It is *The Rainbow*, together with *Women in Love* (1920) and the best of the tales, on which Dr F. R. Leavis, in his study of Lawrence, has chosen to lay the main stress.[1] And whether or not we can go all or most of the way with Dr Leavis in what he says about Lawrence in general, I am sure his selection here is right. And out of this selection *Women in Love* seems a suitable particular choice to illustrate Lawrence's mature art. Lawrence seems to have thought it, together with *The Rainbow*, his greatest work – though in later years his preoccupation with the Chatterley book may have caused him to alter his judgement. Dr Leavis, having given good reasons for treating it (despite the carry-over of names of characters) as a separate work from *The Rainbow*, ranks it above the earlier novel. Whether this is so or not, it seems clear that it is best considered as a separate work (though one initial problem that confronts the reader of *Women in Love*, the uncertainty about the social status of the two girls Ursula and Gudrun whom he meets in the first chapter, is cleared up if we come to the later novel from the earlier). Perhaps it is a pity that Lawrence did not change the names of the characters who are carried over when he separated out the two works from the originally envisaged single novel of *The Sisters*. The Ursula of *Women in Love* is not like the Ursula of *The Rainbow*. To simplify for the moment, Ursula of *The Rainbow*, though quite convincingly dramatized and a girl, lives mainly out of the experience of the young Lawrence himself. The Ursula of *Women in Love* has much more in her of Lawrence's wife Frieda. Any effort by the reader to fuse the two Ursulas in his reading of *Women in Love* would lead to difficulties. It is true that the later part of *The Rainbow* – what bears on the failure of the affair between Ursula and Skrebensky – contains germinally some of the substance of *Women in Love*. But the connexion is thematic, rather than narrative. *Women in Love* is thus best treated separately.

There are two reasons for choosing it, rather than its predecessor, for discussion. First, the cyclical, repetitive method of *The Rainbow* is not hard to grasp, once it is seen for what it is. The book contains patches of local obscurity (as often with Lawrence, the love-scenes are obscure), but it has not on the whole been found so radically puzzling as *Women in Love*. But above all *Women in Love* is the more 'modern' of the two, the one in which Lawrence is more concerned with what we recognize as contemporary life. There is something of a pastoral, idealizing, idyllic quality about *The Rainbow* – at any rate, in the earlier part, before the advent of 'modern' life in the story of the childhood and youth of the girl Ursula. That earlier part has a certain epic spaciousness which is unlike anything else in Lawrence. *The Rainbow* compares with *Women in Love*, in this respect, as *War and Peace* does with *Anna Karenina*. Its idyllic quality is beautiful. But that quality is only possible because of the background to the story, the older England which has gone for ever; it is the work of the Lawrence whom Dr Leavis can see as the successor to the George Eliot of *The Mill on the Floss*. *Women in Love*, then, is chosen here as the more complex, difficult, and 'modern' of the two novels of Lawrence's creative prime – not necessarily as the better.

This novel can be, and has been, used (as in Dr Leavis's treatment of it) to show how prose fiction takes over, in Lawrence's hands, the thematic and symbolic method of poetry. Such things as Gerald's treatment of his mare (in Chapter IX) or the episode of the cats (in Chapter XIII) will strike the reader even at a first reading as essentially poetic in this sense. But, effective as they are, they do not go far beyond the devices of previous fiction, in that they are the economical and vivid summing-up of a significance that has already been made explicit. In chapters like that called 'Rabbit' (XVIII), and most of all in the wonderful chapter called 'Moony' (XIX), where Birkin, watched by Ursula without his knowledge, throws stones into the water to shatter the moon's reflection, we seem to reach deeper levels. Their significance is not that they sum up what has gone before, but that they extend and deepen our awareness of what is happening in the novel. In chapters like these Lawrence justifies the claims that have been made for him as a formal innovator who extends the range of the art of fiction.

Dr Leavis's method of analysing this novel has been to select representative themes and characters to illustrate its content and significance. But this analysis, though illuminating, does not bring out the total structure of the book. An account of the structure does indeed support and reinforce, to some extent, the critic's claims for Lawrence's artistry. But it also seems to me to reveal weaknesses which the critic's more selective analysis passes over.

What is *Women in Love* about? It is natural (though not, I think, best) to set about answering this question by beginning at the beginning of the novel, with the conversation between the two sisters, Ursula and Gudrun Brangwen. This opening scene impressively illustrates Lawrence's power of suggesting undercurrents of feeling and atmosphere: in this case the suppressed sexual tension and, more dimly in the background, the social unease of the girls – yet all is done dramatically, through the conversation, picking up and fading out in an apparently casual, natural way. Their conversation is about marriage; and there presently follows a description of a wedding at which the two are present, and during which we are introduced to most of the principal characters of the novel. All this is simply but adroitly done, and as the book gets going we are ready to assume that it is to be about marriage, and the varying attitudes of the two girls (who are already contrasted) to men in marriage. We are thus tempted to regard the girls as central characters. And indeed Gudrun's attitude to Gerald Crich in this chapter, the nature of her attraction to him, does point forward to what their relationship is to become. But it soon becomes clear that the organizing principle of the novel is not to be found in the difference between the two girls nor in the theme of marriage. True, we are given to understand at the end that Ursula, the more sympathetic of the two girls, does marry Birkin. But this marriage has no climactic effect. If, then, we begin our analysis of *Women in Love* from what seems the natural starting-point, we soon get into difficulties, such as have made less analytically minded readers in the past give up the book in exasperation.

It seems to me, then, that the structure – and hence the total meaning – of the book is better understood not by beginning at the natural starting-point suggested by the book's title and the first chapter, but by beginning at what might be called the logical starting-point, which is Birkin. This is not to assume that as an actual fact of composition Lawrence himself began here – though it seems significant that in an early draft of *Women in Love* the book did begin with Birkin's meeting with Gerald on holiday on the Continent. All that is claimed is that the effective structure of the book is more clearly revealed by taking Birkin to be the principal centre of interest. It may well turn out – indeed in my view it does – that Birkin does not in the end have quite the kind of central and standard-supplying role in the book which Lawrence may have intended. But he is, after all, virtually a self-portrait of Lawrence, and as such he carries whatever weight of doctrine about the relations of men and women is to be found in the novel. And it will be seen that all the other principal characters and themes of the book are in a sense causally dependent on the conception of Birkin.

Though modelled on the author, Birkin is definitely a character *in* the book and not overshadowing it. He is exasperating and touching, protean, sometimes unpleasant, sometimes likeable, in a credible way. If his peculiarities are Lawrence's own, they are presented by Lawrence quite objectively. It is not even clear that when Birkin and Ursula are in conflict the reader's sympathy is automatically presupposed to be with Birkin. This objectivity is comparatively rare in Lawrence. The passage in Chapter XIX, in which the two sisters discuss Birkin, suggests how this effect is obtained:

> 'Of course,' she [Gudrun] said easily, 'there is a quality of life in Birkin which is quite remarkable. There is an extraordinary rich spring of life in him, really amazing, the way he can give himself to things. But there are so many things in life that he simply doesn't know. Either he is not aware of their existence at all, or he dismisses them as merely negligible – things which are vital to the other person. In a way he is not clever enough, he is too intense in spots.'
>
> 'Yes,' cried Ursula, 'too much of a preacher. He is really a priest.'
>
> 'Exactly! He can't hear what anybody else has to say – he simply cannot hear. His own voice is too loud.'
>
> 'Yes. He cries you down.'
>
> 'He cries you down,' repeated Gudrun. 'And by mere force of violence. And of course it is hopeless. Nobody is convinced by violence. It makes talking to him impossible – and living with him I should think would be more than impossible.'
>
> 'You don't think one could live with him?' asked Ursula.
>
> 'I should think it would be too wearing, too exhausting. One would be shouted down every time, and rushed into his way without any choice. He would want to control you entirely. He cannot allow that there is any other mind but his own. And then the real clumsiness of his mind is its lack of self-criticism. No, I think it would be perfectly intolerable.'

Ursula 'assents vaguely' to this, but she 'only half agrees', and presently she feels 'a revulsion from Gudrun'.

> She finished life off so thoroughly, she made things so ugly and so final. As a matter of fact, even if it were as Gudrun said, about Birkin, other things were true as well. But Gudrun would draw two lines under him and cross him out like an account that is settled. There he was, summed up, paid for, settled, done with. And it was such a lie. This finality of Gudrun's, this dispatching of people and things in a sentence, was such a lie.

It is a measure of the success in the presentation of Birkin that we are made both to feel the applicability of what Gudrun says and the understandableness of Ursula's reaction to it. We see him often as Ursula does in Chapter XI, where we hear of

> ... this duality of feeling which he created in her ... his wonderful life-rapidity, the rare quality of an utterly desirable man: and there was at the same time this ridiculous, mean effacement into a Salvator Mundi and a Sunday-school teacher, a prig of the stiffest type.

In this treatment of his self-dramatization Lawrence shows himself one of the great realists of literature. Not that he is always convincing in his treatment of material facts, settings, and milieux: anyone who has read much of Lawrence will know that that is not so. But when he is at his best he can give expression in the most effective way – in the dramatic treatment of character – to the refutation of that 'finality' which Ursula here imputes to Gudrun: the moralist's wish for the ultimate and definitive 'placing' of live human creatures in their life and growth, in relation to some static and preconceived notion of purpose and value. And correspondingly the novelist's positive achievement is the communication of a sense of life as it is lived, not merely in the day-by-day or moment-by-moment fluctuations of perception and emotion, but in the shifts of judgement and attitude which are inevitable in any live human relationship. The result is that we are involved in the experiences described in a fuller way than as mere spectators, because we are made to feel that it is continuous with ours. Sometimes, indeed, the involvement is too great, as in the quarrels between Mr and Mrs Morel in *Sons and Lovers*, or Birkin's obscure battles with Ursula in this novel; the 'frame' of the book is broken and we are drawn into the quarrel as if it were real life, forced to take sides, to want to intervene. This is a serious fault in the art, but it shows the strength of Lawrence's conceptions: a strength which in his best work is surprisingly compatible with the 'distancing' that good art requires. But this compatibility would not be possible without the dual nature of the character Birkin. Lawrence is personally involved in him but – in the best passages anyway – without this interfering with our sense of Birkin as a dramatic character, open to objections which are forcibly put, either by himself or by the tenacious Ursula.

Birkin, then, is a spokesman for Lawrence's changing moods. He is also, just credibly, a school-inspector; this enables Lawrence both to give some trace of plausibility to the restless wandering which seems to characterize his form of life, and to put him in touch with Ursula in her fictional capacity as a school-mistress. But he is above all the opportunity for Lawrence to imagine an experiment in life. Birkin is a man of religious temperament who cannot believe in the God of Christianity, or in any formal religion. He feels a revulsion from the mechanized wilderness of the modern world, the loss of supernatural sanctions, the disappearance of clear significance and purpose in living from every class of society. This revulsion is accompanied by a deep repugnance for the whole social structure of England. Birkin has no clear positive idea of just what he wants changed, and what he wants to put in its place. This no doubt deprives his jeremiads of any definite political significance; but it does not invalidate them as expressions of his state of soul. He evinces the same passionate dislike of the bourgeoisie among whom he lives (with Bohemian intervals) as the clever cultivated Gudrun does for the working-class life in which she has grown up and from which she has broken away. The book ends, as Lawrence's stories so often do (*The Fox*, *The Daughters of the Vicar*, and others), with the 'fugue', the flight abroad of the Lawrence-character with the woman he loves, into a social void. But although Birkin can find no general practical cure for the social disease that disgusts him, he seeks for a personal way of salvation for himself. He wants to try to live by a religion of love. This 'love' is not to be interpreted in a romantic or Christian sense. It is to be a relationship between 'fulfilled' individuals, who remain individuals (Birkin shrinks in horror from the idea of any kind of 'merging', loss of individuality in the union of love) but who each achieve through the other some contact with a hitherto unknown, non-human, and trans-human power. One lover is to be the 'door' of the other to this unknown power, the life-source to which Christianity (as Birkin–Lawrence understands, it), and still more modern humanitarianism and democracy, have no access.

The Birkin theme is thus mainly concerned with his choice of Ursula as the woman with whom he is to try this 'way of freedom' in love, and to whom he preaches – against her understandable resistance – a curious doctrine of sexual *Apartheid* that goes with it. His failure with another woman, Hermione, which we learn about early in the novel, and the consequent embarrassing, embittered, and prolonged epilogue to their love-affair, represent the wrong kind of relationship between a man and a woman. Birkin has to escape from this. He has also to escape from an inner temptation which he feels very strongly towards a cult of purely sensual, 'mindless' experience evoked in the novel by a West African statuette which is introduced, with effective dramatic symbolism, in the chapter called 'Totem'. Here, of course, we have an instance of Lawrence's famous primitivism. But we note that in the book it is a temptation which Birkin sees as such. That sensual mindlessness, which he calls the 'African way', is a sort of barbaric equivalent to the sentimental Western idea of love which he feels to be decadent: but it too he supposes to be a product of decadence. But Birkin also thinks he must educate Ursula out of the sentimental and romantic love-ideal which she wants to impose on their relationship. He senses behind it that devouring and essentially egocentric maternal possessiveness which readers of Lawrence will not be surprised to learn that he regards as the enemy of human life and growth. It is this would-be 'education' of Ursula which makes up the main positive part of the Birkin theme.

This purpose of Birkin's can be taken as the logical starting-point of the novel. We have it foreshadowed in Chapter v, in a conversation between Birkin and his friend Gerald Crich, in which Birkin asks Gerald the characteristically Laurentian question: 'What do you think is the aim and object of your life?' It is a characteristic question, because it demands, and permits, only a certain kind of answer, the kind that is suggested when Birkin says presently: 'I find that one needs some one *really* pure single activity.' It is also characteristic because it seems to be as much a question asked of himself as of Gerald. Gerald finds some difficulty in answering, and finally admits that he has no answer to it, or to the equivalent question: 'Wherein does life centre for you?' 'It doesn't centre at all. It is artifically held *together* by the social mechanism', is what he eventually has to say. Birkin agrees, but presses his view that 'there remains only this perfect union with a woman – sort of ultimate marriage – and there isn't anything else'. Gerald's rejection of this idea of 'ultimate marriage', a rejection which expresses his essential nature, and the psychological consequences of that rejection, underlie the extended story of his relations with *his* chosen woman right down to its disastrous close, his extinction in an inhuman world of snow and ice.

The Gerald theme is thus both complementary and contrasting to the Birkin theme. It is so much easier to work out analytically, after reading the book, that to some readers it seems to be the main 'story' in *Women in Love*. But this is not its place in the intended structure of the work. The two men, Gerald and Birkin, show a kind of contrast which is familiar to all readers of Lawrence. No subject does he write about more, whether well or badly, in his fiction. It is a contrast easier to illustrate than describe: the contrast between what is meant to be represented, in their different ways, by the gamekeeper in *Lady Chatterley*, by Count Dionys in *The Ladybird*, or by Alexander Hepburn in *The Captain's Doll*, and on the other hand by Sir Clifford Chatterley, by Rico in *St Mawr*, or by the Bricknells in *Aaron's Rod*. One says 'meant to be represented', because sometimes confusions and contradictions vitiate Lawrence's handling of it. But in its outlines the nature of the contrast is clear: that between the man who has the right kind of human naturalness, showing itself in a play of emotional spontaneity and mobility and a capacity for tenderness – a man whose form of life grows from that 'life-centre' without which Lawrence thought modern living was mere automatism; and the man who lets 'will-power', 'personality', and 'ideals', in the strongly derogatory sense Lawrence gives to such words, interfere with his proper relation to other men and women and the universe, and who thus lacks the emotional depth and the capacity for sincere relationships and tenderness which for Lawrence were the evidence of a connexion with some power above and beyond the individual. In his various novels and tales Lawrence sees people's superficially different or unconnected characteristics – such as executive or intellectual domineering, sentimentality, aestheticism, flirtatiousness, smart flippancy – as all symptoms of living at too shallow a level, excessive 'consciousness' (as Lawrence likes to call it) drawing its perverse power from thwarted and misdirected emotional forces. He is apt to weight the scales against such people by representing them as sexual failures, but it is clear that this is only the sign or symbol of a more general failure. And Lawrence in his later years came with an increasing bitterness to see people of Gerald's *Weltanschauung* as the real rulers of the modern world.

Now we may argue that Lawrence's sense of proportion, and at times his sense of reality, desert him in some of his treatments of this theme. Rico and Sir Clifford Chatterley, for example, are too slight as characters to bear the symbolic weight which their part in the chosen fable imposes on them. Worse than that, many of them, like Rico (though unlike Sir Clifford), are badly drawn, unconvincing, and presented with such obvious animosity as to invalidate their functioning as art. But one of the notable things about *Women in Love* is that the treatment of the Gerald theme is wholly convincing; Gerald as a character does really enact the symbolic role which he is assigned. He is done from within as almost no other characters of this kind are done in Lawrence: Lawrence *is* Gerald in important ways, and this identification is reflected in the strong and deep relation that there is in the book between Birkin and Gerald, who are close friends, ambivalent, intermittent, and obscure as the presentment of their friendship is in chapters like 'Man to Man' and 'Gladiatorial'. Lawrence is not weighting the scales this time; as a result he realizes much more fully the potentialities of the Gerald theme.

So thoroughly, indeed, is the Gerald theme worked out that Dr Leavis is able to base on it the greater part of his account of *Women in Love*. Once the intention behind the creation of Gerald is grasped his drama is felt to unfold itself convincingly. Gerald's strength is a mechanical strength, a strength of 'will-power' and 'ideals'. He has not the inner reserves to meet the mounting crisis of his life, and the strain in him is felt like the tighter and tighter winding-up of a mechanical toy which at last flies loose and bounds away to its final destruction. It is worth noting that Gerald's realistic status in the novel, as an efficient colliery-owner, does not (whatever Lawrence may have intended) derive its validity from any faithfulness to social history. The judgement on Gerald would still be valid even if there were in fact no general correlation between the qualities needed for success in industry and the particular *malaise* of which he is the victim. The point of making him an industrial tycoon is symbolic: he is a man who makes the machine his god, and it is a god that fails.

Yet Gerald himself is not a machine, but a human being, and by no means an unsympathetic one. Lawrence gives a pretty full account of his previous life and his background – his father, his mother with her significant 'queerness', due to the ruining of her life by her husband's 'idealism', the childhood in which he accidentally killed his brother. When he grows up his knowledge of his father's inefficient paternalism as 'industrial magnate' spurs him on to improve on and supersede his father. He makes himself efficient and ruthless, and though the colliers hate him they respect him as they did not respect his father, because even if he despises them and they know it, they are slaves themselves to the 'values' which he seems so successfully to embody. But his strength is not true strength. He has limitations. The machine fails him already in the 'Water-Party' chapter, where he 'assumed responsibility for the amusements on the water' – lest this 'responsibility' for what happens, the drowning of his sister, should seem too tenuous, the point is driven home by the failure of his attempt at rescue. And ironically this cruel expression of his limitations comes just at the moment when he has been able to achieve one of the rare moments of 'apartness' and peace with the woman he loves. It is not Lawrence's purpose to show that strength and tenderness are incompatible. On the contrary, it is Gerald's inner weakness which is the corollary of his incapacity for true love. The slow disintegration and death of his father brings sickeningly home to him the void in his life which 'will-power' is powerless to fill. He turns in his need to the woman, Gudrun. But it is part of the dialectic of their relationship – their similar incapacity for true love – that this need should call out in Gudrun the mocking, destructive, malicious side of her nature. This has throughout been shown as a possible development in Gudrun, and it is one of the ways in which the two sisters are shown as different types of woman. The dramatic consequences of the conflict between the lovers are worked out in the long chapter called 'Snowed Up'. The final death of Gerald in the snow is only the symbolic expression of the inexorable consequence of his life-defeating idealism. Lawrence often uses the contrast of warmth and cold in a symbolic way: human warmth is a spiritual reviving-power in stories like *The Horse-Dealer's Daughter* or *The Virgin and the Gipsy*. Here the intense cold is the symbol of spiritual death.

Everything in *Women in Love* that bears on this theme is finely organized. And it is noteworthy that, although the drama of Gerald and Gudrun mostly happens on an esoteric plane, most of it is made to happen also on a plane where the ordinary criteria for successful fiction can be employed. In spite of some *avant-garde* critics, a general credibility of characters and setting is necessary for successful fiction. 'People don't do such things' remains a valid adverse criticism of a novel. Now, once the total structure of *Women in Love* has been understood – and it is this on the whole that has been found difficult – the characters do affect us as belonging to a life we know, and behaving in keeping with it (given a certain amount of poetic licence in the presentation of the social setting).

This keeping in touch with ordinary reality is a remarkable achievement. It broadens the scope of the novel. It enables Lawrence to introduce, quite naturally, characters like Gerald's father and mother – indeed the whole of the Crich family – who are very relevant to the Gerald theme, and yet are given the kind of dramatic presence, natural dialogue, and ordinary credibility which the novel-reader expects. Some of them may be 'odd', but they are odd as people in real life are odd. Lawrence takes similar opportunities in depicting Birkin's relation to Hermione. Much of this is on an esoteric level, half-conscious swirls of emotion, since Hermione is a sort of feminine counterpart of Gerald, in her blend of domineering will-power and inner weakness, just as her need for Birkin, which he knows he cannot meet, is a counterpart of Gerald's need for Gudrun. Yet Hermione is vividly depicted as a picturesque serio-comic character, and her house-party makes the appropriate occasion for Lawrence to bring in some satire both on the 'Establishment' of the day and the sophisticated radical intelligentsia he had encountered in such quarters (he takes the chance to pay off an old score against Bertrand Russell). Even the chapters describing artistic Bohemian life, though their relevance is less obvious, have a function in making the Bohemian side of Birkin's and Gerald's life more real, and in one place at least – the night Gerald spends with Halliday's mistress – their bearing on the Gerald theme is important, as illustrating the superficiality of Gerald's attitude to sex. And there is no need to emphasize the functional importance of minor characters like the artist Loerke, who plays his part in the climax of Gerald's tragedy. Thus *Women in Love* has a structure which arises naturally from Lawrence's firm grasp of his dual theme. The filling-up and population of the book seems thereby also to be accomplished with inevitability and naturalness.

Women in Love, then, does seem in part to justify the unusualness of its formal conception: a novel whose 'plot', if it is to be so called, does not answer to the usual account of 'character in action'. There is development, but it is at a deeper level than that of 'personality'. If the whole book had a convincingness equal to what we find in the treatment of the Gerald theme, it could be judged an assured artistic success. But it suffers from a grave central weakness. The book's strong pattern derives from the contrast between the destinies of the two couples, and the subsidiary, though important, masculine relationship between Birkin and Gerald. (We may compare the strong pattern given to *Anna Karenina* by Tolstoy's use of the three marriages of Anna, Dolly, and Kitty, the 'unhappy', the 'ordinary', and the 'happy' marriages respectively.) But what is the significance of this pattern in expressing the intended total meaning of *Women in Love*? Dr Leavis would have us believe that the Birkin–Ursula relationship sets up a standard – or at least moves towards a standard – from which the Gerald–Gudrun experience is a deviation. But do we feel this in reading the novel? Surely what we feel in reading the novel is that Birkin too is a sick and tortured man, who does not (except at a few ideal moments which give rise to some of the worst writing in the book) achieve with Ursula the kind of fulfilment which he has made his *raison d'être*. Perhaps if Lawrence had conveyed the positive quality of those moments – as distinct from the mere feeling of repose and relief after fighting and tension, which as always he conveys wonderfully – our sense of Birkin's 'normative' standing in the novel would have been induced. But as it is, those ideal moments – as in Chapter XXIII, 'Excurse' – are among the weaknesses of the book. Lawrence expresses the ineffable no better here by his obscure, repetitious, periphrastic style than he does in the notoriously direct passages of *Lady Chatterley's Lover*. And if it is urged that, given the nature of the experience in question, those portentous wordinesses are all he could do, that is enough to prove the enterprise mistaken.

But this is not the most radical question. To understand Birkin fully we must understand the state of mind of the Lawrence who wrote of him. It is true that *Women in Love*, as part of *The Sisters*, was presumably conceived before the horror of the war-years had closed down on Lawrence: conceived during the happy interval between the break with 'Miriam' and the coming of the war. But it is hard not to see in Birkin the Lawrence of 1916, amid the penury and misery of his life in Cornwall, and in his mind always the horror of the war and the nightmare of suspicion and persecution. How else can we explain Birkin's hatred of human life? 'Mankind is a dead tree, covered with fine brilliant galls of people', he says, and there is much in the same strain. But this is a defect in a work of imagination. Birkin's hatred is not clearly accounted for in particular terms. It remains in the book just a *donnée*, an idiosyncrasy, which is so strongly rendered that it seriously limits Birkin's value as a representative of the normal man. No doubt it is unfair to attack *Women in Love* on the ground that Birkin himself is obviously not a normal man. Some imaginative licence must be granted in the presentation of this experiment in love: for the character who thinks of making it to be at all convincing, he would have to be rather unusual. But it is clear that Lawrence intended Birkin to be searching for, and perhaps even eventually reaching, conclusions about the relations of men and women in marriage which *could* be held to be valid for normal men.

This suggests a more serious criticism. For we cannot ignore Birkin's own sense of his failure. After all, the last chapter, in which Birkin gazes down at the dead Gerald, is a final taking-up of the issues first proposed between them in the chapter called 'In the Train'. Birkin has come to realize that his ideal of 'ultimate marriage' was not sufficient. It needed completion by the male relationship with Gerald. But this too has failed. What makes Gerald's death tragic – and there is an unmistakable note of tragedy in Birkin's thoughts as he turns away – is not the death itself (Gerald is not a figure of tragic stature) but its effect on Birkin. And the whole effect of the book – though Birkin even at the end will not directly admit this to Ursula – is to show that the kind of love he wanted is illusory. And to say this is not to bring extrinsic standards to bear on a work of imagination. It is what the work itself seems to say: pointing a moral of its own, which is not the author's.

NOTES

1. *D. H. Lawrence, Novelist*, by F. R. Leavis (London, 1955).

THE CONSISTENCY OF JAMES JOYCE

ARNOLD KETTLE

Professor of Literature, The Open University

JAMES JOYCE (1882–1941) was no flincher. There is a consistency about his life and development as a writer, a coherence and a completeness which has the sort of aesthetic rightness at which he aimed with such single-mindedness in his work.

From the writing of the first stories of *Dubliners* (1914, p. 545) to the moment when, the extraordinary work at last complete, its progress rounded off with an unending sentence, he announced the title of *Finnegans Wake* (1939), he seems to have known precisely what he was doing. If there is a false start amidst his *œuvre*, a cul-de-sac leading off the Vico road, it is the two volumes of lyric poetry. Looking back at the total achievement these do seem, with their rather pale refinement and sometimes crude effects, to be expendable. This particular use of language was not in reality Joyce's forte. If it is as a poet that he is to be remembered it is not by this kind of poetry.

Everywhere else – in *Dubliners, A Portrait of the Artist* (1916), even *Exiles* (1918), as well as *Ulysses* (1922) and *Finnegans Wake* – the organization of words and the final effect of the whole has the stamp and intensity of poetry, successful or not. *Stephen Hero* (published posthumously, 1944) for all its interest, has not this quality to anything like the same degree, and Joyce was right, from his point of view, to reject it.

From *Stephen Hero* we get, explicity, the theory of epiphanies:

> ... By an epiphany he meant a sudden spiritual manifestation, whether in the vulgarity of speech or of gesture or in a memorable phase of the mind itself. He believed that it was for the man of letters to record these epiphanies with extreme care, seeing that they themselves are the most delicate and evanescent of moments. He told Cranly that the clock of the Ballast Office was capable of an epiphany. Cranly questioned the inscrutable dial of the Ballast Office with his no less inscrutable countenance.

'Yes,' said Stephen. 'I will pass it time after time, allude to it, refer to it, catch a glimpse of it. It is only an item in the catalogue of Dublin's street furniture. Then all at once I see it and I know at once what it is: epiphany.'

'What?'

'Imagine my glimpses at that clock as the gropings of a spiritual eye which seeks to adjust its vision to an exact focus. The moment the focus is reached the object is epiphanised. It is just in this epiphany I find the third, the supreme quality of beauty.'

'Yes?' said Cranly absently.[1]

I do not think Joyce ever again expressed more clearly in analytical terms what he was after. This passage and the whole, more highly-wrought discussion on aesthetics in *A Portrait of the Artist* is worth reading in conjunction with Virginia Woolf's well-known essays on modern fiction and worth considering too, as Mrs Woolf does, in relation to the aims and achievements of contemporary French painting. Joyce is a far bigger figure than Virginia Woolf – his work bristles with an intellectual and moral toughness which hers lacks – and it is the measure of his superiority as a writer that his concern with the texture of reality should exercise itself in verbal and intellectual rather than merely visual or descriptive terms. Even if his emphasis on the word was to be, in the end, destructive, it was also his incomparable strength.

It is right at this point to emphasize also the importance of the theory expounded by Stephen of 'esthetic stasis':

An esthetic image is presented to us either in space or in time. What is audible is presented in time, what is visible is presented in space. But, temporal or spatial, the esthetic image is first luminously apprehended as self-bounded and self-contained upon the immeasurable background of space and time which is not it. You apprehend it as *one* thing. You see it as one whole. You apprehend its wholeness. That is *integritas*...

... The radiance of which [Aquinas] speaks is the scholastic *quidditas*, the whatness of a thing. This supreme quality is felt by the artist when the esthetic image is first conceived in his imagination. The mind in that mysterious instant Shelley likened beautifully to a fading coal. The instant wherein that

> supreme quality of beauty, the clear radiance of the esthetic image, is apprehended luminously by the mind which has been arrested by its wholeness and fascinated by its harmony is the luminous silent stasis of esthetic pleasure, a spiritual state very like to that cardiac condition which the Italian physiologist Luigi Galvani, using a phrase almost as beautiful as Shelley's, called the enchantment of the heart.[2]

Stephen goes on, incidentally, to develop a theory of the depersonalization of the artist which reminds us that Mr Eliot was not, in 1917, a lone voice calling. But what is particularly interesting is, first, the remarkable emotional force which in their context in the *Portrait* these apparently abstract passages have – they are part and parcel of Stephen's own life-adventure – and, secondly, their connexion with the famous climax of the book in which Stephen, having uttered his devil's vow of 'non serviam' and rejected utterly the claims of church and state, sets forth upon his life of silence, exile, and cunning to encounter 'the reality of experience and to forge in the smithy of my soul the uncreated conscience of my race'.

The contradiction so powerfully expressed at the conclusion of *A Portrait of the Artist* is embedded deep in the whole of Joyce's life and achievement. He leaves Dublin in 1904, to return to the city endlessly in every page he writes. It is the non-juring exile, indifferent, paring his fingernails, so insistently outside the struggle that two world wars and the achievement of his country's independence fail to arouse his comment, who takes upon himself the task of expressing the uncreated conscience of his race. It is the writer whose work, above all others, gives an impression of self-sufficiency to the point of isolation, the least extraverted of all artists, who develops not only a more than Rabelaisian humour but a style – if that is the word – more cosmopolitan than any in modern literature.

Ulysses begins straightforwardly enough. No one has evoked more richly and movingly the awakening hours of a city and its people. These wonderful pages – the Telemachaia – which act as lead-in to the epic of Bloomsday and as a bridge between *A Portrait of the Artist* and Joyce's later work combine also the Chehovian naturalism of *Dubliners*, the passionate intellectual argumentation of the *Portrait*, and the techniques of complex *leit-motiv* and verbal association upon which Joyce was more and more to concentrate. They form therefore a remarkably convenient starting-point for the would-be initiate and one which requires the minimum of outside support. The reader need not know or worry that Stephen is to be Telemachus; he will grasp soon enough what is at this stage of the book far more important, that Stephen is his mother's son and that the mother, though she is one and unique, is also something more impersonal, Irish and Catholic, and so linked – not just arbitrarily but in the complex inter-relations of life itself – with mother-figures more pervasive; and Stephen, though he is Stephen Dedalus, student and artist, mummer and pedant, is a little boy lost, partaking of the problems and nature of Hamlet and of Jesus, as well as of Parnell and Ulysses' son. Ireland-Island is also all islands, the sea all seas, and the key in Stephen's pocket has not just in the ordinary sense 'dramatic significance' but is the archetype of all keys, locking, unlocking ...

Ulysses can be approached from a whole number of directions. One of the best, as Richard Ellmann's fine biography indicates, is through an awareness of Joyce's own life.[3] The Homeric parallels, though too heavy weather can be made of them, are important. 'Homer is my example and his unchristened heart.' No less than Yeats, Joyce turned to epic and mythology as a release from the tyranny of abstract ideas. *Ulysses*, like *Joseph Andrews*, is a comic epic poem in prose, and the framework is no more arbitrary than that of Fielding or Cervantes. It is an epic with a difference and the difference is conveyed partially in the word comic, which Joyce in his later years would doubtless have found some means of linking verbally with cosmic.

Bloom's journey through a Dublin day, easier to plot geographically than Ulysses' Odyssey, is given form by being seen – with all rules broken – from behind Homer. But one should most certainly not conclude that Joyce's interest in his hero is therefore schematic or second-hand. He does not just exist for the pattern. Frank Budgen, who saw Joyce frequently while *Ulysses* was being written and read passages as they were completed, relates that the author's first question, on getting back a section of the manuscript, almost always bore on the convincingness of Bloom as a 'character', not on the effectiveness or subtlety of the presentation or method which appeared to be his first concern in composition. Bloom was to be the first complete all-round character presented by any writer, an advance on Homer's Ulysses. And the extraordinary thing is that, in a sense, the ambition was fulfilled. 'He's a cultured all-round man, Bloom is.' With him, human manysidedness achieves a new level of literary expression. Which is not to say that he makes a more vivid or convincing impression than, say, Falstaff or Mr Boffin or Isabel Archer. What one can confidently say is that one knows more about Bloom than about these others.[4]

Ulysses is at the same time a triumphant piece of 'realism' – a book about convincingly 'real' people in an actual city, presented with a regard for detail that would have made a French naturalist envious – and a microcosmic representation of certain themes and patterns in human life. Thus Leopold Bloom, middle-aged, Jewish, kind, abused, unheroic is at the same time Ulysses the Wanderer, an archetypal Father searching for a Son, an Exile homing (the word is applied to a sailing ship entering Dublin Bay) in a hostile and yet not unfriendly world. In the conversation of medical students in a hospital where a woman is having a baby all human history – or at least chronology – is implied through a series of literary parodies. When Molly Bloom thinks of tomorrow's breakfast as she lies in bed the whole flux and continuity of life is involved.

The difference between the significance of theme and symbol in *Ulysses* and in, say, Dickens's *Bleak House* is worth emphasizing. The fog which shrouds *Bleak House* is often called, for want of a better word, symbolic. That is to say, it has a significance in the novel which is more than a part of the realistic description of London: it is bound up with and illuminates (in the way poetic images do) Dickens's vision of a whole society and the fog of Chancery is moral and mental as well as physical. Yet although this image of fog is so pervasive, so extraordinarily 'significant' in *Bleak House*, there is nothing mystical or metaphysical about Dickens's use of it, no implication that the image is somehow or other touching the bounds of cosmic processes as such. One never feels the need to put a capital letter to the fog. But the father-son theme in *Ulysses*, for instance, like the theme of exile, has, in a subtle but essential sense, a quite different status. Between Bloom and Stephen, who do not meet until the last third of the book, late in the evening of Bloomsday, there is throughout the whole day a tenuous but insistent *rapport*, achieved by a sort of literary counterpoint, which is quite different from the sort of significance Dickens achieves through his inter-connected images and subtly complicated plot. You cannot usefully compare the relationship of Esther and Lady Deadlock, even though they are in a very important sense searching for one another and are indeed daughter and mother, with the relationship of Bloom and Stephen. Nor does the word 'psychological', in its more workaday sense, help us much in defining this new significance which Joyce expresses. Bloom's need for a son is not to be thought of primarily in terms of an individual 'psychological' need. All the time it is such concepts as the 'collective unconscious' that are the relevant ones. I think the continued influence of Roman Catholicism on Joyce has been somewhat exaggerated. I do not see his later work as guilt-ridden. But certainly one of the inheritances of his Catholic youth was to be a life-long suspicion of liberal scepticism as an alternative to a philosophy.

That is why, although Bloom's Odyssey is rightly to be seen as an epic of disintegration, it is at the same time (before *Finnegans Wake*) the most consciously integrated book in history. The disintegration is – to make a division which can only be temporarily and perilously maintained – in the content of the book, the integration is in the form. 'It is not my fault that the odour of ashpits and old weeds and offal hangs round my stories'[5] Joyce had written of *Dubliners*, sixteen years before the publication of *Ulysses*, and had referred to Dublin as 'the centre of paralysis'. In *Ulysses* the odour remains: Bloom's first waking act is to collect offal from the butcher's; Stephen (and later Bloom) watches the writhing weeds lift languidly on the Dublin shore as he waits for his ash-plant to float away, the ash-plant (did it grow in an ashpit?) which is to be one of the key symbols in the climactic moments of the scene at Bella Cohen's. And the paralysis remains too, deep in the book. Mr Levin makes the point well:

> Streets intersect, shops advertise, homes have party walls and fellow-citizens depend upon the same water supply; but there is no co-operation between human beings. The individual stands motionless, like Odysseus becalmed in the doldrums.[6]

In this crowded Dublin, at least as full of *leit-motivs* and symbolic phrases as it is of human beings, nothing is achieved but a series of epiphanies.[7] Things and people 'belong' only in the sense that they are there and willy-nilly mingle with one another. No work – one might almost say nothing productive whatever – is done. This lack of a productive material basis in the Joyce world is very significant. It is what leads ultimately to the arbitrariness of Joyce's verbal associations, for as he goes on he becomes progressively less interested in words as symbols for real things and actions and more interested in the word as such. As Mr Alick West in a very perceptive essay has pointed out:

> What Joyce spends most care on is the formal side, watching that a phrase used on one page has the right echoes with phrases used on fifty other pages. But this sovereign importance of the verbal phrase is in contradiction to the life of the book. For it implies that the fabric is stable, and that its surface can be decorated with the most subtle intricacy, like the Book of Kells ... It assumes something as permanent as the church was for its monks. Yet Stephen and Bloom are both drawn as symbols of humanity in the eternal flux. On the other hand the sense of change in the book is so strong that this static formal decoration is felt to be a mechanism of defence against the change, and only valuable to Joyce as such defence. Joyce seems to play with the two styles of change and stability as he plays with his two chief characters. He plays with the contradictions; he does not resolve them. Where in Milton there is advancing movement, Joyce only shifts from one foot to the other, while he sinks deeper into the sand-flats.[8]

What is good about *Ulysses* is the enormous vitality and human insight, as opposed to mere virtuosity, of many of the parts, the poetic evocation of the city itself, the inter-relationships which Joyce's *leitmotivs* establish and illuminate often with a power as intellectually stimulating as it is sensuously haunting. What is unsatisfying about the book is perhaps best pinpointed by the words that almost everyone writing about Joyce finds himself coming back to: the words 'play with'.

They are not arbitrary words, for they take one to the heart of Joyce's mystery, and it is a mystery in the old craft sense, with Joyce the artificer. It we call Joyce an aesthete (and I think we should) we must be conscious of just what the word implies for worse and for better. The better side is expressed in the joy and vigour and mastery of play, done beautifully and, more nearly than almost any activity, for its own sake. If would be naïve to imagine that Joyce, the admirer of Ibsen, believed that the activity of the artist ignored morality. When he wrote of forging the uncreated conscience of his race he meant what he said and knew as well as James or Conrad or Hamlet the ramifications of the word conscience. 'I believe that in composing my chapter of moral history in exactly the way I have composed it I have taken the first step towards the spiritual liberation of my country.'[9] But Joyce the liberator worked in his own way, the exile's way, through art, a conception of art not only above but also below and around all other struggles, as many-worded as many-sided, reaching for the kind of ultimate involved in the word he used about Bloom – all-round.

It is not by chance that *Ulysses* ends with Molly Bloom's half-awake reverie. The final chapter pushes to the furthest extent the 'stream of consciousness' method – the attempt to find a verbal equivalent for the inner thought-processes of a character. ('I try to give the unspoken, unacted thoughts of people in the way they occur.'[10]) Joyce's purpose in developing this method is primarily to enrich his objective evocation of a total situation by adding a new dimension, another side to the many-sidedness of complex life. This attempt, though it has often been associated historically with the development of psychology as a science, is no more 'scientific' than any other literary attempt to give the impression of reality. You cannot in the nature of things find a precise verbal equivalent for unformulated thoughts; the interior monologue may give the *impression* of an actual thought-track, but it cannot do more than that.

Joyce knew plenty about contemporary developments in psychiatric research. He knew what it was to be jung and easily freudened.[11] He did not live in Zürich for nothing. But while he *used* the material of modern psychology for his purposes (just as he used among much else a considerable knowledge of anthropology and scholastic philosophy and a life-long passion for vocal music), his aim was not that of the analyst, the scientist. And he was bound to run up against an outstanding difficulty: you cannot isolate the individual's consciousness from what is happening around and to him. Hence, throughout most of *Ulysses*, 'stream of consciousness' is mingled continuously and sometimes uneasily with objective narrative and the description of outside fact.

In the final chapter 'stream of consciousness' finally comes into its own and for the simple reason that Molly Bloom is half-asleep. She is *doing* nothing and can therefore dispense with punctuation. Joyce, in this remarkable chapter, seems to have stumbled – not that one normally thinks of him as stumbling – on one ideal possibility in his constant battle against the fact of time and its implications. By concentrating on the moment of sleep he defeats his enemy; but it is at the cost of presenting consciousness not as an active apprehension of the present (and therefore involving the challenge of action and the possibility of progress) but passively as a mode of recollection and impulse divorced from actual activity. The only affirmation that Molly Bloom is permitted is in fact the sort of affirmation associated with a principle rather than a person. Her yes, like Anna Livia's, is the yes of the Eternal Feminine, no more an act of volition than the journey of the river to the sea, without which life would stop altogether, a possibility which even Joyce does not seem seriously to contemplate.

Finnegans Wake follows *Ulysses* inevitably. If Bloom is an all-round character, *Finnegans Wake* is an all-round book. I think it is unrealistic not to recognize it as – for better or worse – Joyce's masterpiece and one of the great odd masterpieces of all literature. That it is 'difficult', more difficult than any novel ever written, cannot be denied; but most of the general theoretical rejections of it, because it is hard or queer or private, seem to be beside the point. The commonly expressed view that it is a 'private' book, in the sense of involving a rejection of the artist's obligation to communicate, is simply untrue. Whatever Joyce was up to he was not bogged down in the subjective theory of 'self-expression'. The language of *Finnegans Wake* is not a private language, it is a very extraordinary development of public language, involving a use of the resources of half a dozen different tongues, though fundamentally it is English, with the spoken (or sometimes sung) note of Dublin guiding its cadences. Every sentence, indeed every word, can be logically explained. It is true that for any one person to be in a position to give such an explanation is virtually impossible; and like some other truths this may properly be held to be a pity. It is also true that there is a kind of cosmic pedantry about Joyce's total achievement which is in the end perhaps its most vulnerable quality. I am not arguing that *Finnegans Wake* can be regarded as popular literature or is ever likely to be. I am arguing, however, that the book is not to be dismissed as a mere private eccentricity, a gigantic mistake, least of all the product of a charlatan.

The case for *Finnegans Wake* is that it can, in its parts perhaps more than its whole, delight the reader, acting in such a way that 'it awakens and enlarges the mind itself by rendering it the receptacle of a thousand unapprehended combinations of thought', and that these combinations are not just arbitrary and casual but very often intimately connected with the actual experiencing and interpreting of reality.

It is not easy, in a few words, to substantiate this claim and one can only propose to the sceptical reader that he should, duly armed with some of the essential information garnered by Messrs Campbell and Robinson,[12] take the plunge into one of the more accessible areas of the book – say the opening of the 'Shem the Penman' passage (p. 169 ff.) – assured at least that in this of all books he will not be cheating by starting in the middle. Better still, that he should listen, if he can find means of acquiring it, to the gramophone record in which Joyce himself reads a part of 'Anna Livia Plurabelle'. It should perhaps be mentioned, however, that this particular passage is unusually lyrically 'attractive' and may possibly raise false expectations. Those passages, both in *Ulysses* and *Finnegans Wake*, in which the author indulges – rivers and seas seem to tempt him to it – in somewhat lush and easy rhythms do not show Joyce at his best.

The core of the method of *Finnegans Wake* is contained in a famous anecdote related by Frank Budgen:

> I enquired about *Ulysses*. Was it progressing?
>
> 'I have been working hard on it all day,' said Joyce.
>
> 'Does that mean that you have written a great deal?' I said.
>
> 'Two sentences,' said Joyce.
>
> I looked sideways but Joyce was not smiling. I thought of Flaubert.
>
> 'You have been seeking the *mot juste*?' I said.
>
> 'No,' said Joyce, 'I have the words already. What I am seeking is the perfect order of words in the sentence. There is an order in every way appropriate. I think I have it.'
>
> 'What are the words?' I asked.
>
> 'I believe I told you,' said Joyce, 'that my book is a modern Odyssey. Every episode in it corresponds to an adventure of Ulysses. I am now writing the *Lestrygonians* episode, which corresponds to the adventure of Ulysses with the cannibals. My hero is going to lunch. But there is a seduction motive in the Odyssey, the cannibal king's daughter. Seduction appears

> in my book as women's silk petticoats hanging in a shop window. The words through which I express the effect of it on my hungry hero are: "Perfume of embraces all him assailed. With hungered flesh obscurely, he mutely craved to adore." You can see for yourself in how many different ways they might be arranged.'[13]

This tells us a great deal about Joyce's use of language, as well as about his method of work in general. By putting 'assailed' at the end of its sentence, the physical impact of the word is allowed, so to speak, to pile up: by putting the object before the verb a suggestion comes through of a possible reversal of object and subject. The position of 'all' in the sentence gives it a maximum effect, referring back to 'embraces' and forward to 'him'. This last would be lost, or weakened, if Joyce had written 'all of him', and at the same time the maleness of 'him' would have been less potent too. Just as the perfume, placed anywhere else in the sentence, would have impregnated it less thoroughly.

What Joyce is up to here is not anything very extraordinary. He is playing the game all poets play. There is nothing sacred about the order of words. Poets arrange them in the way that will make them work best for their particular purposes, organizing, if they can, their every reverberation, controlling the fall-out of any verbal explosion.

No one – not even Shakespeare or Rabelais – has carried the experiment as far as Joyce did, but in its essence the method of *Finnegans Wake* is not really so different from that of, say, *Paradise Lost* or *The Waste Land*. And neither, if it comes to that, is a good deal of the subject-matter. It is no more misleading than any other statement about that extraordinary book to say that it is about the Fall.

What is new technically, of course, is the extent to which Joyce plays around with words including non-English ones, syllables, rhymes, half-rhymes, inventions, anagrams, and every kind of associative device. It is this that makes his rhetoric uniquely rich. Compare Fielding on the subject of Tom Jones's lowness, social and literary, with Joyce on Shem:

> How is that for low, laities and gentlenuns? Why, dog of the Crostiguns, whole continents rang with this Kairokorran

> lowness! Sheols of houris in chems upon divans (revolted stellas vespertine vesamong them) at a bare (O!) mention of the scaly rybald explained: Poisse![14]

In *Finnegans Wake*, narrative, in the more orthodox sense, which presumes a beginning and an end and implies, if not progress, at least development or decay, is dispensed with. Since this is a circular book the usual kinds of criticism are rendered more or less impossible, for ultimately all evaluation must depend on some objective reality against which the thing concerned will be judged, and this is precisely what Joyce denies us. It is impossible to be quite sure how far, or indeed whether, *Finnegans Wake* is Earwicker's dream, for the question is, in the light of Joyce's preoccupations, irrelevant. If time, in the usual sense of the term, is unimportant or illusory, judgements which involve the assumption that it is basic are automatically undermined.

Similarly, it seems implicit in Joyce's method that judgements of the more usual sort about the success or failure of specific images are inapplicable to his book. The very word image comes uneasily. L. A. G. Strong, who writes sympathetically about Joyce, suggests as the primary defect of *Finnegans Wake* that

> the two processes, from association to object, from object to association, seldom harmonise, and often create serious confusion.[15]

I think one is bound to come to this conclusion if one attempts to evaluate Joyce's imagery by any objective criteria whatever. For example, in the passage (p. 528 ff.) in which Earwicker is copulating with his wife images from cricket abound. But why? What, apart from some purely verbal fun, do they give or add to the passage? Indeed so visually irrelevant do these cricketing images seem that one would be tempted to assume, were it not for biographical evidence, that Joyce had never seen a cricket match in his life and had merely collected the terms from a study of Wisden. Judged by a normally acceptable objective standard I do not see how the conclusion can be avoided that this group of images is arbitrary and unsuccessful; but the snag about making such a judgement is that one has in the end no means of knowing what Joyce is *basically* trying to do. The ambiguities do not, as in a speech of Shakespeare, enrich and modify the meaning; they are the book itself. That is why it is so hard to discuss, let alone judge, *Finnegans Wake*. What, one is constantly brought up against the question, is relevant to what? Huckleberry Finn's significance in *Finnegans Wake*, for instance, seems to depend entirely on the chance of his name – or are we to imply that names are got by something more than chance? Always in the later Joyce there is hovering in the air the suspicion that words have *in themselves* some mystic significance. Because of Joyce's refusal to commit himself to the proposition that dream is less real than reality he ends up, it sometimes seems, with the implication that nothing is real except words.

Finnegans Wake can only be read and enjoyed in its own terms, i.e. by an acceptance for the purposes of the book of the whole Joycean bag of tricks (Vico, collective unconscious, Dublin geography, Norse etymology, street-ballads, and all). And because reality is more important and pervasive than theories about it, the great odd book has a way of breaking through many of the objections which commonsense consideration will plausibly erect. That is why, while L. A. G. Strong is right in pointing out that *Finnegans Wake* is 'a book written to a theory', with the problems that this implies, it would be wrong to regard this judgement as a dismissal.

A reader – or, perhaps better still, a group of readers – prepared to play seriously but not too solemnly the game of reading *Finnegans Wake* is likely to get from it a great deal of fun and information and a new sense not only of the possibilities of language but of the interconnexions of things. One who is not an out-and-out Joycean hesitates to make a larger claim than that, for there remains a deeply based scepticism. Does Joyce the writer succeed all in all in releasing language and emotion as, for instance, Rabelais does? Certainly he does things with words that no one previously had done, but is the final predominant effect one of liberation and enrichment or of a stupendous yet ultimately rather arid *tour de force*? Certainly in the best of Joyce laughter and tears assert themselves as a humanizing force, counteracting with their sanity any tendencies towards pedantry and isolation. Yet the very consistency of his total effort, the very completeness of the structure he creates has in it something inhuman, leaving one in the end with the feeling that he who accepted so boldly all the implications of his exile – poorjoist unctuous to polise nopebobbies – had flinched at nothing except life itself.

NOTES

1. *Stephen Hero* (1944), p. 188. See also *Introduction*, p. 13 ff., by Theodore Spencer.

2. *A Portrait of the Artist as a Young Man* (Travellers Library, 1930) p. 241 ff. See also the discussion of this point in *James Joyce* by Harry Levin (1944), especially Part I, Chapter 3 and Part II, Chapter 3.

3. Mr Ellmann (*James Joyce*, 1959) shows very clearly the direct autobiographical basis of almost all Joyce's literary preoccupations. It is a fruitful emphasis not only because it explains much in the two major books that is otherwise almost incomprehensible, but also because it counteracts the over-metaphysical approach to Joyce which many of his admirers (including Messrs Campbell and Robinson) have encouraged.

4. Richard Ellmann discusses in a most illuminating way the significance of Bloom.

5. *Letters*, ed. Stuart Gilbert (1957), p. 64.

6. Op. cit., p. 96.

7. Mr Ellmann's description of *Ulysses* (op. cit., p. 370) as 'pacifist' seems to me suggestive and useful but not quite satisfactory. 'The theme of *Ulysses* is simple ... Casual kindness overcomes unconscionable power' (p. 390). But does it?

8. Alick West, *Crisis and Criticism* (1937), p. 178.

9. *Letters*, pp. 62–3.

10. Frank Budgen, *James Joyce and the Making of Ulysses* (1934), p. 94.

11. *Finnegans Wake*, p. 115.

12. *A Skeleton Key to Finnegans Wake* (1947).

13. Op. cit., p. 20.

14. *Finnegans Wake*, p. 177.

15. *The Sacred River* (1947), p. 147.

EZRA POUND'S *HUGH SELWYN MAUBERLEY*

DONALD DAVIE

Professor of English, University of Stanford, California

THE name of Ezra Pound (b. 1885)* undoubtedly belongs in the first place to the history of American rather than English poetry. Nevertheless his personality and his activities during at least one phase of his long career, together with the poems he then wrote, cannot be ignored in any survey, however selective, of twentieth-century English poetry. From 1908 until 1920, he made London his headquarters, playing a militant and decisive part in the crucial literary and artistic battles then being fought out on the English scene; in particular over several of these years he acted as at once mentor and sponsor of the youthful T. S. Eliot. Moreover, two of his major works of that period, *Homage to Sextus Propertius* (1917) and *Hugh Selwyn Mauberley* (1920), are explicitly attempts to portray and diagnose the state of British (not at all of American) culture at the historical moment which, for instance, D. H. Lawrence in *Women in Love* similarly took to be for England a tragically momentous turning-point. But the conclusive reason why Pound cannot be ignored is that *Hugh Selwyn Mauberley* at any rate has been accepted into the English poetic tradition, in the sense that every subsequent British poet at all serious about his vocation has found it necessary to come to terms with this work, accepting or else quarrelling with its conclusions about British culture no less than with its revolutionary strategies and methods.

Because Eliot has thrown in his lot with Britain as Pound has not, the British reader will probably come to *Hugh Selwyn Mauberley* only after reading Eliot's poetry up to and including *The Waste Land*. Yet as Eliot has been the first to insist, in respect of many of the poetic methods common to both poets it was Pound who was the pioneer. Moreover, where the poets make use of a device common to both, there is every danger of not realizing that Pound's intention is different from Eliot's in profoundly important ways.

* Ezra Pound died in 1972.

A conspicuous example of this is the strategy which is common to *Hugh Selwyn Mauberley* and to *The Waste Land* – the extensive use of interlarded and unacknowledged quotations from poets and poems of the past, and of more or less devious references and allusions to these sources. When the reader recognizes that in Pound's poem such references are sown more thickly than in *The Waste Land*, and that the allusions are sometimes more devious, it is easy to decide irritably that Pound's use of the device is less serious than Eliot's, and open to objections which Eliot escapes:

> Turned from the 'eau-forte
> Par Jacquemart'
> To the strait head
> Of Messalina:
>
> 'His true Penelope
> Was Flaubert',
> And his tool
> The engraver's.
>
> Firmness,
> Not the full smile,
> His art, but an art
> In profile;
>
> Colourless
> Pier Francesca,
> Pisanello lacking the skill
> To forge Achaia.

A good French dictionary will reveal that '*eau-forte*' means an etching; and the context then makes it clear that the fictitious minor poet, Mauberley (whose career we are following as in a biography), is at this point turning in his art from the relatively full and detailed richness of the etcher's rendering of reality to the severely selective art 'In profile' of the engraver of medallions. A very little knowledge of Flaubert will reveal that the French novelist differs from his English contemporaries, at least in intention, in rather the same way, as throwing his emphasis upon selection of the one telling detail rather than on accumulation of many details and instances. And in the art of the Italian Renaissance, the medallist Pisanello can be opposed in just the same way to the painter Piero della Francesca, master of composition and colour. This is entirely and sufficiently intelligible. But the reader may well protest that the point could have been made more directly, without all this 'name-dropping'. It is easy to protest that this is pretentious, a parade of recondite expertise for its own sake – a charge which at one time was often brought against Eliot. In fact, in the course of answering this objection, we not only distinguish Pound's attitude and achievement from Eliot's, we uncover what is uniquely valuable in Pound's work as a whole, and in this poem in particular.

In the first place Pound would say that to talk of 'recondite expertise' begs the whole question: if knowledge of the art of the medallion, of paintings by Piero della Francesca, and of novels by Flaubert, is out-of-the-way knowledge for us, it shouldn't be. For Pound these names represent experiences which should be familiar to any educated man, and he is arguing, in particular, that neither we nor the Americans can see our own cultural traditions in proper perspective except in the context of achievements in other languages or by other cultures. He would be happy if our reading of these lines sent us to the Victoria and Albert Museum, the British Museum, and the National Gallery to look at late Roman or Italian Renaissance coins, and at Italian paintings. Pound in fact, while he shares with Eliot the wish to attain by these vivid juxtapositions an unexampled conciseness of especially ironic expression, has a further intention which Eliot does not share. He has never ceased to be the pedagogue. Just as in his London years he sought to instruct (apparently to good effect) all of his contemporaries whom he respected – Eliot, the novelists Percy Wyndham Lewis and James Joyce, even the much older and already illustrious W. B. Yeats – so in all his writings he is trying to instruct his readers, telling them what buildings and paintings they should look at and what books they ought to read. For instance, concealed behind the cryptic reference to the etching by Jacquemart is the name of the French poet Théophile Gautier, who is pointed to much more explicitly elsewhere in the poem. Pound alludes to Gautier as Eliot does, because Gautier suits his purposes, but also because he is sure he fits ours too, if we only knew it.

In fact Pound is much more interested than Eliot in the spectacle of human events and affairs for their own sake, not merely as somehow reflecting his own predicament. It is this interest which he shares with Robert Browning, whom he has consistently honoured as his own first master; and it is what distinguishes him not only from Eliot but from his other great contemporary and associate, W. B. Yeats. Whereas Eliot's diagnosis of the state of Western Christian culture is not of the sort that can be abstracted from *The Waste Land* and argued over, Pound's diagnosis in *Hugh Selwyn Mauberley* asks to be treated, and *can* be treated, in just this way. Pound's view of history is put forward in all seriousness; so in *Hugh Selwyn Mauberley*, if Pound has misgauged the temper of the period he is dealing with, the poem must suffer thereby, as Yeats's poem 'The Second Coming' doesn't suffer for all its very odd view of history. In fact, Pound's reading of English cultural history from about 1860 to 1920 is a wonderfully accurate register of the temper of those times, and squares with the facts as we know them from other sources.

And yet, so far are we from conceiving of a poetry that asks to be measured against commonly observable reality, that even those readers who recognize and applaud Pound's historical insight will not rest content with this, but probe further to find in *Hugh Selwyn Mauberley* a diagnosis by the poet of his own state of mind and his own predicament. Though Pound has said, 'Of course I'm no more Mauberley than Eliot is Prufrock',[1] the poem is commonly read as if H. S. Mauberley, the fictitious poet whose representative biography the poem presents, is no more than a transparent disguise for Pound himself. Yet Mauberley, as the poem presents him, an apprehensive and diffident aesthete, all too tremulously aware of the various artistic achievements of the past (herein, incidentally, another reason – a dramatic one – for the 'name-dropping' in the poem) and of niceties of nuance in social encounters, ever less capable (as the poem proceeds) of coming to terms with the vulgarity of his age, and therefore defensively withdrawing into an always more restricted world of exquisite private perceptions – what has this figure in common with Pound, the poet, who alone among his associates and contemporaries had Browning's (or Chaucer's) zestful appetite for the multifarious variety of human personality and human activity?

The misreading arises from the first five stanzas of the poem. For this poem about Mauberley begins with a section not about Mauberley, but about E. P., that is, Pound himself:

E.P. Ode pour L'Election de Son Sepulchre

For three years, out of key with his time,
He strove to resuscitate the dead art
Of poetry: to maintain 'the sublime'
In the old sense. Wrong from the start –

No, hardly, but seeing he had been born
In a half-savage country, out of date;
Bent resolutely on wringing lilies from the acorn;
Capaneus; trout for factitious bait;

"Ἴδμεν γάρ τοι πάνθ', ὅσ' ἐνὶ Τροίῃ
Caught in the unstopped ear;
Giving the rocks small lee-way
The chopped seas held him, therefore, that year.

His true Penelope was Flaubert,
He fished by obstinate isles;
Observed the elegance of Circe's hair
Rather than the mottoes on sun-dials.

Unaffected by 'the march of events',
He passed from men's memory in *l'an trentiesme*
De son eage; the case presents
No adjunct to the Muses' diadem.

This has been taken as Pound's judgement upon himself, but in fact it presents Pound as he knows he must appear to some others. It was the French poet of the Middle Ages, François Villon, a most distinguished 'adjunct to the Muses' diadem', who in the first line of his *Grand Testament* described himself as passing from sight in his thirtieth year, in '*l'an trentiesme De son eage*'; Pound, in his ironic and entirely characteristic use of this inserted quotation, is deriding, in effect, the confidence with which the speaker so conclusively consigns him also to oblivion. Similarly, the earlier reference to Pound's native America as 'a half-savage country' is an example of the Englishman's misplaced condescension. All the same, this fictitious Englishman is no fool. By introducing the line from Homer's *Odyssey*, 'For we know all the things that are in Troy', the speaker of this poem wittily makes Odysseus's own story of Troy into the siren-song which Pound heard and was seduced by. And in fact Pound had already started his version of the story of Odysseus, the long epic poem which has occupied him ever since. In the speaker's view, Circe, representing Pound's epic aspirations, had beguiled him from pursuing his voyage home to his faithful wife, Penelope, to his true objective, which was Flaubertian. The irony of this famous line 'His true Penelope was Flaubert' (which is echoed, as we have seen, in a later section) has been well disentangled by a transatlantic critic. For Pound, he says,

> Flaubert represents the ideal of disciplined self-immolation from which English poetry has been too long estranged, only to be rejoined by apparently circuitous voyaging. For the writer of the epitaph, on the other hand, Flaubert is conceded to be E.P.'s 'true' (= equivalent) Penelope only in deprecation: Flaubert being for the English literary mind of the first quarter of the present century a foreign, feminine, rather comically earnest indulger in quite un-British preciosity; ... a suitable Penelope for this energetic American.[2]

Thus the speaker of the poem says what is true while meaning to say (in identical words) what is false.

Pound has lately said, of commentators on *Hugh Selwyn Mauberley*, 'The worst muddle they make is in failing to see that Mauberley buries E. P. in the first poem; gets rid of all his troublesome energies.'[3] But though we have been obtuse if we suppose that the speaker of this epitaph is Pound himself, there is no way of knowing that the speaker in fact is Mauberley. Moreover Pound's comment implies, what it is not easy to discover within the poetry itself, that subsequent sections of the poem are also to be understood as spoken not by Pound himself but by the imaginary Mauberley. This is indicated by further examples of the same stilted and precious diction as 'the case presents No adjunct to the Muses' diadem'. (The model for this sort of language, incidentally, is another Frenchman, Jules Laforgue.) Section III, for instance, is written in this style and expresses the views of Walter Pater in one place and of Swinburne in others, more wholeheartedly than Pound himself might choose to do. But this mannered language can be taken, and has been taken, as indicating a degree of ironical detachment in the poet, without supposing that the detachment goes so far as to require another speaker altogether. Again, Section V, the beautiful and bitter comment on the First

World War, reduces the value of European civilization to 'two gross of broken statues', in a way that doubtless Pound would not endorse, though he might sympathize with the anger at waste and loss which thus expresses itself. But from a lyric one doesn't anyway expect considered judgements; so that the dramatic fiction, Mauberley, isn't necessary here, either. The section where it is essential to realize that Mauberley and not Pound is speaking is Section II, where Mauberley acknowledges that if Pound's epic pretensions were not what 'The age demanded', still less does it demand his own 'Attic grace', his 'inward gaze', his 'classics in paraphrase'. Having talked of how Pound is out of step with his age, he now talks of how he himself is out of step with it, though in a quite different way. If readers have found themselves incapable of this rapid change of stance (preferring instead an impossible compound poet, of epic and sublime pretensions in Section I yet vowed in Section II to Attic grace and Gautier's 'sculpture of rhyme'), the poet is partly to blame; he is trying to make ironical detachment and slight shifts of tone do more than they can do, by way of directing and redirecting the reader's attention.

The admirable sixth and seventh sections, entitled respectively 'Yeux Glauques' and (a line from Dante) 'Siena mi fe'; Disfecemi Maremma', are those which provide a tart and yet indulgent capsulated history of late-Victorian literary culture. 'Yeux Glauques' establishes the milieu of, for instance, D. G. Rossetti, in the 1870s:

> The Burne-Jones cartons
> Have preserved her eyes;
> Still, at the Tate, they teach
> Cophetua to rhapsodize;
>
> Thin like brook-water,
> With a vacant gaze.
> The English Rubaiyat was still-born
> In those days.

The masterly compression here is all a matter of punctuation and grammar played against the structure of the quatrain. Grammar makes 'Thin like brook-water, With a vacant gaze' refer to the distinctively Pre-Raphaelite ideal of feminine beauty, as embodied in several women (the most famous is Rossetti's Elizabeth Eleanor Siddall) who were at once these painters' models and their mistresses, but embodied also in the paintings of the school, of which one of the most famous is 'King Cophetua and the Beggar Maid'. But metre and rhyme make 'Thin like brook-water' refer also, in defiance of grammar, to Edward Fitzgerald's translation of Omar Khayyám's *Rubá'iyát*, which went unnoticed for years until discovered by Rossetti, remaindered on a bookstall. Such ('Thin like brook-water') is Mauberley's view of the Pre-Raphaelite ideals, of the painting and poetry in which those ideals were embodied, and of the public taste which indiscriminately overlooked or applauded them. In the next poem, the focus has shifted to the later literary generation of 'the nineties', and it covers the same ground as the chapter 'The Tragic Generation' from *The Trembling of the Veil*, among Yeats's *Autobiographies*; Pound's immediate source is a more obscure book, *Ernest Dowson* by Victor Gustave Plarr, who is concealed in the poem under the fictitious name, 'Monsieur Verog'. To read these two poems as spoken by Mauberley rather than Pound turns the edge of the otherwise weighty objection[4] that Pound's irony here is of the unfocused kind which enables him to have it both ways, so that the tartness and the indulgence, the mockery and the affection, lie side by side without modifying each other. If Mauberley is the speaker, however, this unresolved attitude is dramatically appropriate and effective, and helps to account for his own subsequent failure.

After this sketch of a historical development comes a survey of the state of affairs it produced, concentrated into five acrid portraits – of 'Brennbaum' (perhaps Max Beerbohm); of 'Mr Nixon', the successful best-seller (perhaps Arnold Bennett); of 'the stylist'; of modern woman; and of the patron, 'the Lady Valentine'. Again Mauberley is speaking, for in Section XII the speaker, waiting upon the Lady Valentine, describes himself in terms more appropriate to Eliot's Prufrock than to the ebullient and assertive Pound. The first stanza of this poem is another splendid example of Pound's witty compactness:

> 'Daphne with her thighs in bark
> Stretches toward me her leafy hands', –
> Subjectively. In the stuffed-satin drawing-room
> I await the Lady Valentine's commands.

The quotation-marks are Pound's acknowledgement that the first two lines are an adaptation from *Le Château du Souvenir* by Gautier.

But the borrowing is made utterly Poundian by the deflating word 'Subjectively', which meets the reader as he swings around the line-ending, thus achieving the maximum surprise and shock. In the Greek legend the river-nymph Daphne was saved from ravishment by the amorous god Apollo, when her father, the river-deity, transformed her on the instant into a laurel-tree. The sexual connotation is present here, as in other episodes of Mauberley's career. But more important is the allegorical meaning by which Apollo the god of poetry figures, sensationally diminished, as the poet waiting humbly upon his patroness. What the poet wants from her is the traditional acknowledgement of poetic prowess, the laurel-wreath; but when she seems to hold this out to him ('her leafy hands') he reminds himself that she does so only 'subjectively', only in his private fantasy, for in objective fact she represents no such respectable body or principle of taste as could permit the poet to value her approval. It would require nothing less than a divine miracle to metamorphose her in this way, from a false patroness to a true one!

We have to say that this whole sequence of twelve short poems reads better, that several difficulties are ironed out, if they are taken as spoken by the fictional Mauberley. Yet many of them can be read as if spoken directly by Pound. The limitation involved here is inherent in any use of a created character standing between the poet and the reader. This device, by which the poet speaks in an assumed character, was first exploited consistently by Browning in his dramatic monologues. What Pound called the 'persona' and what Yeats called the 'mask' are refinements upon Browning's model. Eliot's Prufrock and Gerontion, and his Tiresias who speaks *The Waste Land*, correspond to Pound's Mauberley, and so (though with certain important differences) do Yeats's Michael Robartes, his Ribh, and his Crazy Jane. To all three poets the device recommended itself because it helped them to what, at different times and perhaps for different reasons, they all desired, the effect of impersonality. But the device appears to work only if the persona is sufficiently differentiated from the poet himself–otherwise the irony lapses, and the reader overlooks the presence of the persona. If this happens with Pound's Mauberley, it seems to me to happen too, and more calamitously, with Eliot's Gerontion.

How closely at this period Pound and Eliot were working in

concert can be seen from a comment made by Pound many years later (in 1932, in *The Criterion*):

> at a particular time in a particular room, two authors, neither engaged in picking the other's pocket, decided that the dilutation of *vers libre* ... had gone too far and that some countercurrent must be set going. Parallel situation years ago in China. Remedy prescribed '*Émaux et Camées*' (or the Bay State Hymn Book). Rhyme and regular strophes.
>
> Results: Poems in Mr Eliot's *second* volume, not contained in his first ..., also H. S. Mauberley.

Pound the pedagogue is characteristically evident. But the central point is clear: Pound and Eliot, the two poets who had done most to familiarize free verse in English, had seen the necessity, at least as early as 1918, to revert to writing in rhyming stanzas, and if necessary to find their models in something so unfashionable as a provincial hymn-book. The model they adopted (Gautier, author of *Émaux et Camées*) was not much less unfashionable.

To be sure, there could be no question of simply putting the clock back. The large-scale rhythms of free verse, with its roving stresses, inform Pound's quatrains, which cannot be scanned by traditional principles, and similarly the rhymes are only approximate rhymes much of the time; still, the pattern of the rhyming stanza imposes itself, and the result is, to the ear, a peculiarly pleasant one – powerful surges of expansive rhythm never quite given their head, but reined back and cut short. On the other hand, there are quite different patterns, as in one of the sections on the Great War:

> These fought in any case
> and some believing,
>   pro domo, in any case ...
>
> Some quick to arm,
> some for adventure,
> some from fear of weakness,
> some from fear of censure,
> some for love of slaughter, in imagination,
> learning later ...
> some in fear, learning love of slaughter;

This may look like free verse; in fact it is a learned imitation of the measures of the late-Greek pastoral poet, Bion.

On the list of contents in the first English and American printings of *Hugh Selwyn Mauberley*, the first and much the longer part of the poem, specifically sub-titled 'Part I', consists of the pieces we have so far considered. Standing on its own, between Part I and Part II, is the poem headed 'Envoi (1919)'. This is one place where there is no doubt who is speaking. It is Pound himself, suddenly stepping from behind the wavering figure of Mauberley and all the veils of irony, to speak out personally, even confessionally, into a situation which he had seemed to contrive just so as not to speak in his own person at all. This wonderfully dramatic moment is signalized by the sudden appearance of a wholly unexpected metre and style, flowing, plangent, and *cantabile*, so wholly traditional in every respect that the voice of the poet seems to be the anonymous voice of the tradition of English song:

> Go, dumb-born book,
> Tell her that sang me once that song of Lawes:
> Hadst thou but song
> As thou hast subjects known,
> Then were there cause in thee that should condone
> Even my faults that heavy upon me lie,
> And build her glories their longevity.

The tradition that here utters itself is the tradition that is invoked in the name of Henry Lawes, who composed the music for Milton's *Comus*; it is the tradition not of English poetry, but of English song, English poetry for singing.

> Tell her that sheds
> Such treasure in the air,
> Recking naught else but that her graces give
> Life to the moment,
> I would bid them live
> As roses might, in magic amber laid,
> Red overwrought with orange and all made
> One substance and one colour
> Braving time.

We are now enough acclimatized to this unexpected, poignantly archaic convention, to perceive that in its different way it is still dealing with matters that the earlier sections, out of their chilly smiling poise, have already canvassed. The last section of Part I, for instance, spoke of 'Fleet St, where/Dr Johnson flourished', and remarked:

> Beside this thoroughfare
> The sale of half-hose has
> Long since superseded the cultivation
> Of Pierian roses.

These Pierian roses have become the roses which, if sealed in amber, would be 'Red overwrought with orange' and saved from the ravages of time. Thus, the 'she' whom the book must address is surely the England that Pound is preparing to leave. In an American edition of *Hugh Selwyn Mauberley*, the title-page carried a note, reading, 'The sequence is so distinctly a farewell to London that the reader who chooses to regard this as an exclusively American edition may as well omit it...' It seems plain that this second stanza of the 'Envoi' conveys with beautiful tenderness Pound's ambiguous attitude to an England which he sees as full of poetic beauties yet regardless of them:

> Tell her that goes
> With song upon her lips
> But sings not out the song, nor knows
> The maker of it, some other mouth
> May be as fair as hers,
> Might, in new ages, gain her worshippers,
> When our two dusts with Waller's shall be laid,
> Siftings on siftings in oblivion,
> Till change hath broken down
> All things save Beauty alone

It is impossible to read this, if one is an Englishman, without real distress. Only Lawrence, in letters written about this time, registers the death of England as a live cultural tradition with such sorrow and with the added poignancy that comes of being English. (Nearly thirty years later, in Canto LXXX written in the Pisan prison-camp, Pound reverts to the theme, using the same imagery, in three beautiful quatrains beginning, 'Tudor indeed is gone and every rose...') The name of Waller locks in with that of Lawes, as one who wrote words for the other's music. The 'two dusts' that will lie with Waller's are those of the poet and of his book. And the 'other mouth' than England's, which may in new ages gain England new worshippers, may well be the mouth of the English-speaking nations in North America. The ambitious and poignant perspectives which have been opened before us underline the irony by which the poet who was so conclusively dismissed at the end of the 'Ode pour l'Election de son Sepulchre' is the same who, twelve poems later, here recaptures the tradition of English song at its most sonorous and plangent.

Only now, with Part II, does Mauberley, the titular hero of the whole work, emerge for our scrutiny, his emergence signalized by a new cross-heading 'Mauberley (1920)'. As with Eliot's Prufrock, so with Mauberley, the inability to come to grips with the world for the sake of art is symbolized in the inability to meet the sexual challenge, to 'force the moment to its crisis'. Mauberley, like (apparently) Prufrock, allows the moment of choice to drift by without recognizing it, and is left with

> mandate
> Of Eros, a retrospect.

The last stanza of this section – about 'The still stone dogs' – is a reference to a story from Ovid's *Metamorphoses*, but for once this doesn't matter, since the biting mouths immobilized in stone are an obviously apt metaphor for impotence which is partly but not exclusively sexual.

Sections III and IV of Part II trace Mauberley's degeneration, his gradual withdrawal into an ever more private world, until he becomes

> Incapable of the least utterance or composition,
> Emendation, conservation of the 'better tradition',
> Refinement of medium, elimination of superfluities,
> August attraction or concentration.
>
> Nothing, in brief, but maudlin confession,
> Irresponse to human aggression,
> Amid the precipitation, down-float
> Of insubstantial manna,
> Lifting the faint susurrus
> Of his subjective hosannah.

As Mauberley in the very first section of the poem damned Pound with compassionate condescension as Flaubertian, and used Homeric parallels to do it with, so here Pound takes his revenge. The Simoon and 'the juridical Flamingoes' (that epithet a Flaubertian *mot juste*) are taken from Flaubert's exotic novel *Salammbô*, and used (with lordly disregard for geography, which would protest that they are inappropriate to the Moluccas) to stand as metaphors from the physical world for the spiritual state of abstracted passivity which is now Mauberley's condition. As for Homer:

> Coracle of Pacific voyages,
> The unforecasted beach;
> Then on an oar
> Read this:
>
> 'I was
> And I no more exist;
> Here drifted
> An hedonist.'

In the *Odyssey* one of Odysseus's ship-mates, Elpenor, killed by accident, is buried on the sea-shore, and his oar is set in the sand to mark his grave, with a noble inscription which Pound, in Canto I, renders as 'a man of no fortune, and with a name to come'. The contrast with Mauberley's epitaph is clear and damning.

The troublesome question of who is to be imagined as the speaker does not arise with these first four poems of Section II. It crops up again, however, in respect of the last section of the whole poem. Since we have learned that Mauberley, at a relatively early stage of his disastrous career, attempted in poetry something analogous to the severe and limited art of the medallist, the title 'Medallion' given to these last quatrains must mean that here again Mauberley is speaking, that this is one of his poems, closing the sequence just as another of his poems opened it. The poem is symptomatic of Mauberley's degeneration in its externality, its fixity and rhythmical inertness. It shows too how Pound was aware of just these dangers in a too unqualified acceptance of the Flaubertian doctrine of '*le mot juste*', as also in the programmes of the Imagists. The poem is not without distinction; it shows exactness of observation, clarity of order, and compact economy in the phrasing. For Mauberley is no fool, as we realized from the first; he is a man of principle, as well as a man of true poetic ability. The judgement is all the more damning: his principles and his abilities go for nothing because they are not informed by any vitality. All his scrupulous search for *le mot juste* to describe the braids of hair only transforms the hair with all its organic expressiveness into the inertness of metal. Venus Anadyomene, the mythological expression of how sexual and other vitality is renewed, hardens under Mauberley's hand into the glazed frontispiece to a book on Comparative Religion. (We note that it is the head which, for Mauberley, is rising Venus-like from the sea, not the breasts or the loins.) And not just the 'amber' but also the 'clear soprano' invite a damning comparison with the 'Envoi', a poem just as formal, but with a formality expressive of vital response. Mauberley's deficiencies as a writer are identical with his deficiencies as a human being. For there appears no reason to doubt that the woman here described is the same figure whose challenge earlier Mauberley could only evade. Everything that is hard, metallic, and ominous in Mauberley's description of her as an image in a poem symbolizes his fear of her as a person, and his inability to meet her with any sort of human response.

But the most chastening reflection for a British reader is what Pound implies very plainly, that in a culture so riddled with commercialism and false values as English culture is (or was, in 1920), no English artist is likely to do any better than Mauberley did.

NOTES

1. *The Letters of Ezra Pound, 1907–1941*, edited by D. D. Paige (London, 1951), p. 248.
2. Hugh Kenner, *The Poetry of Ezra Pound* (London, 1951), pp. 170–1.
3. See Thomas E. Connolly, in *Accent* (Winter, 1956).
4. See Yvor Winters, *In Defense of Reason*, p. 68.

T. S. ELIOT: POET AND CRITIC

L. G. SALINGAR

Lecturer in English, the University of Cambridge

SINCE he published his first volume of poems in 1917, T. S. Eliot (b. 1888)* has gradually overcome the incomprehension or dislike of critics bound by nineteenth-century literary conventions and has won an authority such as no other poet in English has enjoyed since Tennyson – an authority as a poet seconded by his prestige as a critic, publicist, and playwright. He has restored the intellectual dignity of English poetry; at a time when few people would take it seriously, he formed a means of expression in poetry for the surface and the depths of a representative modern mind, intensely aware of his surroundings, their place in history, and his intimate reaction to them. And with his sensitive, multi-lingual scholarship he has contributed more than any other modern writer to the framework of ideas within which English poetry, past as well as present, is read and interpreted. A decisive literary achievement; yet one that, by its very power, drives the reader to ask whether it has not been gained at a heavy cost, the cost of ignoring or suppressing a great deal of common feeling and experience. Precisely because of his great influence on modern literature, it is important for us to try to judge Eliot's work clearly and in perspective.

Two impressions stand out from Eliot's first volume, *Prufrock and Other Observations* (written 1909–15). One is the impression of a remarkable technique, already flexible and accomplished. The other is that the poet is usually dealing with involved or obscure or painful states of mind. And the special question raised by this poetry of 'observations', written in some sense from the outside, is whether the accomplishment is serving to elucidate the states of mind, or doing something else instead.

The flexible technique springs largely, as Eliot has told us, from his early study of Jacobean stage verse and the free verse of Jules Laforgue (1860–87)[1] (though to these should perhaps be added the influence of

* T. S. Eliot died in 1965.

Browning and of Henry James.) Webster and Laforgue speak together, for example, in lines such as these from the *Portrait of a Lady* (written 1910):

> I feel like one who smiles, and turning shall remark
> Suddenly, his expression in a glass.
> My self-possession gutters; we are really in the dark.

It is a sign of Eliot's originality and insight that he should have turned to these two models in verse and studied them together; and especially that he should have been one of the first English writers to respond to the most significant developments in modern French poetry. For the prevailing influence in these early poems is that of Laforgue, with Baudelaire behind him. From this source, besides his fluid metre, Eliot has adapted his urban settings, with their burden of tedium and nostalgia, and his notation of feelings by mean of fugitive and intermingled sense-impressions, diversified with literary allusions or ironic asides:

> You will see me any morning in the park
> Reading the comics and the sporting page ...
>
> I keep my countenance,
> I remain self-possessed
> Except when a street piano, mechanical and tired
> Reiterates some worn-out common song
> With the smell of hyacinths across the garden
> Recalling things that other people have desired.
> Are these ideas right or wrong?

This is very like Laforgue; so, too, is Prufrock's 'No! I am not Prince Hamlet, nor was meant to be'. But whereas Laforgue's verse, with its 'sentimental irony', is concentrated on himself – *pauvre, pâle et piètre individu* [poor, pale and paltry individual] – Eliot's monologues remain 'observations', detached from the imagined speaker and reaching beyond him. The origin of disturbance within his poetry appears to be, not merely the sense that the feelings imagined are inadequate (as with Laforgue), but the more radical intimation that they are somehow unreal. F. R. Leavis has pointed out how Eliot's mature poetry carries the effect of a 'de-realizing of the routine common-sense world' while hinting at the same time at a hidden spiritual reality[2]; and this description brings out the central preoccupation and the central problem of Eliot's work from the outset. Imagining characters whose feelings are insubstantial or puzzling to themselves, the poet moves swiftly – and often too swiftly – from asking what these feelings are worth on the plane of personal living to asking what their status is in relation to the absolute. In the long run the feelings are left even emptier than at first.

The Love Song of J. Alfred Prufrock (finished in 1911, when he was twenty-three) already shows Eliot's distinctive manner and indicates the range of his wit in the quizzical title followed by a sombre epigraph from Dante. His break from Victorian poetry comes out in the opening lines, where colloquial language presents a situation at once distinct and mystifying:

> Let us go then, you and I,
> When the evening is spread out against the sky
> Like a patient etherised upon a table;
> Let us go, through certain half-deserted streets,
> The muttering retreats
> Of restless nights in one-night cheap hotels
> And sawdust restaurants with oyster-shells:
> Streets that follow like a tedious argument
> Of insidious intent
> To lead you to an overwhelming question ...
> Oh, do not ask, 'What is it?'
> Let us go and make our visit.
>
> In the room the women come and go
> Talking of Michelangelo.

The speaker is vague, but the images he uses are distinct, acutely so; and the precise movement of these irregular lines tells us directly how Prufrock feels: they reach forward only to fall back. The two striking lines ending in 'table' and 'question' are left without the support of rhyme, but when Prufrock clinches his words in rhyming couplets he only seems to be losing balance. Similarly, there is a continuous undercurrent of half-audible images from the 'muttering' streets with their 'tedious argument' to the thought of the women talking, where it peters out, for the moment, in irrelevance and anti-climax. Eliot has said that the most interesting verse is that which constantly approaches a fixed pattern without quite settling into it: 'it is this contrast between fixity and flux, this unperceived evasion of monotony, which is the very life of verse' (*Reflections on 'Vers Libre'*, 1917[3]). This is an apt and fundamental comment on his own practice.

And contrast between fixity and flux applies to much more than the versification of these lines. Prufrock's surroundings consist of hard, gritty objects; his thoughts are fluctuating and evasive. He is witty, nervous, self-important, and illogical. With a side-glance at romantic sunsets, he merges the evening into his own state of trepidation. The 'retreats' he notices are neither calm nor silent. He reads 'an overwhelming question' into the layout of the city blocks. What that question is – a proposal of marriage? the question of human dignity? – is not put into words; but the way it emerges expresses the condition of seeing a problem and shrinking away from it.

Beyond Prufrock's vacillation, moreover, there are hints of something permanent which he can dimly perceive but cannot grasp. The sky and the table are more enduring than the presence of any single evening or any single patient; and by a striking and characteristic compression of meanings, 'etherised' suggests 'going under' and 'spiritualized' at the same time. Oyster-shells and Michelangelo recall high values, however empty of content at present; conversely, 'restless nights in one-night cheap hotels' and again the image of the women talking suggest a coming-and-going of many lives across fixed points of loneliness or boredom. Prufrock's irony is made to reflect a general human predicament besides being directed against himself. But if Eliot's attitude here is already more complex than that of Laforgue, it is hardly as yet more mature: Prufrock's fear of ordinary living is measured by his own standards.

Eliot's *Prufrock* volume belongs to Boston and Paris. His next group of poems was written in London about the end of the war. Here (acting on Ezra Pound's advice) he turns from free verse to the strict rhyming quatrains of Gautier. With the new form of verse goes a sharper satiric edge, but also a more startling conjunction of images and ideas, as if Eliot were compensating for more fixity in one direction by more elasticity in another. In his disconcerting wit we seem to feel the pulse of the generation for whom (as he wrote soon after) 'the dissolution of value had in itself a positive value'.[4] These poems are dry, fantastic, astringent. But they leave the poet's essential attitude to life still unresolved.

Sweeney Among the Nightingales (1918) illustrates the method of the rhyming poems. The narrative is kept obscure but it appears that in a tavern somewhere in South America a number of shady characters are plotting against Apeneck Sweeney. Possibly he escapes. But at the end, as if in a film, the images of the present scene are transposed into others emerging from a remote and tragic past:

> The host with someone indistinct
> Converses at the door apart,
> The nightingales are singing near
> The Convent of the Sacred Heart,
>
> And sang within the bloody wood
> When Agamemnon cried aloud,
> And let their liquid siftings fall
> To stain the stiff dishonoured shroud.

Agamemnon and Sweeney, and music, blood and droppings, are coupled together; religion and poetry (the Convent and the nightingales) have always been witnesses of the same squalid agony. And yet what these lines emphasize most is not the horror of the spectacle but its monotony, with an overriding sense of the neatness of the versification. Technique here is not a means of clarifying the tangle of human experience but of withdrawing from it towards an artificial objectivity.

Although this passage is not one of Eliot's best, it reveals the purpose behind his finest poetry. His central purpose can be described as a search for detachment, or impersonality (as Eliot calls it in his programmatic essay of 1917 on *Tradition and the Individual Talent*). Detachment is the counterpoise to his deep sense of unreality, or equivocal reality, in personal emotions. The people he creates in his early work embody detachment in the negative sense that they have no satisfying hold on life. They have no personal roots or affections and cannot trust their own impulses. They are acutely conscious of some spiritual absolute, but only in the form of a privation, as 'the Shadow' that falls 'Between the emotion And the response' in *The Hollow Men* (1925). Or they feel they are exiles in the midst of life, somewhat like Orestes, because of their contact with a dreadful but unidentifiable guilt – as with the heroes of *Sweeney Agonistes* (1924–6) and *The Family Reunion* (1939). Eliot speaks of a poet's desire to escape from the burden of private emotion; and he comes to recognize that the name of impersonality may cover a variety of attitudes to life, from self-discipline to indifference or revulsion. His ideal of impersonality is ambiguous. But at its clearest, it stands for an intense effort to pass through a baffling, oppressive sense of unreality, to free himself of it by converting it into a mode of detached contemplation.

In the same essay, Eliot insists on a poet's obligation to transcend his private self by loyalty to the tradition of European literature as a whole – for which he needs 'the historical sense'. The historical sense is not antiquarian; for Eliot, it means a constant attention to changes in literary styles and values, but also to continuity and permanence; a sense of fixity together with flux; and further, 'a sense of the timeless as well as of the temporal and of the timeless and of the temporal together'. In his reaching out from America to the tradition of Europe, Eliot resembles Henry James.[5] But he goes far beyond James; and, especially in his sense of the relativity of values, he speaks for the general mind of his own age, imbued with the historical and evolutionary thought of the nineteenth century and at the same time perplexed by the problem of discontinuity in culture and belief. From Eliot's sense of history and his search for a metaphysical reality beyond the self come a series of meditations in his poetry on the idea of Time – time as an aspect of individual lives or the succession of generations, time in relation to the discredited idea of progress, time in relation to eternity. In Eliot's poetry, the idea of Time has the same kind of prominence as the idea of Nature in the poetry of the romantics. It is latent there from the beginning (for instance, in Prufrock's references to Michelangelo and Hamlet or in the coupling of Agamemnon with Sweeney). It comes to the forefront in *Gerontion* (1919), the most important poem in his second volume. And thereafter meditation on time remains an essential aspect of his poetry, from *The Waste Land* to *Four Quartets*, where it supplies both a subject and a method.

Gerontion is important in other respects as well. Gerontion ('the little old man') is apparently a former seaman or business man at the end of his tether, 'an old man driven by the Trades To a sleepy corner'. He is blind; he lives in 'a decayed house' which is not his own; as he considers his possible future and the memories left by his travels he realizes with anguish that he has no genuine life behind him, no achievements, 'no ghosts', no faith, no passions. In *Prufrock*, Eliot had made the speaker confuse his sensations with his thoughts; in *Gerontion*, he makes the effort of thinking itself almost a physical sensation, a straining to grasp at elusiveness and illusion:

> After such knowledge, what forgiveness? Think now
> History has many cunning passages, contrived corridors
> And issues, deceives with whispering ambitions,
> Guides us by vanities. Think now
> She gives when our attention is distracted
> And what she gives, gives with such supple confusions
> That the giving famishes the craving. Gives too late
> What's not believed in, or if still believed,
> In memory only, reconsidered passion. Gives too soon
> Into weak hands, what's thought can be dispensed with
> Till the refusal propagates a fear. Think
> Neither fear nor courage saves us. Unnatural vices
> Are fathered by our heroism. Virtues
> Are forced upon us by our impudent crimes.
> These tears are shaken from the wrath-bearing tree.

This passage, with its quick interplay between sound, metaphor, and idea, shows Eliot triumphantly applying his study of the Jacobean dramatists. And it shows what he means in his own practice by a 'metaphysical' quality or texture in verse, the quality he describes as 'a direct sensuous apprehension of thought, or a recreation of thought into feeling'. His dramatizing tendency works together with his tendency to seize ideas at their point of contact with sensations.

Yet the poem as a whole is unbalanced precisely where it is most obviously dramatic. The concentration in Gerontion's mind, the urgent rhetorical 'Think now', gives way to an impulse to hypnotize himself with his own despair; the 'corridors' lead him to a private nightmare (like the streets in *Prufrock*), a maze where he loses his identity. He merges himself with the whole of mankind, with the failures imposed by history or else – the argument shifts – resulting from original sin. But there is no clear relation between the private and the universal phases of Gerontion's despair, for the personal memories he has just recalled (the immediate objects of his guilty 'knowledge') are no more, in themselves, than provocative but trivial fragments; in the phrase Eliot himself applies to *Hamlet*, they do not constitute an 'objective correlative' to Gerontion's feelings about history.[6] Nevertheless, his despair is presented as something more weighty than a personal outburst. The intimate and the rhetorical elements in the poem are brought together by force.

Eliot might have left a different impression if he had been willing to treat Gerontion as a character with particular qualities and a particular story. But he is evidently reluctant to shape a narrative, with its chain of proximate causes and effects. He dismisses these as predetermined by or in History –

> while the world moves
> In appetency, on its metalled ways
> Of time past and time future.
> (*Burnt Norton*, 124; 1935)

And when he praises *Ulysses* for giving 'a significance to the immense panorama of futility and anarchy which is contemporary history', the point of his admiration is that Joyce uses analogies drawn from myths 'instead of narrative method'.[7] Eliot's indifference to narrative in his own work is another aspect of his search for impersonality.

* * *

In his critical essays, especially the early ones, Eliot is deeply (and rightly) concerned with his practical interests as a poet. He is brilliant and illuminating when he declares his own taste or when he deals with versification and certain aspects of poetic language. But he becomes evasive and inconsistent when he touches on poetic composition as a whole or on a poet's attitude to life, although he regularly assumes an incisive and even dogmatic tone. Hence his critical pronouncements form a tricky instrument to use for the understanding of his own poetry and still more for that of other poets.[8]

Although he once proclaimed himself a classicist, his view of poetry derives from the nineteenth century, not from the seventeenth or the eighteenth; it comes from Flaubert and Baudelaire and their French successors and from the more direct influence of Irving Babbitt and Santayana at Harvard and Ezra Pound and T. E. Hulme in London. The Flaubertian strain in his doctrine of impersonality comes out where he argues (as in his essay on tradition) that a poet's mind should remain 'inert' and 'neutral' towards his subject-matter, keeping a gulf between 'the man who suffers and the mind which creates'; or again, where he tries to equate literature with science (comparing the method of *Ulysses*, for example, to 'a scientific discovery'). The influence of Baudelaire and his successors is powerful both in the moral colouring of Eliot's poetry and in his views on poetic symbolism, on the use of mythological or literary parallels and allusions, on the music in poetry, and on sensibility.

The poetic world of Baudelaire contains 'forests of symbols'. His images blend the resonance of differing sense-impressions; they signify a hidden unity between matter and spirit, or else disclose an ironic contrast-in-resemblance between the actual and the ideal. And Mallarmé claims that a poet can evoke the ultimate mystery of things in and through the non-conceptual properties of words, especially their music. Eliot takes the same direction. He admires in Baudelaire the power of bringing 'imagery of the sordid life of a great metropolis' to a pitch of 'the *first intensity* – presenting it as it is, and yet making it represent something more than itself'; and in Dante he emphasizes the physical immediacy of the allegory – 'Dante's is a *visual* imagination ... in the sense that he lived in an age in which men still saw visions.'[9] The important factor here is rather sensory apprehension than the visual as such, for elsewhere Eliot claims, rather like Mallarmé, that a poet's 'auditory imagination' can pass through the conventions of language accumulated by history to return to 'the most primitive', 'penetrating far below the conscious levels ... seeking the beginning and the end'. Similarly, he holds that the true function of the poetry in poetic drama is to 'touch the border of those feelings which only music can express' – thus preparing the audience for a religious insight transcending the spectacle of human action.[10] Here Eliot differs from Mallarmé and the cult of pure poetry, in that he considers poetry an auxiliary to religion and not a substitute for it. As to poetry in its own sphere, however, he sketches out a similar view: the poet apprehends what is below or above the plane of practical consciousness through a heightened activity of his senses, which includes his response to language. And this perception, crystallized in language, is as much independent of the writer's everyday personality as the vision of a mystic or the discovery of a scientist. What Eliot leaves unclear in his statements is the part he assigns to the poet's intelligence.

At first sight, it appears that he values the intellect and the senses together – the 'recreation of thought into feeling'. But he repeatedly implies that the senses are both vital and trustworthy for a poet, whereas the intellect is irrelevant. In one place he writes that 'the keenest ideas' have 'the quality of a sense-perception'; elsewhere, that poets like Donne and Mallarmé pursue philosophical speculation simply in order to 'develop their power of sensibility' – without believing in their ideas or even thinking consecutively.[11] In his essay on *Shakespeare and the Stoicism of Seneca* (1927) he maintains that 'the poet who "thinks" is merely the poet who can express the emotional equivalent of thought' – which looks plausible. 'But' (Eliot goes on) 'he is not necessarily interested in the thought itself' – which is almost nonsense. However, 'in truth neither Shakespeare nor Dante did any real thinking'; although Dante relied on a superior philosophy, the philosophy of St Thomas, 'that was just his luck'; and the so-called thinking of both poets is simply 'the thought current at their time, the material enforced upon each to use as the vehicle of his feeling'. Now, it is one thing to say that a poet is not a systematic philosopher; quite another to suggest that he merely drifts on the stream of his age. It is difficult to see how Eliot supposes Dante leaned on St Thomas, or Shakespeare leaned on Seneca to the neglect of St Thomas (who, after all, was pretty much as accessible to him as to Eliot); or how Dante or Donne or Shakespeare could have represented their feelings coherently at all. But his theory maintains that during the process of composition a poet's mind is inert or neutral towards his experience (including his reading and his emotions alike), while the real work of creation is done by his sensibility; as, for example, in a now famous passage in his essay on *The Metaphysical Poets* (1921):

> Tennyson and Browning are poets, and they think; but they do not feel their thought as immediately as the odour of a rose. A thought to Donne was an experience; it modified his sensibility. When a poet's mind is perfectly equipped for its work, it is constantly amalgamating disparate experience; the ordinary man's experience is chaotic, irregular, fragmentary. The latter falls in love, or reads Spinoza, and these two experiences have nothing to do with each other, or with the noise of the typewriter or the smell of cooking; in the mind of the poet these experiences are always forming new wholes. ... The

> poets of the seventeenth century, the successors of the dramatists of the sixteenth, possessed a mechanism of sensibility which could devour any kind of experience.

When Eliot wrote these words, it required a highly creative taste to bring home the difference between Browning and Donne; but his general statement is another matter. What is valuable or suggestive in it comes, directly or indirectly, from previous critics – the concept of the poet's amalgamating power from Coleridge, the concept of multiple sensibility from Baudelaire and Rémy de Gourmont.[12] What Eliot has contributed is the stark alternative between order and chaos and the notion that a poet achieves order through some privileged internal 'mechanism'. Instead of fastening upon the real strength of such a poet as Donne – his power of sensitive concentration – Eliot reduces the writing of poetry to a sort of conjuring trick. Apparently he does so because of his dislike of romantic opinions; on one occasion, he says he prefers to think of poetry as 'a superior amusement'. But it surely comes nearer to our understanding of good poetry (and nearer to the classical tradition as well) to say, with Wordsworth, that it is 'the spontaneous overflow of powerful feelings' in a man 'who, being possessed of more than usual organic sensibility, had also thought long and deeply'; or even, with Arnold, that it is 'a criticism of life'.

* * *

The essential vision for a poet, Eliot has also said, is a vision of 'the boredom, and the horror, and the glory' (*The Use of Poetry*, ch. vi, 1933). His own poetry is defective as a criticism of life because he is too deeply occupied with horror and boredom. He shares very little of Baudelaire's moral passion or the human sympathy of Gerard Manley Hopkins. But his greatness as a poet lies in his striving to grasp a metaphysical reality – to maintain a detachment resembling that of the mystics against the pressure of his own scepticism. There is no parallel in English to the poetry of sustained and strenuous contemplation in *Four Quartets*. Eliot there does not define his metaphysical reality or describe a contemplative experience, so much as recreate the experience dramatically, in a new form of monologue which embodies a logical conclusion to his previous work. Here, more completely than anywhere else in his writing, the resolution of tensions, the experience of achieving detachment, takes place within the poetry itself.

His dramatic impulse, inadequate to the action of a play, finds a natural outlet in the poetic monologue, focused on the awareness of shifting and irreconcilable values within a single perception or state of mind. Through all his poetry there runs the same constructive principle of dramatized meditation, of searching for fixity in and through the flux of time. As Eliot himself suggests, this is the principle behind his masterly handling of verse, which is more sensitive to fine shades of feeling in irregular forms hinting at a pattern than it is, as a rule, in regular stanzas with rhyme. And this is the principle behind his treatment of images – behind his 'sensuous apprehension of thought' and 'recreation of thought into feeling'. In his 'de-realizing of the routine common-sense world' (to revert to Leavis's defining phrase), Eliot breaks down habits of sentiment, moral or literary, breaks down the comforting sensation that mind and feelings are resting on something solid, and exposes himself to a profoundly dismaying experience of disintegration. His development has been a progress from treating experiences of such a nature with indecisive irony or contained horror to the hard-won composure of *Four Quartets*.

Prufrock shrinks away from definite consciousness, Gerontion is quivering with it. *The Waste Land* (1922) is an amazing anthology of indeterminate states of mind and being, of 'memory and desire' resisting present awareness, of vivid perception passing over into hallucination, of phrases, situations, personalities blended and superimposed across the boundaries of time and place. Reluctance and bewilderment, as between sleep and waking, are given, for example, in the very rhythm of the first lines, with their dragging participial endings suggesting life and immobility together:

> April is the cruellest month, breeding
> Lilacs out of the dead land, mixing
> Memory and desire, stirring
> Dull roots with spring rain.

This in-between state, neither spring nor winter, neither dull nor alert, but straining between the two, provides the model of everything that follows. Sometimes it rises to fever-pitch, as in these lines (352–8), where the absence of punctuation contributes to the sense of lurching hopelessly forward:

> If there were the sound of water only
> Not the cicada
> And dry grass singing
> But sound of water over a rock
> Where the hermit-thrush sings in the pine trees
> Drip drop drip drop drop drop drop
> But there is no water.

Or else the sense of hovering between consciousness and unconsciousness is made part of a complex synthetic image, as in the lines (215 ff.) introducing the scene of the typist's seduction (or rather, mechanical surrender):

> At the violet hour, when the eyes and back
> Turn upward from the desk, when the human engine waits
> Like a taxi throbbing waiting,
> I Tiresias, though blind, throbbing between two lives ...

The light, the moment of city routine, the feel of the engine, all work together – and against each other; and Tiresias, who, 'though blind', is to 'see' the seduction, belongs to the same mode of being. He is both male and female, time-bound and timeless, a withered demi-god, a prophet hypnotized by an eternal machine.

In *The Waste Land* Eliot has applied the 'mythical method' he admires in *Ulysses* with brilliant but finally incoherent results.[13] All the fragmentary passages seem to belong to one voice, recalling memories, meditating, crossing spoken and unspoken thoughts; but the one voice pertains to a multiple personality beyond time and place. He is Tiresias (who resembles Gerontion) and, as such, suffers with the women he observes; he is the knight from the Grail legend; he moves through London ('Unreal City') and Baudelaire's Paris and a phantasmal post-war Middle Europe; he is Ferdinand from *The Tempest* and a Phoenician sailor anticipating his own shipwreck (and hence, conceivably, Dante's Ulysses as well). But the moral sequence or development is lost in this tangle of myths. Early in the poem, for instance, there is a striking and poignant moment (35 ff.):

'You gave me hyacinths first a year ago;
'They called me the hyacinth girl.'
– Yet when we came back, late, from the Hyacinth garden,
Your arms full, and your hair wet, I could not
Speak, and my eyes failed, I was neither
Living nor dead, and I knew nothing,
Looking into the heart of light, the silence.

The moment of ecstasy has been ambiguous, and the memory of it now is followed by passages of hallucination, boredom, or disgust; but nothing is gained for the understanding of this crucial phase in the poem by accumulating parallels and multiplying costumes and dates. Eliot relies on allusion and analogy to do more work than they can. At another important passage (307 ff.) he explains in a footnote that he is echoing both St Augustine and Buddha –

To Carthage then I came

Burning burning burning burning
O Lord Thou pluckest me out
O Lord Thou pluckest

burning

– but the words are quite insufficient for the constructive effect intended, while at the same time 'burning' seems excessively violent to describe the emotions of the people in the Waste Land. Instead of reducing these emotions to order, the 'mythical method' reflects their confusion.

The Hollow Men (1925) forms a sardonic elegy on the unreal beings in the previous poems; *Ash-Wednesday* (1927–30) marks a decisive 'turning' to religious faith. Nevertheless, the *Four Quartets* can still be described as a return to early themes and symbols, a return to the garden glimpsed in *The Waste Land* and to 'the heart of light, the silence'.[14] The central problem, both personal and universal, is still the unreality of time, the unreality of human life so governed by time that the present dissolves into memories of the past and desires for the future; and each of the *Quartets* follows a pattern foreshadowed in the earlier work. Each introduces the central problem by means of a meditation aroused by a particular season and place – the vanished rose garden in *Burnt Norton* (1935), the country lane in *East Coker* (1940), the Mississippi and the New England coast in *The Dry Salvages* (1941), the chapel with its Civil War associations visited during war-time in *Little Gidding* (1942). The second section re-states the opening themes, first lyrically and then in more abstract terms; the third describes a revulsion or withdrawal from the world, a kind of negative ecstasy; the fourth, a short lyric, forms a prayer; and the last section suggests a resolution, in 'hints and guesses', supported by reference to the satisfaction of creating a work of art or responding to it. As in the earlier poems Eliot dwells on indeterminate states of mind, dissolving common-sense reality: for instance, the introduction of *Burnt Norton*, delicately hovering between actuality, memory, and speculation; or the powerful opening of *The Dry Salvages*, where the throb of the lines evoking the river calls up the menace 'of what men choose to forget' and yet blends with cheerful memories of boyhood; or the 'midwinter spring' at Little Gidding, where 'the soul's sap quivers'. But there is a surer control in such passages than before, and a firmer progression of thought through the *Quartets* as a group. *Burnt Norton* presents the themes in a general, abstract form (the half-historical, half-imaginary garden representing both childhood and the Garden of Eden). The middle poems deal more concretely with history and the lessons of experience; the mood here comes closer to despair. And *Little Gidding* carries the despair to a climax, changing the general pattern to this effect by bringing forward to its second section the main passage dealing with literature (the meeting with the ghost) and also making it the strongest passage of negative emotion; but on the other hand *Little Gidding* gathers together the positive symbols and affirmations of the whole sequence. In detail and organization, *Four Quartets* is a superb achievement, the masterpiece of modern English poetry.

One sign of Eliot's mastery is his having perfected a new form of verse, resembling Langland's measure and challenging, without being distracting to, a modern ear. It might be called a poised measure, distinct alike from *vers libre* and irregular blank verse. It consists of lines of varying length, commonly with four strong beats, pausing midway as if for deliberation; it upholds that most precarious of poetic flights, calm abstract statement:

Time present and time past
Are both perhaps present in time future,
And time future contained in time past.
If all time is eternally present
All time is unredeemable.

(*Burnt Norton*, I)

The same cadence is heard again at the end of this *Quartet*, but on this occasion with echoes and repetitions seeming to check (or 'contain') the flight of time:

Words move, music moves
Only in time; but that which is only living
Can only die. Words, after speech, reach
Into the silence. Only by the form, the pattern,
Can words or music reach
The stillness, as a Chinese jar still
Moves perpetually in its stillness.

And the same cadence is heard throughout the passages in a longer line:

There are three conditions which often look alike
Yet differ completely, flourish in the same hedgerow:
Attachment to self and to things and to persons, detachment
From self and from things and from persons; and, growing
  between them, indifference
Which resembles the others as death resembles life,
Being between two lives – unflowering, between
The live and the dead nettle ...

(*Little Gidding*, III)

This has the deliberateness of prose, but the effect of poetry – even (in its subdued manner) of dramatic monologue; the verse movement underscores the act of the mind in distinguishing 'between' neighbouring concepts. Eliot has found the exact rhythm and tone of voice for his purpose.

And this tone and rhythm hold at the opposite pole of his 'detachment', where he is contemplating emptiness or disintegration:

I said to my soul, be still, and let the dark come upon you
Which shall be the darkness of God. As, in a theatre,
The lights are extinguished, for the scene to be changed
With a hollow rumble of wings, with a movement of darkness on
  darkness,
And we know that the hills and the trees, the distant panorama
And the bold imposing façade are all being rolled away –
Or as, when an underground train, in the tube, stops too long
  between stations
And the conversation rises and slowly fades into silence
And you see behind every face the mental emptiness deepen
Leaving only the growing terror of nothing to think about;
Or when, under ether, the mind is conscious but conscious of
  nothing –
I said to my soul, be still ...

(*East Coker*, III)

Here the 'going under' is more distinctly and more steadily conveyed than in the earlier poems; it is placed in a clearer framework of experience. So, too, the moving 'Death by Water' from *The Waste Land* is surpassed in the corresponding passage, the sestina in *The Dry Salvages* (II):

Where is the end of them, the fishermen sailing
Into the wind's tail, where the fog cowers?
We cannot think of a time that is oceanless
Or of an ocean not littered with wastage
Or of a future that is not liable
Like the past, to have no destination.

We have to think of them as forever bailing,
Setting and hauling, while the North East lowers
Over shallow banks unchanging and erosionless
Or drawing their money, drying sails at dockage;
Not as making a trip that will be unpayable
For a haul that will not bear examination.

Eliot's verbal invention comes out here in 'oceanless' and 'unpayable', with its compound of opposites – the solemn ('beyond profit or loss') and the sardonic ('priceless'). And his ever-present sense of the futility of human effort is now more compassionate and more objective than before.

The description of the aftermath of an air-raid that introduces the Dantesque episode of the ghost in *Little Gidding* (II) is one of the most sustained passages of tragic intensity in English verse; if nothing else, it is an unforgettable record of war. With extraordinary intimacy, Eliot catches the nervous tension of such a moment, merging together the frightful throbbing of the machines and the ebbing sensations of relief, breathlessness, bewilderment:

> In the uncertain hour before the morning
>   Near the ending of interminable night
>   At the recurrent end of the unending
> After the dark dove with the flickering tongue
>   Had passed below the horizon of his homing
>   While the dead leaves still rattled on like tin
> Over the asphalt where no other sound was
>   Between three districts whence the smoke arose
>   I met one walking, loitering and hurried
> As if blown towards me like the metal leaves
>   Before the urban dawn wind unresisting.

By a daring paradox, the enemy bomber ('the dark dove') suggests the Holy Ghost, and the 'uncertain hour' becomes an 'intersection time' between London and Purgatory. But the paradox emerges from an experience directly met and unflinchingly received. Eliot has not only turned sensation into thought, he has made sensation universal.

In a sense, then, Eliot becomes more impersonal in *Four Quartets* by speaking in the first person. Nevertheless, he still leaves the reader to balance his creative achievement against his scepticism. There are, for example, the relatively mechanical passages of satire on the ordinary mind in *East Coker* (101–11) and *The Dry Salvages* (184–98); and there is the prevailing sense of effort wasted – after which it comes as poor encouragement to be urged to 'fare forward' or to be told that the apprehension of timelessness is 'an occupation for the saint'. The consolatory message from the dead in *Little Gidding* (III) appears to come to no more than that they *are* dead. And this follows the utterance of futility and exasperation on the part of the ghost, who recalls the despair of Gerontion, but with more force and more authority, since Eliot makes him represent the whole European literary tradition. Against such feelings, there is the effect of Eliot's superb command of language and his determination to find a pattern in human experience. The poems rest on a statement of faith. But it is difficult to feel sure how far the total pattern they communicate is due to the mastery of horror and boredom, and how far it is simply an aesthetic ideal.

We owe an immense debt to Eliot for extending the range of English poetry. But it is a chilling reflection on the poet and on his age that so distinguished a writer should have spent so much of his energy in negation.

NOTES

1. See T. S. Eliot's Introduction to *Selected Poems* of Ezra Pound (London, 1928), and 'From Poe to Valéry' (1948: repr. in *Literary Opinion in America*, ed. M. D. Zabel, New York, 1951). For details of French influence on Eliot, see the books of Greene, Smith, and Wilson listed in Part IV below; and cp. Arthur Symons, *The Symbolist Movement in Literature* (London, 1899); G. M. Turnell, 'Jules Laforgue', *Scrutiny*, Vol. V (1936); and P. Mansell Jones, *The Background of Modern French Poetry* (Cambridge, 1951) and *Baudelaire* (Cambridge, 1952).

2. Leavis, *Education*, p. 96 [see Part IV, below].

3. Eliot, *Selected Prose*, pp. 86–91.

4. *The New Criterion* IV (1926), pp. 752–3; cp. Eliot in *A Garland for John Donne*, ed. T. Spencer (Cambridge, Mass., 1931), p. 8.

5. Cp. Van Wyck Brooks, *New England: Indian Summer, 1865–1915* (London, 1940).

6. See Eliot's essay on *Hamlet* (*Selected Essays*), of the same year as *Gerontion*; and cp. Leavis in *Commentary* XXVI, pp. 401–2.

7. Eliot's review of *Ulysses* is repr. from *The Dial* (1923) in *Forms of Modern Fiction*, ed. William Van O'Connor (Univ. of Minnesota, 1948); cp. G. Melchiori, *The Tightrope Walkers* (London, 1956), p. 71.

8. On Eliot's criticism, see Buckley; Leavis, in *The Common Pursuit*, *Commentary* XXVI, and *D. H. Lawrence: Novelist* (London, 1955); and Yvor Winters, *The Anatomy of Nonsense* (Norfolk, Conn., 1943; repr. Unger, pp. 75 ff.).

9. *Selected Essays* (1932 ed.), pp. 229, 374. Cp. Mario Praz, 'T. S. Eliot and Dante', *The Southern Review* II (1937).

10. *The Use of Poetry*, pp. 118–19; *On Poetry*, pp. 30, 86–7; cp. Matthiessen, pp. 89–90, and Ronald Peacock, *The Art of Drama* (London, 1957), ch. IX.

11. Eliot, in *The Athenaeum* (1919), p. 362, and *La Nouvelle Revue Française* (1926: quoted, René Taupin, *L'Influence du symbolisme français sur la poésie américaine, 1910–20* (Paris, 1929), pp. 224–5); cp. *Selected Essays* (1932 ed.), pp. 96, 134 ff.

12. See F. W. Bateson and Eric Thompson in *Essays in Criticism* I–II (1951–2).

13. See Note 7, above, and Smith, pp. 59–60, 71 ff.; cp. Matthiessen, pp. 34–45. For detailed studies of *The Waste Land*, see Leavis (in *New Bearings*) and Brooks.

14. On *Four Quartets*, see Harding and Leavis (*Education*, pp. 87 ff.). Raymond Preston, '*Four Quartets*' *Rehearsed* (London, 1946), Unger, pp. 374 ff. ('T. S. Eliot's Rose Garden'), Philip Wheelwright, 'Eliot's Philosophical Themes' (in *T. S. Eliot: a Study of his Writings by Several Hands*, ed. B. Rajan, London, 1947), and Smith give studies of the imagery; on the versification, see Gardner, ch. 1, and Eliot, *On Poetry*, p. 80.

CRITICISM AND THE READING PUBLIC

ANDOR GOMME

Senior Lecturer in English Literature, University of Keele

> CRITICISM ... must always profess an end in view, which roughly speaking, appears to be the elucidation of works of art and the correction of taste. The critic's task, therefore, appears to be quite clearly cut out for him; and it ought to be comparatively easy to decide whether he performs it satisfactorily, and in general, what kinds of criticism are useful and what are otiose. But on giving the matter a little attention, we perceive that criticism, far from being a simple and orderly field of beneficent activity, from which impostors can be readily ejected, is no better than a Sunday park of contending and contentious orators, who have not even arrived at the articulation of their differences. Here, one would suppose, was a place for quiet cooperative labour. The critic, one would suppose, if he is to justify his existence, should endeavour to discipline his personal prejudices and cranks – tares to which we are all subject – and compose his differences with as many of his fellows as possible, in the common pursuit of true judgment. When we find that quite the contrary prevails, we begin to suspect that the critic owes his livelihood to the violence and extremity of his opposition to other critics, or else to some trifling oddities of his own with which he contrives to season the opinions which men already hold, and which out of vanity or sloth they prefer to maintain. We are tempted to expel the lot.

This famous passage from one of the most distinguished of Mr Eliot's essays, on 'The Function of Criticism', was written in 1923. Reviewing the essay himself thirty-three years later, Mr Eliot said that he found it impossible to recall what all the fuss was about. The facts, so far as the early twenties are concerned, are there to discover simply by looking in the files of the literary and semi-literary magazines of the day. But actually Mr Eliot's words would quite accurately describe the situation today. The most immediately noticeable change is that there has been a certain congealing: a good many differences *have* been composed, though the result has not generally been any advance toward true judgement (and Mr Eliot's present bewilderment may well be the outcome of composing too many differences with the wrong kind of fellow). If there is now a rather less confusing array of contention and dispute, the element of clique and coterie, with its snobbism, its pushing of personal and arbitrary values, is perhaps even more apparent. It remains true, as Arnold said in *Culture and Anarchy* (1869), that

> Each section of the public has its own literary organ, and the mass of the public is without any suspicion that the value of these organs is relative to their being nearer a certain ideal centre of correct information, taste, and intelligence, or farther away from it.

What is not true now is that there would be agreement between those counting themselves educated on the direction in which the ideal centre lies. With much talk of the relativity of values, there is often doubt as to whether the ideal centre exists; and for the rest the idea of the élite, implying a dedication to values that are generously and broadly human, has been superseded by that of the gang,[1] with its motivation derived from private or arbitrary sources. The confusion of critical standards is as marked as ever it was: it has merely become a little more lumpy.

The period has been one of a great general cultural upheaval, in which mass literacy and the enormous increase in the power and range of mass media have been accompanied by an apparently final decay and disintegration of traditional sanctions of belief and behaviour. Thus the literary tradition comes to have a greater importance than ever, as on it alone now depends the possibility of maintaining a link with the past by which we can draw on the collective experience of the race. We are at a stage in civilization which demands more and more consciousness, when the individual cannot be left to be formed by the environment but must be trained to discriminate and resist.

The 'collective experience' sounds now almost an empty phrase, so fragmentary are the relics of any homogeneous culture that we may have had. Yet this is the kind of culture that the person for whom literary criticism seriously matters must strive toward; the culture in which it will be possible to appeal to the common reader as Johnson did, in which individual judgements will be confirmed and amplified in an experience of civilized living which is more than individual, where personal concerns meet in the creation of the standards by which a civilization lives.

Only on the basis of a common reader who can be appealed to in this way, who is part of a homogeneous culture with 'more-than-individual judgement, better-than-individual taste', can literature flourish and perform its function in the community. The 'literary court of appeal', then, which James looked for[2] is the very reverse of an academic preserve of rules of good writing. The appeal must always be from the general judgement to the particular, but to the particular seen as part of a coherent, educated, and influential reading-public, one capable of responding intelligently and making its response felt, for it is only then that 'standards are "there" for the critic to appeal to: only where there is such a public can he invoke them with any effect'. Standards are 'there' only in a community, a coherent (though not necessarily conscious) body of thought and feeling, because the standards appealed to, common to all men, are not created individually; for living is a more-than-individual process.

The absence of adequate standards of intelligence and taste, together with the inflation of private and temporary ones, is naturally seen at its worst in the dance of the reviews. Already in 1893, Henry James could remark that reviewing is 'a practice that in general has nothing in common with the art of criticism'; and his description of the way in which 'the great business of reviewing' carries on 'in its roaring routine' holds admirably for today:

> Periodical literature is a huge open mouth which has to be fed. ... It is like a regular train which starts at an advertised hour, but which is free to start only if every seat be occupied. The seats are many, the train is ponderously long, and hence the manufacture of dummies for the seasons when there are not passengers enough. A stuffed manikin is thrust into the empty seat, where it makes a creditable figure till the end of the journey. It looks sufficiently like a passenger, and you know it is not one only when you perceive that it neither says anything nor gets out. The guard attends to it when the train is shunted, blows the cinders from its wooden face and gives a

> different crook to its elbow, so that it may serve for another run. In this way, in a well-conducted periodical, the blocks of *remplissage* are the dummies of criticism – the recurrent, regulated breakers in the tide of talk.[3]

Yet reviews are the nearest that most people get to most books and that some people get to any books at all; they have become a substitute literature speeding the decay of critical standards, a way of talking about books which obscures and flattens out their differences in adequacy and interest. And in the fairly short run the result is that literature is demoralized. There is a close connexion between the extraordinary thinness of our contemporary literature on the one hand, and on the other the proliferation of nine-day masterpieces, the manufacture of easy reputations based on unsubstantiated promise, and the resulting ambience in which minor but interesting talent is stunted and prevented from developing in the pink haze of admiration without discretion or respect. James's strictures are indeed justified:

> The vulgarity, the crudity, the stupidity which this cherished combination of the offhand review and of our wonderful system of publicity have put into circulation on so vast a scale may be represented ... as an unprecedented invention for darkening counsel. The bewildered spirit may ask itself, without speedy answer, What is the function in the life of man of such a periodicity of platitude and irrelevance? Such a spirit will wonder how the life of man survives it, and, above all, what is much more important, how literature resists it; whether, indeed, literature does resist it and is not speedily going down beneath it. The signs of this catastrophe will not in the case we suppose be found too subtle to be pointed out – the failure of distinction, the failure of style, the failure of knowledge, the failure of thought.

Failure of thought, however, not just among writers but in the nation at large. It isn't merely that literary standards look outwards and reflect – as we make judgements – an attitude to civilization and to day-to-day habits of living; failure to maintain a critical spirit means a decay in the very processes of thought and feeling. The language is kept alive by a living literature and a living commerce with it: the effect of the genuine writers of the time is felt far and wide:

our language goes on changing; our way of life changes, under the pressure of material changes in our environment in all sorts of ways; and unless we have those few men who combine an exceptional sensibility with an exceptional power over words, our own ability, not merely to express, but even to feel any but the crudest emotions, will degenerate.

(Eliot, 'The Social Function of Poetry')

Literature, as Ezra Pound said in one of his manifestos,[4]

has to do with the clarity and vigour of 'any and every' thought and opinion. It has to do with maintaining the very cleanliness of the tools, the health of the very matter of thought itself. Save in the rare and limited instances of invention in the plastic arts, or in mathematics, the individual cannot think and communicate his thought, the governor and legislator cannot act effectively or frame his laws, without words, and the solidity and validity of these words is in the care of the damned and despised *litterati*. When their work goes rotten – by that I do not mean when they express indecorous thoughts – but when their very medium, the very essence of their work, the application of word to thing goes rotten, i.e. becomes slushy and inexact, or excessive or bloated, the whole machinery of social and of individual thought and order goes to pot. This is a lesson of history, and a lesson not yet half learned.

The absence of a responsive and responsible public, and the consequence of not living in 'a current of ideas in the highest degree animating and nourishing to the creative power', will always be felt most tellingly by the artist, who is thereby deprived of the critically healthy and creatively stimulating environment necessary for the making of work which has a value and meaning both in its own time and place, and permanently, acting as 'nutrition of impulse'. Society in Sophocles' and in Shakespeare's time was, says Arnold, 'in the fullest manner permeated by fresh thought, intelligent and alive; and this state of things is the true basis for the creative power's exercise, in this it finds its data, its materials, truly ready for its hand'. And James saw the reverse in his time, commenting that 'to be puerile and untutored' about literature 'is to deprive it of air and light, and the consequence of its keeping bad company is that it loses all heart'. The great artist, the really distinguished individual, will suffer, no doubt, less in his art than others. Yet even he cannot write entirely without an audience; and the want of a reciprocal and health-giving relation between the writer and his public marks – a notable example – much of the late work of James himself, a work clearly and painfully deriving much more from the writer's own intense mental effort than from real commerce with a living environment. On the other hand, coming to too easy terms with an intellectually ingrown and complacent society has led Eliot, in his writing since *Four Quartets*, into modishness and triviality.

The worst effect will unquestionably be seen in the way in which the age makes use of its minor talent, which will always be the majority of talent and has much to do with keeping society 'fresh, intelligent and alive' or letting it become the reverse. And here the history of poetry and of poetical reputations in the last thirty years, a period in which immature talent has again and again been hailed as genius, and caught and held in an atmosphere wholly subversive and hostile to mature development, amply documents the dangers of not living in an animating and nourishing current of ideas. For as Dr F. R. Leavis put it, in discussing this very 'Poetical Renascence',

> Favourable reviews and a reputation are no substitute for the conditions represented by the existence of an intelligent public – the give-and-take that is necessary for self-realization, the pressure that, resisted or yielded to, determines direction, the intercourse that is collaboration (such collaboration as produces language, an analogy that, here as so often when art is in question, will repay a good deal of reflecting upon: the individual artist to-day is asked to do far too much for himself and far too much as an individual).

The resistance always required of the writer to his age is now of a deeper and more exhausting kind: he must write, as it were, against the public potentially so willing to do him the wrong kind of honour. The environment, and its vocal representation in the reading public, is the reverse of nourishing.[5]

It is inevitable, therefore, that for anyone seriously concerned for the function of criticism at the present time, the creation and maintenance of a coherent and responsible reading public must be a matter of the greatest urgency. That there is now an extraordinary amount of writing about writing is no indication that the issue is being faced. A notable aspect of the situation has indeed been the display of new literary organs, the enormous number of reviews, 'little magazines', and book sections whose production has become one of the major small industries of the century. Almost all of these have seen their function as catering for the local interests of small sections of the public, and presenting them as matters of universal concern. Almost none has been devoted to maintaining or re-creating human values in literature, or human criteria of relevance in judgement. An early (and partial) exception was the *Athenaeum*, which kept up an independent existence as a weekly from 1919 to 1921, before being submerged in the *Nation*. Under the lively if uneven editorship of John Middleton Murry, it was responsible (among much that was infuriatingly silly) for a standard of reviewing which at its best – particularly in the regular work of Murry and Katherine Mansfield – was incomparably better than anything in weekly journalism today.

Even the *Athenaeum*, however, was something of a catering agency. The first real attempt this century to create the nucleus of an influential reading public coherent enough to keep the function of criticism served at all came with *The Calendar of Modern Letters* (1925–7), a first-rate review whose early death was one sign of the difficulty of the undertaking. *The Calendar* in fact saw its purpose as the creation of such a body as had (in its own comparison) been represented by *The Quarterly*, *The Edinburgh*, and *Blackwood's*. Its position was stated bluntly in the first editorial:

> In reviewing we shall base our statements on the standards of criticism, since it is only then that one can speak plainly without offence, or give praise with meaning.

That these standards represent – in so far as *The Calendar*'s critics were able to call on them – a mature public attesting to the existence of a 'contemporary sensibility' is evidenced throughout in the continuously high level of response and attention expected from readers,[6] and in the tone of its confident appeal to a judgement embracing far more than the personal reaction of the writer. At its most explicit, *The Calendar*'s relation to its reading public is brought out in Douglas Garman's excellent article on 'Audience', one of the first after Arnold to realize the importance of the audience in the creation of literature and to distinguish between poetry and various types of pseudo-poetry which only exist 'to season the opinions which men already hold, and which out of vanity or sloth they prefer to maintain'.

The strength of *The Calendar* – which in only two years and a half yielded three anthologies of reviews and articles of permanent critical value[7] – is manifested not only in the quality of individual contributions (including the first appearances of Lawrence's 'Art and Morality' and 'Morality and the Novel': Lawrence was a fairly regular reviewer), but in the high level of work maintained by the various writers as a team of reviewers. It comes out at its most characteristically impressive in such a review as Edgell Rickword's of Eliot's *Poems 1909–1925*, an article whose significance lies in an exact appreciation of the importance of Eliot's work – the struggle with technique by which he 'has been able to get closer than any other poet to the physiology of our sensations' – with an insight which can pinpoint the dangerous 'personal' tendencies (the arbitrary or obstinately private collocations) to which Eliot was prone and which lessened the public availability of his poetry. The value of Eliot's contribution is thus all the more surely established and the essay, written in 1925, is an amazing achievement at a time when Eliot was everywhere greeted with bewildered or contemptuous hostility.[8]

The Calendar's weakness – seen from time to time in a rather unthinking acceptance of the counters of the poetical academy (awe in front of *Prometheus Unbound* or *Samson Agonistes*), in a naïveté of tone (as when Muir complains that Eliot doesn't appreciate Milton and Wordsworth as much as Marvell and Dryden), and in occasional uncertainty of judgement with regard to contemporary writers (an over-estimation of Joyce and even Wyndham Lewis at the expense of Lawrence) – seems to come partly from a refusal to attempt live critical judgements of past literature in terms of present needs and aspirations as well as present viewpoint and availability; and partly in a refusal to go outside literature (in the directions in which literature leads), and thus display and strengthen the foundations of literary judgement. Possibly it is this last that lies behind the cryptic hint thrown out in the 'Valediction forbidding Mourning' in the final issue:

> the present situation requires to be met by a different organization, which we are not now in a position to form.

Scrutiny (1932–53), by far the most important and – it will prove – most influential critical review of the century, started not only with the experience of *The Calendar* behind it, but also with the immediate stimulus of Q. D. Leavis's *Fiction and the Reading Public* (1930), a book whose fully documented account of the development of popular reading habits during the hundred years or so in which fiction-reading had become largely responsible for spreading a lazy shoddiness of thought and feeling, represented a new realization of the cultural crisis of mass literacy accompanied by the collapse of a widely held community of taste and judgement. *Scrutiny*'s aim and practice were more widely and firmly grounded than those of *The Calendar*, with a concern not merely for literary values, but that their influence should be felt in a world which hardly holds literature to matter at all: the 'intelligent educated and morally responsible public' which *Scrutiny* sought to nourish was to be one which had, with its experience of a training in sensitive judgement, a real effect in fostering a free play of constructive thought on all the conditions of the human situation:

> *Scrutiny* stands for co-operation in the work of rallying such a public, the problem being to preserve (which is not – need we say? – to fix in a dead arrest) a moral, intellectual and, inclusively, humane tradition, such as is essential if society is to learn to control its machinery and direct it to intelligent, just and humane ends.
>
> (*Scrutiny*, II, iv. 332)

While first place was always given to the importance of literary culture, as the guardian of collective wisdom, the standards discovered in live contact with the literature of the present and that of the past which is vital for us today were applied in criticism of other issues in the contemporary cultural and social scene, and particularly in the educational movement with which *Scrutiny* was associated from the start.[9] Indeed, the whole project of *Scrutiny* involved necessarily a movement towards the resurrection of standards in education to ensure a training of general non-specialist sensibility adequate to meet the pressures of contemporary life – not only for the sake of individual well-being but to lead to a common realization of human ends, unrelated to which practical and political action is likely to be worse than useless.

The bringing of literature, and of the values inherent in it, to bear on the conditions of everyday practical affairs is something that can only happen through a public educated in this way. *Scrutiny*'s main effort, then, was towards the defining – that is, forming – of a 'contemporary sensibility':

> What it should be possible to say of 'the skilled reader of literature' is that he 'will tend, by the nature of his skill', to understand and appreciate contemporary *literature* better than his neighbours. The serious critic's concern with the literature of the past is with its life in the present; it will be informed by the kind of perception that can distinguish intelligently and sensitively the significant new life in contemporary literature.
>
> (XIX, iii. 178)

The function, as an early editorial put it,

> is essentially cooperative – involving cooperation and fostering it ... The critic puts his judgements in the clearest and most unevadable form in order to invite response; to forward that exchange without which there can be no hope of centrality. Centrality is the product of reciprocal pressures, and a healthy criticism is the play of these.
>
> (II, iv)

For if standards are only 'there' in an intelligent, educated, morally responsible public, they are only worked out and displayed in collaborative exchange between critics. In a later article Dr Leavis expanded the conception of the process hinted at above:

> A judgement is a real judgement, or it is nothing. It must, that is, be a sincere personal judgement; but it aspires to be more than personal. Essentially it has the form: 'This is so, is it not?' But the agreement appealed for must be real, or it serves no critical purpose and can bring no satisfaction to the critic. What his activity of its very nature aims at, in fact, is a collaborative exchange or commerce. Without a many-sided real exchange – the collaboration by which the object, the poem (for example), in which the individual minds meet, and at the same time the true judgements concerning it, are established – the function of criticism cannot be said to be working.
>
> (XVIII, iii. 227)

Standards derive from centrality (which is 'the product of reciprocal pressures'), the many-sided exchange working to eliminate the merely personal element of prejudice and eccentricity, which characterizes to some degree the initial individual response, and to develop the genuine individual judgement into an understanding of the significance of the work in the community of values upon which the culture is built. And the kind of exchange found throughout *Scrutiny* is in fact almost the only example we have of a cooperative attempt to discover and make palpable values which are essentially and broadly human and not simply those of a coterie. The initial agreement of its contributors was on *function*, on the nature of the discipline undertaken in literary criticism and its relation outside itself in the influence it can bring to bear in the world at large.[10] They formed in fact a group of highly intelligent common readers (whose intelligence was certainly *not* common in the usual sense), who had trained themselves in the discipline of a central but non-specialist cultural activity: they were, in short, one centre of the élite upon whose existence the survival of humane values has come entirely to depend.

Scrutiny's contribution to the defining of a contemporary sensibility (its firm but sensitive assessing, in the first place, of contemporary writing) depended upon a revaluation of our past literature which was pursued rigorously and intelligently. As one friendly but impartial critic put it, this work amounted to a whole new conception of the English literary tradition; and the same writer's judgement elsewhere may be allowed to stand:

> Richards wrote *Practical Criticism* but *Scrutiny* was practical and criticized. Cleanth Brooks wrote notes for a new history of English poetry but in essay after essay *Scrutiny* accumulated a new history *in extenso*. Burke and Ransom extended the boundaries of critical discussion but *Scrutiny* actually occupied the territory and issued new maps.
>
> (Eric Bentley, in *Kenyon Review*, Autumn 1946)

And as Dr Leavis himself was able to claim, not only have the main *Scrutiny* revaluations become generally current, but all the work of 'affecting radically the prevailing sense of the past' was done in *Scrutiny*.

So impressive was this achievement that it has been implied by the editor of a review with claims towards something of *Scrutiny*'s vigilance that *Scrutiny*'s 'task of revaluation' had been completed, the work done and now safely docketed so that the judgements could be drawn on by those with the more urgent purpose in hand of 'responding' to the contemporary literary scene. The apparent compliment, of course, distorts the place that this radical, critical, and scholarly rewriting of English literary history had in *Scrutiny*'s programme. Revaluation is not something that is done once for all, the judgements being established for all time: it is the discovery of how the literature of the past is alive in the present. As such – and because the present is always changing – no revaluation is ever final, however much permanent conditions may be pointed to: the many differences within *Scrutiny* itself testify to an understanding of this.

Scrutiny lasted for twenty-one years – in itself something remarkable. Its final decline and death came not directly from the hostility and neglect with which it was normally treated in more institutional quarters so much as from the dislocation caused by the war, which dispersed the contributors and destroyed the network of collaboration which had been made. *Scrutiny* outlasted the war by eight years, but 'never again was it possible', as the valedictory editorial says, 'to form anything like an adequate nucleus of steady collaborators'. This way of putting it shows immediately how important to the whole scheme was essential agreement among contributors on the function of the discipline they were engaged in. *Scrutiny* was never a haphazard collection of articles on literary matters. A breadth of interest and concern was implicit in the conception from the start; and the marked narrowing of attention which is so plain in the later issues is a sign that to some degree the world had triumphed, and the literary critic was no longer to be found who could feel that he had anything important to say outside his own 'literary' field. Fewer books were reviewed, and those on a much smaller range of subjects. Moreover articles became longer, more 'exhaustive', and at the same time less stimulating. Where earlier essays (for example, Leavis's on *Othello*) had taken one or two central issues raised by their subject to suggest lines where further inquiry would be profitable, there seemed to be a tendency towards the end to assume that the work had not been properly done unless every possible aspect had been covered, every possible approach explored. Sometimes indeed subject-matter seems to have been embarked on just for the sake of having something new to say. The opening, for example, of D. A. Traversi's essay on *Henry V*[11] must immediately arouse in the reader concerned for relevance a suspicious, defensive attitude:

> There are, among Shakespeare's plays, those which seem to have eluded criticism by their very simplicity. ...

The implication (alas, borne out in the sequel) seems to be that Mr Traversi will now set out to remedy not only the shortage of criticism but also the simplicity. Indeed the heavyweight treatment that Shakespeare received at the hands of Mr Traversi and others seems to lead away altogether from an interest in the plays as live literature and to find its significance in the tracing of patterns of imagery almost for its own sake – an activity which is pursued quite intensively enough in universities and academic journals as it is. This kind of treatment is at times only too close in feeling and intention to such an offering (to take an example conveniently to hand) as appeared in a recent number of *Essays in Criticism*, where a contributor has ploughed through 'the structure of imagery in *Harry Richmond*' – an undertaking which immediately demonstrates the futility of engaging in literary business without a live critical sense: for the right critical deduction would have shown at the start that the subject itself couldn't maintain the interest required of the reader or rightfully demand his spending time and attention on it.

Mention of *Essays in Criticism* (founded 1950) in connexion with *Scrutiny*, however, can only be made in order to establish their essential difference, which is the difference, in general, between academic literariness uncontrolled by critical insight, and the benefit of working with a sense of relevance, always in sight of Arnold's 'central, truly human point of view'. And *Scrutiny*'s limitations and shortcomings seem in retrospect a small thing compared with the entire failure of any other journal to maintain anything like a true perception of the function of criticism at the present time.

* * *

For the function of criticism to be properly served the media must be created in which individuals can carry on 'the common pursuit of true judgement'. But there must, too, be distinguished critics ready to use the occasion to its best advantage. In this, our age has been peculiarly fortunate; it isn't possible here to do more than point to four critics whose work seems now to have the greatest permanent value as well as being significant in the development of the general cultural state during the last eighty years. Inevitably this is unfair to a number of critics whose work is not considered and yet has much value. Of the four writers whom I glance at here three are among the greatest creative writers of our time, and the relation of their main work to their criticism is what gives the latter its largest interest. Among these, Eliot – especially in his early work – has had so notable an influence in the spreading abroad of certain literary ideas that his inconsistencies and loosenesses of thought may be historically as significant as his more assured successes.

Of the most recent of the four, F. R. Leavis, it is only necessary to say in introduction that of all the critics in our period he has been the most actively and continuously concerned for the creation of a worthy and stimulating critical environment, as well as providing in his own work a body of criticism of the utmost consistency and distinction. It is impossible to separate a discussion of *Scrutiny* from that of his own contribution to it, for one cannot doubt that the review's incisiveness, centrality, and sense of relevance were the mark more than anything of his genius, and that without this its continuance for even half its actual lifetime would have been out of the question.

'A sense of relevance' has not only led Leavis to see in a continuance of Arnold's spirit the critic's true business in the world, to see criticism as essentially practical and theory as subservient and secondary to practice, but also to find in values stemming from a fine sense of the whole breadth of life the standards by which literature must be judged. The truly relevant criteria – the futility, also, of ignoring them – come out admirably in a passage where he is discussing Jane Austen's position at the start of the great tradition of the English novel:

> As a matter of fact, when we examine the formal perfection of *Emma*, we find that it can be appreciated only in terms of the moral preoccupations that characterize the novelist's peculiar interest in life. Those who suppose it to be an 'aesthetic matter', a beauty of 'composition' that is combined, miraculously, with 'truth to life', can give no adequate reason

for the view that *Emma* is a great novel, and no intelligent account of its perfection of form. It is in the same way true of the other great English novelists that their interest in their art gives them the opposite of an affinity with Pater and George Moore; it is, brought to an intense focus, an unusually developed interest in life. For, far from having anything of Flaubert's disgust or disdain or boredom, they are all distinguished by a vital capacity for experience, a kind of reverent openness before life, and a marked moral intensity.

(*The Great Tradition*, pp. 8–9)

This grasp of criteria is what enabled Leavis to map out and define the significant tradition of the English novel from Jane Austen, through George Eliot, James, and Conrad, to Lawrence – which, as Leavis himself says, 'has become a fact of general acceptance ... with the implication that it has always been so'.

The appropriateness of these criteria in criticism of the novel would now perhaps be generally granted. But, as Leavis has shown in the course of practical analysis and revaluation of English poetry, they carry over into all literature, remain central to our judgement. In the sensitive and penetrating analysis of verse Leavis has certainly no master, but always his concern for 'practical criticism', for close attention to 'the words on the page', is a concern for something which far transcends the limits usually implied by these phrases: the accuracy arises out of a need to establish the relevance of a passage in the work as a whole and, by extension, the place which the work should take up in our cultural consciousness.[12]

Technique, in short, 'can be studied and judged only in terms of the sensibility it expresses'. The need to find and realize our contemporary sensibility should lie behind all discussions of technique, and justifies, in Leavis's case, the attention given to it.

The *locus classicus* for inquiry into the relation between technique and the feelings and attitudes which it expresses has been for the last thirty years a passage from one of the finest of Eliot's essays which has been reprinted as 'Poetry in the Eighteenth Century', in Volume IV of the present series (*From Dryden to Johnson*):

after Pope there was no one who thought and felt nearly enough like Pope to be able to use his language quite successfully; but a good many second-rate writers tried to write

> something like it, unaware of the fact that the change of sensibility demanded a change of idiom. Sensibility alters from generation to generation in everybody, whether we will or no; but expression is only altered by a man of genius. A great many second-rate poets, in fact, are second-rate just for this reason, that they have not the sensitiveness and consciousness to perceive that they feel differently from the preceding generation, and therefore must use words differently.

Eliot's own work as the man of genius who altered expression is intimately bound up with that of the critic who saw that 'every vital development in language is a development of feeling as well'. The technique that has mattered in our day is the outcome of

> an intense and highly conscious work of critical intelligence [which] necessarily preceded and accompanied the discovery of the new uses of words, the means of expressing or creating the new feelings and modes of thought, the new rhythms, the new versification. This is the critical intelligence manifested in those early essays: Eliot's best, his important, criticism has an immediate relation to his technical problems as the poet who, at that moment in history, was faced with 'altering expression'.[13]

'Never', Leavis has said, 'had criticism a more decisive influence.' The intimate connexion between Eliot's poetry and criticism was what drew attention to the truly classical statements that his early essays contain. In 'The Perfect Critic', which came out first of all in *The Athenaeum* and was reprinted in *The Sacred Wood*, Eliot noted the likelihood that the critic and the creative artist should frequently be the same person. And more recently he rightly said of his own best criticism that it consists of essays on poets and poetic dramatists who had influenced him. The essay on Marvell, for example, is a model of critical conciseness, accuracy, and suggestiveness – evaluating (with a little helpful practical analysis by the way) Marvell's own personal distinction, generalizing to probe the nature of the quality (wit) which he shared with the earlier metaphysicals and with Dryden and Pope, then back again to isolate the precise tone of its appearance in Marvell. No better introduction to a poet could be found; it leaves most of the work to be done by the reader himself, while making clear the lines which can profitably be followed up. And in so doing it makes generalizations which open up new ways of approach to English poetry as a whole. It is hardly too much to say that this essay and its two companions in the pamphlet *Homage to John Dryden* began the whole movement of re-appraisal in which *Scrutiny* later played the most important part.

But the connexion between Eliot's decline as a poet (decline, that is, from *Four Quartets* to the subsequent plays in verse) and the frequency with which he has come to produce arbitrary and unsubstantiated critical dogmas will not seem a chance one. And just as there are forced and unrealized collocations in *The Waste Land*, as Edgell Rickword pointed out, so even in the early criticism appear ideas and doctrines (among them some that have been widely influential) which are arbitrary, being unrelated to his general critical insights or to the creative successes that seemed to lend them force. The dogma of impersonality, which began its career in 'Tradition and the Individual Talent' (see in *Selected Essays*) is the most notorious of these. In this essay, Eliot, extending the idea of the poet as the supreme representative of consciousness in his time, expels the poet's mind and individuality from having any part in the poetic process. The poet's mind is represented as

> a receptacle for seizing and storing up numberless feelings, phrases, images, which remain there until all the particles which can unite to form a new compound are present together.

How this uniting happens we never learn – only that 'floating feelings' come together:

> The ode of Keats contains a number of feelings which have nothing particular to do with the nightingale, but which the nightingale, partly perhaps because of its attractive name, and partly because of its reputation, served to bring together.

The mind of the poet is said during this process to be as unaffected as the shred of platinum used as a catalyst (even though somehow it 'digests' and 'transmutes' 'the passions which are its material'). We hear a good deal – here and throughout Eliot's work – of the business of poetry being to express emotions, though whose or what must remain in doubt. In the end the complete divorce postulated between 'the man who suffers and the mind which creates' opens the door for a determinism in which the distinguished individual has no part and the poet is a mere mouthpiece of his age, whose business is

> to express the greatest emotional intensity of his time, based on whatever his time happened to think.

It is difficult to make short statements about Eliot's criticism because of the radical inconsistency which it so often displays, a habit which moved Yvor Winters to exclaim that 'at any time he can speak with equal firmness and dignity on both sides of almost any question, and with no realization of the difficulties in which he is involved'. But a generalization about his more recent work would be bound to take note of the increasing (but possibly always deep-seated) conventionality of his judgement, curiously contradicting his very real achievement. His record (inconsistencies and all) with regard to his contemporaries has all along been very unhappy; rather less to be foreseen has been his acceptance of academic or even Book Society standards and attitudes, maintained without a substantiating relation to the work in hand and upheld, one feels (especially in the proposal of interest in Kipling as a 'great verse-writer'), for reasons other than those of a literary critic.

Eliot's best – his lasting – criticism, then, is 'a by-product of his poetry workshop'. It in a sense codified the 'change of expression' which his poetry had made to correspond with the change of sensibility that he had found. It was the poetry, as Leavis has said, that drew attention to the criticism, and not the other way round; inevitably the poetic achievement, with its so notably new distinction, lent speciousness to much in the criticism that has since seemed hollow or arbitrary.

The same qualifications do not need to be made about the two other great practitioner-critics, in whom nonetheless a close link between the two sides of their work is always apparent: Henry James and D. H. Lawrence. Both wrote much about the fiction of their own and earlier periods, and related it to the problems, opportunities, and challenges which faced them as novelists; but both also have produced judgements on novelists and novels which achieve classical rank in their accuracy and the keenness of their understanding as well of the particular concerns of their subject as of the general conditions under which the novel can be met, and against which it is to be judged. James's book on Hawthorne, his essays on Flaubert, Maupassant, and Zola, and on Arnold, Lawrence's on Galsworthy and Verga, his 'Morality and the Novel', and his *Study of Thomas Hardy* are classics of criticism which should have far more recognition than they have received.[14]

The parallels can be interestingly extended. Both did much practical criticism in the way of reviewing: for James and Lawrence at least, a review was an occasion for delicate and precise judgement; and the valuations they then directly made have remained astonishingly secure. James's review of *Our Mutual Friend* is in its way a masterpiece, a model of accurate and refined judgement, excellent in its tone, in the seriousness with which it treats its subject, in the way in which, while condemning Dickens's work, it enables one to see by what high standards it is being, and must be, judged. James's poise at the age of twenty-two is amazing:

> Insight is perhaps too strong a word [for Dickens]; for we are convinced that it is one of the chief conditions of his genius not to see beneath the surface of things. If we might hazard a definition of his literary character, we should, accordingly, call him the greatest of superficial novelists. We are aware that this definition confines him to an inferior rank in the department of letters which he adorns; but we accept the consequence of our proposition. It were, in our opinion, an offence against humanity to place Mr Dickens among the greatest novelists. For, to repeat what we have already intimated, he has created nothing but figures. He has added nothing to our understanding of human character.

The assurance with which these generalizations are made and grounded on accurate and pertinent observations of detail in the novel is entirely convincing. An even more impressive case is the review, written nine years later, of Flaubert's *La Tentation de Saint Antoine*, particularly its magnificent ending in which James fixes permanently the deficiencies of the society which produced the book, in such a way as to make quite clear the measures against which it is found wanting:

> His book being, with its great effort and its strangely absent charm, the really painful failure it seems to us, it would not have been worth while to call attention to it if it were not

> that it pointed to more things than the author's own deficiencies. It seems to us to throw a tolerably vivid light on the present condition of the French literary intellect. M. Flaubert and his contemporaries have pushed so far the education of the senses and the cultivation of the grotesque in literature and the arts that it has left them morally stranded and helpless. In the perception of the materially curious, in fantastic refinement of taste and marked ingenuity of expression, they seem to us now to have reached the limits of the possible. Behind M. Flaubert stands a whole society of aesthetic *raffinés*, demanding stronger and stronger spices in its intellectual diet. But we doubt whether he or any of his companions can permanently satisfy their public, for the simple reason that the human mind, even in indifferent health, does after all need to be *nourished*, and thrives but scantily on a regimen of pigments and sauces. It needs sooner or later – to prolong the metaphor – to detect a body-flavor, and we shall be very surprised if it ever detects one in 'La Tentation de Saint Antoine'.

This measure James to a great extent found in the American society for whom he was writing (most of the best reviews were for *The Atlantic Monthly* and the American *Nation*), and which evidently provided him with an intelligence and responsiveness of a high order, on which he could continuously count. There is, in his early criticism, a sense of being secure among values which were accepted as the natural basis of a civilized society: for James's poise and self-confidence are more than personal – they are those of a distinguished individual who is nonetheless closely related to a poised and confident society (though one which he understood well enough to criticize shrewdly – see especially *The Europeans* and *Washington Square* – and which in the end failed to provide him with what, as a novelist, he needed). This feeling of knowing for whom he was writing disappears in some degree from James's later work. The criticism which James wrote at the same time as his last novels has something of the same air of having been written in unread loneliness, so strained and involved is the very process of writing. And the work is correspondingly more cautious, more hesitant even – and more distant from us. Even in the essay on Flaubert, one of his best, which has all James's admirable perceptiveness and understanding, he doesn't push his judgements to their logical conclusions:

> Emma Bovary, in spite of the nature of her consciousness and in spite of her reflecting so much that of her creator, is really too small an affair. ... Why did Flaubert choose, as special conduits of the life he proposed to depict, such inferior and in the case of Frédéric such abject human specimens? I insist only in respect of the latter, the perfection of *Madame Bovary* scarce leaving one much warrant for wishing anything other. Even here, however, the general scale and size of Emma, who is small even of her sort, should be a warning to hyperbole. If I say that in the matter of Frédéric at all events the answer is inevitably detrimental I mean that it weighs heavily on our author's general credit. He wished in each case to make a picture of experience – middling experience, it is true – and of the world close to him; but if he imagined nothing better for his purpose than such a heroine and such a hero, both such limited reflectors and registers, we are forced to believe it to have been by a defect of his mind. And that sign of weakness remains even if it be objected that the images in question were addressed to his purpose better than others would have been: the purpose itself then shows as inferior.

This is excellent, not only in the directness with which the individual judgements are made, but, again, in their grounding. How fine a sense James has of what it is relevant to bring in, and how delicate a feeling for the life to which Flaubert seems to offer an insult. But James's perception and honesty have undermined the general judgement: 'the perfection of *Madame Bovary*'. The particular and the general judgements don't hang together, and Flaubert's genius, after James's criticism, is not enough to resolve the contradiction. Much the same applies, rather less obviously because the writing is more confused, to the extremely high rank that James gives to Balzac in face of very severe limiting judgements.

Like Lawrence's, James's competence as a reviewer extends over an extraordinarily wide field: his essay on Arnold remains one of the finest broad assessments we have, as well as being itself a model of taste and discretion. But it is for his work on the novel that one returns to him with most profit, and this again links him to Lawrence, in whose work too the importance of the novel is central. For James the novel must 'represent life', its province is 'all life, all feeling, all observation, all vision', the essence of its 'moral energy' is to 'survey the whole field'. And so for Lawrence the novel is 'the one bright book of life', which 'can make the whole man alive tremble. Which is more than poetry, philosophy, science, or any other book-tremulation can do'. In these terms, the novel was of course more than just prose fiction:

> The Bible – but *all* the Bible – and Homer, and Shakespeare; these are the supreme old novels. These are all things to all men. Which means that in their wholeness they affect the whole man alive, which is the man himself, beyond any part of him. They set the whole tree trembling with a new access of life, they do not just stimulate growth in one direction.
>
> ('Why the Novel Matters')

For Lawrence 'the business of art is to reveal the relation between man and his circumambient universe, at the living moment'. It is the living moment that is all-important: in the novel 'everything is true in its own time, place, circumstance, and untrue outside of its own place, time, circumstance. If you try to nail anything down in the novel, either it kills the novel, or the novel gets up and walks away with the nail. Morality in the novel is the trembling instability of the balance ...' true to the ever-changing relationships between men and between man and the universe, never fixed in one place or one attitude. As the relations change, so the living novel changes, informing and leading 'into new places the flow of our sympathetic consciousness, and [leading] our sympathy away in recoil from things gone dead'.

This clearly is something very different from the poor conventional accounts which even quite distinguished critics give of the business of the novel, and its relation to the life it celebrates or describes. The acuteness and originality of Lawrence's criticism, so much a piece with his actual practice of the novel, are natural products of his deep feeling (a religious feeling, he would have called it) of the need to be fully alive, which means not being 'nailed down', not reacting by convention or out of part of oneself, but with one's whole being, seeing the living moment as it really is in all its changing aspects. And the novel will be true to this only if it presents life whole and openly: so its morality is never a fixed counter, but always draws its validity from the conditions of the time and place. Or when the novelist denies this and forgets the demand of honesty and has an axe to grind, 'when the novelist has his thumb in the pan, the novel becomes an unparalleled perverter of men and women'.

The relevance of these passages to Lawrence's own work is very clear. But the insight they show – the insight of a novelist of supreme moral openness and integrity – acts also as a marvellously sure foundation for his criticism of other novelists, and enables him to go to the heart, for instance, of the fatal weakness which makes Galsworthy so palpably second-rate, while it also accounts for his continuing popularity:

> Why do we feel so instinctively that [the Forsytes] are inferiors?
>
> It is because they seem to us to have lost caste as human beings, and to have sunk to the level of the social being, that peculiar creature that takes the place in our civilization of the slave in the old civilizations. The human individual is a queer animal, always changing. But the fatal change to-day is the collapse from the psychology of the free human individual into the psychology of the social being, just as the fatal change in the past was a collapse from the freeman's psyche to the psyche of the slave. The free moral and the social moral: these are the abiding antitheses.

Lawrence, then, all the time traces the links between the books he writes of and the wider interests that they raise, and which he brings relevantly to bear, generalizing to their presence and significance in the world itself. The relation of the novel to the life it serves is always the criterion. So it is in the brilliant short essays on Verga, where so much is said, so many openings made, Verga himself sensitively placed and the value of his work surely indicated, while the issues that his books bring to the fore are further explored and generalized; and so, on a larger scale, in the *Study of Thomas Hardy*, where the novels provide the natural occasion for some of Lawrence's most daring and impressive statements on the morality of art and the morality of life.

Lawrence's genius as a critic is one with his genius as a novelist; there is in him no division of personality: everything he deals with he approaches as 'whole man alive'. It is this which enabled him to write the finest brief statement on the nature of criticism that we have:

Literary criticism can be no more than a reasoned account of the feeling produced upon the critic by the book he is criticizing. Criticism can never be a science: it is, in the first place, much too personal, and in the second, it is concerned with values that science ignores. The touchstone is emotion, not reason. We judge a work of art by its effect on our sincere and vital emotion, and nothing else. All the critical twiddle-twaddle about style and form, all this pseudo-scientific classifying and analysing of books in an imitation-botanical fashion, is mere impertinence and mostly dull jargon.

A critic must be able to *feel* the impact of a work of art in all its complexity and force. To do so, he must be a man of force and complexity himself, which few critics are ...

More than this, even an artistically and emotionally educated man must be a man of good faith. He must have the courage to admit what he feels, as well as the flexibility to *know* what he feels. So Sainte-Beuve remains, to me, a great critic. And a man like Macaulay, brilliant as he is, is unsatisfactory, because he is not honest. He is emotionally very alive, but he juggles his feelings. He prefers a fine effect to the sincere statement of the aesthetic and emotional reaction. He is quite intellectually capable of giving us a true account of what he feels. But not morally. A critic must be emotionally alive in every fibre, intellectually capable and skilful in essential logic, and then morally very honest.

(Essay on Galsworthy)

* * *

In a short chapter it isn't possible to do more than sketch a few lines of approach. One cannot possibly include all those critics whose work has been influential in one way or another, or even all those to whom one can now return with some prospect of profiting by the journey. For since Eliot wrote the polemic quoted at the start, there have emphatically been 'certain books, certain essays, certain sentences, certain men, who have been "useful" to us'. So much so, indeed, that one can only be appalled at the forces at large in the world which have prevented their making the great impression on contemporary life – or even on the literary scene – which one might expect, and which comparable or lesser critics of earlier periods could certainly count on making. In the early eighteenth century, the thought of the *Spectator* and *Tatler* reviewers *was* the thought of the common reader ('who *were* common, because to live in a homogeneous culture is to move among signs of limited variety'); the influence of the incisive critical insight of Johnson was great; Coleridge's presence was felt very impressively. By the end of the nineteenth century, the effect of Arnold, of James, of Leslie Stephen, was a very much less substantial affair and had tended to become almost exclusively literary: that it had not been so before the influence of Coleridge on Mill testifies. But the situation today is very much worse than ever Arnold or James conceived. During the period covered by this book we have had the astonishing good fortune of at least three and a half great critics: it is not too much to say that their influence on the larger issues of contemporary life has been negligible. Yet this influence is something that we do without at our peril.

NOTES

1. 'The gang' – a term used of themselves by prominent members of 'the poetical renascence', who, amongst other things, had the run of Eliot's review, *The Criterion*. Spender's autobiography, *World Within World*, is, from its title onwards, a revealing document of the operation of a metropolitan literary clique. It can hardly be recommended on other grounds.

2. In 'The Lesson of Balzac', reprinted in Edel, *The House of Fiction* (London, 1957). '... the appeal I think of is precisely from the general judgement, and not to it; it is to the particular judgement altogether: by which I mean to that quantity of opinion, very small at all times, but at all times infinitely precious, that is capable of giving some intelligible account of itself.'

3. 'Criticism', included in *The Art of Fiction*, edited by Morris Roberts (New York, 1948). Orwell's essay, 'Politics and the English Language' (reprinted in the Penguin *Selected Essays*), is an interesting extension of this theme.

4. *How to Read*, reprinted in *Literary Essays of Ezra Pound* (London, 1954). This and other of Pound's manifestos have useful propaganda material (especially 'The Teacher's Mission'), though what active criticism they contain is generally perverse. Pound's frequent impercipience and irresponsibility make even the use of his propaganda a dangerous business and liable to misinterpretation. See Leavis, *How to Teach Reading*, reprinted as Appendix II to *Education and the University* (2nd. ed.) (London, 1948).

5. 'If a poet gets a large audience very quickly, that is a rather suspicious circumstance: for it leads us to fear that he is not really doing anything new, that he is only giving people what they are already used to.' (Eliot, 'The Social Function of Poetry'.) Eliot had said in his essay on the Metaphysical Poets (1921) that 'it appears likely that poets in our civilization, as it exists at present, must be *difficult*. Our civilization comprehends great variety and complexity, and

this variety and complexity, playing upon a refined sensibility, must produce various and complex results.' An interesting comparison can be made between the reception of Eliot's own (admittedly difficult) poetry and that of more recent 'modern' poets, who have had it far too much their own way. And cf. a review by Edwin Muir in *The Calendar:* 'The writer who does not resist his age, defending himself against all its claims crowding in upon him and overwhelming him, will belong to the literature of fashion. The writer who refuses to realize his age is not likely to belong to literature at all.'

6. Muir's review already cited is a good – and typical – example. The difference between work like this and the reviews that Muir later wrote for *The Observer* is a significant and distressing one: it reflects very largely on what the two journals expect in their readers.

7. *Scrutinies I* and *II*, edited by Edgell Rickword; *Towards Standards of Criticism*, edited by F. R. Leavis.

8. 'The impression we have always had of Mr Eliot's work ... may be analyzed into two coincident but not quite simultaneous impressions. The first is the urgency of the personality, which seems sometimes oppressive, and comes near to breaking through the so finely-spun aesthetic fabric; the second is the technique which spins this fabric and to which this slender volume owes its curious ascendancy over the bulky monsters of our time. For it is by his struggle with technique that Mr Eliot has been able to get closer than any other poet to the physiology of our sensations (a poet does not speak merely for himself) to explore and make palpable the more intimate distresses of a generation for which all the romantic escapes had been blocked. And, though this may seem a heavy burden to lay on the back of technique, we can watch with the deepening of the consciousness, a much finer realization of language...' (*Calendar*, II, pp. 278–9).

9. A glance at the contents of a typical issue illustrates the range tackled: for instance, Vol. II, No. 4 contains essays on Burns (John Speirs) and on Swift (Leavis); on the Scientific Best Seller (J. L. Russell); 'What shall we teach?' (Denys Thompson); 'Fleet Street and Pierian Roses' (Q. D. Leavis). The books reviewed included three popular books on art, *Music and the Community*, Baden Powell's autobiography, *Change in the Farm*, and books on anthropology, history, and sociology as well as a number on more strictly literary topics. Nor was this variety ever allowed to become indiscriminate.

The most important product of this educational movement was Leavis's *Education and the University*, a book of great and central significance.

10. Cf. 'The Kenyon Review and Scrutiny', *Scrutiny* XIV. ii. 136: '*Scrutiny* has no orthodoxy and no system to which it expects its contributors to subscribe. But its contributors do, for all the variety represented by their own positions, share a common conception of the kind of discipline of intelligence literary criticism should be, a measure of agreement about the kind of relation literary criticism should bear to "non-literary" matters, and, further, a common conception of the function of a non-specialist intellectual review in contemporary England. They are, in fact, collaborators.'

The work of Yvor Winters, as being that of an impressive intelligence apparently isolated from collaborative exchange, is the most notable case of a fresh and vigorous taste and judgement, which, while aspiring to be much more than individual, have too often remained obstinately personal and idiosyncratic. His work is however of great interest, strikingly original and often penetrating, particularly noteworthy in a scene in which reputations are too easily made and taken for granted.

11. Vol. IX, No. iv. His *Coriolanus* essay (VI. i) is a different matter. I owe to Mr J. M. Newton much of my understanding of these trends in *Scrutiny* and elsewhere.

12. '... to insist that literary criticism is, or should be, a specific discipline of intelligence is not to suggest that a serious interest in literature can confine itself to the kind of intensive local analysis associated with "practical criticism" – to the scrutiny of the "words on the page" in their minute relations, their effects of imagery, and so on: a real literary interest is an interest in man, society and civilization, and its boundaries cannot be drawn.' Leavis, *Scrutiny*, XIII, i, 78.

13. Leavis, 'T. S. Eliot's Stature as Critic', *Commentary* (New York), Vol. 26, No. 5, November 1958, a valuable essay from the point of view of both its author and its subject. It contains a very fine treatment of the whole doctrine of 'Impersonality'.

14. James's and Lawrence's criticism has never been properly collected, though in Lawrence's case there is a useful volume edited by Anthony Beal, *Selected Literary Criticism* (London, 1955), which contains all the essays mentioned in this chapter as well as much of the *Hardy* and the *Studies in Classic American Literature*. The Galsworthy essay and one or two others are in the Penguin *Selected Essays;* many more appear in *Phoenix* (new edition, London, 1961). James's *Hawthorne* (and Lawrence's *Studies*) is reprinted in Wilson, *The Shock of Recognition* (London, 1956). James's own collections *French Poets and Novelists*, *Partial Portraits*, and *Notes on Novelists* have long been out of print; and the only readily available work now is in Mordell, ed., *Literary Reviews and Essays* (a compendious anthology of James's excellent early reviews) (Grove Press, 1957), Edel, *The House of Fiction* (London, 1957), and perhaps still Roberts, *The Art of Fiction* (London, 1948).

THE POETRY OF W. H. AUDEN

R. G. COX

Senior Lecturer in English Literature, The University of Manchester

ONE could expect fairly general assent to the statement that of living poets Auden (b. 1907) ranks next in importance to Eliot. When, however, we ask just how near is 'next' and what is the precise nature of the importance, opinions at once diverge. He has no universally accepted masterpieces, nothing as central as *The Waste Land* or *The Tower*, and there is little agreement either about the relative success of his poems or the best way to describe their nature. Auden, we hear, is the Picasso of verse; Auden is mainly a poet of general ideas; Auden is primarily a satirist; Auden's poetry is fundamentally romantic; Auden is most successful in light verse. Some of this is due to the variety of stages that his thought and feeling have passed through in thirty years and to the immediate sensitiveness with which he has registered the changing moods and opinions of his time. For many of his contemporaries there is a sense of being directly and personally implicated in his poetry. Such topical urgency may lend a spurious liveliness to work which later appears dated and ephemeral, and it would seem that Auden's younger readers today show some tendency to be bored by the social and political concerns of the thirties and to question their permanent interest as poetic themes. With the problem of sifting out the mere journalism from Auden's work go fundamental questions of pre-suppositions and belief – psychological, moral, political, and religious. At a more technical level there is a constant experimenting with new forms and manners. And perhaps most essentially confusing to the critic is the presence throughout of a peculiarly deep-seated inequality and unevenness, cutting across all the changes in thought, subject-matter, and general atritude.[1] Having regard to the variety of stages through which Auden s work has passed, it seems best to take a broadly chronological view of his development.

Auden's first volume, published in 1930 when he was twenty-three, made an immediate impact. Here was unquestionably a new talent, the voice of an individual sensibility alive in its own time and capable of vigorous expression. Everywhere there were striking and memorable phrases: 'gradual ruin spreading like a stain', 'spring's green Preliminary shiver', 'Events not actual In time's unlenient will', 'brave sent home Hermetically sealed with shame'. Imagery of unusual force was often matched with expressive and moving rhythms:

O watcher in the dark, you wake
Our dream of waking, we feel
Your finger on the flesh that has been skinned. ...

The song, the varied action of the blood
Would drown the warning from the iron wood
Would cancel the inertia of the buried:

Travelling by daylight on from house to house
The longest way to the intrinsic peace,
With love's fidelity and with love's weakness.

The originality was of course tempered by a normal proportion of the derivative: it is easy to find echoes here of Eliot, Edward Thomas, Wilfred Owen, Emily Dickinson, Robert Graves, Laura Riding, and perhaps the Pound of *Mauberley*:

Issued all the orders expedient
In this kind of case:
Most, as was expected, were obedient,
Though there were murmurs, of course;

as well as of Skelton, Old English poetry, and the sagas. Less healthy signs were an excessive dependence on purely personal associations and a frequent use of private jokes and allusions. The difficulty of some of these poems seems far beyond what is demanded by the depth or complexity of the thought to be expressed. Some of it is a trick of over-elliptical grammar and syntax: some of it can be cleared up by reading the psycho-analytical writings in which Auden was so deeply interested at this time, but there remains much that looks merely irresponsible. Christopher Isherwood has recorded[2] Auden's early habit of constructing poems out of good lines salvaged from poems that his friends had condemned, 'entirely regardless of grammar or sense'. We need not take this too literally, but the suggested attitude is revealing. However, this was, after all, a first volume and it still seems reasonable that its positive originality and its promise should have received the main stress. If the feeling for words and imagery could be controlled by a fuller and profounder organization of experience there was every reason to expect a great deal.

Meanwhile the themes and atmosphere were new and exciting, however much the genuine feeling might seem mixed with adolescent elements. The sense of a doomed civilization, the references to disease and the death-wish symbolized as a mysterious Enemy, the imagery of guerilla warfare, ruined industry, railheads, and frontiers, had not yet become the stock-in-trade of all up-to-date verse as they were to a few years later – a point that modern readers may easily forget. And in *Paid on Both Sides*, the 'charade' which so curiously mingles the heroic and modern worlds, the sagas, and the spy-story, Auden seems to penetrate at times to a level of something like universal human tragedy. The most successful of the *Poems* are perhaps XI, the typical landscape with symbolic overtones subsequently called 'The Watershed'; II, the archetypal quest poem now entitled 'The Wanderer'; III, the address of the Life Force to modern man later given the whimsical caption 'Venus Will Now Say a Few Words'; and XVI, the long personal meditation on the element of dissolution in modern culture, which, in spite of some awkward passages of elliptical grammar not unfairly described by Mr John Bayley as 'pidgin English', has an unusual accent of personal sincerity and maturity in its better parts. The opening paragraph arrests the attention with a powerful contrast:

> It was Easter as I walked in the public gardens
> Hearing the frogs exhaling from the pond,
> Watching traffic of magnificent cloud
> Moving without anxiety on open sky –
> Season when lovers and writers find
> An altering speech for altering things,
> An emphasis on new names, on the arm
> A fresh hand with fresh power.
> But thinking so I came at once
> Where solitary man sat weeping on a bench,
> Hanging his head down, with his mouth distorted
> Helpless and ugly as an embryo chicken.

and the rest of the poem develops the relation between death and growth with, for the most part, a sense of complexity, a refusal of easy simplification often lacking in later work.[3] The characteristic unevenness of these early poems appears most strikingly in the concluding sonnet ('Petition' in the collected volume). It has the arresting phrases – 'a sovereign touch Curing the intolerable neural itch'; the psychological insight and moral urgency – 'Prohibit sharply the rehearsed response'; the private allusions – 'the liar's quinsy'; the throw-away bathos of 'country houses at the end of drives'; and the queer Kipling-Wells uplift of 'look shining at New styles of architecture, a change of heart'. No wonder the late Edwin Muir remarked that it was hard to tell whether the person addressed was 'the Head of the universe or of the school'.[4]

This inequality is accentuated in *The Orators* (1932), that curious experiment, largely in prose, which Auden now thinks a good idea imperfectly executed. Here a great part is played by the theories of Groddeck and Homer Lane, especially that of the psychological origin of disease. Once more inertia, ossification, fear, and death in the individual consciousness and in society generally are symbolized as the Enemy, and there is a constant atmosphere of military campaigns, conspiracy, and intrigue, that is continually slipping back into the world of scouting, O.T.C. field-days, and the schoolboy thriller. It is as if the author has never quite made up his mind whether he is really concerned with more than amusing his friends. The brilliance appears chiefly in the more intelligibly satirical prose sketches, 'Address for a Prize Day' and 'Letter to a Wound': the verse marks no advance on *Poems* and sometimes drops to the level of popular lampoon ('Beethameer') or undergraduate parody, as when the stanza of *The Wreck of the Deutschland* is ingeniously used to celebrate a Rugger victory.

In the more political phase which followed, Auden often exploited popular light verse, partly in an attempt to reach a wider public, and much of this is associated with writing for the stage. An extreme instance is *The Dance of Death* (1933): with more direct Marxist propaganda and more sheer doggerel than any other work, it is the only one from which recent collections have salvaged nothing. The three later plays in collaboration with Isherwood had a more varied scope, and although they all contain passages looking like attempts to beat Noel Coward on his own ground, they also include quite ambitious serious verse, for which Auden is generally assumed to be responsible. The best of this is choric, and it often picks up that technique of the cinematic survey interspersed by vivid close-ups of typical detail that had already been developed in *Poems* (the use in Poem XXIX of the view of the hawk or 'helmeted airman' has been discussed by a number of critics):[5]

> The Summer holds: upon its glittering lake
> Lie Europe and the islands; many rivers
> Wrinkling its surface like a ploughman's palm ...
> We would show you at first an English village ...
> A parish bounded by the wreckers' cliff: or meadows where
> browse the Shorthorn and the map-like Frisian
> As at Trent Junction where the Soar comes gliding out of green
> Leicestershire to swell the ampler current.

Sometimes this choric verse lapses into preaching on Marxist and psycho-analytical texts, either solemnly and directly or through satire whose force tends to be blunted by a facile knowingness. As in *The Orators*, almost anything may be a symptom:

> Beware of those with no obvious vices; of the chaste, the non-
> smoker and drinker, the vegetarian
> Beware of those who show no inclination towards making money:
> there are even less innocent forms of power ...

When in *The Ascent of F6* (1936) verse is used for serious dialogue it tends to be rather heavy, and Ransom's climactic soliloquy is an extraordinary piece of imitation Shakespeare: not surprisingly it can hardly stand up to the invited comparison.

The problem of the popular song manner as used by a serious poet is that too often his nature is subdued to what it works in. The banal rhythms and language simply cannot carry effectively the more sophisticated meanings and deeper intentions. Where in Auden's revue lyrics and doggerel ballads these are attempted, the result is too often a peculiarly distasteful air of smartness. The section of

'Lighter poems' in *Another Time* (1940) provides instances: why in volume after volume should Auden have gone on reprinting 'Victor' and 'Miss Gee'? He has always championed light verse – even editing an Oxford Book of it in 1938 – as a proper use of talent and an antidote to Victorian over-solemnity about poetry, but it has often betrayed him into a peculiar uncertainty of tone and recourse to irony of the self-protective kind.[6] 'The Witnesses', an early poem which survives in the short version used in *The Dog Beneath the Skin* (1935), seems to me typically unsure how serious it intends to be. An allied uncertainty affects some of the political satire: the once popular 'A Communist to Others' (reprinted without title in *Look, Stranger!* (1936) but dropped from later collections) is typical in its hesitation between virulent intensity and facetious exuberance.

Auden's more serious poetic output of the thirties is to be found in the two volumes *Look, Stranger!* (entitled in the U.S.A. *On this Island*) and *Another Time*, with the verse sections of *Journey to a War* (1939). As compared with the first poems these show less taut bareness of language, less elliptical compression, and less awkwardness; but at the same time something has been lost in pressure and urgency of feeling. The technique has more surface competence, and this can give at its best a greater ease and fluency, but it sometimes emerges as a smooth slickness which provides a ready mask for irresponsibility or the absence of a deeper organization. That often-quoted song 'Our hunting fathers', for example, owes rather too much to sheer rhetorical vigour and assurance (borrowed, perhaps, partly from Yeats). It appears to combine subtle complexity with epigrammatic logic in a way that analysis cannot quite substantiate:[7]

> Our hunting fathers told the story
>   Of the sadness of the creatures,
> Pitied the limits and the lack
>   Set in their finished features;
> Saw in the lion's intolerant look
>   Behind the quarry's dying glare,
> Love raging for the personal glory
>   That reason's gift would add,
> The liberal appetite and power,
>   The rightness of a god.

Who nurtured in that fine tradition
   Predicted the result,
Guessed love by nature suited to
   The intricate ways of guilt?
That human ligaments could so
His southern gestures modify,
And make it his mature ambition
   To think no thought but ours,
To hunger, work illegally
   And be anonymous?

The general meaning is fairly clear: 'Love' must of course be taken as something like instinctive energy, or the Life Force: it has vague overtones from psycho-analytical theory and constitutes the main positive value explicitly recognized in Auden's earlier work. The 'result' in the second stanza is presumably the result of the tradition, not the result of love's achievement of reason's gift, but why then insist on the modification of love's southern gestures by 'human ligaments'? The important contrast would seem to be that between the 'fathers' and the present generations, and surely 'love' must have been embodied in 'human ligaments' in both? One may find answers to these questions individually, but the fact is there are, throughout, various loose ends of possible meaning not completely organized. If we rule them out the poem becomes a simpler statement of Marxist or Freudian doctrine than it appears at first: if not, it must be seen as a less unified whole.

Technical facility, indeed, comes to seem Auden's chief danger henceforward. Poem after poem contains brilliant or powerful lines but is less successful as a whole because he has not been able to resist the irrelevant elaboration, the chasing of too many hares at once, the smart epigram, or the multiplication of self-conscious ironies. Too many possibilities present themselves as he writes, and he accepts them without adequate discrimination. Some of his methods lend themselves particularly to these dangers. The illustration, for example, of a general state or mood by a series of revealing details or particular instances can sometimes become a mere catalogue. The acknowledged inequality of 'Spain' arises chiefly from the list of activities typical of the present and future, where almost any item, one feels, might have something else substituted for it, yet at its best the poem focuses sharply on the immediate crisis:

On that arid square, that fragment nipped off from hot
Africa, soldered so crudely to inventive Europe,
  On that tableland scored by rivers,
Our fever's menacing shapes are precise and alive.

Other technical mannerisms which sometimes get out of hand are the surprising simile and epithet. The first, which is often an effective source of expressive vitality:

such a longing as will make his thought
Alive like patterns a murmuration of starlings
Rising in joy over wolds unwittingly weave

sometimes degenerates into a kind of compulsive nervous tic: 'And lie apart like epochs from each other', 'Encased in talent like a uniform', 'Anxiety receives them like a grand hotel', 'added meaning like a comma'. The second is that peculiar feature of Auden's style which often concentrates all the more striking part of his meaning into the adjectives, or into the tension between an adjective and the noun it qualifies. Edwin Muir, reviewing *Another Time*,[8] objected that Auden used the adjective to express a controversial attitude to things rather than the qualities of things, but Mr Hoggart[9] has reasonably argued that this adjectival comment may function as a play of wit and irony bringing experiences into new relationships – as perhaps in 'the habit-forming pain', 'eternal and unremarkable gestures Like ploughing or soldiers' songs', 'Death's coercive rumour', 'the low recessive houses of the poor'. It must be admitted, however, that often the adjective adds nothing or merely injects a perfunctory sophistication: 'the necessary lovers touch', 'the striped and vigorous tiger', 'the luscious lateral blossoming of woe', 'the flower's soundless hunger'.

With an increasing tendency in the later thirties to general intellectual comment, there went a remarkable fondness for personifying abstract qualities. Some lines in 'A Summer Night 1933' evoking

evenings when
  Fear gave his watch no look:
The lion griefs loped from the shade
And on our knees their muzzles laid
  And Death put down his book

show the gain in concreteness achieved by this incarnation in vivid gestures, but also the temptation to excessive ingenuity and the difficulty of control, since Death's movement might in itself be equally well taken as ominous. 'August for the People' provides a list of personified ills (emulating Shakespeare's Sonnet LXVI) which ranges from 'Courage to his leaking ship appointed' through the over-smart 'Greed showing shamelessly her naked money' to the flat bathos of 'Freedom by power shockingly maltreated'. Later poems up to *New Year Letter* (1941) tend to make personification an automatic habit:[10]

> Violence successful like a new disease
> And Wrong a charmer everywhere invited ...
>
> And when Truth met him and put out her hand
> He clung in panic to his tall belief ...

To an easy mastery of free verse there is increasingly added in the later thirties a fluent use of regular forms. Sometimes this contributes to a new lyrical quality, as in the title poem of *Look, Stranger!* or some of the love songs – 'May with its light behaving', 'Fish in the unruffled lakes', 'Lay your sleeping head', 'Underneath the leaves of life'. Sometimes it is recognizably another poet's music that is reproduced, and difficult problems arise as to how far the pastiche is deliberate and how far it can be justified in the total effect – the use of Housman and Blake, for example, in 'Now the leaves are falling fast' or of Blake in the elegy on Yeats:

> Intellectual disgrace
> Stares from every human face,
> And the seas of pity lie
> Locked and frozen in each eye.

Monroe K. Spears[11] has defended this device as a deliberate use of a *persona*, but it seems doubtful whether it can always be accepted so easily. Yeats himself is laid under contribution in a number of poems, not perhaps always consciously, but Auden has generally contrived to make the characteristic trimeter his own and to marry the Yeatsian rhetoric to a new moral content:

What mad Nijinsky wrote
About Diaghilev
Is true of the normal heart;
For the error bred in the bone
Of each woman and each man
Craves what it cannot have,
Not universal love
But to be loved alone.

This comes from 'September 1st, 1939' a poem in which world events precipitate a more than usually mature blending of Auden's psychological and political concerns. Here the self-consciousness falls away and the feeling is conveyed with sufficient conviction to avoid the opposite fault of propagandist solemnity. The poems of this period which have worn best are those showing a somewhat similar balance: in the best of the lyrical group mentioned above (say, 'Underneath the leaves of Life') the emotion controls the technique and the eye is less on the audience: elsewhere in a number of poems dealing with personal experiences certain urgent needs of self-analysis and understanding seem to have had the same effect, as in 'Through the Looking Glass', 'Two Worlds', and, in part, 'Birthday Poem'. One characteristic vein which generally results in a more convincing tone and feeling is that of general meditation linking the mood of a place with comment on the general drift of the world: 'Perhaps', 'The Malverns', 'Dover 1937', 'Oxford', and the 'Commentary' concluding 'In Time of War': with these may be mentioned one or two reflections in a loose discursive manner such as 'Musée des Beaux Arts'. Space does not permit the full quotation that would be desirable here, but I hope the reader will be able to follow up these references.

Two groups not yet mentioned deserve a brief note. The first is a series of critical essays or epigrams, sometimes obituary, but including past writers back to Voltaire and Pascal. At their worst these run to glib reach-me-down psycho-analysis (on Housman, Arnold, Edward Lear); at their best they provide distinguished reflective verse as in most of the elegy on Freud. The second group consists of the poems, mostly sonnets, written under the influence of Rilke. Professor Enright, who has discussed this influence in some detail,[12] thinks that it 'encouraged Auden's gift for the brief dramatic situation', and notes that Auden applies Rilke's symbols and techniques to his own anti-aesthetic ends and emphatically human concerns. Even here he remains the generalizing moralist:

> We envy streams and houses that are sure
> But we are articled to error; we
> Were never nude and calm like a great door,
>
> And never will be perfect like the fountains;
> We live in freedom by necessity,
> A mountain people dwelling among mountains.

These lines from the last sonnet 'In Time of War' call to mind a technical device present in Auden from the first but strongly confirmed by Rilke's influence – the use of geography and landscape to symbolize spiritual and mental states:

> Lost in my wake the archipelago
> Islands of self through which I sailed all day ...
>
> To settle in this village of the heart ...

This, too, is a device that can be overworked:

> Our money sang like streams on the aloof peaks
> Of our thinking ...
>
> He hugged his sorrow like a plot of land ...

but in a wider development it leads on to one of the more successful aspects of Auden's later work.

The second Rilkean sonnet sequence, *The Quest*, was published in the same volume as *New Year Letter* (called in the U.S.A. *The Double Man*) which is the first of the group of longer poems constituting Auden's chief work of the forties. The years of his emigration to America and the beginning of the Second World War saw a considerable change in his intellectual outlook, principally towards a much more serious and more explicit concern with religion. The influence of Marx and Freud gives way to that of Kierkegaard and modern Protestant theologians, and there is an increasing employment of orthodox Christian doctrines. *New Year Letter* records in octosyllabic couplets, with a remarkable proliferation of notes, references and appended after-thoughts, part of the intellectual debate accompanying this change. The critic who called it 'a kind of Hundred Points of Good Husbandry for contemporary intellectuals'[13] presumably had his eye on the verse style as well as the matter and it must be admitted that much of the poem is near doggerel in its loose prosaic informality. Critics have not usually tried to defend it as a whole; they have been content to discuss the new developments of thought in the abstract, especially the new recognition that 'Art is not life, and cannot be A midwife to society', to note the instances of frank self-criticism:

> Time and again have slubbered through
> With slip and slapdash what I do,
> Adopted what I would disown,
> The preacher's loose immodest tone ...

and to point to the occasional passages of greater life and sensitiveness such as the last lines of the concluding affirmation of faith or the description of man and his development in terms of remembered Northumbrian landscape.

The next volume, *For the Time Being* (English edition 1945), contained also *The Sea and the Mirror*, a 'commentary' on *The Tempest* in the form of verse monologues by the chief characters, all except Caliban who has a mannered prose which starts as a close imitation of later Henry James. The main theme of this work seems to be the relation between art and life, and its treatment brings in a wide range of religious and philosophical problems and perceptions, but the result is hardly a complete artistic success. The symbolic possibilities tend to become too wide for adequate control, and the attempts at profounder analysis to be dissipated in surface brilliance, so that we are left with a number of effective fragments that look rather more impressive out of their context. The title piece of the volume is described as a 'Christmas Oratorio': it has a Narrator, Chorus, and allegorical characters, as well as the persons of the Nativity story. Two sections, the meditation of Simeon and the speech of Herod, are in prose, the first a complex theological statement and the second a kind of Shavian soliloquy. The verse seems in general to rehearse the whole gamut of Auden's previous manners. We find a particularly unfortunate instance of the personification trick – 'tortured Horror roaring for a bride' – and at times there is a general effect of self-parody:

Our plans have all gone awry
The rains will arrive too late,
Our resourceful general
Fell down dead as he drank ...

Elsewhere there occur some jarring transitions of tone: it is difficult to see what is gained by the Gilbertian element in the song of the Wise Men or the excessively exuberant nastiness of the Voices of the Desert. Among the more impressive parts are the Annunciation song and Mary's lullaby in the Manger scene, but on the whole the apparent intellectual and doctrinal intention is far from being adequately realized.

The Age of Anxiety, the 'Baroque Eclogue' of 1948, is again experimental both in substance and style. Through the minds of four characters meeting by chance in a New York bar in wartime Auden attempts to create a general modern consciousness – rootless, isolated, insecure, obscurely dominated by fear, guilt, and the awareness of failure. The verse throughout is highly artificial, an adaptation of old alliterative forms, handled as usual with great virtuosity, but seldom appearing inevitable or unselfconscious, and often showing signs of strain in the choice of words to maintain the sound-pattern ('our dream-wishes Vert and volant, unvetoed our song'). As always there are striking phrases ('the light collaborates with a land of ease') and the occasional memorable expression of a profounder insight:

We would rather be ruined than changed,
We would rather die in our dread
Than climb the cross of the moment
And let our illusions die

But the general unsatisfactoriness remains: as Mr G. S. Fraser has remarked, in this poem 'the theme of our awkward malaise was all too faithfully mirrored in the elaborate maladroit handling'.[14]

Auden's work of the fifties is found in the two partly overlapping volumes *Nones* (1951) and *The Shield of Achilles* (1955). These give a later rendering of most of the moods and qualities of his earlier work. The technical ingenuity continues in a number of experiments with assonance and internal rhyme and in the appearance of a new long line, rather loose and informal, mostly used for discursive reflection and lending itself rather too readily to diffuseness. It is even found linked with the manner of an essay or broadcast talk, so that a poem will begin 'I know a retired dentist who only paints mountains'. The example comes from the sequence of 'Bucolics', meditations on 'Winds', 'Mountains', and so on which are sometimes witty but sometimes sink to the merely whimsical. More than one poem tails off into an uneasy flippancy like the last line of 'Lakes': 'Just reeling off their names is ever so comfy'. More effective use of landscape and 'the spirit of place' is found in the Horatian *tour de force* 'Ischia', or 'Air Port' with its expression of modern rootlessness, or in what is perhaps the best-known poem of this group, 'In Praise of Limestone'. This uses a favourite geographical symbol to convey insights into psychology, history, and man's place in the scheme of things:

> Not to be left behind, not, please! to resemble
> The beasts who repeat themselves, or a thing like water
> Or stone whose conduct can be predicted, these
> Are our Common Prayer ...

and the limestone landscape becomes finally a symbolic aid to imagining 'a faultless love Or the life to come'.

Auden is still fond of the generalizing aerial view of civilization, as in the 'Ode to Gaea' or 'Memorial to the City' with its vision seen by the 'eyes of the crow and the eye of the camera'. Unfortunately the crow has to be 'on the crematorium chimney' and the sketches of historical epochs in terms of the ideal city of each have the facile quality of some of the earlier biographical epigrams. Similarly the old difficulty of pastiche appears once more: in 'The Proof', for instance, the bemused reader, catching some echoes and suspecting more, wonders what a parody of Tennyson imitating Shakespeare ('When stinking Chaos lifts the latch') has to do with Pamina and Tamino. Something of a new quality appears in the title poem of *The Shield of Achilles*, where Thetis, looking over Hephaestos's shoulder with traditional expectations as he engraves the shield, is confronted with a vision of modern inhumanity stated with considerable directness and force:

The mass and majesty of this world, all
  That carries weight and always weighs the same
Lay in the hands of others; they were small
  And could not hope for help and no help came ...

This poem is unusual in presenting tragedy without comment: in these volumes an orthodox Christian view is usually in the background if not explicit. The most ambitious attempt at poetry directly on Christian themes is the sequence *Horae Canonicae*, where the seven traditional Church offices provide the framework for a Good Friday meditation on the modern world and the human situation generally. Inevitably there are echoes of Eliot, suggesting comparisons which tend to be damaging:

This mutilated flesh, our victim,
  Explains too nakedly, too well,
The spell of the asparagus garden,
  The aim of our chalk-pit game; stamps,
Birds' eggs are not the same, behind the wonder
  Of tow-paths and sunken lanes,
Behind the rapture on the spiral stair,
  We shall always now be aware
Of the deed into which they lead ...

Here the restless internal rhyming, too, is typical of the general over-conscious experimenting. It is only occasionally that we feel this to be properly controlled by the profounder thoughts and concerns that the poet is clearly trying to express, and the tone is frequently as uncertain as ever: in the culminating stanza of 'Compline', for example, we find:

... *libera*
  Me, libera C (dear C)
And all poor s-o-b's who never
  Do anything properly, spare
Us in the youngest day when all are
  Shaken awake ...

No more than any other of the longer works can the *Horae Canonicae* sequence be said to succeed as a whole.

The three volumes of the sixties do not make any outstandingly new departures. *Homage to Clio* (1960) contains, notably in the title-poem and 'Good-bye to the Mezzogiorno', some wittily allusive meditations in the loose colloquial manner which seems to have become Auden's most characteristic later vein; but there is also much laboured whimsy, and the volume is eked out with mere trivia. The chief technical experimenting now runs to syllabic verse in the style of Marianne Moore, and this continues in *About the House* (1966), half of which is a sequence of reflections suggested by different aspects of the poet's country cottage in Austria, and half a miscellaneous collection whose variety follows lines predictable from the time of *Nones*. 'Whitsunday in Kirchstetten', with which Auden bows himself out of this volume, is the familiar kind of musing, epigrammatic, serious and whimsical by turns, on politics, religion, and the human situation. *City Without Walls* (1969) is a miscellany on lines very similar to the second part of *About the House*.

Auden's latest work, in fact, leaves us with the same problem of unevenness on our hands that has arisen at every stage in his career. It comes to seem a fundamental quality of his talent, almost a necessary condition of his creative activity. He can always be relied on to be more interesting, lively, provocative, wide-ranging, psychologically penetrating, technically skilful, and ingenious than most of his contemporaries. He has given us a small number of successful poems and a great many incidental and fragmentary brilliances. But he has never gathered up and concentrated all his powers in a major achievement, and never quite fulfilled the promise of the first volumes. This is not merely the obstinate prejudice of those who, in the special Auden number of *New Verse* over thirty years ago, were taken to task for refusing to recognize that a poet's development might be twisted and obscure and that 'a wet day in April is not the end of summer'. It is often Auden's most sympathetic interpreters today whom we find doubting, even after the fullest possible survey of his poetic range and quality, whether he can be claimed as a major artist.[15] He remains a peculiarly representative figure whose work and career raise the important question: what is it in the present relation of the poet, his critics, and his public which apparently makes it more difficult than at any earlier time for genuine talent to grow to its full stature?

NOTES

1. A further grave complication is Auden's habit of making numerous textual alterations and revisions at different re-printings. The whole question has been investigated in detail by Joseph Warren Beach in *The Making of the Auden Canon*. References to titles added to earlier poems at a later date are taken from the volume of *Collected Shorter Poems, 1930–44* (1950).

2. In a contribution to the *New Verse* special Auden number (November 1937).

3. An interesting analysis of this poem appeared in an article on 'Marxism and English Poetry' by D. A. Traversi, *Arena* I, p. 199 (1937).

4. In *The Present Age from 1914*, p. 121.

5. E.g. John Bayley in *The Romantic Survival*, A. Alvarez in *The Shaping Spirit*.

6. The point was discussed in a number of reviews of Auden's early work by F. R. Leavis (*Scrutiny* III, 76; V, 323; IX, 200, and see also 'This Poetical Renascence' in *For Continuity*).

7. Richard Hoggart, in his *Auden, an Introductory Essay*, gives a helpful commentary on the poem but does not, I think, quite solve the problem.

8. In *Purpose* XII, 149 (1940). The same number contains an essay by Auden on Thomas Hardy, whom he claims as his 'poetical father'.

9. *Auden, an Introductory Essay*, pp. 90–2. I am indebted to the whole chapter on Auden's technique, which raises many interesting points.

10. See the review by R. O. C. Winkler, *Scrutiny* X, 206.

11. In an article 'Late Auden: the satiristas lunatic clergy man', *Sewanee Review*, Winter, 1951.

12. See the essay 'Reluctant Admiration' in *The Apothecary's Shop*.

13. L. C. Knights in an essay on Bacon (*Explorations*, p. 110).

14. See 'Auden's Later Manner', in *Vision and Rhetoric*.

15. E.g. Richard Hoggart in his British Council pamphlet (1957): 'We cannot claim that Auden is now a major artist or seems likely to become one'. For a more favourable opinion generally of Auden's achievement, see Monroe K. Spears: *The Poetry of W. H. Auden. The Disenchanted Island* (1963). This book also gives useful and comprehensive factual information about the whole of the poet's work, including his opera libretti and his critical and miscellaneous prose.

NOVELISTS OF THREE DECADES: EVELYN WAUGH, GRAHAM GREENE, C. P. SNOW

GRAHAM MARTIN

Reader in Literature, The Open University

In any discussion of minor writers, you really want to say two things: why you think they are minor, and then, given the limitation, what their achievement amounts to. But in a short essay about prolific novelists like Waugh, Greene, and Snow – together they have written nearly forty novels – it is impossible to deal fairly with both points. It seems better, then, to concentrate on the second, and hope that a suggestive definition will serve to enforce the undiscussed general assessment. With these writers, this is the more worthwhile, because since each speaks from a distinct social situation, their juxtaposition underlines major changes in the structure of English society between the late 1920s and the present day. Moreover, since at least one of the ways in which novelists matter arises from their ability to interpret their social preoccupations more or less penetratingly, a basis already exists for the view that they *are* limited. None of these novelists, that is, seems completely in control of his material; or at least, of the kind of issues which his presentation of the material raises. Greene's awareness is certainly more acute and more arresting than that of either Waugh or Snow, and he is, correspondingly, a more considerable figure. Snow, of course, has the special interest of a contemporary whose retrospective view of the period could never be inferred from any acquaintance with Waugh or Greene. Waugh, on the other hand, even though he still writes, offers mainly a period interest. He is essentially a pre-war novelist, and the post-war interest in him is a kind of hang-over, a nostalgic reaction, socially, but not critically, interesting. Greene spans the gap between Waugh and Snow. His deeper penetration releases him from the strictures of both 'pre-war' and 'post-war'. (But he is not any more a contemporary, as he was ten years ago.) This judgement coincides with the strikingly different social settings favoured by each novelist: Waugh's upper-middle class, Greene's middle-middle, and Snow's professional and working or lower-middle class. Simply in that shift, the process of social change is plain enough. Snow, of course, is not the only witness to the results of the process – one needs *Anglo-Saxon Attitudes* and *Lucky Jim* as well – but he does effectively qualify the complacent, Forward-With-The-People, version of it, without obliging us to accept Waugh's helpless disgust. (See the opening pages of *Brideshead Revisited*.) As Edward Hyams remarks, 'People forget that the Managers began their revolution in the second year of the war'.[1]

Evelyn Waugh (b. 1903)*

Evelyn Waugh's first novel, *Decline and Fall*, appeared in 1928. In 1964 he was the author of fourteen novels, a collection of short stories (1936), several travel books in the thirties, a study of Rossetti (1928), and a biography of Edmund Campion (1935). The novels fall into two well-defined groups: up to and including *Put Out More Flags* (1942); and from *Brideshead Revisited* (1945) forwards. The second group is less homogeneous than the first. There are one or two satires in the earlier manner of which *The Loved One* (1948) is the best known; two novels in a trilogy about the war; and a historical novel, *Helena* (1950), in which the author's Roman Catholicism prominently figures. For reasons which will appear, it is possible to discuss Waugh as a pre-war novelist. It is certainly necessary to do so in this chapter.

Waugh has objected to the common description of his early work as social satire on the ground that this is impossible in a society which provides the satirist with no acceptable norms of behaviour, attitude, and belief.[2] The analysis is arguable, though, in view of the negative emphasis of the novels themselves, it is worth bearing in mind. But in the first instance, 'satire' is hard to do without. The kind of observation – 'Mrs Ape watched them benignly, then, squaring her shoulders and looking (except that she had really no beard to speak of) every inch a sailor, strode resolutely to the first-class bar' – the recourse to parody – 'you will find that my school is built upon an ideal – an ideal of service and fellowship. Many of the boys come from the very best families' – the stretches of dead-pan quotation from real speech, the sequence of fantastic and grotesque events, run in the end to an impression reasonably described in the Penguin editions as 'pungent satire upon the coteries of Mayfair'. It seems pointless to

* Evelyn Waugh died in 1966.

wonder whether this is *really* satire because it lacks moral indignation – it doesn't – or farce, or comedy of manners, or a peculiar amalgam of all three. These terms have no precise modern application. With the exception of *A Handful of Dust* (1934), 'social satire' provides at least a starting point for discussion of Waugh's novels from *Decline and Fall* to *Put Out More Flags*.

As a narrator, Waugh is usually neutral, concealing his attitude behind a front of impersonal reporting. Sometimes, however, he is more open, and the result is interesting.

> Various courageous Europeans, in the seventies of the last century, came to Ishmaelia, or near it, furnished with suitable equipment of cuckoo clocks, phonographs, opera hats, draft-treaties and flags of the nations which they had been obliged to leave. They came as missionaries, ambassadors, tradesmen, prospectors, natural scientists. None returned. They were eaten, every one of them; some raw, others stewed and seasoned – according to local usage and the calendar (for the better sort of Ishmaelites have been Christian for many centuries and will not publicly eat human flesh, uncooked, in Lent, without special and costly dispensation from their bishop). Punitive expeditions suffered more harm than they inflicted, and in the nineties humane counsels prevailed. The European powers independently decided that they did not want that profitless piece of territory; that the one thing less desirable than seeing a neighbour established there was the trouble of taking it themselves. Accordingly, by general consent, it was ruled off the maps and its immunity guaranteed. As there was no form of government common to the peoples thus segregated, nor tie of language, history, habit or belief, they were called a Republic.
>
> (*Scoop*, pp. 74–5)*

This attack on the benefits of 'civilization' typifies the spirit of much of *Scoop* (1938), of *Black Mischief* (1932), and of many incidental gibes at 'humanism' elsewhere; yet in neither of the novels can we point to any alternative position in whose terms the attack can be understood. Moreover, in the details of the passage itself, the novelist deliberately withdraws, at the actual moment of utterance, the only morality to which the paragraph might successfully have appealed

* Page references to the Penguin editions in this and subsequent cases.

(see the sentence in brackets, above). If the passage accepts anything, it is only the honest Ishmaelites who ate the European colonists raw.

Scoop and *Black Mischief* move into a slightly different world from that represented by Lady Metroland and the coteries of Mayfair, though the two are not unconnected, of course. But in doing this, they only extended to new material a manner and an attitude already characteristic.

> It was called a Savage party, that is to say that Johnnie Hoop had written on the invitation that they were to come dressed as savages. Numbers of them had done so; Johnnie himself in a mask and black gloves represented the Maharanee of Pukkapore, somewhat to the annoyance of the Maharajah, who happened to drop in. The real aristocracy, the younger members of the two or three great brewing families which rule London, had done nothing about it. They had come on from a dance and stood in a little group by themselves, aloof, amused but not amusing. Pit-a-pat went the heart of Miss Mouse. How she longed to tear down her dazzling frock to her hips and dance like a Bacchante before them all. One day she would surprise them all, thought Miss Mouse.
>
> (*Vile Bodies*, p. 53)

The *nouveau riche* Miss Mouse is at one point the object of the satire – she is a social climber into *this* society – and at another, the focus of a satirical comment upon it. She innocently longs for the real barbarism of which the Mayfair party provides a bored, decadent imitation. Waugh does not exactly accept her (comparative) sincerity – as he accepts the honesty of the more frank of the Ishmaelian cannibals – but, by implying this alternative, and at the same time mocking its foolishness, he complicates the simpler attack of the rest of the paragraph. This is more of a piece with the manner dominating most of the novel.

> There was a famous actor making jokes (but it was not so much what he said as the way he said it that made the people laugh who did laugh). 'I've come to the party as a wild widower,' he said. They were that kind of joke – but, of course, he made a droll face when he said it.

> Miss Runcible had changed into Hawaiian costume and was the life and soul of the evening.
>
> She had heard someone say something about an Independent Labour Party, and was furious that she not been asked.
>
> (Ibid.)

The cumulative effect of this is actually to dissipate the greater satirical energy of the passage about Miss Mouse. (The same is true of *Scoop*.) But that passage still does represent something important about the whole novel, because the series of accidents which make up 'the story' is no more successful in establishing a secure point of view than this, or any other, seeming confession of one. The satirical bias, which we begin by assuming is simply hidden from view by the parodic report, turns out to have no definable status. When Waugh appears to offer one, it is only a trick. He lures the reader into a judgement – in the context of neutral narration we are eager to accept one – and then leaves him there, the target of a hostility more supple and more deep-seated than he had guessed. In both a local and a general view, this is more important than the dissection of Mayfair high life. It commits Waugh to his so-called (but the word is misleading) dramatic presentation. The world is disliked, but it is not understood; the report on it must therefore communicate a generalized unselective distaste. To angle the view (as, for example, Angus Wilson does) would be to expose a particular animus, and so a criterion of judgement. But there is no criterion. And, as a consequence, the neutral manner is not simply a satirist's tactic, but the statement of what we have to call, for lack of another term, an attitude.

If this is largely true of all Waugh's satires, it applies more exactly to the two earliest: *Decline and Fall* (1928) and *Vile Bodies* (1930). *Black Mischief* (1932) and *Scoop* (1938) offer (in part at least) a contrast between types of social and political folly and a *relative* normality. *Put Out More Flags* (1942) opposes the job-hunting of the phoney war to the patriotic realities of personal sacrifice (though the presentation of Basil Seal and the 'comic' victimization of Ambrose Silk are deeply ambiguous). It is, then, the earlier pair that best represent the 'pure' Waugh statement. In each, the novelist organizes the social report around the story of young man's adventures in Society. Each is, formally speaking, the hero, presented on the whole more sympathetically than his milieu. But neither is allowed to focus upon that milieu anything like a criticism. In *Decline*, Paul Pennyfeather is very explicitly *not* allowed to do so (see pp. 187–8). In *Vile Bodies*, Adam Fenwick-Symes is, like his predecessor, the passive victim of his group, but in a subtler way. He belongs to the coterie, but even though he suffers from the trivializing folly of its attitudes, he still accepts them. The action details his unsuccessful attempts to get rich so that he can marry Nina. With her, he shares a feeling towards which we are expected to be sympathetic. Yet neither this feeling (nor even the old Edwardian order represented by Anchorage House) is set up in opposition to the demonstrated meaningless of their social life. Adam fails to get rich, Nina marries someone who is, and Adam ingeniously cuckolds her husband by pretending to be that husband on a Christmas visit to Nina's home. War interrupts this idyll, and the novel concludes ('Happy Ending') with Adam reading a letter from Nina in the midst of 'the biggest battlefield in the history of the world'.

As a sort of reason for all this misery, Waugh offers in the mysterious person of Father Rothschild, S.J. this comment on the Bright Young Things: 'But these people have got hold of another end of the stick, and for all we know it may be the right one. They say, "If a thing's not worth doing well, it's not worth doing at all." It makes everything very difficult for them' (p. 132). And an exchange between Adam and Nina at a crisis in their fortunes appears to make the 'difficulty' more general:

> 'Adam, darling, what's the matter?'
> 'I don't know ... Nina, do you ever feel that things simply can't go on much longer?'
> 'What d' you mean by things ... us or everything?'
> 'Everything.'
>
> (p. 192)

It would, of course, be impressive to describe this as an intimation of class-decadence, but the view is so restricted, the analysis so slight, and the treatment so external, that 'class' is not a possible term. It is never more than a question of Society.

We have to conclude, I think, that in these two novels the writer is reporting a situation which, strictly, he cannot interpret. His feeling towards its particular meaninglessness is one of half-fascinated, half-indulgent horror. He makes gestures of protest, but does not follow them through. On the other hand, he is far from a ruthlessly amoral exploration. The neutral assurance again and again exposes sudden crystallizations of hatred and disgust; and the story moves easily towards the grotesque and the nightmarish. But one thing distinguishes the two earlier satires: a quality of nihilistic acceptance which refuses to escape into the general securities – the country-house, patriotism, 'culture' – hinted at (though never wholly accepted) in the later ones. This makes for a peculiar tension which, already slackening in *Scoop* and *Put Out More Flags*, disappears altogether from the post-war writing (except in *The Loved One*). Waugh now allows himself to take up attitudes for which in the early period he had nothing but distaste.

Waugh's only novel of the decade, not merely satirical, is *A Handful of Dust* (1934). It is not possible to discuss it in detail, but since it is sometimes referred to as a minor classic, one comment is necessary. We seem to be reading about a typical relationship of upper-middle-class society in the thirties. Yet when we explore for the real substance of the marriage and its breakdown, try to realize the motives and sympathies of wife, lover, and husband, as the seriousness of their situation appears to invite us, we run up against a blank silence. The neutral presentation seems designed to baffle and confuse the development of those very responses it begins by invoking. Our sympathies are engaged, but never exactly. We are manipulated into accepting as 'real' characterizations and substantial moral involvements people and a story that are scarcely there at all. Except in a kind of brilliant faking, Waugh never goes beyond the external accuracy of observation which served him in the satires. We are left, as a result, with an extreme statement of personal disillusion, but masked as an impersonal analysis and an objective account.

Waugh then represents the pre-war period in a peculiar way. His novels do not provide insights into the special aspect of his time that he knows, but they recognize its symptoms. (Compare *Vile Bodies* with Greene's *A Gun For Sale*.) The situation he speaks about is a fragmentary social experience scarcely related at all to the encompassing society and culture to which it belonged. Auden and Huxley, writing from a comparable condition, generalize and interpret in a way that sometimes disguises and even falsifies. Waugh avoids this. He seems admirably careful to submit to the discipline of a faithful report. But the report itself is really serving the rigidities of fixed emotion ('those vile bodies'); a state of affairs which can obstruct 'meaning' quite as effectively as an over-zealous pursuit of it.

Graham Greene (b. 1904)

Graham Greene's writing career is almost exactly contemporaneous with Evelyn Waugh's. His first novel, *The Man Within*, was published in 1929; and he is still writing today. In 1959, he is the author of seventeen novels; or, excluding the first three – which the author himself described as *juvenilia* – and starting with *Stamboul Train* (1932), fourteen main titles. Six of these belong to the thirties, three to the forties, and five to the fifties. Full novels alternate with 'entertainments' (Greene's name for his less serious works) more or less evenly over the whole thirty years. There is an early volume of poems (1925). There are collections of short stories, essays critical and autobiographical, travel books, and, recently, plays.

Unlike Waugh, Greene has always been a highly topical writer. The depression, international capitalist monopolies, war-scare, survivors from torpedoed ships, diamond-smuggling by neutrals, spy-scare, the Cold War, anti-Americanism – this list of headlines comes only from *England Made Me* (1935), *The Heart of the Matter* (1948), and *The Quiet American* (1955); and even if Greene's topicality extended only to the sensations of the national dailies, it would still be worth stressing. This is one of the ways in which Greene has been popular, without being any the less serious. But the sense for news penetrates more deeply than this. Greene is also very sensitive to climates of opinion, and in his novels these emerge, not through spokesmen for (quaintly) period-views, but through their mood, their general feeling about the topical events made use of by the plots. In *A Gun For Sale* (1936), for example, the fear of war is neither simply a device for the story, nor an emotion certain people experience: it emerges also from the way the scene of the action is presented, from the buildings, the streets, the anonymous crowds who fill them. Its presence 'in the air' of the novel is underlined in a contrast with *Vile Bodies*, whose conclusion adopts the same topical fact of war-scare, without any of Greene's compelling social actuality. Waugh's 'biggest battlefield in the history of the world' belongs to a nightmare appropriate enough to his novel, but remote from the thing itself. Again, *The Ministry of Fear* (1943), *The Heart of the Matter* (1948), and *The End of the Affair* (1951) all recognize the presence of the war, less as something to be fought, or stopped, or worried about, than as a social fact to be lived with, and put up with, like some chronic but not fatal disease. Simply as social history, 'topicality' at this level is not to be despised. And the question it immediately raises, i.e. how does it relate to Greene's serious themes? is central to Greene's importance.

Kenneth Allott, in his discussion of the way Greene establishes in each novel his characteristic attitudes and interpolations, has stressed the dominant role of his metaphorical prose.[3] Now this (through scene-setting and the detailed response of key-characters to the scene) is also the source of the topical mood, so that between Greene's peculiar sensibility and his topical sense, there must be a very close connexion; and a connexion, moreover, which rules out two common views of Greene's social observation. Neither the view which confines the *value* of this to the novels of the thirties (where it is certainly more obvious), nor the view which commends it as a superior kind of social-documentary padding really accounts for the character of Greene's prose. This implies that Greene's 'social consciousness' is both more extensive and more important than that, and at the same time calls for very careful definition. For if the topicality is always more than a record, if, then, it does verge on explicit social comment, it is never easy to decide what this comment amounts to. The fact is that none of Greene's novels from any period ever succeeds in challenging, much less in revising the rough social images of the different periods which we already possess. As far as its social insight goes, each novel remains an isolated statement. There is no sense in which, collectively, 'the world of Greene's novels' outlines the significant experience of an epoch. With Greene or without him, we still experience the three decades of his career as three, as a still-to-be-interpreted sequence of roughly known facts and partial insights. Greene's topicality, therefore, remains ambiguous, however pervasive, however deep-seated. On the one hand, whatever social insight it portends seems locked within the parochial details of the thirties, the forties, the fifties. On the other hand, the fact of its persistence points to an equally persistent social condition which Greene's sensibility is particularly able to express. The only way to identify this condition, and at the same time to account for its literal obscurity, is to consider the actual art which is its vehicle.

In *Brighton Rock* (1938), the first of Greene's Catholic novels, the corrupt lawyer, Mr Drewitt, to whom Pinkie applies for advice about his marriage, fittingly quotes Mephistopheles. 'Why, this is Hell,' he says, 'nor are we out of it', and the remark applies, of course, to the career of the damned Pinkie. But it also indicates a feature of the novel less explicit than its theology. The presentation of Brighton, full as it is of convincing period detail, can be called 'realistic', but 'hell' is also a very fair description. Apart from Ida – and the novel's argument sets her apart – Pinkie's individual response to the scene is completely endorsed throughout the novel, even when the viewer is Hale. The novel's 'realism', that is, cooperates with Pinkie's state of mind by the language it uses and the currents of feeling this sets going, through, in a word, its mood. This mood has been compared with the relevant sections of *The Waste Land*, and the comparison underlines not only a common emphasis on seediness, sterility, and despair, but a common method of establishing it. Like Eliot, Greene works through metaphor to convey a particular range of feeling which ratifies, almost proves, an unstated general view of life. (E.g. 'Jug, jug to *dirty ears*' – the last two words overpower the whole implication of what has gone before, and somehow exclude protest or dissent.) Yet unlike the poem's, the novel's mood emerges not within a formal poetic organization (with all the reservations that that brings into play), but underwritten by the apparently unquestionable guarantees of 'realism'. This is not to imply that in *Brighton Rock* Greene is 'a poet' trying to be 'a novelist' and failing. *Brighton Rock* is a successful novel, and this part of its structure contributes to that success. Greene's earliest work, *Stamboul Train* for example, is over-metaphorical, but as he develops, Greene turns not to the 'symbolist' inventions of Lawrence, but to the analytical procedures of James and Conrad: distanced characterization, significant description, multiple point-of-view narrative, 'credible' plots. The ambiguous 'realism' is, in a sense, Greene's particular addition to these methods. In *Brighton Rock* the effect of this is to objectify Pinkie's moral condition. Brighton/Hell exists both in its own right, and as a vehicle for Pinkie's character, a projection of his sterile guilt. This balance works both ways, so that the personal guilt and the particular character define themselves in 'real' social environments. Neither environment nor moral condition predominates; neither is the cause of the other; and as a result, both together, Pinkie *and* Brighton, combine in the novel to suggest an absolute human condition, of no particular social or historical identity. The modified 'realism' helps both to make topical *and* to generalize Pinkie's total estrangement from the meaning of his life. Greene, of course, goes on to interpret this condition theologically. But novels can be more socially conscious than novelists, and this is the case here and with a number of Greene's novels; Pinkie's condition is socially meaningful, not because he is the victim of a particular kind of social outrage which Greene, blinkered by his religion, refuses to name. It is his failure to belong to his own experience that matters. Loss of meaning, loss of control, loss of contact, not simply with others, but, except in crude glimmerings, with one's own actual experience – there is no need to elaborate the reasons for this having been felt more generally, more acutely, and more persistently in our society between 1930 and 1945. What Greene diagnoses as an absolute human condition – 'why, this is hell, nor are we out of it' – existed as an experienced social fact. And as a result, Greene's sense for topical mood was able to connect, and connect significantly, with his own themes. The same reason may account in his more recent work for the falling-off in relevance of this kind.

What, of course, makes it hard to identify the social consciousness of Greene's novels is either the exclusion in the early ones of any explicit comment, or, in the later ones, the insistence of the theology. More and more, this works to convert the novels into parables with just sufficient contemporary detail to make them apply. That does not mean that *ipso facto* the Catholic novels fail; or that their theses can, either for agreement or dismissal, be disengaged from the situations they interpret. But it does make possible two critical questions: does the official interpretation evade or confuse the meaning of the novel's situation? or if it does not, *as an argument*, how seriously is it being offered? The first question applies to *The Heart of the Matter*, which I discuss below, but since *The Power and The Glory* (1940) is also a candidate for Greene's best novel, it is worth applying the second question there. Clearly, its thesis is appropriate enough to the situation, but in at least one instance it seems disingenuously offered. The 'radical' policeman is completely routed in his arguments with the 'reactionary' priest, but only for two reasons which have little to do with the real content of the argument. The policeman's position is a parody of what it is supposed to be, and the priest's arguments get their real force from the priest's experience. That experience, especially in the prison scene, is so much finer, so much more vivid than the hollow interchanges of the subsequent argument, that it seems to justify the novelist's glaring partiality for the priest's view of the case. In a slightly different way, the same holds for some of the earlier novels of the thirties. Admittedly there is no thesis there, but the richness of scene and characterization accumulates an effect powerful enough to underline the novelist's refusal to be explicit about it.* *It's A Battlefield* (1934) and *England Made Me* (1935), certainly studies in the moral absolutes of betrayal, guilt, and loneliness, are also novels about identifiable social and political conditions. But these conditions are never identified in the novels, and this withholding portends the cruder juggling of the issues in *The Power and The Glory*. The final stage in this process seems to be *The End of the Affair*, where an over-articulate thesis dominates characters and setting so completely that 'social-documentary padding' does seem the correct description for the presence of the blitz, and wartime London. From this point of view, then, *The Heart of the Matter* is Greene's most successful novel because it best coordinates argument and example; better even than *Brighton Rock*, where the plan is more unevenly realized, perhaps because it is only an 'entertainment'. Thus, the West African colony is familiar enough in being English, because a colony; but strange, because for the same reason it is not England. The scene is better able to provide Scobie's tragedy with its objective guarantee; yet the details of this successfully inhibit any irrelevantly 'social' interpretation of his state of mind. (Put Scobie in London, and his troubles either dissolve, or generalize themselves into recognizable social tensions. Compare the Assistant Commissioner in *It's A Battlefield*.)

Scobie's experience hovers in a kind of no-place between the condition of personal nightmare, subdued only because he feels he has chosen it; and that of a general waste land in which, though they do not know it so thoroughly as Scobie, all human beings share.

* But perhaps the climate of literary opinion in the thirties accounts for this reticence.

> Why, he wondered, swerving to avoid a dead pye-dog, do I love this place so much? Is it because here human nature hasn't had time to disguise itself? Nobody here could ever talk about a heaven on earth. Heaven remained rigidly in its proper place on the other side of death, and on this side flourished the injustices, the cruelties, the meanness that elsewhere people so cleverly hushed up. Here you could love human beings nearly as God loved them, knowing the worst: you didn't love a pose, a pretty dress, a sentiment artfully assumed.
>
> (pp. 33–4)*

Evidently, 'here' is crucial to the argument, and it supports it both by being offered as 'real', and at the same time as being the projection of the attitudes and assumptions on which the argument really depends. The point of the 'dead pye-dog', not the only one to be picked out in this way, is to mobilize the support of earlier examples of such projections, and such arguments. This early description of the police-station, for example:

> In the dark narrow passage behind, in the charge-room and the cells, Scobie could always detect the odour of human meanness and injustice – it was the smell of a zoo, of sawdust, excrement, ammonia, and lack of liberty. The place was scrubbed daily, but you could never eliminate the smell. Prisoners and policemen carried it in their clothing like cigarette smoke.
>
> (p. 6)

Or the description of Scobie's wife Louise:

> He saw the fist open and close, the damp inefficient powder lying like snow in the ridges of the knuckles ... He lifted the moist hand and kissed the palm: he was bound by the pathos of her unattractiveness.
>
> (p. 23)

Even Wilson's seemingly casual perceptions are laid under contribution:

> A vulture flapped and shifted on the iron roof and Wilson looked at Scobie. He looked without interest in obedience to a stranger's direction, and it seemed to him that no particular interest attached to the squat grey-haired man walking alone

*Page references to the 1951 Uniform Edition by William Heinemann.

> up Bond Street. He couldn't tell that this was one of those occasions a man never forgets: a small cicatrice had been made on the memory, a wound that would ache whenever certain things combined – the taste of gin at midday, the smell of flowers under a balcony, the clang of corrugated iron, an ugly bird flopping from perch to perch.
>
> (p. 4)

In each case, a combination of physical accidents generates a mood and a point of view whose main consciousness is Scobie. Thus because the prison's 'lack of liberty' is, by metaphor, an actual smell, it emerges not as a particular social condition with particular causes, but as an irreducible fact of life. The argument of the first quotation grows, therefore, from a context which makes it seem the only possible one. It is in this way that Scobie's personal morality is projected on to an environment from which, at the same time, it seems inevitably to grow. In the most extreme cases, the result is nightmare. Here is Scobie's act of self-damnation:

> Father Rank came down the steps from the altar bearing God. The saliva had dried in Scobie's mouth: it was as though his veins had dried. He couldn't look up: he saw only the priest's skirt like the skirt of the mediaeval war-horse bearing down upon him: the flapping of feet: the charge of God. If only the archers would let fly from ambush ... But with open mouth (the time had come) he made one last attempt at prayer, 'O God, I offer up my damnation to you. Take it. Use it for them', and was aware of the pale papery taste of his eternal sentence on the tongue.
>
> (p. 272)

As well as being a poetic statement of mood and attitude, *The Heart of the Matter* narrates the history of certain human relationships. Scobie's isolation, his sense of being moral in relation to a world which is immoral, and yet immoral in relation to the morality of God, has to be proved there as well. And since he is, in a sense, an Everyman, the voice of the moral man's complaint against the nature of life itself, his story must protect him from over-specific charges against his character as an individual man. Here Greene runs into difficulties: the story purports to be an unbiased record, concealing nothing significant to the moral situation. Yet there is more than one point at which the record seems to have been too carefully arranged. In an account of actual relationships, selective 'realism' is only a possible method if the basis of the selection (as in satire) is fully confessed. Yet Greene's method, his generalizing intention, necessarily conceals this basis. Thus, Scobie's mistrust of Ali, his only real friend, leads to the latter's brutal death. The narration makes this seem an inevitable tragedy arising from Scobie's quixotic surrender to Helen Roth's demands upon him – Scobie's 'responsibility' perhaps, but not his fault. But in fact, either this catastrophe *does* reveal a moral fault in Scobie which particularizes his condition; or, if not, then it is imposed on to his likely behaviour to 'prove' how brutally meaningless life really is. The novel very skilfully refuses to choose: the first would affect Scobie's general significance; the second the inevitability which the 'realism' of behaviour attempts to convey. So, the incident counts against him only in the way that Scobie allows it to count. We are forced to accept his vague self-contempt. There is no other standard to go by. In the same way, Scobie's relationship with his wife seems less than fully declared. What he calls his 'pity' for her can be more simply described as lack of love. In fact, Louise actually says this, but the effect is merely to prevent us saying it, because the structure of the novel carefully allows her no moral rights. Scobie's is the only effective view. In both relationships, then, Greene covertly indulges his hero's faults, and in the case of the two women, his 'pity' for them is allowed to attract the same kind of admiration (despite the results of his bungling) as his feeling for the survivors of the torpedoed ships, or of the dying child. The attitudes within such terms as 'pity' and 'responsibility' are, in fact, more complex than the author lets us think. Scobie is both more and less admirable than the formal view of him which the novel offers. This view, which the contrivance of the plot works for with great skill, explains Scobie's suicide by the nature of life itself, rather than by the nature of Scobie's life. But many different causes cooperate in Scobie's damnation: the significantly obscure failure of his marriage, the place he works in, the heat, the war, money, his job, and so forth. This makes it 'realistic' of course, but it proves nothing absolute about the human condition. It is one thing to detail a particular story, and invite sympathy for it – 'Here was a man who ..., etc.' It is quite another to manipulate the presentation so that the story proves a hidden argument. The argument may be right or wrong – that is not the point – but to insinuate it into Scobie's story by way of plot-contrivance (however subtly and skilfully) is to invite at least the charge of limited seriousness. Put beside the more candid intensities of local feeling and particular vision (e.g. the last of the above quotations, Scobie's reaction to the dying child, or to the dawn-sea) the argument of the plot seems rather shabby.

The point is impossible to discuss fairly in short space, but because it emerges so intimately from Greene's method as a novelist, it has to be mentioned. Greene's art attempts to reconcile the narrow strength of a very specialized vision – Kenneth Allott has described Greene's world as 'an underworld' – with an easily accessible novel structure whose purpose is to generalize the vision. At the level of what I have called 'mood', the reconciliation succeeds, but beyond that it begins to involve serious evasions and ambiguities. And this is certainly one of the ways in which Greene is a minor novelist. A 'major' treatment of his underworld would involve either a different quality in the supporting argument or a fuller commitment to the special vision – in either case, a very different kind of novel. On the other hand, the ambiguities evidently spring from the writer's belief that the condition he diagnoses *is* absolute, and demands an expression of itself which says so. So, at this point, the discussion can only go forward by questioning the belief, i.e. by going beyond the currently accepted limits of criticism.

C. P. Snow (b. 1905)

In 1959, C. P. Snow was the author of seven novels in a sequence not then completed, whose title will be that of the first published member of the sequence, *Strangers and Brothers* (1940). (*The Search*, which first appeared in 1934 and was reprinted in 1958, does not belong to this sequence.) In the preface to the novel, *The Conscience of the Rich* (1958), Snow describes the series as having two aims: to give 'some insights into society' by relating the stories of several individuals over a period of time, roughly 1920 to 1950; and to follow the moral growth of Lewis Eliot, the narrator of these stories, as he experiences the struggle for power, both private and public, within his own life and in that of his friends. Each novel can be separately read, but they are all closely linked, not only by their common themes, but by the persons, incidents, and places used in the narration. Eliot's presence is of course the main link, and even where, as in *The Masters* (1951), his part in the story is marginal, he is still more than a narrative convenience. Eliot is not exactly a Jamesian 'consciousness', but the experience related is very certainly his, whether its ostensible interest is social history as in *The New Men* (1954), or personal biography as in *A Time of Hope* (1949). He is the only character in the whole sequence with whom we feel any degree of intimacy.

The scheme is ambitious, and though for a reason which I will suggest it is not really successful, it makes Snow interesting as no other contemporary writer is. Quite apart from the social history it recounts, Eliot's own career – provincial clerk, rising barrister, Cambridge don, industrial legal consultant, upper civil servant – is a significant one. (It is, in fact, A Career.) The road from the working or lower-middle class to Whitehall is never likely to be very busy; but the spirit in which successful travellers journey, the kind of experience the journey brings, the kinds of observation it encourages – and discourages – these have a general relevance (to other kinds of contemporary social travelling) which it is difficult to overrate. More especially, perhaps only Eliot's career could make available the classic pattern of English society and at the same time display so clearly its altered significance. 'Society' (in the Waugh sense) is no longer the place where the ambitious man, having arrived at the summit, begins to enjoy his reward. Society has become 'contacts', something to be made use of on the way to the top. The goal to be achieved (in Eliot's case to be renounced) is not social elevation, but effective power; and the criteria of judgement not finally manners or culture, though these help, but ability, weightiness, acumen, and, above all, an instinct for backing the winning side.

As an observer, Snow is accurate and painstaking rather than sensitive (cp. Greene). He has little success in conveying any mood or atmosphere which does not fall within the reflective sensibility of Lewis Eliot, so that between us and the portrayal there is a certain remoteness. But the accuracy is convincing.

> [After the war] we had to recognize that English society had become more rigid, not less, since our youths. Its forms were crystallizing under our eyes into an elaborate and codified Byzantinism, decent enough, tolerable to live in, but not

blown through by the winds of scepticism or individual protest or sense of outrage which were our native air. And those forms were not only too cut-and-dried for us: they would have seemed altogether too rigid for nineteenth-century Englishmen. The evidence was all about us, even at that wedding-party: quite little things had, under our eyes, got fixed, and, except for catastrophes, fixed for good.

(*Homecomings*, 1956, p. 283)

He was propounding the normal Foreign Office view that, since the amount of material was not large, it was the sensible thing to distribute it in small portions, so that no one should be quite left out; we should thus lay up credit in days to come. The extreme alternative view was to see nothing but the immediate benefit to the war, get a purely military judgment, and throw all this material there without any side-glances. There was a whole spectrum of shades between the two, but on the whole Eggar tended to be isolated in that company and had to work very hard for small returns. It was so that day. But he was surprisingly effective in committee; he was not particularly clever, but he spoke with clarity, enthusiasm, pertinacity and above all weight. Even among sophisticated men, weight counted immeasurably more than subtlety or finesse.

(*The Light and The Dark*, 1947, pp. 333–4)

There was a chance, how good I could not guess, that the [atomic] pile would still work quickly; it meant giving Luke even more money, even more men.

'If you're not prepared for that,' I said, hearing my voice sound remote, 'I should be against any compromise. You've either got to show some faith now – or give the whole thing up in this country.'

'Double or quits,' said Rose, 'if I haven't misunderstood you, my dear chap?'

I nodded my head.

'And again, if I haven't misunderstood you, you'd have a shade of preference, but not a very decided shade, for doubling?'

I nodded my head once more.

Rose considered, assembling the threads of the problem,

the scientific forecasts, the struggles on his committees, the Ministerial views.

'This is rather an awkward one,' he said. He stood up and gave his polite youthful bow.

'Well,' he said, 'I'm most indebted to you and I'm sorry to have taken so much of your valuable time. I must think this out, but I'm extremely grateful for your suggestions.'

(*The New Men*, 1954, pp. 123–4)

This social documentation is only one aspect of these three novels. Into each account of public events Snow interweaves a personal story; and this structure roughly corresponds on the one hand to the social insights, and on the other to the struggle for power. But the private histories are the least successful parts of these novels. Snow's powers of characterization, limited chiefly to speech-style, and very often amounting to little more than a few typical phrases per character, are scarcely adequate to the demands of his scheme. The novels are very thin in their physical and emotional life. Thus, Eliot's difficult relationship with his first wife as told in *Homecomings* (1956), or equally difficult friendship with Roy Calvert (*The Light and The Dark*, 1947) are present in the novels only through Eliot's personal account of his own feelings. His responses are 'there', but not the objects which are supposed to account for them. This failure in realization is important enough in itself, but it extends farther, to the narration of the public events as well. The various incidents, considered apart from the local use that Eliot makes of them, resolve into mere aggregate of social-documentary detail. Eliot is therefore the only explicit source of each novel's judgements, so that a contradiction between his essential attitudes and the ostensible scheme of the novels cannot be compensated elsewhere. The success of the scheme stands or falls by Eliot's ability to unify and interpret its material. In two ways it seems to me that he fails to do this, so that the necessary connexion between his history and the social insights he mobilizes is never forged.

The first dissonance between Eliot and 'the material' concerns the theme of power. On this issue, Eliot is principally an interested observer, who rarely passes judgements, except in the special cases of his own renunciations (see *A Time of Hope* and *Homecomings*). Ostensibly, the illustrative incidents are left to speak for themselves, and on a number of occasions it is possible to discern the submerged workings of an attitude which, since it is not Eliot's, can only be the novelist's. This attitude can be described as a quickened feeling for the actual process of decision-taking, as distinct, that is, from the content or the meaning of the decision. In, for example, *The Light and The Dark*, Snow recounts the arguments for and against the decision to launch regular night-bombing against the Germans. Bomber Command's view is that it will boost civilian morale in such a way that the great expense in men and materials will be worthwhile. Eliot and, more importantly, his friend Francis Getliffe think the expense too great. Getliffe is an influential man because of his war-work on radar, and he throws himself into the business of pressuring and lobbying the appropriate committees. However, the decision goes against him, and because he continues the fight to the very last moment, he hopelessly identifies himself with a losing cause. As a result, he is relegated to unimportant work. Now, in the meanwhile, Eliot's friend Roy Calvert, who already knows about the heavy losses from conversations with Eliot, decides to become a bomber pilot. His personal life (whose tensions the novel is mainly concerned with tracing) has reached the point at which he no longer cares whether he lives or dies. Bomber Command provides him with an honourable solution; and so, in due course, he becomes one of the 'losses who might have fought longer' and his friend Eliot is left alone with his memories and grief. This, very briefly, is the point at which the public decision, whose mechanics we know in some detail, interlocks with the private history. But in doing so, its *public* significance disappears, to be replaced by its *private* effect on three individual lives. Calvert dies *privately*, not as a patriot; Eliot mourns him as a friend, not as a type of the heavy losses; Getliffe is demoted; and as everybody knows, the bombing went on. This implies (and I say 'implies' because it is a case of what is not said, rather than what is) that the only kind of individual participation in public life is at the level, not of responsibility, but of power. Eliot's neutrality (unawareness?) at this point offers no other solution. Choice, control, understanding: these ideas are confined to the private histories, which are lived out in a public context determined on quite different principles. In their private lives, some people stoically accept the fact that they are victims of uncontrollable forces. In public, however, other people make decisions which direct these forces one way or another to the more or less severe detriment of many private lives. But the two kinds of decision remain separate, and their meeting in Eliot's narration of his experience only underlines their hiatus. Eliot's attitudes belong to the sphere of private life; the public history remains significantly uninterpreted.

The second dissonance must be more briefly mentioned. Eliot's deepest response to the complexities of personal friendship is that of Arnold: 'Yes! in the sea of life enisled ... We mortal millions live *alone*'. And since Snow is unable to provide Eliot with a context which speaks up for the opposite feeling (i.e. that we mortal millions live socially if we live at all), Eliot's morality dominates the novels, becomes in fact the felt morality of the novelist, and this considerably magnifies the importance of his failure to oppose Eliot through the realization of other and different characters. It is this failure that makes Snow's ambition to show realistic 'insights into society' virtually impossible to achieve – except, that is, in the external manner of the above quotations. Necessarily, the novelist of 'social insights' whose presentation of social experience is so remote and so static as Snow's defeats his own hope. In the last analysis, the sequence seems less to be about society than about Lewis Eliot's personal journey through various sections of the English class-structure.

NOTES

1. *Taking It Easy* (1958), p. 5.
2. F. J. Stopp, *Evelyn Waugh: Portrait of an Artist* (1958), cited pp. 194–5.
3. K. Allott and M. Farris, *The Art of Graham Greene* (1951).

The reader should also refer to the chapter entitled 'The Novel Today', pp. 490–530.

SYLVIA PLATH, PATHOLOGICAL MORALITY, AND THE AVANT-GARDE

DAVID HOLBROOK

Assistant Director of Studies, Downing College, Cambridge

SYLVIA PLATH sets us problems which take us into the heart of the dilemma of the relationship between man and his culture in our time. She certainly challenges all the assumptions of the educator, not least the teacher who believes that the reading of literature is beneficial to the sensibility – in the tradition of Matthew Arnold. For here we have a woman who was capable of writing beautiful poetry, who had profound insights into the inner world – but who was also fascinated by suicide, and became at last encapsulated in a false belief that death represented a pathway to re-birth. Many of her themes lead to this, and are very convincing. If we teach her, may we not be handing on a poisoned chalice to our pupils?

The fashionable *avant-garde*, of course, don't share such doubts, and in this essay I propose to use the work of Sylvia Plath in an attempt to discriminate against their use of this poet's work. I believe they are endorsing a denial of human weakness and ambivalence which is homunculist and which belongs to a 'pathological morality', as Michael Polanyi calls it.[1]

In the essay in which he uses the term 'pathological morality' the latter quotes Simone de Beauvoir on the Marquis de Sade. He is discussing 'moral inversion', a 'condition in which high moral purpose operates only as the hidden force of an openly declared inhumanity'.

> The ... lines of antinomianism meet and mingle in French existentialism. Mme de Beauvoir hails the Marquis de Sade as a great moralist when Sade declares through one of his characters: '... I have destroyed everything in my heart that might have interfered with my pleasures.' And this triumph over conscience, as she calls it, is interpreted in terms of her own Marxism: '... Sade passionately exposes the bourgeois

> hoax which consists of erecting class interests into universal (moral) principles.'[2]

A nihilistic fanaticism arises from such moral inversion, based on a naturalistic view of man, essentially on Freud's pessimistic view of man's make-up. Man is a bundle of appetites, and what is most 'real' about him are his id-instinctual drives. No noble features are ascribed to the id: morality is imposed upon it externally by 'society'. This restraint is condemned because it produces sickness. In consequence, as in Mme de Beauvoir, moral scepticism is combined with moral indignation, despite the logical incompatibility.

The incompatibility becomes absurd, when critics of the *avant-garde* endorse pathological syndromes in individuals as glorious manifestations of the quest for freedom. For instance, discussing the French playwright Jarry, George E. Wellwarth, an American critic, writes:

> Jarry's greatest gesture of rebellion ... was his alcoholism. There can be little doubt that he deliberately drank himself to death. Not long after his arrival in Paris, he must have made up his mind to make the supreme gesture of suicide ... eventually it *freed him from the whole burden of his life.* In a way it was a heroic death, for it was a death for a cause. *It was certainly not an insane or unreasonable death.* Rebellion as Jarry saw it was a quest for total freedom and a protest against the ultimate enslavement which is death. Jarry chose to rebel against the ultimate by systematically destroying himself. In this way he conquered, paradoxically; for, having consciously sentenced himself to death, having decided *to control his own death*, he was able to be *completely at liberty*, completely contemptuous of all manifestations of social order during the period of life that was left to him.[3]
>
> [my italics]

To the reader who is not bewitched by the *avant-garde* persuasion, it will seem absurd to believe that one can 'rebel against the ultimate' by destroying oneself before the natural processes of life do, as will the concept of 'being at liberty' which involves one in being buried by the end of the week.

In consequence we have a dilemma, in the world of culture. Do *avant-garde* works involve us in the delusions of nihilistic fanaticism or not? The question is not yet resolved. The movement typified by

French existentialist literature may be valuable in forcing us to confront ultimate problems of existence: on the other hand it may merely be making things worse, by seducing us into pathological delusions. It is interesting to see how writers outside literary disciplines deal with this problem. An existentialist psycho-analytical writer, Dr Rollo May, for instance, writes of modern drama:

> Many of the contemporary dramas, to be sure, are negations, and some of them tread perilously close to the edge of nihilism. But it is the nihilism which shocks us into confronting the void. And for the one who has ears to hear, there speaks out of this void (the term now speaks of a transcendent quality) a deeper and more immediate apprehension of being.[4]

If there is value in being 'shocked' when we 'confront the void', then it must reside in being forced to discover ourselves, to ask 'What is it to be human?' Nihilism, as Camus pointed out, is itself logically absurd, since the nihilist does not follow the implications of his own philosophy and retreat immediately into death, but rather thrusts his philosophy out into the world, to influence others. Why does he, if everything is as futile as he believes? The energetic moral impulse of the nihilist exposes his own nihilism as absurd.

From the point of view of the 'philosophical anthropology' that seems to be emerging from such disciplines as psycho-analysis and phenomenology[5] today, even the nihilist is engaged, like the rest of us, on a desperate quest to answer the question, 'What is it to be human?', though his answers may be false.

In Sylvia Plath's writings we may find answers to the question of existence which are superbly true, and at the same time answers which are staggeringly false. It would, of course, take longer than a brief essay of this kind to substantiate what is meant by 'true' and 'false' here. But from the point of view I am adopting, which is very different from that of Freud, there is in every individual a 'true self' which yearns to realize its potentialities – and is enabled to do so by the mother's care in the first months of life. By the 'creative reflection' of the mother, a secure self capable of both 'being' and 'doing' evolves, psychically speaking, from the first 'togetherness'. One important aspect of this identity is that, insofar as it is able to realize its nature according to a 'formative principle',[6] it has a natural conscience which is an aspect of the 'normal' healthy individual, and develops from the first stages of 'concern'[7] – that is, the first awareness of the influence of one's actions on others, at a time when one is wholly dependent upon them.[8] Behind these syntonic processes is a fear of emptiness and meaninglessness – the ultimate schizoid problems.[9]

Because everyone is weak and human, and mothers are weak and human, these processes can go wrong. The child may be left with such a lack of a sense of identity that the individual suffers for ever after from what R. D. Laing calls 'ontological insecurity' – a fundamental doubt about the origins of his being.[10] He must resort to false solutions to the problem of being and develop a 'false self'. This false self can be heroic, but it consists largely of 'false doing' – it takes the form of *conforming* to what is demanded of the self by 'society'. Yet this conformism is hated, because it is never the gateway to realization of the true self. Hence, in the schizoid individual, there may be a hatred of 'society' and of conforming to society. It may seem to such an individual that 'society' has 'oppressed' him. From this springs the hostility of schizoid individuals to society, and it explains why so many schizoid individuals are revolutionaries and *avant-gardists*.[11]

Moreover, as Fairbairn indicates, the schizoid individual develops an intensely moral inversion of morality. Because he has never been convinced of the value of love in confirming his humanness, he becomes terrified of love. This observation is confirmed by R. D. Laing's insights in *The Divided Self*. The schizoid individual will have such a feeling of psychic emptiness that he fears that love will 'implode' him, burst into his inner vacancy. Or he may feel so insecure of tegument that it is too easy for others, especially if they come near him in affectionate ways, to empty him of substance. He fears, even, that he can flow into other people, come to merge with them (a phenomenon discussed by Laing, and expressed powerfully by Ted Hughes in 'Love Song' in *Crow*).

Because of this terror of love, the schizoid individual will substitute hate for love. He will try to alienate others, to keep them at arm's length. And he will deal with the world according to two fundamental – and often tragic – moral inversions. Since love is harmful it is better to base one's living on hate, because to deal with the world by love would involve others in dangers. But there is also an immoral motive – which is that, since the joys of loving are forever barred to him, the schizoid might as well give himself up to the joys of hating, and gain what satisfaction he can out of that. From both motives, the schizoid individual declares, 'Evil be thou my good, and Good be thou my Evil.'[11]

Once one has taken in Fairbairn's illuminating observation about such individuals who suffer the deepest 'existential frustration', one can see why many of those who are most energetic in culture in our time tend to be fanatical nihilists: the analysis above applies, for instance, plainly to the whole following of Sartre, and his elevation of de Sade and Genet to the status of martyrdom. Fairbairn's analysis explains how there can be a pathological moralism in our culture, which at the same time is driven by an intense moral conviction. The aim of the *avant-garde* everywhere is to 'make evil my good', and to destroy normal values (as a 'bourgeois hoax') in order to open the way for the destruction of all values based on love and normal human development.

The cult of violence in such a writer as Sylvia Plath belongs to the same pathological syndrome. This poet may be said to stand at the parting of the ways. One must make a choice when reading her. Some of her poems move towards a deep and anguished recognition of the ambivalence and agony of being human, with love and hate commingled in one's weakness. This recognition links us with all the guilt and existential frustration of man. Other poems take a different path – they renounce human solutions, and take to those of hate and the anti-human. The knife-edge on which she balances is one on which she must have teetered all her life. It is perhaps most easily examined in terms of the dreadful problem she had, over whether or not to destroy her own children, when she committed suicide. To take this problem alone will perhaps raise the problem of her poetry in such a way as to invoke undeniable ethical values. One must not, surely, live at the expense of others, to the extent that they are destroyed? Whatever one's right to destroy oneself, an adult's right to annihilate her own children, as if they were an extension of herself, cannot be admitted? An impulse to such an anti-human action must surely be rejected as pathological, immoral, and socially impermissible? If we agree, then we can perhaps recognize the necessity of invoking standards of sanity, morality, and social right and wrong, even in the field of culture?

To pursue the best of Sylvia Plath, we may begin with her poem *You're*,[12] written to her unborn baby. It is full of joyful and amused expectancy. The mother is waiting to reflect the face of a new being – who as yet has no face:

> A clean slate, with your own face on ...

The 'clean slate' will have 'its own face'. But what kind of a creature it will be depends upon its 'otherness': the baby is a 'high-riser, my little loaf', expected mail, a 'creel of eels, all ripples' – it could take any form, and there is a joy at the very fact of its unknown immanence. The thrust of the baby to be born is

> a common-sense
> Thumbs-down on the dodo's mode ...

It wants to be born, to be, for the sake of the continuity of life.

The mother herself, however, as Louis Ames says, thought that her baby would 'confirm her own identity'.[13] She herself has not, if we are to take her poetry and her novel to refer to her own psychic experience, felt sufficiently 'reflected' in her being in her formative years. Everywhere throughout Sylvia Plath's writing there are images of blank-faced moons, pools, mirrors, and globules of mercury, which offer no meaningful reflection – and offer often only hate: 'the moon's crackling blacks'. When she looks into a glass case in a museum (*All the Dead Dears*)[14] she sees only a whole sequence of mother, grandmother, and female imagos of her family past who threaten to drag her down, as if into a pool, rather than reflect her independent existence. In the glass case is an ancient skeleton, which has been gnawed by an animal. Behind the poem lurks the 'gross eating game' which is death, that swallows us all. But death merges with the aspects of love – family ties, links between individuals, even *mothering itself*, which seem forms of incorporation.

Her poems about babies, and passages in the novel *The Bell Jar* about babies, are often therefore about 'blankness' in response to a child's need to be reflected. Babies are impersonal lumps of stuff which come from within: and a repeated image is that of a 'baby in a bell jar' or a foetus in a bottle. In the symbolism of her work this baby is not a baby 'out there' in the world, so much as the psychic baby inside oneself that has never been born (Guntrip relates how, in his schizoid patients, he has often encountered the kind of dream which sees a baby 'in a steel drawer' – locked away, and never to be brought to birth.)[15] In *Morning Song*,[16] which is a delightful poem about a new baby, the baby is 'set going like a fat gold watch', but in response to it

> We stand round blankly as walls ...

Sylvia Plath is fascinated by the evanescent quality of the child's existence:

> All night your moth-breath
> Flickers ...

But in this poem she responds in a natural way, as a mother does:

> One cry, and I stumble from bed, cow-heavy and floral
> In my Victorian night-gown ...

Elsewhere, however, she records a terrible inability to respond. Here one of her most profound and original poems is *The Night Dances*.[17] Whenever this poem is discussed in, say, a university class it is fascinating to watch the readers groping for the meaning: they are, like her, groping to 'find' the baby. After a while we find it:

> the gift
> Of your small breath, the drenched grass
> Smell of your sleeps ...

We pick the baby up, as it were! But the poem is about how the crucial relationship between mother and infant – that relationship on which everything of human identity depends – is a matter of throwing off gestures over a gulf between creatures. The mother should catch these gestures – but they seem to dissolve before she can receive them:

> So your gestures flake off –
> Warm and human, then their pink light
> Bleeding and peeling
> Through the black amnesias of heaven.

The mother here on her part is uncertain that she can accept and give back these gestures – yet she sees that she does get richness from her baby. But in a terrifying way the offered smiles and gestures remain on the outside of her existence like snowflakes on the skin, and the poem ends with the terrifying word 'Nowhere'.

Why am I given
These lamps, these planets,
Falling like blessings, like flakes
Six-sided, white
On my eyes, my lips, my hair
Touching and melting
Nowhere.

Not only is there for her a problem of 'meeting' and 'finding' the baby. Any baby reminds Sylvia Plath of the 'inner' baby that hungers to exist. This 'regressed libidinal ego' is described in *Elm*.[18]

I am inhabited by a cry,
Nightly it flaps out
Looking, with its hooks, for something to love.

I am terrified by this dark thing
That sleeps in me;
All day I feel its soft, feathery turnings, its malignity.

In trying to find and embrace this inner danger she had uncanny insights, but could never get further;

I am incapable of more knowledge.
What is this, this face
So murderous in its strangle of branches? –
It petrifies the will. These are the
isolate, slow faults
That kill, that kill, that kill ...

In this poem, *Elm*, I believe we can see a turning point. The future became hopeless – because the baby within, despite all kinds of attempts to bring it to birth, including attempted suicide, could not be released from its glass-walled encapsulation. So, she turned towards suicide again, and a week before her death wrote the terrifying poem *Edge*:[19]

The woman is perfected.
Her dead

Body wears the smile of accomplishment ...

Each dead child coiled, a white serpent.
One at each little

Pitcher of milk, now empty.
She has folded

Them back into her body as petals
Of a rose close ...

The moon 'is used to this sort of thing' and 'has nothing to be sad about'. The (imago) mother needn't complain – 'her blacks crackle and drag': she can only give a kind of hate-cackle. The children are both asps, killing the mother at her will, and at the same time emanations from her inner substance which she has folded back into her own (dead) body, in a perfection obtained only in death – because she has taken to the final false solution, in

the illusion of a Greek necessity.

Even here she sees the 'solution' as an 'illusion': and in real life Sylvia Plath recognized the separate existence of her children sufficiently to leave them alive.

Before she became involved in the 'illusion of necessity' that destroyed her, Sylvia Plath used her uncanny insights into existential problems and the problem of hate to produce some poems which offer profound comments on the predicament of present-day existence. One of these is *The Thin People*,[20] a poem which emerges out of her own thin sense of identity, her capacity to identify with the victim of persecution, and her paranoia. We saw the concentration camp victims on the film, she says – but they didn't stay there, nor did they stay in our dreams or memories. They have actually streamed out, to affect our perception, so that we cannot look at the world without seeing them, among the trees, threatening to take the meaning out of that which we see. By contrast with Christ, they present us with meaninglessness:

so thin
So weedy a race could not remain in dreams,
Could not remain outlandish victims
In the contracted country of the head ...
... They persist in the sunlit room ...

The poem verges on the psychopathological: but it is also a poem which reveals to us our own involvement in the psychopathological disasters which have threatened the significance of all human life, and made it impossible for us ever to feel unalloyed joy or happy perception of our world, without guilt.

Another such poem is *The Swarm*,[21] in which the protagonist sleepily hears shooting in the street. As she goes to the window she confuses in her mind the story of Napoleon with the dawning realization that a man is shooting down a swarm of bees. The phantasy of the collective 'mind' of the swarm is compared with the hate that drove Napoleon to seek to melt the domes of Russia into his phantasies of schizoid envy. The poem maintains a fascinating ambivalence: do we admire the dreams, or do we prefer the practical reality? Are we better pleased that Wellington defeated Napoleon? Do we approve the docility of the defeated bees? Or were the dreams, of a united Europe, of a 'ton of honey', more admirable? The poem leaves one with a valuable sense of the suffering and dangers that can emerge from a collective delusion of a 'pack' of 'everybody' – and yet aware that the 'schizoid revolutionary' also creates history, and a kind of glory. But, in the end, the glory becomes nothing more than the busts of generals working themselves into niches in a mausoleum like grubs in a hive, and the swarm being 'knocked into a cocked hat, – a straw skip – by the practical man in asbestos gloves.

The latter is the 'keeper of bees', and a version of Sylvia Plath's imago of her father, who died when she was ten. There is a great deal to say about him for he was an expert on bumble-bees, and in her phantasies a focus of 'beeing'. He had to be that, because

> The mother of mouths didn't love me ...[22]

The 'bee' poems, which are among her most fascinating, are about the verb 'to be(e)'. She seems to believe that her difficulties of identity originated in a failure of the 'mothering' process. Whatever the realities of her early life she is always looking for the 'queen bee' in herself. But

> The old man shrank to a doll ...

Daddy proved not quite adequate to be a basis of her identity, because he was a man and died in her childhood. There is a terrible hatred of him for dying and leaving her, combined with a desperate need to build a kind of pseudo-male identity round his image. He recurs in her work, therefore, as a cracked colossus, to whom she is attached by strangely ambivalent impulses.

In the end, she tried to reject this Daddy-centre of her being, and to declare that the 'telephone was cut off at the root'. She would communicate with Daddy in his grave no more. He was a Nazi: he had oppressed her. So, in a jaunty tone borrowed from children's abusive rhymes, she writes a hate-poem rejecting Daddy:

> Daddy, daddy, you bastard, I'm through ...

Of this poem, and a number written from despair, such as *Lady Lazarus*,[23] we can, I believe, say, with the psycho-analyst (of a schizoid):

> It is in a state of exhaustion and with a sense of futility that such individuals reach the day when no investigation is worth conducting, no spiritual exercise merits an effort, and no prophet, master, or teacher can command, inform, or instruct the wayfarer. Action of any sort becomes more and more difficult to execute. Ideation may be refuted as a way of life. But now it seems to have a life of its own, like dreams. Conceptual activity becomes unbearable but endures – only now in a form apparently separated from conscious control. Fantasies clash, overlap, decompose, and re-emerge in twisted and bizarre (often paranoid) forms, terrifying the sufferer and creating confusion and uncertainty among those who attempt to cope with such an individual's speech and gestures. In this context, incessant symbolizations are sometimes stilled for ever by a man who knows that death is the final truth, the great experiment, the only reasonable subject left for him to investigate.[24]

Interestingly enough, it is the poems of this hopelessness and despair which belong to this period in Sylvia Plath's life that avant-garde critics hail as being her best work. Of *Daddy* Alvarez says:

> Her trick is to tell this horror story in a verse form as insistently jaunty and ritualistic as a nursery rhyme. And this helps her to maintain towards all the protagonists – her father, her husband and herself – a note of hard and sardonic anger, as though she were almost amused that her own suffering should be so extreme, so grotesque.[25]

Alvarez, approaching her as a 'neurotic' whose problem would be guilt, fear of hate, and a need to come to terms with that hate, sees her recognition of 'violence' as strength. As he points out, discussing the poem *Ariel*, in her work there is often something 'curiously "substanceless" – to use her own word'. But of *Ariel* Alvarez says 'the detail is all inward' and is about 'what happens ... when the *violence* of the animal is *unleashed*'. (My italics). His model is obviously the naturalistic one of Freud and conveys no sense of how the 'schizoid diagnosis' would interpret the problem.

To Alvarez, as to much fashionable criticism today (Susan Sontag, Wellwarth), the false solution of 'unleashing violence' is to be acclaimed as the way ahead: 'all the best' poetry (he says) is taking this path. And as he indicates, Sylvia Plath was encouraged to write her later poems, in which she 'might as well give herself over to the joys of hating', by the discovery of other writers who were exploring such extreme inward experience:

> I've been very excited by what I feel in the new break-through that came with, say, Robert Lowell's *Life-Studies*. This intense break-through into very serious, very personal emotional experience, which I feel has been partly taboo. Robert Lowell's poems about his experience in these peculiar private and taboo subjects I feel have been explored in recent American poetry – I think particularly of the poetess Anne Sexton, who writes also about her experience as a mother: as a mother who's had a nervous breakdown . . .[26]

When she turned away from humanness (and ambivalence) Sylvia Plath sought a strange black purity – which is the purity of pathological morality. In *Fever 103°*,[27] says Alvarez,

> The idea of the individual and the world purged of sin is established, and the poem is free to move on to the realm of purification.

Fever 103° is a record of the feelings of dread induced in such a schizoid individual in physical illness (itself an invasion of the tegument). The protagonist feels full of impure inner contents ('the sin, The sin') for which further implosion threatens – 'Hiroshima ash', or even the sheets which are 'heavy as a lecher's kiss'. Every touch of external reality threatens rape of the identity, while the self within seems to be being assayed as in a refiner's fire. She cannot bear to be touched:

> I am too pure for you or anyone ...

The purity here, however, is that of a split-off goodness, from which all badness (i.e. ego-weakness) has been eliminated: moreover, since love is so dangerous and vulnerable, the most pure self is the self of hate. It is the purity of 'being swabbed of my loving associations' (*Tulips*) – of being a 'no un'*,[28] without dependency on love and relationships which are impure. In the poem the protagonist is going up to Paradise, in an incandescent ecstasy of purity:

> My selves dissolving ...

The intellectual detachment is appropriate:

> My head a moon
> Of Japanese paper, my gold beaten skin
> Infinitely delicate and infinitely expensive ...

This yearning goes with the kind of dissociation discussed by Dr Daly above: the anguish of trying to maintain 'control'. In her British Council interview Sylvia Plath said:

> I believe that one should be able to control and manipulate experiences, even the most terrifying – like madness, being tortured, this kind of experience ...
> ... – and one should be able to manipulate these experiences with an informed and intelligent mind. I think that personal experience shouldn't be a kind of shut box and mirror-looking narcissistic experience. I believe it should be generally relevant, to such things as Hiroshima and Dachau, and so on.[29]

Hiroshima and Dachau were themselves terrible acts of ultimate schizoid hate: there is a dreadful relevance in what she says. But her own detached intellect, in its false logic, is itself at times in the same state of dissociation as the minds of those who threw babies into furnaces and extracted the gold teeth from Jews, a pathological morality which involved them in a 'final' quest for solutions to the

*A schizophrenic patient of R. D. Laing's wanted to be a 'no un' – i.e. a no-one, a (pure) nun, a *noun* rather than a person. Note the force of the word 'swabbed' in *Tulips*: love is associated with unpleasant bodily secretions.

problem of existence and for a (hate) purity which would transcend for ever the problem of being human, weak, mixed, and ambivalent.

Sylvia Plath becomes in *Lady Lazarus*, says Alvarez, an 'imaginary Jew'. But insofar as she identifies with an inmate of a concentration camp, Sylvia Plath does so in order to experience, imaginatively, torture, oppression and annihilation, in order to feel real. Alvarez approves of her impulse:

> For anyone whose subject is suffering has a ready-made modern example of hell on earth in the concentration camps. And what matters in them is not so much the physical torture – since Sadism is general and perennial – but that modern, as it were industrial, techniques can be used to destroy utterly the human identity. Individual suffering can be heroic provided it leaves the person who suffers a sense of his own individuality – provided, that is, there is an illusion of choice remaining to him. But when suffering is mass-produced, men and women become as equal and identity-less as objects on an assembly line, and nothing remains – certainly no values, no humanity. This anonymity of pain, which makes all dignity impossible, was Sylvia Plath's subject.[30]

But can Sylvia Plath be said to *oppose* the dreadful dehumanization of the death-camp – or to revel in it? By contrast with the record of the cherishing of scraps of humanness by anyone who was in a death camp (such as Viktor R. Frankl),[31] she seems to revel in dehumanizing herself:

> I have done it again ...
> One year in every day
> I manage it –
> ... my skin
> Bright as a Nazi lampshade,
> My right foot
> A paper weight ...

We feel horror – but her facetiousness is pathological: the integration of the self has broken down, so that the only response to the horror of a lampshade of human skin is a hebephrenic giggle, and an arrogant posture (her voice on the recording moves from a tremble of fear to noisy aggression):

> The big strip tease.
> Gentlemen, ladies ...

Surely, she is merely the victim of 'giving herself up to' the joys of hating', the hate being directed at internal bad objects, like the imago of her father?

To Alvarez, however, these delusions themselves are heroic and to be endorsed as positive:

> ... she seemed convinced, in these last poems, that the root of her suffering was the death of her father, whom she loved, who abandoned her and who dragged her after him into death. And her father was pure German, pure Aryan, pure anti-semite.

Sylvia Plath tries herself to make out that her poem *Daddy* is 'spoken by a girl with an Electra complex. Her father died while she thought he was a god.'

> Her case was complicated by the fact that her father was also a Nazi and her mother very possibly part Jewish. In the daughter the two strains marry and paralyse each other – she has to act out the awful little allegory before she is free of it.[30]

But the compulsion is not so easily rejected:

> I was ten when they buried you.
> At twenty I tried to die ...

– and at thirty she did.

The last sentence above about the allegory is terrifying: Sylvia Plath, speaking of herself with hideous detachment, is saying that the only way to find her 'freedom' is to 'act out the awful little allegory' again – at the third decade.

Yet Alvarez says:

> What comes through most powerfully, I think, is the *terrible unforgivingness* of her verse, the continual sense not so much of violence – although there is a good deal of that – as of violent resentment that this should have been done *to her*. What she does in the poem is, with a weird detachment, to turn the violence against herself so as to show that she can equal her oppressors with her self-inflicted oppression.[30]

But the hate comes to be turned on herself, since the imago Daddy only lives in herself, as an internalized object to which she is libidinally attached as an inadequate source of a sense of identity. The hate of Daddy becomes a closed system, hate turned 'with a weird detachment, against herself, in despair and delusion. Yet Alvarez can say:

> And this is the strategy of the concentration camps. When suffering is there whatever you do, by inflicting it upon yourself you achieve your identity, you set yourself free.[31]

This is not borne out by Frankl's view of how one preserved one's human dignity in Auschwitz, by 'little nameless, unremembered acts of kindness and of love ...' Sylvia Plath's oppression is only imaginary, and her infliction of hate on herself was a delusory way of finding strength. As one of Guntrip's schizoid patients said of suicide, 'If I were man enough I'd do it.' He meant that if he killed himself he would feel real. How absurd! Yet this ultimate delusion is what the avant-garde critic seeks to endorse. As A. R. Jones says in *The Art of Sylvia Plath*, about *Daddy*,

> ... we are persuaded almost to cooperate with the destructive principle – indeed, to love the principle as life itself.[32]

Each such endorsement of pathological morality merely encourages both art and criticism to take flight even further from human dignity and reality – and even from the kind of courage Sylvia Plath showed, in her anguished exploration of her humanness, at best, when she was being true to herself.

NOTES

1. 'Beyond Nihilism' in *Knowing and Being* (Routledge, 1969), p. 18.

2. op. cit., p. 17.

3. George Wellwarth, *The Theatre of Protest and Paradox: Developments in the Avant-garde Drama* (MacGibbon and Kee, 1965), p. 11.

4. Rollo May, *Love and Will* (Souvenir Press, 1969), p. 305.

5. H. Guntrip, *Personality Structure and Human Interaction* (Hogarth Press, 1961); Leslie H. Farber, *The Ways of the Will* (Constable, 1966); Rollo May, op. cit.; Leslie H. Farber, 'Martin Buber and Psychotherapy' in *The Philosophy of Martin Buber*, ed. Schlipp and Friedman (Cambridge, 1969); Marjorie Grene, *The Knower and the Known* (Faber, 1966); *Existence – A New Dimension in Psychiatry and Psychology*, ed. Rollo May, Ernest Angel and Henri F. Ellenberger (Basic Books, 1958).

6. See Marion Milner, *In the Hands of the Living God* (Hogarth Press, 1969), p. 384.

7. See D. W. Winnicott in *Collected Papers* (Tavistock, 1958), p. 262.

8. See Melanie Klein in *Our Adult World and its Roots in Infancy* (Tavistock, 1963), and *passim* in her work.

9. See *Schizoid Phenomena, Object Relations and the Self* (Hogarth, 1969).

10. R. D. Laing, *The Divided Self* (Tavistock, 1960, Penguin Books, 1965).

11. See W. R. D. Fairbairn, *Psychoanalytical Studies of the Personality* (Tavistock, 1952).

12. *Ariel* (Faber, 1965), p. 57.

13. Louis Ames, 'Notes Towards a Biography' in *The Art of Sylvia Plath* (Faber, 1970).

14. *The Colossus* (Faber, 1965), p. 27.

15. See *Schizoid Phenomena, Object Relations and the Self.*

16. *Ariel*, p. 11.

17. *Ariel*, p. 27.

18. *Ariel*, p. 25.

19. *Ariel*, p. 85.

20. *The Colossus*, p. 30.

21. *The Swarm*, published in *Encounter*, October 1963, and in *Winter Trees* (Faber, 1971), p. 37.

22. See *Poem for a Birthday* at the end of *The Colussus.*

23. *Ariel*, p. 16.

24. 'Schizoid Rule-following', Robert W. Daly, *Psychoanalytical Review, U.S.A.* (Fall, 1968), p. 408.

25. Alvarez, *The Art of Sylvia Plath.*

26. British Council Interview.

27. *Ariel*, p. 58.

28. R. D. Laing, *The Divided Self.*

29. British Council Interview.

30. *Evanston Triquarterly*, no. 7 (Fall, 1966).

31. *From Death Camp to Existentialism* (Beacon Press, U.S.A., 1962); see *The Doctor and the Soul* (Souvenir Press, 1970).

32. *The Art of Sylvia Plath*, p. 236.

MASS COMMUNICATIONS IN BRITAIN

RICHARD HOGGART

Assistant Director-General (Social Sciences, Humanities and Culture), U.N.E.S.C.O.

THIS chapter is not about 'serious' or 'good' literature; nor is it about literature alone. It is about that extraordinary and complicated range of recreational activities put out by the media of mass communication, activities which reflect and affect aspects of British 'culture' today. Somewhere outside them stands the work of the novelists, poets, and dramatists discussed elsewhere in this volume; so do older forms of popular urban entertainment such as working-men's club concerts, brass bands, chapel choirs, comic postcards, and *Peg's Paper*; so do officially established cultural organizations and arrangements, such as the Arts Council and the sixpenny rate which local authorities may spend on the arts. But here, in the centre for the moment, are: *Reveille*, *The Golden Shot*, *The News of the World*, *Nationwide*, *The Troubleshooters*, *This Is Your Life*, *The Daily Mirror*, *Crossroads*, *Aquarius*, the advertisements on ITV, *Coronation Street*, *Top of the Pops*, the columnist Marje Proops and 'personalities' such as David Frost and Malcolm Muggeridge, *Panorama*, television Westerns, *Woman*, *The Archers*, *Omnibus*. The relation of all these to literature, and to the 'high culture' of which literature is a part, is not immediately clear. But there is a relationship, direct and important, and one which anyone interested in literature and in society will do well to think about.

Many people have been thinking about it, of course; discussion about mass communications has been persistent, confused, and heated in this century. But it is not essentially new. It is a development in contemporary terms of a larger debate, with a long history. A recent historian and critic of this larger debate, Mr Raymond Williams, begins his examination with Edmund Burke and moves – to name only some major figures – through Coleridge, Newman, Lawrence, and Eliot (if we regard Eliot as British). This list spans more than one hundred and fifty years, and Britain alone. If we look more widely, to European and American writers, we can span a roughly similar period by moving, say, from Alexis De Tocqueville to Ortega y Gasset.

The larger debate is about 'culture' and society, that is, about the quality of the life which democracies offer and encourage. 'Culture' here, then, has to do with the quality of the imaginative and intellectual life these societies express, most obviously though not only through the place they give to the creative arts and to intellectual inquiry. The debate is also, inevitably, about the relation of culture to 'class', to wealth, to work, and to educational provision. What place, if any, do traditional forms of 'high culture' (those arts and inquiries largely produced and sustained, formerly, by members of the middle and upper classes) have in a universally literate and fairly prosperous democracy? What future, if any, have the elements of a differently phrased and local 'working-class' culture? Is a good, widely diffused, 'popular' or demotic culture possible in such democracies? What kinds of persuasion, by government or by non-statutory bodies, are legitimate and desirable?

Such a debate is not expressed only in writing. In nineteenth-century Britain the sustained and devoted efforts by some members of the 'privileged' classes to disseminate the benefits of education and culture to those less fortunately placed is part of the same movement (as in the development of extra-mural teaching by the universities, which was begun by Cambridge). Similarly, many of those resourceful nineteenth-century reformers who were themselves from the working-classes believed that they had a cultural as well as a political and economic mission (to take another example from adult education: the universities did not there plough a virgin field; many grass-roots organizations for the cultural improvement of working-people existed before the universities entered).

This is a very simple outline of a complex background, meant to indicate chiefly that the discussion of mass communications is part of a larger and longer inquiry. But there are sound reasons why the inquiry should be especially active today and should have the particular emphasis we go on to describe. The twentieth century is the first century of the truly *mass* media of communication, and this gives a special emphasis to questions of the kind enumerated above. Is 'high culture' bound to be peripheral to the driving and overriding forces of mass communications? Are all older types of culture likely to be submerged in new substitute forms, in what the Germans call 'kitsch'? What is the relation of the creative arts and of disinterested intellectual activity to these new means of communication?

But, first, what are the mass media and how did they arise? No definition can be precise, but a workable definition can be reached. The chief forms of mass communication, as the phrase is normally used today, are sound and television broadcasting, the press (with certain exceptions), the cinema, and some types of advertising. In general, and this is their distinction, all these activities are addressed regularly to audiences absolutely very large and relatively undifferentiated by class, income, background, or locality (thus, most books are not in this sense mass media). All these activities are products of the last eighty years; before then, broadcasting and the cinema did not exist; the press and advertising existed, but not in forms which would have allowed them properly to be called mass media.

Several social and technological factors combined to produce these modern forms of communication. Two are usually given overriding importance and must be mentioned first. In fact, the illumination they give of the more subtle aspects of the problem – those to do with direction and quality – is not great. These two factors are technological advance and universal literacy. Obviously the two interact and some mass media (especially popular publications) have particularly developed from the interaction; on the other hand, cinema and broadcasting need hardly attend on literacy. The most striking primary cause for the appearance of contemporary mass communications, then, was technical knowledge and its application. The last decades of the nineteenth century, in particular, saw an enormously accelerated development in all parts of this field.

In Britain, it is true and important, these advances roughly coincided with the appearance of a new reading public. Towards the end of the nineteenth century the Registrar-General was able to announce that Britain – no other nation had preceded her – was substantially literate. And the total population was growing, and has continued to grow. There is plenty of evidence, especially in the biographies of the first press-lords, that some energetic men appreciated the commercial opportunities presented by this large, new, literate, but not intellectually cultured, audience.

Three further qualifications have to be made, however, so that universal literacy is not given too much weight in the general development of mass communications. First, it would be wrong to infer that before the late nineteenth century only a tiny minority in Britain could read. Recent research has shown that by the middle of the century a substantial proportion were able to read, even among the working-classes. Second, there was a considerable amount of cheap publication for working-people by, for example, 1840; these productions divide roughly into two types, the 'improving' and the sensational. Third: if too simple a relationship is assumed between statutory education for the body of the people and the rise of certain types of mass communication, then one more easily assumes that these productions are addressed chiefly to working-people, that working-people, almost alone, are affected by them. This was never substantially true and is daily losing some of its relevance.

Two other factors lie behind the rise of mass communications and tell more about their nature and quality. The first is the development, in both democracies and totalitarian states, of centralized social planning. In almost all societies, and especially in those which are becoming increasingly industrialized, a kind of national self-consciousness is greater today than ever before. This does not necessarily mean that what is commonly called a 'nationalist spirit' is more powerful, but that these societies need more and more to speak to their citizens as a body, to persuade them in certain directions. This is the public or governmental pressure behind mass communications and can be seen in a great number of forms: in authoritarian countries as a support to state ideologies (Mussolini's Italy, Hitler's Germany, Soviet Russia, Communist China); in democratic countries chiefly in time of war or 'cold war'; but increasingly in the day-to-day peacetime life of any technologically advanced state. It would be difficult to decide the relative importance of various factors when comparing the *speed* with which the means of mass-communication have been adopted in different countries. In the democracies we tend to overestimate the effect of commercial forces. We should give more importance to larger social forces, to public and governmental pressures.

Still, there are important commercial pressures in the democracies. In spite of the damage of two major wars and in spite of the increases in population, the last half-century has seen a considerable increase in the real wealth of many Western countries. Many more things are being made and have to be sold, competitively. Thus in Britain a large body of people who previously spent almost the whole of their income in providing, and often barely providing, for necessities now have money to spend on goods which are not essential – though they may be pleasant to have. This is generally true, though not evenly spread throughout society. Since the war marginal spending by teenagers, in particular, has encouraged, and been encouraged by, substantial businesses; by contrast, pensioners and others past working age have not so much benefited from post-war prosperity (compare the attention paid by commercial television to 'youth' with that to the aged). This general improvement may or may not accompany a levelling of incomes within a society. The crucial element is the over-all rise in real wealth which has ensured that a large number of people who were previously below the level at which they attracted serious and concerted attention from the makers of non-essential consumer goods are now above that level. These are what market-research specialists call 'new markets', especially for tastes previously enjoyed chiefly by middle- and upper-class groups, or 'potential markets' where a more novel taste or invented 'need' has to be encouraged.

In Russia and China the mass media are substantially arms of government, with positive and comparatively single-minded functions. In different democracies their use differs, according to the structure and underlying assumptions of each society. We can say roughly that in America the main emphasis is on the commercial use of the means of mass communication – they tend to be aids to selling, or profit-making organizations in their own right. In Britain, which is both a stratified society with a responsible and still fairly powerful Establishment and yet a commercial 'open' democracy, the use of mass communications reflects this piebald character. The British like to use direct governmental controls as little as possible, but their strong tradition of public service and public responsibility causes them (where it is not possible or relevant to support existing voluntary agencies) to establish semi-autonomous chartered bodies under regular, but not day-by-day, government surveillance. The Universities Grants Committee and the Arts Council are typical of such bodies. This tradition helped to ensure that, once broadcasting had begun to show its powers, in the middle 1920s, a new chartered body was created – the British Broadcasting Corporation – charged with the responsibility for public service broadcasting. After the appearance of television there was considerable pressure for a commercial channel – strengthened by the country's increased prosperity – and so in 1954 the Independent Television Authority was created, to run a second channel from the proceeds of advertisements. (In 1972 it was renamed the Independent Broadcasting Authority when the newly-founded commercial radio stations were also placed under its control.) Advocates of ITV always point out that programmes on this channel are not 'sponsored' by the advertisers as they are in the United States. This is true, but the similarities between American television and British television on ITV are greater than the differences. And the general tendencies of both are markedly different from those of the BBC It would be more accurate to call the British second channel 'commercial television' rather than 'independent television'. In media so centralized and which reach instantaneously so large an audience there can be no full independence: one chooses to try to fulfil, as objectively as possible, one's public service responsibilities; or one is pulled by the pervasive general requirements of those who pay for the advertisements. The BBC was subsequently granted control of the third national channel and started BBC2 in 1964, but the main competition remained that between the original two channels, BBC1 and ITV. With each fighting for the attention of the British people, and each representing one main form of 'dependence' they offer now the most striking evidence for the two themes of this essay: the intrinsic power and importance of the organs of mass communication; and the curiously piebald relationship of Great Britain to the use of these organs – a relationship decided partly by history and tradition, and partly by newly emerging commercial and cultural pressures.

In Great Britain, particularly during the last thirty years, these four factors – technological advances, universal literacy, increased public self-consciousness, and increased consumption of goods – have encouraged two striking changes in almost all forms of public communication. To some extent these changes, towards centralization and concentration, must develop as the means of communication become means of mass communication; in Britain they have developed very quickly.

Centralization denotes the tendency for local or regional sources of communication to give way to one metropolitan source. The metropolitan area itself progressively subdivides into segments, each providing nationally most of the popular material within a given branch (e.g. Denmark Street and its environs for popular songs). There are a number of reasons why this process should have moved particularly quickly in Britain. The country is highly industrialized, densely populated, small in area, and has good communications. Practically everyone can be reached instantaneously by sound or television broadcasting, or within a few hours by a national newspaper. The United States has roughly three-and-a-half times the population of Britain but thirty times her land area. Holland and Belgium have most of the characteristics listed above, but the relative smallness of their populations makes it less likely that really massive organizations can be founded in the field of communications. Nor has Britain any strong regional centres of cultural and intellectual activity. Edinburgh and Manchester can make some claim, but a comparison with, say, Naples or Milan shows how limited the claim is.

Centralization in communications reflects the centralization in commerce and industry. Similarly, concentration reflects larger economic movements. If centralization makes for the production of almost all material of one kind from one source, concentration makes for a reduction in variety within each kind. In industry, the production of motor cars is an obvious instance. Several kinds of car are available (family saloon, sports car, limousine, estate car) but the number of different makes and so of models within each kind is small. The large markets thus ensured bring obvious advantages: lower price, relative stability of employment, concentration of resources for research. Occasionally, some of these advantages can be usefully taken in the *distribution* of good intellectual and imaginative works, as in the issue of excellent books in paper-back form which now flourishes in the United States and Britain. But this is chiefly a matter of 'marketing' an existing product of good quality (and for every publication of this sort the same machines produce several of an exceptional poorness). The real problems which concentration in cultural matters poses lie here: that concentration does not simply distribute existing material but to a large extent decides the form and nature of all new material, reduces variety in approach and attitudes, seeks manners which will gain a mass audience most of the time. Motor cars are not really very important; if by centralizing and concentrating their production we get workable models cheaply we may well be satisfied. But cheapness, speed, modernity, smartness are all profoundly irrelevant to intellectual and imaginative affairs and, worse, are often bought at the cost of what is relevant to them.

Sound and television broadcasting are products of a highly technological period and have been since their birth both centralized and concentrated. The cinema, since it is almost entirely a profit-making industry, has been centralized and concentrated almost since its beginning, and our pleasure when something even mildly exploratory is attempted in a film sufficiently suggests what a loss this has meant. But changes in the British press and in periodical publication during the last thirty years show most clearly the trend towards centralization and concentration, since these types of production originally had a great variety of outlets and attitudes.

The number of provincial papers still published might seem to suggest that here at least centralization and concentration have not gone far. Certainly the evening provincial papers sometimes have more independent life than those published in the morning. But a close reading of most provincial papers reveals that centralization and concentration are here too. Ostensibly a paper may belong to a provincial town and the editor live in its suburbs. But in most important respects these papers are often no more than provincial outlets, printing offices, for large London combines and, though they include a moderate amount of local news and views (rather after the manner of the local insets in a parish magazine), the major comment and editorials, the background articles, the judgements on all topics other than those of a purely local interest, are likely to be issued by teletype from London each day and so syndicated in papers under the same central control all over Britain.

Concentration is even more striking here. Many people still think that Britain has seven national popular daily newspapers, of roughly equal effect. Seven there certainly are, but a glance at the differences in their circulations shows how far concentration has advanced. Among the popular national morning dailies, two alone account for about two-thirds of all sales on any one day. The position is similar in popular Sunday newspapers and in weekly family magazines, and is even more marked in women's magazines.

It is simply not sufficient to say, as some do, that the mass media are only means of communication, channels for the large-scale distribution of material whose character is not affected by the manner in which it is distributed. Yet there is some truth in the claim, and it underlines the undoubted advantages mass communications can bring. Television, it is true and we are told often enough, can suggest a range of worthwhile interests and pleasures far wider than most of us would otherwise have known. It can give millions the chance to see at the same time a really informed discussion on some matter of public interest; it can occasionally give an unusually close sense of the characters of admirably impressive individuals who would otherwise have been no more than names to us; it can present from month to month plays, well acted and produced, which most of us would have passed a lifetime without seeing. In all this television is acting as a transmitter, a multiple transmitter; and it can be extremely valuable.

Some other forms of mass communication also seem to be acting as 'straight' transmitters, in less obvious or simple ways. They appear to have taken over from scattered and varied oral agencies the work of sustaining an elementary folklore. In this shadowy but powerful symbolic world some of the strip-cartoons now work alongside and are probably beginning to replace a dark network of urban stories and myths.

Most of the work of the mass media, however, is done in a more self-conscious light. And the fact that this work is produced for a mass audience radically affects its character. Its situation almost always forces certain qualities upon it; and these are weakenings of the qualities of those established arts on which mass communications must feed.

Mass communications are usually led, first, to avoid clear psychological and social definition. Sharp definition is possible in 'high art', and concrete definition of a certain kind is possible in 'low' art, since each depends on a limiting of the audience. The first audience is nowadays largely self-selected, without overriding reference to social or geographic factors. This is, for want of a better term, the 'highbrow' audience composed of people who, during the times that they are being 'highbrows', are not in a disabling sense also clerks in Sheffield, mechanics in Manchester, or stockbrokers in Croydon – though these may be their everyday occupations and should reinforce their reading. Yet they are, whilst forming this audience, in a certain sense disinterested. A clerk can read *Anna Karenina* with essentially the same kind of attention as a stockbroker or a mechanic, though the life of upper-class Russian civil servants in the nineteenth century has little social similarity with any of theirs.

The second audience is limited by class or geography or both. It can allow a kind of definition within a specific way of life because this way of life is local or socially accepted. This was the audience of, say, *Peg's Paper* or the *Tatler*.

The mass media can only occasionally accept either of these types of audience. The first is too small to be of much use; the second is a *series* of audiences, of roughly the same type though divided by habit and custom. Essentially the job of the mass media is to weld this second series of audiences into one very much larger group. There is an immediate loss. Compare only the texture of working-class life embodied in Lawrence's *Sons and Lovers*, or even the particularity and denseness of working-class life assumed in an old-fashioned working-class women's magazine, with the life embodied and assumed in one of the newer classless women's magazines, or that in the posters and pamphlets issued by either of the main political parties in Britain.

The overwhelming use of the 'realist' or photographic method in mass art underlines this situation. The mass media, especially in a commercial society, dare not genuinely disturb or call in question the *status quo*. Basically their function is to reinforce the given life of the time, to help their new or emerging mass audience to accept the 'reality' that is offered them. Everything has to be shown as 'interesting' and yet as equally interesting, since to do otherwise would be to inspire distinctions and so create minorities. By this means most of existence is presented as a succession of entertaining items, each as significant as the next: a television 'magazine' programme or a weekly illustrated magazine will successively give the same sort of treatment – the visual, the novel, the interesting – to a film actress, a nuclear physicist, a teenage singing star, a great 'man of letters'; or similar treatment will be given to close-up photographs of a personal tragedy or a new technique for building roads. Order and significance give way to sheer spectacle, the endlessly fragmented curiousness of brute experience.

So, though they are exceptionally aware of their huge audience as a huge audience, the mass media dare not have a real closeness to the individuals who compose that audience. They can rarely be so precise and particular as to inspire any one of that audience to say, 'There, but for the grace of God ...' or, 'This attitude I cannot accept ...' They retreat from the dramatic immediate presentations of art to the sterilized world of the 'documentary', where the close detail of individual existence is reduced by being generalized to the status of 'problems which concern us all', problems which are examined in a 'neutral', a 'fair-minded' and 'objective' way. This is the foundation of that standardization, that stereotyping, of character which marks almost all works produced expressly for the mass media.

We are told that the mass media are the greatest organs for enlightenment that the world has yet seen, that in Britain, for instance, several million people see each issue of *Panorama* and several million each issue of *Nationwide*. We have already agreed that the claim has some foundation. Yet it is not extensive. It is true that never in human history were so many people so often and so much exposed to so many intimations about societies, forms of life, attitudes other than those which obtain in their own local societies. This kind of exposure may well be a point of departure for acquiring certain important intellectual and imaginative qualities; width of judgement, a sense of the variety of possible attitudes. Yet in itself such an exposure does not bring intellectual or imaginative development. It is no more than the masses of stone which lie around in a quarry and which may, conceivably, go to the making of a cathedral. But the mass media cannot build the cathedral, and their way of showing the stones does not always prompt others to build. For the stones are presented within a self-contained and self-sufficient world in which, it is implied, simply to look at them, to observe – fleetingly – individually interesting points of difference between them, is sufficient in itself.

Life is indeed full of problems on which we have – or feel we should try – to make decisions, as citizens or as private individuals. But neither the real difficulty of these decisions nor their true and disturbing challenge to each individual can often be communicated through the mass media. The disinclination to suggest real choice, individual decision, which is to be found in the mass media is not simply the product of a commercial desire to keep the customers happy. It is within the grain of *mass* communications. The Establishments, however well-intentioned they may be and whatever their form (the State, the Church, voluntary agencies, political parties), have a vested interest in ensuring that the public boat is not violently rocked, and will so affect those who work within the mass media that they will be led insensibly towards forms of production which, though they go through the motions of dispute and inquiry, do not break through the skin to where such inquiries might really hurt. They will tend to move, when exposing problems, well within the accepted cliché-assumptions of democratic society and will tend neither radically to question those clichés nor to make a disturbing application of them to features of contemporary life; they will stress the 'stimulation' the programmes give, but this soon becomes an agitation of problems for the sake of the interestingness of that agitation in itself; they will therefore, again, assist a form of acceptance of the *status quo*. There are exceptions to this tendency, but they are uncharacteristic.

The result can be seen in a hundred radio and television programmes as plainly as in the normal treatment of public issues in the popular press. Different levels of background in the readers or viewers may be assumed, but what usually takes place is a substitute for the process of arriving at judgement. Programmes such as this – they occur on all television channels – are important less for the 'stimulation' they offer than for the fact that that stimulation (repeated at regular intervals) may become a substitute for and so a hindrance to judgements carefully arrived at and tested in the mind and on the pulses. Mass communications, then, do not ignore intellectual matters; they tend to castrate them, to allow them to sit on one side of the fireplace, sleek and useless, a family plaything.

Similarly, mass communications do not ignore imaginative art. They must feed upon it, since it is the source of much of their material and approaches; but they must also seek to *exploit* it. They tend to cut the nerve which gives it life – that questioning, with all the imaginative and intellectual resources an artist can muster, of the texture and meaning of his experience; but they find the body both interesting and useful. Towards art, therefore, the mass media are the purest aesthetes; they want its forms and styles but not its possible meanings and significance. Since they are mass communications they have both a pressing awareness of their audience and a pressing uncertainty about that audience. There is a sense in which we may say that a serious artist ignores his audience (assuming that they will share his interest in exploring the subject); or in which we may say that a popular artist with a defined audience simply assumes that audience because his work is embedded in, and expresses, attitudes which are never called in question. But the worker in the mass media is not primarily trying to explore anything or express anything: he is trying to capture and hold an audience. Manner is more important than matter. The fact that very often there is not one writer on a specific programme but a 'team', each member contributing his tactical items, underlines how far is this process from the serious artist's single strategy towards his recalcitrant imaginative material.

If an artist will cooperate with the mass media on their terms (to their credit some artists go on working with the media for the sake of such success as they can gain in their own imaginative terms), then he may have exceptional rewards. For in the age of mass communications art becomes one of the most elusive and therefore most sought-after forms of 'marginal differentiation'. Culture becomes a commodity. And just as the dilemmas of experience are reduced to a series of equally interesting but equally non-significant snapshots, or to the status of documentary 'problems', so the products of art become an eclectic shiny museum of styles, each of them divorced from its roots in a man or men suffering and rejoicing in certain times and places. You may buy by subscription and renew, as often as you renew the flowers in your sitting room, examples of Aztec art or African art or Post-Impressionist painting or Cubist painting or the latest book (probably about the horrors of mass-society) which a panel of well-publicized authorities have selected for you. And all have the same effect as the last instalment of the television magazine. You have sipped and looked and tasted; but nothing has happened. Culture has become a thing for display not for exploration; a presentation not a challenge. It has become a thing to be consumed, like the latest cocktail biscuit.

The above point needs to be especially stressed because it is altogether too easy to think that the mass media affect only 'them'; that the 'masses' are some large body of people in an outer uncultured darkness. There are probably no masses at all – only operators in the mass media trying to form masses and all of us from time to time allowing them. But these 'masses' cannot be identified with one social class or even with our usual picture of the lowbrows and the middlebrows (against the highbrows). Not everyone who reads the book page of the *Observer* is automatically free from mass persuasions, even in his cultural interests.

For, as we have persistently noted, one primary need of mass communications is to reach as wide an audience as possible. Class divides. Where the mass media are commercially influenced this need is all the stronger. To sell their centralized and concentrated goods they must seek a centralized and concentrated audience. In this, therefore, the mass media are both reflecting and encouraging much wider social changes. Centralized production, changes in the nature of work (partly through more effective automatic processes), the higher general level of incomes, greater social mobility, educational changes – all these are helping to alter the local and class lines of British life. In part those lines are also related to divisions in types of cultural activity. British society may well be forming new stratifications, by brains, education, and occupation rather than by birth and money. But such a society will need, if it is not to be irritated by constant inner dissent, a sort of common meeting ground of acceptable attitudes. In democracies this assent has to be brought about by a winning persuasion. In commercially powerful and densely populated democracies the acceptable attitudes can include a wide range of seemingly varying attitudes. There is room there for the *Daily Mirror* as much as for *Vogue*, for the *Miss Great Britain Competitions* as much as for the *Book of the Month Club*. But the variety is only apparent; the texture of the experience they offer is not significantly different at any point in the spectrum. You have then arrived at a sort of cultural classlessness.

This need to reach a large and (whilst they are listening) classless audience ensures that the mass media can take little for granted. What sort of furniture, of reactions, of assertions may be used here? How far dare one go on this line without running the risk of alienating some group? It follows that mass communications tend to flatter, since they will take the more plainly winning attitude before the one which may disconcert. Much more important, they have little opportunity for exploring a living relationship towards their material. Some existing attitudes they may use, after a fashion; others they must freshly introduce, with great care. This explains the strange and limited narcissism of the mass media towards attitudes which have been traditionally acceptable to large numbers of people, especially towards attitudes which can be made to assist in creating the most suitable atmosphere in mass media themselves. Thus, they will accept certain well-established working-class attitudes such as tolerance, lack of meanness, generosity – and extend them into a friendly public buyers' and sellers' world in which – like stuck flowers – they look the same but may soon wither, for want of the soil (of difficulty and tension) in which they had first been nurtured. Programmes such as *This Is Your Life* and *Opportunity Knocks* are typical instances of this kind of process – so is the whole tone of much popular journalism, especially that in the gossip columns and correspondence columns.

This kind of extension can only go so far and soon risks foundering on the reefs of excessive generality (over-extending the stereotype) or excessive particularity (alienating part of the audience). Therefore, in a society marked with the fine complicated lines of class distinction, mass communications have to move towards a world which is not too specifically recognizable by any one group or class but is acceptable to all. They have to invent a world which most of us, in the times that we are consumers, are happy to inhabit. This is the origin of the glossy advertising copywriters' world, a world with a fixed grin which most of us at some times could imagine inhabiting, but which is artificial, 'dreamed-up'. Such is the sophistication of mass communications (they are rarely naïve) that there are also built into this world allowances for idiosyncrasy, for the old 'highbrow', and even for the 'bloody-minded' individual. But all will have in the process been effectively neutered. Mass communications naturally tend towards a bland, a nice, a harmless but bodiless range of attitudes. For more and more of the time more and more of us become consumers of more and more things – from material goods to human relations.

Here we come to the overriding danger of mass communications, unless they are constantly criticized and checked against individual judgement. We are not primarily concerned with whether 'highbrow' books will be read in a society dominated by mass communications (as we have seen, they will still be read, in a certain way); we have to ask what will be the quality of the life expressed through all the arts and at all levels in such a society. It may be that literature will have relatively a much smaller place in the society which is now emerging than most people who read this chapter have assumed and hoped.

The intricate social pattern which produced, among much else, the 'high culture' that is normally recognized is being changed. At the same time great numbers of people are in some respects freer than before. In a changed society the best qualities which inform 'high culture' may have to find other ways of expressing themselves; so will the best qualities in the old local and oral life of people who were not in a position to make much contribution to 'high culture'. At the moment the one seems likely to be bypassed and the other eroded by the impact of massively generalized communications. There is a considerable fund of common imaginative strength in all parts of society. If a thinner consumers' culture is not to spread over all much more care will have to be taken in seeking relevant connections, genuine links between things which show this strength (some features of day-to-day life, some work in the arts today, some social organizations, some forms of recreation). It is not possible to define in advance the nature of a decent demotic culture. Unless one believes that such a culture is not possible, one has to try to keep open all lines which may allow for good development as well as to oppose those which are likely to lead to a dead smartness. At present most people with literary interests are less effective at keeping lines open than they are at opposition.

POSTSCRIPT

ROSALIND BRUNT

Centre for Contemporary Cultural Studies, University of Birmingham

THE reference point of the preceding essay is the English 'culture and society' tradition. This provides a context for posing questions about the nature of mass communications. Accordingly, forms of popular culture, for instance, or various literary modes and the ways in which they have traditionally handled and explored the material of experience, are offered as standards of comparison for evaluating what the modern media have to communicate. Here the prevailing concern is with the authenticity of individual judgement and discrimination, the possibility of making real choices, and the scope of artistic response. Against the touchstone 'quality of life', the communications of the media are seen to be lacking in imaginative power, stereotypical, and of tightly limited range. In the widest literary-critical and humanist sense, then, the criteria of evaluation are essentially 'moral' ones.

However, since this essay was first written (in 1961 – with subsequent revisions mainly on matters of detail), the argument about mass communications has altered its focus. From the late sixties onwards, it has been conducted within a broadly *political* context. While the terms of moral evaluation have remained actively in currency, they have come to be applied in a much more restricted sense. Not only is their usage being debased by a strand of conservative opportunism, but also they are now commonly understood as pertaining to (especially sexual) 'morals' and 'morality'. Thus anxiety is keenly expressed about the mass media's presentation and implied promotion of, say, 'the permissive society', 'gratuitous sex and violence', and what is taken to be pornographic, blasphemous, or obscene. In this case, the conviction is widespread among those who are termed, and term themselves, 'ordinary decent people' or 'the silent majority', that previously-held 'standards' derived particularly from religious and family behaviour are being undermined: and since the media function as the most obviously and massively 'visible' carriers of cultural values, they tend to be understood as straightforwardly *deliberate* purveyors, or, indeed, the immediate cause of an erosion effect.

But even this tendency of strong moralistic concern can also be seen as but a specific expression of a more generalized disquiet that is based on an increasing awareness of the monolithic and unilateral nature of modern communications in 'mass' society. Their centralized powers of transmission are set against the relative powerlessness of their various receiving publics, who are granted, in the main, only negative forms of response. The so-called 'power' of the switch, for example, the institution of letters-to-the-editor or phoned-in complaints are increasingly reckoned merely to provide managed channels of behaviouristic 'feedback', always following, and dependent on, the original event of transmission.

Although such awareness is often inchoate, or crudely expressed in conspiracy terms, it is this perceived disparity between the few who control the mass media and maintain them as relatively closed systems, and the many 'outside' who lack a 'voice' in transmission or even some controlling representation, which has contributed to the current 'mass media debate' and the generally political direction it has taken. This change in direction of course reflects a growing tendency in the whole 'climate of opinion' in Britain and elsewhere: widespread criticism of the institutional order, now increasingly linked with the articulation of political 'demands'. Thus Stuart Hood's formulation, '*access, accountability and participation*', serves to indicate the main platform of demands around which discussion of the mass media takes place. In the ensuing arguments, the common shorthand expression, 'the media', is often used to refer specifically and almost exclusively to the dominant instrument of communications, broadcasting, because this is the one most *sensitively* placed within a complex institutional network. And here, particularly, the BBC is designated as the crucial battle-area, because of its special role as a 'national institution' and the historical associations of its existence as a 'public service' corporation. So, for example, Mary Whitehouse, of the National Viewers' and Listeners' Association, demands the accountability of the BBC by pointing to the classical inscription on the wall of Broadcasting House: if the BBC is no longer dedicated to the ethos of civilizing Christianity there proclaimed, she asks, where indeed does it now stand? The question remains pertinent for those who generally hold views different from hers: in a highly differentiated and fragmented society, where consensual views, of whatever complexion, are increasingly open to challenge, according to what frame of reference does broadcasting now operate?

Demands for accountability come to focus most urgently, then, on the 'documentary' presentation of a society to itself, the area of special concern being that of news and current affairs coverage. As it is increasingly recognized that journalism, in the press as well as broadcasting, is not 'presuppositionless', questions about the origin of 'news values', their 'unwitting bias', and the underlying 'views of the world' that they represent become more insistent. Currently, they form the focus of interest for research into the 'effects' of the mass media, for instance, in the kind of work being done at Leicester under James Halloran. But the main initiative comes particularly from groups who are themselves involved in various kinds of societal conflict. Seeing their actions reported in terms which do not accord with their own experience and 'definition of the situation', they are led to question their 'media identification': for instance, who or what says they are acting 'against the public interest'?

Hence arises the demand for 'access'. Opportunities are sought to state a case in the most 'unmediated' way possible, as a particular group sees fit, and with adequate resources for exposition. At the same time, the attainment of such conditions is often thought to be beyond the capability of the existing order of communication. The attempts of the broadcasting authorities, for example, to mark off special programme-areas for 'talkback' and 'grassroots' discussion are generally deemed pre-emptive and potentially 'assimilating'. In this context, the popularized arguments of the Frankfurt School of Philosophy, and of Herbert Marcuse in particular, have been influential. For the pervasive notion that formally democratic societies are implicitly irrational and 'totalitarian' places significant weight on the role played by the mass media as pacifiers, agents of 'repressive tolerance' and 'social control'. And from another perspective, that of the Situationists, comes the notion, derived from Henri Lefebvre, that the media serve to promote the world of 'the spectacle', wherein ideological 'displays of reality' are manufactured as cultural commodities, mere exchangeable units of 'appearance'. Such views are translated into the frequently expressed fear that to participate in the production of mass communications, at any level, is to risk 'incorporation by the spectacle'.

One of the effects of such a withdrawal has been the growth and rapid proliferation since the late sixties of the 'alternative media'. From the 'free' and 'street' presses, attached to specific local constituencies or fractions of the counter-culture, to film co-operatives, and 'video' groups experimenting with community television, the thinking behind such developments is the concern to provide 'other' communications – 'all the news that isn't fit to print' – and to demonstrate that there are different methods of producing them than the established, so-called 'straight', media can acknowledge. Thus, the emphasis is on decentralization and collective production; the attempted aim, the breakdown of the existing receiver/transmitter dichotomy. And hence, the insistence on 'demystifying' the élitist preserves of professionalism, for, it is maintained, modern developments in electronics now make it possible for everybody to learn how to manipulate the equipment of communication. Although legal and financial difficulties frequently combine to curtail their existence, the alternative media do still serve as an active critique of the mass media organizations. Particularly, they offer a certain 'counter-acting' response to the sort of structural tendencies that Richard Hoggart notes in his essay. For the twin processes of 'concentration' and 'centralization', that he describes, are crucial to a proper understanding of how the mass media work, especially when they are seen in relation to ownership and control. And indeed, since he wrote, these developments have intensified to a point where the examination and discussion of 'structures' *necessarily* becomes an integral aspect of the mass media debate. From this point of view, 'accountability' begins to involve questions about the nature of present economic and institutional trends and how these may affect the range and content of communications. For instance, attention has focused on the rapid growth of 'monopoly ownership' of the means of communication – more accurately described, though, as a situation of 'oligopoly' – as exemplified by the succession of mergers and takeovers that magazine and newspaper publishing went through in the sixties. Another recent development causing concern has been the appearance of 'multi-media' organizations which extend their sphere of interests throughout what is now known as 'the leisure industry'. Thus a television company might 'diversify' into publishing, cinemas, bowling alleys, hotel and motorway catering, television rentals, and possibly commercial radio; or an electronics company produce records and manufacture film equipment, control cinemas, film distribution, and a television station.

The scale of such operations requires coherent integration and planning at every stage, in order to minimize financial risk and maximize profit. The techniques of *marketing* and *management* thus become a structural necessity for the efficient functioning of media organizations. Now, when such techniques are critically examined, it is realized that, far from their being merely 'neutral' and 'instrumental' in application, they actually serve to generate professional and institutional 'ideologies', ways of thinking about communication that specifically shape and define it. Subject to most criticism recently have been the economic and ideological practices associated with '*rationalization*', for these have involved a marked delimitation of communication-content. In the name of streamlining and the most effective 'capture' and 'penetration' of markets, rationalization promotes increasingly narrow and specialized 'channels' of communication 'catering' for predetermined 'target' audiences, more and more finely graded by market-research on the basis of supposed 'consumer-interest'.

The vocabulary of passivity and victimization is notable, and as market-categorization and exchange-value take precedence over the intrinsic 'use-value' of communications, it is asked what has happened to the notion of actively engaging the interest of an audience by offering 'the widest possible range and choice of subject-matter'. It used to be thought that, as a non-commercial organization, the B.B.C., at least, embodied this principle. But, following the tendency of all 'public service' corporations in mixed economies, it too has been subject to the commercial logic. Indeed, the recent changes in B.B.C. radio provide a virtual paradigm of rationalization, for here, on the advice of management consultants, the tradition of 'mixed' programming, of varied, popular appeal, was ended and 'a cleaner separation' of the airways instituted, with 'generic' networks 'offering a continuous stream of one particular type of programme, meeting one particular interest'. Meanwhile, intensified competition between the two television systems makes for a situation where scheduling procedures geared to 'the ratings' militate against the production of programmes that allow for experiment and risk-taking, and subject-matter is increasingly rationalized into predictable series and serial formats. Every such development, transforming 'quality into quantity', has of course always been dignified under the rubric of '*giving the public what it wants*'. The present force of the media debate is, finally, to open that notion to challenge.

POETRY TODAY

CHARLES TOMLINSON

Reader in English Poetry, University of Bristol

ANYONE attempting to write on poetry today must inevitably feel the shifting of the ground under his feet: tomorrow is already here, and the arrival of a new poet or the republication of a neglected one has altered the sense of priorities. That modification of an accepted order 'by the introduction of the new (the really new) work of art', which Eliot speaks of in 'Tradition and the Individual Talent', accounts for one of the difficulties. Another lies in the fact that 'the silent celerity of time' is itself needful for a true perspective on the present moment. An earlier draft of this chapter was prepared in 1959. It was composed polemically from a standpoint that felt itself challenged by the publication, in 1955, of a number of verse manifestoes, from the group known as the Movement, in D. J. Enright's *Poets of the 1950s*. These included Kingsley Amis's

> ... Nobody wants any more poems about philosophers or paintings or novelists or art galleries or mythology or foreign cities or other poems. At least I hope nobody wants them.

and Philip Larkin's

> [I] have no belief in 'tradition' or a common myth-kitty or casual allusions in poems to other poems or poets.

English empiricism had narrowed with a vengeance: if this was to be the whole extent of a poet's wisdom, then a counter possibility had to be established. In his introduction to *New Lines* (1956), Robert Conquest announced that the poetry of the fifties, at least that part of it represented by the Movement, 'is empirical in its attitude to all that comes'. But how much was *allowed* to come before the poet? Hadn't the deliberate narrowing – in some part a healthy reaction against the gestures of neo-romantic poetry of the forties – been merely an excuse, one asked oneself, for the British philistine and was not the need still the Arnoldian one – 'to pull out a few more stops in that powerful but at present somewhat narrow-toned organ, the modern Englishman'? In 1957 appeared a German anthology of poetry and prose since 1945: it contained Paul Celan's astonishing *Todesfuge*. Pondering this poem, one came to feel one was being forbidden to write at that level. Years later, in 1964, Philip Larkin was still saying: '... to me the whole of the ancient world, the whole of classical and biblical mythology means very little, and I think that using them today not only fills poems full of dead spots but dodges the writer's duty to be original'. ('Four Conversations', *The London Magazine*, Vol. 4, No. 8.) So Eliot, Pound, Cavafy, Seferis, Pasternak had dodged their duty? England seemed, in all senses, to be becoming an island, adrift from Europe and the past.

Yet it was precisely in the fifties that David Jones, Hugh MacDiarmid, Austin Clarke and Basil Bunting were beginning a re-emergence. To take first MacDiarmid and Clarke, one could say that it was only in the fifties that one came to be aware of work they had accomplished as far back as the late twenties and thirties, though not until *Collected Poems* (1962) in MacDiarmid's case and *Later Poems* (1961) in Clarke's was their work readily available. MacDiarmid (b. 1892) had fought Scottish philistinism (even more single-minded than English) from the beginnings of his career and perhaps it left him with something of its own steely intransigence. MacDiarmid's *Collected Poems* revealed, particularly in its early stretches, something of what may be won by conscious determination supported by poetic ability. MacDiarmid does not resemble Eliot technically, but like the latter he has retained in his best verse the presence of 'the mind of Europe' and like him he has worked in the full knowledge of what he was about. His aim has been to resurrect the Scottish tradition that petered out with Burns; his achievement has been to forge a Scots verse, neither antiquarian nor provincial, but one in which a modern awareness can nourish itself on the Scottish past, and that can absorb into itself Chaucer, Dunbar, Villon. The *Second Hymn to Lenin*, *The Seamless Garment*, *The Parrot Cry*, a body of lyrics which would include the early *Sangschaw*, *Penny Wheep*, *A Drunk Man Looks at the Thistle* (particularly, *O Wha's Been Here Afore Me Lass*) represent something of MacDiarmid's harvest. His range extends from the short lyric as in *The Eemis Stane*:

I' the how-dumb-deid o' the cauld hairst nicht
The warl' like an eemis stane
Wags i' the lift;
An' my eerie memories fa'
  Like a yowdendrift.

Like a yowdendrift so's I couldna read
The words cut oot i' the stane
Had the fug o' fame
An history's hazelraw
No' yirdit thaim.

(Eemis = insecure; hairst = harvest; yowdendrift = snowdrift; hazelraw = a lichen; yirdit = buried.)

to rich and strange explorations of unfamiliar words as in *On a Raised Beach*:

All is lithogenesis – or lochia,
Carpolite fruit of the forbidden tree,
Stones blacker than any in the Caaba,
Cream-coloured caen-stone, chatoyant pieces,
Celadon and corbeau, bistre and beige,
Glaucous, hoar, enfouldered, cyathiform,
Making mere faculae of the sun and moon,
I study you glout and gloss, but have
No cadrans to adjust you with, but turn again
From optik to haptik and like a blind man run
My fingers over you, arris by arris, burr by burr,
Slickensides, truité, rugas, foveoles,
Bringing my aesthesia in vain to bear,
An angle-titch to all your corrugations and coigns,
Hatched foraminous cavo-rilieva of the world,
Diectic, fiducial stones, chiliad by chiliad
What bricole piled you here, stupendous cairn?

Subsequent collections of MacDiarmid (*A Clyack Sheaf*, 1969, *Selected Poems*, 1970, *More Collected Poems*, 1970) still leave one with the impression that, for all the interest and ambition of late poems like *In Memoriam James Joyce* (1956), the essential work was done in the twenties and thirties. It was thirty to forty years later that its nature was assimilable because re-available.[1] A comparable time-lag affects Austin Clarke (b. 1896).

Another reason for juxtaposing the later poetry of Austin Clarke and MacDiarmid would be to illustrate the way a sense of nationality can deepen a comparatively narrow talent. Clarke is Irish. Yeats wrote of one of his prose romances to Olivia Shakespear in 1932: 'Read it and tell me should I make him an Academician.' Clarke was made an Academician, but Yeats's subsequent hesitations about him and his backing of the far weaker poetic abilities of F. R. Higgins have resulted in his neglect. *Later Collected Poems* (1961) – these, in fact, contain a selection from the *Collected Poems* of 1936 – show Clarke, particularly in *Ancient Lights* (1955) and *Too Great a Vine* (1957), to be an epigrammatist, satirist, and autobiographer of remarkable individuality. *Flight to Africa* (1963) confirmed all this; *Mnemosyne Lay in Dust* (1966) attempts to extend the range into narrative, *Tiresias* (1972) into myth. *Twice Round the Black Church* (1962) and *A Penny in the Clouds* (1968) fill out the picture in prose. A sense of not only what Ireland is, but what it was, enables Clarke to speak with a national voice that, like MacDiarmid's at his very fragmentary best, represents not the inertia of chauvinism, but a labour of recovery. Clarke's skill in using traditional Irish rhyming patterns is similarly not merely a technical recovery, but the measure of a worked-for relation with the past. His poem on the death of orphanage children by fire accomplishes what in intention Dylan Thomas sets out to do in *A Refusal to Mourn the Death, by Fire, of a Child in London*:

> Martyr and heretic
> Have been the shrieking wick.
> But smoke of faith on fire
> Can hide us from enquiry
> And trust in Providence
> Rid us of vain expense.
> So why should pity uncage
> A burning orphanage,
> Bar flight to little souls
> That set no church bell tolling?
> Cast-iron step and rail
> Could but prolong the wailing;
> Has not a bishop declared

That flame-wrapped babes are spared
Our life-time of temptation?
Leap, mind, in consolation
For heart can only lodge
Itself, plucked out by logic.
Those children, charred in Cavan,
Pass straight through Hell to Heaven.

The work of Ezra Pound (1885–1972) continued to appear throughout the fifties, and it was then that a gradual reassessment of his achievement began with that first, courageous study of his poetry, Hugh Kenner's *The Poetry of Ezra Pound* (1951). To pass from the assured, narrow national strength of Clarke to the vaster resources of an expatriate like Ezra Pound is to realize, as in the case of MacDiarmid, the extent to which the *déracinement* of our century can ultimately entail great unevenness and loss of creative power and balance of tone, even in the finest writers. The continued appearance of Pound's Cantos – *The Pisan Cantos* (1949), *Section: Rock-Drill* (1957), *Thrones* (1959), *Drafts and Fragments of Cantos CX–CXVII* (1969) – return one to that criticism which Yeats made of Pound in his preface to *The Oxford Book of Modern Verse* in 1936: 'When I consider his work as a whole', writes Yeats, 'I find more style than form: at moments more style, more deliberate nobility and the means to convey it than in any contemporary poet known to me but it is constantly interrupted, broken, twisted into nothing by its direct opposite, nervous obsession, nightmare, stammering confusion; he is an economist, poet, politician, raging at malignants with inexplicable characters and motives, grotesque figures out of a child's book of beasts.' Yeats's criticisms, when due qualifications have been made, are still often valid after the passage of over thirty years, but having endorsed them we should do wrong to follow common English opinion and to relegate the Cantos to that total neglect they by no means deserve. As Ronald Bottrall contended in one of the first lengthy appraisals of *A Draft of XXX Cantos* in 1933 (*Scrutiny* II) and as Donald Davie has since argued, the finest work in the Cantos is both nobly impressive and of extraordinary beauty.[2] 'More deliberate nobility and the means to convey it...': Yeats's words still apply to those passages of processional magnificence in *The Pisan Cantos* – 79 (O Lynx keep watch on my fire .../O puma sacred to Hermes),

80 (the lyric, Tudor is gone and every rose), 81 (Yet/Ere the season died a-cold .../all in the diffidence which faltered) – and in *Rock-Drill* – Cantos 90–93 – where Pound evokes the paradisal elements of myth and folk-memory, as in the earlier and splendid Cantos 17 and 47. Cantos 99 and 106 in *Thrones* are relevant here. This recurrence to the ceremonial aspects of past cultures (see Canto 52, Know then:/Toward summer when the sun is in Hyades ...) links the Pound of the Cantos to Pound the translator (*The Classic Anthology Defined by Confucius*, 1955). A reader who experiences the rhythmic tact of the 'Envoi' in *Mauberley* will recognize that a comparable power is at work in this later volume:

1

For deep deer-copse beneath Mount Han
hazel and arrow-thorn make an even, orderly wood;
A deferent prince
seeks rents in fraternal mood.

2

The great jade cup holds yellow wine,
a fraternal prince can pour
blessing on all his line.

3

High flies the hawk a-sky,
deep dives the fish,
far, far, even thus amid distant men
shall a deferent prince have his wish.

4

The red bull stands ready, and
clear wine is poured,
may such rite augment the felicity
of this deferent lord.

5

Thick oaks and thorn give folk fuel to spare,
a brotherly prince shall energize
the powers of air.

6

And as no chink is between vine-grip and tree
thick leaf over bough to press,
so a fraternal lord seeks abundance
only in equity;
in his mode is no crookedness.

Sensuous exactness becomes in this translation the defining equivalent for a moral distinction: 'And as no chink is between vine-grip and tree/thick leaf over bough to press ...' And not only have we the power of the sensuous image: the first of these lines, riding forward on its stresses, enacts the vigour of the moral directness which is being recommended. The didactic element and the poetic element are at one, whereas in the weaker sections of the Cantos the morals, whether economic or political, are too much a matter of *a priori* formulation, nakedly and shrilly dogmatic without organic relation to their context. The Cantos can degenerate into abuse; whereas the moral scheme of the Confucian translations unites compellingly with imagery and rhythm. In Pound's *Classic Anthology* is to be found some of the most impressive verse of the fifties. Of his contribution to modern dramatic verse in *Women of Trachis* (first published 1954), a 'version' of Sophocles' *Trachiniae*, suffice it to say that Pound has given us one of the very few readable (and actable) translations of Greek drama.[3]

Pound remains a looming presence, an active irritant in a way that only the major figure can. Thus it is not my intention to deal here with those smaller but excellent poets of an older generation, Robert Graves and William Empson. The best work of Graves has long been a model for poems that combine formal grace and masculinity of expression. Empson's compressed and inimitable poems *were* imitated by several members and fellow-travellers of the Movement,[4] that miscellaneous group chiefly united by their rejection of the neo-romanticism of the nineteen-forties. Empson has himself expressed the opinion that it is his criticism which stays 'developable' and not his verse. I share that opinion. Nor is it my intention to re-create the poetic climate of the forties against certain tendencies of which period several poets, today in their maturity, forcefully reacted. A fair account of this phase exists already in John Press's *A Map of Modern English Verse*. A critical book, very pertinent to the reaction of the fifties, was Donald Davie's *Purity of Diction in English Verse* (1952): it sought primarily to cleanse diction of excess and inanity and it pointed us back to the achievements of the great Augustan figures. In a postscript to the edition of 1967, Davie admits the existence of that streak of philistinism I have noted among the Movementeers, but attempts to measure what was seriously in question:

> In my book this vulgar streak shows up where I declare myself indifferent to any poem or poetic effect that cannot be shown to be moral. Nowadays this strikes me as strident and silly. And yet I can see clearly enough how it came about, as an angry reaction from the tawdry amoralism of a London Bohemia which had destroyed Dylan Thomas, the greatest talent of the generation before ours, and had helped some journalists to cast a facile glamour over the wasted squalor of Thomas's last years. Some years later, in his learned and mordantly witty poem, *Antecedents*,* Charles Tomlinson wrote of the Bohemianism which grew up around the figure of Thomas as only a vulgarized reach-me-down version of the more justifiable Bohemias of the nineteenth century in France. Tomlinson was a poet right outside the Movement and opposed to it, though not opposed, I am glad to say, to the thesis of *Purity of Diction in English Verse*. It seems to me now that the poems of Tomlinson, the poems of Amis and others, my own poems and this essay in poetics, have at least this continuing relevance and importance – that they represent an originally passionate rejection, by one generation of British poets, of all the values of Bohemia ... That there is no necessary connection between the poetic vocation on the one hand, and on the other exhibitionism, egotism and licence – this was what my book was contending for, even when it seemed most 'technical'. The Bohemians hit back by calling it 'puritan' or, more cleverly, 'genteel'.

The poet whom common consent has chosen as the most significant of the Movement is Philip Larkin, born 1922 (*The North Ship*, 1945, *The Less Deceived*, 1955, *The Whitsun Weddings*, 1964). Larkin's talents work hand in hand with a wry and sometimes tenderly nursed sense of

* In *Seeing Is Believing* (1958). Tomlinson's work also includes *The Way of a World* (1969) and *Written on Water* (1972), and he certainly would have figured more prominently in this chapter had it been written by someone else. – *Editor.*

defeat. He sings, often with humour, the unlived life of the English provinces. Adept, and with what one critic has called 'a fundamental lugubriousness', he writes poem after poem where one waits for the dying fall: 'Nothing to be said', 'It had not done so then, and could not now', 'Never such innocence again'. We are impelled to register things 'out of reach' or experience 'a sense of falling'. With his knowing humility ('Hatless I take off/My cycle clips in awkward reverence') and his naughty jokes (a bathing photograph to be snaffled from a girl's album, an Irish sixpence put in the church collecting box), we are seldom far from the sense of a formula. When the formula works, as it does in many of the poems of *The Less Deceived* and in the title poem of *The Whitsun Weddings*, Larkin earns his dejected laurels. One is tantalized to wonder what might have happened had he followed the path suggested by an early and attractive poem, *Wedding-Wind*, where he goes so far as to acknowledge the possibilities of human fulfilment. Not that one is asking for facile optimism – defeat can also come to sound facile. Larkin's narrowness suits the English perfectly. They recognize their own abysmal urban landscapes, skilfully caught with just a whiff of English films *circa* 1950. The stepped-down version of human possibilities (no Renaissances, please), the joke that hesitates just on this side of nihilism, are national vices.

One attempt to confront Larkin's poetry occurs in Davie's *Thomas Hardy and British Poetry* (1972). In the same volume Davie argues the merits of Roy Fisher (*Collected Poems*, 1968). Fisher's *City*, a work consisting of poems in verse and prose, first appeared in 1961: Larkin, facing the urban scene, smothers both its vulgarity and its warmth in his own dejection; Fisher recognizes its lacks, but his vision of Birmingham has a factuality and geographic exactness that give it a more than personal authority:

> In the century that has passed since this city has become great, it has twice laid itself out in the shape of a wheel. The ghost of the older one still lies among the spokes of the new, those dozen highways that thread constricted ways through the inner suburbs, then thrust out, twice as wide, across the housing estates and into the countryside, dragging moraines of buildings with them. Sixty or seventy years ago there were other main roads, quite as important as these were then, but lying between their paths. By day they are simply alternatives,

short cuts, lined solidly with parked cars and crammed with delivery vans. They look merely like side-streets, heartlessly overblown in some excess of Victorian expansion. By night, or on a Sunday, you can see them for what they are. They are still lit meagrely, and the long rows of houses, three and four storeys high, rear black above the lamps enclosing the roadways, clamping them off from whatever surrounds them. From these pavements you can sometimes see the sky at night, not obscured as it is in most parts of the city by the greenish-blue haze of light that steams out of the mercury vapour lamps. These streets are not worth lighting. The houses have not been turned into shops – they are not villas either that might have become offices, but simply tall dwellings, opening straight off the street, with cavernous entries leading into back courts.

A poet who has ridden alongside Larkin in Movement anthologies is Thom Gunn (b. 1929), a very different kind of writer, and one early resolved to seek out the heroic in the experience of nihilism. Gunn startled poetry readers by writing, while still an undergraduate, *Fighting Terms* (1954). His uneasy energy and admiration for a Hemingway-like muscularity in situations of a Sartrean tortuousness (the spirit of the age seemed as consciously courted as all that implies) left one uncertain whether he would develop a moral sensitivity equal to his concerns. *The Sense of Movement* (1957) and *My Sad Captains* (1961), for all their range and skill, still left one, as do two more recent collections, with unresolved doubts. In an early poem he writes of those who, like Byron and like 'strong swimmers, fishermen, explorers', 'Dignify death by thriftless violence–/Squandering all their little left to spend.' Precisely the same uncritically rhetorical gestures turn up in later poetry where, in those symbols he draws from the world of James Dean and Marlon Brando, Gunn often seems committed to a kind of nihilistic glamour for which he cannot always convincingly apologize. Elsewhere, as in *In Santa Maria del Popolo*, the poet's stance is far more convincing and so is his diction. Yvor Winters has compared him with Donne while admitting that 'as a rule, he has a dead ear, and the fact makes much of his work either mechanical or lax in its movement ...'. Gunn continues to add to an uneven but always individual body of work (see *Poems 1950–66*, 1969, *Moly* 1971).

I have mentioned already the criticism of Donald Davie (b. 1922). Its impact on our day and our own sense of poetry is comparable in scope to that of William Empson's at the height of his powers. Some time ago Davie was writing verse close to that of Yvor Winters and, though he is to return to this earlier mode (see *Against Confidences* in *New and Selected Poems*, 1961, and compare it with *Creon's Mouse*, one of his best pieces from *Brides of Reason*, 1955), he has developed since then a more various and ample style. Indeed, one of the effects of reading Davie's *Collected Poems* (1972) is to be reminded of the many styles in which he has written. The variety of attack and the pulsation of energies ranging from tenderness to anger leave one in no doubt of the demands Davie makes on his craft: he is not the merely careful, 'academic' poet some critics have mistaken him for. Rather, he is incautious, drawn to extremes of fret and exacerbation, always in search of forms adequate to contain and qualify his troubled feelings. *Collected Poems* contains a note by the poet himself which defines the sort of writer he is:

> It is true that I am not a poet by nature, only by inclination; for my mind moves most easily and happily among abstractions, it relates ideas far more readily than it relates experiences. I have little appetite, only profound admiration, for sensous fullness and immediacy; I have not the poet's need of concreteness. I have resisted this admission for so long, chiefly because a natural poet was above all what I wanted to be, but partly because I mistook my English empiricism for the poet's concreteness, and so thought my mind was unphilosophical, whereas it is philosophical but in a peculiarly English way.
>
> Most of the poems I have written are not natural poems, in one sense not truly poems, simply because the thought in them could have been expressed – at whatever cost in terseness and point – in a non-poetic way. This does not mean however that they are worthless or that they are shams; for as much can be said of much of the poetry of the past that by common consent is worth reading and remembering ...

Some of the stylistic virtues that Davie admires were anticipated in the work of an earlier poet, Keith Douglas[5] (1920–44), but a poet who was not readily obtainable until *Selected Poems* (1965). He still seems contemporary in a way that, say, George Barker or Edith Sitwell do not. Douglas, who was killed in the war at the age of twenty-four, belonged to the generation of Sidney Keyes. It was Keyes who received the public recognition which in terms of comparative achievement is so evidently the due of the other poet. For that of a poet who died in his twentieth year, Keyes's work, self-consciously over-literary as it was, showed a great deal of promise (see *Paul Klee*, *Kestrels*, *Seascape*), but more than that one cannot say. Douglas's *Collected Poems* did not appear until 1951. The wartime poetry boom which had made possible three editions of Keyes was over. The fashion was on the point of change – from the excessive verbal luxuriance of neo-romanticism to the slick formalism of Empson's successors. Douglas, like any original poet, did not fit the picture and although his collection was well received, it seems to have left but little trace on a literary consciousness that swings so readily to journalistic extremes. Its contents, despite the immaturities, suggest that here was a poet whose death was a serious loss for English literature. Take, for example, these lines from *Time Eating* (1941):

> But as he makes he eats; the very part
> Where he began, even the elusive heart,
> Time's ruminative tongue will wash
> and slow juice masticate all flesh.
>
> That volatile huge intestine holds
> material and abstract in its folds:
> thought and ambition melt and even the world
> will alter, in that catholic belly curled.

Here one has something of the linguistic compactness and steady cumulative attack Douglas brings to his awareness of mutability. Death may be the chief factor behind his verse, but it focuses rather than blurs the vision. Sensuous detail grows compact in its presence; life takes on an edge, as in *The Sea Bird*, *Syria I*, *Egyptian Sentry*, *Cairo Jag*, *Words*, and as in the view of the wrecked houses in *Mersa*:

> faces with sightless doors
> for eyes, with cracks like tears,
> oozing at corners. A dead tank alone
> leans where the gossips stood.

I see my feet like stones
underwater. The logical little fish
converge and nip the flesh
imagining I am one of the dead.

What one finds impressive in Douglas, even in those poems where the idiom is not yet equal to the vision, is the intrinsically poetic nature of that vision. In *The Marvel*, for instance, a dead swordfish has 'yielded to the sharp enquiring blade/the eye which guided him' past dead mariners 'digested by the gluttonous tides'; and a live sailor, using the eye for a magnifying glass, burns into the deck of his ship the name of a harlot in his last port. The incident welds into a poetic unity the worlds of life and death, of time and nature.

'To be sentimental or emotional now is dangerous to oneself and to others', Douglas wrote in 1943, and the fruit of this realization is the firm yet malleable tone which can encompass the charmingly satirical *Behaviour of Fish in an Egyptian Tea Garden*, the satiric yet good-natured *Aristocrats*, and the ironically ambitious *Vergissmeinnicht*. The refusal to *force* himself into stylistic neatness (which in effect has been the attempt of many of the poets of the fifties) meant a certain unevenness and want of finish in his later poems; yet even this is evidence of Douglas's integrity.

It was a subsequent poet, Ted Hughes, who, in a fine selection of Douglas's work, *Selected Poems* (1965), isolated most succinctly the latter's qualities and their relation to the war:

> The war brought his gift to maturity, or to a first maturity. In a sense, war was his ideal subject: the burning away of all human pretensions in the ray cast by death. This was the vision, the unifying generalization that shed the meaning and urgency into all his observations and particulars: not truth is beauty only, but truth kills everybody. The truth of a man is the doomed man in him or his dead body. Poem after poem circles this idea, as if his mind were tethered. At the bottom of it, perhaps, is his private muse, not a romantic symbol of danger and temptation, but the plain foreknowledge of his own rapidly-approaching end – a foreknowledge of which he becomes fully conscious in two of his finest poems.

Hughes comments on this achievement:

> ... he has invented a style that seems able to deal poetically with whatever it comes up against. It is not an exalted verbal activity to be attained for short periods, through abstinence, or a submerged dream treasure to be fished up when the every-day brain is half-drugged. It is a language for the whole mind, at its most wakeful, and in all situations.

It is no accident that Ted Hughes (b. 1930) was a poet who recognized Douglas as potentially one of the most powerful writers of his generation. Hughes also circles the idea of death in poem after poem:

> I drown in the drumming ploughland, I drag up
> Heel after heel from the swallowing of the earth's mouth,
> From clay that clutches my each step to the ankle
> With the habit of the dogged grave, but the hawk
>
> Effortlessly at height hangs his still eye.
> His wings hold all creation in a weightless quiet,
> Steady as a hallucination in the streaming air.
> While banging wind kills these stubborn hedges,
>
> Thumbs my eyes, throws my breath, tackles my heart,
> And rain hacks my head to the bone, the hawk hangs
> The diamond point of will that polestars
> The sea drowner's endurance: and I,
>
> Bloodily grabbed dazed last-moment-counting
> Morsel in the earth's mouth, strain towards the master-
> Fulcrum of violence where the hawk hangs still.
> That maybe in his own time meets the weather
>
> Coming the wrong way, suffers the air, hurled upside down,
> Fall from his eye, the ponderous shires crash on him,
> The horizon trap him; the round angelic eye
> Smashed, mix his heart's blood with the mire of the land.
>
> (*The Hawk in the Rain*)

He emerged, already an impressive talent, with *The Hawk in the Rain* (1957), a book where his own voice blends a little too easily at times into that of Dylan Thomas. Two experiences seem to have dominated him – firstly, the mythos of World War I and that sense of dislocation it brought to 'the mind of Europe', secondly an awareness of nature, of that other England which the London-bound writer has forgotten about. *Lupercal* (1960) extends these two worlds of violence – that of men and that of animals – and it is *Lupercal* that makes one conscious of Hughes's primary literary allegiance, the work of Henry Williamson. Williamson's *Tarka the Otter* and *Salar the Salmon* find poetic equivalents among poems in Hughes's second book, particularly in *An Otter* and *Pike*. His obsession with the first world war is preluded by Williamson's own, exhaustively pursued in his novels. Hughes's successes in his first two books and in *Woodwo* (1967) force one to ask, without precisely formulating the questions themselves, what exactly could be the relation between the intelligence, the life of mind, and this universe of blind energies? Again, the same critical question is unconsciously proposed by Williamson. He, too, portrays animal life and, following his master Richard Jefferies, writes with great intimacy about the details of nature, but once human beings appear on the scene, fails at any finally convincing analysis of their doings. When, in *Thrushes*, Hughes equates the 'bullet and automatic purpose' of thrushes with Mozart's artistic instinct and then Mozart with sharks ('Mozart's brain had it, and the shark's mouth...'), one begins to wonder if Hughes's powerful evocation of primitive forces is not bought at the cost of knowing what civilization is. If you isolate Mozart's musical *savoir faire* in this way, between the amoral automatism of the thrush and the shark's lust for blood, you work a false rhetoric which prevents the reader asking in what ways human civilization and the centuries-long traditions of music were essential before Mozart could write a note. Hughes once attempted to contrast man and beast when he said of his portrayal of animals: 'Each one is living the redeemed life of joy. They're in a state of energy which men only have when they have gone mad. This strength arises from their complete unity with whatever divinity they have' (*Manchester Guardian*, 23 March 1965). I do not know if Hughes, on reflection, would wish to equate animal energy and human madness in this way, but it is clearly a stripped-down version of man – man thrown back on unthinking reflexes – that fascinates him. His version of Seneca's *Oedipus* (1969), the most interesting of his experiments with dramatic form, includes in its preface a contrast between Sophocles' *Oedipus* and Seneca's play: Seneca's protagonists, says Hughes, 'are more primitive than aboriginals. They are a spider people, scuttling among hot stones.' This aboriginal quality, occurring in Nero's Rome, attracts Hughes's imagination because of the buried mystery play he finds in Seneca, a kind of '[groping] towards salvation'. The groping and the blindness are of a piece with Hughes's own poetry and Seneca, like Hughes, ran the risk of unpacking his heart with words. *Crow* (1970) seems to shelve the implicit dilemmas of earlier volumes. Its rhetoric – somewhere between Seneca and the music-hall – settles for easier solutions than Hughes's poised sense of the universe's challenge to man and the Douglas-like contemplation of the destructiveness around him.

Geoffrey Hill, born two years later than Hughes, in 1932, is a poet who has reflected on men's awareness of divinity and its reverberation in history. It is as if he had taken a route proposed by Hughes's own *The Martyrdom of Bishop Farrar* in *The Hawk in the Rain* – a route Hughes did not follow. There the resemblance ends. Hill's own style is dense and, at its least effective, clotted, yet the clotting seems less the result of an easy rhetoric than the failure of a magnificent attempt to notate the antiphonal ironies of history: the attempt stretches Hill's resources and the reader's capacities defeatingly in many poems. His successes in *For the Unfallen* (1959), number the fine *Martyrdom of Saint Sebastian* and *Requiem for the Plantagenet Kings*:

> For whom the possessed sea littered, on both shores,
> Ruinous arms; being fired, and for good,
> To sound the constitution of just wars,
> Men, in their eloquent fashion, understood.
>
> Relieved of soul, the dropping-back of dust,
> Their usage, pride, admitted within doors;
> At home, under caved chantries, set in trust,
> With well-dressed alabaster and proved spurs
> They lie; they lie; secure in the decay
> Of blood, blood-marks, crowns hacked and coveted,
> Before the scouring fires of trial-day
> Alight on men; before sleeked groin, gored head,
> Budge through the clay and gravel, and the sea
> Across daubed rock evacuates its dead.

The vindication of Hill's methods appears in the sequence *Funeral Music*, 'a florid grim music broken by grunts and shrieks', in *King Log* (1968). *Mercian Hymns* (1971) is a book of poems in prose in which King Offa, who reigned over Mercia in the eighth century A.D., is taken as a recurrent psychological type of human tyranny, reappearing in the schoolboy bully and the twentieth-century magistrate.

In a characteristically rich and subtle essay, 'Redeeming the Time' (*Agenda*, Vol. 10, No. 4) Hill reflects on Coleridge's attachment to what he called 'the moral copula', by which he meant the action of the humanizing intellect as against the merely prudential or circumstantial reasoning of those who judge history by what is termed results. The moral copula, according to Coleridge, would 'take from history its accidentality and from science its fatalism'. Hill himself is concerned to keep vivid our sense of that moral copula in face of the brutalities of history which he so painfully records. Thus, he will have none of the scholarly detachment that sees in the Wars of the Roses merely dynastic skirmishes 'without much effect on the economic routines of the kingdom'. In the essay which accompanies *Funeral Music* he retorts: 'Statistically, this may be arguable; imaginatively, the Battle of Towton itself commands one's belated witness.' The poem provides the witness of imagination as against statistics, in accordance with the Coleridgean imperative. Again, Coleridge defends his use of parentheses for their enactment of 'the drama of reason', one thing held in balance over against another. Hill, by a typical flight of mind, makes us see this drama in terms of the uses of rhythm and even the antiphonal responses of the Anglican church service. This sense of 'the other voice' demanding to be heard is central to Hill's own poetic style in its renovation of clichés, its punning density and its grim humour. *Mercian Hymns* is full of splendid examples of compacted dualities.

These poems in prose are headed by an epigraph from C. H. Sisson: 'The conduct of government rests upon the same foundation and encounters the same difficulties as the conduct of private persons...' The quotation is from Sisson's privately printed *Essays* (1967). Sisson (b. 1914) has never received his due as a poet. Both Hill and Sisson are deeply responsive to the traditions of Christian thought, Sisson far more doctrinally so than Hill. His *Numbers* (1965) and *Metamorphoses* (1968) reveal a writer both wry and haunted – haunted by original sin and curiously determined to make the ironic best of a bad lot.

Peter Porter (b. 1929), whose two most interesting volumes, *Preaching to the Converted* and *After Martial*, both appeared in 1972, also bears witness to the strength of a residually Christian imagination.

Porter is an outstanding 'performer', technically adept, morally conservative. We are always being told of the death of Christianity, and yet Christian belief and ethics temper the imagination of a number of poets, from Sisson to the minor, but justly admired, R. S. Thomas (b. 1913). It is evidently still easier to be a Christian than a Jew in present English society: the strain shows in some of Jon Silkin's committed poems. Silkin (b. 1930) seems to me almost invariably at his best when he is least self-conscious of his Jewishness. Michael Schmidt has written well on Silkin in *Poetry* (Vol. 120, No. 3) where he says:

> Many, if not most, of his poems are technically flawed. There are recurrent obscurities of diction – an elaborate, often archaic or poetical diction; there is excessive punctuation, a blurred syntactical line. These qualities make the poems hard reading, but what is flawed in Silkin is still substantial. The humanity of the poems, their concern with situations of relationship, suffering, and death, and the strong tone of voice with an 'I' not self-assertive but perceptive, redeem the frequent clumsiness.

A useful choice of Silkin appears in *Poems New and Selected* (1966). He is to be found at his most ambitious in *Amana Grass* (1971).

The most remarkable re-emergence of the nineteen sixties is that of Basil Bunting. *The Spoils*, written in 1951, was not generally available until 1965; *Briggflatts* (1966) is a poem that makes contact with our traditions at a level that had not seemed possible in many years. For too long Bunting's work had been lost to all but a few readers and was to be found in any bulk only in the rare Cleaners' Press edition of *Poems* (1950). His verse, now united in *Collected Poems* (1968), should clearly have penetrated the anthologies long ago: *The Well of Lycopolis*, *Chomei at Toyama*, *Vestiges*, *The Orotava Road*, *Villon*, *Attis* often confess their Poundian provenance, but they are intricate and interesting poems. *The Spoils*, with its experiences of semitic culture and its return to 'Cold northern clear sea-gardens' leads directly to the richness of *Briggflatts*, the most authoritative long poem of the sixties. Here Bunting comes back to the Northumbrian landscape and tongue ('Southrons would mawl the music of many lines in *Briggflatts*') where monosyllables combine to produce a music new to modern verse. The sense of mortality, the vision of landscape, the repeated motifs are densely but lucidly orchestrated in a

> Flexible, unrepetitive line
> to sing, not paint: sing, sing
> laying the tune frankly on the air.

The music of Byrd, Monteverdi, Scarlatti and Schoenberg are some of Bunting's analogies for what he is after in terms of structure. One of the measures of the poem's success is his right to such analogies.

Bunting instances the sixth-century bard, Aneurin, who celebrated in *Y Gododdin* the deaths of warriors at the battle of Catterick. Aneurin is also a central instance for another poet, David Jones. Jones has produced a striking series of poems on the Roman–Celtic past (written 1955–65). The most readily approachable of these is perhaps *The Wall* (1955), the most recent, *The Fatigue* (1965) and *The Tribune's Visitation* (1969). All are a further growth beyond the exasperating and intriguing *Anathemata* (1952), a poem of great ambition and often impenetrable scholarship. 'The work of David Jones,' wrote T. S. Eliot, 'has some affinity with that of James Joyce ... and with the later work of Ezra Pound, and with my own.' Indeed, as Eliot points out, Jones belongs to the literary generation of these men and his ambition marks him as one of their fraternity. What remains impressive about *The Anathemata* is its penetration of pre-history, and to my own mind its opening section, *Rite and Fore-Time*, is unique in post-war writing. A difficult work to assess with finality, *The Anathemata* points us back to Jones' incontrovertible masterpiece, the prose book *In Parenthesis* (1937). Here he was able to convey a range of reference without burying the text in footnotes, as too frequently happens later on.

NOTES

1. For an early discussion of MacDiarmid's work see John Speir's *The Scots Literary Tradition* (1940).

2. Donald Davie, 'Form and Concept in Ezra Pound's Cantos', *Irish Writing*, 36, and 'Adrian Stokes and Pound's *Cantos*', *Twentieth Century* (November 1956). The material of these essays appears in a later form in *Ezra Pound, Poet as Sculptor* (1964).

3. See 'Ezra Pound and *Women of Trachis*', in Denis Donoghue's *The Third Voice* (1959).

4. For a history of the Movement see my 'The Middlebrow Muse', *Essays in Criticism*, VII, No. 2.

5. See G. S. Fraser's *Keith Douglas* (British Academy, 1956).

THE NOVEL TODAY

GILBERT PHELPS

WHEN we recall the scope and variety of English fiction in the earlier years of this century in the hands of such writers as Henry James, Joseph Conrad, E. M. Forster, D. H. Lawrence, and Virginia Woolf, it is difficult not to feel that there has been a decline. The trend of the English novel since the Second World War has, on the whole, been analogous to that of the poetry – a turning aside from the mainstream of European literature, and a tendency to retreat into parochialism or defeatism – attended, it is true, by outstanding moments of protest, defiance, honesty or insight, but rarely by anything approaching a unified vision. It is doubtful, for example, whether any single English novel of the period can bear comparison with Boris Pasternak's *Dr Zhivago* (English translation, 1958) either in profundity of theme or power of creative imagination (and this itself is of a lower order than the greatest of the nineteenth-century Russian novels). At the same time, despite a number of gloomy prognostications, the English novel is far from dead.

In a limited space it is impossible to do more than indicate some of the more important or characteristic English novels written during the period – and inevitably this means distortion and over-simplification, considerable licence to individual preferences, and an exclusion, in consequence, of names and titles that may well strike the reader as inexcusable.

In attempting, therefore, what is meant to be a very general picture of post-war developments, it is convenient to divide novelists roughly into four main categories: the survivors of the thirties (that is, writers who were already in the forefront of the literary scene between the wars); novelists who were writing during the same period, but who either did not achieve maturity or failed to gain full recognition until after the Second World War; the so-called 'Angry Young Men', or those related to them in theme or approach; and (obviously a particularly amorphous grouping) those writers who have also achieved considerable reputations in the period under consideration but have little in common with any of the other categories.

The general point to be made about the first of these groups is that the majority of them found it difficult to make the transition successfully to the post-war world. Some of them, of course, tried to grapple with the fact of war itself. Charles Morgan, for example, in *The River Line* (1949) wrote about airmen shot down in enemy territory and escaping with the help of the Resistance: but the mood and atmosphere are almost identical with those in his earlier novels such as *Sparkenbroke* and the presence of the war merely serves to underline the dated and essentially vapid nature of the philosophizing. Many of the old 'writers of sensibility', in fact, failed to make any fundamental adjustment to new realities: they went on writing as if they were denizens of Chehov's Cherry Orchard, hanging on long after the trees had been chopped down. They tended to retreat farther and farther, into the world of reverie, nostalgic reminiscence, self-contemplation, and fine writing. Their attitude of mind is perhaps summed up by Cyril Connolly's valediction in the last issue of *Horizon*:

> It is closing-time in the gardens of the West and from now on an artist will be judged only by the resonance of his solitude or the quality of his despair.[1]

It is hardly surprising that the post-war young reacted against this attitude to life and literature.

Even those novelists of the thirties who, between the wars, were most committed to the task of registering or interpreting contemporary reality and the historical forces making for change for the most part preferred to stand aside from the challenges of the post-war world. Rex Warner, for example, author of *The Wild Goose Chase* (1937), which was more or less prescribed reading for the ardent young leftists of the day, after his Kafkaesque (and often compelling) allegory *The Aerodrome* (1941) turned to the historical novel and the distant past in *The Young Caesar* (1958), *Imperial Caesar* (1960), and *Pericles, the Athenian* (1963). The urgent, immediate tone that had made Christopher Isherwood's pre-war Berlin stories genuine transcripts of the times seemed to desert him as soon as he went to America, though some of it lingered in *Prater Violet* (1946). The most interesting of his later novels has been *Down There on a Visit* (1962), largely because with the return of 'Herr Issyvoo' as narrator, and the return visit, too, in one section of the novel, to Berlin some of the 'I Am a

Camera' sharpness of vision and rightness of tone also returned. But for the most part the private hells which Isherwood explores in many of his post-war novels have little universal human significance, while the excursions into Oriental philosophies, as in *A Meeting by the River* (1967), are not, as far as the reader is concerned, always morally convincing.

The ideas of Aldous Huxley (who died in 1963), another typical novelist of the thirties, did of course change over the years. *Ape and Essence* (1949) envisaged a California of the future after a nuclear war, in which nothing remains of human civilization, except its squalor, taboos, and the conscious worship of evil. The first part of *Island* (1962) showed the reverse side of the coin – a genuine Utopia where the 'good life' really does exist (because man's limitations and potentialities have at last been properly understood) – until it is destroyed by a brutal materialistic dictator. But ideas by themselves do not make a novel and (though there is never any doubt of Huxley's personal humanity) his books have tended to be in effect a series of set-pieces illustrating a thesis, rather than works of imaginative creation. On the whole, indeed, there is much more vitality in Huxley's novels of the thirties – *Brave New World* (1932) among them – largely because they succeeded in capturing a part, even if it was a particularly negative and destructive part, of the spirit of the times.

As for George Orwell's *1984*, it is surely by now apparent that a good deal of the excitement it aroused when it was first published (in 1949) was related to Cold War fever. Although it can still produce its *frissons* of horror, the writing is frequently slack and tired compared to that of Orwell's earlier books (including the far more vital and effective fable, *Animal Farm*, published in 1945), the tone is frequently shrill and hysterical, and the characterization notably wooden.

The dilemma of many of the uneasy survivors of the thirties is admirably symbolized by Evelyn Waugh's novel *The Ordeal of Gilbert Pinfold* (1957). In the first chapter, entitled 'Portrait of the Artist in Middle Age', we are shown that little of passion is left to men like Mr Pinfold beyond a few testy prejudices:

> ... His strongest tastes were negative. He abhorred plastics, Picasso, sunbathing and jazz – everything in fact that had happened in his own life-time. The tiny kindling of charity which came to him through his religion sufficed only to temper his

> disgust and change it to boredom ... He wished no one ill, but he looked at the world *sub specie aeternitatis* and he found it flat as a map; except when, rather often, personal arrogance intruded. Then he would come tumbling from his exalted point of observation. Shocked by a bad bottle of wine, an impertinent stranger, or a fault in syntax ...

The candour and wit of the portrait undoubtedly make this one of the most successful novels in this particular group. But although Waugh's satire in *The Loved One* (1948) of the Californian way of death (and, by implication, way of life too) in the vast and bizarre cemetery of Forest Lawn revived, and in some respects improved on, that of his typical thirties novels, his war trilogy *Sword of Honour* (*Men at Arms*, 1952; *Officers and Gentlemen*, 1955; and *Unconditional Surrender*, 1961), despite some brilliantly funny scenes, is more a vehicle for the author's quirks and prejudices and for his particular and somewhat exclusive brand of Roman Catholicism than an imaginative fictional rendering of the impact of war upon real human beings. In this vital respect it compares unfavourably with Ford Madox Ford's 'Tietjens' sequence about the First World War.

One other point must be made in this connection – that it has become increasingly evident that little of the experimentation of the twenties and thirties has borne fruit. It is true that the influence of James Joyce can be detected in a number of novelists, among them Joyce Cary and Samuel Beckett. Cary we shall be coming to in a moment. In a limited inquiry of this nature Beckett, whose only three novels to be written in English were published before the war, can be regarded as belonging primarily to French fiction – though he does his own translating into English, and his is obviously an original contribution to European literature as a whole. Whether his studies of the null or twilight areas of human experience, and the stark techniques he has evolved for them, represent a growing-point themselves is a different matter. 'My characters have nothing', he has told us. 'I'm working with impotence, ignorance ... My little exploration is that whole zone of being that has always been set aside by artists as something unusable – as something by definition incompatible with art.' In his 'novels' (they demand the inverted commas because they are rapidly – and of course by intention – shrinking in size) and his plays alike, Beckett has shown that this zone is certainly not incompatible with his own art, but one cannot help suspecting that it is a triumph accessible only to his rare and unusual genius, and one that could not possibly be repeated or even imitated successfully.

But apart from these exceptions there are no real heirs to James Joyce, and *Finnegans Wake* (1939) appears to have presented an evolutionary dead-end as far as English fiction is concerned, while Virginia Woolf's last novel, *Between the Acts* (1941), was essentially a repetition, at a lower level of achievement, of techniques and attitudes that had little relevance to the emotional climate of the times. It has to be admitted, too, that save for a very few honourable exceptions the more radical challenge, for a kind of fiction that would get to the heart of the modern social and spiritual *malaise* and in the process evolve new techniques to embody new aspects of being, has also largely gone unanswered.

There is, however, one writer who once seemed the most representative of all the novelists of the thirties, in the sense that he more than any other captured their peculiar atmosphere and 'feel', who *has* adapted himself without any loss of power to the world this side of the war. Graham Greene's work is discussed elsewhere in this volume, so it is only necessary here to stress some of the more important points about him – and the first is that the feeling for the contemporary scene that informed his earlier novels has never deserted him, though some people would argue that the peak of his achievement was reached in *The Heart of the Matter* (1948). Greene's sense of topicality is not simply the result of a good journalistic eye or of a sharp ear for the idiom of a particular place or period; it is a deeper response that pervades the style and characterization of each novel. Thus in *The End of the Affair* (1951) the atmosphere of war-time London is present in the reader's imagination in a far more fundamental way than in, say, Elizabeth Bowen's *The Heat of the Day* (1949), poetically evocative though that novel is: it seeps into the bones, so so speak. Similarly in *The Quiet American* (1955) the Cold War, in its particular context of the war of liberation against the French in Indo-China, is absorbed into the very texture of the novel in a way that recalls the integration of politics, character and setting in Joseph Conrad's *Under Western Eyes*.

In addition, of course, everything Greene writes, including the lighter 'entertainments', such as *Our Man in Havana* (1958) and *Travels with My Aunt* (1969), has embedded in it a concern for the human condition. This is not only due to his religion. As A. C. Capey says, comparing Greene and Waugh:

> If Greene's world is also a Catholic world, it encompasses more of the world to justify the assumption; and the problems set ... are more searching. Greene at his best can show something of the grandeur underlying the sorriest things.[2]

In the Greene world, it is true, the 'grandeur' is usually implied rather than revealed, and it is the 'sorry' side of life that is most in evidence. The central character in nearly all Greene's post-war novels is, in some respect or other, 'a burned-out case' – to borrow the title of the novel set in a leper colony in the Congo and published in 1961 (a better novel, incidentally, than has been generally allowed). There is, in fact, some change of direction here, in that the typical protagonist of pre-war novels like *England Made Me* (1935) was, as a rule, simply 'seamy' – an empty squib that never contained any combustible material *to* burn out.

It is true, too, that disgust, depression, and defeat lie heavy on Graham Greene's novels, sometimes submerging the creative affirmation – and that characters like the naïve and futile Pyle of *The Quiet American* or the cranky American couple of *The Comedians* (1966) are hardly inspiriting examples of the more 'positive' values. On the other hand, it can be argued that this is an accurate reflection of a world in which these values *are* almost overwhelmed, to flicker up only occasionally and in the most unlikely places, and that the miracle of human goodness is that it obstinately persists, even if it is forced to choose the most unlikely receptacles. At least Greene does not surrender to or glorify the chaos and anarchy of our times, as so many other post-war novelists have done – or retreat inside a narrow doctrinal fortress, even when refusal to do so means quarrelling with his own Church. In *The Comedians* in particular – set against the especially nasty and sordid background of 'Papa Doc's' Haiti at a time when revolt seemed imminent (another instance of Greene's astonishing news sense) – the distinction between those who opt out into a selfish detachment and indifference (the 'comedians') and those who, however grotesque and indeed 'comic' (like the vegetarian American professor and his wife), hold on to their integrity, is firmly and uncompromisingly brought out, while even the squalid 'comedian' narrator is shown to contain the seeds of spiritual regeneration. There is an element of courage and honesty about *The Comedians* which makes it one of Graham Greene's most satisfactory books, and which is caught in the tone (however chilling we may find the content) of the brave and dedicated Communist doctor:

> Catholics and Communists have committed great crimes, but at least they have not stood aside, like an established society, and been indifferent. I would rather have blood on my hands than water like Pilate.

Henry Green (born in 1905, a year after his near-namesake) has displayed consistency of a different sort, conveyed by his use of single-word titles, from *Blindness* (1926), which was written while he was still at school, to *Doting* (1952). These titles express the economy and directness natural to Henry Green's fictional mode from the beginning. It is significant, too, that most of them are in the form of participles – and most of them in the present tense: it is not merely that these set the themes, but that they indicate the separate poetic entities of the novels. The characters and backgrounds, of course, vary – *Living* (1929), for example is about workers in a Midlands factory; *Loving* (1948) is set in Ireland; *Concluding* (1948) takes place in a mythical future, and so on. The art in the later novels (and it is to be hoped that another one will not be too long delayed) has become richer and more controlled – and above all, perhaps, in *Concluding* – but each of Green's novels, early or late, offers a self-contained imaginative world: each of them could be described (to make use of Green's own method of nomenclature) by the word 'being' – the particular state of being, that is, appropriate to the chosen plot and cast of characters. It will be apparent from this that the titles have a symbolic significance: but it is symbol – used almost in an Imagist sense – strictly controlled by the necessities of each separate 'being' (or the more up-to-date 'happening'), very different from the clumsy and portentous symbolism common in so many other contemporary novels.

One more novelist might be mentioned in this group, though he really falls outside the scope of this chapter. Wyndham Lewis published *The Childermass* in 1928, but the sequels, *Monstre Gai* and *Malign Fiesta* (which together with the unfinished *Trial of Man* were to form a sequence entitled *The Human Age*), did not appear until 1955. Lewis published other works of fiction too after the war, including the novel *Self-Condemned* (1954) and a collection of short stories. But the date of *Childermass* has some significance, for Wyndham Lewis really belongs to the more robust ethos of the twenties. His vision of human society (in his painting as well as in his fiction) was formed in the explosion of anger that succeeded the First World War. It is pessimistic and largely destructive, expressed, as far as the sequence of novels is concerned, in terms of fable rather than realistic fiction, and marred by long digressions and clumsiness of technique. But at the same time it is a unified and dynamic vision of twentieth-century man and his predicament as a member of a mass civilization, as victim and participant in the Age of the Machine. It was the very scale of this conception that provided the impetus that carried it without any relaxation of purpose beyond the 1930s; but there was little development in Lewis's basic attitudes, most of which were already apparent in his early novel *Tarr* (1918).

* * *

The most unusual novelist of the second group is Ivy Compton-Burnett.* A superficial reading of one of her books might lead one to classify her as a brilliant but narrow eccentric, somewhat in the manner of Ronald Firbank, and she is the kind of writer who tends to attract either the distorting attentions of the cult, or the equally distorting ones of the parodist. Her material is peculiarly, not to say idiosyncratically, selective; for she deals almost exclusively with upper-middle-class society of the Edwardian era. She is quite explicit about this:

> I do not feel that I have any real organic knowledge later than 1910. I should not write of later times with enough grasp or confidence.[3]

Moreover, her treatment of the Edwardian world is the reverse of naturalistic. She does not consider descriptions of persons or scenes essential to a novel. 'They are not of a play,' she has said, 'and both deal with imaginary human beings and their lives.'[4] And her highly melodramatic plots are conducted almost entirely by means of stylized conversations.

This brief account suggests two obvious considerations: first, that

* Ivy Compton-Burnett died in 1969.

Ivy Compton-Burnett is clear in her own mind what she is doing and why: and second, that in doing it she has imposed upon herself a set of conventions that one might well assume would be utterly inhibiting. They *do*, of course, restrict her scope – but it is the scope she wants and it is the limitations, so clearly recognized and accepted, that give her strength. The fictional world she presents is consistent, with its own laws of being and its own credibility. It is this consistency and self-sufficiency that tempt one to compare her with Jane Austen. For one thing she has a genuine wit – as distinct from smartness and stylistic ornament – proceeding from a critical but humane assessment of the standards and values of her creations. The comparison of course immediately emphasizes the differences. Jane Austen was writing about a way of life that was a present and stable reality: her vision was both more profound and more vital, and her humour has a radiance, a redeeming quality that Ivy Compton-Burnett's lacks. She was not deliberately building up a set of conventions: they sprang from a milieu in which she was an active participant. Ivy Compton-Burnett, on the other hand, in order to achieve her effects is forced to isolate her characters in a setting that has already passed away. She may be right when she says her own connection with it is 'organic', but her success is to a very large extent dependent upon its historical unreality as far as her readers are concerned (it is real enough artistically of course, within the bounds of each novel). The country house (usually of the 1890s) provides her, in fact, with a laboratory in which she is able to make her observations upon human behaviour. She makes this clear in the course of an argument designed to show that people today, because of the wider sphere in which their lives take place, are less 'individualized' than their forebears: they may, she says:

> ... be better and do less harm, but they afford less interest as a study ... Imagine a Winston Churchill, untaught and untrained in the sense we mean, and then immured in an isolated life in a narrow community, and think what might have happened, what would have happened to it.[5]

The temptations of power are indeed one of her major preoccupations, and in order to demonstrate it she has placed it in the hot-house of the Edwardian, or patriarchal family. Here, too, she differs from Jane Austen, for she has little concern for normal human relationships or for romantic passion, and her world is a narrower and more sombre one in consequence. Many of her novels are about domestic tyrants; sometimes men – as in *A House and Its Head* (1935), *Parents and Children* (1941), *Manservant and Maidservant* (1947) and *A God and his Gifts* (1963); sometimes women – as in *Daughters and Sons* (1937) and *Elders and Betters* (1944).

The plots usually depend for their resolution upon violent climaxes, either the actual committing of a crime or the revelation of some skeleton in the cupboard. The crimes include incest in *Brothers and Sisters* (1929), matricide in *Men and Wives* (1931), sundry thefts and fornications in *Darkness and Day* (1951), and attempted suicide in *The Present and the Past* (1953). There is here an interest in violence that in a lesser writer could have degenerated into morbid sensationalism or unconscious farce. She is saved from both by her sureness of touch and the complete freedom from sentimentality in her view of human nature. 'I think', she has said, 'there are signs that strange things happen, though they do not emerge. I believe it would go ill with many of us if we were faced with temptation, and I suspect that with some of us it does go ill.'[6] And when she was criticized (in connection with *Elders and Betters*) on the grounds that she often allowed the wicked to flourish she argued that her whole point was that wickedness frequently did *not* get punished, 'and that is why it is natural to be guilty of it. When it is likely to be punished, most of us avoid it.'[7]

This does not mean that there is a lack of human values in her work: the absence of sentimentality is indeed a guarantee of their presence. Like Jane Austen she has no illusions about human nature and makes no concessions to complacency or wishful thinking; like her she is distrustful of moral generalizations. But a sympathy and understanding for the victims of human wickedness – the evil-doers included – emerge unmistakably from the drift and texture of the conventionalized dialogues and in the tensions they generate.

It is perhaps surprising that a novelist who consistently wrote about a vanished era should have attracted a following in the post-war world. But modernity is not a matter of surface detail: it belongs to the depth and quality of the response that a writer makes to the society in which he lives, and if these are present it hardly matters in what period the actual 'fable' is cast. Most of the human passions with which Ivy Compton-Burnett deals belong to no particular age or society – though it is true that some of them have a special relevance in acquisitive ones – and in depicting them she is in fact doing so in full awareness of the modern world. She writes mostly about Edwardians; but she would have written quite differently if she had been living among them. One cannot doubt, for example, that she was conscious, however indirectly, of a cultural climate that includes Ibsen, Dostoyevsky, and Freud. Her triumph may be a precarious one depending as it does upon the maintenance of a rather peculiar set of conventions and of a corresponding precision of verbal stylization. There were signs in *Mother and Son* (1955) that she might have been paying too much attention to critics who had urged her to be more 'compassionate'. But the subsequent novels – and in particular *A Heritage and its History* (1959), *The Mighty and their Fall* (1961), and *A God and his Gifts* (1963), her last and one of her best books – show her once more in precise control. This precision was, of course, vital for what was in the nature of a razor-edge triumph: but there can be no doubt at all that it was a genuine one.

Another of the outstanding members of this second group is L. P. Hartley.* In some respects he is less original than Ivy Compton-Burnett, in so far as he has literary debts, notably to Henry James, which are more obvious and sometimes become obtrusive. At times, when inspiration flags, he falls back on Jamesian flourishes of style, as in this passage from *My Fellow Devils* (1951):

> 'If you loved me,' Colum said, as though divining her thoughts, 'you would believe me.' But he had put the cart before the horse. If she had believed him she would have loved him.

A review of L. P. Hartley's first novel, *Simonetta Perkins* (1925), in the *Calendar of Letters*[8] accurately assessed his equipment – the cool and lucid style, the firm intelligence, the 'observant, neat, and graceful exercises upon a "situation" ', the 'ironic and comprehensive attitude'. It is an equipment that has limitations as well as virtues. It serves him best when, like Ivy Compton-Burnett, he distances his characters. *The Shrimp and the Anemone* (1944), the first of a trilogy, is set against the background of an East coast seaside resort at the turn of the century. It is a beautiful evocation of childhood – and for once that well-worn phrase really is applicable. What distinguishes it from

* L. P. Hartley died in 1973.

the explorations of childhood conducted by most of his contemporaries is the fact that there are so few sentimental distortions. The scene, almost in spite of the gracefully modulated style with its suggestion of an English water-colour, is solidly set, and the emotions and behaviour of the characters are directly and concretely related to it. A measure of Hartley's control of his material is that one can accept the symbolic relationship of shrimp and anemone to the gentle and rather ineffectual Eustace and his vivid, dominating sister Hilda in the same compassionate and ironical spirit in which it is offered.

The Sixth Heaven (1946), the second novel of the trilogy, is not as successful, reading in places as if the author regarded it as a dumping ground for the machinery of the plot, which he isn't really interested in but which has to be disposed of so that he can get on to the sequel. *Eustace and Hilda*, which finally reveals the underlying nature of the relationship between brother and sister and carries it to its tragic conclusion, in which Eustace in effect opts out of life in order to release his sister from the attachment, is an impressive work. It is a theme which few English novelists have tackled, but Hartley encompasses it with surprising ease. His style is in fact tougher than it looks at first sight: it can achieve depth as well as subtlety. Eustace's gradual realization of the situation, his sudden understanding of the intensity of emotion pent up inside his sister, and the wilting of his own spirit before it, constitute some of the most effective scenes in contemporary English fiction.

When Hartley ventures outside the areas of experience he knows well, the results are not always as happy. *The Boat* (1949), for example, is long and, for Hartley, surprisingly confused. The characters outside the author's own social sphere do not convince: the 'lower orders' appear mostly as figures of fun. The climax, too, is harsh and contrived and the symbolism of the boat is thrust down our throats by one of the characters:

> 'It was a death-wish. He couldn't face modern life ... and the boat was his way out, a symbol of absolute peace, where no-one could get at him ...'

In some of the novels we feel that Hartley himself is aware of a reluctance to 'face modern life' and that as a kind of self-discipline he is forcing himself to deal with aspects of it that are basically repugnant to him and which he cannot properly assimilate. The film world in *My Fellow Devils* (1951), suburbia in *A Perfect Woman* (1955) – though this is also a delicate enough study in personal relationships – and the changes in the class system in *The Hireling* (1957) – perhaps the most contrived of his novels – are examples, while *Facial Justice* (1960), his excursion into fantasy of the 'Brave New World' type, is ingenious but disappointing.

The most successful novel since his trilogy has been *The Go-Between* (1953), which is set in the same period and rendered with something of the same rich concreteness of detail. In some ways Leo, the boy who in ignorance of the implications acts as go-between for the lovers, resembles the Eustace of the earlier novels, for he too is the innocent cause of emotional upheavals which he is too weak to sustain. He is, in the words he uses when years later he looks back on the experiences that had blighted his whole life, 'a foreigner in the world of emotions, ignorant of their language but compelled to listen to it'. The novel does not possess quite the assurance of *The Shrimp and the Anemone* and *Eustace and Hilda*, but the tumult of emotions and the long, hot summer against which they are enacted are communicated vividly and sensuously.

There have been signs in the more recent novels of some slackening of tension, a demonstration perhaps that sensibility of this rather rarefied kind might eventually be tapped dry – or simply that Hartley has been over-producing. *The Brickfield* (1964), for example, although it contains evocations of Edwardian childhood as brilliant as those in *The Go-Between*, echoes the themes and treatment of the latter too closely. Moreover the querulous and rather sad-sack old writer Mardick, the central character of *The Brickfield*, has not enough substance to him to sustain the sequel, which is entitled *The Betrayal* (1966) and which seems to be drawing too directly on private disappointments and dissatisfactions. *Poor Clare* (1968) and *The Love Adept* (1969) – though they contain some excellent writing and some shrewd perceptions of human folly and perverseness – somehow feel dated and literary. All the same, L. P. Hartley possesses a genuine interest in problems of moral discrimination and a concern for humane and civilized values that make it possible to relate him at his best to the tradition represented by Henry James, inherited perhaps by way of E. M. Forster.

Neither Ivy Compton-Burnett nor L. P. Hartley, in spite of the inherent vitality that carried them beyond the thirties where so many of their contemporaries had remained transfixed, set out to be 'historians of their times' in the same way as Anthony Powell and C. P. Snow, the two most distinguished contemporary exponents of the large-scale fictional sequence. Anthony Powell's first novel, *Afternoon Men*, published in 1931, was a satire of the chic world of fashion and the arts, somewhat in the manner of Evelyn Waugh. Several other novels followed during the 1930s, but it was not until 1951, with the publication of *A Question of Upbringing*, that he launched his long sequence 'The Music of Time'. Since then he has been producing the 'instalments' every two years or so – *A Buyer's Market* (1952); *The Acceptance World* (1955); *At Lady Molly's* (1957); *Casanova's Chinese Restaurant* (1960); *The Kindly Ones* (1962); *The Valley of the Bones* (1964); *The Soldier's Art* (1966); and *The Military Philosophers* (1968). The last of these carries Powell's ingrown, cliquish, but oddly vital cast of eccentrics up to the end of the war, and a tenth novel, *Books Do Furnish a Room* (1971), beyond it, while two more novels are planned, to bring the total up to twelve. The over-all title of the sequence obviously invites comparison with Proust's *À la recherche du temps perdu*, and in some respects this is unfortunate because it serves to underline the fact that the sequence has so far revealed little in the way of a commanding structural design or pattern. The plots, locations, and attitudes change, but there is always the feeling that the books, in spite of slightly different shapes and flavours, have all been cut, roughly to the same size, from the same interminable length of material (they do in fact all run to practically the same number of words). The style, too, is not suited to sustained flights, and certainly not to the ambitious musical analogies suggested by the title of the sequence. The style, in fact, is a medium for short bursts of description, for sudden stabs of insight and characterization, for vignette, metaphor and epigram rather than for the slow unfolding of a theme. At the same time it has a kind of garrulous energy and toughness (at times recalling the best passages of Huxley's *Crome Yellow*) as well as a remarkable consistency.

It is a curious paradox that it should so often be an obsessive attachment to a narrow and restricted coterie or area of experience that provides the most voluminous material – in Proust's case as well as that of Anthony Powell. It calls for gifts of an unusual order to vivify such material into more than a coterie significance. Anthony Powell's sequence depends rather too much on cast-marks and passwords that are often meaningless outside a closed circle: but it does convince us that it is based on values that are fundamentally decent and humane, and that it is a genuinely created world of the imagination.

As far as pattern and design are concerned C. P. Snow's sequence is much more successful, in that there are carefully regulated themes, large and small, running through it, all closely related to the personal destinies of his characters. *Strangers and Brothers*, the title-novel of the series, appeared in 1940, and Snow had also published two other novels during the 1930s: but it was not until 1951, with the publication of what is probably his most popular novel, *The Masters*, that the scope and determination of his purpose began to be fully appreciated. This study of the in-fighting at a Cambridge college over the election of a new Master, although in some respects it is not in the mainstream of the series, sharply focused Snow's overriding preoccupation – the analysis of the centres of power in post-war English society, in both their public and their private manifestations. Snow's approach has been aptly summed up by Michael Ratcliffe:

> Each novel is a panorama of moral attitudes and social behaviour, invariably heightened by a crisis within a closed society.[9]

And the more closed the society, the more successful the approach usually is: certainly next to *The Masters* the most gripping of the novels from a narrative point of view have been *The Affair* (1960) – also set in a Cambridge college, with an indiscreet 'Red' don presenting the central moral problem – and *The Corridors of Power* (1964) – which is about the workings of the upper echelons of the Civil Service.

The adoption of the latter title into our popular idiom is a measure of its contemporary relevance. With the decay of the pre-war liberal idealism, the absence of any large political passions, the apparent stalemate in our democratic processes during the era of 'Butskellism', it certainly seemed as if the real 'decision-making', together with the assessment of the moral issues involved, was carried out in the way Snow describes and by the kind of people he presents.

Not that he adopts an Establishment view or dodges the major challenges: in *The New Men* (1954), for example, the narrator-participant Lewis Eliot shares the horror of many of his fellow-scientists at the implications of official policies on the nuclear deterrent – among them his own brother, who, in effect, gives up his career because of his principles. Neither, of course, is Snow unaware of the temptations and dangers, public and private, implicit in the kind of world he portrays: in *A Sleep of Reason* (1968), for example, Lewis Eliot returns to his home-town to find that a horrifying child-murder trial is taking place there (obviously based on the 'Moors' case) – and this raises the whole question of the spirit of sadistic violence that had attended so many of the events of the 1960s and which, by implication, permeates the whole of our society.

These are all big and important questions, and Snow is the only contemporary novelist who has consistently set out to be their chronicler. The measure of his success is analysed in some detail by Graham Martin in an earlier chapter of this volume, but three points might be usefully made here. The first is that Snow's topicality, in spite of its thoroughness, intelligence, and authenticity, does not possess the kind of imaginative urgency and commitment which distinguishes that of Graham Greene. The second is that the private lives of the characters do not always offer satisfactory correlatives to the public themes – as they do so triumphantly, for example in Joseph Conrad's *Nostromo* – and this applies even to the most convincing and likeable of them, Lewis Eliot himself. There is some truth in Mr Capey's description of him as 'an establishment figure – cautious, committed only as far as his communications will allow, content to achieve a tidy compromise', and in his accusation that his creator has identified himself so closely with 'this recurrent representative of clean hands and stability in the corridors of power' that he 'cannot see the latent possibilities in his material for ironic and detached art'.[10]

It is a curious fact that although Anthony Powell is in one sense more obsessively committed to his world – in itself much narrower than that of Snow – in another he seems more detached, and is more successful, too, in conveying that 'felt life' which Henry James thought so vital to a novel.

And, thirdly, there is the often commented on lack of 'poetry' in

Snow's work. As Anthony Burgess (himself a compelling and often rewarding novelist) has put it, with particular reference to *The Corridors of Power*:

> Snow seems to have robbed the novel-form of its power to feed the senses. The world of colour and texture and scent has disappeared ... and life seems reduced to a number of paradigms, as though this were a grammar-book and not a novel.[11]

All the same, this is too sweeping. The concluding novel of the sequence, *Last Things* (1970), is certainly an apt and characteristic summing-up of the main themes and preoccupations. The sense of contemporary involvement is preserved through Charles, son of the narrator (now Sir Lewis Eliot), who belongs to a student activist group – and the compromise element is undoubtedly present in that Charles, in spite of his anti-Establishment views and ideals, clearly reserves for himself the possibility of a position of power at some future date. On the other hand, Eliot himself has, to some extent at any rate, seen through the power-game, renouncing both an important ministerial post and a seat in the House of Lords, and convincing us of his essential goodness. There is perhaps a greater sense of 'felt life' in the description of Eliot's physical crisis (with its spiritual lessons), when during an operation for correcting a detached retina his heart temporarily stops beating, than anywhere else in the sequence, while Eliot's personal relationship with his son comes over in simple and moving terms.

Ivy Compton-Burnett, L. P. Hartley, Anthony Powell, and C. P. Snow, then, are novelists who, at varying levels of achievement, have established their reputations in the post-war world, and have had something of real value to say to it. It is doubtful, though, whether any of them could be thought of as a 'growing point' in the English novel. The only writer in this group who makes one aware of any really powerful release of fresh forces is Joyce Cary. The source lies to a considerable extent in Cary's own personality, which was vigorous, extrovert, and tough: tough, that is, in the sense that it contained a hard core of integrity that never dissolves into self-pity or self-justification – the reverse in fact of that kind of toughness we find in some American writers such as Hemingway or in some of the 'Angry

Young Men' of the 1950s, a toughness which is so often inverted sentimentality and a fear of deep feeling. Cary, one feels, was afraid of nothing and his personal bravery gets into his characters. Sara in *Herself Surprised* (1941), Gulley Jimson in *The Horse's Mouth* (1944), and Nina in *Prisoner of Grace* (1952), for example, have something of that simple courage that we find in Joseph Conrad's novels.

The other source of Cary's freshness and strength is that he was able to return to the older tradition of the English novel in a far more radical way than any of his contemporaries; he returns, moreover, with a kind of joyousness, as if he is tapping a life-giving spring. There are signs in his work that he was influenced by James Joyce (for example in his use of interior monologue) and perhaps also by Virginia Woolf and Dorothy Richardson, but his vital attachment was to the most robust part of the English tradition, that represented by the great moral writers such as Joseph Conrad and George Eliot, and beyond them to the Evangelical and Protestant traditions, leading through Defoe back to Bunyan.

Joyce Cary's early novels, with the exception of *Castle Corner* (1938), drew on his experiences as an administrator in Nigeria. The first of them was the much re-written *Aissa Saved* (1932), but the best of this group is *Mister Johnson* (1939), the story of an ill-fated African clerk, told with humour and compassion, and already displaying that power of absorption in his characters' desires and destinies which constitutes one of his greatest strengths. The same objectivity is apparent in his novels about children, particularly perhaps in *Charley is My Darling* (1940), which is about slum children evacuated to a Devonshire village at the beginning of the war. His major work, however, consists of two trilogies (though the novels are independent of each other). In the first, consisting of *Herself Surprised* (1941), *To Be A Pilgrim* (1942), and *The Horse's Mouth* (1944), his ostensible aim was to deal with 'English history, through English eyes, for the last sixty years'.[12] A similar purpose lies behind the second trilogy, which consists of *Prisoner of Grace* (1952), *Except the Lord* (1953), and *Not Honour More* (1955). There is more history, in the political sense, in the second trilogy, as one of the central characters is Chester Nimmo, a radical politician of working-class origins – and strict Nonconformist upbringing – who becomes Prime Minister during the First World War and an Elder Statesman after it, and whose career is related with such calm conviction that it is often difficult to remember that it is not an actual biographical study.

In both trilogies the grasp of historical processes, the sense of gradual change within the social structure, of the interlocking of political events with sectional and individual destinies, of subtle shifts in public and private morality with their accompanying changes in dress, idiom, and *mores*, are conveyed in vivid and concrete detail. In this respect alone Cary's is an outstanding achievement. But there is nothing of the *roman à thèse* in his work: all the issues are conveyed through the destinies of fully realized individuals and there is none of that thinness of the imaginative and emotional life that spoils most other contemporary attempts at depicting the history of our times. Thus in spite of the all-pervading presence of the Protestant conscience in these novels we are offered no easy moral conclusions. In reading *Herself Surprised* our sympathies are fully engaged with Sara: but in its sequel, *To Be A Pilgrim* (the title comes from one of Bunyan's hymns), we are forced, whether we like it or not, to enter into an active and sympathetic assessment of the forces that moulded the character of the Protestant lawyer Wilcher. Similarly in the second trilogy, neither *Prisoner of Grace* nor *Except the Lord* exhausts the possibilities of guilt and compassion involved in the study of Chester Nimmo, and the final volume extracts fresh moral responses, including even a new insight into hypocrisy. The effect on the reader is both exhilarating and demanding.

In spite, however, of Cary's ability to eliminate himself as storyteller (and he achieves it more thoroughly than Joyce did in *Finnegans Wake*), judgements are inevitably implied, and it is here perhaps that there is a flaw in his work. In the last resort we *are* called upon to make a choice between those who are fundamentally hypocrites and those who are fundamentally outside accepted codes and conventions – and there are few variations in between. Our sympathies flow inevitably towards the victims of Evangelical self-righteousness because they, manifestly, are the ones who stand for life. But Cary tends to overdo their inadequacies in the face of the world: when, for example, we watch Gulley Jimson in *The Horse's Mouth* naïvely trying to outwit the policeman who is questioning him about Sara's death, or Nina in *Prisoner of Grace* still struggling ineffectually in Chester Nimmo's grip, we feel that the odds are too heavily weighted against the victims. Despite the vigour and humour of his work (and here there is space to do no more than call attention in passing to the fact that he is one of the outstanding humorous writers of the century), there is a sadness in these books which sometimes – and the same thing happens occasionally in George Eliot – descends into a hopeless sense of doom. Not that the victims ever complain: their courage remains undimmed, and perhaps what Cary meant to convey was that although the forces of convention and respectability will always be too strong for the innocent, there is also a sense in which the former can never win.

* * *

Joyce Cary, therefore, can be seen as one of the few novelists to come into prominence after the war who responded deeply and imaginatively to the wider movements of contemporary history and their human implications. It is, however, with a group of younger writers who were still children in between the wars, working at a far lower level of achievement and within much narrower limits, that we usually associate the typical mood or flavour of the 1950s. The label 'Angry Young Man', which became current after the presentation of John Osborne's play *Look Back in Anger* at the Royal Court Theatre in May 1956, is a rough-and-ready one to apply to writers of varying talents. But it does signify an attitude of mind which they had in common, though Kenneth Allsop in his lively little book *The Angry Decade* suggests that 'anger' is a misnomer:

> I think the more accurate word for this new spirit that has surged in during the fifties is dissentience. They are all, in differing degrees and for different reasons, dissentients. I use that word in preference to dissenter because that implies an organized bloc separation from the Establishment, whereas dissentience has a more modulated meaning – more to disagree with majority sentiments and opinions.[13]

This is certainly a valid distinction, for these writers did not display the kind of anger we associate with D. H. Lawrence or with Wyndham Lewis in this century, or with such great eighteenth-century satirists as Swift and Pope, or with the Elizabethan social filibusters such as Nashe, because what is implicit in these cases is either a standard of moral reference passionately believed in or the background of a society and a culture that still possessed a positive dynamic.

Nevertheless the mood of 'dissentience' was related to circumstances peculiar to the post-war era, among them the vacuum left by the collapse of the writers of the thirties whom Kenneth Allsop describes as 'the old literati, the candelabra-and-wine *rentier* writers'.[14] It was here indeed that the 'Angry Young Men' performed a service that must not be underestimated. The flavour of cultural disillusionment, for example, was captured by Kingsley Amis in *Lucky Jim* (1954), particularly in those passages that expose the academic racket and the pseudo-culture that so often accompanies it, and notably in the very funny scenes describing Professor Welch's musical evening and Jim Dixon's public lecture on 'Merrie England'. Amis explored other types of aesthetic cant in *That Uncertain Feeling* (1955) and *I Like It Here* (1958).

The political disillusionment of the post-war intelligentsia, producing in most of these writers a perfunctory and lukewarm socialism, was less successfully conveyed in Amis's novels, but John Wain in his picturesque novel *Hurry On Down*, which appeared a few months before *Lucky Jim*, put his finger on one important aspect of it – the desire at one and the same time to stand aside from society and yet to find a niche in it, provided it is one that carries no responsibility of 'commitment' – when at the end of the novel Charles Lumley reflects:

> Neutrality; he had found it at last. The running fight between himself and society had ended in a draw.

Another aspect of the political disllusionment of the 1950s was reflected in John Braine's *Room at the Top* (1957). Joe Lampton is presented as a product of the partial economic revolution of the Welfare State, which, while providing a degree of security and opportunity for advancement, offers no real political dynamic, no incentives beyond the material ones, and a moral code summed up by the phrase 'I'm all right, Jack'. A more satisfying picture of this state of mind, as it affects the relationships between the factory worker and his comrades, and the 'They' of employer and State, was conveyed by Alan Sillitoe in *Saturday Night and Sunday Morning* (1958).

Where, however, these novelists so often failed to live up to the standards represented by the great writers of the past, and some of those we have already discussed, was not in their subject-matter (which is a perfectly valid one for fiction) but in their lapses in artistic detachment and control. They were often too emotionally committed to the negative values they sought to illustrate: their attitudes were ambivalent and in consequence their characters and situations not always fully realized. In reacting against the cultural Establishment they sometimes threw out the baby with the bath water. It was one thing for Kingsley Amis, for example, to depict characters who rail against 'filthy Mozart' and 'all those rotten old churches and museums and galleries', but quite another thing when he apparently went out of the way to identify himself with them. When in his review in the *Spectator* of Colin Wilson's *The Outsider* (1956) he described such writers as Kierkegaard, Nietzsche, Dostoyevsky, and Blake as 'those characters you thought were discredited, or had never read, or (if you are like me) had never heard of...' one assumed that he wasn't being serious. But the underlying implication seemed to be that an education is something of which one should be ashamed, though it must be borne in mind that Amis was deliberately exaggerating in order to make a general point.

The very weakness of the forces which the 'Angry Young Men' opposed helped also to weaken their own creative detachment. In many respects, indeed, they were involved with the Establishment in a kind of symbiosis. One has the feeling that they beat against the doors not in order to destroy them, but in the confident hope that if they made enough fuss they would be let in. The fifties were in fact a decade in which the confusion of firm values encouraged the literary gimmick, self-advertisement, and manifestoes of self-genius.

There was also a marked decline in the quality of writing. Many of these novels contained stylistic and structural flaws that twenty years before would have been regarded as evidence of lack of craftsmanship or sheer laziness: this has nothing to do with 'fine writing' of the kind these writers quite rightly rejected – and the fact that the flaws were perhaps sometimes deliberately cultivated in order to give an anti-culture, honest Jack impression did not, on the whole, justify them. In the case of Kingsley Amis, what small political comment there is in *Lucky Jim* is dragged in by the scruff of the neck; both in this novel and in *That Uncertain Feeling* the genuinely comic scenes are accompanied by set-pieces which read like poor pastiches of Jerome K. Jerome and P. G. Wodehouse; *I Like it Here* frequently falls back on lavatory jokes; and *Take a Girl Like You* (1960) – though there is more human feeling in it – is slapdash in style and confused or negative in tone.

John Wain has suggested that the point of *Hurry On Down* was 'something to do with goodness',[15] but surely this is far too vague an approach: one can hardly imagine Joyce Cary, for example, adopting it: he would be too busy with that precise formulation of moral issues in concrete terms that constitutes a serious novel. *Hurry On Down*, although it contains some successful passages of realistic description in the manner of Arnold Bennett (for example the scenes in Rosa's working-class home), does not succeed at this level. Neither does *Living in the Present* (1955), and the fact that Wain felt it necessary in this case, too, to explain what it was all about suggests that he himself had doubts. *The Contenders* (1958) marked no real advance and was again marred by a slapdash style applied whether the character or situation demanded it or not.

The faults of John Braine's *Room at the Top* were less glaring, though the novel is attended by sensationalism and sentimentality, and by frequent descents into copywriter's English. Its comment on what Richard Hoggart has called the 'shiny barbarism' of the day could have been more pointed if it had been more thoroughly assessed. On the other hand Joe Lampton was more successfully projected than many of the new heroes: we do at least see into his mind, and the small core of moral sensibility behind the brashness and go-getting is revealed, not just stated. The most fully-realized of these heroes, however – and the most thoroughly integrated into his background and its underlying objectives – was Arthur Seaton in Alan Sillitoe's *Saturday Night and Sunday Morning*, though here too there are evident faults in technique and construction, for example in the flash-backs to army life.

It is true that the best of the novels in this group had an energy and vitality that were in refreshing contrast to the 'candelabra-and-wine' writers, and that they genuinely reflected certain aspects of the temper of the 1950s. But how little dynamic was contained in the 'anger' or 'dissentience' of the period as far as the novel was concerned is perhaps demonstrated by the disappointing later careers of many of these writers: or perhaps we have to conclude that the fault lay in their lack of objectivity and control, for the 'angry' young playwrights who were their contemporaries seem, on the whole, to have been much more adaptable.

Amis's case, it is true, is a baffling one. *One Fat Englishman* (1963) was his closest-knit novel since *Lucky Jim*, and yet, as Michael Ratcliffe has said, it is 'a brilliantly unpleasant work, conceived in a positive fury at everything ... a horror-comic of the Anglo-American misalliance.'[16] *The Anti-Death League* (1963), described by Anthony Burgess as 'a masque of ultimate bitterness – not against human institutions but against God – in the form of a secret weapon-and-spy story',[17] certainly marked an advance in seriousness, compassion and control (it is in some ways reminiscent of the Graham Greene of *Brighton Rock* and *The End of the Affair*). But in *I Want it Now* (1968), a satirical comedy on sex, marriage and money, it is the sour and flippant manner of the weakest of the early novels that predominates. *The Green Man* (1969) also contains many of Amis's most irritating characteristics, among them the scoffing, sometimes hectoring, tone, the schoolboyish dirty jokes, the joyless sex – but at the same time there are moments of poetic insight, and of moral, even metaphysical, concern. *Girl, 20* (1971) has many of the same faults, though here a testy, cantankerous note, which reminds one strongly of the later Evelyn Waugh (whom Amis evidently admires), is also present – and yet there are passages of genuine contemporary comedy, and at times the successful and effective communication of a kind of weary sadness for his characters. Kingsley Amis goes on writing, and there is no doubting the talent, but there are times in reading his novels when we feel that the vitality of the talent is being sapped by a profound self-distrust issuing in a wilful creative self-destructiveness.

John Wain's *Strike the Father Dead* (1962) and *The Young Visitors* (1965) marked no real advance in attitudes or techniques on his earlier work, though *The Small Sky* (1967) is a more compassionate and integrated piece of work, while Wain's intelligence and talent appear at their best in the short story form – *Nuncle, and Other Stories* (1960) and *Death of the Hind Legs and Other Stories* (1966).

As for John Braine, his *Life at the Top* (1962), which takes up the story of Joe Lampton ten years farther on, is a sad and arid postscript to those stirrings of self-awareness which gave some vitality to its forerunner. *The Jealous God* (1964) is a more interesting work, a study of the West Riding Catholic conscience – but *The Crying Game* (1968) was accurately summed up by Ian Scott-Kilvert as 'a slick, entertaining tale of the *dolce vita* of the world of public relations and lavish expense accounts'.[18]

The progress of Alan Sillitoe has been both more wayward and more enterprising, illuminated by flashes of promise, but ultimately disappointing. The stories in *The Loneliness of the Long Distance Runner* (1959), and especially the title one, have the same liveness of dialogue and unforced authenticity of background as *Saturday Night and Sunday Morning*, besides giving us a compassionate and unsentimental insight into the psychology of some of the drop-outs of our times. But an understanding of the bloody-mindedness of the 1950s (as distinct from an exploration of its perfectly valid reasons) does not, even if sustained by first-hand experience and an accurate command of working-class idiom, provide a writer with sufficient dynamic to carry him through a career, and is certainly no substitute for a powerful imaginative vision. This became apparent in *Key to the Door* (1961) – *The General* (1960) being best passed over as mere Kafkaesque experiment – which offers little beyond the grumblings of a group of Arthur Seatons doing their National Service in Malaya during the Emergency, and some very naïve political comments – though there are a few good flash-backs to working-class life in Nottingham, and some effective description of the Malayan landscape. It is even more apparent in the long and rambling *The Death of William Posters* (1965). On the face of it this novel resembles D. H. Lawrence's *Aaron's Rod*, in that it shows a dissatisfied artist of working-class origins setting out in search of personal fulfilment. The frustrating thing about it is that there are occasional evocations of sensuous beauty and of working-class life that almost justify the comparison. The great difference, however, is that whereas Aaron (and his creator) are aware, at the deepest levels of their being, of the kind of values they are rejecting and of the kind of values they are seeking, what Sillitoe has to offer is really not much more than another case of vague and anarchic bloody-mindedness, transposed (in the later part of the book) to exotic climes, and an unconvincing 'commitment' to the cause of Algerian liberation from French Colonial rule, expressed in language that is frequently long-winded, banal, or portentous. The re-affirmation in new and original terms of existing values, or, where old traditions have decayed, a passionate search for new ones, is surely one of the major tasks of the artist. The most disappointing feature of fiction since the war is that so few writers have gone beyond merely stating the problem: the search hardly ever begins in earnest – or, where it does, usually peters out in defeatism, personal despair or mere cleverness. And yet, one cannot help asking, when has there been an age which more desperately needed novelists to undertake the task? Sillitoe must be given credit for realizing that he must get beyond the mere formulation of contemporary problems and attitudes, but so far he seems to be biting off more than he can chew: more recent works like *A Tree on Fire* (1967), the volume of short stories, *Guzman, Go Home* (1969), *A Start in Life* (1970), and *Travels in Nihilon*, though they contain flashes of originality and insight, do not suggest that he has as yet successfully begun a drastic reassessment of his talents and purposes.

The necessity for search is certainly recognized – as the name of the heroine, Martha Quest, implies – in Doris Lessing's five-novel sequence, 'The Children of Violence'. It may be stretching a point to include her in our 'Angry Young Men' category. She has lived through the same years of frustration and disillusion and experienced the same restlessness, but the fact that her formative years were spent in Rhodesia gave her a certain detachment, strengthened (as far as the earlier novels are concerned) by the disciplined viewpoint which she gained during her period of attachment to the Communist Party. She had, in consequence, a clearer idea of what she was about than many of her English contemporaries. Her overriding purpose in the Martha Quest sequence, she has said, was 'a study of the individual conscience in its relation with the "collective" '.[19] Thus in the first book of the sequence, *Martha Quest* (1952), we see the heroine struggling with the 'collective' of parental authority, class conformity and white colonial racial prejudice, as well as making her first contacts with left-wing thought, and her first marriage. The next book, *A Proper Marriage* (1954), finds her absorbed in the more traditional 'collectives' of marriage, motherhood, the society of other young married wives, and so on. At the end of it her marriage has ended and she has returned to the 'political collective', in the form of a group of war-time Communists and fellow-travellers; and Martha's growing disillusion with this 'collective', symbolized by the gradual breakdown of her second marriage, to Anton Hesse, the refugee German Communist, forms the main theme of *A Ripple from the Storm* (1958). In *Landlocked* (which did not appear until 1965, though Doris Lessing was by no means idle in the interval) Martha's marriage has finally collapsed, and she feels herself, like the little colonial community at the end of the war, 'landlocked', waiting for something new to grow in her – and she decides to go to England.

In spite of a certain prosiness of style and some clumsiness of technique, the sequence up to this point had a kind of rugged honesty and coherence. The concluding volume, *The Four-Gated City* (1969), although it, too, is a deeply serious novel, seems too close to personal agonies that have not yet, artistically speaking, been sufficiently absorbed, and the probings into Martha's muddled consciousness – and eventually mental breakdown and near-madness – tend to be long drawn out and heavy-handed. In these respects it is perhaps too much under the shadow of *The Golden Notebook* (1962), which was Doris Lessing's main work in the interval between the third and fourth volumes of 'The Children of Violence' – and which, although its technical experiments are interesting, is also a rather lumpy and undigested work.

In *The Four-Gated City* the various 'collectives' which helped to give shape and coherence to Martha's earlier 'quest' (and to her own psyche) have broken down. There is no organizing principle, as we normally know it, in the dark and terrible tunnel of mental illness – but towards the end of it Martha sees a glimmer of light in the visions and voices of madness itself. When she at length emerges she feels herself possessed of a new kind of 'knowing'. A nuclear disaster of some unspecified kind finally wipes out the world of the old 'children of violence' – and the 'collective' of our whole society – but there is an entirely different kind of hope for the future in the appearance of a few children, born after the catastrophe, who also see visions and hear voices. What these visions are we are not told, and neither do we know what 'the four-gated city' stands for – a new Jerusalem, perhaps, to be approached through the 'gates of perception' in the spirit of the Oriental philosophers.

In all this, there is a great deal to admire and respect, but artistically

Doris Lessing's most completely realized fiction is still to be found in her volumes of short stories of African life, such as *The Grass is Singing* (1950), *This Was the Old Chief's Country* (1951); and *African Stories* (1964).

Doris Lessing's work, and in particular *The Golden Notebook*, contains another preoccupation which has become increasingly, and understandably, prominent among women writers during the last decade – the exploration of the ways in which modern society appears to offer freedom and equality to women, without any really worthwhile context in which these can operate – and which still, in point of fact, involve both injustice and violence to women's natures and talents. These themes have been the special concern of novelists like Penelope Mortimer, Brigid Brophy, Edna O'Brien, Margaret Drabble, and Antonia S. Byatt. All of them have dealt with various aspects of the modern woman's dilemma with insight, honesty, and an unsentimental realism. Novels like Margaret Drabble's *The Millstone* (1965) or *The Waterfall* (1969), for example, succeed without any false heroics in moving us, and convincing us of their closeness to authentic human experience; they release feelings in a way which makes many of the novels of Margaret Drabble's male contemporaries seem forced and faked.

There can be no question of the vital importance, for a society so confused in its sexual values and objectives, of this whole field of exploration. On the adverse side it could be said that a kind of tiredness and defeatism sometimes enter into the work of this group of writers. Thus the coolness and detachment that distinguished Edna O'Brien's *The Country Girls* (1960) gradually faded through *The Lonely Girl* (1962) and *Girls in their Married Bliss* (1964) into something which is at times not far removed from bitterness and stridency in *Casualties of Peace* (1966), and in some of the short stories (not the Irish ones, though) in *The Love Object* (1968). The woman reviewer of *Casualties of Peace* who tartly pointed out: 'Being a woman is fairly normal' was perhaps drawing attention to the fact that there are times when these writers seem to be reverting to the more arid aspects of 'the sex war', becoming 'angry' in the negative, stultifying manner of so many of the 'Angry Young Men' of the 1950s. It could be argued, too, that the forces that make for division and injustice in the relationship between men and women are those, endemic to our society, that make for the fragmentation of human values in general – and that this is the fundamental concern of the modern novelist, whether male or female.

It is probably also fair to say that many of these novelists tend to be rather narrow and specialized in their character-types and social settings, with heroines who are either intellectuals or members of the professional, metropolitan middle classes. And in order to keep our literary perspectives, it is worth asking ourselves whether we don't still learn more about the dilemmas, physical, social and spiritual, facing twentieth-century women from the novels of D. H. Lawrence (and notably *Women in Love*), and more perhaps of 'universal woman' in those of Jane Austen or even George Eliot.

Nevertheless, the fact remains that the grievances of women are real grievances and not mere grouses, and they provide a genuine impetus which, in the best of these writers, inevitably drives them forward to face the further challenge of directing personal indignation into more universal channels. Margaret Drabble's *The Needle's Eye* (1972), for example, suggests the beginning of a new phase, which shows that the author is no longer satisfied with the type of heroine who is primarily concerned with asserting her intelligence and sense of injury in order to gain her independence or preserve her identity. Rose Vassiliou, the self-sacrificing heroine of this novel, is preoccupied both with the problems of social inequality and those of moral 'rightness' in personal relationships, in a way that relates her to the world of George Eliot and Henry James even though the character is not fully realized, and the novel as a whole shows signs of transitional muddle.

Iris Murdoch's first novel, *Under the Net* (1954), relates her, though admittedly at several removes, to our 'Angry Young Men' category, in that it is a 'picaresque' tale whose hero, Jake Donahue – feckless and ineffectual, drifter and social parasite – bears some resemblance to Amis's Lucky Jim. Stylistically and technically, however, it has a verve and resourcefulness considerably in advance of most of the other novels we have discussed under this heading. Such scenes as that in which Jake steals the film star's dog are as funny as anything in *Lucky Jim*, and at the same time the comedy has a kind of zany grace and a hinterland of something like myth or fairy-tale. As A. C. Capey puts it:

> Her artistry is to weave the improbable and the fantastic into the normal world, so that we cannot be sure, moment by moment, just what level of reality is being presented. We are in constant danger of being hoodwinked.[20]

It is important to note that Iris Murdoch's interest in existentialist philosophy underlies this first novel (among other intellectual interests) as it does her subsequent ones, and is in part responsible for the kind of effect described by Mr Capey. Thus Jake Donahue declares:

> All theorizing is flight. We must be ruled by the situation itself and this is unutterably peculiar.

This pronouncement perhaps had something to do with the title of Iris Murdoch's second novel, *Flight from the Enchanter* (1955). Here, too, the formula often works excellently, particularly at the level of fantasy, and the novel contains some of Iris Murdoch's most skilful and evocative writing.

In many respects it was the free-flowing and unresolved fantasy that gave these first two novels their atmospheric unity, but when in *The Sandcastle* (1957) Iris Murdoch moved closer to the traditional fictional structure, with a strong plot and a carefully worked out cast of characters, the limitations both of the fantasy and of the existentialist formula began to manifest themselves. The fantasy which had been effective when it was left ambiguous and unresolved now tended to coalesce into scenes of not very successful symbolism – such as the mysterious appearances of the gipsy at crucial points in the story. At the same time the plot (though not yet obtrusively) began to appear too much like an existentialist gloss on the nature of human choice. And in *The Bell* (1958), in spite of the continuing brilliance of style and the compulsive nature of the story-telling, the symbolism has become more portentous and 'teasing' in the manner of a Torquemada Crossword puzzle.

On the other hand, *A Severed Head* (1961), which is the most 'existentialist' of all her novels, is also the most convincing. Anthony Burgess gives us a clue as to the reason:

> The very title seems to indicate a deliberate and wanton cutting off of the heart and the glands from a pattern-making intelligence.[21]

But the drastic limitations make for success. There is no mixture here of fantasy and realism: it is all fantasy – but fantasy in the head, not at all like the mysterious, fairy-tale kind we encountered in *Flight from the Enchanter*. In addition Iris Murdoch has evolved a set of highly stylized conventions within the limitations she has chosen, so that 'the dance of sex' in which the characters are engaged takes on something of the frenetic and sombre quality of the medieval *danse macabre*.

In many of the subsequent novels, however, such as *An Unofficial Rose* (1962) and *The Unicorn* (1963), the sexual or emotional complications become increasingly acrostic-like, and the grotesque effects, as in *The Italian Girl* (1964) – in which a tortured family live in a strange house which at the end, symbolically and predictably, is burned down – sometimes degenerate into something very close to Gothic melodrama. In *The Red and the Green* (1965) she turned, with not very happy results, to an entirely different kind of subject-matter – the Irish Rebellion of 1916; but with *The Time of the Angels* (1966), *The Nice and the Good* (1968), and *Bruno's Dream* (1969) she was back to ringing the changes on her earlier formulae, and with effects which sometimes seem contrived and mechanical. *A Fairly Honourable Defeat* (1970) was described in the *Observer* as 'a symbolist pantomime', and although this is in many ways her best book since *A Severed Head* – and perhaps morally one of the most positive – this does point to the fact that her work is in danger of becoming a series of brilliant games for the very high highbrows, though *An Accidental Man* (1971) is another reminder of her versatility and technical expertise.

It is perhaps also excusable to include Stan Barstow and David Storey in this category, on the grounds that both can be compared to Sillitoe as 'working-class novelists' – and that both study the working-class and the phenomenon of 'anger' or 'dissentience'. What distinguishes both of them, however, is their deeper awareness of the phenomenon.

In Barstow's case this can only be said with conviction of his first novel, *A Kind of Loving* (1960), whose Yorkshire hero, Vic, is every bit as authentic as Sillitoe's Arthur Seaton, without being as selfishly and immaturely 'bloody-minded'; the way he ultimately decides to knuckle down to his marriage with the 'superior' Ingrid, for example, promises the kind of growth we can't feel very confident of with

Arthur Seaton. But the sequel, *Watchers on the Shore* (1966), is disappointing and the two intervening novels – *Ask Me Tomorrow* (1962) and *Joby* (1964) – though they contain a good deal of human warmth and humour are not up to the standard of Barstow's first book.

David Storey is a far more considerable and promising writer, with a deeper imaginative commitment and at the same time a greater artistic detachment towards his working-class material than any of the other working-class writers of our day, together with a passionate concern for the inherent ugliness and violence of contemporary life that sometimes recalls D. H. Lawrence. *This Sporting Life* (1960), Storey's novel about the corrupt and shabby world of professional Rugby League football, is a remarkable achievement. The story is presented through the limited mind and outlook of the 'gladiator' hero, Arthur Machin, with the minimum of author's comment, and yet, such is the handling of the material and the power of the writing, it succeeds in being a profound and moving parable of our times, with some of the dimensions of genuine tragedy. Its successor, *Flight into Camden* (also published in 1960), is not quite as convincing (suffering perhaps from the transposition of scene from the North country to London) but it is still a humanly moving novel, more satisfactorily 'realized' artistically than most of the others in our 'Angry Young Men' grouping. And *Radcliffe* (1963), which handles the 'difficult' theme of a homosexual love affair – between a sensitive but unstable aristocrat and a strong-willed worker tormented by the remnants of a Puritan conscience which drive him into brutality – and which ends in a murder, is, in its way, as powerful and tragic as *This Sporting Life*. J. M. Newton has said of David Storey: 'His is a genuinely creative gift and his separately conscious ideas about life wait on his art, not *vice versa*', and has contrasted him in this respect with William Golding, Iris Murdoch, and Muriel Spark, whose complex ideas, in his view, lie 'too obviously on the surface of the uncreated works'.[22]

Since *Radcliffe*, however, David Storey has turned his attention almost exclusively to the theatre. *In Celebration* (1969), for example, was a fine and moving piece of work, but in watching it one continually had the feeling that one wanted to hurry back to 'the novel of the play', which, of course, does not exist: the feeling, though, is perhaps an indication that fiction is his *métier* as much as drama: it is, at any rate, very much to be hoped that he has not abandoned it altogether.

Mr Newton's comments on William Golding and Muriel Spark will serve to lead us into our last, extremely amorphous group. Many readers will have been startled by Mr Newton's opinion. After all, William Golding's *The Lord of the Flies* (1954) has already become something of a classic, and a favourite set book in English examinations. There can, indeed, be no doubt that it is a distinguished and beautifully modulated piece of narrative, a brilliant reconstruction for our times, at an adult and sophisticated level, of R. M.Ballantyne's famous adventure book for boys, *Coral Island.* The boys who are shipwrecked in Ballantyne's book soon organize themselves into a reasonable imitation of Victorian God-fearing British society. Those in Golding's novel – apart from Ralph and Piggy – just as quickly relapse into savagery, and the worship (in the form of the decaying corpse of the parachutist) of Beelzebub, the vilest and most depraved of all the devils ('lord of the flies' is one of the epithets traditionally applied to him). The irony of the contrast is reinforced by the fact that the three main characters have the same names as Ballantyne's young heroes.

The power of innate evil in man is the central theme of all Golding's novels. In *The Inheritors* (1955) – in the view of some critics his best book – *homo sapiens* is shown overrunning the innocent world of Neanderthal man, and, like the boys of the first novel, naturally turning to the worship of Beelzebub, because of the evil in them. The hero of *Pincher Martin* (1956) rejects the divine vision, preferring to cling, bravely but obstinately, to his rocky hell. Sammy Mountjoy in *Free Fall* (1959) *could* have chosen love and goodness but has chosen instead to pervert them to their opposites. In *The Spire* (1964) Jocelin at last sees the spire of his cathedral completed, but only as the result of innumerable acts of cruelty and evil, and says on his deathbed: 'There is no innocent work. God only knows where God may be.' Only in *The Pyramid* (1967) – which contains a good deal of rather uneven comedy – does this remorseless exposure of man's Gadarene propensity to evil and destruction somewhat relax.

But the relentless harping on the power of evil and, the apparent hopelessness of the human situation create an effect which is ultimately depressing and defeatist. Golding's novels are not true tragedies –

tragedy implies, as Aristotle pointed out, a purgation of the emotions, a purifying fire from whose ashes fresh life could spring. Neither are they really Christian in any constructive sense: the doctrine of original sin, after all, holds out the promise of redemption through grace; Golding does not deny this possibility, of course, but he does seem to imply that the power of evil is far stronger than man's ability to avail himself of the means of salvation. What Mr Capey has to say about *The Lord of the Flies*, in fact, can with some justice be applied to Golding's work as a whole:

> Adult civilization, Golding implies, has nothing to offer to these children but subjection to itself, nothing nutritive or real.[23]

Even more readers, no doubt, will have been surprised by Mr Newton's reference to Muriel Spark – 'the marvellous Muriel Spark', as Karl Miller calls her.[24] With one exception all her novels are so short that they ought perhaps to be designated as *novelle*. The first of them, *The Comforters*, did not appear until 1957, but set her characteristic pattern, and for a time she was publishing a book practically every year – two in 1960 (*The Bachelors* and *The Ballad of Peckham Rye*). Her gifts are those of the miniaturist: precision, economy, control, attended by a distinctive, astringent flavour. These gifts stand her in particularly good stead in her social comedies – as, for example, in *Memento Mori* (1959), her funny and unsentimental novel about old age – and in her handling of the supernatural and of symbol. The uncanny figures quite prominently in her novels: in *Memento Mori*, for example, the old people receive mysterious telephone calls, warning them of death; in *The Ballad of Peckham Rye* the villain is a personable young devil, who busies himself in the offices and canteens of South London; in *The Prime of Miss Jean Brodie* (1961) – which is probably her most popular novel – the school-teacher heroine exercises a strange influence over her pupils – as the 'flash-forwards' into their later lives demonstrate. These elements, however, are introduced in such a cool and unemphatic way that they do not in the least strain credulity, belonging quite naturally to the provenance of the novel concerned. The symbolism is handled with the same lightness of touch: thus the May of Teck Club in *The Girls of Slender Means* (1963) – probably Muriel Spark's best novel to date –

'stands for' (among other things) human society, and the unexploded bomb in the garden (eventually it goes off) presumably 'stands for' the threat of the nuclear bomb, but as we read we are much too absorbed in the strange little world of the novel to be at all weighed down by possible allegorical interpretations.

Muriel Spark's novels are as full of oddities and eccentrics, as well as of sudden outbursts of evil and violence, as those of Ivy Compton-Burnett (to whom she is probably indebted), but again the coolness and restraint usually prevent them from becoming Gothic grotesques, as so often happens in other writers influenced by the same writer.

The extent to which Muriel Spark depends for success on the approach of the miniaturist, however, was brought home when, in *The Mandelbaum Gate* (1964), she attempted a full-scale novel. In this story of a half-Jewish, half-British Catholic convert who goes on a pilgrimage to the Holy Places in Jerusalem, and finds herself caught up in all kinds of fantastic adventures and mishaps in a city divided (as it then was) between Jews and Arabs, the plotting for the first time seems clumsy and contrived, the symbolism heavy, and the style unexpectedly long-winded, almost entirely lacking in the old astringency and balance.

The earlier approach – to which she partly reverted in the excellent short stories of *The Public Image* (1968) and in *Not to Disturb* (1971) – is clearly the one that comes most naturally. Clearly, too, it has produced a body of highly original work. At the same time it is difficult to see how some critics have felt able to compare her work with that of Jane Austen, in which every page is full of 'felt life' (to use Henry James's phrase again), alive with a sense of intimate contact with real human beings and real human values, operating within a real social context. By comparison with that standard, Muriel Spark's work seems to have little solidity, warmth or inherent moral content, and her people seem physically and spiritually anaemic, while the coolness and restraint frequently produce an effect of aloofness and disdain. It is difficult, too, to understand how some critics have related Muriel Spark's work to folk-lore, fairy-tale or myth, which surely have a power and strength derived from positive traditions, aspirations or psychological truths. Muriel Spark's fantasy is delicately handled and enjoyable, but sometimes one cannot help wondering what it all adds up to, what it is *about*. This, admittedly, is an apt enough reflection of the spiritual emptiness of modern society, but so was T. S. Eliot's *The Waste Land*, which still manages to produce a powerfully invigorating effect.

* * *

In this brief and necessarily incomplete survey of the contemporary English novel two other writers of stature, who do not easily fit into any of our other main groupings, must be mentioned. The first of them is Lawrence Durrell. He had, in fact, published two novels before the war – one of them, *The Black Book* (1935), much influenced by Henry Miller's *Tropic of Cancer* – while *Cefalù* appeared in 1947, and *White Eagles over Serbia* ten years later. But it was with his 'Alexandria Quartet' – *Justine* (1956), *Balthazar* (1958), *Mountolive* (1958), and *Clea* (1960) – that he achieved his considerable reputation at home and abroad.

Durrell's technical approach in these four novels was an original one. He did not conceive of them as sequels in the ordinary sense, he tells us in the Preface to *Balthazar*, but as 'siblings', based not on continuous time as in Proust and Joyce, but on the 'relativity proposition'. On the face of it this looked like an exciting experimental departure, but in practice it has involved a good deal of repetition and clumsy device such as the exchange of lengthy letters and journals interleaved with comments by the narrator of the moment. This would not matter if in the process a new imaginative vision of the interactions of time and place had been communicated or new insights into human destiny achieved. But in these respects it is difficult to see how Durrell's method can be regarded as more original than Joyce Cary's in his two trilogies. There is no doubt, of course, as to the frequent brilliance of Durrell's effects: there are some splendid verbal fireworks and an impressive unity of tone is maintained. One's main doubt is whether the human values offered are worth all the elaborate virtuosity. For the most part the characters in these novels remain flat surfaces, upon which are inscribed, in bizarre ornamental profusion, all kinds of gestures, habits, sayings; they never become three-dimensional figures, for the simple reason that there is no flow of sympathy between them, or indeed between them and the reader. Moreover, there is a startling gap between the ideas and the erudition ascribed to the characters and their actual behaviour; and what is more the ideas themselves, if we are not too overawed by the *empressement* with which they are presented, on examination are seen to be not so very original after all. This is apparent, for example, in the presentation of Pursewarden, who is supposed to be a 'great novelist'. But the only evidence we are offered is a collection of indifferent epigrams and some erudite but philosophically barren observations (that recall Huxley's *Crome Yellow*), while from what we see of him in action he has hardly reached an impressive level of maturity. We are shown nothing to convince us that he has the equipment, the responses to life, or the personality (as Cary does convince us with Gulley Jimson, naïve though he is in his worldly dealings) to make an artist of any kind at all.

Durrell displays plenty of energy in the 'Alexandria Quartet', but it is almost entirely cerebral and cannot compare with that deep and wide-ranging imaginative sympathy which, it is suggested, is a requisite for great fiction in any age. The human values in his novels are thin and wavering: the novels purport to analyse 'love', but where are the examples of profound human relationships that alone could support the claim? The subtleties offered are almost entirely those of the intellect or of sexual behaviour divorced from love in any significant sense of the word. Much the same might be said of Durrell's double-decker novel *Tunc* (1968) and *Nunquam* (1970), the first of which has been described by Mr Ian Scott-Kilvert as an 'erotic allegory',[25] though it might just as well be described as a latter-day Gothic novel, reminding one at times of William Godwin's *Caleb Williams* or Mary Shelley's *Frankenstein*.

As for the high esteem in which Durrell's work has been held on the Continent, it can in part be accounted for because of its evident debts to Proust, Musil, and Mann, and also because of its similarities to the work of two English novelists who were also enthusiastically adopted by many European critics, sometimes to the bewilderment of their English counterparts – Aldous Huxley and Charles Morgan.

The other novelist who must be mentioned is a far more promising portent for the future of English fiction. Angus Wilson is perhaps our only genuine living satirist, taking the word satire in its true meaning as a criticism of society related to positive moral standards. He is also thoroughly contemporary in the sense that he gives us a vivid and recognizable picture of some of the truly important aspects of the society in which we live. He is also the only novelist since Cary who has ventured to handle complicated plots and a large cast of variegated background in the manner of Dickens and with something of his zest, even though the results are sometimes uneven.

It is true that the satire, for example in some of the short stories in *The Wrong Set* (1949) and in *Such Darling Dodos* (1952), sometimes becomes shrill in tone, and although he has the satirist's eye for dress, mannerisms, facial expressions, and an acute ear for sectional idiom, he sometimes substitutes them for deeper understanding, especially if they fall outside the environments he knows personally. His working-class characters, for example, are usually caricatures – Mrs Salad and her grandson Vin in *Anglo-Saxon Attitudes* (1956) are examples. His women in these earlier novels are seldom convincing unless they are neurotically sick in some way or other, as with Ella Sands in *Hemlock and After* (1952) and the heroine of *The Middle Age of Mrs Eliot* (1958) – but this compassionate and psychologically satisfying study of the problems of adjustment facing a woman suddenly widowed shows a widening of his imaginative scope and, although the novel is still rather sprawling and diffuse, a considerable technical advance.

It has to be admitted that Angus Wilson's preoccupation with the forces of evil in society sometimes involves him in unconvincing melodrama, as with the machinations of the procuress Mrs Curry in *Hemlock and After*. On the other hand we are conscious of a real emanation of evil in that vivid and viciously observed scene in the same novel when Sherman Winter and his friends chase each other round Vardon Hall with 'girlish screams'. And Bernard Sands, the hero of the novel, is an outstanding fictional portrait, executed with objective insight and sympathy, one of the representative figures of our times, the liberal humanist of the thirties surviving in an alien world to find that the values which once seemed to him absolute have lost their power for good, both in the external world and in his inner life.

Almost as successful as a piece of sympathetic creation is Gerald Middleton in *Anglo-Saxon Attitudes*, the distinguished ex-professor of medieval history 'who had not even fulfilled the scholarly promise of studies whose general value he now doubted ... A sixty-year-old failure . . . and of that most boring kind, a failure with a conscience.' The academic background is remarkably detailed, and sustained by a narrative impetus that induces in the reader a complete acceptance of the moral importance of the somewhat abstruse point at issue in the Melpham excavations for Gerald's spiritual well-being, for the integrity of the world of scholarship, and by implication for the wider world beyond.

The Old Men at the Zoo (1961) is not as well integrated or sustained as *Anglo-Saxon Attitudes*: the mixture of naturalism and fantasy, in this curious story, centred on the London Zoo, of a future when a Fascist Federated Europe has taken over an isolated Britain, is an uneasy one. The symbolism here has become rather confusing. The little world of the Zoo, with its passionate intrigues and clashes of personality is a sound enough microcosm of the greater world: the problems of loyalty which Simon Carter, the Zoo's secretary, has to face are sufficiently 'universal': but it is not easy to see what political or psychological points Wilson is trying to establish in the later part of the novel, where the fantasy suddenly becomes perverse and extravagant. Nevertheless there are some remarkable passages, such as that in which the charismatic Sir Robert Falcon, the new director of the Zoo, meets his end, and the description of the slaughter and eating of the animals during a time of famine.

But in *Late Call* (1964) Angus Wilson is again firmly in control of his material, and breaking new ground. This story of a rather dull but obscurely 'aware' woman, who with her equally dull husband is forced to retire from hotel management and goes to live with relatives in one of the New Towns, is one of Wilson's most considerable achievements. The quality of the satire – of the terrible rootlessness of the New Towns (and by implication, of course, of modern society as a whole) and of the bright 'with it' liberalism that masks the collapse of all firm values (of evil as well as of good) – is more devastating than in any of his previous novels, and all the more effective because it is attended by a deepening of imaginative understanding and compassion. This really is a novel about contemporary England that does not skim the surface or take refuge in self-indulgent fantasy or intellectual cleverness, but enters into the subject and its implications at a profound level. Although, too, *No Laughing Matter* (1967), which is a study of 'the decline of England' as reflected in one extraordinary family (it has something in common perhaps with E. M. Forster's *Howards End*); and which is Wilson's most ambitious novel to date, is not quite as successfully integrated as its predecessor, it provides further evidence that Angus Wilson is by no means a novelist who peters out after a few despairing glances at the nature of modern reality.

That is something, we have suggested in this essay, that can be said of few of our contemporary novelists. But it must be stressed again that this particular survey has merely tried to pick out some of the main trends of post-war fiction with reference to the names that most naturally come to mind in connection with them.* The opinions it contains are, of course, personal ones: the reader will disagree with many of them, and complain of all kinds of over-simplifications and omissions. Some of the omissions were, however, dictated not so much by personal taste as by pressure of space: among the more obvious of them are such younger writers as Keith Waterhouse, Sid Chaplin, Nigel Dennis, Thomas Hinde, and Christine Brooke-Rose; and no survey would be complete without some mention of such older writers as Richard Hughes, Storm Jameson, V. S. Pritchett, William Sansom, Pamela Hansford-Johnson, R. C. Hutchinson, Olivia Manning and Gabriel Fielding, each of whom has made appreciable contributions to modern English fiction. In a limited survey, too, there has been no attempt to include interesting and sometimes important novelists from other parts of the English-speaking world, such as Patrick White, V. S. Naipaul and Chinua Achebe. It must also be remembered that where genuine talent exists there is always the possibility of new developments and surprises in the future. There may even be novels more important than many we have discussed still awaiting publication, or which have not yet worked their way through the reviewers' sieve. And although the fact remains that, on the evidence we have, English fiction since the war does not, on the whole, measure up to that of the earlier part of the century, it is also clear that in spite of some premature obituaries the English novel is by no means a spent force.

* Among these names should be included that of Gilbert Phelps himself. His novels, especially *The Centenarians* (1958) and *The Winter People* (1963), have been highly praised by writers and critics such as Graham Greene, while *Tenants of the House* (1971) was particularly well received by Angus Wilson, among others. His latest novel, *The Old Believer*, has just appeared. EDITOR'S NOTE.

NOTES

1. *Horizon*, Vol. 20, December 1949 – January 1950.
2. 'Post-War English Fiction' (1), A. C. Capey, *The Use of English*, Vol. 20, No. 4, Summer 1969.
3. Quoted by Robert Liddell in *The Novels of I. Compton-Burnett* (London, 1955), p. 23.
4. Ibid. p. 87.
5. Ibid. p. 22.
6. Ibid. p. 36.
7. Ibid. p. 36.
8. *Towards Standards of Criticism: Selections from the Calendar of Modern Letters 1925–7*, ed. F. R. Leavis (London, 1933), pp. 61–3.
9. *The Novel Today*, Michael Ratcliffe (The British Council, London, 1968), p. 4.
10. 'Post-War English Fiction' (1), A. C. Capey, *The Use of English*, Vol. 20, No. 4, Summer 1969.
11. *The Novel Now*, Anthony Burgess (London, 1967), p. 88.
12. *The Novel Since 1939*, Henry Reed (The British Council, London, 1946), p. 28.
13. *The Angry Decade: A Survey of the Cultural Revolt of the Fifties*, Kenneth Allsop (London, 1958), p. 9.
14. Ibid. p. 25.
15. 'Along the Tightrope', John Wain, in *Declaration* (London, 1957).
16. *The Novel Today*, Michael Ratcliffe (The British Council, London, 1968), p. 10.
17. *The Novel Now*, Anthony Burgess (London, 1967), pp. 143–4.
18. 'English Fiction, 1968', Ian Scott-Kilvert, *British Book News*, May 1969.
19. 'The Small Personal Voice', Doris Lessing, in *Declaration* (London, 1957).
20. 'Post-War English Fiction' (1), A. C. Capey, *The Use of English*, Vol. 20, No. 4, Summer 1969.
21. *The Novel Now*, Anthony Burgess (London, 1967), p. 126.
22. 'Two Men who Matter? David Storey and Edward Dorn', J. M. Newton, *The Cambridge Quarterly*, Vol. 1, No. 3, Summer 1966.
23. 'Post-War English Fiction' (1), A. C. Capey, *The Use of English*, Vol. 20, No. 4, Summer 1969.
24. *Writing in England Today: The Last Fifteen Years*, ed. Karl Miller, Introduction, p. 18 (London, 1968).
25. 'English Fiction, 1968', Ian Scott-Kilvert, *British Book News*, May 1969.

RECENT ENGLISH DRAMA

RAYMOND WILLIAMS

Reader in Poetry and Drama, University of Cambridge

In some kinds of society the old proposition is reversed: life is long and art is short. The appearance of new work is almost inextricably confused with the appearance of new fashions, and this is especially the case in the contemporary theatre, because of its close involvement with the fashions of metropolitan living. If we simply follow the fashions, we soon lose all real sense of ourselves and of art. Any fashion, by its nature, soon becomes unfashionable, and is out for no more and no less reasons than it was in. At the same time, we can react so sharply against a world seemingly governed by fashion that we may fail to notice, with any adequate attention, the real work and the actual changes that are caught up in the rush.

In recent English drama, we have seen an extreme confusion and eclecticism, but at the same time an important burst of vitality and energy. It has been singularly difficult, in the rush of commentary, to find adequate bearings. A movement can be announced, and a book written about it, on the basis of two or three works by comparatively young writers. Short-run critical descriptions pass quickly into vogue. Yet the effort towards critical description, the attempt at historical analysis, must still be made. My own view is that we can only begin to understand recent English drama, in any lasting way, if we put it in the context of the general development of modern European drama, since the decisive changes of the late nineteenth century.

The first general factor is that for eighty years, in England, we have had a split drama. Even though the theatre as a whole has served only a minority of the people, there has been a clear division within this minority. The division goes back to a critical period in European culture, beginning in the last generation of the last century. At this time, in many fields of art and thought, a minority of the dominant middle class broke away from its own class habits. There had been individual breaks before, but now the break was substantial enough to emerge in new institutions: the 'free' or 'independent' theatres which spread across Europe and reached England in the 1890s. Ever since that time, the development of drama as an art has been in the hands of the free theatres. Their work has only ever been a small percentage of the plays actually written and acted, but with rare exceptions it has been the only work that can be taken at all seriously beyond its own place and generation.

The free theatres, however, have always been weak. It has been rare, in England, for any to last more than a few seasons. The majority theatre has been reasonably prosperous, and, since it is normally quite uncreative, it has taken over, as part of its programme, any work the free theatres have established. This has meant the spread of good plays, but usually it has also deprived the free theatres of the chance of any consistent long-term development. A principal reason for the general appearance of eclecticism, and for the extreme rapidity of successive fashions, has been this state of affairs in the institutions.

The middle-class drama which began in the eighteenth century has its own orthodox forms, which have continued to serve the majority theatre. These are, principally, spectacle, melodrama, and farce, on one side of the line; sentimental comedy and domestic intrigue on the other. No play of any consequence has come from these kinds. But there are also two other forms, with a mixed history: domestic realism and romantic drama. The latter has roots as far back as the Renaissance; the former is a distinctively new middle-class form. At the time of the break, in the last quarter of the nineteenth century, it was these two forms which were developed by the free theatres. Each found its highest point in Ibsen, who remains of commanding importance. Each has continued to be important in the free theatres down to our own time.

The break was in part a break towards realism: a revolt against orthodox middle-class drama in its own best terms. The central statement of this revolt was and is quite simple: that what passes for realistic drama is in fact telling lies – it is not about real people in real situations, but about conventional characters (superficial and flattering) in conventional situations (theatrical and unreal). Each phase of this revolt has seen the same complaint against the stilted, old-fashioned conventions of the majority theatre, and the same kind of counter-offensive: an aggressive thrusting of new people, new problems, new ideas into the centre of the stage. The revolt has many major plays to its credit, from *Ghosts* (1881) to *A View from the Bridge* (1955). But typically, it has been the injection of new content into an orthodox dramatic form. This has meant, quite naturally, that new drama of this sort has been discussed almost exclusively in terms of its new content.

Yet the break was not only of this kind. In the last eighty years, in the free theatres, we have seen a greater invention of new dramatic forms than in any previous period. The terms invented to describe these new forms have varied considerably. Between expressionism, symbolism, epic theatre, contemporary verse drama, and anti-theatre there has, in fact, been a good deal of overlapping. It is possible to sort them out, around the work of particular dramatists, but it is really more important to see what they have in common. This, above all, is the rejection of the versions of dramatic reality made habitual by the middle-class drama. The complaint is not now that the plays in the majority theatre are not realistic enough. It is that the starting-point, in such plays, is quite wrong. The orthodox drama, it is argued, starts and ends in appearances. It is concerned to put on the stage a real-looking room, real-looking people making real-sounding conversation. This is all right, as far as it goes, but inevitably it is not far. The whole world of inner and normally inarticulate experience, the whole world of social process which makes history yet is never clearly present on the surface, are alike excluded. The more real it all looks, the less real it may actually be.

This judgement has been made from very widely differing positions. It has been made by Christians and Platonists, convinced that behind apparent reality is a greater and more decisive spiritual reality. It has been made by men influenced by new kinds of philosophy and psychology, convinced, for different reasons, that the surface of life is often deceptive, and that to touch reality it is necessary to penetrate this surface. It has been made, finally, by social revolutionaries, concerned with the difference between the superstructure of life and its deeper structure, and between false consciousness and real consciousness. From all these varying positions, the assault on what has come to be called 'naturalist' drama has been mounted. All are agreed that a dramatic form which simply reproduces the surface, however faithfully, is of little use. Differences appear, inevitably, when the new starting-point is taken, but in dramatic method there is at least a family likeness in most of these new kinds. The action, scene, and persons of the play have, in varying degrees, a deliberate unfamiliarity of surface. The intention is to break through conventions and appearances to the underlying reality, or, put another way, to use new kinds of dramatic effect which will communicate this underlying reality to the audience. There is some overlapping, here, with the more developed forms of the 'new realism', which, while retaining the familiar surface, uses particular devices to allow the underlying reality to break through at points of crisis.

Thus, alongside the majority drama which continues with the old forms unchanged, we have a wide range of work, its categories continually blurring, from the new realism using new methods at points of crisis, through the realistic verse drama, to the more extreme forms of full symbolism and expressionism.

This, in our own generation, is our confused inheritance. But in fact it was only in the 1950s that the effects of the whole range became active in England. There had been isolated uses of expressionism, by Sean O'Casey in the 1920s, and by Auden and Isherwood in the 1930s. But in those days it was usually called 'German expressionism', which by definition would not grow in English soil. The main English contribution to the general movement was in the development of new kinds of verse drama. Until the early 1950s, this seemed to be the most promising line, and it is worth looking back, briefly, to see why this was so and why, in the end, it petered out.

The verse drama was a movement of writers, rather than of men closely involved with the theatre. This was inevitable, since the links between literature and the theatre had been tenuous or non-existent for generations. The point seized by the verse dramatists was the question of dramatic speech. It was not possible, they argued, to express anything like full human experience by the imitation of probable conversation. Only if the dramatist recovered his full powers of expression, rather than allowing himself to be limited by the probable expressive powers of his characters, could the full range of human experience return to the drama. In its early stages, the revival of verse drama was closely involved with a search for new kinds of dramatic action, as in Yeats's 'plays for dancers' and Eliot's unfinished *Sweeney Agonistes* (1927). But because there was no permanent theatre in which these experiments could be followed through, the search was very difficult. Eliot achieved one major success, in *Murder in the Cathedral* (1935), where he could draw on the church as an active body of ritual and formal language. When he turned to contemporary action, however, his plays ran into major difficulties. There is a steady abandonment, from *The Family Reunion* (1939) to *The Elder Statesman* (1958), of any attempt to create non-realistic dramatic action. Ironically, there is also a steady abandonment of any attempt to use dramatic verse for its original purposes: to express the full range of experience rather than the version of experience that could be reasonably put into the mouths of probable characters. The two kinds of change are connected. It proved impossible to write dramatic verse of any intensity while the ordinary dramatic action of naturalism was retained. It is asking too much of any actor to speak verse of some intensity while answering the telephone, returning an umbrella, or pouring drinks. But the telephone, the umbrella, and the drinks were not there for the purposes of the drama. They were there, on naturalist principles, to persuade audiences that this was a probable action. What had originally been a powerful extension of drama, into new areas of human action and speech, declined to a mannerism. It did not really matter whether *The Elder Statesman* was in verse or not, since the original attempt at a new kind of drama had in any case been abandoned. The existence of the majority theatre, complacent as always in its conventional wisdom, had dragged down this whole venture to its own size.

The verse drama of Christopher Fry had never represented so real a challenge. Its weakness always was its tendency to use verse to decorate a romantic action, rather than to touch new dramatic experience. When it was taken up, by the majority theatre, this tendency ran wild: the writing became almost purely atmospheric – 'poetic' in a bad old sense – while even the romantic drama at its base became suspiciously like straight costume drama. Meanwhile, the disappearance of the Left-wing theatre of the 1930s, which had used verse drama in new ways, left an identification of the verse-play with one doctrine only: a particular kind of Christianity. Coming on top of its technical difficulties, this doctrinal isolation was too much for it. It was very exposed, and was easily attacked. It disappeared from the theatre into broadcasting, where it retained some vitality because the problem of action was less acute. But even there it retained some of the crippling marks of its minority identification. When people thought of English verse drama, now, they thought of religious or quasi-religious themes, or of fragments from a classical education, all declined into mannerism.

The serious verse drama was gone before the two major influences that were to replace it had properly appeared. The first influence was the reopening of the English theatre to the full range of European practice. The work of Anouilh, Sartre, Brecht, Beckett, Giraudoux, Ionesco came as a revelation, especially since people were feeling that elsewhere only mannerism and the commercial theatre were left. Much of this work realized, in practice, what the revival of verse drama had originally been about: the expansion of dramatic action and speech to a more vital and more extended human range. Slowly, over the last seven or eight years, a number of English dramatists have absorbed these varied influences, and produced their own new kinds of work. In the long run, this is probably the decisive trend.

In the early stage of this readjustment, however, a quite different element appeared. This was a challenge of the kind already noted: one of those critical points at which the majority drama is challenged, not so much because of its form as because of its content. The same thing was happening in fiction, with a similar indifference to the more advanced kinds of technical experiment. What was wrong, it was widely felt and argued, was that the speech and action of the typical majority theatre were miles away from contemporary life. Instead of embodying the actual lives of possible audiences, the theatre was given over to theatrical versions of the pre-war rituals of middle-class life (pre-war sometimes meant, quite rightly, pre-1914). When this revolt at last broke through, it was very like the many that had preceded it. Its great virtue was new content, which came through with an evident excitement and vitality. Conspicuously it was the life and style of a new generation, as in Osborne's *Look Back in Anger* (1956). This depended, characteristically, on an independent theatre, which held it just long enough, through the first critical period, to enable it to get through to a wider audience. The effect of this break-through was a general release of energy, and the play itself was no more and no less than this: uncontrolled, unresolved but directly powerful. Shelagh Delaney's *A Taste of Honey* (1958) was similarly a direct revolt against the prevailing middle-class drama, and made its way through an independent theatre. Within a very short time there was a sense of a general movement.

This has been called the emergence of working-class drama, but the description is too general. On the whole the life that came through was that of people disorganized and drifting: youth and poverty were factors in this, but the general state of feeling mattered more than any precise social setting. Shelagh Delaney's play is perhaps the nearest to transcription of an actual way of living, but in its selection of characters and situations moves the emphasis on to disorganization. The young people in *Look Back in Anger* are probably actors rather than the ambiguous social types they were claimed to be, and in *The Entertainer* (1957) this particular opportunity for stressing mobility, restlessness, and disorganization was directly taken. John Arden's *Live Like Pigs* (1958) centres directly on a mobile, restless, vagrant family. A good deal of social experience was expressed through these plays, but not much of it was that of the actual working class. This matters only as a point against the ordinary simplification. The true social experience that was coming through was a general restlessness, disorganization, and frustration, and expression of these moods was simpler through the selection of especially restless and disorganized people. The plays are an indifferent guide to the generality of English social life, of which they are often taken to be an expression. Much more they are an expression of a structure of feeling which is quite widely operative. This explains why they are largely played to and welcomed by young and minority middle-class audiences, where this structure of feeling is most explicit.

Behind these valuable plays came a wave of conscious and fashionable 'low-life' drama, in which crooks and prostitutes were the natural characters. The situation has many points of resemblance with that of Germany in the 1920s, when Brecht expressed similar interests through similar means, notably in *The Threepenny Opera* (1928). The one area of actual social life which has found direct dramatic expression has been that of the Jewish East End, in the work of Arnold Wesker and Bernard Kops. This has qualities of vitality and expressiveness which makes it dramatically easier to handle, but it is not quite the exception it appears, for again it is in part the drama of an inherently mobile minority, and the sense of disorganization, restlessness, and frustration comes very powerfully through Wesker's plays. Behan used a particular facet of Irish life in the same way, in *The Hostage* (1959) which is interesting not so much as a continuation of the Irish drama which in Synge and O'Casey has been so important in this century, but as a contrast with it. *The Hostage* is not so much an Irish scene as a microcosm of disorganization and restlessness; more like Wesker's *The Kitchen* (1961) than like O'Casey.

What came through, then, was not so much a new area of life, in the ordinary descriptive sense, as a new wave of feeling. In fact it had some elements in common with the drama it evidently replaced; in Eliot and Fry, also, the dominating themes had been restlessness and loss of direction. But these were now expressed in new voices, and with a different edge. In the late plays of Eliot, and in the decorated sentences of Fry, there had been a sense of indulgence in these emotional states, for their own sake. There was again indulgence, in several of the new plays, but in the best of them there was a new sound: that of ordinary human voices trying to live through the despair. This is perhaps at its most effective in *A Taste of Honey*, where, almost without artifice, the language of care and love keeps counterpointing the convincing bitterness, and where the play ends in a rooted disorder yet one through which a new life is coming and is given a blessing. The idea of a new life, in a more generalized and consciously political way, comes clearly through Wesker, and the voice of the political aspiration is new in that it is presented primarily as the sudden articulation of individual energy.

What was first noticed, however, was the new edge: the bitter, almost inarticulate rage at the general condition. Dramatically, *Look Back in Anger* is mainly this kind of declaration, and the most effective points in Wesker's plays are declarations of the same kind. It is not a doctrine that is declared, as in Shaw or in Ibsen's *Enemy of the People*; it is a primarily emotional protest, barely articulate, with an intensity beyond its nominal causes. The cry was recognized, in this form, by its immediate audiences.

We have then the curious situation of a revival of naturalist drama which, when its structure of feeling is analysed, is only intermittently consistent with naturalism. This new work is less the drama of social description and probability than the drama of a state of mind. It has used naturalism, consciously or unconsciously, mainly as a means of expressing this state of mind. This is why it is so stupid to call it 'kitchen-sink drama', which is a phrase that could only have got currency in a state of dramatic ignorance. That kind of work is at least eighty years old (perhaps a fair period for a phrase to get through to some of our newspapers), and the new work is not at all like it. We have not had documentaries of youth and poverty, but a number of intensely personal cries in the dark: a lyrical and romantic drama turned bitter and almost hopeless; a set of blues rhythms rather than a set of social problem plays.

This is where the other new factor of the 1950s, the renewed contacts with European drama, is so important. Beckett, particularly in *Waiting for Godot* (1952) and *All That Fall* (1958), fitted this mood exactly. I remember reading in the programme of *Waiting for Godot* that it was a kind of documentary about a very interesting kind of French vagrant; the point is no more and no less sensible than descriptions of *A Taste of Honey*, *Roots*, *Look Back in Anger* in similar pseudo-objective social terms. A style of living, theatrically communicable, is used to express a state of mind, by Beckett as plainly as by our own young dramatists; though in Beckett much more powerfully, and with much greater skill. In the plays of Ionesco, this kind of action has been developed into a distinctly anti-realistic convention, to express, however, basically similar feelings. A play like Pinter's *The Dumb Waiter* (1960) reflects quite directly and identifiably the methods and even the rhythms of Beckett and Ionesco, yet it is not far in texture from the new naturalism of the other young dramatists. The typical failure to communicate with other persons, the anxious and at times hysterical struggle to establish personal identity in a world where betrayal is not only particular but general, as the sense of a common reality declines to illusion or to conventional catchphrases: this structure of feeling belongs as much to the 'social' as to the 'psychological' dramatists, and determines the forms of the new naturalism – an articulate hero in an otherwise inarticulate world – as much as it determines the literal cross-talk, the insignificant silences in which meaning is groped for, the dramatization of inaction, of the later expressionist and anti-theatre productions.

In this confused situation, we need a clear sense of dramatic history and development. What looked at first like simple archaism, a throwback to naturalism, is not turning out that way at all. Perhaps even some of the dramatists have been misled, by descriptions of their work in terms of social content (and thence, by old formulas, of naturalism), even where it is clear that the driving force is quite different. There is an evident reaching beyond the resource of ordinary conversation, by the use of music, songs, speeches. The immediate tradition of formal verse drama has been thoroughly rejected, but the tensions which originally led to it have all reappeared. In forty years of experiment the formal verse drama had reached a high level of technical skill, though it had never solved the problems of action. The new drama of recent years, rejecting that particular tradition, has had to start all over again, and is often, inevitably, crude and unfinished in its actual writing. Contact with the wider European tradition has restored the possibility of a new and more mature direction, with stylization of quite different kinds.

During the 1960s, however, another important factor became evident. Since Artaud and, in different ways, Pirandello, there has often been a latent distrust of conventional theatre, in any of its set forms, and some part of this distrust has been expressed in the theatre itself. The concept of the author creating an action which others perform has been increasingly challenged by other concepts of theatrical creation. The most orthodox form of this challenge has been the emphasis on a producer's theatre, in which the written structure of the play has been at best the basis, but sometimes only the occasion, for what is seen as the independent exercise of theatrical art. Tensions between dramatists and producers have been common throughout the period of the European revival of the last ninety years, and it was indeed only at the beginning of this period that the now characteristic figure of the producer or director became common. In recent years, especially, there has been considerable confusion about the nature of conventions, within this division and tension of creative processes. For if a style of production can be applied *to* a play, rather than developed from its internal conventions, experiment is seen as a primarily theatrical rather than a primarily dramatic fact.

Yet the figure of the creative director can, after a time, seem merely to replace, to stand in for, the dramatic author. It is against this kind of direction, which whether from author or producer is seen as external, that another version of free theatre has been attempted. Some of the most lively work of the sixties has been in group theatre, in which the actors as a group are the only creators, discovering in movement and relationship, sometimes improvised, sometimes rehearsed, new theatrical or dramatic patterns. This has been part of a general cultural emphasis on creative performers, as most evidently in the groups in popular music. Words, which had been the dramatist's contribution, are often less important in this kind of theatre than the elements of movement and design. A number of experiments have been directed towards what is seen as a mixing of media: with song, dance, movement, lighting integrated, or offered to be integrated, into new total forms. But there have been other cases where this new kind of group theatre has been directly engaged with by dramatists. Among many names, John Arden, in his later work, has been consciously moving in this direction.

Meanwhile the range of drama has come to be permanently altered by the extension from the theatre to cinema and television. Indeed, some part of the emphasis on group creation is undoubtedly related to this, since the character of the new media involves continuing collaboration in the creative process. The traditional situation, in which a play is written in its final form, in words, and is then available for many and usually different kinds of performance, has been replaced, in cinema and television, by a situation in which the 'performance' is also the final creation of the work: not the written but the acted work standing as the real artefact. British cinema has been at a low ebb during the sixties, with only occasional new work of a serious kind. But it can reasonably be argued that the important successors to the new theatre dramatists of the fifties have been the new television dramatists of the sixties: David Mercer, Dennis Potter, Alun Owen and others.

In the theatre, because of these developments, there has indeed been some narrowing of scope. The dominant English influence has been Pinter, rather than Osborne or Wesker, and there has been persistent experiment in that variant of naturalism in which a stylized flatness of speech is combined with the creation of a bizarre or terrifying situation (a method reaching back, ultimately, to Ionesco). The coexistence of a seemingly arbitrary and permanent violence with a sense of deprivation and limited human resources has become, within this tendency, almost orthodox. Yet it is important to notice that the tone of this work is only occasionally resigned; more characteristically it is lively, boisterous, often openly comic; a paradox of feeling within what is ordinarily seen as not so much the human condition as the human trap. Indeed this fusion of comedy and violence, in a whole series of plays, has become so general that it can properly be called the dominant theatrical experience of the sixties.

Perhaps the most important new theatre dramatist of the sixties has been Edward Bond (*Saved*). Other plays to notice are David Rudkin's *Afore Night Come* and Joe Orton's *Loot* and *Entertaining Mr Sloane*.

At the same time, another kind of play has been regularly attempted since the period of change and revival in the mid-1950s. Whereas the play of contemporary life has been a series of variants on naturalism, other conventions have been used, as by Brecht, for historical themes. The problem of the resources of speech is less pressing, when the obligation to reproduce contemporary actuality is thus removed. Still, we must make distinctions about these uses of history. There is a kind of historical play – well exemplified by Bolt's *A Man for All Seasons* (1960) – which is really a kind of ante-dated naturalism: the characters talk and feel in the twentieth century, but for action and interest are based in the sixteenth. This is often a strong form, in part because of the external interest of its historical material. Overlapping with this, but in certain respects going into a new kind, is the play of romantic intrigue – well illustrated by Whiting's *The Devils* (1961). Here the external interest is again evident, but the opportunity is taken – as only incidentally in historical naturalism – to create new kinds of theatrical effect: the colour and excitement of costume, the patterns of old rituals, the exhibition of torture and possession. Fry made romantic comedies out of this kind of material: Whiting has made a psychological drama. It has great theatrical attraction, because of its colour and movement, and it can usually be effectively produced and played, because it can draw directly on contemporary methods of acting and producing Shakespeare (as distinct from Shakespeare's own dramatic methods, where all these elements are directed by the verse).

Again overlapping with this, but in certain respects going beyond it into a new kind, is the historical play which Brecht has taught us to call 'epic drama'. The point here is that while external historical interest is sometimes used (as in *Galileo*, 1943), and while full opportunity is taken of theatrical colour and movement (as in *The Caucasian*

Chalk Circle, 1945), the centre of the play is quite different; its primary interest is in a definition of meaning, belonging more to the present than to the past, which the action is quite consciously used to act out. A comparable British play is John Arden's *Serjeant Musgrave's Dance* (1960), deliberately not located in any precise history, though consciously using the past for theatrical colour and action, but centred in an examination of the meaning of violence, using the action as an image. In its richness and concentration of theme and in its remarkable control of action and language, *Serjeant Musgrave's Dance* is almost certainly the most important English play of its generation. John Osborne's *Luther* (1961) looks at first sight a similar kind of play, but in fact it is wholly different from the Brechtian epic drama. In Brecht, a historical action becomes a dramatic action, of a public kind. In Osborne, a historical action is reduced to a historical personality, who is then made the centre of a private psychological play. In feeling, *Luther* belongs with Lytton Strachey and Aldous Huxley rather than with Brecht.

What we have then is not, in any textbook sense, a movement, with common aims and methods. We are in a confused and eclectic phase, which has valuably caught up elements of our own immediate tensions (the particular and recognizable tensions of Britain in the late 1950s and 1960s) but which belongs, finally, to the period of European dramatic experiment which began more than ninety years ago. We are now taking part in this again, with exceptional energy, through an unusually strong generation of young dramatists who have turned to the theatre as a primary form. We have one new advantage: that in the performance of recent European drama, and from direct observation and contact with it, our producers, actors, and audiences are much better equipped for experiment than in the period when the verse drama revival was beginning. Solid naturalist habits need not drag this generation back in the same way.

Yet also we have one continuing disadvantage: the split theatre. The minority theatres will continue to be the main channels of this work, but while they are financially insecure, and consequently subject all the time to the pressures of the commercial theatre, it will be difficult for any experiment to get enough time and resources for it to be properly carried through. Nothing is now more urgent than the creation of securely based professional companies, with real guarantees for their future, to carry forward, in several different ways, the possibilities now sensed. The weaknesses of our new drama are realized nowhere more clearly than among those working in it, and the confusion is not easy to bear when the practical opportunities to work through it are not easy to come by. It is of course true that the theatre is now not the only important dramatic institution. The expansion of television drama has provided vital new outlets, and there has been, most significantly, a corresponding expansion of the audience for serious drama. Some important new plays have gone directly to audiences of between five and ten million people, and writers seeking to overcome the disadvantages of the minority theatre have often turned to television for just this reason. Yet the deep social and cultural reasons for the split are in the end perhaps even more evident in the development of the television institutions. Periods of really experimental television drama have in practice been as short as the periods in which the experimental free theatres have flourished, and the commercial pressures against them have been large-scale and severe.

The effect of these pressures, and of the ways in which they distort our dramatic institutions, may be seen as simply practical: a limitation of the possibilities for serious work. But there are deeper effects, from this pressure and consequent sense of impermanence and isolation, on the nature of the drama itself. The preoccupation with themes of isolation, breakdown, failure to communicate, and relationships seen as illusion has indeed been part of a general crisis in our culture, and has led to much brilliant expression and experiment.

Yet the point can be reached when this particular preoccupation is in danger of disintegrating rather than merely changing the forms of dramatic action. No simple judgement is possible, for many tendencies, in method and feeling, are now interwoven, in very complicated ways, even within the work of individual writers. Yet we can remind ourselves of this larger context by noting how much Pinter and Osborne, for example, have in common with Eliot and Fry, in matters of feeling, even though their immediate dramatic methods differ widely and can be charted as separate movements. Drama often shows, more clearly and more quickly than other arts, the deep patterns and changes in our general ideas of reality. We have one example, in Brecht, of a major dramatist changing from one view of reality to another, within the pressures of a radically changing society. The early Brecht is like the early Eliot in feeling, and like Osborne and others in the 1950s. The later Brecht belongs to a different, more mature, and I think more dramatic world. But again we have to notice how complicated this change was, in its social bearings: a move from psychological exile, through political commitment, to actual exile. This is not a simple or repeatable journey. Yet the reference, finally, is right, when it forces us to consider the minority theatre as more than a technical or professional problem. The point can be reached (and in some recent English drama has been clearly reached) when the forms of the minority theatre become acceptable and even popular in an otherwise moribund majority theatre, mainly because their kinds of feeling, their versions of reality, are coming, under crisis, to dominate the society as a whole. This emergence has then to be seen, not simply as an extension of art, but as a fact about the whole society.

Nothing is now more striking than the *resemblance* between minority and popular art, over very wide areas including much of our actual drama (especially if we include work done in the cinema and in television as well as in the theatre). The contrast between minority and majority drama, first made in the closing decades of the nineteenth century, rested not only on the experiments of the minority that was breaking away, but also on the traditional and conventional confidence of the persistent majority. This confidence has now largely gone: disintegration, disillusion, and the struggle to break away have become, in large part, the imaginative themes of popular as well as experimental art. This fact further confuses contemporary understanding, in that the conscious originality of some of our minority dramatists is now, in plain terms, the merest commonplace. The attempt to create a new imaginative world, in the public terms and spoken and acted relationships of drama, has then to be carried on in a context wider than that of drama itself, though depending always on the most precise and direct knowledge of its experiments and its traditions.*

* A revised version of an article originally published in the *Twentieth Century* (Vol. 170, No. 1011).

PART IV

BIBLIOGRAPHY

COMPILED BY JOAN BLACK

THE lists which follow are intended as a guide to the literature written in the British Isles in the period, and to the background of that literature. Section A.1 (The Writers and their Works) concentrates mainly on British writers, though it includes such other major writers in the English language as T. S. Eliot and Ezra Pound. Section B.2 includes a list of foreign writers and thinkers whose work has been influential on that of the major British writers in the first section. In the case of major authors a fairly comprehensive list of titles (with dates of first publication) is given, together with selected bibliographies and commentaries on their work. For a large number of minor writers, a collected edition of their work (if published), or a selection of titles, is noted.

For easy reference, a list of the sections of the bibliography follows:

A: *The Literature*

1. The Writers and their Works
2. Collections and Anthologies; Periodicals
3. History, Criticism and Bibliographies of the Literature
4. Major Critical Writings and Theories of Literature of the Period

B: *The Background*

1. History – Major Historians; Documentary Sources; Constitutional, Social, and Economic Histories
2. Intellectual Background – Major Philosophers, and a selected list of Foreign Thinkers; Political, Social and Cultural Issues; Education
3. The Arts (excluding literature)

A: The Literature

1. THE WRITERS AND THEIR WORKS

AE: See RUSSELL, George William (1867–1935).

AMIS, KINGSLEY (b. 1922): Novelist, critic and poet.
Novels: *Lucky Jim*, 1954; *That Uncertain Feeling*, 1955; *I Like it Here*,

1958; *Take a Girl Like You*, 1960; *My Enemy's Enemy*, 1962; *One Fat Englishman*, 1963; *I Want It Now*, 1968; *Girl '70*, 1971.

Poems: *Bright November*, 1947; *A Frame of Mind*, 1953; *Poems*, 1954; *A Case of Samples*, 1956; *A Look around the Estate*, 1967.

Critical writings: *New Maps of Hell*, 1960; *The James Bond Dossier*, 1967.

See D. Lodge: 'The Modern, the Contemporary and the Importance of being Amis', *Critical Quarterly*, Vol. 5, 1963.

ARDEN, JOHN (b. 1930): Playwright.

Plays: *Serjeant Musgrave's Dance*, 1959; *Ironhand*, 1963; *The Workhouse Donkey*, 1964; *Left-handed Liberty*, 1965; *Armstrong's Last Goodnight*, 1965; *Soldier, Soldier*, 1967.

AUDEN, WYSTAN HUGH (b. 1907): Poet, verse dramatist, critic, translator, librettist.

Poems: *Collected Shorter Poems, 1927–1957*, 1966; *Collected Longer Poems*, 1968; *Look, Stranger!*, 1936; *New Year Letter*, 1941; *For the Time Being*, 1945; *The Age of Anxiety*, 1948; *The Shield of Achilles*, 1955; *Homage to Clio*, 1960; *About the House*, 1965; *City Without Walls*, 1969.

Plays: (with Christopher Isherwood) *The Dog Beneath the Skin*, 1935; *The Ascent of F6*, 1937; *On the Frontier*, 1938.

Essays, criticism: *The Dyer's Hand*, 1948, rev. 1962; *The Enchafèd Flood*, 1951; *Making, Knowing and Judging*, 1956; *Secondary Worlds*, 1968.

Other writings: *Letters from Iceland* (with L. MacNeice), 1937; Words for Britten's music: *Ballad of Heroes*, 1939, and *Hymn to St Cecilia*, 1942; Libretto for Stravinsky's *The Rake's Progress* (with Chester Kallman), 1951; English version of libretto for *The Magic Flute*; verse narrative for *The Play of Daniel*, 1958; translations of Goethe's *Italian Journey* (with E. Mayer), 1962, of Brecht's *The Caucasian Chalk Circle* (with others), 1963; *A Certain World: a commonplace book*, 1971.

See B. C. Bloomfield: *W. H. Auden, a Bibliography* (to 1955), 1965; J. W. Beach, *The Making of the Auden Canon*, 1957; J. G. Blair, *The Poetic Art of W. H. Auden*, 1965; B. Everett, *Auden*, 1964; J. A. Fuller, *A Reader's Guide to W. H. Auden*, 1970; M. K. Spears, *The Poetry of W. H. Auden: the Disenchanted Island*, 1963.

BARKER, GEORGE GRANVILLE (b. 1913): Poet and novelist.

Poems: *Thirty Preliminary Poems*, 1933; *Poems*, 1935; *Elegy on Spain*, 1939; *Lament and Triumph*, 1940; *Sacred and Secular Elegies*, 1941; *Eros in Dogma*, 1944; *Love Poems*, 1947; *News of the World*, 1950; *Collected Poems, 1930–1955*, 1957; *The View from a Blind I*, 1962; *Dreams of a*

Summer Night, 1966; *The Golden Chains*, 1968; *At Thurgarton Church*, 1969; *Poems of Places and People*, 1971.

Novel: *The Dead Seagull*, 1950.

Verse autobiography: *The True Confession of George Barker*, Book I, 1950, Book II, 1965.

BEARDSLEY, AUBREY VINCENT (1872–98):

Art editor of the first four volumes of *The Yellow Book*, 1894–7.

See S. Weintraub, *Beardsley*, rev. edn, 1972.

BECKETT, SAMUEL BARCLAY (b. 1906). Born in Dublin. Novelist, playwright (stage and radio), story writer. Much of Beckett's work was originally written in French and later translated by himself into English.

Plays: *En attendant Godot*, 1952 (*Waiting for Godot*, 1954); *All that Fall*, 1957; *Fin de partie suivi de Acte sans paroles*, 1957 (*Endgame and Act Without Words*, 1958); *Krapp's Last Tape*, 1958; *Embers*, 1959; *Happy Days*, 1961 (*Oh! les beaux jours*, 1963); *Play and Two Short Pieces for Radio* (*Words and Music; Cascanda*), 1965; *Eh Joe, and Other Writings* (*Act Without Words II; Film.*) 1967; *Not I*, 1973.

Novels, short stories and essays: *More Pricks than Kicks*, 1934; *Murphy*, 1938 (in French, 1947); *Molloy* (in French), 1951 (in English, 1955); *Malone meurt*, 1951 (*Malone Dies*, 1956); *L'innommable*, 1953 (*The Unnamable*, 1958); *Watt*, 1953; *Nouvelles et Textes pour rien*, 1955; *Comment c'est*, 1961 (*How It Is*, 1961); *Imagination Dead Imagine*, 1966; *No's Knife*, 1967; *Lessness*, 1969; *Mercier et Camier*, 1970; *Premier amour*, 1970.

Beckett's 1930 poems, *Whoroscope*, have been reprinted with *Three Dialogues with Georges Duthuit* (on modern painting), 1965.

See *Beckett at 60: a Festschrift*, 1967; R. Coe, *Beckett*, 1964; R. Federman, *Journey to Chaos: Samuel Beckett's early fiction* (includes bibliography), 1966; J. Fletcher, *Samuel Beckett's Art*, 1967; H. Kenner, *Samuel Beckett, a critical study*, 1961; M. Robinson, *The Long Sonata of the Dead*, 1969.

BEERBOHM, SIR MAX (1872–1956): Essayist, short story writer, theatre critic, broadcaster.

See Beerbohm's writings throughout the *Yellow Book* and the *Saturday Review*; *A Christmas Garland*, 1895, enl. edn, 1950; *The Works of Max Beerbohm*, 1896; *More*, 1899; *Yet again*, 1909; *Around Theatres*, 2 vols, 1924; *Lytton Strachey*, 1943; *Mainly on the Air*, enl. edn, 1957; *Selected Essays*, 1958.

Novel: *Zuleika Dobson*, 1911; Short stories: *The Happy Hypocrite*, 1897; *Seven Men*, 1919; *The Dreadful Dragon of Hay Hill*, 1928.

See A. E. Gallatin and L. M. Oliver, *A Bibliography of the Works of Max Beerbohm*, 1952.

Lord David Cecil, *Max, a Biography*, 1964.

BEHAN, BRENDAN (1922–64): Irish novelist, essayist and playwright.

Plays: *The Quare Fellow*, 1956; *The Hostage*, 1958 (produced in Gaelic and English).

Novel: *The Scarperer*, 1964. *Autobiography: Borstal Boy*, 1958.

Essays and travel notes: *Island, an Irish sketch book*, 1962; *Hold Your Hour* and *Have Another*, 1963; *Brendan Behan's New York*, 1964.

See D. Behan, *My Brother Behan*, 1965.

BELLOC, JOSEPH HILAIRE PETER (1870–1953): Born in Paris. Historian, essayist, novelist, poet.

Verse collections: *Cautionary Verse*, 1940; *The Verse of Hilaire Belloc*, 1954.

Other writings include: *The Path to Rome*, 1902; *The French Revolution*, 1911; *The Servile State*, 1912; *A Companion to Mr Wells's Outline of History*, 1926.

Novels include: *Mr Clutterbuck's Election*, 1908; *The Green Overcoat*, 1912.

BENNETT, ENOCH ARNOLD (1867–1931): Novelist, playwright.

Novels: *Anna of the Five Towns*, 1902 (dramatized as *Cupid and Commonsense*, 1909); *Buried Alive*, 1908; *The Old Wives' Tale*, 1908; The Clayhanger Trilogy: *Clayhanger*, 1910, *Hilda Lessways*, 1911, *These Twain*, 1915; *Riceyman Steps*, 1923; *Imperial Palace*, 1930.

Plays: *Milestones* (with E. Knoblock), 1912; *London Life*, 1924; *Mr Prohack*, 1927.

Other writings: *Journals*, ed. N. Flower, 3 vols, 1932–3; *Letters*, ed. J. Hepburn, 3 vols, 1966–70; *The Author's Craft and other critical writings*, ed. S. Hynes, 1968.

See D. Barker, *Writer by Trade*, 1966; J. Hepburn, *The Art of Arnold Bennett*, 1965; G. Lafourcade, *Bennett: a Study*, 1939.

BETJEMAN, SIR JOHN (b. 1906): Poet, writer on architecture. Poet Laureate, 1972.

Collected Poems, 1958; *Summoned by Bells: an Autobiography in Verse*, 1960; *Ghastly Good Taste*, 1933; *The English Towns in the Last Hundred Years*, 1956.

BOND, EDWARD (b. 1934): Playwright.

Plays: *Saved*, 1966; *Early Morning*, 1968; *Narrow Road to the Deep North*, 1968.

BOWEN, ELIZABETH (b. 1889): Born in Dublin. Novelist, short story writer.

Novels: *The Last September*, 1929; *The House in Paris*, 1935; *The Death of the Heart*, 1938; *The Heat of the Day*, 1949; *A World of Love*, 1955; *The Little Girls*, 1964.

Short stories: *Encounters*, 1923; *Joining Charles*, 1929; *Look at All Those Roses*, 1941; *The Demon Lover*, 1945; *A Day in the Dark*, 1965.

See J. Brooke, *Elizabeth Bowen*, 1952; W. W. Heath, *Elizabeth Bowen, an Introduction to her Novels*, 1961.

BRAINE, JOHN (b. 1922): Novelist.

Novels: *Room at the Top*, 1957; *The Vodi*, 1959; *Life at the Top*, 1962; *The Crying Game*, 1968; *Stay with me till Morning*, 1970.

BRIDGES, ROBERT (1844–1930): Poet. Editor of G. M. Hopkins' poetry. Poet Laureate, 1913–30.

Poetical Works, 6 vols, 1898–1905; *Collected Essays and Papers*, 30 vols, 1927–36.

BROOKE, RUPERT CHAWNER (1887–1915): Poet.

Poetical Works, ed. G. Keynes, 1946.

Other writings: *John Webster and Elizabethan Drama* (dissertation), 1916; *Letter from America*, 1916; *Democracy and the Arts*, 1946; *The Prose of Rupert Brooke*, ed. C. Hassall, 1956; *Letters*, ed. G. Keynes, 1968.

See G. Keynes, *A Bibliography of the Works of Rupert Brooke*, 1956; W. de la Mare, *Rupert Brooke and the Intellectual Imagination*, 1919; C. Hassall, *Rupert Brooke*, 1963; T. Rogers, *Rupert Brooke, a selection and a re-appraisal*, 1971.

BUNTING, BASIL (b. 1900): Poet.

Poems: *Poems*, 1950; *The Spoils*, 1955; *Loquitur*, 1965; *Briggflatts*, 1966; *Collected Poems*, 1970.

BURGESS, ANTHONY (b. 1917): Novelist, composer, critic.

Novels include: *Time for a Tiger*, 1956; *The Enemy in the Blanket*, 1958; *The Doctor is Sick*, 1960; *The Worm and the Ring*, 1961; *A Clockwork Orange*, 1962; *Honey for the Bears*, 1963; *Inside Mr Enderby*, 1963; *Enderby Outside*, 1968; *MF*, 1971.

CAMPBELL, ROY (1901–57): Born in Natal. Poet and translator.

Poems: *Adamastor*, 1930; *Pomegranates*, 1932; *Flowering Rifle*, 1939; *Talking Bronco*, 1946; *Collected Poems*, 3 vols, 1949–60.

Translations of: St John of the Cross, Baudelaire, Calderón, Cervantes, Lope de Vega.

Autobiography: *Light on a Dark Horse, 1901–1935*, 1951.

See D. Wright, *Roy Campbell*.

CARY, ARTHUR JOYCE LUNEL (1887–1957): Born in Londonderry. Novelist, essayist.

Novels: *Mister Johnson*, 1939; *Charley is my Darling*, 1940, *A House of Children* (autobiographical), 1941; Trilogy: *Herself Surprised*, 1941, *To be a Pilgrim*, 1942, *The Horse's Mouth*, 1944; *A Fearful Joy*, 1949; Trilogy: *Prisoner of Grace*, 1952, *Except the Lord*, 1953, *Not Honour More*, 1955; *The Captive and the Free*, 1959.

Short stories: *Spring Song*, 1960.

Other writings include: *Power in Men*, 1939; *The Case for African Freedom*, 1941, rev. 1944; *Art and Reality*, 1958.

Poems: *Verse*, 1908; *Marching Soldier*, 1945.

See R. Bloom, *The Indeterminate World*, 1962; J. Holloway, 'Joyce Cary's Fiction', *Times Literary Supplement*, 7 August, 1959; G. L. Larsen, *The Dark Descent*, 1965; M. Mahood, *Joyce Cary's Africa*, 1964; A. Wright, *Joyce Cary: A Preface to his Novels*, 1958.

CAUDWELL, CHRISTOPHER (pseud. of Christopher St John Sprigg) (1907–37): Critic, novelist and poet.

Criticism: *Studies in a Dying Culture*, 1938; *Illusion and Reality*, 1939; *Romance and Realism*, ed. S. Hynes, 1970.

Poems: *Poems*, 1939.

CHESTERTON, GILBERT KEITH (1874–1936): Essayist, critic, novelist, poet.

Novels and short stories include: *The Napoleon of Notting Hill*, 1904; *The Man who was Thursday*, 1908; *The Ball and Cross*, 1909; *The Flying Inn*, 1914; The 'Father Brown' stories, collected edns, 1929, 1935.

Poems: *Collected Poems*, 1933.

Literary criticism includes: *Browning*, 1903; *Thackeray*, 1908; *Shaw*, 1910; *William Blake*, 1910; *Dickens*, 1911; *The Victorian Age in Literature*, 1913; *Chaucer*, 1932.

See C. Hollis, *G. K. Chesterton*, 1950.

COMPTON-BURNETT, IVY (1892–1969): Novelist.

Novels include: *Dolores*, 1911; *Pastors and Masters*, 1925; *Brothers and Sisters*, 1929; *Men and Wives*, 1931; *More Women than Men*, 1933; *A House and its Head*, 1935; *A Family and its Fortune*, 1939; *Parents and Children*, 1941; *Darkness and Day*, 1951; *A Heritage and its History*, 1959; *A God and his Gifts*, 1963.

See C. Burkhart, ed., *The Art of I. Compton-Burnett*, 1972; R. Liddell, *The Novels of Ivy Compton-Burnett*, 1955.

CONNOLLY, CYRIL VERNON (b. 1903): Pseud. 'Palinurus'. Essayist, critic, editor, novelist.

Edited *Horizon* (see p. 589 below), 1939–45; literary editor of the *Observer*, 1942–3.

Novel: *The Rock Pool*, 1935.

Critical essays include: *Enemies of Promise*, 1938, rev. 1949; *The Unquiet Grave*, 1944; *The Condemned Playground: Essays, 1927–44*, 1945; *Previous Convictions*, 1963; *The Modern Movement, 1880–1920*, 1965.

CONRAD, JOSEPH – Josef Teodor Konrad Korzeniowski – (1857–1924): Polish-born novelist and short story writer. Settled in England 1896.

Novels: *Almayer's Folly*, 1895; *An Outcast of the Islands*, 1896; *The Nigger of the 'Narcissus'*, 1897; *Lord Jim*, 1900; *Heart of Darkness*, 1902; *Nostromo*, 1904; *The Secret Agent*, 1907 (dramatized, 1923); *Under Western Eyes*, 1911; *Chance*, 1913; *Victory*, 1915; *The Shadow-Line* 1917; *The Arrow of Gold*, 1919; *The Rover*, 1923; *Suspense*, 1925.

Stories: *Tales of Unrest*, 1898; *Typhoon*, 1902; *Youth*, 1902; *'Twixt Land and Sea*, 1912; *Within the Tides*, 1915; *Tales of Hearsay*, 1925.

Autobiography: *The Mirror of the Sea*, 1906; *A Personal Record*, 1916.

Essays: *Notes on Life and Letters*, 1921; *Last Essays*, 1926; *Joseph Conrad on Fiction*, ed. W. F. Wright, 1964.

Collections of letters: To his wife, 1927; to Richard Curle, 1928; to M. Porodowska, 1940; to William Blackwood and D. S. Meldrum, 1966; to R. B. Cunninghame Graham, 1969; *Letters, 1895–1924*, ed. E. Garnett, 1928; *Conrad's Polish Background*, ed. Z. Nayder, 1964.

See G. Jean-Aubry, *Conrad, Life and Letters*, 2 vols, 1927, and *The Sea-Dreamer: A Definitive Biography*, 1957; Jessie Conrad, *Joseph Conrad as I knew him*, 1926; A. J. Guerard, *Conrad the Novelist*, 1959; E. Hay, *The Political Novels of Joseph Conrad*, 1963; F. R. Karl, *A Readers' Guide to Joseph Conrad*, 1960; F. R. Leavis in *The Great Tradition*, rev. 1960; M. Mudrick, ed., *Conrad: a Collection of Critical Essays*, 1966; N. Sherry, *Conrad's Eastern World*, 1966, and *Conrad's Western World*, 1971; T. Tanner, *Conrad: Lord Jim*, 1963.

DAVIE, DONALD (b. 1922): Poet and critic.

Poems: *Events and Wisdoms, 1957–63*, 1964; *Essex Poems, 1963–7*, 1969; *Six Epistles to Eva Hesse*, 1970.

Criticism: *Purity of Diction in English Verse*, 1952, 1957; *Articulate Energy*, 1957.

DAVIES, WILLIAM HENRY (1871–1940): Poet, miscellaneous prose writer.

Poems: *The Complete Poems*, intro. O. Sitwell, 1963.

Autobiography: *The Autobiography of a Super-Tramp*, 1908; *Beggars*, 1909; *Later Days*, 1925.

Travel writings include: *The True Traveller*, 1912; *The Adventures of Johnny Walker, Tramp*, 1926.

See R. Church, *Eight for Immortality*, 1941; R. J. Stonesifer, *W. H. Davies, a Critical Biography*, 1963.

DE LA MARE, WALTER (1873–1956): Poet, anthologist, essayist, critic.

Poems include: *Songs of Childhood*, 1902; *The Listeners*, 1912; *Peacock Pie*, 1913; *The Old Man*, 1913; *Down-adown-derry*, 1922; *Never More Sailor*, 1925; *Alone*, 1927; *Poems for Children*, 1930; *This Year, next Year*, 1937. *A Choice of De La Mare's Verse*, ed. W. H. Auden, 1963; *Complete Poems*, 1969.

Anthologies include: *Behold this Dreamer*, 1939.

Stories include: *Henry Brocken*, 1904; *The Three Mulla-mulgars*, 1910; *The Riddle*, 1923; *The Hostage*, 1930; *The Nap*, 1936; *Animal Stories*, 1939; *A Beginning*, 1955.

See H. C. Duffin, *Walter de la Mare*, 1953; K. Hopkins, *Walter de la Mare*, 1953; F. R. Leavis in *New Bearings in English Poetry*, rev. 1950; F. Reid, *Walter de la Mare, a Critical Study*, 1929.

DOUGHTY, CHARLES MONTAGU (1843–1926): Poet and traveller.

Poems include: *The Dawn in Britain*, 6 vols, 1906; *Mansoul*, 1920, rev. 1923.

Travel: *Travels in Arabia Deserta*, 2 vols, 1888.

DOUGLAS, GEORGE NORMAN (1868–1952): Novelist, essayist, travel-writer.

Novels: *South Wind*, 1917; *They Went*, 1920; *In the Beginning*, 1927, complete edn by C. Fitzgibbon, 1953; *The Angel of Manfredonia*, 1929.

Essays: *London Street Games*, 1916; *Birds and Beasts of the Greek Anthology*, 1927; *Footnotes on East and West*, 1929.

Travel writing: *Siren Land*, 1911; *Fountains in the Sand* (Tunisia), 1912; *Old Calabria*, 1915; *Alone*, 1921; *Together*, 1923; *Capri*, collected edn, 1930.

Autobiography: *Looking Back*, 1933; *Late Harvest*, 1946.

See C. Woolf, *A Bibliography of Norman Douglas*, 1954. H. M. Tomlinson, *Norman Douglas*, 1952.

DURRELL, LAWRENCE GEORGE (b. 1912): Indian-born poet and novelist.

Poems: *A Private Country*, 1943; *Cities, Plains and People*, 1946; *On Seeming to Presume*, 1948; *Private Drafts*, 1955; *The Tree of Idleness*, 1955; *Collected Poems*, 1960, 2nd edn, 1968.

Verse plays: *Sappho*, 1950; *An Irish Faustus*, 1963.

Novels: *Pied Piper of Lovers*, 1935; *Panic Spring*, 1935; *The Alexandrian Quartet*: *Justine*, 1957, *Balthazar*, 1958, *Mountolive*, 1958, *Clea*, 1960; *Tunc*, 1968; *Nunquam*, 1970; *The Black Book*, 1973.

Travel writing: *Reflections on a Marine Venus* (Rhodes), 1953; *Bitter Lemons*, 1957.

Criticism: *A Key to Modern Poetry*, 1952; *Art and Outrage*, 1959.

Letters, *Lawrence Durrell and Henry Miller: A Private Correspondence*, ed. G. Wickes, 1963.

See H. T. Moore, *The World of Lawrence Durrell*, 1962, rev. edn, 1964; G. Steiner, in *Language and Silence*, 1967; J. Unterecker, *Lawrence Durrell*, 1954.

ELIOT, THOMAS STEARNS (1888–1965): American poet, critic, dramatist. Editor of *The Egoist* 1917–19; established and edited *Criterion* 1923–39.

Poems: *Prufrock and Other Observations*, 1917; *Poems*, 1919; *The Waste Land*, 1922; *Ash Wednesday*, 1930; *Old Possum's Book of Practical Cats*, 1939; *Four Quartets*, 1943, the collected edn of *East Coker*, 1940, *Burnt Norton*, 1941, *The Dry Salvages*, 1941 and *Little Gidding*, 1942; *The Complete Poems and Plays, 1909–1950*, 1952; *The Cultivation of Christmas Trees*, 1959; *Poems Written in Early Youth*, ed. J. Hayward, 1957; *Complete Poems and Plays*, 1969; *Facsimile of the Early Drafts of the Waste Land*, ed. V. Eliot, 1971.

Plays: *Sweeney Agonistes*, 1932; *The Rock*, 1934; *Murder in the Cathedral*, 1935; *The Family Reunion*, 1939; *The Cocktail Party*, 1949; *The Confidential Clerk*, 1954; *The Elder Statesman*, 1959; *Collected Plays*, 1962; *Complete Poems and Plays*, 1969.

Critical writings: *Ezra Pound, his Metric and Poetry*, 1917; *The Sacred Wood*, 1920; *For Lancelot Andrewes*, 1928; *Selected Essays, 1917–1932*, 1932, enl. edn., 1951; *The Use of Poetry and the Use of Criticism*, 1933; *After Strange Gods*, 1934; *Elizabethan Essays*, 1934; *Essays Ancient and Modern*, 1936; *The Idea of a Christian Society*, 1939; *What is a Classic?*, 1945; *Notes Towards a Definition of Culture*, 1948; *The Three Voices of Poetry*, 1953; *Essays on Elizabethan Drama*, 1956; *On Poetry and Poets*, 1957; *Knowledge and Experience in the Philosophy of F. H. Bradley*, 1964; *To Criticize the Critic*, 1965.

See D. C. Gallup, *T. S. Eliot, a Bibliography*, rev. edn, 1952.

C. Brooks, *Modern Poetry and the Tradition*, 1948; *Encounter*, Vol.

24, 1965; N. Frye, *T. S. Eliot*, 1963; H. Gardner, *The Art of T. S. Eliot*, 1949; D. E. Jones, *The Plays of T. S. Eliot*, 1960; H. Kenner, *The Invisible Poet, T. S. Eliot*, 1959; R. Kojecky, *T. S. Eliot's Social Criticism*, 1971; F. R. Leavis, *New Bearings in English Poetry*, rev. 1950; D. E. S. Maxwell, *The Poetry of T. S. Eliot*, 1952; F. O. Matthiessen, *The Achievement of T. S. Eliot*, rev. by C. L. Barber, 1958; Tate, A., ed., *T. S. Eliot, The Man and His Work*, 1967; G. Williamson, *A Reader's Guide to T. S. Eliot*, 1955.

EMPSON, WILLIAM (b. 1906): Poet and critic.

Poems: *Letter IV*, 1929; *Poems*, 1935; *The Gathering Storm*, 1940; *Collected Poems*, 1955.

Critical writings: *Seven Types of Ambiguity*, 1930, rev. 1947; *Some Versions of Pastoral*, 1935; *English Pastoral Poetry*, 1938; *The Structure of Complex Words*, 1951; *Milton's God*, 1961, rev. 1965.

See G. S. Fraser, *Vision and Rhetoric*, 1959; *The Review* (Empson number) June, 1963; J. Wain, *Preliminary Essays*, 1957.

FIRBANK, RONALD (1886–1926): Novelist.

Novels: *Vainglory*, 1915; *Inclinations*, 1916; *Valmouth*, 1919; *Sorrow in Sunlight* (also called *Prancing Nigger*), 1924; *Concerning the Eccentricities of Cardinal Pirelli*, 1926; *The Artificial Princess*, 1934.

Collected Writings: *The Complete Ronald Firbank*, pref. A. Powell, 1961; *The New Rythum* (posthumous collection), 1962.

See M. Benkowitz, *Ronald Firbank, a Bibliography*, 1963; J. Brooke, *Ronald Firbank*, 1951.

FORD, FORD MADOX – Ford Madox Hueffer – (1873–1939): Novelist, critic, editor; collaborated on three novels (*The Inheritors*, 1901, *Romance*, 1903, and *The Nature of a Crime*, 1924) with Joseph Conrad. Founded the *English Review*, 1908 and *Transatlantic Review*, 1924.

Novels: *The Benefactor*, 1905; *An English Girl*, 1907; *Mr Apollo*, 1908; *The Young Lovell*, 1913; *The Good Soldier*, 1915; The 'Tietjens Tetralogy': (*Some Do Not*, 1924, *No More Parades*, 1925, *A Man Could Stand Up*, 1926, *Last Post*, 1928 – collected as *Parade's End*, 1950); *The Bodley Head Ford Madox Ford*, ed. G. Greene, 4 vols, 1962–5.

Critical writings: *Rossetti*, 1902; *The Spirit of the People: Analysis of the English Mind*, 1907; *The Pre-Raphaelite Brotherhood*, 1907; *The Critical Attitude*, 1911; *Henry James*, 1913; *A Mirror to France*, 1926; *New York Essays*, 1927; *The English Novel*, 1929; *The Critical Writings of Ford Madox Ford*, ed. F. MacShane, 1964.

Other writings: *Collected Poems*, 1914, 1936; *Thus to Revisit*, 1921; *No Enemy*, 1929; *It was the Nightingale*, 1933; *Mightier than the Sword* (reminiscence and autobiography), 1938; *Joseph Conrad, a Personal Remembrance*, 1924; *Letters*, ed. R. M. Ludwig, 1965.

See D. D. Harvey, *Ford Madox Ford, 1873–1939: A Bibliography*, 1962; D. Goldring, *The Last Pre-Raphaelite*, 1948; A. G. Hill, 'The Literary Career of Ford Madox Ford', *Critical Quarterly*, Vol. 5, 1963; F. MacShane, *The Life and Work of Ford Madox Ford*, 1965; A. Mizener, *The Saddest Story*, 1972.

FORSTER, EDWARD MORGAN (1879–1970): Novelist, short story writer, critic.

Novels: *Where Angels Fear to Tread*, 1905; *The Longest Journey*, 1907; *A Room with a View*, 1908; *Howards End*, 1910; *A Passage to India*, 1924; *Maurice*, 1971.

Short stories: *The Celestial Omnibus*, 1911; *The Eternal Moment*, 1928; *Collected Short Stories*, 1948, 1965; *The Life to Come, and Other Stories*, ed. O. Stallybrass, 1972.

Criticism and essays: *Aspects of the Novel*, 1927; *G. L. Dickinson*, 1934; *Abinger Harvest*, 1936; *Reading as Usual*, 1939; *Virginia Woolf*, 1942; *The Development of English Prose between 1918 and 1939*, 1945; *Two Cheers for Democracy*, 1951; *The Hill of Devi*, 1953; *Marianne Thornton*, 1956.

See B. J. Kirkpatrick, *A Bibliography of E. M. Forster*, 1965; J. B. Beer, *The Achievement of E. M. Forster*, 1962; M. Bradbury, ed., *E. M. Forster: A Collection of Critical Essays*, 1966; L. Brander, *E. M. Forster, a Critical Study*, 1968; K. W. Gransden, *E. M. Forster*, 1962; F. R. Leavis, in *The Common Pursuit*, 1952; W. Stone, *The Cave and the Mountain*, 1966; L. Trilling, *E. M. Forster*, 1944.

FOWLES, JOHN (b. 1926): Novelist.

Novels: *The Collector*, 1963; *The Magus*, 1966; *The French Lieutenant's Woman*, 1969.

FRY, CHRISTOPHER (b. 1907): Verse dramatist, translator.

Plays include: *A Phoenix Too Frequent*, 1946; *The Lady's Not For Burning*, 1949; *Venus Observed*, 1950; *A Sleep of Prisoners*, 1951; *The Dark is Light Enough*, 1954; *Curtmantle*, 1961, rev. 1965; *A Yard of Sun*, 1970.

Translations of Anouilh: *Ring around the Moon*, 1950, and *The Lark*, 1955; of Giraudoux: *Tiger at the Gates*, 1955, and *Duel of Angels*, 1958.

See D. Stanford, *Christopher Fry*, rev. edn, 1962.

FULLER, ROY (b. 1912): Poet and novelist.

Poems: *Poems*, 1940; *The Middle of a War*, 1942; *A Lost Season*, 1944;

Epitaphs and Occasions, 1949; *Counterparts*, 1954; *Brutus's Orchard*, 1957; *Collected Poems, 1936–1961*, 1962; *Buff*, 1965; *New Poems*, 1968.

Novels: *Full Measure*, 1936; *Savage Gold*, 1946; *With My Little Eye*, 1948; *The Second Curtain*, 1953; *Fantasy and Fugue*, 1954; *The Ruined Boys*, 1959; *The Father's Comedy*, 1961; *The Perfect Fool*, 1963; *My Child, My Sister*, 1965.

GALSWORTHY, JOHN (1867–1933): Novelist, playwright and essayist.

Novels: Three 'Forsyte' trilogies:

1. *The Forsyte Saga: The Man of Property*, 1906, *In Chancery*, 1920, and *To Let*, 1921; collected, 1922, with two connecting narratives *The Indian Summer of a Forsyte* and *Awakening*, 1920.
2. *A Modern Comedy: The White Monkey*, 1924; *The Silver Spoon*, 1926, and *Swan Song*, 1928; collected in 1929.
3. *End of the Chapter: Maid in Waiting*, 1931, *Flowering Wilderness*, 1932, *Over the River*, 1933; collected in 1934.

Plays: *The Silver Box, Joy, Strife*, 1909; *Justice*, 1910; *The Eldest Son*, 1912; *The Fugitive*, 1913; *The Skin Game*, 1920; *A Family Man*, 1922; *Escape*, 1926; *Exiled*, 1929.

Other writings include: *Collected Poems*, 1934; *Letters from John Galsworthy, 1900–1932*, ed. E. Garnett, 1934.

See H. V. Marrot, *A Bibliography of the Works of John Galsworthy*, 1928; D. Barker, *A Man of Principle*, 1963; D. H. Lawrence in *Phoenix*, 1936; H. V. Marrot, *The Life and Letters of John Galsworthy*, 1935.

GASCOYNE, DAVID EMERY (b. 1916): Poet and translator.

Poems: *Roman Balcony*, 1932; *Man's Life is this Meat*, 1936; *Hölderlin's Madness*, 1938; *Poems, 1937–1942*, 1943; *A Vagrant*, 1950; *Night Thoughts*, 1956; *Collected Poems*, ed. R. Skelton, 1965; *Sun at Midnight*, 1970.

Translations: *Collected Verse Translations*, ed. R. Skelton and A. Clodd, 1970.

GOLDING, WILLIAM (b. 1911): Novelist.

Novels: *Lord of the Flies*, 1954; *The Inheritors*, 1955; *Pincher Martin*, 1956; *Free Fall*, 1959; *The Spire*, 1964; *The Pyramid*, 1967; *The Scorpion God* (3 novels), 1971.

Play: *The Brass Butterfly*, 1958.

Essays and reminiscences: *The Hot Gates*, 1965.

See M. Kinkead-Weekes and I. Gregor, *William Golding, a Critical Study*, 1967; J. Peter, 'The Fables of William Golding', *Kenyon Review*, Vol. 19, 1957; J. Whitley, *Golding: Lord of the Flies*, 1970.

GRAHAME, KENNETH (1859–1932): Children's writer.

Stories: *The Golden Age*, 1895; *Dream Days*, 1898; *The Wind in the Willows*, 1908.

GRAVES, ROBERT RANKE (b. 1895): Poet, novelist, critic, translator, essayist.

Poems: Various issues of *Poems* from 1927 to 1968; and of *Selected Poems*, 1940, 1943, 1957; *New Poems*, 1962; *Collected Poems*, 1965; *Seventeen Poems*, 1966, *Poems, 1965–68*, 1970.

Novels and shorter fiction: *No Decency Left*, 1932; *I, Claudius*, 1934; *Claudius the God*, 1934, *Count Belisarius*, 1938; *King Jesus*, 1946; *Hercules my Shipmate*, 1951; *Homer's Daughter*, 1944; *Collected Stories*, 1964.

Essays and critical writings include: *Contemporary Techniques of Poetry: A Political Analogy*, 1925; *Poetic Unreason and other Studies*, 1925; *A Survey of Modernist Poetry* (with Laura Riding), 1927; *Goodbye to All That*, 1929, enl., 1951; *The Long Weekend: Social History of Great Britain, 1918–1939* (with Alan Hodge), 1940; *The White Goddess*, 1948, rev. 1952; *Oxford Addresses on Poetry*, 1962; *The Greek Myths*, 2 vols, 1955, rev. as *Greek Gods and Heroes*, 1962.

Translations include: Apuleius's *The Golden Ass*, 1951, and Homer's *Iliad* in *The Anger of Achilles*, 1959.

See F. H. Higginson, *A Bibliography of the Works of Robert Graves*, 1966; J. M. Cohen, *Robert Graves*, 1960; D. Day, *Swifter than Reason*, 1963; D. J. Enright, 'Robert Graves and the Decline of Modernism', *Essays in Criticism*, Vol. XI, 1961.

GREEN, HENRY – Henry Vincent Yorke – (b. 1905): Novelist.

Novels: *Blindness*, 1926; *Living*, 1929; *Party Going*, 1939; *Caught*, 1943; *Loving*, 1945; *Back*, 1946; *Concluding*, 1948; *Nothing*, 1950; *Doting*, 1952.

Autobiography: *Pack my Bag*, 1940.

See E. Stokes, *The Novels of Henry Green*, 1959.

GREENE, HENRY GRAHAM (b. 1904): Novelist, playwright and journalist.

Novels: *The Man Within*, 1929; *Stamboul Train*, 1932; *It's a Battlefield*, 1934, rev. 1948; *England Made Me*, 1935; *A Gun for Sale*, 1936; *Brighton Rock*, 1938; *The Power and the Glory*, 1940; *The Ministry of Fear*, 1943; *The Heart of the Matter*, 1948; *The Third Man*, 1950; *The End of the Affair*, 1951; *The Quiet American*, 1956; *Our Man in Havana*, 1958; *A Burnt-out Case*, 1961; *The Comedians*, 1966; *Travels with my Aunt*, 1969.

Plays: *The Living Room*, 1953, *The Potting Shed*, 1957; *The Complaisant Lover*, 1959; *Carving a Statue*, 1964.

Short stories: Collections published in 1935, 1954, 1963; *May we borrow your Husband?*, 1967.

Other writings: *Journey without Maps* (French Guinea, Liberia), 1936; *British Dramatists*, 1942; *The Lost Childhood*, 1951; *Collected Essays*, 1969; *A Sort of Life: Autobiography*, 1971.

See K. Allott and M. Farris, *The Art of Graham Greene*, 1951; L. Lerner, 'Graham Greene' in *Critical Quarterly*, Vol. 5, 1963; M. D. Zabel, *Craft and Character in Modern Fiction*, 1957.

GREENWOOD, WALTER (b. 1903): Novelist and playwright.

Novels include: *Love on the Dole*, 1933; *His Worship the Mayor*, 1934; *Standing Room Only*, 1936; *The Secret Kingdom*, 1938; *Only Mugs Work*, 1938; *How the Other Man Lives*, 1939.

Short stories: *The Cleft Stick*, 1937.

Play: Dramatization of *Love on the Dole*, 1934.

Autobiography: *There was a Time*, 1967.

GREGORY, ISABELLA AUGUSTA – Lady Gregory – (1852–1932): Playwright, co-founder (with W. B. Yeats in 1899) and manager of the Abbey Theatre, translator of Douglas Hyde's Irish writings.

Plays: *Spreading the News*, 1904; *The White Cockade*, 1905; *The Rising of the Moon* (with Hyde), 1906; *The Unicorn from the Stars* (with Yeats), 1908; *The Full Moon*, 1911; *Irish Folk History Plays*, 1912; *Three Wonder Plays*, 1922; *The Story brought by Brigit*, 1924; *Selected Plays*, ed. E. Coxhead, 1962.

Other writings and anthologies: *Our Irish Theatre: A Chapter of Autobiography*, 1941; *The Kiltartan Poetry Book: Prose Translations from the Irish*, 1919; *Visions and Beliefs in the West of Ireland*, 1920; *Journals, 1916–1930*, ed. L. Robinson, 1946.

See E. Coxhead, *Lady Gregory: A Literary Portrait*, rev. 1966; A. Saddlemyer, *In Defense of Lady Gregory, Playwright*, 1966.

GUNN, THOM (b. 1929): Poet.

Poems: *Fighting Terms*, 1954, rev. 1962; *Poems*, 1954; *The Sense of Movement*, 1957; *My Sad Captains*, 1961; *Touch*, 1967; *Moly*, 1971.

See G. S. Fraser, 'The Poetry of Thom Gunn', *Critical Quarterly*, Vol. 3, 1961.

HARDY, THOMAS (1840–1928): Poet and novelist.

Novels: *Desperate Remedies*, 1871; *Under the Greenwood Tree*, 1872; *A Pair of Blue Eyes*, 1873; *Far from the Madding Crowd*, 1874; *The Return of the Native*, 1878; *A Laodicean*, 1881; *Two on a Tower*, 1882;

The Mayor of Casterbridge, 1886; *The Trumpet-Major*, 1888; *Tess of the d'Urbervilles*, 1891; *Jude the Obscure*, 1896; *The Well-Beloved*, 1897.

Short Stories: *A Group of Noble Dames*, 1891; *Life's Little Ironies*, 1894; *A Changed Man*, 1913.

Poems: *Wessex Poems*, 1898; *Poems of the Past and the Present*, 1902; *The Dynasts* (poetic drama in three parts) 1903, 1906, 1908; *Time's Laughingstocks*, 1909; *Satires of Circumstance*, 1914; *Late Lyrics and Earlier*, 1922; *Human Shows*, 1925; *Winter Words*, 1928; *Collected Poems*, 1919, 1930; *Selected Poems*, ed. G. M. Young, 1940; *Selected Shorter Poems*, ed. J. Wain, 1967.

Other writings: *Life and Art: Essays, Notes and Letters*, coll. E. Brennecke, 1925; *Thomas Hardy's Notebooks*, ed. E. Hardy, 1955; *The Architectural Notebook of Thomas Hardy*, intro. C. J. P. Beatty, 1966.

See R. L. Purdy, *Thomas Hardy: A Bibliographical Study*, 1954. E. Blunden, *Thomas Hardy*, 1941; H. C. Duffin, *Hardy: A Study of the Wessex Novels, the Poems and The Dynasts*, 3rd edn, 1967; A. J. Guerard, *Hardy: The Novels and the Stories*, 1949; Emma Hardy, *Some Recollections*, 1961; J. Holloway in *The Charted Mirror*, 1960; P. Larkin, 'Wanted: Good Hardy Critic', in *Critical Quarterly*, Vol. 8, 1966; D. H. Lawrence in *Phoenix*, 1936; F. R. Leavis in *New Bearings in English Poetry*, rev. 1950; L. Lerner and J. Holmstrom, eds., *Thomas Hardy and his Readers*, 1968; J. H. Miller, *Thomas Hardy: Distance and Desire*, 1970; M. Millgate, *Thomas Hardy: His Career as a Novelist*, 1971; J. M. Murry, in *Aspects of Literature*, 1920; F. B. Pinion, *A Hardy Companion*, 1968; C. J. Weber, *Hardy of Wessex*, rev. 1966; M. Williams, *Thomas Hardy and Rural England*, 1972; G. Wing, *Thomas Hardy*, 1963.

HARTLEY, LESLIE POLES (b. 1895): Novelist, critic and short story writer.

Novels: *The Shrimp and the Anemone*, 1944; *The Sixth Heaven*, 1946; *Eustace and Hilda*, 1946; *The Go-Between*, 1953; *The Hireling*, 1957; *The Brickfield*, 1964; *The Betrayal*, 1966.

Stories: *The Killing Bottle*, 1932; *Two for the River and other Stories*, 1961; *Collected Stories*, 1968.

Criticism: *The Novelist's Responsibility*, 1968.

HILL, GEOFFREY (b. 1932): Poet.

Poems: *King Log*, 1968; *Mercian Hymns*, 1971.

HOLLOWAY, JOHN (b. 1920): Poet, critic.

Poems: *The Minute*, 1956; *The Fugue*, 1960; *The Landfallers*, 1962; *Wood and Windfall*, 1965; *New Poems*, 1970.

Criticism includes: *The Victorian Sage*, 1953; *The Charted Mirror*, 1960; *The Story of the Night: Studies in Shakespeare's Major Tragedies*, 1961; *The Colours of Clarity*, 1964; *The Lion Hunt*, 1964; *Widening Horizons in English Verse*, 1966; *Blake: The Lyric Poetry*, 1968.

Other writings: *Language and Intelligence*, 1951; *A London Childhood*, 1966.

HOUSMAN, ALFRED EDWARD (1859–1939): Poet and classical scholar.

Poems: *A Shropshire Lad*, 1896; *Last Poems*, 1922; *More Poems*, ed. L. Housman, 1936; *Collected Poems*, 1939, 1953, 1956; *Complete Poems*, 1966.

Other writings: *The Name and Nature of Poetry*, 1933; *Selected Prose*, ed. J. Carter, 1961.

See L. Housman, *My Brother, A. E. Housman*, 1938.

HUGHES, TED (b. 1930) : Poet.

Poems: *The Hawk in the Rain*, 1957; *Lupercal*, 1960; *Selected Poems* (with Thom Gunn) 1962; *Wodwo*, 1967; *Crow*, 1970, enl. edn, 1972.

Short stories: *Meet my Folks!*, 1961, *The Earth Owl*, 1963.

See *London Magazine* (articles on Hughes), January 1971.

HUXLEY, ALDOUS LEONARD (1894–1963): Novelist and essayist.

Novels: *Crome Yellow*, 1921; *Antic Hay*, 1923; *Those Barren Leaves*, 1925; *Point Counter Point*, 1928; *Brave New World*, 1932; *Eyeless in Gaza*, 1936; *After Many a Summer*, 1939; *Island*, 1962.

Short stories: *Limbo*, 1920; *Mortal Coils*, 1922; *Brief Candles*, 1930; *Beyond the Mexique Bay*, 1934; *The Gioconda Smile*, 1938.

Essays include: *On the Margin*, 1923; *Jesting Pilate*, 1926; *Vulgarity in Literature*, 1930; *Music at Night*, 1931; *Texts and Pretexts*, 1932; *Ends and Means*, 1937; *Grey Eminence*, 1941; *The Perennial Philosophy*, 1945; *Ape and Essence*, 1948; *Themes and Variations*, 1950; *The Doors of Perception*, 1954; *Adonis and the Alphabet*, 1956; *Heaven and Hell*, 1956; *Brave New World Revisited*, 1958; *Literature and Science*, 1963.

Other writings: *Letters*, ed. Grover Smith, 1969.

See C. J. Eschelbach, *Aldous Huxley: A Bibliography, 1916–1959*, 1961. J. Atkins, *Aldous Huxley; A Literary Study*, 1956; P. Bowering, *Aldous Huxley: A Study of the Major Novels*, 1969; J. Brooke, *Aldous Huxley*, 1954; J. Huxley, ed. *Aldous Huxley, 1894–1963*, a memorial volume, 1965.

ISHERWOOD, CHRISTOPHER WILLIAM (b. 1904): Novelist, essayist.

Novels: *All the Conspirators*, 1928; *Mr Norris Changes Trains*, 1935; *Sally Bowles*, 1937; *Goodbye to Berlin*, 1939; *Prater Violet*, 1945; *The*

World in the Evening, 1952; *Down There on a Visit*, 1962; *A Meeting by the River*, 1970.

Plays: With W. H. Auden, *q.v.*

Travel and essays: *Journey to a War*, 1939; *Vedanta for Modern Man*, 1951; *Exhumations*, 1966; *Lions and Shadows*, autobiography, 1938.

See F. R. Karl, *A Reader's Guide to the Contemporary English Novel*, 1962.

JAMES, HENRY (1843–1916). American novelist, playwright and critic. Settled in England, 1876, and became British subject in 1915.

Novels: *Roderick Hudson*, 1875; *The American*, 1877; *The Europeans*, 1878; *Daisy Miller*, 1879; *Washington Square*, 1880; *The Portrait of a Lady*, 1881; *The Bostonians*, 1886; *The Princess Casamassima*, 1886; *The Reverberator*, 1888; *The Tragic Muse*, 1890; *The Spoils of Poynton*, 1897; *What Maisie Knew*, 1897; *In the Cage*, 1898; *The Awkward Age*, 1899; *The Sacred Fount*, 1901; *The Wings of a Dove*, 1902; *The Ambassadors*, 1903; *The Golden Bowl*, 1904; *The Outcry*, 1911; *The Ivory Tower*, 1917; *The Sense of the Past*, 1917.

Plays and Stories: *The Turn of the Screw*, 1898; *Complete Plays*, ed. L. Edel, 1949; *Complete Tales*, ed. L. Edel, 12 vols, 1962–4.

Critical writings include: *French Poets and Novelists*, 1878; *Hawthorne*, 1879; *Partial Portraits*, 1888; *Notes on Novelists*, 1914; *The Art of the Novel* (prefaces to novels), ed. R. P. Blackmur, 1934; *The Scenic Art*, ed. A. Wade, 1948; *The Art of Fiction and Other Essays*, ed. M. Roberts, 1948; *The House of Fiction*, ed. L. Edel, 1957; *Selected Literary Criticism*, ed. M. Shapira, 1964.

Autobiographical writings: *A Small Boy and Others*, 1913; *Notes of a Son and Brother*, 1914; *The Middle Years*, 1917; these three collected and ed. by F. W. Dupée as *Henry James: An Autobiography*, 1956.

Other writings: *Letters*, ed. P. Lubbock, 2 vols, 1920; *Selected Letters*, ed. L. Edel, 1956; *Notebooks*, ed. F. O. Matthiessen and K. B. Murdock, 1947.

See L. Edel and D. H. Laurence, *A Bibliography of Henry James*, rev., 1961. Q. Anderson, *The American Henry James*, 1958; M. Bewley, in *The Complex Fate*, 1952 and *The Eccentric Design*, 1959; F. W. Dupée, *Henry James*, 1951; L. Edel, *Henry James*, 5 vols, 1953–7; R. Gard, ed., *Henry James: The Critical Heritage*, 1968; D. W. Jefferson, *Henry James and the Modern Reader*, 1964; L. C. Knights, in *Explorations*, 1946; D. Krook, *The Ordeal of Consciousness in Henry James*, 1962; F. R. Leavis in *The Great Tradition*, rev. edn, 1960; F. O. Matthiessen, *Henry James: The Major Phase*, 1946; Ezra Pound, in *Literary Essays*, 1954; S. G. Putt, *A Reader's Guide to*

Henry James, 1966; L. Trilling in *The Opposing Self*, 1955, and *The Liberal Imagination*, 1951; E. Wilson in *The Triple Thinkers*, 1952.

JELLICOE, ANN (b. 1927): Playwright.

Plays: *The Sport of my Mad Mother*, 1964; *The Knack*, 1964; *The Giveaway*, 1970.

Other writings: *Shelley or The Idealist*: A Tragi-comedy, 1966; *Some Unconscious Influences in the Theatre*, 1967.

JENNINGS, ELIZABETH (b. 1926): Poet.

Poems: *A Way of Looking*, 1955; *Song for a Birth or a Death*, 1961; *Recoveries*, 1964; *The Mind Has Mountains*, 1966; *Lucidities*, 1970.

Essays, etc.: *Poetry Today*, 1961; *Every Changing Hope*, 1961; *Christianity and Poetry*, 1965.

JONES, DAVID (b. 1895): Born in Wales. Poet and painter.

Poems/prose: *In Parenthesis*, 1937, new ed., intro. T. S. Eliot, 1961; *The Anathemata*, 1951; *The Tribune's Visitation*, 1969.

Essays: *Epoch and Artist*, ed. H. Grisewood, 1959.

See *Agenda* (special Jones issue) Vol. 5, 1–3, 1967; D. Blamires, *David Jones, Artist and Writer*, 1971; J. Holloway, in *The Charted Mirror*, 1960; *Poetry Wales* (special Jones issue), vol. 8, no. 3, 1972.

JOYCE, JAMES AUGUSTINE ALOYSIUS (1882–1941): Irish novelist and poet.

Novels: *A Portrait of the Artist as a Young Man*, 1916, new edn, 1968; *Ulysses*, Paris, 1922, London, 1936; *Finnegans Wake*, 1939, corr. edn, New York, 1945. *Finnegans Wake* is the completed title of *Work in Progress*, which appeared in the following extracts from 1928 to 1937: *Anna Livia Plurabelle*, 1928; *Haveth Children Everywhere*, 1928; *Tales Told of Shem and Shaun*, 1929; *The Mime of Mick, Nick and the Maggies*, 1934; *Storiello as she is syung*, 1937. Later publications concerned with *Finnegans Wake* are: *Scribbledehobble: the Ur-Workbook for Finnegans Wake*, ed. T. E. Connolly, 1961; *A First Draft of Finnegans Wake*, ed. D. Hayman, 1963; and *A Shorter Finnegans Wake*, ed. A. Burgess, 1966. *Stephen Hero*, ed. from manuscript by T. Spencer, 1944, enl. edn by J. J. Slocum and H. Cahoon, 1955.

Stories: *Dubliners*, 1914.

Play: *Exiles*, 1918.

Poems: *Chamber Music*, 1907, ed. W. Y. Tindall, 1954; *Gas from a Burner*, 1912, *Pomes Penyeach*, 1927; *Collected Poems*, 1936.

Criticism: *The Critical Writings of James Joyce*, ed. E. Mason and R. Ellmann, 1959.

Letters, 3 vols: Vol. I, ed. S. Gilbert, 1957, rev. 1966; Vols II and III, ed. R. Ellmann, 1966.

See J. J. Slocum and H. Cahoon, *A Bibliography of Joyce*, 1953. R. Deming, ed., *Joyce: The Critical Heritage*, 2 vols, 1970; R. Ellmann, *James Joyce*, 1959 and *Ulysses on the Liffey*, 1972; S. Gilbert, *James Joyce's Ulysses: A Study*, rev. 1952; S. Goldberg, *The Classical Temper: A Study of Ulysses*, 1961; H. Kenner, *Dublin's Joyce*, 1956; H. Levin, *James Joyce: A Critical Introduction*, 1941; A. W. Litz, *The Art of James Joyce*, 1961; W. T. Noon, *Joyce and Aquinas*, 1957; W. Y. Tindall, *A Reader's Guide to James Joyce*, 1959.

KIPLING, JOSEPH RUDYARD (1865–1936): Poet, novelist, short story writer.

Poems: *Departmental Ditties*, 1886; *Barrack-room Ballads*, 1892; *The Seven Seas*, 1896; *The Ballad of East and West*, 1899; *The White Man's Burden*, 1899; *Rudyard Kipling's Verse*, 1919, 1927, 1933, definitive edn, 1940; *A Choice of Kipling's Verse*, ed. T. S. Eliot, 1941.

Stories: *Soldiers Three*, 1888; *The Jungle Book*, 1894; *Stalky and Co.*, 1899, *Just So Stories for Little Children*, 1902; *Puck of Pook's Hill*, 1906; *Rewards and Fairies*, 1910; *The Complete Stalky and Co.*, 1930; *All the Mowgli Stories*, 1933.

Novels: *The Light that Failed*, 1890; *Kim*, 1901.

See C. Carrington, *Kipling: His Life and Work*, 1955 (Penguin edn, 1970); L. L. Cornell, *Kipling in India*, 1966; J. I. M. Stewart, *Rudyard Kipling*, 1966; J. M. S. Tompkins, *The Art of Rudyard Kipling*, rev. 1965.

LARKIN, PHILIP (b. 1922): Poet, novelist and critic.

Poems: *The North Ship*, 1945; *Poems*, 1951, *Poems*, 1954, *The Less Deceived*, 1955; *The Whitsun Weddings*, 1964.

Novels: *Jill*, 1946; *A Girl in Winter*, 1947.

Criticism: *All What Jazz?: A Record Diary, 1961–68*, 1970.

LAWRENCE, DAVID HERBERT (1885–1930): Novelist, poet, playwright, story writer, critic.

Novels: *The White Peacock*, 1911; *The Trespasser*, 1912; *Sons and Lovers*, 1913; *The Rainbow*, 1915; *Women in Love*, 1920; *The Lost Girl*, 1920; *Aaron's Rod*, 1922; *Kangaroo*, 1923; *The Plumed Serpent*, 1926; *The Woman who Rode Away*, 1928; *Lady Chatterley's Lover*, 1928, first authorized expurgated edn, 1932, first authorized unexpurgated edn, 1961, *The First Lady Chatterley* (the First Version), 1972, *John Thomas and Lady Jane* (the Second Version), 1972; *The Virgin and the Gypsy*, 1930; *The Man who Died*, 1931.

Stories: *The Prussian Officer*, 1914; *England, my England*, 1922; *The Ladybird*, 1923; *St Mawr*, 1925; *Glad Ghosts*, 1926; *Rawdon's Roof*, 1928; *Love among the Haystacks*, 1930; *Apocalypse*, 1930; *The Lovely Lady*, 1933; *The Tales*, 1934; *A Modern Lover*, 1934; *Complete Short Stories*, 3 vols, 1955.

Poems: *Love Poems*, 1913; *Look! we have come through*, 1917; *Bay*, 1919; *Birds, Beasts and Flowers*, 1923; *Selected Poems*, 1928; *Pansies*, 1929; *Nettles*, 1930; *Last Poems*, ed. R. Aldington and G. Orioli, 1932; *Poems*, collected edn, 2 vols, 1939; *Complete Poems*, 3 vols, 1957, and, ed. V. de Sola Pinto and W. Roberts, 2 vols, 1964, rev., 1972; *Selected Poems*, ed. K. Sagar, 1972.

Plays; *Touch and Go*, 1920; *David*, 1926; *The Plays*, 1934; *A Collier's Friday Night*, 1934; *Complete Plays*, 1965.

Critical writings and essays: *Psychoanalysis and the Unconscious*, 1921; *Fantasia of the Unconscious*, 1922; *Studies in Classic American Literature*, 1923; *Reflections on the Death of a Porcupine*, 1925; *Pornography and Obscenity*, 1929; *Phoenix*, posthumous papers, ed. E. D. MacDonald, 1936; *Selected Essays*, ed. R. Aldington, 1950; *Selected Literary Criticism*, ed. A. Beal, 1955; *The Symbolic Meaning*. ed. A. Arnold, 1962; *Phoenix II*, 1966.

Travel writings: *Twilight in Italy*, 1916; *Sea and Sardinia*, 1921; *Mornings in Mexico*, 1927; *Etruscan Places*, 1932.

Letters: *Collected Letters*, ed. H. T. Moore, 2 vols, 1962; *Selected Letters*, ed. D. Trilling, 1958; *Lawrence in Love: Letters to Louie Burrowe*, ed. J. T. Boulton, 1968.

Paintings: Lawrence's paintings were first reproduced in 1929; a collected edn by M. Levy, published in 1964.

See W. Roberts, *A Bibliography of D. H. Lawrence*, 1963. C. Clarke, *River of Dissolution: D. H. Lawrence and English Romanticism*, 1969; H. M. Daleski, *The Forked Flame*, 1965; R. P. Draper, ed., *D. H. Lawrence, the Critical Heritage*, 1970; E. Goodheart, *The Utopian Vision of D. H. Lawrence*, 1963; D. J. Gordon, *D. H. Lawrence as a Literary Critic*, 1966; G. G. Hough, *The Dark Sun*, 1966; F. R. Leavis, *D. H. Lawrence, Novelist*, 1955; J. M. Murry, *Son of Woman*, 1931; E. Nehls, comp. and ed., *D. H. Lawrence: A Composite Biography*, 3 vols, 1957–58; K. Sagar, *The Art of D. H. Lawrence* (includes bibliography), 1966; H. Talon, *D. H. Lawrence*, Paris, 1966; E. Vivas, *D. H. Lawrence: The Failure and the Triumph of Art*, 1961.

LESSING, DORIS (b. 1919): Born in Persia. South African novelist and short story writer. Settled in England 1949.

Novels: *The Grass is Singing*, 1950; The 'Children of Violence' series: *Martha Quest*, 1952, *A Proper Marriage*, 1954, *A Ripple from the Storm*, 1959, *The Golden Notebook*, 1962; *Landlocked*, 1965; *The Four-Gated City*, 1969; *The Summer Before the Dark*, 1973.

Stories: *This was the Old Chief's Country*, 1951; *The Habit of Loving*, 1960; *A Man and Two Women*, 1963; *African Stories*, 1964; *The Story of a Non-Marrying Man, and Other Stories*, 1972.

LEWIS, CECIL DAY (1904–72): Poet, critic, and under pseud. of Nicholas Blake, detective story writer. Poet Laureat 1968–72.

Poems: *Beechen Vigil*, 1925; *From Feathers to Iron*, 1931; *The Magnetic Mountain*, 1933; *Child of Misfortune*, 1939; *Word over All*, 1943; *Collected Poems, 1929–1936*, 1948; *Poems, 1943–47*, 1948; *An Italian Visit*, 1953, *Collected Poems*, 1954; *Pegasus*, 1957; *Requiem for the Living*, 1964; *The Room and other Poems*, 1966.

Critical writings include: *A Hope for Poetry*, 1934; *Revolution in Writing*, 1935; *The Colloquial Element in English Poetry*, 1947; *The Poetic Image*, 1947; *The Poet's Task*, 1951; *The Lyrical Poetry of Thomas Hardy*, 1953; *The Lyrical Impulse*, 1965.

See C. Dyment, *C. Day Lewis*, 1955.

LEWIS, PERCY WYNDHAM (1886–1957): American-born essayist, novelist, painter. Edited *Blast*: review of the great English vortex (with Ezra Pound) 1914–15; *The Tyro* (painting and sculpture review) I and II, 1921–2; *The Enemy* (literary review), 1927–9.

Novels: *Tarr*, 1918, rev. 1928; *The Childermass*, Vol. I, 1928; *The Apes of God*, 1930; *Snooty Baronet*, 1932; *The Revenge for Love*, 1937; *Self-Condemned*, 1955; *The Human Age*: Book I, a revision of *Childermass*; Book II, *Monstre Gai*, and Book III, *Malign Fiesta*, 1955; *The Red Priest*, 1956.

Essays and criticism: *The Caliph's Design*, 1919; *The Art of Being Ruled*, 1926; *The Lion and the Fox: The Role of the Hero in Shakespeare*, 1927; *Time and Western Man*, 1927; *Paleface: The Philosophy of the Melting Pot*, 1929; *Satire and Fiction*, 1930; *The Wild Body*, 1932; *The Enemy of the Stars*, 1932; *Men without Art*, 1934; *Left Wings over Europe*, 1936; *Blasting and Bombardiering* (autobiographical essays), 1937; *The Jews, are they human?*, 1939; *The Writer and the Absolute*, 1952; *The Demon of Progress in the Arts*, 1954; *Wyndham Lewis on Art: Collected Writings, 1913–1956*, ed. W. Michel and C. J. Fox, 1969.

Letters: *The Letters of Wyndham Lewis*, ed. W. K. Rose, 1963.

See *Agenda* (Lewis special issue), Vol. 7, iii–Vol. 8, i, 1969–70; T. Armstrong, *Apes, Japes, and Hitlerism: Study and Bibliography of Wyndham Lewis*, 1932; W. Allen, 'The Achievement of Wyndham

Lewis', *Encounter*, Vol. 21, 1963; T. S. Eliot, 'Wyndham Lewis', *Hudson Review*, Vol. 10, 1957; N. Frye, 'Neo-classical agony', *Hudson Review*, Vol. 10, 1957; J. Holloway, in *The Charted Mirror*, 1960 and 'Wyndham Lewis on Art', *Critical Quarterly*, Winter, 1971; H. Kenner, *Wyndham Lewis*, 1954; E. W. F. Tomlin, *Wyndham Lewis*, 1955.

LIVINGS, HENRY (b. 1929): Playwright.

Plays: *Eh?*, 1965; *Good Grief*, 1968; *Honour and Offer*, 1969; *Pongo Plays*, 1–6, 1971.

LOGUE, CHRISTOPHER (b. 1926): Poet.

Poems: *Patrocleia*: adaptation of Book XVI of the *Iliad*, 1962; *Logue's ABC*, 1966; *Pax*: translation of Book XIX of the *Iliad*, 1967; *New Numbers*, 1969.

MACDIARMID, HUGH (pseud. of Christopher Murray Grieve, b. 1892): Scottish nationalist poet and critic.

Poems: *Sangschaw*, 1925; *A Drunk Man Looks at the Thistle*, 1926; *Tarras*, 1932; *Scots Unbound*, 1932; *Stony Limits*, 1934; *Selected Poems*, 1934; *Direadh*, 1938; *Cornish Heroic Song for Valda*, 1943; *A Kist of Whistles*, 1947; *Three Hymns to Lenin*, 1957; *The Battle Continues*, 1957; *Collected Poems*, 1962; *Poetry like the Hawthorn*, 1963; *The Terrible Crystal: A Vision of Scotland*, 1964; *The Ministry of Water*, 1965; *The Fire of the Spirit*, 1965; *A Lap of Honour*, 1967; *Early Lyrics*, ed. J. K. Annand, 1968; *A Clyack Sheaf*, 1969; *Selected Poems*, ed. D. Craig, 1970; *More Collected Poems*, 1970.

Essays, critical writings: *Contemporary Scottish Studies*, 1926; *Albyn, or Scotland and the Future*, 1927; *Scotland in 1980*, 1930; *Warning Democracy*, 1931; *Scottish Scene*, 1934; *At the Sign of the Thistle*, 1934; *In Memoriam James Joyce*, 1955; *Burns Today and Tomorrow*, 1959; *The Ugly Birds without Wings*, 1962; *Selected Essays*, ed. D. Glen, 1969.

Autobiography: *Lucky Poet*, 1943; *The Company I've Kept*, 1966.

See *Agenda* (special MacDiarmid and Scottish issue) Vol. 5, iv–Vol. 6, i, 1967–8; K. Buthlay, *Hugh MacDiarmid*, 1954; D. Glen, *Hugh MacDiarmid and the Scottish Renaissance*, 1964.

MACNEICE, LOUIS (1907–63): Born in Belfast. Poet, script writer for radio.

Poems: *Blind Fireworks*, 1929; *Poems*, 1935; *The Earth Compels*, 1938; *Autumn Journal*, 1939; *The Last Ditch*, 1940; *Plant and Phantom*, 1941; *Springboard: Poems 1941–44*, 1944; *Holes in the Sky: Poems 1944–47*, 1948; *Ten Burnt Offerings*, 1952, *Autumn Sequel*, 1954; *The Other Wing*, 1954; *Visitations*, 1957; *Solstices*, 1961, *The Burning Perch*, 1963; *Col-*

lected Poems, 1925–1948, 1949; *Selected Poems*, ed. W. H. Auden, 1964; *Collected Poems*, ed. E. R. Dodds, 1966.

Radio plays: *Christopher Columbus*, 1944; *The Dark Tower*, 1947; *The Mad Islands* and *The Administrator*, 1964.

Translations: from Aeschylus and Goethe.

Travel writing: *Letters from Iceland* (with W. H. Auden), 1937; *I Crossed the Minch*, 1938.

Critical writings: *Modern poetry*, 1938; *The Poetry of W. B. Yeats*, 1941; *Varieties of Parable*, 1965.

Autobiography: *The Strings are False* (unfinished), 1965.

See G. G. Hough, 'MacNeice and Auden', *Critical Quarterly*, Vol. 9, 1967; J. Press, *Louis MacNeice*, 1965.

MANSFIELD, KATHERINE – Kathleen Mansfield Beauchamp – (1888–1923): New Zealand short story writer, lived in England from 1908 to her death.

Stories: *In a German Pension*, 1911; *Prelude*, 1918; *Je ne parle pas français*, 1918; *Bliss*, 1920; *The Garden Party*, 1922; *The Dove's Nest*, 1923; *Something Childish*, 1924; *Collected Stories*, 1945.

Poems: 1923.

Personal writings: all ed. by J. M. Murry: *Journal*, 1927, enl. 1954; *Letters*, 1928; *The Scrapbook of Katherine Mansfield*, 1938; *Letters to J. M. Murry, 1913–1922*, 1951.

See A. Alpers, *Katherine Mansfield*, 1954.

MASEFIELD, JOHN EDWARD (1878–1967): Poet, playwright, novelist; Poet Laureate, 1930–67.

Poems: *Ballads*, 1903, enl. 1910; *A Mainsail Haul*, 1905, rev. 1954; *The Widow in the Bye Street*, 1912; *Lollingdon Downs*, 1917; *Enslaved*, 1920; *The Dream*, 1922; *End and Beginning*, 1933; *The Country Scene*, 1937; *Land Workers*, 1942; *Complete Poems*, 1963.

Novels: *Martin Hyde, the Duke's Messenger*, 1910; *Sard Harker*, 1924; *The Midnight Folk*, 1927; *The Bird of Dawning*, 1933; *The Box of Delights*, 1935; *Basilissa*, 1940.

Plays: *The Tragedy of Nan*, 1909; *The Faithful*, 1915; *Melloney Hotspur*, 1922; *Easter*, 1929; *Plays*, 2 vols, 1938.

Masefield's *Collected Works* were published in 10 vols, 1935–8.

See C. H. Simmons, *A Bibliography of John Masefield*, 1930.

MAUGHAM, WILLIAM SOMERSET (1874–1965): Novelist, playwright, short story writer.

Collected Works, 20 vols, 1934–50; *Complete Short Stories*, 3 vols, 1951.

Novels include: *Liza of Lambeth*, 1897; *Of Human Bondage*, 1915;

The Moon and Sixpence, 1919; *Cakes and Ale*, 1930; *The Razor's Edge*, 1944.

Plays include: *The Circle*, 1921; *East of Suez*, 1922; *The Letter*, 1925.

Travel writings: *A Writer's Notebook*, 1949.

See L. Brander: *Somerset Maugham: A Guide*, rev. 1965.

MERCER, DAVID (b. 1928): Playwright.

Plays include: *The Generations*, a trilogy, 1964; *Belcher's Luck*, 1967; *The Parachute* and two more TV plays, 1967; *After Haggerty*, 1970; *Flint*, 1970; *On the Eve of Publication*, 1970.

MONRO, HAROLD EDWARD (1879–1932): Poet. In 1912 founded the Poetry Bookshop. Editor of *Poetry Review* and *Poetry and Drama*.

Collected Poems, ed. A. Monro, 1933.

See J. Grant, *Harold Monro and the Poetry Bookshop*, 1967.

MOORE, GEORGE (1852–1933): Irish novelist and essayist associated with the Irish literary revival.

The Works of George Moore, 20 vols, 1937.

Novels include: *A Modern Lover*, 1883; *Esther Waters*, 1894; *Celibates*, 1895; *The Brook Kerith*, 1916; *Aphrodite in Aulis*,1930.

Autobiography: *Hail and Farewell*, a trilogy, 1911–14.

MUIR, EDWIN (1887–1959). Poet, critic, novelist, translator (with Willa Muir). Born in the Orkney Islands. Assistant editor of *The New Age*, 1919.

Poems: *First poems*, 1925; *Chorus of the Newly Dead*, 1926; *Variations on a Time Theme*, 1934; *Journeys and Places*, 1925; *The Narrow Place*, 1943; *The Voyage*, 1946; *The Labyrinth*, 1949; *Prometheus*, 1954; *One Foot in Eden*, 1956; *Collected Poems, 1921–51*, ed. J. C. Hall, 1952; *Collected Poems, 1921–1958*, 1960; *Selected Poems*, ed. T. S. Eliot, 1965.

Essays and critical writings include: *Enigmas and Guesses*, 1918; *Latitudes*, 1924; *Transition*, essays on contemporary literature, 1926; *The Structure of the Novel*, 1928; *Scott and Scotland: The Predicament of the Scottish Writer*, 1936; *The Present Age from 1914*, 1939; *The Scots and their Country*, 1946; *Essays on Literature and Society*, 1949, rev. 1966.

Translations (with Willa Muir) of: Kafka, *The Castle*, 1930; *The Great Wall of China*, 1933; *The Trial*, 1937; *America*, 1949; *In the Penal Settlement*, 1949; and Feuchtwanger, Hauptmann, Heuser, Sholem Asch.

Autobiography: *The Story and the Fable*, 1940, rev. 1954 as *An Autobiography*.

See E. W. Mellown, *A Bibliography of the Writings of Edwin Muir*, rev.

1966. R. P. Blackmur, 'Edwin Muir', in *Four Poets on Poetry*, ed. D. C. Allen, 1959; E. Butter, *Edwin Muir*, 1962, and *Edwin Muir, Man and Poet*, 1966; J. Holloway, 'The Modernity of Edwin Muir', in *The Colours of Clarity*, 1964; Willa Muir, *Belonging*, 1968; K. Raine, in *Defending Ancient Springs*, 1967.

MUNRO, HECTOR HUGH – 'Saki' – (1870–1916): Born in Burma. Novelist and playwright.

Novels include: *Reginald*, 1904; *The Chronicles of Clovis*, 1911; *The Unbearable Bassington*, 1912.

Collected Works: *The Novels and Plays of Saki*, 1933.

MURDOCH, IRIS (b. 1919): Born in Dublin. Novelist.

Novels: *Under the Net*, 1954; *The Flight from the Enchanter*, 1956; *The Sandcastle*, 1957; *The Bell*, 1958; *A Severed Head*, 1961; *An Unofficial Rose*, 1962; *The Unicorn*, 1963; *The Italian Girl*, 1964; *The Red and the Green*, 1965; *The Time of the Angels*, 1966; *The Nice and the Good*, 1968; *Bruno's Dream*, 1969; *A Fairly Honourable Defeat*, 1970; *An Accidental Man*, 1971; *The Black Prince*, 1973.

Criticism: *Sartre*, 1953.

See M. Bradbury, 'Iris Murdoch's *Under the Net*', *Critical Quarterly*, Vol. 4, 1962; A. S. Byatt, *Degrees of Freedom: The Novels of Iris Murdoch*, 1965.

MYERS, LEOPOLD HAMILTON (1881–1944): Novelist.

Novels: *The Orissers*, 1922; *The Clio*, 1925; *The Near and the Far*, 1929, with its sequel *Prince Jali*, 1931, and *Rajah Amar*, appeared as *The Root and the Flower*, 1935; *Strange Glory*, 1936; *The Pool of Vishnu*, 1940, republished with *The Root and the Flower* as *The Near and the Far*, 1943.

See G. H. Bantock, *L. H. Myers: A Critical Study*, 1956.

NOYES, ALFRED (1880–1958): Poet.

Poems include: *Drake*, 1906–1908; *The Torchbearers*, 3rd edn, 1937; *Collected Poems*, 1950.

O'CASEY, SEAN (1880–1964): Irish playwright.

Plays: *Juno and the Paycock* and *The Shadow of a Gunman*, 1925; *The Plough and the Stars*, 1926; *The Silver Tassie*, 1928; *Within the Gates*, 1933; *Five Irish Plays*, 1935; *The Star turns Red*, 1940; *Purple Dust*, 1940; *Red Roses for Me*, 1942; *Cock-a-doodle-dandy*, 1949; *The Bishop's Bonfire*, 1955; *The Drums of Father Ned*, 1960; *Collected Plays*, 4 vols, 1951–2.

Autobiography: *I Knock at the Door*, 1939; *Pictures in the Hallway*, 1942; *Drums Under the Window*, 1945; *Inishfallen, Fare Thee Well*, 1949; *Sunset and Evening Star*, 1954; *Mirror in my House*, 1958.

Selections from O'Casey's writings: *Feathers from the Green Crow, 1905–25*, ed. R. Hogan, 1952; *Blasts and Benedictions*, ed. R. Ayling, 1967.

See S. Cowasjee, *O'Casey*, 1966.

O'CONNOR, FRANK – Michael Francis O'Donovan – (1903–67): Irish short story writer, critic and translator from the Irish.

Stories: *Guests of the Nation*, 1931; *The Saint and Mary Kate*, 1932; *Crab Apple Jelly*, 1944; *Selected Stories*, 1946; *The Common Chord*, 1947; *Traveller's Samples*, 1951; *Domestic Relations*, 1957; *My Oedipus Complex*, 1963; *Collection Two*, 1964; *Collection Three*, 1969.

Critical writings: *Towards an Appreciation of Literature*, 1945; *The Art of the Theatre*, 1947; *The Mirror in the Roadway: Study of the Modern Novel*, 1957; *Shakespeare's Progress*, 1960; *The Lonely Voice: Study of the Short Story*, 1963.

Novel: *Dutch Interior*, 1940.

Plays, *In the Train*, 1937; *The Invincibles*, 1937; *Moses' Rock*, 1938.

Translations of Irish poetry: *The Wild Bird's Nest*, 1932; *Kings, Lords, and Commons*, 1959; *The Little Monasteries*, 1963.

See T. Flanagan, 'Frank O'Connor, 1903–1966', *Kenyon Review*, Vol. 28, 1966.

ORWELL, GEORGE – Eric Blair – (1903–50): Indian-born novelist, essayist, critic.

Novels: *Burmese Days*, 1934; *A Clergyman's Daughter*, 1935; *Keep the Aspidistra Flying*, 1936; *Coming up for Air*, 1939; *Animal Farm: A Fairy Story*, 1945; *Nineteen Eighty-four*, 1949.

Essays and criticism include: *The Road to Wigan Pier*, 1937; *Homage to Catalonia*, 1938, ed. L. Trilling, 1952; *Inside the Whale*, 1940; *The Lion and the Unicorn: Socialism and the English Genius*, 1941; *Critical Essays*, 1946; *The English People*, 1947; *Shooting an Elephant*, 1950; *England, your England*, 1953; *Collected Essays, Journalism and Letters*, ed. S. Orwell and I. Angus, 4 vols, 1968.

Autobiography: *Down and Out in Paris and London*, 1933.

See J. Atkins, *George Orwell* (a literary and biographical study), 1965; M. Gross, ed. *The World of George Orwell*, 1971; C. Hollis, *A Study of George Orwell*, 1956; E. M. Thomas, *Orwell*, 1965; R. Williams, *Orwell*, 1971; G. Woodcock, *The Crystal Spirit: A Study of George Orwell*, 1967.

OSBORNE, JOHN (b. 1929). Playwright for stage and television.

Plays: *Look Back in Anger*, 1957; *The Entertainer*, 1957; *Epitaph for George Dillon* (with A. Creighton), 1958; *Luther*, 1961; *A Subject for*

Scandal and Concern, 1961; *Plays for England: The Blood of the Bambergs, Under Plain Cover*, 1963; *Inadmissible Evidence*, 1965; *A Patriot for Me*, 1966; *A Bond Honoured* (from Lope de Vega), 1966; *Time Present*, and *A Hotel in Amsterdam*, 1968; *The Right Prospectus*, 1970; *Very Like a Whale*, 1971; *West of Suez*, 1971.

Musical comedy: *The World of Paul Slickey*, 1959. Osborne also wrote the filmscript for a production of Fielding's *Tom Jones*, 1964.

OWEN, WILFRED (1893–1918). Poet.

Only four poems published, in periodicals, during Owen's lifetime. Seven poems were included in E. Sitwell's *Wheels, Fourth Cycle*, 1919; a further selection in *Poems*, ed. S. Sassoon, 1920; Collected editions: ed. E. Blunden, 1931; ed. C. Day Lewis, 1963; ed. E. Blunden, 1966.

Collected Letters, ed. H. Owen and J. Bell, 1967.

See H. Owen, *Journey from Obscurity: Wilfred Owen, 1893–1918*, 3 vols, 1963–5; D. S. R. Welland, *Wilfred Owen: A Critical Study*, 1960.

PINTER, HAROLD (b. 1930): Playwright.

Plays: *The Dumb Waiter*, 1960; *The Room*, 1960; *The Birthday Party*, 1960, rev. 1965; *The Caretaker*, 1960; *A Slight Ache and Other Plays*, 1961; *Three Plays*, 1962; The collection: *The Lover*, 1963; *A Night Out*, 1963; *The Homecoming*, 1965; *The Tea Party and Other Plays*, 1967; *Landscape and Silence*, *Night*, 1969.

Poems: *Poems*, 1968.

See J. R. Brown, 'Dialogue in Pinter and others', *Critical Quarterly*, Vol. 7, 1965; M. Esslin, *The Peopled Wound*, 1970.

PLATH, SYLVIA (1932–63): American poet, novelist, short story writer. Married to the poet Ted Hughes (see above).

Poems: *The Colossus and Other Poems*, 1960; *Ariel*, 1965; *Uncollected poems*, 1965.

Novel: *The Bell Jar*, 1963.

Radio Play: *Three Women* (first broadcast, 1962), 1968.

See E. Homberger, *A chronological checklist of the periodical publications of Sylvia Plath*, 1970; C. Newman, ed., *The Art of Sylvia Plath: A Symposium*, 1970 (includes bibliography).

POUND, EZRA LOOMIS (1885–1972): American poet; lived in London 1908–20.

Poems: *A lume spento*, 1908; *Personae*, 1909; *Canzoni*, 1911; *Ripostes*, 1912; *Lustra*, 1916; *Homage to Sextus Propertius*, 1917; *Quia pauper amavi*, 1919; *Hugh Selwyn Mauberley*, 1920; *Poems*, 1918–21; Pound's

Cantos were published at intervals, 1919, 1925, 1928, 1930, 1934, 1937, 1940 and as *Cantos 1–84* in 1948; Section: *Rock Drill*, 1956, is *Cantos 85–95*; drafts and fragments of *Cantos CX–CXVII* appeared in 1969; *Collected Shorter Poems*, 1968.

Essays and critical writings include: *The Spirit of Romance*, 1910, rev. 1953; *Gaudier-Brzeska: A Memoir*, 1916; *Antheil and the Treatise on Harmony*, 1924; *How to Read*, 1931; *ABC of Reading*, 1934; *Make it New*, 1934; *Jefferson and/or Mussolini*, 1935; *Guide to Kulchur*, 1938, rev. 1951; *Patria mia* (written in 1913), 1950; *The Literary Essays of Ezra Pound*, ed. T. S. Eliot, 1954; *Selected Prose, 1909–65*, ed. W. Cookson, 1973.

Pound's translations include works by Cavalcanti, Confucius, Fenollosa, Fontenelle, Gourmont, and translations of the Japanese Noh plays.

Letters: *The Letters of Ezra Pound*, ed. D. D. Paige, 1950; *Pound/Joyce Letters*, ed. F. Read, 1969.

See D. Gallup, *A Bibliography of Ezra Pound*, 1963; D. Davie, *Ezra Pound: Poet as Sculptor*, 1964; E. Hesse, ed. *New Approaches to Ezra Pound*, 1969; E. Homberger, ed., *Ezra Pound, the Critical Heritage*, 1972; H. Kenner, *The Poetry of Ezra Pound*, 1951, *The Pound Era*, 1972; N. Stock, *Reading the Cantos*, 1967, and *The Life of Ezra Pound*, 1970; M. de Rachewiltz, *Discretions*, 1971.

POWELL, ANTHONY (b. 1905): Novelist.

Novels: The 'Music of Time' series: *A Question of Upbringing*, 1951; *A Buyer's Market*, 1952; *The Acceptance World*, 1955; *At Lady Molly's*, 1957; *Casanova's Chinese Restaurant*, 1960; *The Kindly Ones*, 1962; *The Valley of Bones*, 1964; *The Soldier's Art*, 1966; *Books Do Furnish a Room*, 1971; other novels include: *Afternoon Men*, 1931; *From a View to a Death*, 1933.

POWYS, JOHN COWPER (1872–1963): Novelist, poet, critic.

Novels: *Wood and Stone*, 1915; *Rodmoor*, 1916; *Ducdame*, 1925; *Wolf Solent*, 1929; *A Glastonbury Romance*, 1932; *Jobber Skald*, 1935, rev. 1963, American edn, 1934 with title, *Weymouth Sands*; *Maiden Castle*, 1938; *Morwyn, or The Vengeance of God*, 1937; *Owen Glendower*, 1940; *Porius: A Romance of the Dark Ages*, 1951; *The Inmates*, 1952; *Atlantis*, 1954; *The Brazen Head*, 1956; *All or Nothing*, 1960.

Poems: *Odes*, 1896; *Poems*, 1899; *Wolf's Bane: Rhymes*, 1916; *Mandragon*, 1917; *Samphire*, 1922; *Lucifer*, 1956; *Selected Poems*, ed. K. Hopkins, 1964.

Essays and critical writings: *Visions and Revisions*, 1915, rev. 1955; *Suspended Judgments*, 1916; *Psychoanalysis and Morality*, 1923; *The*

Meaning of Culture, 1929; *Dorothy M. Richardson*, 1931; *A Philosophy of Solitude*, 1933; *The Art of Happiness*, 1935; *The Enjoyment of Literature*, 1938; *Obstinate Cymric: Essays, 1935–47*, 1947.

Autobiography: *Autobiography*, 1934.

See H. P. Collins, *John Cowper Powys, Old Earth Man*, 1966; G. W. Knight, *The Saturnian Quest*, 1964.

POWYS, LLEWELYN (1884–1939): Essayist and short story writer.

Writings include: *Ebony and Ivory*, 1923; *Black Laughter*, 1925; *Verdict of Bridlegoose*, 1927; *Impassioned Clay*, 1931; *Dorset Essays*, 1935; *Somerset Essays: A Pagan's Pilgrimage*, 1937.

POWYS, THEODORE FRANCIS (1875–1953): Novelist and short story writer.

Novels: *Black Bryony*, 1923; *Mark Only*, 1924; *Mr Tasker's Gods*, 1925; *Mockery Gap*, 1925; *Innocent Birds*, 1926; *Mr Weston's Good Wine*, 1927; *Kindness in a Corner*, 1930; *Unclay*, 1931.

Stories include: *The Left Leg*, 1923; *Feed my Swine*, 1926; *A Strong Girl, The Bride*, 1926; *The Rival Pastors*, 1926; *The Dewpond*, 1928; *Fables*, 1929; *Uncle Dottery*, 1930; *The Only Penitent*, 1931; *The Two Thieves*, 1932; *Bottle's Path*, 1946.

See H. Coombes, *T. F. Powys*, 1960; W. Hunter, *The Novels and Stories of T. F. Powys*, 1930.

THE POWYS BROTHERS.

See R. C. Churchill, *The Powys Brothers*, 1962; K. Hopkins, *The Powys Brothers*, 1967; L. Marlow, *Welsh Ambassadors*, rev. ed., intro. K. Hopkins, 1971.

PRIESTLEY, JOHN BOYNTON (b. 1894): Novelist, playwright, essayist.

Novels include: *The Good Companions*, 1929; *Angel Pavement*, 1930; *Let the People Sing*, 1939.

Plays include: *Dangerous Corner*, 1932; *Laburnum Grove*, 1933; *When we are Married*, 1938; *An Inspector Calls*, 1945.

Essays and critical writings include: *The English Comic Characters*, 1925; *The English Novel*, 1927; *Literature and Western Man*, 1960.

RICHARDSON, DOROTHY MILLER (1872–1957). Novelist.

Novels have the collective title 'Pilgrimage': *Pointed Roofs*, 1915; *Backwater*, 1916; *Honeycomb*, 1917; *Tunnel*, 1919; *Interim*, 1919; *Deadlock*, 1921; *Revolving Lights*, 1923; *Trap*, 1925; *Oberland*, 1927; *Dawn's Left Hand*, 1931; *Clear Horizon*, 1935; *Dimple Hill*, 1938; *Pilgrimage*, new ed., intro. W. Allen, 4 vols, 1967.

See J. C. Powys, *Dorothy M. Richardson*, 1931.

ROLFE, FREDERICK WILLIAM – 'Baron Corvo' – (1860–1913): Novelist.

Works include: *Stories Toto told Me*, 1898; *Hadrian VII*, 1904; *Don Tarquinio*, 1905.

See A. J. A. Symons, *The Quest for Corvo*, 1934.

ROSENBERG, ISAAC (1890–1918): Poet.

Poems: *Night and Day*, 1912; *Youth*, 1915; *Collected Poems*, ed. G. Bottomley and D. Harding, 1949.

See D. W. Harding, in *Experience into Words*, 1963.

RUSSELL, GEORGE WILLIAM – 'AE' – (1867–1935): Irish poet and journalist. Editor of *Irish Homestead*, 1906–23 and *Irish Statesman*, 1923–30.

Poems: *Homeward*, 1894; *The Divine Vision*, 1903; *Collected Poems*, 1913, 2nd edn, 1926; *Midsummer Eve*, 1928; *Vale*, 1931; *The House of the Titans*, 1934.

Essays and critical writings include: *Literary Ideals in Ireland*, 1899; *Controversy in Ireland*, 1904; *The Renewal of Youth*, 1911; *The Candle of Vision*, 1918; *The Interpreters*, 1922.

Correspondence with W. B. Yeats, 1936.

RUTHERFORD, MARK – William Hale White – (1831–1913): Novelist, critic and philosopher.

Novels: *The Autobiography of Mark Rutherford*, 1881; *Mark Rutherford's Deliverance*, 1885; *The Revolution in Tanner's Lane*, 1887; *Catharine Furze*, 1893; *Clara Hopgood*, 1896.

See J. Stone, *Mark Rutherford*, 1955.

SASSOON, SIEGFRIED LORRAINE (1886–1967): Poet, novelist, journalist.

Poems: *Poems*, 1906; *An Ode for Music*, 1912; *Discoveries*, 1915; *The War Poems*, 1919; *Satirical Poems*, 1926, enl. 1933; *To the Red Rose*, 1931; *Vigils*, 1934; *Selected Poems*, 1943; *Common Chords*, 1950; *The Path to Peace*, 1960; *Collected Poems, 1908–56*, 1961.

Novels: *Memoirs of a Fox-hunting Man*, 1928; *Memoirs of an Infantry Officer*, 1930 – these two published together as *The Complete Memoirs of George Sherston*, 1937.

Autobiography: *The Weald of Youth*, 1942; *Siegfried's Journey, 1916–1920*, 1945.

See G. Keynes, *A Bibliography of Siegfried Sassoon*, 1962; M. Thorpe, *Siegfried Sassoon*, 1966.

SHAW, GEORGE BERNARD (1856–1950): Born in Dublin. Playwright, essayist, critic.

Plays: *Plays Pleasant and Unpleasant*, 1898 (Pleasant: *Arms and the Man, Candida, The Man of Destiny, You Never Can Tell*; Unpleasant: *Widowers' Houses, The Philanderer, Mrs Warren's Profession*); *Three Plays for Puritans*, 1901 (*The Devil's Disciple, Caesar and Cleopatra, Captain Brassbound's Conversion*); *Man and Superman*, 1903; *Major Barbara*, 1907; *Misalliance*, 1910; *The Doctor's Dilemma*, 1911; *Androcles and the Lion*, 1914; *Pygmalion*, 1916; *Heartbreak House*, 1917; *Great Catherine*, 1919; *Back to Methuselah*, 1921; *St Joan*, 1924; *The Apple Cart*, 1930; *Too True To Be Good*, 1934; *In Good King Charles's Golden Days*, 1939; *Complete plays with prefaces*, 1962; *Collected plays with prefaces*, ed. D. H. Laurence, 1970–.

Essays, critical writings: Collections – *The Quintessence of Bernard Shaw*, ed. H. C. Duffin, rev. 1939; *Platform and Pulpit*, ed. D. H. Laurence, 1962; *Shaw on Shakespeare*, ed. E. Wilson, 1961; *The Matter with Ireland*, ed. D. H. Laurence and D. H. Green, 1962; *Religious Speeches*, ed. W. Smith, 1963; *The Complete Prefaces*, 1965; *Selected Non-Dramatic Writings*, ed. D. H. Laurence, 1965; *Shaw's Ready Reckoner*, ed. N. H. Leigh-Taylor, 1966.

Letters: *Florence Farr, Shaw and Yeats: Letters*, ed. C. Box, 1941; *Letters to Ellen Terry*, ed. C. St John, 1949; *Bernard Shaw and Mrs Patrick Campbell: Correspondence*, ed. A. Dent, 1952; *Advice to a Young Critic*, 1955; *Bernard Shaw's Letters to Granville Barker*, ed. C. B. Purdom, 1956; *To a Young Actress, Letters to Molly Tompkins*, ed. P. Tompkins, 1961; *Collected Letters*, 1874–97, ed. D. H. Laurence, 1966–.

See E. Bentley, *Shaw: A Reconsideration*, 1947, rev. 1957; W. Irvine, *The Universe of G. B. Shaw*, 1949; R. J. Kaufmann, ed. *G. B. Shaw: A Collection of Critical Essays*, 1965; M. Meisel, *Shaw and the Nineteenth Century Theater*, 1963; C. B. Purdom, *A Guide to the Plays of Bernard Shaw*, 1961; E. Strauss, *Shaw: Art and Socialism*, 1942; R. Williams, in *Drama from Ibsen to Brecht*, 1968; E. Wilson in *The Triple Thinkers*, 1952.

SILLITOE, ALAN (b. 1928): Novelist, short story writer, poet.

Novels: *Saturday Night and Sunday Morning*, 1958; *The General*, 1960; *Key to the Door*, 1961; *The Death of William Posters*, 1965.

Stories: *The Loneliness of the Long-distance Runner*, 1959; *The Ragman's Daughter*, 1963.

Poems: *Without Beer or Bread*, 1957; *The Rats*, 1960; *A Falling Out of Love*, 1965.

SIMPSON, NORMAN FREDERICK (b. 1919): Playwright.
Plays: *One Way Pendulum*, 1960; *The Hole and other plays*, 1964; *The Cresta Run*, 1966; *Some Tall Tinkles*, TV plays, 1968.

SITWELL, DAME EDITH (1887–1964): Poet and critic.
Poems: *The Mother*, 1915; *Façade*, 1922, enl. 1950; *The Sleeping Beauty*, 1924; *Rustic Elegies*, 1927; *Collected Poems*, 1930; *Five Variations on a Theme*, 1933; *Poems New and Old*, 1940; *Green Song*, 1944; *Poor Men's Music*, 1950; *Gardeners and Astronomers*, 1953; *The Collected Poems*, 1957; *Selected Poems*, 1965.
Essays and critical writings: *Poetry and Criticism*, 1925; *Alexander Pope*, 1930; *Aspects of Modern Poetry*, 1934; *A Poet's Notebook*, 1943; *A Notebook on William Shakespeare*, 1948.
Autobiography: *Taken Care Of*, 1965.
See R. Fifoot, *A Bibliography of Edith, Osbert and Sacheverell Sitwell*, 1963; M. Moore, in *Four Poets on Poetry*, ed. D. C. Allen, 1959.

SMITH, STEVIE (1905–71): Poet and novelist.
Novels: *Novel on Yellow Paper*, 1936; *Over the Frontier*, 1938; *The Holiday*, 1949.
Poems: *Selected Poems*, 1962; *More Selected Poems*, 1966.

SPARK, MURIEL (b. 1918): Novelist, short story writer.
Novels: *The Comforters*, 1957; *Robinson*, 1958; *Memento Mori*, 1959; *The Bachelors*, 1960; *The Ballad of Peckham Rye*, 1960; *The Prime of Miss Jean Brodie*, 1961; *The Girls of Slender Means*, 1963; *The Mandelbaum Gate*, 1965; *The Public Image*, 1968.
Stories: *The Go-Away Bird*, 1958; *Voices at Play*, 1961 (includes playscripts); *Doctors of Philosophy*, 1963 (includes four playscripts).

SPENDER, STEPHEN (b. 1909): Poet and critic. Jointly editor of *Horizon*, 1939–41 and *Encounter*, 1953–1965.
Poems: *Nine Entertainments*, 1928; *Vienna*, 1934; *The Still Centre*, 1939; *Poems for Spain*, 1939; *Ruins and Visions*, 1942; *Poems of Dedication*, 1947; *The Edge of Being*, 1949; *Collected Poems, 1928–1953*, 1955; *Selected Poems*, 1965; *The Generous Days*, 1971.
Essays and critical writings: *The Destructive Element*, 1935; *Forward from Liberalism*, 1937; *The New Realism*, 1939; *Poetry since 1939*, 1946; *Shelley*, 1952; *The Creative Element*, 1953; *The Making of a Poem*, 1955; *The Struggle of the Modern*, 1963.
Autobiography: *World within World*, 1951.
See G. S. Fraser, in *The Modern Writer and his World*, rev. 1964.

SPRIGG, CHRISTOPHER ST JOHN: See CAUDWELL, Christopher.

STOREY, DAVID (b. 1933): Novelist and playwright.

Novels: *This Sporting Life*, 1962; *Flight into Camden*, 1964; *Radcliffe*, 1965; *The Restoration of Arnold Middleton*, 1967.

Plays: *In Celebration*, 1969; *The Contractor*, 1970; *Home*, 1970.

STRACHEY, GILES LYTTON (1880–1932): Essayist.

Writings include: *Landmarks in French Literature*, 1912; *Eminent Victorians*, 1918; *Queen Victoria*, 1921; *Books and Characters*, 1922; *Elizabeth and Essex: a Tragic History*, 1928.

Letters: *Virginia Woolf and Lytton Strachey: Letters*, ed. L. Woolf and J. Strachey, 1956.

See M. Holroyd, *Lytton Strachey, a Critical Biography*, 2 vols, 1967–8; J. K. Johnstone, *The Bloomsbury Group*, 1954.

SYNGE, JOHN MILLINGTON (1871–1909): Irish playwright.

Plays: *In the Shadow of the Glen, Riders to the Sea*, 1905; *The Well of the Saints*, 1905; *The Playboy of the Western World*, 1907; *The Tinker's Wedding*, 1908; *Deirdre of the Sorrows*, 1910.

Collected works: Vol. I, *Poems*, ed. R. Skelton, 1962, Vol. II, *The Aran Island, In Wicklow, West Kerry, Connemara*, essays, ed. A. Price, 1966; Vols III and IV, *Plays*, ed. A. Saddlemyer, 1968.

See D. H. Greene and E. M. Stephens, *J. M. Synge, 1871–1909*, a bibliography, 1959. D. Corkery, *Synge and Anglo-Irish Literature*, 1966; A. Price, *Synge and Anglo-Irish Drama*, 1961.

THOMAS, DYLAN MARLAIS (1914–1953): Welsh poet.

Poems: *Eighteen Poems*, 1934; *The Map of Love*, 1939, *New Poems*, 1943; *Deaths and Entrances*, 1946; *In Country Sleep*, 1953; *Collected Poems, 1934–1952*, 1952.

Stories: *Portrait of the Artist as a Young Dog*, 1940; *Adventures in the Skin Trade*, 1955; *Quite Early One Morning* (broadcast talks), 1954.

Verse play: *Under Milk Wood*, 1954.

Other writings: *A Child's Christmas in Wales*, 1954, rev. 1959; *A Prospect of the Sea*, ed. D. Jones, 1955; *Miscellany*, 1963.

Letters: *Letters to Vernon Watkins*, 1957; *Selected Letters*, ed. C. Fitzgibbon, 1966.

See J. A. Rolph, *Dylan Thomas: A Bibliography*, 1956. J. M. Brinnin, *Dylan Thomas in America*, 1955; C. Fitzgibbon, *The Life of Dylan Thomas*, 1966; D. Holbrook, *Llareggub Revisited*, 1962; W. J. Moynihan, *The Craft and Art of Dylan Thomas*, 1966; W. Y. Tindall, *A Reader's Guide to Dylan Thomas*, 1962.

THOMAS, PHILIP EDWARD (1878–1917): Poet, critic, essayist.

Poems: *Poems* (by 'Edward Eastaway'), 1917; *Last Poems*, 1918; *Collected Poems*, 1920, new ed., 1936.

Essays: *Horae Solitariae*, 1902; *Richard Jefferies*, 1909; *Rest and Unrest*, 1910; *The Feminine Influence on the Poets*, 1910; *The Country*, 1913; *Walter Pater*, 1913; *A Literary Pilgrim in England*, 1917; *Cloud Castle*, 1922; *The Prose of Edward Thomas*, ed. T. Grant, 1948.

Autobiography: *The Childhood of Edward Thomas*, 1938.

See R. P. Eckert, *Edward Thomas: A Biography and a Bibliography*, 1937. H. Coombes, *Edward Thomas*, 1956; F. R. Leavis, in *New Bearings in English Poetry*, rev. 1950; J. M. Murry in *Aspects of Literature*, 1920; V. Scannell, *Edward Thomas*, 1965.

THOMAS, RONALD STUART (b. 1913): Poet.

Poems: *The Stones of the Field*, 1946; *An Acre of Land*, 1952; *The Minister*, 1953; *Song at the Year's Turning: Poems 1942–54*, 1955; *Poetry for Supper*, 1958; *Tares*, 1961; *The Bread of Truth*, 1963; *Pièta*, 1966; *Not that he brought Flowers*, 1968.

Essays: *Words and the Poet*, 1964.

See *Poetry Wales* (special Thomas issue), vol. 7, no. 4, 1972; R. G. Thomas, *R. S. Thomas*, 1964.

TOMLINSON, CHARLES (b. 1927): Poet.

Poems: *Seeing is Believing*, 1958; *American Scenes*, 1966; *The Way of a World*, 1969; *Written on Water*, 1972.

WAIN, JOHN (b. 1925): Novelist and critic.

Novels: *Hurry on Down*, 1953; *Living in the Present*, 1955; *The Contenders*, 1958; *A Travelling Woman*, 1959; *Strike the Father Dead*, 1962; *The Young Visitors*, 1965.

Stories: *Nuncle*, 1960; *Death of the Hind Legs*, 1966.

Poems: *A Word Carved on a Sill*, 1956; *Wildtrack*, 1965.

Essays, critical writings: *Preliminary Essays*, 1957; *Essays on Literature and Ideas*, 1963; *The Living World of Shakespeare*, 1964.

Autobiography: *Sprightly Running*, 1962, rev. 1965.

WALPOLE, HUGH SEYMOUR (1884–1941): Novelist. Born in New Zealand.

Novels include: *Maradick at Forty*, 1910; *Mr Perrin and Mr Traill*, 1911; *The Dark Forest*, 1916; *Jeremy*, 1919; *The Captives*, 1920; *The Old Ladies*, 1924; *Wintersmoon*, 1928; *The Herries Chronicle*: I, 1930, II, 1931, III, 1931, IV, 1933, collected, 1939; *The Sea Tower*, 1939.

Criticism: *Joseph Conrad*, 1916; *The English Novel*, 1925; *Anthony Trollope*, 1928.

See R. Hart-Davis, *Hugh Walpole*, 1952.

WATKINS, VERNON (1906–67): Welsh poet.

Poems: *Ballad of the Mari Lwyd*, 1941; *The Lamp and the Veil*, 1945; *The Lady with the Unicorn*, 1948; *Selected Poems*, 1948; *The Death Bell*, 1954; *Cypress and Acacia*, 1959; *Affinities*, 1962; *Fidelities*, 1968.

See L. Norris, ed. *Vernon Watkins, 1906–1966*, 1970; K. Raine, in *Defending Ancient Springs*, 1967.

WAUGH, EVELYN ARTHUR (1903–66): Novelist.

Novels: *Decline and Fall*, 1928; *Vile Bodies*, 1930; *Black Mischief*, 1932; *A Handful of Dust*, 1934; *Scoop*, 1938; *Work Suspended*: two chapters of an unfinished novel, 1942; *Put Out More Flags*, 1942; *Brideshead Revisited*, 1945; *The Loved One*, 1948; *Helena*, 1950; War trilogy: *Men at Arms*, 1952, *Officers and Gentlemen*, 1955, *Unconditional Surrender*, 1961, rev. as *Sword of Honour*, 1965; *Love among the Ruins*, 1953; *The Ordeal of Gilbert Pinfold*, 1957.

Travel writings include: *When the Going was Good*, 1946.

Criticism, biography: *Rossetti: His Life and Works*, 1928; *The Life of Ronald Knox*, 1959.

See M. Bradbury, *Evelyn Waugh*, 1964; J. F. Carens, *The Satiric Art of Evelyn Waugh*, 1966; F. J. Stopp, *Evelyn Waugh*, 1958.

WELLS, HERBERT GEORGE (1866–1946): Novelist, short story writer, essayist.

Novels: *The Time Machine*, 1895; *The Wonderful Visit*, 1895; *The Island of Doctor Moreau*, 1896; *The Invisible Man*, 1897; *The War of the Worlds*, 1898; *When the Sleeper Wakes*, 1899, rev. as *The Sleeper Wakes*, 1910; *Love and Mr Lewisham*, 1900; *The First Men in the Moon*, 1901; *The Sea Lady*, 1902; *The Food of the Gods*, 1904; *Kipps*, 1905; *A Modern Utopia*, 1905; *Ann Veronica*, 1909; *Tono-Bungay*, 1909; *The History of Mr Polly*, 1910; *The New Machiavelli*, 1911; *The Passionate Friends*, 1913; *Mr Britling Sees it Through*, 1916; *The Secret Places of the Heart*, 1922; *Men like Gods*, 1923; *The World of William Clissold*, 1926; *The Autobiography of Mr Parham*, 1930; *The Holy Terror*, 1939.

Wells's short stories are collected in the editions of 1927, 1948 and 1964 (*The Valley of the Spiders*).

Essays and critical writings include: *Mankind in the Making*, 1903; *Socialism and the Family*, 1906; *Faults of the Fabians*, 1906; *New Worlds for Old*, 1908; *The Great State*, 1912; *An Englishman Looks at the World*, 1914; *What Is Coming*, 1916; *Democracy under Revision*, 1927; *The Work,*

Wealth and Happiness of Mankind, 1931; *The Shape of Things to Come*, 1933; *The Fate of Homo Sapiens*, 1939; *The Rights of Man*, 1940; *Journalism and Prophecy*, ed. W. Wager, 1966.

Autobiography: *Experiment in Autobiography*, 2 vols, 1966.

Letters: *Henry James and H. G. Wells*, ed. L. Edel and G. N. Ray, 1958; *Arnold Bennett and H. G. Wells*, ed. H. Wilson, 1960; *George Gissing and H. G. Wells*, ed. R. A. Gettmann, 1961.

See M. Belgion, *H. G. Wells*, 1953; B. Bergonzi, *The Early H. G. Wells*, 1961; M. K. Hillegas, *The Future as Nightmare: H. G. Wells and the Anti-Utopians*, 1967; J. Kagarlitski, *Life and Thought of H. G. Wells*, trans. M. Budberg, 1966; I. Raknem, *H. G. Wells and his Critics*, 1962.

WESKER, ARNOLD (b. 1932): Playwright.

Plays: The Wesker trilogy: *Chicken Soup with Barley*, 1959, *Roots*, 1959, *I'm Talking about Jerusalem*, 1960; *The Kitchen*, 1961; *Chips with Everything*, 1962; *Their Very Own and Golden City*, 1966; *The Four Seasons*, 1966; *The Friends*, 1970.

Other writings: *Fears of Fragmentation*, 1970.

WILSON, ANGUS (b. 1913): Novelist, short story writer, essayist.

Novels: *Hemlock and After*, 1952; *Anglo-Saxon Attitudes*, 1956; *The Middle Age of Mrs Eliot*, 1958; *The Old Men at the Zoo*, 1961; *Late Call*, 1964.

Stories: *The Wrong Set*, 1949; *Such Darling Dodos*, 1950.

Essays, critical writings: *Emile Zola*, 1952; *For Whom the Cloche Tolls: Scrapbook of the Twenties* (with P. Jullian), 1963; *A Bit off the Map*, 1957; *The Wild Garden, or, Speaking of Writing*, 1963.

Play: *The Mulberry Bush*, 1956.

See J. L. Halio, *Angus Wilson*, 1966.

WOOLF, VIRGINIA (1882–1941): Novelist and critic.

Novels: *The Voyage Out*, 1915; *Night and Day*, 1919; *Jacob's Room*, 1922; *Mrs Dalloway*, 1925; *To the Lighthouse*, 1927; *Orlando*, 1928; *The Waves*, 1931; *The Years*, 1937; *Between the Acts*, 1941.

Essays and critical writings: *Mr Bennett and Mrs Brown*, 1924; *The Common Reader*, 1925; *A Room of One's Own*, 1929; *The Common Reader*, 2nd series, 1932; *A Letter to a Young Poet*, 1932; *Walter Sickert: A Conversation*, 1934; *Three Guineas*, 1938; *The Death of the Moth*, 1942; *The Moment*, 1947; *The Captain's Death Bed*, ed. L. Woolf, 1950; *Granite and Rainbow*, 1958; *Contemporary Writers*, 1965; *Collected Essays*, ed. L. Woolf, 4 vols, 1966.

Stories: *Two Stories* (with L. Woolf), 1917; *Kew Gardens*, 1919; *A Haunted House*, 1943.

Sketches: *The Mark on the Wall*, 1917; *Monday or Tuesday*, 1921.

Children's story: *Nurse Lugton's Golden Thimble*, 1966.

Biography: *Roger Fry*, 1940; *Flush* (Elizabeth Barrett Browning's dog), 1933.

Letters: *The Letters of Virginia Woolf and Lytton Strachey*, ed. L. Woolf and J. Strachey, 1956.

See B. J. Kirkpatrick, *A Bibliography of Virginia Woolf*, 1957. Q. Bell, *Virginia Woolf, a Biography*, 2 vols, 1972; J. Bennett, *Virginia Woolf: Her Art as a Novelist*, 1945, rev. 1964; B. Blackstone, *Virginia Woolf: A Commentary*, 1949; D. Daiches, *Virginia Woolf*, 1945; E. M. Forster, *Virginia Woolf*, 1954; J. Guiguet, *Virginia Woolf and her Works*, 1965; J. K. Johnstone, in *The Bloomsbury Group*, 1954; H. Richter, *Virginia Woolf, the Inward Voyage*, 1970; N. C. Thakur, *The Symbolism of Virginia Woolf*, 1965; L. Woolf, Vol. III and IV of his autobiography, *Beginning Again, 1911–1918*, 1964 and *Downhill All the Way, 1918–1939*, 1967.

YEATS, WILLIAM BUTLER (1865–1939): Irish poet, playwright and critic. Edited, *Samhain* and *Beltaine*, periodicals, 1901–1908, on the Irish literary theatre.

Poems: *Mosada*, 1886; *The Wanderings of Oisin*, 1889; *Poems*, 1895; *The Wind among the Reeds*, 1899; *The Shadowy Waters*, 1900; *In the Seven Woods*, 1903; *Poems, 1899–1905*, 1906; *The Poetical Works*, 2 vols, 1906–1907; *The Green Helmet*, 1910; *Responsibilities*, 1914; *Michael Robartes and the Dancer*, 1920; *Later Poems*, 1922; *The Cat and the Moon and certain poems*, 1924; *October Blast*, 1927; *The Tower*, 1928; *The Winding Stair*, 1929; *Words for Music, perhaps*, 1932; (poems in) *The King of the Great Clocktower*, 1934; *New Poems*, 1938; *Last Poems* (and two plays), 1939; *The Collected Poems*, 1950; *Complete Poems, Variorum*, ed. by P. Allt and R. K. Alspach, 1957.

Verse dramas and plays: *The Countess Cathleen*, 1892; *The Land of Heart's Desire*, 1894; *Cathleen ni Houlihan*, 1902; *Where There Is Nothing*, 1902; *The Hourglass*, 1903; *The King's Threshold, On Baile's Strand*, 1904; *Deirdre*, 1907; *The Golden Helmet*, 1908; *The Unicorn from the Stars* (with Lady Gregory), 1908; (Plays in) *Responsibilities*, 1914; *The Wild Swans at Coole*, 1917; *Two Plays for Dancers*, 1919; *Four Plays for Dancers*, 1921; *The Player Queen*, 1922; *The Herne's Egg*, 1938; *Diarmuid and Grania* (with George Moore), 1951; *The Collected Plays*, 1952; *Complete Plays, Variorum*, ed. by R. K. Alspach, 1966.

Stories: *The Secret Rose*, 1897; *Tables of the Law, The Adoration of the Magi*, 1897; *Stories of Red Hanrahan*, 1904.

Essays, critical writings: *Ideas of Good and Evil*, 1903; *Discoveries*, 1907; *Poetry and Ireland* (with Lionel Johnson) 1908; *Synge and the Ireland of His Time*, 1911; *The Cutting of an Agate*, 1912; *Per Amica Silentia Lunae*, 1918; *The Bounty of Sweden*, 1925; *A Vision*, 1925, rev. 1937; *A Packet for Ezra Pound*, 1929; *St Patrick's Breastplate*, 1929; *Wheels and Butterflies*, 1934; *Letters to the New Island*, 1934; *Modern Poetry*, 1936; *Essays, 1931–36*, 1937; *If I were Four-and-twenty*, 1940; *Mythologies*, 1959; *Essays and Introductions*, 1961; *Selected Criticism*, ed. A. N. Jeffares, 1964; *Uncollected Prose, Vol. 1: First Reviews and Articles, 1886–96*, ed. J. P. Frayne, 1970.

Autobiography and reminiscence: *Reveries over Childhood and Youth*, 1915; reprinted with *The Trembling of the Veil* under the title, *Autobiographies*, 1926; which, with *Dramatis Personae*, was in turn reprinted as *The Autobiography*, 1938; *Pages from a Diary*, 1944; *Memoirs: Autobiography – First Draft; Journal*, ed. D. Donoghue, 1972.

Letters: *W. B. Yeats and T. S. Moore: Their Correspondence*, ed. U. Bridge, 1953; *Letters to Katharine Tynan*, ed. R. McHugh, 1953; *Letters*, ed. A. Wade, 1954; *Letters on Poetry to Dorothy Wellesley*, 1965.

Other: *The Senate Speeches of W. B. Yeats*, ed. D. R. Pearce, 1960.

See A. Wade, *A Bibliography of the Writings of W. B. Yeats*, 3rd edn, rev. by R. K. Alspach, 1968. Collections of critical writings: *The Dolmen Press Centenary Papers*, I–10, 1965–8; D. Donoghue, ed. *The Integrity of Yeats*, 1964; D. Donoghue and J. R. Mulryne, eds, *An Honoured Guest*, 1965; A. N. Jeffares and K. G. W. Cross, eds, *In Excited Reverie: A Centenary Tribute to W. B. Yeats*, 1965; D. E. S. Maxwell and S. B. Bushrui, eds, *W. B. Yeats: Centenary Essays*, 1965; J. Unterecker, ed., *Yeats: A Collection of Critical Essays*, 1963. Individual critics: D. Donoghue, *Yeats*, 1971; R. Ellmann, *Yeats, the Man and the Masks*, 1948, and *The Identity of Yeats*, 1954; E. Engelberg, *The Vast Design: Patterns in Yeats's Aesthetic*, 1964; T. R. Henn, *The Lonely Tower*, 1960, rev. 1965; J. Holloway, 'Yeats and the Penal Age', *Critical Quarterly*, Vol. 8, 1966; J. Hone, *W. B. Yeats, 1865–1939*, 2nd edn, 1965; A. N. Jeffares, *W. B. Yeats: Man and Poet*, 1949; G. Melchiori, *The Whole Mystery of Art*, 1960; M. L. Rosenthal, 'On Yeats and the Cultural Symbolism of Modern Poetry', *Yale Review*, Vol. 49, 1960; G. B. Saul, *Prolegomena to the Study of Yeats's Poems*, 1957, and *Prolegomena to the Study of Yeats's Plays*, 1958; J. Stallworthy, *Between the lines: Yeats's Poetry in the Making*, 1963 and *Vision and*

Revision in Yeats's Last Poems, 1969; J. Unterecker, *A Reader's Guide to W. B. Yeats*, 1959; P. Ure, *Yeats*, 1963; F. A. C. Wilson, *Yeats's Iconography*, 1960 and *W. B. Yeats and Tradition*, 1958.

2. Collections and Anthologies; Periodicals

POETRY:

Allott, K. (ed.) *The Penguin Book of Contemporary Verse*, rev. 1962.
Alvarez, A. (ed.) *The New Poetry*, rev. 1966.
Bolt, S. (ed.) *Poetry of the 1920s*, 1967.
Brophy, J., and Partridge, E. (eds.) *The Long Trail: What the British Soldier Said and Sang, 1914–1918*, 1965.
Bruce, G., *et al. Scottish Poetry*, 1, 1966, 2, 1967.
Cecil, D., and Tate, A. (eds.) *Modern Verse in English, 1900–1950*, 1958.
Church, R. (ed.) *Poems of Our Time, 1900–1960*, enl. ed., 1960.
Conquest, R. (ed.) *New Lines*, 1956.
Davies, W. H. (ed.) *Shorter Lyrics of the 20th Century, 1900–1919*, 1922.
Enright, D. J. (ed.) *Poets of the 1950s*, 1955.
Finn, F. E. S. (ed.) *Poems of the Sixties*, 1970.
Freer, A., and Andrew, J. M. Y. (eds.) *Cambridge Book of English Verse, 1900–1939*, 1970.
Gardner, B. (ed.) *Up the Line to Death* (World War I), 1964.
Gardner, B. (ed.) *The Terrible Rain: The War Poets, 1939–1945*, 1966.
Griffiths, B. (ed.) *Welsh Voices: An Anthology of New Poets from Wales*, 1967.
The Guinness Books of Poetry, 1–5, 1956/57–1960/61, 1957–62.
Hall, D., and Pack, R. (eds.) *The New Poets of England and America*, 1962.
Hamilton, I. (ed.) *The Poetry of War, 1939–45*, 1965.
Heath-Stubbs, J., and Wright, D. (eds.) *The Faber Book of Twentieth Century Verse*, 2nd ed., 1965.
Holloway, J. (ed.) *Poems of the Mid-Century*, 1957.
Horovitz, M. (ed.) *Children of Albion: Poetry of the Underground in Britain*, 1969.
Jennings, E. (ed.) *Modern Verse, 1940–1960*, 1961.
Lehmann, J. (ed.) *Poems from 'New Writing' 1936–1946*, 1946.
Lewis, C. Day, and Lehmann, J. (eds.) *The Chatto Book of Modern Poetry, 1915–1951*, 1955.
Lindsay, M. (ed.) *Modern Scottish Poetry*, 2nd ed., 1967.
Oxford Book of Twentieth-Century English Verse, ed. P. Larkin, 1973.

Parsons, I. M. (ed.) *Men who March Away* (World War I), 1965.
Penguin Modern Poets, 1–21, 1962–72.
Penguin Book of Georgian Poetry, 1962.
Peschmann, H. (ed.) *The Voice of Poetry: An Anthology from 1930 to the Present Day*, 2nd ed., 1969.
Poetry Book Society Supplements, 1956–72.
Roberts, M. (ed.) *The Faber Book of Modern Verse*, rev. ed., 1951.
Rodway, A. E. (ed.) *Poetry of the 1930s*, 1967.
Rosenthal, M. (ed.) *The New Poets: British and American Poetry since World War II*, 1967; rev. ed. with title *The New Modern Poetry*, 1969.
Skelton, R. (ed.) *Poetry of the Thirties*, 1964.
Thornton, R. K. R. (ed.) *Poetry of the Nineties*, 1970.
Williams, J. S. (ed.) *The Lilting House: Anglo-Welsh Poetry, 1917–1967*, 1969.
Williams, O. (ed.) *The Little Treasury of Modern Poetry*, rev. 1950.
Wright, D. (ed.) *Longer Contemporary Poems*, 1966.
Yeats, W. B. (ed.) *The Oxford Book of Modern Verse*, 1936.
Young, D. (ed.) *Scottish Verse, 1851–1951*, 1952.

PROSE

Davin, D. (ed.) *English Short Stories of Today*, 2nd series, 1958.
Hadfield, J. (ed.) *Modern Short Stories*, 1939.
Hendry, J. F. (ed.) *The Penguin Book of Scottish Short Stories*, 1970.
Hudson, D. (ed.) *English Short Stories: Modern*, 2nd series, 1952.
Jones, P. M. (ed.) *English Short Stories: Modern*, 1939.
Keating, P. J. (ed.) *Working Class Stories of the 1890s*, 1971.
Lehmann, J. (ed.) *English Short Stories from 'New Writing'*, 1952.
Milford, H. (ed.) *English Short Stories*, 1927.
O'Connor, F. (ed.) *Modern Irish Short Stories*, 1957.
Penguin Modern Stories, 1–12, 1969–72 (include English writers).
Rhys, E. (ed.) *Modern English Essays, 1870–1920*, 5 vols, 1923.

PLAYS

Armstrong, W. A. (ed.) *Classic Irish Drama*, 1964.
Four Modern Verse Plays (Eliot/Fry/Williams/MacDonagh), 1957.
Maxwell, B. (ed.) *New Radio Drama*, 1966.
New English Dramatists (Penguin), 1–14, 1959–72.
Rowell, G. (ed.) *Late Victorian Plays, 1890–1914*, 1968.
Three Plays (Shaffer/Wesker/Kops), 1968.
Three Plays (Hall/Lessing/Hastings), 1968.

PERIODICALS: Some influential literary and critical periodicals of the period:

Blast: A Review of the Great English Vortex, ed. W. Lewis, 1914–15.
The Bookman, 1891–1934, ed. W. R. Nicholl and A. St Adcock.
The Calendar of Modern Letters, ed. Rickword and D. Garman, 3 vols, 1925–7; see: *Selections*, ed. F. R. Leavis, 1960: *Towards Standards of Criticism*.
Coterie: Art, prose and literature quarterly, 1919–21.
The Criterion, ed. T. S. Eliot, 1923–39.
The Critical Quarterly, 1959–.
The Egoist, ed. R. Aldington, 1914–17.
Encounter, 1953–.
The Enemy, ed. Wyndham Lewis, 1927–9.
English, the Magazine of the English Association, 1936–.
The English Review, 1908–37.
Essays and Studies by members of the English Association, Vols 1–32, 1910–46; new series, 1948–.
Essays in Criticism, ed. F. W. Bateson, 1951–.
Horizon, ed. C. Connolly, 1940–50.
The Mask, a theatre quarterly, ed. E. G. Craig, 1908–29.
The Modern Language Review, 1906–.
The New Age, new series, 1907–38.
Nine, Vols 1–4, 1949–56.
Poetry and Drama, 1913–14.
Poetry Review, 1912–.
The Review of English Literature, 1960.
Review of English Studies, Vol. 1–25, 1925–49; new series, 1950–.
Scrutiny, Vols 1–19, 1932–53, reprinted 1963 with a 'Retrospect' by F. R. Leavis. See: 'A Symposium on *Scrutiny*', *Essays in Criticism*, Vol. 1, 1964.
The Times Literary Supplement, 1902–.
Twentieth Century Verse, 1937–9.

3. History, Criticism and Bibliographies of the Literature

BIBLIOGRAPHIES:

Batho, E., and Dobrée, B. *The Victorians and After, 1830–1914*, 1938.
The English Association: *The Year's Work in English Studies*, 1919–.
Ireland, N. *Index to full length plays, 1895–1964*, 1965.

Millett, F. B. *Contemporary British Literature*, 3rd rev. ed. of Manly and Rickert's edition, 1935.

Modern Humanities Research Association: *Annual Bibliography of English Language and Literature*, 1921–.

Modern Language Association of America: *Annual Bibliography* (English section), 1919–.

Muir, E. *The Present Age, from 1914*, 1939, revised 1958 by D. Daiches as *The Present Age, after 1920.*

The New Cambridge Bibliography of English Literature, vol. 3, 1800–1900, ed. G. Watson, 1969 (revision of F. Bateson's 1940 edn); vol. 4, 1900–1950, ed. I. R. Willison, 1972.

The *Penguin Companion to Literature, 1: British and Commonwealth Literature*, ed. D. Daiches, 1971.

Temple, R. S., comp., *Twentieth Century British Literature: A Reference Guide*, 1968.

GENERAL HISTORY AND CRITICISM OF THE LITERATURE:

Bell, Q. *Bloomsbury*, 1968.

Bergonzi, B. *Heroes' Twilight: A Study of the Literature of the Great War*, 1965.

Bowra, C. M. *Poetry and Politics, 1900–1960*, 1966.

Bradbury, M. *The Social Context of Modern English Literature*, 1971.

Chapple, J. A. V. *Documentary and Imaginative Literature*, 1970.

Clarke, A. *The Celtic Twilight and the Nineties*, intro. R. McHugh, 1969.

Dobrée, B. *The Lamp and the Lute*, 1929.

Donoghue, D. *The Ordinary Universe: Soundings in Modern Literature*, 1968.

Eagleton, T. *Exiles and Emigrés*, 1970.

Ellmann, R. *Eminent Domain: Yeats among Wilde, Joyce, Pound, Eliot and Auden*, 1967.

Enright, D. J. *The Apothecary's Shop: Essays on Literature*, 1957.

Fraser, G. S. *The Modern Writer and his World*, rev. 1964.

Harrison, J. R. *The Reactionaries, Yeats, Lewis, Pound, Eliot, Lawrence: A Study of the Anti-Democratic Intelligence*, 1966.

Hartman, C. *et al. Approaches to the Study of 20th Century Literature*, 1964.

Hoggart, Richard. *Speaking to Each Other*, 2 vols, 1970.

Holloway, J. *The Colours of Clarity*, 1964.

Hough, G. *Image and Experience*, 1960.

Isaacs, J. *An Assessment of 20th Century Literature*, 1951.

Johnstone, J. K. *The Bloomsbury Group*, 1954.

Kermode, F. *Continuities*, 1968; *Modern Essays*, 1971.

Lester, J. A. *Journey through Despair: Transformations in British Literary Culture, 1880–1914*, 1968.

Levin, H. (ed.) *Perspectives of Criticism*, 1950.

Melchiori, G. *The Tightrope Walkers: Studies of Mannerism in Modern English Literature*, 1956.

O'Brien, C. C. *Writers and Politics*, 1966.

The *Review*, Nos 11, 12, 1964: 'The Thirties'.

Robson, W. W. *Critical Essays*, 1966; *Modern English Literature*, 1970.

Ross, R. H. *The Georgian Revolt: the Decline of a Literary Ideal?* 1966.

Routh, H. V. *English Literature and Ideas in the 20th Century*, 3rd edn, 1950.

Scott-James, R. A. *Fifty Years of English Literature, 1900–1950*, 2nd edn, enl. to *1955*, 1955.

Steiner, G. *Language and Silence*, 1967.

Swinnerton, F. *The Georgian Literary Scene, 1910–1935*, rev. 1950.

Tindall, W. Y. *Forces in Modern British Literature, 1885–1956*, 1956.

Walsh, W. *A Human Idiom: Literature and Humanity*, 1964.

Ward, A. C. *Twentieth Century Literature, 1901–1950*, 1956.

Wilson, E. *Axel's Castle: A Study of the Imaginative Literature of 1870 to 1930*, 1936; *The Shores of Light: A Literary Chronicle of the Twenties and Thirties*, 1952.

POETRY:

Aldington, R. *Poetry of the English-Speaking World*, 1956.

Allen, D. C. (ed.) *Four Poets on Poetry*, 1959.

Alvarez, A. *The Shaping Spirit*, 1958.

Baker, W. E. *Syntax in English Poetry, 1870–1930*, 1967.

Bowra, C. M. *The Heritage of Symbolism*, 1943; *The Creative Experiment*, 1949.

Bullough, G. *The Trend of Modern Poetry*, 3rd edn, 1949.

Cohen, J. M. *Poetry of This Age, 1908–1965*, 1966.

Cox, C. B. *Modern Poetry*, 1963.

Cronin, A. *A Question of Modernity*, 1965.

Davie, D. *Thomas Hardy and British Poetry*, 1973.

Duncan, J. E. *The Revival of Metaphysical Poetry*, 1959.

Ford, H. D. *A Poet's War* (Spanish Civil War), 1965.

Fraser, G. S. *Vision and Rhetoric: Studies in Modern Poetry*, 1959.

Graves, R. and Riding, L. *A Survey of Modernist Poetry*, 1927.

Grubb, F. *A Vision of Reality: Liberalism in 20th Century Verse*, 1965.

Hoffman, D. G. *Barbarous Knowledge: Myth in Yeats, Graves and Muir*, 1967.
Jennings, E. *Poetry Today*, 1961.
Johnstone, J. H. *English Poetry of the First World War*, 1964.
Kermode, F. *Romantic Image*, 1967.
Leavis, F. R.: See LITERARY CRITICS section.
Maxwell, D. E. S. *Poets of the Thirties*, 1969.
Miller, J. H. *Poets of Reality: Six 20th Century Writers*, 1966.
Pinto, V. de S. *Crisis in English Poetry, 1880–1940*, 1951.
Press, J. *Rule and Energy*, 1963; *A Map of Modern Verse*, 1969.
Rosenthal, M. L. *The Modern Poets: A Critical Introduction*, 1960.
Savage, D. S. *The Personal Principle*, 1944.
Schmidt, M., ed., *British Poetry Since 1960: a Critical Survey*, 1972.
Silkin, J. *Out of Battle: the Poetry of the Great War*, 1972.
Stead, C. K. *The New Poetic: Yeats to Eliot*, 1964.
Wright, G. *The Poet in the Poem, the Personae of Eliot, Yeats and Pound*, 1960.

PROSE FORMS:

Allen, W. *Tradition and Dream*, 1965.
Burgess, A. *The Novel Now*, 1971.
Craig, D. *The British Working Class Novel Today*, 1963.
Daiches, D. *The Novel and the Modern World*, rev. 1960.
Davie, D. (ed.) *Russian Literature and Modern English Fiction*, 1966.
Dobrée, B. *Modern Prose Style*, 1934.
Edel, L. *The Psychological Novel, 1900–1950*, 1955.
Forster, E. M. *Aspects of the Novel*, 1927; *The Development of English Prose between 1918 and 1939*, 1945.
Friedman, A. *The Turn of the Novel*, 1966.
Gindin, J. *Post-war British Fiction*, 1962.
Hardy, B. *The Appropriate Form*, 1964.
Karl, F. R. *A Reader's Guide to the Contemporary English Novel*, 1963.
Lodge, D. *The Language of Fiction*, 1965; *The Novel at the Crossroads*, 1971.
Muir, E. *The Structure of the Novel*, 1932. See also AUTHOR entry.
O'Connor, F. *The Mirror in the Roadway*, 1956; *The Lonely Voice*, 1963.
O'Faolain, S. *The Vanishing Hero: Studies in Novelists of the Twenties*, 1956.
Raban, J. *The Technique of Modern Fiction*, 1968.
Rabinowitz, R. *The Reaction against Experiment in the English Novel, 1950–1960*, 1967.

Rippier, J. S. *Some Post-war British Novelists*, 1965.
Rodway, A. *The Truths of Fiction*, 1970.
Sandison, A. *The Wheel of Empire: The Imperial Idea in Late 19th Century and Early 20th Century Fiction*, 1967.
Savage, D. S. *The Withered Branch: Studies in the Modern Novel*, 1950.
Schorer, M. (ed.) *Modern British Fiction: Essays in Criticism*, 1961.
Stewart, J. I. M. *Eight Modern Writers*, 1963.
Van Ghent, D. *The English Novel: Form and Function*, 1953.
Walcutt, C. C. *Man's Changing Mask: Modes and Methods of Characterization in Fiction*, 1966.
West, P. *The Wine of Absurdity*, 1966.
Williams, R. *The English Novel from Dickens to Lawrence*, 1970.

PLAYS:

Archer, W. *The Old Drama and the New*, 1923.
Beerbohm, M. *Around Theatres: Reviews, 1898–1910*, rev. edn, 1953.
Bogard, T. and W. I. Oliver. *Modern Drama: Essays in Criticism*, 1965.
Bentley, E. R. *The Playwright as Thinker: A Study of Drama in Modern Times*, 1946; *The Modern Theatre*, 1948; *In Search of Theatre*, 1954; *The Theatre of Commitment*, 1968.
Brown, J. R. (ed.) *Contemporary Theatre*, 1962.
Browne, M. *Verse in the Modern English Theatre*, 1963.
Cole, T., and Chinoy, H. K. (eds.) *Directors on Directing: A Source Book for the Modern Theatre*, rev. 1964.
Donoghue, D. *The Third Voice: Modern British and American Verse Drama*, 1959.
Eliot, T. S. See AUTHOR entry.
Ellis-Fermor, U. *The Irish Dramatic Movement*, 1954.
Esslin, M. *The Theatre of the Absurd*, 1962.
Gasgoigne, B. *Twentieth Century Drama*, 1962.
Gassner, J. *Ideas in the Drama*, 1964.
Kitchin, L. *Mid-century Drama*, 1960; *Drama in the Sixties: Form and Interpretation*, 1966.
MacNamara, B. *Abbey Plays, 1899–1948*, 1949.
Peacock, R. *The Poet in the Theatre*, 1946.
Robinson, L. *Ireland's Abbey Theatre, 1899–1951*, 1951.
Shaw, G. B. *Plays and Players*, ed. A. C. Ward, 1952. See also AUTHOR entry.
Taylor, J. R. *Anger and After*, 1962, rev. 1964; *The Rise and Fall of the Well-made Play*, 1967; *The Second Wave: British Drama for the Seventies*, 1971.

Weales, G. *Religion in Modern English Drama*, 1961.

Weygandt, C. *Irish Plays and Playwrights*, 1913.

Wickham, G. *Drama in a World of Science*, 1962.

Williams, R. *Modern Tragedy*, 1966; *Drama in Performance*, enl. edn, 1968; *Drama from Ibsen to Brecht*, 1968 (enl. edn of *Drama from Ibsen to Eliot*, 1952).

4. Major Literary Critics and Historians of the Period (with selected works), and some Important Works on the Theory and Criticism of Literature

Bradley, A. C. *Shakespearian Tragedy*, 1904; *Oxford Lectures on Poetry*, 1909.

Daiches, D. *Critical Approaches to Literature*, 1956; *Critical History of English Literature*, 1960.

Eliot, T. S. See Author entry.

Empson, W. See Author entry.

Gardner, H. *The Business of Criticism*, 1959.

Holloway, J. See Author entry.

Hough, G. *The Last Romantics*, 1949; *An Essay on Criticism*, 1966.

Kermode, F. *Continuities*, 1968; *Romantic Image*, 1957.

Knights, L. C. *Drama and Society in the Age of Jonson*, 1937; *Explorations*, 1946; *An Approach to Hamlet*, 1960; *Further Explorations*, 1965.

Lawrence, D. H. See Author entry.

Leavis, F. R. *D. H. Lawrence*, 1930; *Mass Civilization and Minority Culture*, 1930; *How to Teach Reading*; *A Primer for Ezra Pound*, 1932; *New Bearings in English Poetry*, 1932, rev. 1950; *Culture and Environment* (with D. Thompson), 1933; *Revaluation*, 1936; *Education and the University*, 1943; *The Great Tradition*, 1948, rev. 1960; *The Common Pursuit*, 1952; Edited *Scrutiny*, 1932–53.

Lewis, C. S. *The Allegory of Love*, 1936; *A Preface to Paradise Lost*, 1942; *English Literature in the 16th Century*, 1954.

Muir, E. See Author entry.

Murry, J. Middleton. *The Problem of Style*, 1922; *Keats and Shakespeare*, 1925.

Pound, Ezra. See Author entry.

Quiller-Couch, A. ('Q'). Edited *The Oxford Book of English Verse*, 1900; *On the Art of Writing*, 1916; *On the Art of Reading*, 1920.

Richards, I. A. *The Meaning of Meaning* (with C. K. Ogden) 1923;

Principles of Literary Criticism, 1925; *Practical Criticism*, 1929; *Science and Poetry*, 1926, rev. 1935, rev. 1971 as *Poetries and Sciences*; *The Philosophy of Rhetoric*, 1936; *Speculative Instruments*, 1955.

Saintsbury, G. E. B. *A Short History of English Literature*, 1898; *A History of Criticism and Literary Taste in Europe*, 3 vols, 1900–1904; *A History of English Prosody*, 3 vols, 1906–10.

Spurgeon, C. *Shakespeare's Imagery and What it Tells Us*, 1935.

Steiner, G. *The Death of Tragedy*, 1961; *Language and Silence*, 1967.

Tillyard, E. M. W. *The Personal Heresy* (with C. S. Lewis), 1939; *The Elizabethan World Picture*, 1943.

Williams, R. *Culture and Society, 1780–1950*, rev. ed., 1963. See also criticism of the drama above (p. 594).

Wilson, J. D. Edited the *New Cambridge Shakespeare*. *What Happens in Hamlet*, 1935; *The Fortunes of Falstaff*, 1943.

B. The Background to the Literature

1. History

MAJOR BRITISH HISTORIANS OF THE PERIOD: SELECTED WORKS:

Berlin, I. *The Hedgehog and the Fox*, 1953, rev. 1967; *Two Concepts of History*, 1958; *Karl Marx*, 3rd edn, 1963.

Butterfield, H. *The Whig Interpretation of History*, 1931; *The Study of Modern History*, 1944; *Christianity and History*, 1949; *George III and the Historians*, 1957.

Laski, H. J. *The Rise of European Liberalism*, 1936; *A Grammar of Politics*, 4th edn., 1938; *The Decline of Liberalism*, 1940.

Namier, L. B. *The Structure of Politics at the Accession of George III*, 2nd edn, 1957; *England in the Age of the American Revolution*, 2nd edn, 1961.

Tawney, R. H. *The Acquisitive Society*, 1920; *Religion and the Rise of Capitalism*, 1926; *Equality*, 1931, 4th edn, 1952.

Toynbee, A. J. *A Study of History*, 12 vols, 1934–61; *Christianity and Civilization*, 1940; *A Historian's Approach to Religion*, 1956.

Trevelyan, G. M. *British History in the 19th Century*, 1922; *History of England*, 1926; *English Social History*, 1942.

DOCUMENTARY SOURCES:

Bettey, J. H., ed. *English Historical Documents, 1906–39*, 1967.

Ford, P., and Ford, G. (eds.) *A Breviate of Parliamentary Papers, 1900–1954*, 3 vols, 1957–61.

SELECTED JOURNALS OF THE PERIOD:

Economic History Review, 1927–.

English Historical Review, 1889–.

History: The Quarterly Journal of the Historical Association, new series, 1912–.

History Today, 1951–.

The Journal of Contemporary History, 1966–.

BIBLIOGRAPHIES OF THE HISTORY OF THE PERIOD:

Elton, G. R. *Modern Historians on British History, 1485–1945: A Critical Bibliography*, 1970.

Marriott, J. A. R. *Modern England, 1885–1932*, 1934.

Mowatt, C. L. *British History since 1926*, 1960.

The Oxford History of England, Vol. XIV, 1936; Vol. XV, 1965.

Roach, J. (ed.) *A Bibliography of Modern History*, 1968.

GENERAL POLITICAL, ECONOMIC, SOCIAL AND INDUSTRIAL HISTORIES OF THE PERIOD:

Amery, L. S. (ed.) *The Times History of the War in South Africa*, 7 vols, 1900–1909.

Ashworth, W. *An Economic History of England, 1870–1939*, 1960.

Booth, Charles. *Life and Labour of the People in London*, 17 vols, 1889–1903.

Bott, A. *Our Fathers (1870–1900)*, 1931; (with I. Clephane) *Our Mothers (1870–1900)*, 1932.

Burnett, J. *Plenty and Want: A Social History of Diet, 1815 to the Present Day*, 1966.

Butler, D. E. *The Electoral System in Britain, 1918–1951*, 1951.

Carr-Saunders, A. M., and Jones, D. C. *Social Conditions in England and Wales*, 1958.

Churchill, W. S. *The World Crisis, 1911–1918*, 6 vols, 1923–31; *The Second World War*, 6 vols, 1948–54.

Clapham, J. H. *An Economic History of Modern Britain*, 3 vols, 1930–38.
Clegg, H. A. *et al. History of British Trade Unions since 1889*, Vol. I: *1889–1910*, 1966.
Cole, G. H. D. *History of the Labour Party from 1914*, 1948; (with M. Cole) *The Postwar Condition of Britain*, 1956; (with R. Postgate) *The Common People, 1746–1946*, rev. 1946.
Collier, J., and Lang I., *Just the Other Day: An Informal History of Great Britain since the War*, 1932.
Dibelius, W. *England*, 1930.
Ensor, R. C. K. *England, 1870–1914* (*Oxford History of England*, Vol. XIV), 1936.
Foot, M. R. D. *British Foreign Policy since 1898*, 1956.
Graves, R., and Hodge, A. *The Long Weekend: A Social History of Great Britain, 1918–1939*, 1940.
Gregg, P. *A Social and Economic History of Britain, 1760–1950*, 1950.
Halévy, E. *The Rule of Democracy, 1905–1915*, 2 vols, 1953.
Hartley, A. A. *A State of England*, 1963.
Hinde, R. S. E. *The British Penal System, 1773–1950*, 1951.
The History of the T.U.C., 1868–1967: A Pictorial Survey of a Social Revolution, 1968.
Hopkins, H. *The New Look: A Social History of the Forties and Fifties in Britain*, 1963.
Hopkinson, Tom (ed.) *Picture Post, 1938–1950*, 1970.
Hutt, A. *Postwar History of the British Working Class*, 1937.
Jackson, W. E. *Local Government in England and Wales*, 1949.
Jennings, I. *The British Constitution*, 1941, 4th edn, 1966; *The Queen's Government*, 1954.
Jones, G. P., and Pool, A. P. G. *A Hundred Years of Economic Development in Great Britain*, 1940.
Kaldor, N. *The Causes of the Slow Rate of Economic Growth in the United Kingdom*, 1966.
Laver, J. *The Age of Optimism: Manners and Morals, 1848–1914*, 1966.
Lewis, W. A. *Economic Survey, 1919–1939*, 1949.
Lichnowsky, Prince Karl Maximilian. *My Mission to London*, 1918.
Lynd, H. *England in the 1880s*, 1945.
Macfarlane, L. J. *The British Communist Party* (to 1929), 1966.
Marsh, D. C. *The Changing Social Structure of England and Wales, 1871–1951*, 1958.
Masterman, C. F. E. *The Condition of England*, 1909; *How England is Governed*, 1921, rev. by D. Foot, 1937.
Mowatt, C. L. *Britain between the Wars, 1918–1940*, 1962.
Murray, J. *The General Strike of 1926*, 1951.

Namier, L. B. *Europe in Decay, 1936–1940*, 1950.
Nowell-Smith, S. (ed.) *Edwardian England, 1901–1914*, 1964.
Pelling, H. *The Origins of the Labour Party, 1881–1900*, 1954.
Pollard, S. *The Development of the British Economy, 1914–1950*, 1966.
Reynolds, E. E. and Brasher, N. H. *Britain in the 20th Century*, 1966.
Robbins, L. *The Great Depression*, 1934.
Sampson, A. *Anatomy of Britain*, 1962; *Anatomy of Britain Today*, 1971.
Seaman, L. C. B. *Post-Victorian Britain, 1902–1951*, 1966.
Smellie, K. B. *A Hundred Years of English Government*, rev. 1951.
Somervell, D. C. *British Politics since 1900*, 1950.
Taylor, A. J. P. *English History, 1914–1945* (*Oxford History of England*, Vol. XV), 1965.
Thomson, D. *England in the Twentieth Century, 1914–1963*, 1965.
Webb, S. and Webb, B. *The History of Trades Unionism*, rev. edn, 1950.
Williams, F. *Magnificent Journey: The Rise of the Trade Unions*, 1954.
Woodhouse, C. M. *Post-war Britain*, 1966.
Zweig, F. *Labour, Life and Poverty*, 1948; *Women's Life and Labour*, 1952; *The British Worker*, 1952.

2. The Intellectual Background: Philosophy; Political, Economic and Social Theory, Education, Cultural Issues

MAJOR BRITISH THINKERS OF THE PERIOD: SELECTED WORKS.

(See also Sections on Literary Theory and Major Historians above)

Austin, J. L. *Sense and Sensibilia*, 1962; *How to do Things with Words*, 1962.
Ayer, A. J. *Language, Truth and Logic*, 1936, 2nd ed., 1949; *The Foundations of Empirical Knowledge*, 1940; *The Problem of Knowledge*, 1956.
Bradley, F. H. *Ethical Studies*, 1876, rev. 1927; *Appearance and Reality*, 1893.
Collingwood, R. G. (See also ARTS Section below.) *Religion and Philosophy*, 1916; *Essay on Philosophical Method*, 1933; *The Philosophy of History*, 1934; *The New Leviathan*, 1942.
Emmet, D. M. *Philosophy and Faith*, 1936; *The Nature of Metaphysical Thinking*, 1945; *Rules, Roles and Relations*, 1966.
Findlay, J. N. *Hegel: A Re-examination*, 1958; *Values and Intentions*, 1961; *Language, Mind and Value*, 1963; *The Discipline of the Cave*, 1966; *The Transcendence of the Cave*, 1967.

Frazer, O. G. *The Golden Bough*, 12 vols, 1890–1915.

Hulme, T. E. *Speculations*, ed. H. Read, 1924. *Further Speculations*, ed. S. Hynes, 1955.

Keynes, J. M. *A Treatise on Money*, 1930; *The General Theory of Employment, Interest and Money*, 1936.

McTaggart, J. M. E. *The Nature of Existence*, 2 vols, 1921–7.

Moore, G. E. *Principia Ethica*, 1903; *Ethics*, 1912; *Philosophical Studies*, 1922.

Price, H. H. *Perception*, 1932; *Thinking and Experience*, 1961.

Russell, B. *Principia Mathematica* (with A. N. Whitehead) 1903, 2nd edn, 1925; *Problems of Philosophy*, 1912; *Our Knowledge of the External World*, 1914; *Sceptical Essays*, 1928; *Conquest of Happiness*, 1930; *An Inquiry into Meaning and Truth*, 1940; *A History of Western Philosophy*, 1946; *The Wisdom of the West*, 1959.

Ryle, G. *The Concept of Mind*, 1949.

Sidgwick, H. *Methods of Ethics*, 1875.

Whitehead, A. N. *Process and Reality*, 1929; See also Russell, B.

Wittgenstein, L. *Tractatus Logico-Philosophicus*, 1922; *Philosophical Investigations (1936–1949)*, ed. G. Anscombe, 1953; *The Blue and Brown Books* (lectures 1933–5), 1958.

PHILOSOPHY: HISTORIES AND STUDIES

Selected Journals of the period:

Aristotelian Society Proceedings, new series, 1900– ; *Supplementary Papers*, 1918–.

Mind, 1876–91; new series, 1892–.

Philosophy, 1926–.

Philosophical Quarterly, 1950–.

Davies, H. *Worship and Theology in England*, Vol. V: *The Ecumenical Century, 1900–1965*, 1966.

Elton, W. (ed.) *Aesthetics and Language*, 1954.

Flew, A. G. N. (ed.) *Logic and Language*, first and second series, 1951, 1953.

Lewis, H. D. (ed.) *Contemporary British Philosophy*, 1956.

Mace, C. A. (ed.) *British Philosophy at Mid-Century*, 1966.

Mackintosh, H. R. *Types of Modern Theology*, 1937.

Passmore, J. A. *A Hundred Years of Philosophy*, 1957.

Pears, D. *Bertrand Russell and the British Tradition in Philosophy*, 1967.

Pryce-Jones, A. (ed.) *A New Outline of Modern Knowledge*, 1956.

Ryle, G. (ed.) *The Revolution in Philosophy*, 1956.

Urmson, J. O. *Philosophical Analysis: Its Development between the Two World Wars*, 1956.

Warnock, G. J. *English Philosophy since 1900*, 1958.

Williams, B. and Montefiore, A. (ed.) *British Analytical Philosophy*, 1966.

SOCIAL, POLITICAL AND ECONOMIC THOUGHT: HISTORIES AND STUDIES:

Annan, N. *The Curious Strength of Positivism in English Political Thought*, 1959.

Benn, S. I., and Peters, R. S. *Social Principles and the Democratic State*, 1959.

Brown, J. A. C. *The Social Psychology of Industry*, 1954.

Burnham, J. *The Managerial Revolution*, 1942.

Crossman, R. H. S. (ed.) *The God that Failed*, 1950.

Drucker, P. *The End of Economic Man*, 1938.

Ellis, H. *A Study of British Genius*, 1904; *Studies in the Psychology of Sex*, 6 vols, 1897–1910; Vol. 7, 1928.

Flugel, J. C. *Man, Morals and Society*, 1954.

Ginsberg, M. *Reason and Unreason in Society*, 1947.

Harding, D. W. *Social Psychology and Individual Values*, 1953.

Huxley, A. See AUTHOR entry above.

Koestler, A. *The Yogi and the Commissar*, 1945; *The Sleepwalkers*, 1959.

Lewis, Wyndham. See AUTHOR entry above.

Mishan, E. J. *The Costs of Economic Growth*, 1967.

Mumford, L. See entry in ARTS section below.

Oakeshott, M. *Political Education*, 1951.

Orwell, G. *The Road to Wigan Pier*, 1937. See also AUTHOR entry above.

Russell, B. *Roads to Freedom: Socialism, Anarchism and Syndicalism*, 1918; *The Prospects of Industrial Civilization*, 1923; *Authority and the Individual*, 1949. See also Section on MAJOR THINKERS above.

Shaw, G. B. *The Intelligent Woman's Guide to Socialism, Capitalism, Sovietism and Fascism*, rev. 1937; *Essays in Fabian Socialism*, 1937. See also AUTHOR entry above.

Wallas, G. *Human Nature in Politics*, 1920.

Webb, Beatrice. *My Apprenticeship*, 1926; *Our Partnership*, 1948.

Wells, H. G. See AUTHOR entry above.

Whitehead, A. N. *Science and the Modern World*, 1925.

Wootton, B. *Plan or No Plan*, 1934; *Social Science and Social Pathology*, 1959.

EDUCATION: HISTORIES AND STUDIES:

Selected Reports from official organizations:

Adult Education Committee, eleven papers, 1922–33.

Board of Education Consultative Committee: *The Teaching of English in England*, 1921; *The Education of Adolescents*, 1927; *Primary Education*, 1930; *Education in Grammar and Technical High Schools*, 1938.

Central Advisory Council for Education: *Fifteen to Eighteen* (Crowther) 1959; *Half our Future* (Newsom), 1963; *On Higher Education* (Robbins), 1963; *Children and Their Primary Schools* (Plowden), 1967; *The Government of Colleges of Education* (Weaver), 1966.

Ministry of Education: *Education, 1900–1950*, 1950–51; *Report on Education*, 9, 1960; *On the Training and Supply of Teachers*, 1951, 1953, 1954.

Nuffield Foundation: *Nineteenth Report, 1963–64*.

Parliamentary and Scientific Committee: *Research in Education*, 1961.

University Grants Commission: *Annual Survey*, 1948–; *Reports on 5-yearly Periods*, 1935/47–; *University Teaching Methods* (Hale), 1964.

White Paper on educational reconstruction, 1942–3.

Selected journals of the period:

The Times Educational Supplement, 1910–.

The Times Higher Educational Supplement, 1971–.

University Quarterly, 1946–.

Adler, A. *The Education of Children*, 1930.

Armytage, W. H. G. *Civic Universities*, 1955.

Ashby, E. 'Investment in man' (in *Listener*, August 1963).

Bantock, G. H. *Freedom and Authority in Education*, 1952.

Barnard, H. C. *A Short History of English Education*, 2nd edn, 1961. (Study concludes at 1902.)

Bolt, S. *The Right Response*, 1966.

Cox, C. B., and Dyson, A. E. (eds.) *Fight for Education: A Black Paper*, 1969; *Black Paper Two: The Crisis in Education*, 1970.

Cox, E. *Changing Aims in Religious Education*, 1966.

Dancy, J. *The Public Schools and the Future*, rev. 1966.

English Association series of pamphlets, including:
R. W. Chambers: *The Teaching of English in the Universities of England*, 1922; R. B. McKerrow, *Note on the Teaching of English Language and Literature*, 1921.

Floud, J. *et al. Social Change and Educational Opportunity*, 1956.

Ford, B. (ed.) *Young Writers: Young Readers*, 1960.
Holbrook, D. *English for Maturity*, 1961.
Isaacs, S. *The Intellectual Growth of Young Children*, 1930.
Jackson, B., and Marsden, D. *Education and the Working Class*, 1962.
Jenkins, D. *The Educated Society*, 1968.
Lambert, D. *The Hothouse Society*, 1968.
Leavis, F. R. *Education and the University*, rev. 1948.
Lewis, C. S. *The Abolition of Man*, 1943.
Lowndes, G. A. N. *The Silent Social Revolution: Public Education in England and Wales, 1895–1935*, 1937.
Marris, P. *The Experience of Higher Education*, 1964.
Marshall, S. *An Experiment in Education*, 1963.
Palmer, D. J. *The Rise of English Studies*, 1965.
Potter, S. *The Muse in Chains: A Study in Education*, 1937.
Robbins, L. *The University in the Modern World*, 1966.
Sampson, G. *English for the English*, rev. 1952.
Stock, M. *The W.E.A.: The First Fifty Years*, 1953.
Tillyard, E. M. W. *The Muse Unchained*, 1958.
Whitehead, A. N. *The Aims of Education*, 1929.
Whitehead, F. *The Disappearing Dais*, 1966.

CULTURAL ISSUES, MASS COMMUNICATIONS, ETC.: HISTORIES AND STUDIES. See also AUTHOR entries – e.g. D. H. Lawrence, George Orwell, Aldous Huxley, etc.; also section on the ARTS below.

General:

Allsop, K. *The Angry Decade: A Survey of the Cultural Revolt of the 1950s*, 1958.
Anderson, P. 'Components of the National Culture' (*New Left Review*, July–August, 1968).
The Arts Council of Great Britain. *Annual Reports*, 1945/46–.
Churchill, R. C. *Disagreements: A Polemic on Culture in the English Democracy*, 1950.
Forster, E. M. *Two Cheers for Democracy*, 1951. See also AUTHOR entry.
Groombridge, B. *Popular Culture and Personal Responsibility*, 1961.
Harris, J. S. *Government Patronage of the Arts in Great Britain*, 1970.
Hoggart, Richard. *The Uses of Literacy*, 1957.
Holloway, J. 'English culture' (*Listener*, January 1967).
Leavis, Q. D. *Fiction and the Reading Public*, 1932.
Lewis, C. D. (ed.) *The Mind in Chains: Socialism and the Cultural Revolution*, 1937.

Mumford, L. *The Culture of Cities*, 1940. See also ARTS Section below.

O'Brien, C. C. *Writers and Politics*, 1965.

Spender, S. 'The Obsessive Situation' (*Listener*, October 1962); *The Struggle of the Modern*, 1963.

Thompson, D. (ed.) *Discrimination and Popular Culture*, 1964; *Culture and Environment* (with F. R. Leavis), 1933.

The 'Two Cultures' Controversy:

Snow, C. P. *The Two Cultures and the Scientific Revolution*, 1962.

Leavis, F. R. *Two Cultures?: The Significance of C.P. Snow*, 1962.

Snow, C. P. 'The Two Cultures: A Second Look' (*Times Literary Supplement*, October 1963).

Green, M. 'A Literary Defence of the Two Cultures' (*Critical Quarterly*, Vol. 4, 1962).

Trilling, L. 'The Leavis-Snow Controversy' (in *Beyond Culture*, 1966).

Green, M. 'Lionel Trilling and the Two Cultures' (*Essays in Criticism*, 1963).

Williams, R. *Culture and Society, 1780–1950*, 1958; *The Long Revolution*, 1961; ed. *May Day Manifesto, 1968*, 1968. See also following section.

Mass communications, radio, television, film, press, etc.

Angell, N. *The Press and the Organization of Society*, rev. 1933.

Beavan, J. *The Press and the Public*, 1962.

Black. P. *The Mirror in the Corner: People's Television*, 1972.

Boston, R. ed. *The Press We Deserve*, 1970.

Briggs, A. *A History of Broadcasting in the United Kingdom*, 3 vols, 1961–70.

British Broadcasting Corporation. Publications, including Annual Handbook; *Facts and figures about viewing and listening*, 1961; *Broadcasting in the seventies*, 1970.

Crosland, A. R. 'The mass media' (*Encounter*, November, 1962).

Crossman, R. H. 'Thoughts of a Captive Viewer' (*Encounter*, August 1962).

Hall, S., and Whannell, P. *The Popular Arts*, 1964.

Halloran, J. D. *The Effects of Mass Communication*, 1964.

Himmelweit, H. T., ed. *Television and the Child*, 1958.

Hood, S. *A Survey of Television*, 1967.

Houston, P. *The Contemporary Cinema*, 1965.

Independent Television Authority. *Programmes: Facts and Figures*, 1961.

Jackson, I. *The Provincial Press and the Community*, 1971.

Journal of Social Issues, no. 2, 1942 (R. Williams, H. Himmelweit *et al.* on British broadcasting).

Manvell, Roger. *On the Air: A Study of Broadcasting in Sound and Tele-*

vision, 1953; *What is a Film?*, 1965; *This Age of Communication*, 1966; *New Cinema in Britain*, 1969.
Martin, Kingsley. *The Press the Public Wants*, 1947.
Paulu, B. *British Broadcasting in Transition*, 1961.
Reports: Committees on broadcasting (Ullswater, 1935), (Beveridge, 1950, 1951), (Pilkington, 1960, 1962); Committee on the Press (Ross, 1948–9); Royal Commission on the Press (Shawcross, 1962).
Scupham, J. *Broadcasting and the Community*, 1967.
Thompson, D. *Voices of Civilization*, 1943.
Williams, R. *Preface to Film* (with M. Orrom), 1954; *Communications*, 1962, rev. 1966.
Worsley, T. C. *Television, the Ephemeral Art*, 1970.

SELECT LIST OF FOREIGN (INCLUDING AMERICAN) THINKERS OF THE PERIOD WHOSE WORK HAS SUBSTANTIALLY INFLUENCED BRITISH WRITERS (the list includes literary and linguistic theorists):

Adams, Henry
Adler, Alfred
Auerbach, Erich
Barth, Karl
Barthes, Roland
Barzun, Jacques
Buber, Martin
Burke, Kenneth
Camus, Albert
Cassirer, Ernst
Chomsky, Noam
Crane, Ronald S.
Croce, Benedetto
Dewey, John
Eliade, Mircea
Fischer, Ernst
Foucault, Michel
Freud, Sigmund
Fromm, Erich
Frye, Northrop
Goldmann, Lucien
Gombrich, E. H.
Jakobson, Roman
Jaspers, Karl
Jespersen, Otto
Jung, Carl G.
Kaufmann, Walter
Langer, Susanne K.
Lévi-Strauss, Claude
Lorenz, Konrad
Lukács, Georg
McLuhan, H. Marshall
Manheim, Karl
Marcuse, Herbert
Maritain, Jacques
Niebuhr, Reinhold
Ortega y Gasset, José
Otto, Rudolf
Piaget, Jean
Popper, Karl
Reich, Wilhelm
Santayana, George
Sartre, Jean-Paul
Spitzer, Leo
Trilling, Lionel
Unamuno, Miguel de
Veblen, Thorstein
Wellek, René
Wimsatt, W. K

3. THE ARTS EXCLUDING LITERATURE

HISTORIES AND STUDIES (includes some major writings of the period though these do not refer to the period):

Bacharach, A. L. (ed.) *British Music of Our Time*, 1946.
Battersby, M. *The Decorative Twenties*, 1969.

Behrendt, W. C. *Modern Building*, 1937.

Bell, Clive. *Art*, 1914.

Bertram, A. *A Century of British Painting*, 1951.

Blom, E. *Music in England*, 1942.

Bowness, A. (ed.) *Recent British Painting*, 1968.

Briggs, M. *Building Today*, 1944.

Clark, K. *The Gothic Revival*, 1928, 3rd edn, 1962; *Leonardo da Vinci*, 1939; *Civilization*, 1970.

Collingwood, R. G. *The Principles of Art*, 1938.

Crowe, S. *The Landscape of Power*, 1959.

Farr, F. *Design on British Industry: A Mid-Century Survey*, 1965.

Finch, C. *Image as Language: Aspects of British Art 1950–1968*, 1969.

Fry, R. *Vision and Design*, 1920; *Reflections on British Painting*, 1934.

Gropius, W. *The New Architecture and the Bauhaus*, English trans., 1965.

Hamilton, G. H. *Painting and Sculpture in Europe, 1880–1940* (Pelican History of Art), 1967.

Hitchcock, H. R. *Architecture, 19th and 20th Centuries*, 1958.

Hodeir, A. *Jazz: Its Evolution and Essence*, 1956.

Hubbard, H. A. *A Hundred Years of British Painting, 1851–1951*, 1951.

Inglis, C. E. *The Aesthetic Aspect of Civil Engineering*, 1944.

Ironside, R. *Painting since 1939*, 1947.

Laing, D. *The Sound of our Time*, 1969.

Lambert, C. *Music Ho!*, 1934.

Landau, R. *New Directions in British Architecture*, 1968.

Larkin, P. *All What Jazz? A Record Diary 1961–68*, 1970.

Lippard, L. *Pop Art*, 1966.

Lucie-Smith, E. *Movements in Art Since 1945*, 1969.

McGrath, R. *Twentieth Century Houses*, 1934.

Maufe, E. (ed.) *Modern Church Architecture*, 1948.

Mellers, W. *Music and Society*, 1946.

Mitchell, D. *The Language of Modern Music*, 1966.

Nairn, I. *Counter-attack against Subtopia*, 1956; *Britain's Changing Towns*, 1967.

Pevsner, N. *Pioneers of Modern Design from William Morris to Walter Gropius*, rev. 1960; *The Englishness of English Art*, 1964; ed. *The Pelican History of Art*; *The Buildings of England* series.

Read, Herbert. *The Meaning of Art*, 1931; *Art Now*, 1933, rev. 1961; *Art and Industry*, 1934; *Art and Society*, 1937; *Education Through Art*, 1943; *Contemporary British Art*, 1951; *The Philosophy of Modern Art*, 1952; *The Art of Sculpture*, 1956; *A Concise History of Modern Painting*, 1959; *The Origins of Form in Art*, 1965; ed. *Surrealism*, 1936.

Richards, J. M. *Introduction to Modern Architecture*, 1940.

Rothenstein, J. *Modern Painters*, 2 vols, 1962.
Stephen, D. *et al. British Buildings, 1960–64*, 1965.
Stokes, A. *The Quattro Cento*, 1932; *Stones of Rimini*, 1934; *Colour and Form*, 1937; *Smooth and Rough*, 1951.
Summerson, J. *Heavenly Mansions*, 1949.
Whittick, A. *European Architecture in the Twentieth Century*, 2 vols, 1953.
Wilenski, R. H. *English Painting*, rev. 1954.
Williams, R. Vaughan. *National Music*, 1934.

ACKNOWLEDGEMENTS

FOR permission to reprint copyright matter, the following acknowledgements are made: for extracts from the *Collected Poems* of W. H. Auden to Faber & Faber and to Random House in U.S.A.; for poems from the *Collected Poems* of Rupert Brook ('The Soldier' and 'Safety') to Sidgwick & Jackson, to Dodd, Mead & Co. in U.S.A., and to McClelland & Stewart in Canada; for a poem by Austin Clark ('Martyr and Heretic') to the author; for extracts from *Heart of Darkness* by Joseph Conrad to the trustees of the Joseph Conrad Estate and J. M. Dent & Sons, and to Doubleday & Co. in U.S.A.; for extracts from poems by Walter de la Mare to his literary trustees and the Society of Authors as their representative; for extracts from T. S. Eliot's *Collected Poems, Four Quartets* and *Notes towards the Definition of Culture* to Faber & Faber and to Harcourt, Brace & World, New York; for part of a poem by William Empson ('Villanelle') to Chatto & Windus and to Harcourt, Brace & World, New York; for extracts from *The Longest Journey, Where Angels Fear to Tread, A Room with a View*, and *A Passage to India* by E. M. Forster to Edward Arnold, and to Alfred A. Knopf, Inc. and Harcourt, Brace & World, New York; for extracts from *The Collected Poems of Thomas Hardy* to Macmillan & Co. and the trustees of the Hardy Estate, and to the Macmillan Co. in U.S.A.; for a poem by Hugh MacDiarmid ('Lourd on My Hert') to the author; for poems by Wilfred Owen ('The Chances', 'Futility', 'Anthem for Doomed Youth') to Chatto & Windus and to New Directions in U.S.A.; for extracts from poetry by Ezra Pound to the author; for extract from *The Concept of Mind* by Gilbert Ryle to the author and Hutchinson & Co.; for poems by Siegfried Sassoon ('Dreamers', 'The General', 'Suicide in the Trenches', '*They*', 'On Passing the Menin Gate, 1927', 'An Unveiling', 'Disabled') to the author; for part of a poem by Dylan Thomas to J. M. Dent & Sons and to New Directions in U.S.A.; for poems by Edward Thomas ('A Tale', 'March', 'The Glory') to Mrs Thomas and Faber & Faber; for extracts from the Uniform Edition of the Works of Virginia Woolf and from her critical writings to the Hogarth Press and to Harcourt, Brace & World, New York; and for extracts from poems by W. B. Yeats to Mrs Yeats and Macmillan & Co., and to the Macmillan Co. in U.S.A.

INDEX OF NAMES

MORE ABOUT PENGUINS AND PELICANS

Penguinews, which appears every month, contains details of all the new books issued by Penguins as they are published. From time to time it is supplemented by *Penguins in Print*, which is a complete list of all titles available. (There are some five thousand of these.)

A specimen copy of *Penguinews* will be sent to you free on request. For a year's issues (including the complete lists) please send 50p if you live in the British Isles, or 75p if you live elsewhere. Just write to Dept EP, Penguin Books Ltd, Harmondsworth, Middlesex, enclosing a cheque or postal order, and your name will be added to the mailing list.

In the U.S.A.: For a complete list of books available from Penguin in the United States write to Dept CS, Penguin Books Inc., 7110 Ambassador Road, Baltimore, Maryland 21207.

In Canada: For a complete list of books available from Penguin in Canada write to Penguin Books Canada Ltd, 41 Steelcase Road West, Markham, Ontario.

THE PELICAN GUIDE TO ENGLISH LITERATURE

Edited by Boris Ford

What this work sets out to offer is a guide to the history and traditions of English literature, a contour-map of the literary scene in England. It attempts, in other words, to draw up an ordered account of literature that is concerned, first and foremost, with value for the present, and this as direct encouragement to people to read for themselves.

Each volume presents the reader with four kinds of related material:

(i) An account of the social context of literature in each period.

(ii) A literary survey of the period.

(iii) Detailed studies of some of the chief writers and works in the period.

(iv) An appendix of essential facts for reference purposes.

The *Guide* consists of seven volumes, as follows:

1. *The Age of Chaucer*
2. *The Age of Shakespeare*
3. *From Donne to Marvell*
4. *From Dryden to Johnson*
5. *From Blake to Byron*
6. *From Dickens to Hardy*
7. *The Modern Age*